DATE DUE

Lord Randolph Churchill

Lord Randolph Churchill in the early 1880s

LORD RANDOLPH CHURCHILL

A Political Life

R. F. FOSTER

CLARENDON PRESS · OXFORD
1981

Oxford University Press, Walton Street, Oxford OX2 6DP

London Glasgow New York Toronto
Delhi Bombay Calcutta Madras Karachi
Kuala Lumpur Singapore Hong Kong Tokyo
Nairobi Dar es Salaam Cape Town
Melbourne Auckland
and associate companies in
Beirut Berlin Ibadan Mexico City

Published in the United States by
Oxford University Press, New York

British Library Cataloguing in Publication Data

Foster, R. F.
    Lord Randolph Churchill.
    1. Churchill, Lord Randolph—Biography
    I. Title
941.08′1092′4   DA565.C6

ISBN 0-19-822679-9

Filmset in 'Monophoto' Baskerville
by Eta Services (Typesetters) Ltd., Beccles, Suffolk
Printed in Great Britain at the
University Press, Oxford
by Eric Buckley,
Printer to the University

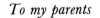

To my parents

Acknowledgements

I owe thanks to many people for help received in the course of writing this book. The following are some outstanding obligations but there should, I know, be many more.

I am indebted to the gracious permission of Her Majesty the Queen for allowing me to consult the Royal Archives at Windsor and to cite certain passages. For access to other manuscript collections and permission to quote from them I am grateful to the Controller of Her Majesty's Stationery Office (for citation of unpublished Crown-copyright material in the India Office Records and the Public Record Office), the Trustees of the British Library, the National Trust and the Bodleian Library (Disraeli Papers), the National Army Museum, the Earl of Rosebery and the Trustees of the National Library of Scotland, the Trustees of the Chatsworth Settlement, Lord Hambleden (for papers in custody of W. H. Smith and Son Ltd.), the Earl of Balfour, the Kent Archives Office and the Administrative Trustees of the Chevening Estate, the Harrowby MSS Trust, H. W. S. Churchill, Esq., Winston Churchill, MP and the Chartwell Trust, Churchill College, Cambridge, the Earl of Cranbrook and the Suffolk Record Office, Viscount Knebworth, the Hon. David Lytton Cobbold and the Hertfordshire Record Office, the Syndics of the Fitzwilliam Museum, Cambridge, Gerald FitzGibbon, Esq., Lord Rothschild and the Trustees of N. M. Rothschild and Sons, the Hon. Miriam Rothschild and Dr Charles Lane, the Marquess of Salisbury, the Duke of Marlborough, Earl St. Aldwyn and the Gloucestershire Record Office, P. Gwynne James, Esq., and the Hereford Record Office, and the University of Birmingham. Quotations from *Winston S. Churchill* appear by permission of William Heinemann, Ltd., from Winston Churchill's *Lord Randolph Churchill* by permission of the Hamlyn Group, Ltd., from *The New Machiavelli* by permission of A. P. Watt and Sons Ltd. Every effort has been made to get in touch with the holders of copyright material; if any oversights have occurred, I apologize and hope this general acknowledgement will be taken as sufficient.

I should like to extend my thanks to the staff of the many

archives and libraries where I worked, especially Patricia Ackerman and Marion Stewart at Churchill College, Elizabeth Thomas at Blenheim, T. W. Baker-Jones at W. H. Smith, and Gershon Knight at N. M. Rothschild. I also enjoyed illuminating conversations and correspondence with Gerald FitzGibbon, Peregrine Churchill, Anita Leslie, the Hon. Miriam Rothschild, and Robert Rhodes James. Those who helped by criticism, advice, and tracing material include James Sturgis, Paul Addison, Alistair Cooke, Owen Dudley Edwards, Duncan Catterall, Adolf Wood, Andrew Harrison, Avis von Herder, Ianthe Ruthven, Colin Matthew, and Leland Lyons; my thanks to them all. I am especially grateful to those who read the whole manuscript: John Vincent (who provided inspiration from the beginning), Stephen Koss, and Marina Warner. Their criticism supplied stimulation and correction; what irregularities remain are my responsibility alone. Annabel Gregory and Judy Collingwood were invaluable research assistants in the final stages and Marie-Anne Bastide, Seana Cahill, and Valerie Hogg gave unstinting secretarial help. I am indebted to Ivon Asquith and Gill Wigglesworth at the Oxford University Press for invaluable advice and sympathetic editing.

The consultation of materials in England and Scotland was made a pleasant task by the hospitality of many friends; notably Andrew and Veronica Tod in Edinburgh, Tom and Giti Paulin in Nottingham, Lynn Geldof in Bristol, Toby Barnard and Anthony O'Connor in Oxford, Charles and Kate Townshend in Staffordshire, and most of all Richard and Julia Heffer in Cambridge. Other problems were circumvented with financial aid from the Central Research Fund of the University of London, the British Academy, and Birkbeck College; my warm thanks to them all. The final job of writing was eased considerably by my election as Alistair Horne Research Fellow at St. Antony's College, Oxford; I should like to record my gratitude to Mr Horne, the Warden, and Fellows for a very pleasant year, and to Birkbeck College for making it possible.

What I owe to my wife Aisling, for her criticism as well as her support, is no mere matter for prefaces; but it must be recorded here. The dedication is an inadequate acknowledgement of another outstanding debt.

R. F. Foster
Birkbeck College,
February 1981.   University of London.

Contents

List of Illustrations

Abbreviations used in the Notes

CHAR: Chartwell Trust papers, held at Churchill College, Cambridge.

DVP: Dufferin Viceregal papers, at India Office Library, London.

EHJ: Edward Hamilton's Journal, in British Library (references to published version—Dudley W. R. Bahlman (ed.), *The Diary of Sir Edward Walter Hamilton* (2 vols., Oxford, 1972)—appear as Bahlman, *Hamilton Diary*).

LHJ: Lewis Harcourt's Journal, in Harcourt MSS B at Bodleian Library, Oxford.

RCHL: Political papers of Lord Randolph Churchill, held at Churchill College, Cambridge

Hatfield House MSS 3M: Papers of 3rd Marquis of Salisbury at Hatfield House.

Introduction:

A Character in a Political Novel

Piety is the besetting weakness of most biography, and a pious imputation of consistency the besetting fault of most political biography. Lord Randolph Churchill has been treated with more than his fair share of both; and such treatment consorted uneasily with the kind of man he was, and the kind of politician he aspired to be. His political ghost only fitfully inhabits the immense, whitewashed shrine erected by his son Winston out of carefully selected materials, which was revealed to the world in 1906; yet it was this filial monument, which cannot be surpassed as a study of Churchill's life and times, that dominated most detailed historiographical treatment of him ever since.[1]

The interest of his career, however, lies in the extent to which his own inconsistency reflected the instability of his political times. 'That Lord Randolph is given to contradicting himself is indeed indisputable and notorious,' wrote the Liberal but sympathetic *Pall Mall Gazette* in 1886; 'the collection of his inconsistencies has been the stock-in-trade of every Liberal hack for years. But where the world is wrong is in attributing this double-sidedness to personal flightiness on Lord Randolph's part, instead of to the permanent ambiguity in his position.' This represented the thesis advanced twenty years later by Winston Churchill, of his father as a Liberal *manqué*, preaching a saving message to an ungrateful Tory party; and this will not stand the test of close examination. 'Personal flightiness', however, can be reinterpreted; the history of a political operator, moving in a time of flux, has its own compelling interest.

This raises larger questions of political biography. The effort is not often made to relate English politicians to the ideas of their times (though an interesting if unconvincing attempt has been made in the case of Chamberlain);[2] but it is not an experiment that need be made in Churchill's case. 'Randolph Churchill

---

[1] Exceptions are E. J. Feuchtwanger, *Disraeli, Democracy and the Tory Party* (Oxford, 1968) and, most notably, A. B. Cooke and J. R. Vincent, *The Governing Passion: Cabinet Government and Party Politics in Britain, 1885–6* (Hassocks, 1974).

[2] P. Fraser, *Joseph Chamberlain* (London, 1966).

exclaimed to me one day', recalled John Morley, ' "Ah, but then Balfour and you are men who believe in the solution of political questions." This belief may or may not be a weakness, yet the alternative, that the statesman is a man who does not believe in the solution of political questions, was startling.'[3] And Churchill duly startled his contemporaries. Nor could it be said of him, as Morley also said of Chamberlain, that 'though not of the politicians who are forced into action by an idea, he was quick to associate ideas with his actions'. With tremendous aptitude for learning, he remained as haphazardly self-educated as only a nineteenth-century public-school product could be; his politics remained instinctual, and his interests were visceral.

The alternative biographical treatment that remains is the one to which most English politicians have been subjected: the personal monument, founded on one collection of papers which has probably been laundered to whiteness (or at least a uniform shade of grey). This approach is connected with Victorian *Lives*, but it lives on, and not only in appositely straight-faced recent lives of Aretas Akers-Douglas and W. H. Smith; Sir Oswald Mosley's biographer remarks that the biographer's role is 'somewhere between counsel for the defence and judge'.[4] There is a soothing quality about British historical biography which calms by dint of repetition. A prominent politician is assured of recurrent applications of biographical varnish, borrowing the texture of previous layers to build up a warm and glowing patina: reiteration of anecdotes, judicious but limited reappraisals of character, a general air of comfortable reassurance. Thus Lord Egremont's Balfour in 1980 is that of Mrs Dugdale in 1936, who was in turn Balfour as he saw himself in *Chapters of Autobiography*. It must of course be emphasized that a historian is under no moral obligation to discover anything new; but it is too seldom taken into account how far back the stereotypes of late Victorian politicians date, and how carefully manufactured they were at the time.

Much of this was due to the power of the press, visual and verbal. The most vivid testimony to this is to be found in Max Beerbohm's childhood memories; and the vision that struck him as most abiding was that of Churchill.

[3] J. Morley, *Recollections* (London, 1918), i, 191.
[4] R. Skidelsky, *Oswald Mosley* (London, 1975), p. 11.

By the time I was eleven years old ... I was interested only in politicians—in Statesmen, as they were called at that time. I had already, for some years, been aware of them. I had seen them, two-dimensionally and on a small scale, every Wednesday, in the pages of *Punch*, and had in a remote and tepid way revered them. I had not thought of them as actual, live men. Rather they were, as portrayed in the cartoons of the great John Tenniel, nobly mythical to me. Sometimes they wore togas; but more often they wore chitons and breast-plates, and were wielding or brandishing swords. Their shins were protected by greaves, and their calves were immensely muscular; and in the matter of biceps they were unsurpassable. They were Ajaxes and Hectors and Achilleses. Now and then they rose to greater heights, becoming Herculeses, Vulcans, Marses and the like. *Punch* was firmly Gladstonian in its politics; and therefore the Prime Minister was always more muscular than any of his enemies, re-doubtable though they too were; and the attitudes that he struck were more striking than theirs. I didn't quite like this. For my father was a Conservative and so, accordingly, was I. I wished—though I didn't care enough to pray—for the downfall of Gladstone. Sometime in the year 1883 I read a speech delivered in the House of Commons by Lord Randolph Churchill. I felt that here was the man to compass the downfall; for he was so very rude. Even the best-behaved little boys rejoice in the rudeness of other people. Lord Randolph's rudeness in a good cause refreshed my young heart greatly; nor ever did his future speeches disappoint me. But, much though I delighted in him, I didn't quite think of him as an actual person. I thought of him as Phaeton. Tenniel—or was it Linley Sambourne?—had depicted him as Phaeton, standing ready on the ground while old Sir Stafford Northcote (the leader of the opposition, here depicted as Phoebus Apollo) was driving the chariot of the sun. I resented the cartoonist's analogy. But the physical image abode with me. It was the London Stereoscopic Company that first opened my eyes to the fact that Churchill and Gladstone, Northcote and Harcourt, Chamberlain, Hartington and all those others, were actual, mortal, modern men.[5]

The representations by political cartoonists and correspondents, the anecdotes of contemporaries, the memories of sons and daughters (often their father's first biographer): these build up personal pictures so familiar that historians of the 1880s need barely identify the character of the public figures who cross their path. Reggie Brett, prince of gossips, tried to show W. T. Stead how inadequate was the picture of 'the mythical Hartington:

[5] Quoted in David Cecil, *Max: A Biography* (London, 1964), pp. 16–17.

that is to say; the man who loves pleasure to the exclusion of work, who sacrifices statecraft to racing, who is *altogether* without personal ambition, whose mind turns away from long and serious contemplation of dull subjects. All this is fiction. Apart from politics he has no *real* interest in life; and cut off from them he would be in reality as bored as he appears to be by them.'[6] From Hartington's private secretary, this might carry some conviction, as well as a welcome novelty; but the mythical Hartington remains, solidly established by Bernard Holland. And political biography remains a genre seen as irrelevant by some historians, and despised as a 'voyeur's charter' by others. The worst history is written from the didactic wish to impose a 'new' interpretation; but how pleasant it would be to reverse the stereotypes, and find a mercurial Hartington, a blundering Balfour, a lightweight Salisbury, an obtuse Chamberlain. The cause, however, is doomed; public men become what they seem, and their images are now themselves part of history.

Churchill, however, somehow evades this, largely because his inconsistency was blatant and unashamed. His career has been prospected, with varying degrees of sophistication, in search of constant themes; but recent treatments of him as—for instance—an unreconstructed Tory, however intellectually attractive, cannot be sustained.[7] There is no real profit in a general thematic treatment, because there are no general themes. He makes—and unmakes—sense from day to day; his only considerable speech on general political principles was a devastating demonstration of the death of political thought in the democratic age.[8] A biography may be structured against order to show disorder, like the modern novel. Avoiding the inevitable pattern of a '*Life*' temptingly laid out in the careful arrangement of the Churchill archives raises its own problems. The pained reactions of Austen and Neville Chamberlain on reading their father's correspondence with Labouchere is evidenced in their own letters; Churchill's relations with his political friends produced a similar effect. Did Balfour really 'lose' all his letters from Churchill in the 1880s? Why is there a twenty-year

---

[6] See M. V. Brett (ed.), *Journals and Letters of Reginald Viscount Esher* (London, 1934), i, 123.

[7] See R. E. Quinault, 'The Fourth Party and the Conservative opposition to Bradlaugh', *EHR* (Apr. 1976), pp. 315–40, and 'Lord Randolph Churchill and Tory Democracy', *Hist. Jn.* (Apr. 1979), pp. 141–65.

[8] At Cambridge, 6 June 1885; see Chapter 7.

gap from 1868 to 1888 in Churchill's letters to Rosebery—though
they were always socially intimate, and often geographically
apart? Where are the majority of his letters to his political
intimates Lord Lytton, Lord Rothschild, and Sir Henry
Drummond Wolff? Lytton Strachey's comment that the history
of the Victorian age will never be written because we know too
much about it needs to be adapted for the case of politicians.

A political biography of Churchill need not necessarily retrace
the ground. Much of the personal background is now too well
known to need retelling: the marriage, the family, the anecdotes.
It is a pity to leave out some of the better stories; but they have
been told at least twice before, by books still in print. It is more
important to attempt to see him in the light of contemporary
opinion and contemporary practice, devoting as much attention
to the papers of other politicians, and to political journalism, as
to the massive and beautifully articulated archives in Churchill
College; reading his speeches in the newspapers instead of in the
form prepared by his publicist and political sidekick in 1888;
and trying to penetrate behind the great formal epic of his son's
biography, to discover the figure who always seemed to T. P.
O'Connor a character created by Balzac.[9]

To many, moreover, he seemed more at home in the pages of
a political novel. Some of his contemporaries went so far as to
put him there; like Oswald Mosley's fifty years later, his slightly
disguised figure stalks through the *romans à clef* written in the
decade he dominated. He is Rolfe Bellarmin, the young Tory-
Democrat hero of Justin McCarthy's *The Rebel Rose*,[10] a pugna-
cious debater whose ginger group holds the parliamentary
balance between Liberals and Conservatives. He is Lord
Reginald Woodstock in W. F. Rae's social comedy *An American
Duchess*,[11] an 'unclassed comet' among politicians who worries
his own party by determined and erratic independence. He
appears under his own name in the same author's *Miss Bayle's
Romance*,[12] as an inspiration to an ambitious American heiress

[9] See T. P. O'Connor, *Memories of an Old Parliamentarian* (London, 1929), i, 61–2. The
terms used, however—'that character in one of Balzac's novels who seemed to care for
nothing in the world, not for God nor man, reckless of all things except his own
devouring ambitions and his determined resolve to dominate his fellow-men'—suggest
that O'Connor might have been thinking of Stendhal's Julien Sorel.

[10] J. McCarthy and Mrs Campbell Praed, *The Rebel Rose* (3 vols., London, 1887).
McCarthy later reminded Mrs Praed of how they had taken Churchill as a model: *Our
Book of Memories* (London, 1912), p. 391.

[11] W. F. Rae, *An American Duchess* (3 vols., London, 1890).

[12] W. F. Rae, *Miss Bayle's Romance* (3 vols., London, 1887).

determined to make something of her aristocratic suitor: who obligingly follows his model by learning some politics from 'Lord Beaconsfield's novels' and standing as a Radical Tory. (Often credited with reading Disraeli's novels, Churchill only discovered them later in life; his preferred fiction, at the time of his great success, was Zola.[13]) In more directly political pieces like St. Loe Strachey's anti-Fair Trade squib *The Great Bread Riots*,[14] Churchill appears as the unnamed President of the National Labour Protection League: an opportunistic nobleman who graduates from representing a pocket borough to Birmingham Tory Democracy, and who uses radicals, Irishmen, socialists, journalists, and Jewish financiers to bring the British economy to a state of anarchy by way of populism and Protection.

Such reflections are as good a way as any to recapture a vital dimension of Churchill's contemporary impact. The fact that his decline was faster even than his rise has tended to mask the fact that his future leadership of the Tories was one of the axioms of political calculation during the 1880s. Another indication to be gleaned from the fictional portraits of him by contemporaries is the difficulty of classifying him; all his life he ruthlessly broke down barriers. When considering modes of biography, it is more tempting to treat Churchill as a psychoanalytic case-study than as a paradigm of his times, but both approaches impose unnecessary limitations. At the same time, he had a more complex psyche than has been credited; and he was, on several levels, a more representative figure than he seems. Rather than operating outside the politics of his day, he was fully integrated into them. His shamelessness about intrigue did not mean that he was the only one among his peers to operate in this way; and, in the general picture, the attempted transition from Woodstock to Birmingham as well as the contacts with figures like Hyndman have a vital importance, for Churchill is the key figure in the restabilizing of Britain by the established parties.

Churchill's political career with its comet-like trajectory also raises questions of epistemology with regard to history-writing: not only whether people meant what they said to each other at dinner-parties, but also whether what matters is what happened, or how people behaved in the light of what they

---

[13] See T. H. S. Escott, *Great Victorians* (London, 1916), p. 306. There are several references to Zola's latest novels in Churchill's letters to his wife during the 1880s.

[14] 'S.L.S.' (John St. Loe Strachey), *The Great Bread Riots, or What Became of Fair Trade* (London, 1883).

thought was going to happen. For this reason as well, he belongs in a political novel: where he could be accorded a more appropriate fate than the mundane tragedy of reality. Churchill himself did his best to behave like a character in a classical English political novel, and his career involves all the trappings of romance, opportunism, and triviality characteristic of the genre. But it is no less part of English political history for that.

Chapter 1

Family Politics, 1849–1877

'Revivals and revisions of Toryism have been tried
so often', said Thorns, 'from the Young England
movement onward'.

'Not one but has produced its enduring effects', I
said. 'It's the peculiarity of English conservatism
that it's persistently progressive and rejuvenescent.'
I think it must have been about that point that
Dayton fled our presence, after some clumsy sentence that I decided upon reflection was intended
to remind me of my duty to my party.

Then I remember Thorns firing doubts at me
obliquely across the table. 'You can't run a
country through its spoilt children', he said. 'What
you call aristocrats are really spoilt children.
They've had too much of everything, except
bracing experience.'

'Children can always be educated', said Chipp.

'I said *spoilt* children', said Thorns.

H. G. Wells, *The New Machiavelli* (1911)

I

If the most important thing about Lord Randolph Churchill's
background is that it was ducal, the second most important
thing is that it was impoverished. The seventh Duke of
Marlborough had inherited a patrimony greatly lessened by
extravagance; while his sons went on to inherit the extravagance, he devoted himself to selling off property to keep the
balance even. Security only really came with the American
marriages of succeeding generations; meanwhile the family
thought a good deal about money.

Poverty, then as now, is relative; the seventh Duke himself
had no expensive tastes except yachting but the exigencies of
his position like entertaining the Crown Prince of Germany and
the Prince of Wales and later the expenses of the Lord

Lieutenancy of Ireland, meant that during the last twenty years of his life the Blenheim estate was depleted by a steady series of sales of land, stock, and art treasures. By 1877 he was credited by *Truth* not only with letting out his St. James's Square house at exorbitant rates, but renting out his guest-list to the socially ambitious tenant as well.[1]

During the early youth of Lord Randolph, born in 1849, this was well in the future.[2] But the family lived modestly enough in a small house on the edge of Blenheim Park until his father succeeded in 1857. The seventh Duke and his wife, Frances, the eldest daughter of the third Marquess of Londonderry, had eight surviving children: Lord Randolph and his elder brother, the Marquess of Blandford, and six daughters: Cornelia, Fanny, Anne, Georgiana, Sarah, and Rosamond. They were strong-minded parents, who none the less indulged their sons as emphatically as they disciplined their daughters. The most trenchant remarks are to be found in Lady Randolph Churchill's memoirs; a more respectful picture appears in her son's life of Lord Randolph. Both sources indicate what other evidence bears out: that the family embodied a strong political tradition, on the part of both Duke and Duchess. Before his succession the Duke had been returned for Woodstock, and violently quarrelled with his brother's Liberal inclination over Church Rates when the latter succeeded him. In the Lords, he associated himself with amending the Public Worship Regulation Bill. For her part, the Duchess came from a family with a long political tradition; her mother, a great political hostess, was a close friend of Disraeli's, who came often to

---

[1] *Truth*, 16 Aug. 1877. Oxford papers catalogue a long list of visits from crowned heads in the early 1870s. As regards finance, in 1862 properties in Wiltshire and Shropshire were sold off for six-figure sums (Blenheim MSS, A/VI/32). In 1874 four square miles of Buckinghamshire were sold to Baron Ferdinand de Rothschild for £220,000; round the same time all the stock of the Blenheim home farm was auctioned off, the Duke having 'given up agricultural pursuits' (*Morning Post*, 14 Sept. 1874; also see *Oxon. Weekly Chronicle*, 26 Aug. 1874). A year later the famous family collection of cameos and intaglios, valued by the Duke at £60,000, were bought for £35,000 by Agnews' on behalf of a Mr Brownlow of Battlesden Park, Beds. (*Oxford Times*, 3 July 1879). The Sunderland Library later fetched £45,000. Churchill itemized these sales in a letter to his brother begging him not to follow the tradition by selling off paintings in 1883 (Churchill to eighth Duke, 12 Aug. 1883, Blenheim MSS F/IV/3).

[2] Ample details of Churchill's childhood will be found in W. S. Churchill, *Lord Randolph Churchill* (London, 1906; 2 vols.; hereafter cited as 'W. S. Churchill'), and are retold in R. Rhodes James, *Lord Randolph Churchill* (London, 1959; hereafter cited as 'R. R. James'). My concern in this chapter is to trace out themes which will be encountered throughout the study, rather than rehearse the story once more.

Blenheim. Here he took a warm interest in the possibilities of Lord Randolph and his friend Lord Rosebery ('a nice-looking boy who blushes')[3] and listened to appeals about the desire for ennoblement on the part of Lady Cornelia's social-climbing husband, Sir Ivor Guest. The Duchess had a powerful will and strong convictions, in politics and in Low Church religion: her son described her as 'hating Romish practices like poison'[4] (which may have been associated with the fact that both her sister Lady Portarlington and her sister-in-law Lady Londonderry were converted to Roman Catholicism). While by no means an intellectual ambience, the atmosphere at Blenheim was one where commitments were strongly felt if not deeply analysed.

The effect which this had on the later career of the second son of the house is debatable; but it certainly influenced the way in which his parents tried to direct him. His elder brother, the heir to the Dukedom, was early on characterized as a bad lot, though a talented one; Lord Randolph was from his youth the representative of his parents' hopes regarding public service. His father's letters to him as a boy show a constant effort to guide him from the self-willed path, where early indulgence had led him; they tell a long tale of disgraces, impertinence, thoughtlessness, and quarrels. 'As you get older you will find yourself, if you do not control your tongue, always quarrelling, unpopular and with few friends ... To tell you the truth I fear that you yourself are very impatient and resentful of any control; and while you stand upon some fancied right or injury, you fail to perceive what is your *duty* and allow both your language and manner a very improper scope.'[5]

Contemporaries recalled his effervescent charm, but also his aggressiveness.[6] After a fashionable prep school, he went to Eton, where he cultivated an image of slightly vulgar glamour; by contrast his friend and contemporary, Lord Dalmeny—later Rosebery—was remembered as feline and discreet. In character and, curiously, appearance Churchill was already much as he

---

[3] W. S. Churchill, i, 30. For Rosebery's blushes, see LHJ, 4 Oct. 1881, vol. 348, p. 229.

[4] Churchill to J. Jerome, 12 Dec. 1873, Blenheim MSS A/IV/11.

[5] Quoted in R. R. James, p. 23 (located in Blenheim A/IV/10). For his mother's admission of the effects of early spoiling see W. S. Churchill, i, 14–15.

[6] See for instance Lord Redesdale, *Memories* (London, 1915); J. Brinsley Richards, *Seven Years at Eton* (London, 1883), pp. 372–3; T. H. S. Escott, *Randolph Spencer-Churchill as a Product of his Age, being a Personal and Political Monograph* (London, 1895; hereafter 'Escott'), chapter 2.

would remain for most of his short life. Of normal height, his thinness, restlessness, and prominent, rather hypnotic, eyes would always lay him open to description as a 'schoolboy'; infectious laughter and appalling rudeness compounded the image. The vein of rather theatrical seriousness noted by several boyhood friends may have indicated depths to be plumbed, but it should be remembered that all his life he loved embarrassing people by unexpected behaviour. Capable of changing from blandishing charm to withering abuse, the problem of self-control emphasized by his father was a permanent feature; so was a mental facility to which the word 'genius' was often, if cautiously, applied in later life, but which only manifested itself in erratic bouts of activity, often after long periods of indolence. It is probable that he exaggerated his own ignorance. Stories like Irving's about Churchill discovering Shakespeare—to his own amazement—by a chance visit to a play, and reading *Hamlet* to find out how it ended, are probably apocryphal. But in later life avuncular political friends (with whom he got on better than with his contemporaries) tended to treasure him as a kind of marvellous savage. 'Of course he isn't educated,' said Harcourt to someone who made the point; 'if he were educated he'd be spoiled.'

Not particularly popular at school, he was frequently in trouble and was threatened by his father with removal. Eton was at the time undergoing a period of educational reform, but Churchill's teachers saw little academic potential in him. Lord Randolph himself, as one of them ruefully wrote to his father, was 'rather disposed to set a high estimate on his own powers',[7] and wanted to go to Balliol: however, he failed entrance in 1867 and went to a crammer's near Aylesbury. The tutor, Revd. Lionel Dawson-Damer, was a first cousin of Churchill's uncle, Lord Portarlington's, and travelled abroad with his pupil for two months before the latter's entry into Merton in 1868. (Later he graduated to a living at Wimborne, probably through the good offices of Churchill's brother-in-law, Sir Ivor Guest.) Oxford seems to have been at most an incidental involvement; he spent much of his time at home, passionately hunting. His reading was erratic, and even his son, who loyally claimed the maximum intellectual interest on Lord Randolph's behalf, can only itemize the Bible, Gibbon, and Jorrocks. His interest in

---

[7] Revd. Lionel Damer to Duchess of Marlborough, 19 Mar. 1867 (Blenheim MSS A/IV/9).

chess was celebrated, and his ability evident; but the Myr-
midons dining-club and well-publicized drinking episodes were
more characteristic of his sojourn at Merton. An ability to 'get
up' necessary knowledge at short notice always distinguished
him, however, and a spurt of hard work before his finals in
December 1870 secured him a high second; his tutor, Mandell
Creighton, felt that he could have done even better. (The still
grateful Damer told the Duchess that his second was 'as good as a
first', and suggested that Churchill become a professional historian
and complete the sorting-out of the Record Office.)[8] He then set
off round Europe for nearly a year, a period for which few
records survive. Though he spent some time at Ischl in Austria,
and found the Franco-Prussian war of absorbing interest, his son
summed it up as 'enlarging his fancy and extending education in
various directions beyond the limits of a university curriculum'.

Despite this broadening of horizons, however, Churchill's
interest remained centred on Blenheim and the local town of
Woodstock—as they had done throughout his Oxford career. In
order to work for his finals he had abandoned his celebrated
pack of Harriers, which he credited with giving him 'an interest
and occupation in the county which before I did not possess';
but he remained active in the local Horticultural and
Agricultural Society, of which he became president in 1873, and
he was much involved in the local branch of the Ancient Order of
Foresters, becoming president in 1880. The annual agricultural
show at Woodstock in September owed its existence to the
Duke's patronage; and it was at one such meeting that Churchill
was to make his first controversial speech in 1877. When MP for
the borough he also involved himself in causes like the restoration of Woodstock church; but he had always kept up local
interests, in a dutiful fashion.[9]

Similarly, he sat on the local bench of magistrates from an
early age, though not in a very authoritative way. 'I have been
doing magistrate most of this afternoon in Woodstock,' he wrote
to his fiancée in 1873. 'I daresay you would have laughed if you
had seen me looking very grave and precious wise, really
knowing very little, but fortunately we have a clever lawyer who

[8] Creighton and Damer to Duchess, 14 Nov. and 17 Dec. 1870, Blenheim MSS
A/IV/9.
[9] See many references in 'Woodstock' column of *Oxford Times* (e.g. 30 May 1874, 11
July 1874, 20 Dec. 1874).

keeps us straight. Don't repeat this.'[10] He wrote similar complaining notes about attendance at meetings to do with the town's sanitation and church affairs. By the time he sat for what was in effect the family borough at the general election of 1874, he had done enough to qualify as a local notable with a sense of public duty.

This was more of an achievement than it may seem, for it involved living down a much publicized incident of his Oxford career, dismissed by both his biographers in a sentence, but which set up considerable local reverberations. It began in a characteristic way, with Churchill featuring at a drunken undergraduates' dinner at the Randolph Hotel, Oxford, on 4 March 1870. As they left they encountered two policemen, one of whom was aggressively shoved and harassed by Churchill, and had his helmet stolen in the process. After an altercation Churchill offered the policeman, named Partridge, some money. The affair ended up in court on 15 March, where Churchill conducted his own defence; he was fined 10*s*. for assault, and acquitted of being drunk and disorderly.

Churchill, however, against the wishes of the university, who begged his father to make him withdraw, brought a counter-case against Constable Partridge for perjury. In this case he claimed that he had not attacked the policeman, had not offered Partridge money, and was not drunk (though he admitted a bottle of wine a head had been consumed at the dinner, with much jumping over chairs and breaking of glasses). The evidence of Churchill's friends and companions was directly in conflict with that of the policemen over the disputed points; the balance was tipped by the evidence of Alfred Wren, a waiter at the Randolph, who itemized the large quantity of champagne, hock, sherry, claret, port, and punch consumed and described Churchill spilling wine and threatening him with a wine-cooler. Eventually after five hours' deliberation the charges of perjury against Partridge were dismissed, the judges getting around the question of conflicting evidence by deciding it was a case of mistaken identity.[11]

---

[10] Churchill to J. Jerome, 30 Sept. 1873, CHAR 28/2. Other letters in this series show a regular attendance on the bench throughout this winter.

[11] See first leader, *Oxford Chronicle*, 2 Apr. 1870; *Oxford Times*, 26 Mar., 2 Apr., 30 Apr. 1870. Also see R. Hawkins to Duke, 19 Mar. 1870 (Blenheim A/IV/9): Hawkins affirmed that Churchill and his companions were certainly drunk, and that the case should be let lie, but the Duke refused to withdraw.

By this time the case had received widespread publicity, in *The Times*, the *Daily Telegraph*, and the *Daily News* as well as the local newspapers. Besides furnishing a classic town-and-gown issue, with local opinion ostentatiously on the side of the much maligned police, the Duke's position as local seigneur added piquancy to the whole affair. But worse was to follow. The evidence of the waiter, Alfred Wren, which had been unquestioned, was decisive; and shortly after the trial, he was summarily dismissed from the hotel. The *Oxford Times* carried the story that this was due to Churchill, who had informed the manager that he refused to patronize the Randolph further as long as Wren's services were retained. The story went uncontradicted; Wren became a local martyr, and was at once offered several situations by sympathizers. The Marlborough interest was roundly accused of perverting local justice by the *Oxford Times*, always ready to attack what it saw as sycophantic deference to the ducal authority.[12] The *Oxford Chronicle*, usually more sympathetic, also took up Wren's case, and angrily attacked Churchill in a leading article.

It was at this point that a public dinner was given to Churchill by his sporting acquaintances in Woodstock. It had the official *raison d'être* of the disbandment of his Blenheim Harriers; he had also come of age two months before. But it seems likely to have been also intended as a gesture of solidarity. The *Oxford Times* cynically remarked that no representative of the paper was invited to the proceedings. But the *Chronicle* was, and obliged with an adulatory and slightly defensive editorial:

Lord Randolph Churchill has made his appearance in a character in which he is well fitted to shine. The friends and neighbours who admire him as a country gentleman and sportsman, and who have participated with him in the pleasures of the chase, have adopted the English method of showing the estimation in which he is held by them, by inviting him to a public dinner ... It was perfectly natural that sportsmen should desire to testify in some shape their appreciation of the manly character of their leader, and if a public dinner has none of the charms of novelty to recommend it it is, at least, as appropriate as any other, and it has the further advantage of affording a fitting opportunity for the interchange of kindly feelings and mutual respect. Lord Randolph's speech upon the occasion was a model of good

---

[12] See for instance attacks on the Duke for his meanness over refusing land for a schoolhouse, *Oxford Times*, 26 Mar. 1870; his lack of patronage of Woodstock trade, ibid., 3 Dec. 1870; his attitude towards the local inhabitants, ibid., 4 Dec. 1869.

sense, and shows that he possesses in a high degree those qualities which Englishmen in general, and the British farmer in particular, most admire in those who, from their talents and social position, are likely to exercise great influence in their day and generation.[13]

All was more or less well that ended well; in a mode very different from the dinner at the Randolph six weeks before, the guest of honour made a graceful and humble speech, paying compliments to those who had helped with the Harriers, declaring his commitment to Oxfordshire, and confessing that the future now seemed 'rather a blank'. But as most of the company must have known the blank was to be filled, in the natural order of things, by his eventual return for the borough of Woodstock.

II

The intervening years, from 1870 to 1874, were passed in travel and society. In this Churchill's way was paved by his elder brother, Lord Blandford, with whom he sustained a close relationship marked by violent altercations. Blandford had early on adopted with relish the persona of a depraved rakehell; after his early death the memoirs of his contemporaries apostrophized him in a very gingerly fashion, as someone with a liking for 'eclectic' company who might possibly have gone very far.[14] A less respectful authority, who had evidently suffered from what he described as the 'hereditary rudeness' of both brothers, described Blandford as 'a company-promoter *manqué*'. He was erratically interested in politics, especially foreign affairs; foreign politicians and financiers provided his favourite company. He had stood for parliament, and was more inclined towards Liberalism than anything else; in 1885 he was rumoured to be considering running an opponent against Lord Randolph at Woodstock. However, the brothers were close friends (though Blandford's solicitous visits to his brother's fiancée in Paris had worried Churchill greatly), and they shared many similarities. There is a friendly tone even in the correspondence which led to

---

[13] *Oxford Chronicle*, 30 Apr. 1870.

[14] See for instance Lord Redesdale, *Memories*, ii, 685; Brinsley Richards, *Seven years at Eton*; J. O. Field, *Uncensored Recollections* (London, 1924). Churchill himself told William Grantham that Blandford 'would have risen to the highest position in public life if he had been in any way controlled by his father and that from childhood he had always been allowed to have his own way' (Grantham to W. S. Churchill, 20 Feb. 1902, CHAR 8/24).

the worst difference between them, arising from Blandford's sale of the great Blenheim art collection when he succeeded in 1883. When Churchill told him that the paintings were a public trust Blandford replied silkily: 'I look to your conservative teaching, my dear R, to open to me a vista of careful undertakings and an area of cultivated thought'; but he sold the collection all the same.[15]

Churchill's sisters were less closely connected to him. Several of them also followed Liberal politics; in 1883 Fanny married Edward Marjoribanks, later Lord Tweedmouth, a friend of Lord Randolph's from Eton and Oxford, and a pillar of the Liberal establishment. Lady Fanny became an influential Liberal hostess, and the couple remained close friends of Churchill's; his private correspondence records only one serious quarrel with them, whereas he was rarely on speaking terms with his sister Cornelia and her husband, Sir Ivor Guest: later Lord Wimborne, and also eventually destined for the Liberal party. Guest, a famous social-climber and snob known as 'the paying Guest', was credited with pressing hard for a peerage from 1876; Disraeli, approached by the Marlboroughs on his behalf, could only ask 'what has he done?'[16] When Blandford and Lord Randolph quarrelled with the Court, the Guests immediately and unequivocally took the other side, which created a lasting rift. Of Churchill's other sisters, Anne married his friend the Marquis of Bowmont and became Duchess of Roxburghe; Georgiana married George Curzon, later Earl Howe (not to be confused with the more famous George Nathaniel Curzon), who became a political follower of Lord Randolph's in the latter's decline; Rosamond, the youngest, was close to him, but made a marriage of which he disapproved; Sarah is rarely mentioned until later in his life.

Generally speaking, Churchill's attachment to his parents was deep, but it alternated with violent denunciations of them. This was of a piece with the manic swings of mood characteristic of him from his youth, and remarked on with some trepidation by

---

[15] 14 Aug. 1883, Blenheim MSS, F/IV/3. Churchill stressed the 'howl of execration' that would arise and described the pictures as a trust 'to be used as the Irish Church Surplus, only for the relief of "unavoidable calamity and distress"' (12 Aug. 1883).

[16] Though he added courteously that 'nothing would give me greater pleasure than to place a coronet on the brow of dear Cornelia' (Julia Cartwright (ed.), *Journals of Lady Knightley of Fawsley 1856–1884* (London, 1916), p. 365). Guest's social ambitions are frequently lampooned in *Truth* and *Vanity Fair* in the 1870s.

his fiancée. The best analysis of his character, to be found in Rosebery's thoughtful short study of him, emphasizes this aspect too, as well as his oscillations between gregariousness and solitude, frivolity and pompousness.[17] Characteristically, Rosebery believed this was due to Churchill's habitual practice of irony on a baroque level; the border of self-deception was occasionally crossed. A later generation may infer a more deeply rooted cause. When carefree, he remained ostentatiously so; 'schoolboy' is an image used by practically everyone who has ever written about him. But he was already characterized by ill health and neurosis; his reactions to his background at once were dutiful and rebellious, personally and politically. Nor was that background as secure as it seemed. In this context, his famous and hasty engagement to a vivacious American beauty after a three-day courtship in 1873 is less surprising than it may seem.[18] Jennie Jerome, the nineteen-year-old daughter of a prominent New York entrepreneur, was high-spirited, formidably charming, and more or less dedicated to a life of frivolity. Churchill was credited by some contemporary opinion with having married for money, but this seems unlikely; though Leonard Jerome had been extremely wealthy, he had just lost most of his money in the 1873 crash. Churchill, who made his own enquiries about Jerome's money, certainly emphasized his prospective father-in-law's fortune when attempting to win round his own hostile family, but after sounding out New York contacts about the extent of Jerome's holdings they were unimpressed.[19] Probably more potent was Churchill's argument that marriage would be a chance to escape from the 'idle and

[17] Lord Rosebery, *Lord Randolph Churchill* (London, 1906); also Escott, pp. 72–3: 'no man is so entirely alone and solitary as I am'. This probably reflected the decline of his marriage but he was always prone to severe depression.

[18] The events of this affair have been endlessly rehearsed. See R. R. James, pp. 34–9; Peregrine Churchill and Julian Mitchell, *Jennie, Lady Randolph Churchill: a Portrait with Letters* (London, 1974), ch. 1; Mrs G. Cornwallis-West, *The Reminiscences of Lady Randolph Churchill* (London, 1908), p. 32; W. S. Churchill, i, 43–9. A document by Lady Randolph called 'Early Recollections', in the Blenheim Archives (A/IV/11) is indispensable but not always accurate. The long series of letters between the engaged couple in the Chartwell Trust provide a detailed account. R. S. Churchill, *Winston S. Churchill*, vol. i: *Youth, 1874–1900* is the fullest version. See *Uncensored Recollections*, p. 299; also a rumour in the *Court Journal* about Miss Jerome's 'splendid dower'.

[19] See H. Paule to Churchill, Sept. 1877, regarding Jerome's fortune (Blenheim A/IV/6), and Churchill to his father in W. S. Churchill, i, 40–1: 'He is reputed to be very well off and his daughters, I believe, have very good fortunes...' Also see detailed reports obtained by Francis Knollys, a Churchill family friend and equerry to the Prince of Wales, in Blenheim A/IV/1.

comparatively useless life' into which he had been drifting. (For their part, the Jeromes were informed that Churchill drank too much and kept fast company.[20]) Money, however, dominated the troubled course of the marriage negotiations. Churchill at one point, backed by the Duke, told his future father-in-law that unless all the dowry capital came to him in the event of his wife dying childless, 'all business between us was perfectly impossible and he could do what he liked with his beastly money'. The eventual settlement involved £50,000 of capital, in various government and railway stocks, and a mortgage on a large landed estate, worth $300,000, yielding £2,000 a year to Lord Randolph and his wife. The Duke, who sold all his Buckinghamshire property this year and was rumoured 'quite ruined', added £1,100 a year; this came out of £20,000 in settlement, less the amount needed to pay Lord Randolph's debts.[21] The couple were eventually married at the British Embassy on 15 April 1874, the Duke and Duchess, though giving their blessing, being conspicuously absent. At the end of May they received an 'enthusiastic reception' at Woodstock. By then, moreover, the newly married son of the Palace was also MP for the local borough.

His marriage may have had something to do with this development. Lady Randolph appears strong-minded as well as charming, at this stage of her life; but essentially both were to grow up after their passionate marriage, and after ten years they took to living separate lives. During their engagement, however, she attacked him for saying he would enjoy 'a peaceful happy life with no particular occupation'. 'I should like you to be as ambitious as you are clever, and I am sure you would accomplish great things.'[22] On another tack, Churchill had threatened

---

[20] See undated letters from Churchill to Jennie Jerome, Blenheim A/IV/11, strenuously denying this; also J. Jerome to Churchill, 4 Nov. 1873 (CHAR 28/92). Jerome however eventually decided 'it is magnificent—the greatest match any American has made since the Dutchess of Leeds [*sic*]': Churchill and Mitchell, p. 68. Churchill's bad temper and rudeness provided more tangible fears than intemperance, as far as his fiancée was concerned. Both of these faults he admitted: 'In my short life I have already made a great many enemies, I am afraid, for I never cared to be civil to anybody I did not like' (Churchill to J. Jerome, 24 Oct. 1873, CHAR 28/41).

[21] See settlement in Blenheim A/IV/4; and draft in CHAR 28/94. Also R. R. James, who however says the American money yielded £3,000 p.a. For rumours of ruin, Churchill to J. Jerome, 'Nov. 1874', CHAR 28/4 (loftily denying them). Churchill's correspondence with his father (Blenheim F/IV) shows him promising economy and expecting frequent remittances from his father-in-law.

[22] J. Jerome to Churchill, 26 Sept. 1873, CHAR 28/92. The refrain was repeated in several letters.

to use his refusal to stand for Woodstock as a bargaining counter in the struggles with his parents over his marriage. He had been destined for what was, as he told his fiancée, a 'family borough' since leaving Oxford. The Duke's influence over the parliamentary fortunes of Woodstock was necessarily covert, but no less decisive for that. Liberals who had the temerity to contest it generally used the issue of emancipation from thraldom to Blenheim; the previous member, Henry Barnett, pointed out to the Duke in 1864 that it was therefore most politic for the candidate to do as much as he could with local interest 'on my own hook, and your influence will then come in conclusively to settle the matter'.[23] The correspondence between the Duke and his erring brother, Lord Alfred, shows a strong assumption on both sides of proprietorial right. The Ballot Act intervened before Lord Randolph's return, but it is not likely that it would have made a great difference.

The Duke's influence did not absolutely guarantee a return; if Lord Alfred had defiantly stood in 1864, Barnett expected a stiff contest. But this was because of his own connections with Woodstock; no other Liberal candidate was thought to have a chance. None the less, when the time came in late 1873 for the Duke's son to be groomed for the take-over, his return was expected, despite his ignorance and awkwardness as a candidate. But a dimension of uncertainty was added by the fact that in 1868 the Liberals had run George Brodrick, a brother of the Earl of Midleton and a fellow of Merton College; and he had lost to Barnett by the narrow margin of twenty-one votes. Brodrick, by his own account, campaigned on a broad political platform and studiously avoided 'exciting local animosities against Blenheim Palace',[24] but had become embroiled in a public correspondence with the Duke over alleged coercion of votes by his agent: a controversy in which Lord Randolph briefly involved himself at Merton. In a future election, Brodrick was considered a likely Liberal candidate.

From September 1873, Churchill was presented to his future constituency at suitable junctures like the Agricultural Society dinner, and dutifully described such affairs to his fiancée:

[The newspapers] have cut my speeches rather short, but they were nothing very brilliant as I could not really give my mind to it, or think

---

[23] See Barnett to seventh Duke, 24 Sept. 1864 (Blenheim F/IV/7). Barnett was a well-known London banker.

[24] See G. C. Brodrick, *Memories and Impressions* (London, 1900), p. 151.

much of what I was going to say ... I secured two or three waverers
and conciliated some enemies against the next election ... I think it is
extremely probable that we may have a dissolution of Parliament
before the close of the year. I am quietly doing 'tout mon possible' to
prevent a contest; it has always been contested, as the present member
for Woodstock is a very unpopular man, but I hope from my having
lived here so long now and knowing many of both sides very
intimately and belonging to a family so closely connected with the
borough, that things may pass off quite quietly ... Perhaps your
parents would have a higher opinion of me if I was a member of
Parliament. But however, I never could go in for anything of that
kind now unless I had you to keep me up to the mark and to take an
interest in the thing and encourage me ... But after all a public life has
not great charms for me, as I am naturally very quiet and hate bother
and publicity.[25]

It was at this time that Churchill threatened not to stand at all,
if the Duke insisted upon a year's engagement before his
marriage. When this manoeuvre was executed, he set himself to
persuading Barnett to retire: both by direct appeals, and by
pressure through Hawkins, the local agent. Barnett was pledged
to retire at the next general election, but Churchill feared that
Brodrick might contest the seat again, supported by the
Agricultural Labourers' movement. For the moment, however,
Brodrick was in America, and so was Joseph Arch. 'So perhaps
Mr Barnett may be induced to retire on the grounds that it
would be good for the Conservative Party in the borough.'[26]

But Mr Barnett was not. And as he waited, Churchill kept up
with current politics, as the political tide set against the Liberal
ministry. His opinions, as reflected in his correspondence, were
nothing very unexpected. A speech of Bright's at Birmingham
'did not amuse or edify me much for a more radical communistic
oration I never read, and it nearly made me sick'. Barnett's
eventual refusal to stand down before a general election made
him 'feel rather anxious... it is impossible in these radical days
to feel much confidence in the working classes with the ballot'.
Miss Jerome must read Lord Salisbury on 'the Programme of the
Radicals' in the *Quarterly Review*, which 'will give you in a few
pages a clear insight into parties in this country and will also tell
you what party and policy your Randolph is prepared consistently tooth and nail to oppose'. The constant theme of this

[25] Churchill to J. Jerome, 19 and 22 Sept. 1873, CHAR 28/2.
[26] Same to same, 27 Oct. 1873, ibid.

correspondence is the probable date of the next election, but more because of its connections with their marriage date than for its intrinsic interest. Meanwhile, Churchill paved the way by using his family contacts in political high society; on a visit to Blenheim in December with the Prince of Wales, Disraeli was prevailed upon to tour the local glove factory and the schools with Churchill. 'He was very goodnatured and did not mind it a bit; and it is sure to have a good effect.'[27]

In January 1874 the long-awaited election was suddenly announced, stopping Lord Randolph *en route* to Paris after a protracted attendance at his Aunt Portarlington's deathbed in Ireland. Barnett, not entirely willingly, stood down, leaving the Conservative candidature to Churchill. Some preliminary canvassing at the coursing meeting 'which my father allowed in the Park' was predictably encouraging; but the next day Brodrick arrived in Woodstock to press his candidature, and the contest began. Brodrick was a strong candidate, already being solicited to stand for Evesham. When he chose Woodstock instead, he was adopted by the Agricultural Labourers' Union: whose support, he later felt, probably lost him more votes than it gained. He also felt that the Marlborough influence gave Lord Randolph, who 'relied almost entirely on personal influence', a great advantage. (Brodrick, who knew Churchill from Merton days, paid tribute to his audacious qualities later in life, but decided early on that 'he had that in him which in a horse would be "vice"'.[28])

Churchill's campaign was managed on the domestic front by the hitherto recalcitrant Barnett, the local solicitor Hawkins, local contacts like his intimate Colonel Thomas, society friends like Strange Jocelyn, and the egregious Blandford, whose presence on the hustings may have hindered as much as it helped; his sisters Rosamond and Anne helped canvass the outlying villages on horseback. With this ostentatiously seignorial campaign, it is not surprising that when approached by the Duke the central party organization decided to send down a more modern-minded auxiliary from London. The man chosen was Edward Clarke, one of a circle of young lawyers who in the previous decade had been influenced by Disraeli's writings and

---

[27] Same to same, 23, 24, 26 Oct. 1873, ibid., and 13 Dec. 1873 (28/3).

[28] Brodrick, op. cit., p. 153. Also, for a letter from Brodrick denying that he had ever made wild promises to agricultural labourers and drawing attention to the pocket nature of the borough, see *The Times*, 23 Oct. 1885.

the idea of a revamped Conservatism, which was put into practice through the local Conservative Associations. Others were John Eldon Gorst and Henry Cecil Raikes as well as less well-known names; the *Imperial Review* propagated their ideas, and the National Union represented their strategy, taking as their theme Disraeli's statement that 'none are so interested in maintaining the institutions of the country as the working classes'.[29] Clarke had already set himself to supplying the brains for Tory candidates like Marcus Beresford; he was in 1874 in the position of a professional election-speaker, waiting for the right seat. He had, moreover, just quarrelled with his colleagues in Lambeth, and was free to support Churchill's campaign at Woodstock.

On Clarke's arrival at Woodstock, Barnett met him, explained the general situation, and introduced him to about thirty of Churchill's supporters, who had determined not to have a public meeting due to their candidate's inexperience. Only at Clarke's vehement insistence did they agree. He returned to Woodstock two days later and met Churchill, 'a nervous, rather awkward young man, who certainly seemed to have the most elementary ideas about current politics'.

Brodrick's address, for all his later disclaimers, was directed unequivocally at the agricultural labourers. Their wages must be raised; game laws must be revoked; household suffrage should be introduced in the counties. He added that he was 'no advocate of socialistic measures, nor will I be party to an agitation whereby class may be set against class'; but reminded his prospective constituents that 'under the Ballot your votes are your own'. The *Oxford Times* saw this as a 'brilliant address', epitomizing the fact that the struggle in contemporary politics was no longer between the landed interest and the commercial interest, but 'between labour and capital, church and secularism, indulgence and temperance ... the new, reforming, pragmatical world and the old, stolid, easygoing world'. Churchill's address was 'bald and meagre', issuing too obviously from the Palace and reliant upon expectations of an outmoded deference; 'certain reminiscences not unconnected with the "Randolph Hotel"' were also instanced, though in an ostensibly friendly way. His majorities were expected to be in Woodstock itself and

---

[29] Clarke mentions W. T. Charnley, A. G. Martin, W. C. Henry, Leonard Sedgewick (*The Story of My Life* (London, 1918), p. 97) as being part of the movement.

the village of Kidlington; other hamlets were supposedly opposed to the Blenheim interest. Brodrick was supported by Joseph Arch on his platforms; and also by Godden, the radical glove-manufacturer of Woodstock, whose work-force was a notably independent-minded element. Godden chaired Brodrick's preliminary meeting, and fulminated against the practice of 'sending young noblemen to the House of Commons to learn the routine of political affairs'; Brodrick himself attacked the snobbery and social climbing characteristic of deferential county politics. Organizational support came from the young H. H. Asquith, a volunteer from Oxford; the university also supplied the aid of Goldwin Smith, who implicitly rebuked Churchill and his supporters for their arrogant attitude 'to those beneath them'.[30]

Goldwin Smith also referred slightingly to Churchill's public address: 'they then had an opportunity of judging if he had applied his mind to the great political questions, whether he had studied them, whether he was ripe in judgement or experience, and whether he was fit to take part in the great council of the nation'. Certainly, a judgement based on his performance could not have been very favourable. Clarke had coached him in the subjects to cover, and had planted friendly questions in the audience; however, Churchill's attempts to read from notes concealed in his hat nearly sabotaged the effect. The speech as delivered emphasized local issues, made some gestures towards the agricultural labourers, and attacked 'infidel rationalism'. But Clarke rescued the proceedings by a more decisive speech, to which Churchill later generously attributed the majority of his votes; he also drafted Churchill's short speech before sending it to the national papers. If the candidate's speech had been unenterprising, so was his election address; it desired to ameliorate the condition of the working class, attacked extreme reformers, opposed Disestablishment, promised support for undefined reforms of local taxation, and generally called for gradual and cautious reform within the limits of measures already passed. Without Clarke's insistence on a public meeting, it is probable that the aura of patronage surrounding Churchill would have acted positively against him. As it was, however,

---

[30] See *Oxford Times*, 31 Jan. 1874, for Brodrick's address and the accompanying judgements and *Oxon. Weekly News*, 19 Aug. 1874, for a long report of Joseph Arch's appearance at Oxford on 18 August, along with Thorold Rogers and Godden of Woodstock.

neither radical glovers, agricultural labourers, nor Liberal intellectuals prevailed against the ducal interest. Churchill won by 569 votes to 404.

The result disappointed those who had been expecting the Ballot Act to make a decisive change; some Liberals threatened a petition, repeating the old changes of coercion against the Duke's agent. The candidate himself seems to have felt some surprise at the outcome. He wrote to his fiancée, who had been urging him to succeed and damning 'those abominable radicals', that the excitement and uncertainty of it all had 'made me quite ill ... one's brain gets quite addled'. The day after the victory he went into Oxford to meet his father and on their return to Woodstock, a crowd took the horses out of the carriage and drew them through the town. 'There was nothing more to be done except pay the bill, which I left my father to do. I was very glad to get away, as the place had got on my nerves, and altogether I wanted change of scene.'[31]

III

If an injection of the energy of modern Conservatism had helped return Lord Randolph to Westminster, his early years there were none the less those of an archetypical Junior Carlton drone. Not even those most anxious to trace a coherent pattern of development behind the eventual image of insouciant young tribune have tried to claim anything else. If he and his wife were remarkable for anything in the first three years of his parliamentary career, it was for a life-style of conspicuous and frivolous consumption; and this, given their circumstances, was not remarkable. But their income was not adapted to society life, and ruinously heavy betting at Newmarket; by January 1876 Churchill was raising a £5,000 loan, 'the last we can make on our present resources'.[32] He was, in this as in much else, a figure of the times.

Against the background of the mid-1870s, the parliamentary Tory party appeared even more than before the defenders of

---

[31] J. Jerome to Churchill, n.d., CHAR 28/94, and replies of 1 and 5 Feb., CHAR 28/4.
[32] Churchill to J. Jerome, 20 Jan. 1876, CHAR 28/5. His correspondence the previous autumn records bets of £50 a time at Newmarket, and wins of up to £500 on a single race; his losses are not detailed. Another large loan was raised the following year; delays in payment of the income from his wife's settlement invariably created financial crises.

property and the status quo: there was a general, muted acceptance that this underlay the war-cries of principle, and the platforms of many successful candidates, including that of the member for Woodstock, had been built upon the foundation that change had gone far enough.[33] Some gloomy opinion felt that, while both parties had come to profess the same creed, the workers had hardened into a race apart, who had taken to Republicanism and given up all optimistic expectations of their betters. But at the same time, a rueful Joseph Chamberlain admitted in October 1874 that Conservative working-men had won the election for the Tories. This hinted at a certain ambivalence: and *The Economist* in 1875 had discerned 'three kinds of Conservatism'. There may well have been more: at least one of which called itself Liberalism. But as early as 1879 the same authority decided that 'Tory Democracy' was the kind 'now in the ascendant'.[34] Certainly, the distrust of the Hatfield connection for Disraeli continued; but Salisbury was shortly seen as selling out right-wing Toryism to Disraelian compromise. There had been attempts at Conservative *rapprochement* with labour interests throughout the early 1870s, through Trade Unions and the New Social Movement. Some opinion referred to 'contemporary moralising on the premature extinction of the Young England Party';[35] and charade though that had been, its potential constituency remained.

As regarded the great parties, the general obsession of 1874 was with their similarity: editorial after editorial in the periodicals analysed the nature of the divide between them, and found it at many points almost non-existent, though the post-1867 dispensation enjoined highly coloured contrasts in public. It was at this time that Lord Lytton, encountering Sir William Harcourt at Lord Ripon's, was 'impressed with the cynical lightheartedness revealed in the conversation of those whom he had hitherto looked upon as serious politicians. The time

[33] Cf. a leader in *Vanity Fair*, 26 Dec. 1874: 'Persons are apt to call Mr Disraeli insincere, which he is, and thence to draw the conclusion that he is therefore unfit to lead the Tory party—which he is not. Modern Toryism is itself insincere, and a man who seriously professed to principle could not sit on the Treasury Bench for three weeks ... The one article of belief with Conservatives is Property—Religion, Education and the British Constitution being nothing but useful war-cries.'

[34] See *Morning Post*, 23 Oct. 1874; *Economist*, 15 Jan. 1875; Feuchtwanger, op. cit., p. 21.

[35] *Pall Mall Gazette*, 27 Feb. 1874.

previous to the meeting was spent in ridiculing the fine things they intended to utter from the platform, after the meeting in laughing still more heartily at the fine things that *had* been uttered'.[36] Abroad, the preoccupation of Conservative opinion was as much with the growth of Socialism in Germany and elsewhere as with the extent of Russian ambitions in foreign policy; to the more thinking politicians of the party, this indicated the need for a new departure regarding the working class. Lord Randolph Churchill was not among the thinking politicians of his party; he operated at the level of 'society' so obsessively reported and analysed in the daily press. And yet even a columnist in *Vanity Fair* felt constrained in the London of 1874 to draw attention to the contrast between those dining on strawberries on a Greenwich terrace, and the naked urchins diving for coppers below; or between the simultaneous reports of a royal banquet for the Duchess of Edinburgh and a death from starvation in the East End.

Churchill certainly would have seen no reason to fix his attention further than the diners. He lived in a Mayfair house paid for by his father-in-law; his mother gave large receptions in St. James's Square.[37] His letters to his wife record an ingenuous reaction to the new world of politics, suitable for his twenty-five years. His prime impression of his first day at the House came on his way into St. Stephen's: 'I heard one of the lower orders, who were there in crowds, say "there is a rum specimen", evidently alluding to me. I was so angry and should like to have been an Ashantee king for the moment and executed him summarily.' Once inside, he found Henry Chaplin 'a very good speaker', though he was to spend most of his later career vituperatively attacking him in private. 'I am sure the House of Commons will be very pleasant', he summed up, adding inaccurately, 'I was quite delighted to find myself there at last; I have always longed for it so much, I can hardly realise it.'[38]

Nor were his opinions any more unexpected; even his

[36] Lady Betty Balfour, *Personal and Literary Letters of Lord Lytton* (London, 1898), i, 315. For further remarks, besides *The Economist* references, see *Pall Mall Gazette*, 24 Nov. 1874, 11 Aug. 1877, and *Edinburgh Review*, Apr. 1874.

[37] Faithfully itemized by the *Morning Post*; see also *Journals of Lady Knightley of Fawsley*, p. 259, which records 'a great squash' at the Duchess's on 18 May 1874. Other large receptions at the Marlboroughs' house in St. James's Square are described in the *Morning Post*, 28 June, 6 July 1876, 8 July 1876.

[38] Churchill to J. Jerome, 5 and 6 Mar. 1874, CHAR 28/4.

Marjoribanks relatives were described as 'radical', and Disraeli denounced for 'wishing to toady the radicals'. The first issue upon which he spoke showed a similarly predictable approach. It concerned the attempt to make Oxford a territorial military centre, a part of Cardwell's 1872 reform outline which Salisbury and Auberon Herbert had already tried to block. Beresford Hope's revival of the motion on 22 May 1874 occasioned Churchill's maiden speech. This was an attack upon the idea of perverting Oxford's student population by the addition of 'roistering soldiers and licentious camp followers', not to mention 'railway roughs and navvies'. The city might welcome such elements; but the city was traditionally hostile to the university's interests. And, unlike Dublin or Edinburgh, the behaviour of the locality did not require such an establishment.

Harcourt replied as Liberal member for Oxford in a friendly way: pointing out that a Churchill should not condemn soldiery, and that his other strictures smacked of class bias. The Lord Mayor of Dublin complained of the references to his native city. Disraeli wrote a characteristic letter to the Duchess praising the speech, and also drew attention to its impressive audacity in his nightly letter to the Queen; the Duchess's reply feared for her son's indiscretion and lack of moderation. In Oxford, university opinion saw it as 'foolish' and recalled, inaccurately, that Churchill himself had been sent down for 'roystering'. And middle-class opinion in the town, as reflected in Churchill's old enemy the *Oxford Times*, was outraged, which probably pleased him most of all; the bad taste and offensiveness of the member for Woodstock's maiden speech was deeply deplored.[39] This was probably the kind of effect Churchill wished to make, and he rested content. His wife described his attendance at this time as 'perfunctory' and in early 1875 he raised only a couple of minor questions, and (inaccurately) contradicted a critical reference by O'Connor Power to the first Duke of Marlborough. Perhaps his most symbolic intervention at Westminster was the question raised by him in May 1876: 'whether the attention of the Commissioner of Works had recently been called to the hard and dusty condition of Rotten-Row, and whether he contemplated

---

[39] *Hansard 3*, ccxix, 713–15; Duchess of Marlborough to Disraeli, 23 May 1874, Disraeli MSS B/xx/93; Earl of Midleton, *Records and Reactions, 1856–1939* (London, 1939). Also *Oxford Times* and *Oxford Chronicle*, 30 May 1874.

taking any steps towards rendering Rotten-Row more suitable to horses and their riders'.[40]

The only other speech of Churchill's that attracted attention was a set-piece debate with the rising Radical star, Sir Charles Dilke, over unreformed corporations, a year earlier, with special reference to Woodstock. Dilke had alerted him to this in advance, and the exchange was in the nature of a public display, for general amusement, to which Churchill brought his friend the Prince of Wales. Churchill's light-hearted defence of the supposedly venal mayor of Woodstock, and his claims of independence for the Woodstock inhabitants, were much reported in the Oxford press, which kept up a running campaign against the allegedly closed nature of the Woodstock corporation; and the *Pall Mall Gazette* printed a long and scathing leader emphasizing the sycophancy of the Woodstock political culture. Churchill's irony was probably appreciated not least in Woodstock itself, whose electors the Duke had assiduously kept plied with *douceurs* on Churchill's behalf—even when Marlborough and his son were themselves temporarily not on speaking terms.[41] As with the other causes he chose to take up—the university of Oxford, the owners of foxhound packs, the *habitués* of Rotten Row—the Woodstock debate shewed him as a frivolous and lightweight defender of the *haut monde* in politics and society. Up to 1880, the issues which he supported in parliament tended to the ultra-Tory line. His defence of the state of quiescence in which the country reposed under the 'blessed Morpheus of Conservative reaction' raised appreciative support at the annual Woodstock Agricultural Dinner in 1875, and seems to have accurately reflected his own predilections.

The co-operation with Dilke in preparing their debate, however, is an indication of other interests; and it prompts an examination of those who constituted Churchill's political con-

---

[40] See *Hansard 3*, ccxxix, 672, and *Pall Mall Gazette*, 12 May 1876. (The Row remained in a dangerous state: see *Truth*, 7 Feb. 1878.) Another representative cause he took up in April 1878 was that of the owners of foxhound packs, whom he felt should be allowed compound with the Treasury for a lower dog-tax (*Hansard 3*, ccxxxix, 1158, 1160). The Irish obstructionists joyfully took this up, O'Donnell attempting to turn it into a class question, and Parnell solemnly speaking 'in the interests of the dogs themselves'. In his correction of O'Connor Power Churchill mistakenly said that Marlborough had been awarded his title for the Blenheim victory.

[41] *Pall Mall Gazette*, 3 June 1875, *Oxford Times*, 5 June 1875. For attacks on Woodstock Corporation see ibid., 16 Jan. 1875, 23 Jan. 1875, 9 Sept. 1876, and a series of reports in Nov.–Dec. 1876. Also see R. B. B. Hawkins to Churchill, 22 Dec. 1875, quoted in Churchill and Mitchell, pp. 84–5; further correspondence is in Blenheim L/IV/17.

tacts in these early years. The fondness of Disraeli for this scion of a ducal house is heavily emphasized by his biographers and family; but the Prime Minister was infuriated by what he took to be Churchill's authorship of a letter to *The Times* in July 1875 attacking the parsimonious official arrangements for the Prince of Wales's visit to India, a scrape into which he had been led by Blandford. Later Disraeli felt that Churchill was angry with him because he was not made a Junior Lord of the Treasury (which would certainly have eased his increasingly embarrassed financial position). And several of Churchill's early political contacts were less respectable. Even before his return to parliament, he was dining with Labouchere, *bon viveur*, Radical, professional cynic, and—most importantly—editor of *Truth*. A much more striking alliance was that which Churchill formed with Dilke (a figure whose career bears many resemblances to his own). At the beginning of his career in parliament, Churchill had described Dilke to his wife as 'a horrible extreme radical whom you may have heard of'. By Easter 1875, however, they had become friendly; crossing to France at that time, they encountered each other and Dilke promised to bring Churchill to visit Gambetta. He did so, and Gambetta liked him enough to invite him back to breakfast; where Churchill astounded his host and amused the company when he 'turned to Gambetta and in his most apologetic style, which is extremely taking, said "*Would* you mind telling me who Ledru-Rollin was?"' Only two years before, Churchill had been passionately concerned with the cause of the Royalists in France, and prepared to 'hang the Left *en mass*' [sic] in Paris.[42]

It was a significant episode. For Churchill, still very much a political novice, Dilke was a considerable influence. At this very time, he was attacking the Conservatives on the grounds of their discouragement of independent freelances within the party, and their ignoring of the masses.[43] Disraeli later styled the Churchill of 1880 as 'Dilke and water'; the point was a telling one.

After the trip to Paris, they dined often together; it may well

[42] See Churchill to J. Jerome, 'Wednesday' (Mar. 1874), CHAR 28/4, and 28 Oct. 1873, 9 Nov. 1873, CHAR 28/2; also Gwynn and Tuckwell, *Dilke*, i, 229.

[43] See Dilke to his Chelsea constituents, 24 Jan. 1876 on 'the absence of independent conservatism on their own side of the house . . . Lord Lytton, after he had himself from being a Liberal become a Conservative, defined Conservatism as having for its "ideal aim to elevate the masses in character and feeling to the standard which Conservatism seeks in aristocracy" . . . If that was Conservatism, he was a Conservative, but he saw little trace of true Conservatism in the present government.' *Morning Post*, 25 Jan. 1876.

have been through Dilke, a friend of advanced Tories, that Churchill became intimate with his future ally Gorst. (Dilke also fanned an interest in India by introducing him to Maharajahs.) Moreover, Dilke's intimacy with Gambetta had led him early on to a positive line on Eastern questions. This influence was reinforced by the fact that the Duke of Marlborough took a moderately anti-government line over the Bulgarian atrocities in 1876, feeling that Disraeli should have taken an unequivocal attitude earlier in this affair.[44] Churchill had always denounced those leaders of his party whom he disliked (especially Derby) to Dilke; by 1878 he was using the Eastern Question and his Liberal contacts as a lever to attempt a revolt from within. This was after a complete reversal in his personal and social position which decisively changed the direction of his politics as well; but he had already been displaying impatience with his leaders, a desire for recognition of his qualities (though these had not yet been revealed as anything very remarkable), and a liking for independent political company.

In these years the Churchills' social life had revolved round Mayfair parties, the Prince of Wales's circle, and contacts in Parisian high society: a round of activity lovingly itemized in Edwardian memoirs and latter-day popular biography, and recorded at the time in daily newspaper bulletins. Though their names appear occasionally at Lady Salisbury's indefatigable receptions, the Churchills generally moved in faster, and less political, company. Churchill had always had a taste for the plutocratic society centred round the Rothschilds, with whom he first became friendly when a boy at the Reverend Damer's (who had reported nervously to the Duchess of 'the allegiance he has struck up with the Jews: there is really no-one else in the neighbourhood to visit'). Staying at Aston Clinton in 1873 he wrote to his fiancée: 'Like all Jews' places it is a wonderful house for eating, every kind of food. I must confess I rather like that.'[45] The Rothschilds, Hirsches, Cohens, Wertheimers, and Bischoffsheims became and remained his close friends. In the early 1870s, however, he was easiest identified as being in the Prince of Wales's set: and in this circle, the exposure of scandal

---

[44] See his speech at a Woodstock public dinner, quoted in *Morning Post*, 29 Sept. 1876.
[45] Damer to Duchess, 19 Mar. 1867 (Blenheim A/IV/9); Churchill to J. Jerome, 16 Dec. 1873, CHAR 28/3.

was fatal. In early 1876, both Churchill and his brother became spectacularly involved in such a scandal. The fact that Lord Aylesford's wife had conducted a liaison with Churchill's brother Blandford while her husband was in India with the Prince of Wales was inconsequential; what mattered was Blandford's readiness for an open scandal, which would expose her previous relationship with the Prince, in the course of bringing on a divorce. Churchill entered the affair with great energy, determined to stop Lord Aylesford instituting the divorce proceedings; his method, as is well known, was to threaten the Princess of Wales with the publication of her husband's letters to Lady Aylesford unless he prevented the divorce. In this, he was carrying out the family policy of preventing Blandford from embarking upon a course of divorce and remarriage; and using the traditional family tactic of brutal aggression. The ramifications of the affair defy unravelling: a political dimension arises through the involvement of Lord Hartington as arbiter, with whom Churchill's relations always remained strained afterwards. What mattered at the time was that his misconceived actions were tantamount to social suicide; compounding the felony by the threat of a duel with the Prince was wilful self-destruction.[46] The public was denied full knowledge of the affair until the hearing of a divorce petition in 1878, where collusion was established, and Lord Aylesford's life-style shown to have involved importing negro minstrels to a house in Bognor where 'ladies danced around the room in smoking caps'.[47] But as early as March 1876, *Vanity Fair* carried covert references to Lord and Lady Blandford's position in the unsavoury affair. In April, after the crisis had broken with the royal family, Churchill escorted his brother to Belgium. It is worth pointing out that, rather than taking his brother's part, his intervention was in fact intended to short-circuit Blandford's wish for a divorce; if he was acting, however unwisely, on anyone's behalf, it was that of his parents

---

[46] For an account of this affair from the Churchill point of view see R. S. Churchill, *W. S. Churchill*, i, ch. 2, and documents in Companion volume; also A. Leslie, *Jennie: the Life of Lady Randolph Churhill* (London, 1969) and *Edwardians in Love* (London, 1972), chapter 8; and Churchill and Mitchell, chapter 4. The relevant correspondence is in Blenheim MSS, A/IV. A letter from Lady Aylesford to her mother at the time remarked: 'Lord Randolph Churchill is very sensible, and knows better than I do what should be done' (quoted in lawsuit retailed in *Pall Mall Gazette*, 2 July 1885).

[47] See *Pall Mall Gazette*, 3 July 1878.

and Lady Blandford.[48] Attempts were made at a reconciliation
with the Prince, with the Duke intervening while the Randolph
Churchills retired to America. The apology that was eventually
agreed on, appositely signed by Lord Randolph from Saratoga,
mended no feelings, and the Churchills were excluded from
society at the Prince's fiat. It was, as is well known, this
involvement and this social boycott that led the Duke to accept
the Lord Lieutenancy of Ireland from Disraeli in 1876 and
remove himself and his family there at the beginning of 1877. As
far as Churchill was concerned, he took with him what is
generally described as an animus against high society, but was
focused more specifically into a hatred of the court circle. He left
behind many of his contacts in society, though naturally enough
these were resumed as soon as the social climate became
temperate once more. As for politics, Churchill's tastes for
confrontation tactics, histrionic oratorical effects, and dangerous
company were encouraged by this embroilment, and his more
pompous and predictable opinions correspondingly muted. He
had become, in a sense, *déclassé*: aspects of the alienation that
this meant were to stay with him for the rest of his life.

[48] Blandford, at this stage passionately wanted as extreme and messy a divorce as
possible; see an inimitable letter quoted in R. S. Churchill, *W. S. Churchill*, i, Companion
vol., i, part I, pp. 35–6: 'I hope you have not got into any more bother—to a certain
extent you know you are responsible for a good deal as *you* will insist on preventing A.'s
divorce and this was certain under present circumstances of making a row . . . I must say
though with Edith that it is not worth all the trouble to avoid the divorce court . . . P.S.
One thing strikes me. If A. leaves matters as they are between him and Edith I shall only
wait till H.R.H. comes back to appear on the scene—and then if A. tries to kill me I shall
do my damndest to defend myself and afterwards, if I am all right, I shall lick H.R.H.
within an inch of his life for his conduct generally, and we will have the whole thing up
in the Police Courts!!!'

Chapter 2

Irish Politics, 1877–1880*

Lord Colambre, from his family connexions, had of
course immediate introduction into the best society
in Dublin, or rather into all the good society of
Dublin. In Dublin there is positively good company, and positively bad; but not, as in London,
many degrees of comparison: not innumerable
luminaries of the polite world, moving in different
orbits of fashion; but all the bright planets of note
and name move in the same narrow limits. Lord
Colambre did not find that either his father's or his
mother's representations of society resembled the
reality which he now beheld ... The hospitality of
which the father boasted, the son found in all its
warmth, but meliorated and refined; less convivial,
more social; the fashion of hospitality had improved. To make the stranger eat or drink to
excess, to set before him old wine and old plate,
was no longer the sum of good breeding. The guest
now escaped the pomp of grand entertainments;
was allowed to enjoy ease and conversation, and to
taste some of that feast of reason and that flow of
soul so often talked of, and so seldom enjoyed. Lord
Colambre found a spirit of improvement, a desire
for knowledge, and a taste for science and litera-
ture, in most companies, particularly among
gentlemen belonging to the Irish bar.

Maria Edgeworth, *The Absentee* (1812)

I

On 28 November 1876, Marlborough's appointment as viceroy
was gazetted, amid faint surprise and some snide remarks about
his family's recent embroilments. The Duke had refused once
before to take the post of viceroy, probably because of money,

---

* Some of the substance of this chapter has already appeared in F. S. L. Lyons and
R. A. J. Hawkins (eds.), *Varieties of Tension: Ireland under the Union* (Oxford, 1980).

and he was no better off now: urgent enquiries in Dublin, and a promise from his comptroller to help keep down costs, still left him expecting to spend £30,000 a year.[1] Other intimations of what awaited him were no more reassuring; he was early on deluged with letters from Irish magistrates, and warnings about what businesses it was politic to patronize: 'probably your Grace has not thought of this'.

He probably had not; nor expected the slightly cynical reception afforded him when he arrived in January 1877, though his comptroller had warned him that 'Dublin people have strange ideas, and are curious people to deal with.' Even from the unionist side, the *Irish Times* made condescending remarks about the Marlboroughs' straitened circumstances, and the famous Trinity wit Dr Mahaffy made an unfunny but silencing remark in the Castle drawing-room about his hosts not paying their debts. Nationalist opinion, quite simply, expected Marlborough never to get to know Ireland at all.[2]

There was also the strange, gimcrack world of 'Castle society', all the stranger at a time when the balance of social classes was itself altering. The Duke's papers include Ascendancy jeers at the Lord Mayor's banquet, for the Duchess's amusement, as well as violently angry letters from those whose wives and daughters had not received invitations to Castle functions.[3] These Pooteresque heights of aggrieved gentility were matched by the more lofty pretensions of precedence questions within the Court itself; in January 1878 a protocol crisis reminiscent of a minor German princedom prevented the Crown Prince of Austria dining with the Marlboroughs.

The son of the viceroy, however, could be in a particularly

---

[1] Col. Caulfield to Marlborough, 1 Nov. 1876, Blenheim MSS D/1/3.

[2] See *Weekly Freeman*, 17 Jan. 1877. It expected him to penetrate no further than 'the judges and chief officers of the Queen, the commander of the forces, and a knot of the more prominent military men, the rising men of his own party at the Bar, and the pith of the chief secretary's correspondence with magistrates and provincial potentates'. Also see W. B. Stanford and R. B. McDowell, *Mahaffy: a Portrait of an Anglo-Irishman* (London, 1971), p. 94.

[3] On the rise of the ' commercial classes' in the Dublin bourgeois hierarchy see Anon., *Recollections of Dublin Castle and of Dublin Society by a Native* (London, 1902) and a series of angry articles in the *Weekly Irish Times*, 27 Jan.–17 Mar. 1877. Also see letters in Blenheim D/1/11 complaining about those nowadays received at the Castle: 'Singing apothecaries, cobblers' sons, rowdy attornies, corporation whisky-sellers and seedsmen, judges, registrars, and official dogs in office of low degree.'

interesting position, as others in that situation have recorded:[4] Lord Randolph was to make the most of it. But tortuous issues of status bedevilled the definition of his position. He is generally described as being his father's unofficial private secretary: but the official position had already been offered to one Percy Barnard, who had been private secretary to Abercorn, the previous incumbent. Barnard objected to being subordinate to Churchill and attempted to hold out for an equal footing with the Viceroy's son; in the end, however, he had to cede precedence behind the scenes to Churchill, and also give up the desirable 'Little Lodge' in the Phoenix Park to him. Even after Barnard's submission, Marlborough continued to solicit advice as to how far Churchill's authority might extend; the appointment, in any case, had to remain 'unofficial and unpaid'.

'The prospect,' Marlborough wrote to Disraeli, 'though not without its cares, is also one which has a great deal to interest one in it'. The possibilities for involvement in public affairs were elastic; a viceroy became as involved as he wanted to be.[5] In the years up to 1880, Marlborough managed an even-handed and politically adroit presentation of himself which usually kept him in high favour. He was notably friendly (in marked contrast to the *hauteur* of Abercorn); he took well-publicized Irish holidays; from the beginning of his tenure he took a close interest in questions like the keeping of order at public demonstrations, and followed a firm line against die-hard peers who wanted permanent coercion. His first important public speech, at the Lord Mayor's banquet in February 1877, was taken as an earnest of liberal intentions. And on a visit to Belfast he spoke out strongly against religious discord there, in a speech generally seen as honest and unprejudiced.[6] In 1878 he identified himself with the call for aid to small farmers to enable them to purchase their holdings; he also strongly backed the mooted bill

---

[4] See E. Cadogan, *Before the Deluge* (London, 1961), pp. 50, 55; W. G. Hamilton, *Parliamentary Reminiscences and Reflections 1868–85* (London, 1917), pp. 112–14; W. E. Hamilton, *Old Days and New* (London, 1923), p. 123.

[5] Marlborough to Disraeli, 20 Jan. 1877, Disraeli MSS B/xx/Ch/72. In 1888 Ashbourne wrote about Londonderry, in a tone of pleased surprise: 'He, I think, is interested in his work. He reads all his official papers . . .' (Ashbourne to Churchill, 24 Oct. 1888; RCHL xvi/1921).

[6] 'If there is one serious reflection connected with the North—and you will allow me to say it as standing in the position I do—it is that exhibition which has from time to time shown itself in religious feuds and discords.' See report in ibid., 28 July 1877. (None the less, the riots on the next 12th of July were exceptionally extensive and aggressive.)

for intermediate education. His tour of the south in August 1878 was taken in some quarters to symbolize the end of 'coercion and arrogance' on the part of the Lord Lieutenant and all he stood for; his visit to Newry in 1879, and the equally warm reception accorded him by Protestant and by Catholic factions, struck one resident as indicating the end of 'the miserable and unreasoning party jealousies of Ulster which are such a source of heartbreak and annoyance to those who wish for the prosperity of Ireland'. By 1880 unionist opinion saw him as 'half an Irishman in his love of the country and community of sympathy with the people'.[7]

There was, of course, an alternative tradition. In August 1878, for instance, when the Queenstown Commissioners discussed an impending visit from the Lord Lieutenant, an influential Fenian wrecked proceedings by moving a satirical amendment to the motion, that they 'pay no attention' to the viceregal visitor, and went on to propose a different address

[expressing] disapproval of the system of government to which our country is subjected, and of which the Lord Lieutenant forms a part ... As regards that part of the system manipulated by the Lord Lieutenancy, we express our belief that corruption is its chiefest feature, and that its social ramifications through the country exercise a most baneful influence upon our condition. The cost of it, too, is enormous. Just fancy that nearly two million pounds have been wrung out of the pockets of the Irish people to compensate your Grace and your 22 predecessors for staying with us in the ornamental capacity of Lord Lieutenant. We think it is a large sum for a very questionable benefit.[8]

This amendment was rejected with laughter, and when Marlborough visited Cork he was presented with an impeccably loyal address by the Queenstown Commissioners. But more moderate nationalist opinion still reacted to the Duke with initial caution, seeing gestures like his interest in Irish agriculture as merely representing avarice on the part of the English economy. However, all parties in Ireland appreciated his commitment to the abortive Irish University Bill, introduced by the

---

[7] See leader in *Weekly Irish Times*, 31 Aug. 1878, 8 May 1880; James Richardson to Duchess, 14 Aug. 1879, Blenheim MSS D/1/8; and T. P. O'Connor, *Memories of an Old Parliamentarian*, i, 58 ('a very dexterous, very handsome, and very conciliatory' Lord Lieutenant).

[8] *Weekly Freeman*, 24 Aug. 1878. The proposer was Charles Doran.

O'Conor Don in 1879 but dropped in favour of a more cautious government measure leading to the creation of the Royal University. The fact that both the Intermediate Education Act of 1878 and the eventual University Act of 1879 were passed due to Parnellite tactics as much as anything else made no difference; the Duke had warmly identified himself with both measures, and had conferred with the Catholic hierarchy about education. Even before arriving in Ireland both he and Lord Randolph had corresponded closely with Hicks Beach, the Chief Secretary, about the latter's scheme to allocate surplus church funds to promote intermediate education. The hierarchy warned Marlborough and Hicks Beach that unless a university scheme followed the intermediate plan, the latter would be seen as a plot to feed 'the infidel universities', and the Duke was already being told of the need to broaden educational opportunities for the Irish middle class. Marlborough accepted the idea, warmly conferring with Cardinal Cullen and assuring Beach that now was the time to meet Catholic wishes in higher education, if the Cabinet could be got to agree.[9] The Irish leader Isaac Butt, who first introduced the question in 1877, and saw it as a tactic for regaining the position which the Parnellite obstructionists had wrested from him, co-operated enthusiastically with Beach and Marlborough; Lord Randolph voted with the Irish and the Radicals in favour of the O'Conor Don's motion on the subject in 1878.

The university schemes originating in Ireland came to nothing, and the government accepted only a limited examining body. Marlborough had been closely associated with the more sweeping ideas and threatened his resignation: he was generally seen as having been let down by the administration. On an Irish visit Northcote had, indeed, written to Disraeli from Ireland in a way that implies extreme doubt on the part of Conservative politicians regarding the Viceroy's ideas; although, since the entire subject was generally seen as Gladstone's great failure, a successful initiative would have been of great political

---

[9] See correspondence in Blenheim D/1/2, especially letters from Chancellor and Vice-Chancellor of Queen's University to Marlborough, May 1877; V. Hicks Beach, *Life of Sir Michael Hicks Beach, Earl St. Aldwyn* (London, 1932), i, 54–5; also Marlborough to Beach, 18 Nov. 1879, St. Aldwyn MSS, PCC/65, and Bishop Conway to Beach, 17 Jan. 1877, Blenheim MSS D/1/19. For Marlborough's representations to Disraeli see Disraeli MSS B/xx/Ch/22 (letter of 30 Mar. 1877).

moment.[10] The important aspect of the whole involvement, however, was the *rapprochement* between the Castle and the Catholics. When the government refused to carry through a full Catholic university, the *Freeman's Journal* gloomily concluded: 'the phenomenon of the Irish Catholic Conservative, which was heretofore possible and which would, if the government had settled the education question, have become so common as to cease to be exceptional, is now an impossibility'.[11] But this was not the case. From the beginning of Marlborough's tenure, the Castle had been assured by the hierarchy that 'in Irish politics, the education question has partially displaced even the Home Rule question and the land question'; it was an analysis in which they devoutly wished to believe. Isaac Butt, fighting for his political life against the Parnellites, gave them similar tidings, adding that the Conservatives were natural allies for the Catholic interest. 'Since I returned to Ireland', he confided in May 1878, 'I have been astonished at the number of communications made to me by the Roman Catholics in various positions to the effect that a very general feeling is pervading the Roman Catholic body that their true and natural alliance is with the Conservative party, and a general wish to be able to support them.'[12] Marlborough was under no illusions about Butt's own desperate personal position, and Tory proclivities; but the message was amplified by complaints from Protestant pundits about the Castle's favouritism towards Catholics, and enthusiastic testimonials from the Duchess's friend Sir William Gregory, a Liberal Irish Catholic and landlord: 'by acting cordially with [the bishops] we can secure the only allies who can help us to contest against the disloyal and seditious spirit which sometimes might smoulder but which always may be

[10] Northcote to Disraeli, 21 May 1879 (copy), BL Add. MS 50018, and 12 Oct. 1879, from Ireland, reporting the Duke's ideas about university education; Northcote to Cranbrook, 8 Dec. 1874, Cranbrook MSS HA 43 T501/271 and to Cairns, 13 Jan. 1880, Cairns MSS, PRO 30/51/5, for Orange and ultra annoyance at Marlborough's proposals.

[11] *Weekly Freeman*, 22 Mar. 1879. A Conservative–Catholic alliance had been forecast by the *Pall Mall Gazette* for years (see for instance 16 Dec. 1876 and 14 Sept. 1876) and was actively campaigned for by Irish MPs like Pope-Hennessy.

[12] See Bishop Conway to Beach, 17 Jan. 1877, Blenheim MSS D/1/19; a long correspondence in St. Aldwyn MSS, PCC/66; Butt to Beach, 28 May 1877, ibid. The reasons he gave for *rapprochement* were the Intermediate Education Bill, Beach's liberality, and 'the personal popularity of the Lord Lieutenant'. Also see D. A. Thornley, *Isaac Butt and Home Rule* (London, 1965), pp. 381–2.

fanned into flame'.[13] Beach had long been convinced that full
denominational education was the only way to stop Fenianism:
an analysis not welcomed by Disraeli but a lesson well learned
by the Marlboroughs and their son.

Lord Randolph's mother was, moreover, nearly as prominent
politically as her husband. From the outset she not only
absorbed herself in charitable involvements, but despite her own
predilections set herself to cultivate prominent clerics like
Cullen: 'I have made on my own account great efforts to
propitiate the Roman Catholics,' she confided to Disraeli.[14] A
cynical contemporary observer described her as 'a bit in
advance of her time as regards the benefit of publicity, for her
one idea was that socially and politically the Lord Lieutenant
and herself should have "a good press", and her maxim was
"feed the press": she would wander around at her parties in
Dublin Castle and, tapping an A.D.C. on his arm with her fan,
ask anxiously: "have the press been fed?"'[15] She maintained
her own circle of Irish contacts and correspondents, notably Sir
William Gregory; and she initiated ideas as well as encouraging
them. In November 1877 it was to her that Disraeli's secretary
Montagu Corry offered his congratulations on what he took to
be the administration's success in defusing Gladstone's Irish
tour, and she was also approached about a possible royal visit.
She was much involved in the choosing of personnel for the
Intermediate Education Commission, and was closely advised
by Dr Delany, the Roman Catholic bishop of Cork. Delany, a
firm Conservative, was a close friend of the Duchess's Roman
Catholic relations Lady Londonderry and Lady Portarlington;
through Delany, who frequented Blenheim, the Duchess built
up close contacts with men like Dr Molloy, later Rector of the
Catholic University, and even with the future Archbishop
Walsh.

There were also more conventional spheres of involvement
for a viceroy's wife: the Duchess indefatigably patronized

[13] Gregory to Duchess, 13 Nov. 1877, Blenheim MSS D/1/7. Also see T. Maguire
(Professor of Latin at Queen's University, Galway) to H. Holmes, 9 Jan. 1878, St.
Aldwyn MSS, PCC/65.

[14] Duchess to Disraeli, 28 Mar. 1877, Disraeli MSS B/xx/Ch/80. Also see Burke to
Duchess, 4 Mar. 1877, discussing the politics of inviting him to a levee; Blenheim D/1/6.
Also Cullen to Duchess, 4 Jan. 1878, Blenheim D/1/8.

[15] Maud Wynne, *An Irishman and His Family: Lord Morris and Killanin* (London, 1937),
p. 98.

embroidery classes, campaigned to establish Irish poplin as a fashionable material, and encouraged the Irish lace industry. She also received a great deal of correspondence on her own account. Her later establishment of the Famine Relief Fund increased her political importance; but even before this, she received many letters from Catholic clerics, asking her to intercede with the Chief Secretary over their affairs. When the time came for her to leave Ireland, the shower of farewell addresses included many in Irish, calling blessings upon her head while conventionally decrying 'the curse of Union'.

II

Thus both Lord Randolph's parents occupied themselves in fitting into suitable niches in the Irish environment; and so did he. His wife's memoirs and his son's biography recall many eclectic dinner-parties at the Little Lodge, and hunting all over the country. By and large, the circuit of grand Ascendancy houses was eschewed in favour of Irish friends: and these friends composed a particular group. They were not, despite later assertions, nationalists: they tended to be Dublin professional men, representatives of an exceptional generation at Trinity College—David Plunket, later Lord Rathmore; Michael Morris, who became Lord Killanin; Edward Gibson, later Lord Ashbourne; J. P. Mahaffy, future Provost of Trinity College; and Gerald FitzGibbon. Churchill was quickly adopted by this group; he made his first Irish speech under their auspices at the Trinity College Historical Society, and they continued to set the tone of his Irish experience.

FitzGibbon, by far the closest of Churchill's Irish friends and an intimate for the rest of his life, became Irish Solicitor-General in 1877. He was twelve years older than Churchill, and came from a robustly Tory and Protestant legal family.[16] After a brilliant university career he became known as a formidable lawyer, and was made Lord Justice of Appeal at forty-one. He would probably have enjoyed a political career, but the seat for Dublin University went to his friend Gibson instead in 1875; Hicks Beach felt FitzGibbon had the makings of a very high-

---

[16] On FitzGibbon and his friends see Foster, 'To the Northern Counties Station: Lord Randolph Churchill and the prelude to the Orange card' in F. S. L. Lyons and R. A. J. Hawkins (ed.), *Ireland Under the Union: Varieties of Tension* (Oxford, 1980), pp. 237–87: hereafter 'Northern Counties Station'.

class politician indeed. And while his ideas were superficially
flexible and realistic, he was at bottom intractably unionist,
referring with slight but unmistakable disparagement to the
ideas of 'Gibson, Plunket and other *moderates*'.[17] Though he
had many Catholic friends and worked closely with the Catholic
clergy, he was at bottom deeply committed to the Protestant
interest (his mother was from Belfast, and he himself was an
influential Freemason).

FitzGibbon and Churchill became allies at once: at the first
meeting in Dublin Castle their rapport was immediate, and
shortly afterwards, encountering each other on the mail-boat,
they sat up all night on deck talking. For the rest of Churchill's
life FitzGibbon kept up a flow of gossipy, affectionate, informative, and often wildly funny letters about Irish affairs: one
letter could range from high-level intrigues with bishops to the
abysmal standard of whist played by the Chief Secretary.
FitzGibbon's style of mock-heroic exaggeration and elaborate
irony closely paralleled Churchill's. He favoured his younger
friend with political advice, generally worth taking, and a
running commentary on Churchill's battles and retreats in the
early 1880s; throughout, the style and policies of successive
Irish administrations received merciless deflation. FitzGibbon
committed himself early to keeping Churchill '*au courant* with
the floating notions of the locality'; and though he felt that
advising Churchill was as often as not 'crying in the wilderness
through the privacy of the penny post', this was to under-
estimate his own influence.

The lesson about Ireland which FitzGibbon set himself to
teach Churchill was one to which his own circle bore evidence:
that as regarded unionist feeling, 'there were others than
landowners to be reckoned with'. The FitzGibbon set, unionist
though it was, included no landowners. Plunket, Paymaster-
General under Disraeli and once 'law adviser' to Dublin Castle,
was an archetypical clever moderate; nationalist opinion constantly expected him to cut his losses and change sides. He was
usually grouped with his fellow-member for Trinity, Edward
Gibson, who was more sociable and eloquent (though politicians, especially of his own party, came to hate him).[18] Like

---

[17] FitzGibbon to Churchill, 18 Dec. 1881, RCHL i/62. For a description of
FitzGibbon's approach to legal questions see Sir John Ross, *The Years of my Pilgrimage*
(London, 1924), p. 201.
[18] For a sensitive treatment of Gibson's politics and his failed promise see A. B. Cooke's
introduction to the *Calendar of the Ashbourne Papers* (HMSO (Belfast), 1974).

Plunket and Morris, Gibson had been a protégé of Disraeli: great things were hoped of him by the Conservative party, but he never managed to deliver them. He had a facility for being all things to all men, and members of the FitzGibbon circle tended to bandy unkind stories about him. Churchill was at this stage friendly with Plunket and Gibson, but closer to the abrasive Michael Morris, who later became the first Catholic Lord Chief Justice of Common Pleas in Ireland. Morris came from the Roman Catholic gentry of Galway, and was intransigently unionist; his temperament was at once pessimistic and volcanic, and he disliked most Englishmen: Churchill and Disraeli being two significant exceptions. A lawyer of vast talents, Morris is a good example of someone who transcends most of the hackneyed stereotypes usually applied to nineteenth-century Irish attitudes.

Morris and Churchill had similar interests, having come together over the question of intermediate education, and being linked by the friendship of Sir William Gregory as well as of FitzGibbon: Morris was socially active, spending much time in London, where he was a friend of the Prince of Wales. Other *habitués* of the FitzGibbon circle included Lord Chief Justice Ball, who had begun life as a Radical failure and kept Churchill supplied with unsolicited political advice; Trinity academics like Benjamin Williamson and J. P. Mahaffy; Dr Nedley, a well-known Dublin wit; and the famous parish priest of Little Bray, Father James Healy. Healy, a strong Conservative and a friend of the Marlborough family, frequented London political society, appearing at Gladstone's breakfasts and Salisbury's luncheons, and turning up at Carlsbad with Labouchere. Both the Viceroy and his son are recorded as attending Healy's famous dinners at his little house in Bray, where archbishops, foreign royalties, and Dublin men-about-town met and invariably dined off boiled mutton.[19]

Outside this circle, but also influential in Churchill's network of Irish contacts, was his uncle Lord Portarlington, sometimes

---

[19] On Nedley and Healy see *Recollections of Dublin Castle . . .* and W. J. Fitzpatrick, *Memories of Father Healy of Little Bray* (London, 1896). For Morris, see Wynne, op. cit.; for Mahaffy, see Stanford and McDowell, op. cit. When taxed by Gladstone with the iniquity of the sale of indulgences, Healy asked his host in mock outrage what better value he would expect for his money. On another occasion, required to furnish a defence of the doctrine of purgatory, he replied economically that 'you could travel further and fare worse'.

described by Lord Randolph's later biographers as a disapproving High Tory. He was in fact a landlord of remarkably advanced opinions, who defended Gladstone's 1881 Land Act, admired Archbishop Croke, and had uninterruptedly good relations with his tenants, who assured him none the less that they were 'all Land Leaguers'; his wife, a Roman Catholic, had entertained most of the hierarchy at Emo Park, and Portarlington took a strongly Catholic line on educational questions. He approved of Churchill, advised him by letter, and later welcomed his Irish initiatives.

Seen against this background, it comes as no surprise that Churchill took the opportunity of his annual appearance at the Woodstock Agricultural Show in September 1877 to make a speech attacking the government's policy of neglect towards Ireland. Already increasingly alienated from the party leadership, he simply said in public what intelligent Irish Tories were saying in private. Apropos of obstruction by the Home Rulers at Westminster, Churchill remarked that the Act of Union had been passed to bring the Irish members to Westminster, and they could not be expelled simply because the government did not agree with them.

He had no hesitation in saying that it was inattention to Irish legislation that had produced the obstruction to English legislation. There were great and crying questions which the government had not attended to, did not seem inclined to attend to, and perhaps did not intend to attend to. These were the questions of intermediate and higher education, the assimilation of municipal and parliamentary electoral privileges to English privileges, and other matters which he would not go into. They must remember that England had years of wrong, years of crime, years of tyranny, years of oppression, years of general misgovernment to make amends for in Ireland.[20]

Conciliatory legislation would make sense of the Act of Union. It was a line he would recur to more than once.

The speech was delivered after a banquet, and the Duke excused it to his agonized Chief Secretary by supposing that Lord Randolph had been drunk. Whether or not this was the case, besides repeating the lessons learned from his Tory lawyer friends, Churchill's speech had another purpose. It was designed to put himself between parties, since he contrived to make fun equally of the Conservative and Liberal positions regarding

[20] Report in *Weekly Freeman*, 22 Sept. 1877.

Near Eastern affairs, and to express fervent thanks for party government, since it preserved the country from following either line. An additional logic behind the speech may have been provided by Gladstone's impending visit to Ireland, due in less than a month: Churchill may have been attempting to cut him out. (If so, it was a miscalculation: Gladstone's visit remained restricted to the Ascendancy circuit, his chief impression was that Ireland was socially contented and politically ashamed of herself, and the only sign of turmoil he noted was that someone had pulled up a tree planted by the Prince of Wales.[21])

Public opinion could not be expected to follow the member for Woodstock's calculations. The *Morning Post* traduced Churchill; while 'the small world of Dublin was moved to its depths'. The *Irish Times* evinced embarrassment, while the *Freeman's Journal* ostentatiously claimed Churchill for Home Rule. A letter from the miscreant to the *Morning Post* attempted to mend his fences, claiming that he never even mentioned 'the conduct of the obstructionists'. His exposition of intelligent Toryism to the Trinity College Historical Society in November, much admired at the time, was seen by his mother at least as a calculated act of expiation, and she hastily reported it to Disraeli as such.[22] An impression, however, had been created, and stayed; even four years later, in the debates over the Coercion Bill, the Liberal Home Secretary was able to recall that 'even in the position of Private Secretary to the Lord Lieutenant, the noble Lord astonished Dublin by delivering a speech in favour of Home Rule'. To which Churchill chose only to rejoin: 'I never was Private Secretary to the Lord Lieutenant.'

The Woodstock speech was of a piece with the development of Churchill's politics during his Irish sojourn. Most of the issues which preoccupied him were Irish ones; but he used his

---

[21] See Morley, *Gladstone*, ii, 571; letter to Granville in A. Ramm (ed.), *The Political Correspondence of Mr Gladstone and Lord Granville, 1876–86* (Oxford, 1962), i, 54–6; J. R. Vincent, 'Gladstone and Ireland' in *Proc. Br. Acad.*, lxiii (1977), 206–7. It was, however, a general belief; on 26 Dec. 1877 the *Pall Mall Gazette* reported that in Ireland 'the people are contented, and there is absolutely no political excitement'. The Duchess found Gladstone's visit most 'provoking' and attempted to lure Disraeli over as a rival 'star'; see letter to Corry, 9 Nov. 1877, Disraeli MSS B/xx/Ch/93.

[22] For this speech see W. S. Churchill, i, 80–2; P. J. Keenan to Duchess, 21 Nov. 1877, Disraeli MSS B/xx/Ch/94, declaring it was 'simply astounding' in its 'humour, wit, erudition and criticism'; and Duchess to Corry, n.d., ibid., 87, emphasizing that Churchill was rehabilitating himself.

friendship with Dilke to attempt to sabotage his party's stance on the controversial Eastern Question. He had hopes of a visit to Constantinople in May 1877 and around this time he violently criticized to his wife the Conservatives' 'extreme Turcophilia'.[23] In February 1878 he attempted concerted action with Dilke, looking for support from the Liberals for an anti-Turkish amendment which Churchill wanted to propose. In a stream of letters from Ireland, Churchill confided his preference for independent Republican governments in the Balkans, and his aversion from his party's policy: his views, he stated, were in agreement with Gladstone's, Harcourt's, and Dilke's, and opposed those of Chaplin and Wolff.[24] 'I feel I am awfully young to endeavour to initiate such a line', he confessed; Granville and others felt likewise, and doubted whether he spoke for anyone else on his side of the House. In this they were correct; plans for Churchill's motion subsided when it was discovered that only one doubtful Tory (Spencer Walpole) might support him.

Churchill's hopes of threatening the government had been high. At this stage he made his first celebrated parliamentary onslaught on the President of the Local Government Board, Sclater-Booth, over the County Government Bill: a much quoted personal attack, moving from vituperation against Sclater-Booth to claiming for Churchill himself the monopoly of Tory principles. The party had been polluted by its Eastern policies: there remained now only the final contamination of this 'Brummagem trash'. The deliberate offensiveness of Churchill's language was more striking than the substance of the criticisms. The content of the speech was, as usual with him in these years, ultra-Tory: 'the "defence of our old institutions",

---

[23] See Churchill to Lady Randolph, 11 May 1877, CHAR 28/5, and n.d., CHAR 28/6.

[24] Amendment: 'that in view of the extreme sufferings so long undergone by the Slav, Bulgarian and Hellenic nationalities of Bosnia, Herzegovina, Bulgaria, Thessaly and Epirus, and considering that the Turkish rule over these provinces has now definitely been put an end to, the efforts of Her Majesty's government, in the opinion of the House of Commons, should be principally directed towards the establishment of the complete freedom and independence of the population of these provinces'. For the full correspondence see S. Gwynn and G. Tuckwell, *Life of Sir Charles Dilke* (2 vols, London, 1917), i, 243–8. On 16 Sept. 1880, Labouchere wrote in *Truth* regarding Dilke's foreign policy ideas: 'He is as ambitious for England as any follower of Lord Beaconsfield, and during no period of the Eastern Crisis was he disposed to make light of the schemes of aggrandisement attributed to Russia. He only differed from the Tories as to the manner in which she was to be met.'

by which the masses enfranchised in 1867 meant beer and the Bible, but others more profound understood the church, the House of Lords, the rights of property, the sanctity of the wills of pious founders, the laws of entail, etc.; and certainly in that programme he should have expected to find county government by Quarter Sessions'. But the speech soon resolved itself into an attack on the party rather than the measure: in the second reading of which, indeed, Churchill had quietly acquiesced three weeks before. It can be seen, once more, as a considered attempt to place himself between parties. Political opinion, however, took it as a cheering diversion in a dull debate, and little more.[25] It remains significant that his contacts at this time were as much Liberal as Conservative, dining with Chamberlain, Morley, and Childers as well as with Dilke, and staying with the Marjoribankses on his visits to London. His letters to his wife in 1877 and 1878 are violently against his leaders; Gathorne Hardy is 'obstinate and bad-tempered', and Disraeli prone to 'dirty dodges'; while he gave a glowing account of a speech of Gladstone's.[26] It is all a long way from the sententious condemnations of 'awful Radicals' two years before.

In other ways too his image in London was changing. The social boycott continued: 'we have so few friends', his wife wrote disconsolately in 1877. Though they reappeared in society in 1878, the Churchills could only afford a cramped house in unfashionable Cleveland Square; their finances were increasingly straitened.[27] Churchill reacted by spending more and more time in Ireland, where his family rented a variety of houses all over the country for fishing holidays. Even here, his London disgrace could pursue him. When his sister Cornelia and her husband invited the Duke of Connaught to Careysville on the Blackwater, where Churchill was staying, he was furious: 'a man whom I cannot meet, who with his brother Wales has

---

[25] See for instance *Truth*, 14 Mar. 1878. Churchill's speech is in *Hansard 3*, ccxxxviii, 900 ff. Chaplin suggested he cross the floor, unless he was practical joking.

[26] See Churchill to Lady Randolph, 4 Feb., 6 Feb., 19 Apr. 1878, CHAR 28/6.

[27] See Churchill to his wife, 13 June 1877, CHAR 28/5: once more begging her to ask her trustees to let them have their quarterly payment punctually. Another letter of 23 Dec. shows him raising another loan; in the same month he considered selling his horses (11 Dec. 1877, CHAR 28/6). On 16 Dec. a worrying letter from Coutts' caused him to write: 'I think it is too bad of your father . . . these kind [*sic*] of irregularities make bankers very suspicious of me.' The following month he had to let bills go unpaid. The next year the Marlborough solicitor raised a £2,000 loan for them, 'positively the last we shall be able to make' (24 Jan. 1879, ibid.).

everywhere said that I am not fit to be spoken to'.[28] The house being too small for discretion, Churchill had to return to England. His animus against Connaught was to have an unexpected importance seven eventful years later.

The Irish issues which he took up covered a varied range. In June 1877 he annoyed the government by objecting to the Queen's Plates prize horse-races instituted for encouraging improvement in breeding: Churchill called for direct subsidies instead, engaging in cross-chat about Irish stallions with members like Major O'Gorman and irritating Hicks Beach. His wife, whose sensitive social antennae had heard that their social disgrace was nearly forgotten in the clubs, feared that this cause was an unpopular one, but Irish sportsmen were pleased; and Churchill was at this time taking care to cultivate more influential sectors of Irish opinion too. Speaking on a motion to inquire into the operation of the 1870 Land Act, he ostentatiously refrained from condemning it. He exchanged compliments with the *Freeman's Journal*, which remained warmly disposed towards him: an attitude that even survived Churchill's declared opposition to the extension of the Irish borough franchise in 1879, a cause for which he had previously indicated his support. 'Whilst exonerating the Irish upper classes of the present day from all feelings of resentment against England', Churchill had remarked, 'he maintained that in descending to the lower classes they did come on very distinct traces of an inborn conviction or suspicion ... he did not wish to say anything to annoy the hon. member for Meath, but he must say that he drew his support from the mob.' This may have been still mending his fences after Woodstock: but it can also be seen as just another facet of the language talked at Dublin unionist dinners.

At the same time, though, he was planning an initiative: and he had chosen the issue of Irish intermediate education, which he had been studying even before he arrived in the country. As early as November 1878 he had mentioned the idea to his father, who had replied encouragingly to the idea of Churchill 'taking up the question from an independent point'. (The same letter shows that Churchill had emphasized to the Duke the

---

[28] Churchill to his wife, 28 Apr. 1878, CHAR 28/6. He had previously complained of Cornelia toadying to the Prince and Princess: 'not ordinary enemies, but most bitter foes' (1 May 1877, ibid.).

importance of 'taking up new ground' on the university question, and approaching Cullen about it.) After intensive work he produced in December 1877 a short pamphlet on the subject which, he wrote to his wife, he hoped 'would make a sensation'. It was followed up by a letter to the press.[29] Assiduously using the findings of the 1854 Commission on Irish endowed schools, Churchill attacked the maladministration of these endowments and argued for a drastic extension of Royal Free Grammar Schools, to become a state system of intermediate education, available to Catholics; the implications of his argument being unequivocally denominational education, aimed at the lower-middle classes. A new Board should take over and rationalize the inchoate organization of the endowed schools: the existing Commissioners of Education were to be dismissed, condemned in the brutal language now becoming characteristically Churchillian. A Royal Commission should be set up to remodel the existing administrative structure and redistribute the endowments, further monies coming from the surplus property of the Disestablished Irish Church.[30] It was a provocative and decisive scheme, outlining what Churchill's line of approach was to be on the Endowed Schools Commission which was the next phase of his campaign.

Having attracted attention, including an article in *The Times*, and opened correspondence with a variety of authorities, Churchill pressed ahead with his strategy for the appointment of a Royal Commission—for which he hoped to attract 'extreme Liberal' support.[31] The issue was sensitive, since Beach was at the time already preparing his own measure; Churchill found him 'most gracious and evidently very anxious to dissuade me from interfering with his bill'. The *Times* article focused attention on his campaign rather than on the Chief

---

[29] A memo from Judge Lawson to Hicks Beach on the subject, 22 Nov. 1876 (Blenheim D/I/19), is annotated in Churchill's handwriting. Also Marlborough to Churchill, 4 Nov. 1877, Blenheim F/IV/5, Churchill to *Freeman's Journal*, 31 Dec. 1877, Churchill to his wife, 4 Dec. 1877, CHAR 28/6.

[30] *Intermediate Education in Ireland: a Letter to Sir Bernard Burke, C.B., Ulster, from Lord Randolph Churchill, M.P.* (Dublin, J. Charles and Co., 1878). Churchill's rather simplistic formula was 'that where the great proportion of the population is Roman Catholic where a school is established, the schoolmaster appointed should be a Roman Catholic—where the proportion is non-Catholic, there the schoolmaster should be a Protestant'. There were to be precautions like a conscience clause and competitive examinations for gratuitous instruction—the winners of which could select what school they wished to attend.

[31] Churchill to Morris, 18 Jan. 1878, Wynne, op. cit., p. 207.

Secretary's plans. 'The best of it is', wrote Churchill gleefully to his wife, 'that everyone nearly in the House gives me credit for the government dealing with intermediate education and thinks the promised bill is owing to my pamphlet!'[32] In June 1878 an Intermediate Education Bill was passed, devised by Beach, and resembling Churchill's ideas in several points—though not actually endowing Catholic education and not reorganizing the endowments monopolized by Protestant schools. His speech in parliament on 4 June 1878 in essence repeated the arguments of his pamphlet, appealed to Dilke for support, and was indeed backed by Chamberlain and Forster; the Irish reaction was extremely friendly. But government opinion, as reflected by Lowther, who had replaced Beach as Irish Chief Secretary, was less approving; Churchill was prevailed upon to withdraw his motion pending discussion of the scope of the proposed commission. As it evolved, it was not empowered to recommend compulsory measures, or even to suggest remedies, but only had an investigative basis. It was, however, swiftly commandeered by the circle of progressive Tory thinkers round the Castle—Churchill himself, FitzGibbon, Mahaffy, and others; the Earl of Rosse was Chairman. (Catholic opinion suspected this body of attempting to preserve the Protestant initiative.) The Commission began its labours in April 1879, and its report shows an extremely thorough and wide-ranging examination of the vast and decayed variety of endowed schools in Ireland. Despite their limited brief, the Commissioners provided detailed criticism of the general inefficiency and carelessness of the Board of Commissioners of Education in Ireland, and their financial wastefulness in the management of their estates. The need and desire for denominational education in principle, as well as the way that it had come to operate in practice, also emerged: late Victorian realism had its say against the rationalist and idealized schemes of the 1830s.

Churchill's own attendance on the Commission was frequent, and his questioning notably pertinent and aggressive, especially regarding foundations which he felt had monopolized an endowment intended for wider purposes. He alone of the Commissioners attempted to draw the witnesses into suggesting remedies and alternatives; he had to assure some of them that he was 'not activated by the least unfriendly feeling towards

[32] Churchill to Lady Randolph, 22 Jan. 1878, CHAR 28/6.

you, quite the contrary'.[33] As with every office he ever filled, he was out to make a reputation; and it was most easily done at the expense of those giving evidence.

The Commission's findings bore only indirect fruit, several years later. But in the course of its investigations, Churchill travelled widely over Ireland. What he found out regarding education was in many ways what he had previously determined to find out. But, especially on the question of land management, upon which much of his individual questioning concentrated, he absorbed a lasting impression. His exchanges with agents for estates all over Ireland showed him that land was hardly ever managed efficiently for returns; that rent valuation was too low and too vaguely determined, but in any case bore little relation to economic realities; and that the tenant's legal position needed immediate clarification. Also demonstrated was the overwhelming desire for denominational education, and the increased confidence and power of middle-class Catholicism. For his own part, Churchill's activity on the Commission demonstrated his sympathy with Catholic requirements in education, and with the work of social stabilizing carried out by a school like St. Stanislaus's of Tullamore; and his own impatience with the pretensions of rickety Ascendancy institutions which had outlived their function. The issues raised were to recur more than once in his later career.

III

The issue that provided the Marlboroughs' shining hour during their Irish involvement, and put the coping on the Duchess's careful construction of contacts, was the celebrated fund for relief of distress which she started after the agricultural crisis of 1879 broke. In this Churchill was closely involved from the start. The Duchess had taken soundings about the state of the country from an early stage, and as the state of their tenantry became worse and worse, friends like Gregory and Colonel King-Harman had convinced her of the need for relief. Castle officials were more cautious, suggesting nothing more than a

---

[33] See *H.C. Rep. from Commons*, no. 25 (Endowed Schools: Ireland), vol. 35 (1881). For financial wastefulness, pp. 22–3; for Churchill's aggressive interrogation, ii, 186–7; for his attempt to prod it to conclusions, ii, 246.

ladies' charitable committee.[34] But the Duchess felt the need was for something greater, politically as well as socially; by mid-December 1879 it was well known, as Parnell remarked cynically to William O'Brien, 'that the government is going to fight the famine—or is it the League?—from behind the Duchess's petticoats'. The Relief Committee that emerged was a large-scale affair: Gladstone was asked to sit on it, but refused; Northcote was lined up in the House of Commons to press its interest. And almost at once the Lord Mayor of Dublin and editor of the *Freeman's Journal*, Dwyer Gray, set up the rival Mansion House Relief Fund. Both organizations denied that they were in any sense competitors, but within a month the Duchess was being privately warned not to 'conciliate' the nationalists' fund if it meant alienating potential funds from her own. She was also warned that the flow of English subscriptions organized for her by the Lord Mayor of London, which by April 1880 had produced £31,000, would dry up at once if there was any co-operation with Dwyer Gray. And the majority of the Duchess's collection came from abroad.[35]

Lord Randolph was one of the most influential figures in the involvement from an early stage. He monitored the critical suggestions of King-Harman and others, and drew up a cautious and considered memorandum on the whole undertaking before the Duchess had committed herself. In this Churchill advised his mother to require full details and statistics before entering on such a venture. Otherwise it would be

inadvisable for you to give the great weight of your name and influence to such proposals ... it must not be forgotten that the nature and extent of Irish disorder is a matter on which there is very great difference of opinion, and that those persons who assert that it is extreme are in many cases persons who have connected themselves with land agitation of a serious nature. By engaging in and initiating an appeal to the public to subscribe to the relief of Irish distress, you will entirely corroborate the premises of these agitators and to a certain extent excuse their acts.

---

[34] See Gregory to Duchess, 18 Sept. 1879, Blenheim D/1/11; and memo of a conversation between Churchill and Burke, n.d., in Blenheim D/1/9. The Duke, too, annoyed a deputation of bishops by his underestimation of the severity of the situation; see E. Larkin, *The Roman Catholic Church and the Creation of the Modern Irish State 1878–86* (Dublin, 1975), p. 32.

[35] See Lord Mayor Truscott to Duchess, 4 Mar. 1880, Blenheim MSS D/1/12. Similar organizations collected funds in Belfast, Manchester, and elsewhere. £53,000 of the total £88,575 collected by March 1880 was subscribed in England.

He added some characteristically swingeing criticisms of King-Harman's suggestions about providing agricultural relief, discussed the extent of the government's power to relieve distress, and reviewed the embarrassments that would be incurred by collecting too much money—or too little. The tone of the memorandum was hostile to the whole idea: it infuriated King-Harman by its scepticism.[36] What is most striking about it is its preoccupation with political advantages and appearances, above the actual question of the extent of the famine.

None the less, when the scheme got under way Churchill was one of the secretaries. His more optimistic prognosis was correct: there were large sums to be handled. By early January 1880 £51,000 had been accumulated. £10,000 was to go at once in seed potatoes, and £21,000 on food, fuel, and clothing. An expenditure of £4,000 to £6,000 a week was arrived at. By March 1880, surplus funds were being diverted to projects like pier-building, though the example of wasted effort in the 1840s was constantly held before the committee. Cynical Dublin opinion persisted in believing that the fund's chief difficulty was getting rid of the money they collected.[37] Churchill was responsible for liaison with the local committees; he wrote to bishops to find out the extent of distress in their dioceses, purchased seeds and potatoes, travelled to London to discuss special cases with the Lord Mayor, and charmed large sums from Baroness Burdett-Coutts at dinner.[38]

Increasingly, however, the politics of charity intervened, especially with the appearance of James Gordon Bennett's New York fund as a third contender. Here Churchill was prominent as well, sustaining through the newspapers a violent altercation with Parnell, who was imperturbably claiming that the Marlboroughs only succoured tenants who paid their rent; William Gregory had to console the Duchess with the unencouraging observation that such squabbles were inseparable from Irish life. Forster's donation of £300 to the Mansion House Fund was seen by the Marlborough trustees as a directly political act; the Lord Mayor was constantly accused of

[36] This memorandum is in Blenheim MSS D/1/11 (n.d.). For King-Harman's reaction see his letter to the Duchess, 15 Dec. 1879, ibid.

[37] See *Recollections of Dublin Castle* . . . and 'The true story of the Irish Famine' in Terence McGrath, *Pictures from Ireland* (London, 1880).

[38] She eventually produced £5,000; for Churchill's activities see Blenheim MSS D/1/9, 12. A later offer of £250,000 was made for seed purchase by the Baroness; see Smith to Baroness Burdett-Coutts, 8 Feb. 1880, Hambleden MSS PS 6/545.

diverting funds; the political temperature was raised to a point where bodies like the Society of Friends decided to set up their own, strictly non-party, fund. A quarrel between Dwyer Gray and the Duke over the latter's refusal to attend a Mansion House dinner imposed an added strain: Churchill contributed to this by publicly accusing the *Freeman* of poaching private telegrams from the Castle; he also advised his mother on how to handle direct onslaughts from the Mansion House. By May 1880, the *Freeman* was violently attacking the Marlborough fund for its implication that the back of the distress was broken: which proved, according to nationalist opinion, that all the Castle was after was political capital.[39] All pretence of amity had long collapsed; but the Marlborough fund was at the same time subject to strong criticism from English Protestant opinion for awarding 'special treatment' to Roman Catholics. The Marlboroughs' supposed Catholic sympathies here reacted against them. Churchill had no patience with this, and his public condemnation of Protestant scruples about the Catholic destination of their subscriptions led to further complaints to the Duchess.

The organization was wound up shortly after the Marlboroughs left Ireland in April 1880; its final report was bitterly indicted by the *Freeman's Journal*, and the fund characterized as a self-seeking machine for opportunists and time servers. There had always been an undercurrent of criticism at local levels as well, and some muttered opinions about the desirability of using the Irish Church Surplus Fund rather than private charity. The Duchess's fund had, none the less, raised £135,000. There was a residue of nearly £15,000; and this, the Duchess announced in a farewell address to 'the distressed districts', would be 'left in good hands, to be appropriated among the most destitute ... I wish to explain this to you in order that you should know that England loves Ireland, and is ever ready to help her in her hour of need.' This surplus was eventually used up on an emigration plan, largely organized by Churchill in association with Sir Alexander Galt. This was, in the event, postponed until 1883 because of 'disturbances', meaning the protracted social and political crisis; which may have indicated to the Trustees that, as regarded the course of the distress, Dwyer Gray had the best of the argument.

[39] *Weekly Freeman*, 8 May 1880. The Duchess returned the impeachment in a series of angry letters to Disraeli; see Disraeli MSS, B/xx/Ch.

Meanwhile the London government's Irish line was changing from indolence to intransigence, climaxing in Disraeli's famous open letter to Marlborough on 8 March 1880 about the 'pestilential' nature of the Home Rule movement. As the conflicts over the famine fund escalated, and the political situation became increasingly polarized, the sunny relationship between the Lord Lieutenant and Irish opinion became more and more clouded; by the time Marlborough left, it was in an atmosphere of considerable bitterness. In January 1880 he had refused to dine at the Mansion House because of Gray's presence at a Home Rule meeting 'where resolutions were passed in relation to the opposition in the West of Ireland to the enforcement of the law'. Dwyer Gray magnanimously declared his esteem for Marlborough, and inferred that it was shame at the government's policy that kept the Duke away. But the ensuing rupture between the Castle and the Mansion House had a marked effect on political relations, and was much used by the Parnellites. And after Marlborough's resignation the *Freeman's* charitable hypotheses gave way to violent attacks on the Duke's 'Tory manœuvres': his adoption of a hard line on coercion was seen as pure party opportunism; his 'mischievous and undignified behaviour' was 'a striking instance of the way in which English noblemen are humbugged and bamboozled by the gobemouche stories of Irish officials'. The *Freeman* had reverted to exactly the tone, and to the accusations, with which it had greeted Marlborough's appointment three years before. When the Duke died suddenly in 1883, the Irish nationalist newspapers took the opportunity to retell the stories of these feuds; even the Duchess's fund received some sharp blows. It was an unforeseen end to the high hopes of the 1870s, with her cultivation of Catholic contacts, and dedicated patronage of the press.

As early as January 1880 Marlborough had announced that, whatever the result of the election, he would not be returning.[40] Money probably had something to do with the decision; so had ill health; so had Lord Randolph's partial restoration in the social world. But a bitter note had entered, and the Duke was no longer popular; he had even lost favour with the episcopacy, ostensibly on account of the government's policy over the

---

[40] *Weekly Irish Times*, 13 Jan. 1880. Marlborough travelled to London and had several conferences with Disraeli. For his official request to resign see letter of 1 Apr. 1880, Disraeli MSS, B/xx/Ch/61.

agricultural crisis. (Driving to Westland Row for the last time, his escort was pelted with eggs, and a firecracker thrown from Trinity railings scorched his travelling-rug.) His speeches in the Lords called for coercion and attacked Gladstone's land legislation. The Duchess also believed that the Irish landlords were undergoing 'injustice and spoilation', and likened the atmosphere of 1881–2 to that of the French Revolution.

Though Lord Randolph had far more pleasant memories of Ireland, this partly affected him. (Preparing his die-hard speeches of January and February 1886, he appears to have consulted his father's broadsides of 1880–1.) His wife found the society dull and Castle convention stifling, though she put a brave face on it in her memoirs; she and her sister took to having races on the viceregal lawn in their night-gowns while the servants were at supper. But much of Churchill's Irish experience was formative and positive. It is too seldom realized what a concerted effort the Irish administration made in the late 1870s to press policy in a progressive and conciliatory direction against the dead weight of unimaginative Tories, notably Northcote; Churchill was much involved in this, and he retained his determinedly Catholic line in education as well as his impatience with the Commons leader. He had also developed his idiosyncratically flexible approach to politics, and his use of exaggerated but two-edged rhetoric. He had created an impression, which was a large part of his intention. Progressive unionists were interested in him. Sir William Gregory wrote of him to the Duchess in August 1880:

He is a very clever fellow, but I wish with all my heart that he would take a higher line than skirmishing. Of course, everyone is greatly amused except his victims—and that makes him persevere. Far rather would I see him, now that he has quite gained his position, make two or three steady speeches and let the House see how much thought and good sense too he is possessed of—Forgive my venturing to interfere, but you know how high is my opinion of his ability, and that opinion was not lightly formed. I like him so much moreover that I want the world to rightly estimate him and to see that he can act as well in heavy armour as in light.[41]

Churchill's relations with the normal Irish landlord interest were another matter: he was generally identified as being

---

[41] Gregory to Duchess, 16 Aug. 1880, Blenheim MSS D/1/11. Gregory retained his interest in Churchill (he supplied him with historical references for his speech against the 1886 Home Rule Bill—RCHL xiii/1485).

opposed to them, despite odd set pieces like his speech on the Compensation for Disturbance Bill in 1880. The landlords themselves saw him as an enemy, and told him so. Two years after he left Ireland, there was a slightly ridiculous incident on one of Churchill's many Dublin visits; a landlord organization claimed that he had attempted to infiltrate one of their meetings, and been refused entry.[42] Unimportant as it was, the incident, and the correspondence it generated, indicated a peculiar degree of antipathy.

But this dislike of landlords should not be identified with a nationalist orientation. If Butt attended dinners in the Little Lodge, he did so at a time when his credit with the Irish party was running out, and he was attempting a common front with the Conservatives. And the clerics who befriended the Marlborough family, Father Healy no less than Bishop Delany, were determined Conservatives. Churchill's Irish friends remained in the FitzGibbon circle, which had contributed so much to his enjoyment of the country. FitzGibbon's attitudes towards education, towards national questions, and towards landlords (whom he regarded as a dislikeable and unproductive species, doomed by economic evolution) became Churchill's. And Churchill's link with Ireland was perpetuated by FitzGibbon's annual Christmas house party at Howth, a seaside village outside Dublin, which was invariably attended by Churchill. Here were assembled Plunket, Morris, Gibson, Williamson, Mahaffy, Nedley, and Healy; sometimes with the addition of unlikely figures like John Morley or Archbishop Walsh. They were mens' parties, convivial and informal. (In later years, when Lord Londonderry as Viceroy asked to be included in the party, FitzGibbon wrote vindictively to Churchill: 'his blood be on his own head if he can't eat three suppers in a smoking-suit ... for I won't alter a tittle of the programme!'[43]) As the years went by, these parties became more specifically 'to enable Churchill to meet his Irish friends'. 'He literally loved these parties ... his greatest pleasure for many years.'[44] The activity featured drink-

---

[42] See Churchill to Col. A. L. Tottenham, 2 Jan. 1882, RCHL i/63: the misunderstanding arose because Gorst *had* wanted to be smuggled into the meeting. Also see Lord Castletown to Churchill, 6 May 1884: 'I know you have little feeling or respect for Irish landlords, and I agree with you ...' (RCHL iii/364).

[43] FitzGibbon to Churchill, 1 Nov. 1888, RCHL xvi/1959.

[44] Wynne, op. cit., p. 97: 'Some could only survive a night or two—Lord Randolph, my father and their host survived the week.' Also see Ashbourne's diary/commonplace book, Ashbourne Papers, A/1/1.

ing, talking, and card-playing. Both Churchill's son and Gibson in later years strenuously denied that these parties were 'political', but the company was overwhelmingly so; and FitzGibbon himself described Howth as 'the *haute école* of intelligent Toryism'. Here Churchill had learned many of the lessons that made him the kind of politician he became; and here he frequently returned. In these years of his social disgrace and political apprenticeship, he used Irish issues to gain authority in Westminster, deliberately establishing himself as an 'Irish expert'; and he used 'Irish' tactics to achieve notoriety outside the House. The preconceptions of the narrow social circle in which he grew up, so notable in his first years of public life, had received many jolts; a protean adaptability and a political sensitivity had been added to the arrogance and ruthlessness which were his heritage.

Chapter 3

Publicity Politics, 1880–1882

'I don't want to make a living out of opinions', said
Deronda; 'especially out of borrowed opinions. Not
that I mean to blame other men. I daresay many
better fellows than I don't mind getting on to a
platform to praise themselves, and give their word of
honour for a party.'

'I'll tell you what, Dan', said Sir Hugo, 'a man
who sets his face against every sort of humbug is
simply a three-cornered, impracticable sort of
fellow. There's a bad style of humbug, but there is
also a good style—one that oils the wheels and makes
progress possible. If you are to rule men, you must
rule them through their own ideas; and I agree with
the Archbishop at Naples who had a St. Januarius
procession against the plague. It's no use having an
Order in Council against popular shallowness.
There is no action possible without a little acting.'

George Eliot, *Daniel Deronda* (1876)

I

Churchill's initiatives and activities when he emerged into the
full light of public politics after 1880 have been closely scruti-
nized by historians. But his biographers treated his actions in
isolation and attempted to show a consistent development of
strategy and motivation. This can be misleading, for the story is
not one of linear progression. In the story of Churchill's politics
during the early 1880s there is one break, always emphasized:
his retirement to Blenheim after his father's death in July 1883.
After this came the violent struggle for control of Conservative
party organization. Certainly the Duke's death was in some
senses the removal of a political brake; it also meant temporary
relief of money troubles. But before this, there had been another
sharp break in continuity, in many ways more important. This
was Churchill's complete withdrawal into a mysterious illness

from March to October 1882: mentioned, but barely commented upon, by previous biographers. After this, there was a marked change of tempo: an escalation of activity, and a policy of neck or nothing. It is conceivable that from this date he knew the nature and severity of the illness which eventually, in the form of General Paralysis brought on by syphilis, finished his career: certainly from this period his strategy is identified by a marked impatience, and an inability to wait on results. And the views of his career which take as axiomatic his fixed adherence to consistent priorities—presented by Winston Churchill, and echoed to a large extent by Mr Rhodes James—are no help here.

What *is* evident is a change from the easily influenced, wayward, indolent product of his background who emerges in 1880 into the limelight at Westminster, where his antics are time and again likened to those of a 'schoolboy': the favourite metaphor for House of Commons behaviour, occasionally brutalized to suit Churchill's case (the *Leeds Mercury* once pictured him memorably as a gutter child throwing filth). After his illness of 1882, insubordination turned into a coherent effort to supplant his leaders; and parliamentary larking turned to a distaste for what he had come to see as timewasting at Westminster. Impatience by then may have had a physiological as well as a psychological reason. But up to March 1882—the period of establishment to which we must now turn—his priority was to make a figure.

J. E. Gorst, Churchill's close associate in these years, believed in later life that his friend was 'deeply indebted to others for the information and opportunities of which he took immediate advantage';[1] what was elsewhere less elegantly called his 'simian aptitude for assimilation' stood him in good stead. As he had taken his line from the fashionable *ton* in 1874, and from Irish Tories in 1877–80, so in 1880–2 he fell in with intelligent legal conservatives like Gorst, H. C. Raikes, and Edward Clarke, who felt that the only way to revive party fortunes was to change direction away from the Old Gang's flaccidity and social exclusiveness. In this, it was sometimes politic to appeal to Beaconsfield, and Winston Churchill portrayed his father as inspired by Disraeli and following his early example. This fitted in with Winston's artistic construction, but sits less comfortably with the facts. In 1880–2, Churchill seemed in a sense about to

---

[1] H. Hyndman, *The Record of an Adventurous Life* (London, 1911), p. 410.

be 'run' by those who believed in organizing middle-class Toryism, and wanted an aristocratic front man. But he was too erratic, and also too prone to making gestures of support towards Salisbury. After the summer of 1882, and his long illness, he was to take his own direction, borrowing the ideas of Gorst and Clarke and dressing them up in the language of 'Tory Democracy'. (The appeal to working-class Tories concealed the fact that the Toryism of Manchester, Liverpool, and Birmingham was not working-class: and the disgruntled representatives of the National Union of Conservative Associations, who obligingly provided his power base, were not representative of the Democracy.) The translation from parliamentary frondeur to platform star would add a weight to Churchill's image which enabled him to declare his terms to his leaders in 1884, disembarrass himself of the elements which had helped 'make' him, and depart gracefully for India. To this the events of 1880–2 formed a necessary background but seemed at the time to tend in a different direction.

Churchill's return from Ireland in 1880 coincided with the preparation for a general election; in his case he also discovered a neglected constituency and an apathetic electorate. Joseph Arch had been approached to stand against him, but— fortunately for Churchill—had declined; an unknown candidate called William Hall entered the lists instead. Even the Liberal newspapers expected Churchill to walk over, and the contest was generally amicable; the only heckling at Churchill's meetings came from a stray Primitive Methodist preacher. However, in his address and in his speeches, he had to align himself firmly against Irish nationalism, in view of his previous gaffe; and he also found that he had to make as much capital as possible from his parents' position, as his slack parliamentary record was made much of by his opponent. When he was returned by sixty votes local opinion attributed his victory equally to Marlborough influence and personal popularity; but, it was added, his 'wonderfully clever speeches surprised even his most ardent admirers'.[2]

The 'wonderfully clever speeches' involved taking frequent refuge in violent die-hard rhetoric; he reassured his mother that he was sounding the Jingo note only to avoid 'lukewarmness'. Absence from debates on heartfelt issues like the Agricultural

---

[2] See *Oxford Times*, 30 Mar., 3 Apr., 1880.

Holdings Bill was held against him; 'I think I must attend more regularly this session.' On the hustings, his reaction was violently to accuse the Liberals of pressurizing and harassing voters; it was not an impressively strong argument. Nor was his onslaught on the ambitions of foreign powers, and the weakness of 'milk and water philanthropy'. He accused his opponent of dangerous Home Rule tendencies, and testified to his own purity by quoting a Trinity College academic who likened Irish Parnellism to French Communism and Russian Nihilism: 'Don't let Woodstock be disgraced by returning a member to the House of Commons who will co-operate with these "political desperadoes".'[3] This advice is ironic in the light of Churchill's record in the parliament to come; but his hard line was probably dictated by his utterances of 1877, often brought up against him.

Otherwise, he made capital of the Liberals' rapacious intentions regarding small boroughs and Sunday licences, and emphasized the Conservative record on behalf of the working class. In keeping with this image, he emphasized that he was proud to call Dilke his friend, and supported extending the franchise to agricultural labourers. But the finale to his election speech was an impassioned and histrionic review of British victories in South Africa, India, and the Near East, and a call for imperial expansion: though imperialism, as Lord Rosebery later recalled, was one belief to which he never subscribed.

These striking attitudes did not alter the fact that, besides the traditional accusations of undue influence exerted from Blenheim, his opponent made the telling point that out of the 217 divisions on foreign policy in the last parliament, Churchill had attended only three. Hall went on to rehearse several anti-government remarks of Churchill's in speeches delivered on his visits home from Ireland. And he used these to substantiate a rumour current before the election: that Churchill had been going to stand as a Liberal, and effect a union between the house of Marlborough and the party of Gladstone. (This was not an unlikely supposition, in view of the fact that within a year the irrepressible Blandford would be fulminating in the *Nineteenth Century* against the House of Lords, the land system, and the 'paternal government of clergy and squires'; in February 1881 he approached Harcourt about standing for Oxford and by June

---

[3] *Jackson's Oxford Journal*, 3 Apr. 1880. Churchill liked the phrase 'political desperadoes' and used it again about the Liberals at Portsmouth the following November. For a further speech see *Oxford Times*, 20 Mar. 1880.

he was generally credited with ambitions to appear in parliament as a Liberal.[4])

His election, then, provided some salutary lessons for Churchill. He returned to a metropolitan political world stunned by the great Conservative defeat, and took up residence in St. James's Place with his wife and two young children. He was still exiled from the social world; in the endless society litanies of attendance to be found in the fashionable journals of the time, the Randolph Churchills never appear (though the Blandfords, attempting a reunion, do). The reason for this was an open secret; when the Conservatives of Manchester presented Churchill with a chair in January 1882, Labouchere's *Truth* insidiously remarked that it was carved with the Prince of Wales's feathers: 'Is there a mysterious meaning in them?'; a *Vanity Fair* squib referred to Churchill retiring from politics to become 'polite letter-writer to the Prince of Wales'. In political circles, the affair continued to provide amusement; Dilke recorded the Prince's antipathy to Churchill in his diary, and when Harcourt warned the Queen of threats against her life by 'a person of rank', she acidly riposted that she did not know who could be meant 'unless it were Randolph Churchill'.[5] Money matters also continued problematic. In 1880 special legislation enabled the Duke to sell the entailed Sunderland Library, and the following year the first sale brought in £20,000 of the £100,000 eventually expected. Public opinion, probably unfairly, drew the conclusion that the Churchills simply saw books as 'lumber'; whatever about this, they certainly needed the money, and Churchill's own finances found only temporary relief.

A similar paucity of resources was evident in the political world. The Conservatives in 1880 were in a state of mild trauma, attested to by commentators at the time and by political historians ever since. Nevertheless, too much can be made of the image of lethargy projected in the picture of an ailing Beaconsfield in the Lords, a timid Old Gang in the Commons, and a demoralized organization in the country. The Fourth Party version of events, which was the one to pass to posterity, is too black and white. Others besides discontented young tyros saw the deficiencies of the party, and attempted to come to grips with them. Smith, though one of the favourite Fourth Party targets as representing the ethos of 'Marshall and Snelgrove' suburban attitudes, was instrumental in the attempt to reorganize the constituencies in 1880–1; he approached Stanhope and Percy, as well as Gorst and Balfour, in this sense and was obsessed from the early 1880s with the danger of otherwise 'drifting into radical socialism very fast indeed'.[6] Significantly, he made the contentious barrister J. E. Gorst the avatar in the effort to restructure electoral organization, circulating letters from him to Northcote and others from an early stage, and coming to a formal agreement with him in July 1880. In return for reorganizing the constituencies, Gorst was to be provided with a law officer's appointment. He accepted the appointment with misgivings, complaining of how he had been 'shelved' after undertaking similar work in the early 1870s, and the arrangement was as unhappy as might have been expected. Gorst quarrelled with local Tories, who he claimed expected him to 'fight corruption with corruption',[7] and became rapidly alienated from Smith. In September 1880 he saw him as an alternative leader to Northcote, and wrote to him in terms of devoted affection; but by mid-1881 they were on a footing of angry formality. Gorst, furious about how he had been treated in terms of responsibility and remuneration, only continued in office with a bad grace until the end of 1882.

This was to be one important factor in the genesis of Fourth Party politics; another was the fact that the attempted reorganization of the Conservative party had the incidental effect of alienating some local Conservative 'working-men's' associations, who felt that the new organizational effort would clash with their own responsibilities.[8] Moreover the National Union, representing grass-roots Conservative organization in the

---

[6] Smith to Cranbrook, 23 Jan. 1882, Cranbrook MSS HA 43 T501/260. Also see Smith to Balfour, 5 Oct. 1881, Balfour MSS, BL Add. MS 49695; and, on the whole issue, Feuchtwanger, pp. 48–9.

[7] Gorst and Smith, 8 Sept. 1880, Hambleden MSS PS/6/639. He was always antipathetic to local chiefs; see letters to Disraeli, 10 Nov. 1875, 22 Nov. 1875, in Disraeli MSS, B/xxi/G/253, 255. In a letter to his chief he referred to the hostility of local managers towards him as 'the natural consequence of my steadfast adherence to those popular principles in politics, which you taught me, which won the boroughs in 1874, and which though for the time being in discredit must ultimately prevail'; 4 Apr. 1878, ibid. 259. His correspondence throughout the 1870s breathes grudges and embitterment.

[8] See address from Westminster Workingmen's Conservative Association to Smith, 5 July 1880; Hambleden MSS PS/6/625a.

country, in Gorst's words 'broke out into discord with the Party managers after the General election' and had to be mollified. From this bizarre constituency of local notables and offended party manipulators Churchill and his friends would draw support in the years ahead.

The picture of party organization in the country is one pre-conditioning factor for the initiative Churchill took in 1880–2; the issue more often emphasized is the situation at Westminster where, even before Beaconsfield's death in April 1881, the quality of the leadership to face the revived Liberals and their restored Colossus was at issue. The rivalry of Salisbury and Northcote for this position was neither as covert nor as gentle-manly as is often implied. Salisbury, for instance, not only agreed with Balfour about the weakness of the Opposition front bench in the Commons, while with characteristic fatalism expecting further decay; he also felt strongly about Beaconsfield's shortcomings as a leader, or at least let Balfour think he did.[9] Salisbury's gloominess, cynicism, and grandeur created an impression of removal from the fray, but this underestimated his appreciation of the realities of battle. Nor were the leaders in the Commons as flaccid and accepting as they are often represented; to some extent, it is tempting to think that the Fourth Party invented the Old Gang. Sir Stafford Northcote ('the Goat', in Churchill's cruelly catching patois) was a traditional figure of fun, timid, cautious, and rather dim; but even he was less modest and retiring, and certainly less respectful of Gladstone, than the propaganda of the Young Turks made him out to be. He was, after all, an ambitious politician, if more diffident than most; in the late 1870s he was capable of 'speaking out in a very bold and unexpected manner' to deputations of disquieted Conservatives; after the 1880 election he had written decisively to Smith that Disraeli's political career was ended. Similarly, he fully realized the realities of his position after Disraeli's death; he immediately went to some trouble to establish that the leader elected in the Lords would not automatically be treated as the leader of the party. His translation to aspirant leader, if in some quarters unexpected, was in its own way effective. He had pressed a decisive foreign policy on Disraeli, and later on Salisbury, against their love of drift; about matters like the 'viciousness' of

[9] Salisbury to Balfour, 2 Sept. 1880, and a long memorandum dated Hatfield, May 1880, in Balfour MSS, BL Add. MS 49688.

the Home Rulers he was unequivocal. While rarely clever, Northcote was not always mild.[10]

None the less, when Churchill and his friends appeared as the Fourth Party opposition within the Opposition, angling their attack against the Conservative front bench as much as against the government and posing as the representatives of aggressive Toryism, they suited the purposes of more elements in the party than they appeared to represent. This was clear from the time of the Bradlaugh case, which formed the base for the first concerted parliamentary effort of Wolff and Churchill, backed by Gorst and Balfour.

Several authorities have analysed the events and attitudes which developed round the attempt by Charles Bradlaugh, a Radical agnostic calling himself an atheist, first to take the oath in the House of Commons after stating he did not believe in it, and then to affirm instead of taking that oath.[11] This created an issue in May 1880 which was seized upon by Sir Henry Drummond Wolff, and supported by John Gorst—though unpopular with many Conservatives in the country at large. By 21 May, Wolff had enlisted Churchill's support in preventing Bradlaugh from taking the oath; Bradlaugh's advocacy of birth control becoming a convenient if irrelevant side issue, much cherished by Churchill. Gibson, still friendly with Churchill from his Irish days, joined in. On 24 May Churchill made his famous speech to the House, concentrating on Bradlaugh's attack in *The Impeachment of the House of Brunswick* on the royal family: a histrionic *tour de force*, during which he trampled the pamphlet on the ground. A hare had been started which would run and run. 'Henceforth upon the Bradlaugh question', his son wrote, 'he took his natural place as leader . . .'

The issue was all the more attractive in view of Northcote's initial hesitation, and supposed Liberal inclinations on such issues; accurately or not, political opinion felt that he was being pressed on 'by his more ardent supporters'. If this was the case, he caught up fast; but his view remained characteristically ambivalent. William Grantham, who investigated the consti-

---

[10] See *Vanity Fair*, 26 Jan. 1878, and Northcote to Smith, 4 Apr. 1880, Hambleden MSS PS/6/574. Also T. Kebbel, *Lord Beaconsfield and Other Tory Memories* (London, 1907), pp. 143–4, and Northcote to Disraeli on the Eastern Question, 21 Apr. 1877 and 2 Jan. 1878, Iddesleigh MSS, BL Add. MS 50018. For his firm line against Salisbury's election see Northcote to Cranbrook, 7 May 1881, Cranbrook MSS HA 53 T501/271.

[11] See W. L. Arnstein, *The Bradlaugh Case* (Oxford, 1965); and R. Quinault, 'Fourth Party and the Conservative opposition to Bradlaugh', loc. cit.

tutional position for Wolff and Churchill, found Northcote's influence exerted against any forward policy in the matter. None the less, Northcote had not been as initially dilatory as he is often portrayed; as early as 15 May he asked Smith: 'What are we to do about Bradlaugh? They say he means to take the oath "under protest"; but I doubt whether we ought to consent to such a Mockery as that. Many excellent people will be deeply pained, if we do.'[12]

Churchill also saw the possibilities of such an issue, and the necessity to outbid Northcote. How seriously he took Bradlaugh's ideas, and the threat of what he represented, is dubious.[13] His motives were generally accepted by contemporaries as dictated by expediency; and both his biographers, though always ready to search out a lofty principle, seem to concur. While a different analysis has recently been advanced, this case can only cite as contemporary witnesses the unbalanced and contumacious F. H. O'Donnell, himself involved in the opposition to Bradlaugh, and a surely ironic description by Henry Lucy, the doyen of parliamentary correspondents, of Wolff and Gorst as 'the two champions of religion'.[14] The religious strain in Churchill's family is certainly marked (if uneven), but whether it extended to his own private attitudes can be doubted—as much as whether the seventh Duke's dedicated opposition to the admission of Jews to parliament affected his son's enjoyment of parties given by Rothschild and Hirsch. Certainly he was never an ardent churchgoer; writing to his wife a few years earlier he had ridiculed 'the monotonous exhortations of a clergyman in a white surplice' compared to 'contemplating the beauties of nature'; on another occasion he confided to her that he thought 'all religious differences senseless ... don't say anything about this'.[15] Naturally, he upheld the principle of the Established Church in election addresses and platform speeches; it would have been politically curious, not to say suicidal, had he not. And certainly, at this stage of his career, he was still influenced and hedged by the

---

[12] Northcote to Smith, 11 May 1880, Hambleden MSS PS/6/617.

[13] Cf. the lofty note of *Vanity Fair*, 3 Oct. 1874; 'Most forward boys have passed through Mr Bradlaugh's intellectual stage ...'

[14] See Quinault, op cit. Gorst's son, writing with his father's approbation, implied that it was all undertaken largely for fun (Harold Gorst, *The Fourth Party* (London, 1906), pp. 43–4, 54–5).

[15] Churchill to Lady Randolph, 26 Oct. 1873, 16 Jan. 1874, CHAR 28/2, 4.

example and preferences of his father, to whom he was deeply attached by emotional ties as well as financial dependence.

But the primary attraction of the Bradlaugh case for Churchill was its potential for political creativity reinforced, possibly, by the chance of social rehabilitation through an attack on Bradlaugh's republicanism (though republicanism *per se* had not affected the attraction he felt towards Dilke). This, in fact, had some of the desired effect; Lady Randolph proudly told her sister on 30 May that the Prince 'expressed himself highly pleased' with Churchill's attack on Bradlaugh, and a reconciliation seemed about to follow. This hope was, in fact, premature: but the policy was still worth persevering with. And Churchill had a further personal interest, curiously ignored by both his biographers: Bradlaugh made a special issue of attacking state pensions, particularly the £4,000 p.a. enjoyed by the Duke of Marlborough for his ancestor's services, though this was a cause which came to prominence only after Churchill had advanced to the fore as Bradlaugh's opponent. The Duke's annuity was seen in other Liberal quarters as irrational and indefensible; and Bradlaugh's campaign against it was probably the reason why he was opposed by Churchill's Gladstonian brother-in-law, Edward Marjoribanks.

Churchill therefore had sufficient personal motivation to attack Bradlaugh; but it is probable that his attraction to the issue was primarily dictated by the opportunity it gave for parliamentary effects, its catalysing action within the Tory party, and his recognition of the popularity of the anti-Bradlaugh case among the electorate in Oxfordshire and elsewhere. At a later stage he wrote enthusiastically to T. H. S. Escott about the possibility of publishing his attack on Bradlaugh as a pamphlet: 'it might be widely circulated in the large towns'.[16] Smith had been told in August 1881 that a Conservative electoral victory in Preston was caused not by the Fair Trade cry but by Roman Catholic feeling against Bradlaugh.[17] Within the halls of Westminster, moreover, the possibilities afforded by the case were endless. Churchill used the affair to attack the government for covertly supporting 'mob law'; he accused them of inspiring Bradlaugh himself. Such an approach provided

---

[16] Churchill to Escott, 6 May 1883, Escott MSS, BL Add. MS 58793. Also see Churchill to Gibson, 5 Nov. 1880, Ashbourne Papers catalogue, p. 102 (B 32/1), and Quinault, p. 329.

[17] R. Mowbray to Smith, 10 Aug. 1881, Hambleden MSS, PS/7/80.

more immediate returns than extrapolating from abstract questions of principle, which he avoided. There was an added attraction in the opportunity for a tactical alliance with the Irish Party; Churchill pressed for a large Irish Catholic representation on the select committee formed to consider the question. In later debates, he was to use the Bradlaugh issue much as he used minor Irish questions; playing for laughs, embarrassing the government, proposing time-consuming amendments. It provided great opportunities for pyrotechnical displays of parliamentary knowledge which he was amassing at a surprising rate; and it also gave him the opportunity to tilt at Liberal academics like Thorold Rogers, who had already opposed him on Oxford platforms. But he did not turn up to vote on several of the vital issues regarding this long-drawn-out affair; and his opposition to Bradlaugh often seemed based on tactics more than on principles. In some quarters this opposition was urbanely attributed to Bradlaugh's class and appearance rather than his opinions, which would be—and were—perfectly acceptable in clubland.

The issue was warmly accepted by the party at large; Northcote was probably more equivocal than most, but even he lined up behind Wolff's motion, and publicly approved of Churchill's speech against Bradlaugh (while confiding to Beaconsfield that it 'overshot the mark'). This did not mean a close alliance between Northcote and those in the vanguard of the attack; Gorst's assurance that the Fourth Party would 'back him up warmly' should not be taken at face value, and Balfour's denigration of Northcote to his uncle never faltered. Salisbury himself was equivocal about the usefulness of the Bradlaugh issue to the party; or at least he appeared so in his letters to Northcote, advising him to stay clear and let things slide: the very tactics for which, in other areas, he heard the leader in the Commons denounced. The campaign was deliberately unconcerted; a meeting on 24 June 1880 to consider Conservative tactics towards Bradlaugh was attended by neither Salisbury nor the Fourth Party.

It remains true that Churchill's violent opposition to Northcote post-dates the former's illness in 1882. But this should be considered in its place: as should Churchill's later attitude towards the question of Bradlaugh's right to affirm. In the day-to-day practice of politics, the multiple factors defining responses to a given situation must be seen all together; if it is tempting to construct a pattern by extracting one theme of involvement and following it through the years, in the case of Churchill the resulting picture would bear little resemblance to reality. There were certainly some ideas which remained constant, but these could not always be acknowledged. Health, money, personal ambition, and the vicissitudes of the contest for the leadership must be borne in mind; and all varied from month to month. Perhaps it is for this reason that Winston Churchill omitted from his account of his father's opposition to Bradlaugh not only the issues of royal favour and the Marlborough pension but also Churchill's volte-face in 1887 when he came to support Bradlaugh's Affirmation Bill. What remains relevant is what some political commentators saw at the time, and what various members of his family concurred in long afterwards: that the Bradlaugh case 'made' Lord Randolph (so much so that he was credited with bribing the Northampton electors to keep returning the miscreant).[18]

Most immediately, the striking development was Churchill's speedy adoption of a combination with Gorst and Wolff, and the readiness of all three to dictate a line to Northcote. The alliance was in many ways a logical one. Sir Henry Drummond Wolff was a middle-aged career diplomat and man-about-town. Socially popular, suave, and well-connected, he was a friend of the Marlboroughs and frequently visited Churchill's sisters; he was close to Churchill from the late 1870s, during which period he had advanced his career through Eastern diplomacy and been a notably forceful opponent of Derby. He was much connected with Egyptian affairs in private and in public; his financial reputation was dubious, a fact held against him by respectable politicians. As early as 1876 he was indulging in what would later be called Fourth Party tactics, moving for a select committee to inquire into the duties and responsibilities of various departmental officials, to vociferous Radical approval. He was seen, with Smith and Hicks Beach, as a coming man; in 1879 he had gone on an important mission to Eastern Roumelia. In Near Eastern matters, he called for universal independence for the Turkish principalities, and was therefore resented by the 'thick and thin partisans of Turkey'; this was probably attractive to Churchill, though even so he had once

---

[18] See for instance Leonard Jerome to Lady Randolph, 30 Nov. 1883, CHAR 28/1. Also Tweedmouth to W. S. Churchill, 10 Sept. 1905, ibid. 8/201. For bribery rumour see LHJ, 1 Mar. 1882, vol. 350, p. 45.

seen Wolff as too 'pro-Turkish'. General opinion in the 1870s saw him as preferring the style of parliamentary freelance rather than using his influential connections; he himself felt that he was 'not well treated by the government'. A good-tempered cynic, he was seen six years before the birth of the Fourth Party as being dangerous to his leaders as well as to the opposition, and was noted for his cross-bench friendships—especially with James (soon to become an intimate of Churchill's) and Chamberlain. But equally important was his propensity to cherish grudges, imagine plots, and blame members of his own party for intriguing against him: a characteristic which developed later in his life into a kind of persecution complex.[19]

J. E. Gorst, a career lawyer–politician credited with being the brains behind the Conservative victory of 1874, has lately been paid more attention by historians than used to be his wont: which he would have seen as his due, for his career was interrupted by disappointments and real or imagined slights. Though in 1867 he had tried to form a reactionary cave against Reform, by 1880 he believed that what he took to be Disraelian 'popular principles in politics', while currently discredited, would ultimately prevail. Disraeli for his part declared that Gorst was the only dangerous Fourth Party member, and confessed himself 'quite unable even to guess at the motives which guide him'. Perhaps this was because Gorst's priorities involved ideas rather than tactics. He was, reasonably enough, embittered at being passed over by his chiefs in the 1870s; he had been marked down as 'a trouble to the government' within the ranks. In 1875 he had resigned as party agent in circumstances of extreme acrimony; after his re-engagement in 1880, the way was no smoother. He continued to be vociferously critical, not only of apathy among party organizers, but also of slack attendance in the House.[20] His son wrote at length in *The Fourth*

[19] See Wolff to Corry, Disraeli MSS B/xxi/W/485, for the 'scurvy treatment' and constant attacks to which he was exposed from 'two particular gentlemen' in the party. On his missions to Constantinople, Cairo, and Madrid in the 1880s, his letters constantly described real or imagined machinations against him. Also see *Vanity Fair*, 5 Sept. 1874; Escott, *Society in London*; H. Gorst, *The Fourth Party*, p. 34; H. D. Wolff, *Rambling Recollections* (London, 1908), ii, 252.

[20] See for instance Gorst to Northcote, 13 Mar. 1883; Iddesleigh MSS, BL Add. MS 50041. Gorst to Disraeli, 4 Apr. 1878 (quoted in Feuchtwanger, p. 139); and *Vanity Fair*, 31 July 1875. 'Since his election to parliament he has shown the most alarming disposition to kick over the traces, and to take a line of his own not consistent with that devotion to his party expected of him.' For his complaints about the Conservative performance in parliament see Gorst to Disraeli, 30 Sept. 1880, Disraeli MSS B/xxi/G/260.

Party of his qualities and his colleagues' lack of appreciation; Dilke delivered a more lapidary judgement in table talk. 'Dangerously frank, a nominal Tory, in fact a Radical, ever battering his own side for the mere fun of the operation; old in years, young in activity of brain and body; a poor man all his life.'

A high point of the Fourth Party's public campaign in the winter of 1880 was when Churchill brought Gorst to speak at Woodstock in November, where he criticized Northcote at length;[21] yet at the same time he was schizophrenically involved with the party elders in organization plans, and committed to addressing local worthies on the same platform as Fourth Party butts like Sclater-Booth. Such creative tension was an important element in Fourth Party dynamics. So was the camaraderie engendered by their parliamentary co-operation. A connection with Wolff and Gorst made sense for Churchill; with Wolff he shared common family friendships and an interest in the Eastern Question, with Gorst a shared dislike of party leaders and a feeling of recognition unrewarded. A close relationship with the elegant and detached Arthur Balfour seems less logical; but Balfour was, as is now generally recognized, only ancillary to the Fourth Party alliance, and were it not for a famous 'Spy' cartoon would barely be counted with them. Certainly, his denials in *Chapters of Autobiography* of close association with Churchill were partly dictated by special pleading; but the correspondence of the time suggests that the others were never sure of him.[22] This was only reasonable; as Salisbury's nephew Balfour's interest was inevitably pledged elsewhere, and his consistent line in letters to his uncle from the 1880s was to depreciate Churchill. Churchill himself would have expected no more; for a biographer to find Balfour's behaviour 'repellent' is to miss the point. Even before Beaconsfield's death and the leadership issue, this line was laid down. Balfour was not as often involved in Churchill's intimate dinners at the Turf Club, and, significantly, he was the channel by which the Old Gang approached Gorst.

None the less, there was an unaffected friendship between Churchill and Balfour: both born to the political purple which did not extend to Wolff and Gorst, who had to make their way

---

[21] See *Jackson's Oxford Journal*, 20 Nov. 1880.
[22] See Wolff, *Rambling Recollections*, ii, 258–9; and letters such as Gorst to Churchill, 17 July 1883, RCHL i/143, which emphasize that 'A.J.B. is not to be relied upon'. Also Cornwallis-West, p. 93.

from scratch. This does not alter the fact that Balfour was never entirely happy about Wolff's and Churchill's more aggressive offensives in the country.[23] (And though Gorst, Wolff, and especially Churchill were friendly with H. M. Hyndman, of the Marxist Social Democratic Federation, that Tory revolutionary, to his slight disappointment, never managed to meet Balfour.) In after years, Balfour saw Fourth Party politics as sharply divided by Disraeli's death, and the ensuring indecision about Salisbury's leadership. Before this 'we were four men who had no personal ambitions beyond the ordinary ones of wanting to get on and make our mark in Parliament ... But as soon as the question of party leadership became a practical one, a second phase set in. Randolph himself realised what my attitude would be, and never expected me to act differently from the way I did.'[24] Balfour went on to credit Churchill with a personal ambition to be leader as early as April 1881: which is probably exaggerated. But a year and a half later, after his lengthy illness, such an analysis has a certain validity.

The four were, none the less, publicly identified together from the time of the Bradlaugh debates (though Balfour was barely involved in these), and were welded into a unit by the obstruction of government measures which made, and gave them, their name. In this as in much else, the Fourth Party learned from the Third, or Irish, Party; by the end of the session they were being blamed as much as the Home Rulers for demoralizing the House.

The membership remained limited. First hearing of it in August 1880, Gladstone's secretary Edward Hamilton thought the Fourth Party included Chaplin and Elcho, and certainly the original nucleus were ready to proselytize; but they remained at most four. James Lowther, noted for heterodox opinions, exasperation with Northcote, and aggressiveness in debate, seemed a natural ally, but was antipathetic to Churchill. Eardley Wilmot followed the Fourth Party on many issues, including sympathy for the Irish, but probably took his politics too seriously for them. Edward Clarke was invited to join them in 1880, but declined—again probably through distaste for

---

[23] See Balfour to Churchill, n.d., RCHL i/16, where he advises against attending a meeting at Glasgow. Also same to same, 11 Oct. 1880 and 3 Nov. 1880, ibid. 17, 22. A letter of Churchill's to Wolff about this, quoted in W. S. Churchill, i, 184, is misdated as 1882.

[24] A. J. Balfour, *Chapters of Autobiography* (ed. B. Dugdale, 1930), p. 133.

Churchill—and was soon seen as an enemy by Gorst. Gibson was urged, in a baroque invitation concocted by Wolff and Churchill at Blenheim, to abjure his 'morbid attachment to Smith and Cross', and join them, but nervously categorized the missive as a 'skit'; Gorst from the beginning wrote him off as 'goaty'.[25] Raikes, a critic of Conservative timidity whose earlier career in party organization closely paralleled Gorst's, was an ally of Wolff and seemed logical Fourth Party material; as chairman of the Church Defence Institution he took a prominent part against Bradlaugh, but was alienated from Gorst in 1880 over party organization. W. H. Smith, the self-consciously humble bookstall magnate, was flattered by Gorst, who told him he would be leader in the Commons 'whether you like it or not'; at this stage the two were closely associated in party organization, and Smith expressed friendship to the Fourth Party in return. But this reflects more the sensitivity of Gorst's position: the terms of his appointment, Northcote told Disraeli with relief in July 1880, included 'conforming to our wishes indoors' in return for a *quid pro quo* when the party regained office.[26] Smith was too well advanced in the party hierarchy to need the Fourth Party; and Churchill had antagonized him by characteristic bourgeois-baiting. Chaplin, a Disraelian and a Fair Trader, was invited to meet the Fourth Party at Blenheim, and speak to the Marlborough tenantry; but the National Union controversy would put him firmly on the other side.

During the 1880 session Churchill's grandiose references to 'my friends' became a staple commodity of his debating style, but the intention was, as so often, heavily ironic: the Fourth Party remained strictly limited, though their recruitment ambitions seem to have been wider than is generally allowed.None the less, by February 1881 he and Gorst were prominent speakers at a meeting in Disraeli's house to discuss strategy; by the following year, the *Pall Mall Gazette* could regretfully refer to 'the Woodstock school of politics'. How this had come about has frequently been described. The filibustering and speech-making of Churchill, Gorst, Wolff, and Balfour, the opposition offered to Northcote, the general devil-may-care insouciance and icono-clasm of their contributions to legislation and non-legislation is

[25] A. B. Cooke and A. P. W. Malcolmson (eds.), *The Ashbourne Papers, 1869–1912: a Calendar of the Papers of Edward Gibson, First Lord Ashbourne* (HMSO, Belfast, 1974); also Gorst to Churchill, 5 Nov. 1880, RCHL i/20.

[26] Northcote to Disraeli, 7 July 1880 (copy), Iddesleigh MSS, BL Add. MS 50018.

lovingly detailed by Churchill's biographers; but they do not mention one important aspect of the way the Fourth Party struck contemporary opinion, even well before Beaconsfield's death. This was as a front movement on Salisbury's behalf in the subterranean manœuvrings for the succession. In June 1880, it was remarked that Wolff and his friends, who now 'entirely ignored' Northcote, 'took their orders from Lord Salisbury'; in December Labouchere still saw Salisbury as 'the real leader behind whom the Fourth Party fight'. This was seen as part of a general strategy to wrench the party away from Northcote's tendency to Whiggish coalition. The Fourth Party themselves subscribed to this analysis, as far as Northcote's intentions went: Gorst, Wolff, and Balfour constantly suspected him of truckling to the Whigs. Though Salisbury assured Balfour there was nothing in the idea, the fact remains that correspondents of figures like Smith constantly bemoaned the ill luck that kept them sundered from right-wing Liberals. And coalition was indeed Northcote's cherished ambition, though he was worried that such an impression might become public.[27] Churchill expressed himself less vehemently about the dangers of coalition; he was never averse to ideas of co-operation, though rarely with Whigs. Wolff, indeed, wrote far more virulently of Northcote than did Churchill at this stage. 'He is a loathsome creature', he remarked to Balfour, 'full of small spite and destitute of virility, except in its lowest germ development: a kind of earthworm.'[28]

This was after Beaconsfield's death. But even before the leadership issue, Salisbury was prepared to advise the Fourth Party—not only through Balfour, but also in letters to Gorst, whom he annoyed by advocating 'a flabby resistance to Gladstone, like that of the Turkish empire', in order to maximize internal Liberal dissension. He was, moreover, capable of delicately denigrating Northcote to Balfour and Gorst.[29] Such intercourse began in 1880, and continued through 1881; in July of that year Churchill approached Salisbury over a projected joint parliamentary offensive about French ambitions in North

---

[27] See Northcote's diary, quoted in A. Lang, *Life, Letters and diaries of Sir Stafford Northcote, First Earl of Iddesleigh* (Edinburgh, 1890), ii. 150. For his worry about such coalition ideas becoming public see Northcote to Smith, 27 Sept. 1881; Hambleden MSS, PS/7/88.

[28] Wolff to Balfour, 17 Nov. 1881; Balfour MSS, BL Add. MS. 49830. At the same time he carefully eulogized Salisbury's speech at Bristol: 'it was so quiet, yet hit so hard'.

[29] Salisbury to Balfour, 2 Sept. 1880, Balfour MSS, BL Add. MS 49688, deprecating the weakness of the leadership in the Commons.

Africa, and was ostensibly dissuaded by him. Public opinion supposed that a Salisbury-led Conservative party would mean politics along the old 'confrontation' lines, whereas the choice of Northcote implied an injection of Liberalism; Salisbury's violence, rashness, and supposed dishonesty would make fusion unlikely. A continuing game of parlour politics was provided for onlookers by the uncertain position of Northcote and Salisbury throughout 1881.

In this, the Fourth Party's position was an important counter. Churchill played a starring role at a Portsmouth meeting in November 1880, where Gorst and Wolff spoke as well; obstruction was defended, the Roman Catholic Church attacked, and the Conservative leadership in the Commons not mentioned. The alliance with Salisbury seemed sealed by the latter's appearance as guest speaker at a large Conservative demonstration in Woodstock in December 1880—an idea originating with Churchill, who prevailed upon Balfour to ask his uncle to oblige him (Salisbury would in any case be attending a house party at Blenheim). That their association was more tentative than the public assumed is indicated by the fact that Churchill saw this as an 'audacious request'. But in 1880–2, a Salisbury front group seemed a plausible interpretation of the Fourth Party's activities; and one very possibly subscribed to by Churchill as well as by Balfour.

This, as so much else, was to alter after Churchill's long illness in 1882. But his speech at Woodstock was a fulsome encomium on Salisbury; Salisbury's answering commendation of Churchill, it was gloomily felt by the *Daily News*, would 'add considerably to the importance of that self-satisfied politician'. Certainly the meeting, officially convened to inaugurate a new local Convervative organization, was as lavish and trumped-up as could be managed, with a large attendance of luminaries and much publicity. Churchill spoke in a classic Fourth Party idiom, comparing positive unity to negative unity in opposition, and hailing Salisbury unequivocally as leader of the party (this four months before Beaconsfield's death); Salisbury referred to Northcote's leadership in the Commons, but went no further, and at the end of the meeting proposed a special vote of thanks to Churchill, who by his 'energy and ability' in the last session had 'given hope to the Tory party of a great ornament and support'. It was, as most newspapers interpreted it, a direct endorsement of the upstart Churchill's policy in the Commons.

Immediately after this, Wolff thought he detected a new offensive by Stanhope and Northcote against the Fourth Party and Salisbury: he counselled ostentatious loyalty, though Churchill did not agree. On 20 December he gave at Preston the sort of dazzlingly unrestrained speech for which he was becoming famous: a flow of baroque hyperbole on the subject of Gladstone and Ireland. Taken with the Woodstock meeting, it made for a very productive recess. And Northcote, between these two triumphs, felt it necessary to emphasize to his constituents that '"the Fourth Party" was an expression of a jocular character, and was not a very accurate representation of the sentiments of any party or association in the House of Commons ... [they were] as true and loyal to the great party to which they belonged as any other gentlemen in the House of Commons'.[30] But the fact remained that in 1880 parliamentary circumstances, the fortuitous coincidence of allies, and the innate readiness to outrage respectable opinion which was encouraged by his Irish exile, combined to make Churchill a figure of note at Westminster. These conditions, and his own parliamentary style, were perfectly adapted to opposition politics in the post-1867 world, where powers of demolition were needed rather than of construction. The ultra-Tory opinions which he had articulated under the previous administration showed little sign of moderating as yet; but the Fourth Party's identification with democratic organization and cultivation of the local party base, which was furnished by Gorst, would soon be taken to the country and be presented as a new Conservative ideology.

II

The Fourth Party's remarkably rapid achievement of public recognition by the Christmas recess of 1880 was greatly aided by effective publicity. Churchill's genius for vulgarization came into play here, and so did the more concrete advantage of journalistic allies. Algernon Borthwick of the *Morning Post* was a friend of Churchill's and Thomas Gibson Bowles and his journal, *Vanity Fair*, an influential social and political weekly, also gave the Fourth Party heavy backing from 1880 onwards (both editors having nurtured political ambitions of their own). Strong articles in favour of their initiative, and attacking the bumbling

---

[30] Speaking at Exeter, 15 Dec. 1880 (*Pall Mall Gazette*, 16 Dec. 1880).

and inept Old Gang, appeared from October of that year; the Fourth Party's parodies of cabinet meetings and ministerial fish dinners were faithfully and affectionately reported; a series of inspired letters pleaded their cause. *Vanity Fair* was notably anti-Northcote; it published editorials on Fourth Party speeches in the country; it devoted one of its coveted profiles to Churchill as early as 10 July 1880, describing him as a 'brilliant and witty' speaker. He was supposed by many to contribute anonymous articles to the paper. Finally, in December 1880, the special extra Christmas number featured the celebrated cartoon of the Fourth Party, accompanied by an exceptionally long profile which took the form of an attack on the worn-out cliques of Toryism and the 'superannuated oligarchy' of Cross and Northcote. A corresponding profile of the Opposition front bench some months later attacked them in equally uncompromising terms.[31]

This commitment continued. The liaison between the Fourth Party and the editorial room appears to have been close. In May and October 1880, two short and probably 'inspired' pieces on Conservative organization appeared, which bore the imprint of Gorst.[32] Paternalistic electoral machinery, the indolence and class bias of the Old Gang, their obsession with the landed interest at the expense of the democracy—all this was rehearsed, and the need for Conservative reorganization emphasized. Caucus must be met with caucus, democracy addressed on its own ground, and in its own language; the future issue of property versus redistribution must be squarely faced. *Vanity Fair* continued to be a repository for Fourth Party manifestos. And the magazine made a special cult of Churchill. He was hailed as the coming leader far earlier there than elsewhere. In July 1880 an editorial pointed out admiringly (though inaccurately) how Churchill was modelling himself on Disraeli in his treatment of Gladstone: 'indeed, his talents are in many respects so like those of the Premier that one wonders a little why under the late Administration he was not offered something worth taking'. Praise had to be tempered, and there was a defensive addendum:

He does not care much for facts, it is true, and his blows are not always perfectly legitimate; while he scarcely pretends to be too much in

---

[31] *Vanity Fair*, 5 July 1881.
[32] Ibid., 1 May 1880, 16 Oct. 1880.

earnest; but surely after all he is therein right ... the House of Commons should really be taken to be what it is—that is to say, a club of gentlemen who for the most part have a fair amount of money and no particular occupation in life but that of finding an escape from being bored. If men in that frame of mind come down to the House after their dinners, they want to be made to laugh, and have a profound dislike of heroics, unless when really well acted, and recalling memories of Modjeska or Bernhardt. Lord Randolph Churchill has grasped this fact, and *il ira loin*.[33]

By the following year, Churchill's Hull speech would draw from *Vanity Fair* a new kind of eulogy: the vision of the leader of the future was being made manifest.

The support of the *Morning Post* and *Vanity Fair*, combined with their own talent for publicity, rapidly built up an identifiable Fourth Party image. This was young—though its members were not all youthful, as is frequently pointed out. It was also slightly raffish, frequenting the Turf Club, Jack Straw's Castle on Hampstead Heath, and private rooms above restaurants (sometimes interrupted by unknown women, bent on assignations). Furthermore, it was Salisburian, and deliberately aggressive: occasions like Wolff's meeting his constituents at Portsmouth in November 1880 were enlivened by the addition of Churchill's 'violence and vulgarity', generally directed against what Northcote represented. Hostile opinion saw the Fourth Party as also characterized by opportunism and superficiality: their choice of issues being restricted to 'general or personal questions requiring no preparatory knowledge'.

Not all these identifications applied accurately to Churchill. He was readier than the others for Irish alliances (Gorst realized the lack of interest in Lancashire and Yorkshire about the Irish issue); he was more involved with individual Liberals. If he rhetorically shared Gorst's and Balfour's fears of an impending Whig coalition masterminded by Northcote, he was less appalled by the idea of co-operation with others of the Opposition. (Gorst, too, conferred often with Henry James, who confided in November 1880 not only his own career ambitions, but also the government's intentions regarding Corrupt Practices and procedural alterations; Gorst in return offered Fourth Party aid.[34])

---

[33] Ibid., 10 July 1880.
[34] Gorst to Churchill, 5 Nov. 1880 (RCHL i/20). For Gorst's realization that Lancashire and Yorkshire were uninterested in Ireland see Gorst to Disraeli, 29 Dec. 1880, Disraeli MSS B/xxi/G/263.

Churchill was still, in a manner, restrained by family influence (his father was horrified at his growing friendship with Joseph Chamberlain, still identified as the Radical scourge); this may have helped dictate his early support for Salisbury rather than Northcote, articulated in 1880, and expressed immediately after Disraeli's death in an attempt to spring on the National Union a resolution unequivocally proclaiming Salisbury as leader. None the less, he remained publicly on good terms with Northcote; it was Balfour who attacked the Commons leadership at a Carlton meeting in August 1880, and Wolff who complained of Northcote to Disraeli the month before; indeed, Salisbury put down Northcote's dislike of the Fourth Party to 'the impudence with which *Wolff* talks about him'. Churchill wrote contemptuously of Northcote in private correspondence during late 1880, but publicly avoided contention; and Northcote felt able to assure Smith in December that 'the Fourth Party are pretty friendly with me', despite the evidence of the Woodstock meeting.[35]

This was, to some extent, wishful thinking. Northcote had attempted to bring the Fourth Party to heel when parliament rose in September, which had caused them to appeal to Beaconsfield, whose balance-holding powers were brought into full play in an interview with Gorst at Hughenden. His advice amounted to restrained encouragement, in a generally anti-Northcote spirit. Gorst had already thought of the Fourth Party's ostentatiously taking their places behind Northcote, in order to press him on further: Churchill vetoed the idea, and later regretted it; Wolff was even more opposed. This month, September 1880, was in other respects too a time of reassessment for the Fourth Party; at this point Gorst began to associate their initiative with organizations in the country, a strategy given credence by Churchill's success at Preston that Christmas. It seems likely that Gorst's long-standing preoccupation with a possible Conservative base among the working classes was behind most of his actions from this time on, and that he had optimistically cast Churchill for the tribune role declined by Disraeli in the early 1870s. But Gorst's ideas of where the Fourth Party might go, like his ideas about the ultimate destination of the party at large, were not those of his colleagues.

What the freelances were known for, at this stage, was still

---

[35] See Northcote to Smith, 21 Dec. 1880, Hambleden MSS, PS/6/644.

their parliamentary activity, which deserves some attention. A 'Fourth Party ideology' can hardly be gleaned by analysing the issues to which they devoted attention, for they were guided by tactical priorities. Rosebery's conclusion that the Fourth Party 'embodied nothing but a negative' is not only a party verdict: Balfour readily implied as much too. And Churchill's remark to Beach ten years later, at the end of his active career, that 'parliament exists for no other object than that of wasting time, and we fail when we try to force its nature and divert it from its real purpose' was a summation of Fourth Party principles at their most insouciant.[36] None the less, their activity was constant—if not always interpreted correctly. Winston Churchill discussed at length their opposition to the Employers' Liability Bill, from the opposite side to that of other Conservatives, though he ignored Edward Clarke's part in the campaign; and according to Harold Gorst, this involvement made his father see the 'real feeling and principle' behind Churchill's flashy impetuosity. Both present the Fourth Party line as a revival of Tory Democracy and the ideas of class reconciliation attributed to Disraeli ever since *Sybil*; and Gorst was writing at a time when his father, who stood for parliament next as a Liberal, was preparing his case as a disillusioned democrat. Neither son mentioned that much of Churchill's case against the Bill was that it discriminated against *employers*, denying them 'the protection to which they were entitled': he proposed an insurance scheme whose premiums would be deducted from workmen's wages 'to make them more careful'. When analysing Fourth Party offensives, it should be remembered that more than one intimate used the word 'cynical' to describe both Gorst and Wolff; and it was surely symbolic that when the little group parodied a ministerial dinner at Greenwich at the end of 1880, their single guest was Labouchere.[37]

In initiatives over issues like Ground Game legislation and the Burials Bill, even Winston Churchill admits that Wolff and Balfour took the lead. Churchill concerned himself with questions about the government's conduct of affairs in the Transvaal, while procedural questions, and issues of House business for purely frivolous purposes, were his special province. The allies' activity was not always united. In March 1881 Churchill

---

[36] Churchill to Beach, 14 July 1890, St. Aldwyn MSS, PCC/82.

[37] Balfour, *Chapters of Autobiography*, p. 134; Cornwallis-West, p. 91; H. Lucy, *Memories of Eight Parliaments* (London, 1908), p. 273.

introduced a Small Debts Bill, from which Gorst disassociated himself; public opinion hoped for a split. But by the next month the party were operating together again, opposed by Sclater-Booth, with Churchill once more triumphantly referring to 'myself and my friends'. And it was a month later that the famous exchange came regarding the number of parties in the House, with Churchill capping Healy's correction of Cowen, which is inaccurately supposed to have given the Fourth Party their name.[38]

Churchill made the most of procedural irregularities, like Dodson's application for the Chiltern Hundreds before standing for a second constituency; but he usually spoke briefly, as he himself pointed out when Hartington suavely computed the number of his speeches. However, the exchanges in which he was involved were no less acrimonious for this. In the spring of 1881 he aroused fury by accusing Dilke and Brassey of subscribing to the anarchist journal *Freiheit*, whose editor, Johann Most, was being charged for seditious utterances regarding the Tsar's assassination; he also complained about the treatment of the editor. This issue may have been suggested to him by the Marxist man-about-town Hyndman, whom Churchill knew well; he liked to cross the road from his Connaught Place house to Speaker's Corner and listen to Hyndman's orations. Hyndman told Blunt in after years that he was continually accused by Rosebery of having 'corrupted Churchill in a socialist sense': which was not the case. But his line on this issue led even perceptive political observers to wonder if he was 'taking up with the socialists', and Hyndman's name occurs in FitzGibbon's letters to Churchill as emblematic of Faustian traffickings. A more visceral reason may have lain behind his attack on Dilke, who according to gossip had made advances to Lady Randolph. In any case, it earned Churchill a 'slating' from James, who wrote to Dilke that evening with uncharacteristic violence that Churchill would probably 'return to his vomit' the next day.[39] The affair, much noted in the press, was an embarrassment to the government for reasons beyond Churchill's spurious claim that Dilke sympathized with re-volutionary anarchism; for the question that lay behind it was

[38] *Hansard*, cclxii, 1503.

[39] Hyndman, *An Adventurous Life*, p. 343; Hyndman to Blunt, 7 Mar. 1910, Blunt MSS (Lytton Coll.), 30; LHJ, 31 Mar. 1881 (vol. 348, p. 27), 8 Mar. 1882 (vol. 350, p. 57); James to Dilke, 7 Apr. 1881, BL Add. MS 43892.

the extent to which the government's prosecution of Most had been dictated by Russian pressure. Dilke, who had privately opposed the prosecution of the editor (and been angry with Chamberlain for supporting it), was alienated from Churchill after this; parliamentary correspondents noted the animosity of their exchanges. They had been in the habit of dining together; but social intercourse seems to have stopped after the *Freiheit* incident, though Dilke recorded ironically in June that 'the only two subjects on which the Prince of Wales agrees with any Liberals are 1. Randolph Churchill, 2. The government of London ... as I personally, tho' assaulted by Randolph, do not hate him, there remains only the government of London'. And meeting Clemenceau in December, Dilke could think of no more damning description than 'an inferior Randolph ... a sort of Figaro'.[40]

Dilke was not the only Liberal leader upon whom Churchill made a personal onslaught at this time; Harcourt, another politician with whom he had been friendly, was savaged by him for aggressiveness and stupidity shortly afterwards. In the same month, he threatened Hartington with a duel. These outbursts had a certain logic, in that they obstructed Northcote's hopes of party *rapprochement*, as well as adding to Churchill's reputation in certain quarters. And when he continued his campaign against Dilke with a barrage of questions about Eastern affairs, in the Turkish interest, and the supposed decline of the British position at Tunis, this was in line with Salisbury's traditional emphasis. Harassing the Liberals was usually done with an eye to its effect upon internal Conservative struggles.

Churchill's activities in the sessions of 1881 and 1882 have been fully detailed by his son, but it is worth emphasizing what spectators like Lucy noted: the special attention Gladstone paid Churchill, and the way that the latter's interjections were given a weight they did not deserve by the fact that the Prime Minister so often followed them in debate. This was probably a deliberate encouragement on Gladstone's part of the Opposition's fissiparous tendency. But the attention of older politicians, combined with his own glamour, and his wife's parties, helped Churchill create a kind of alternative society to those circles still barred to him. A light-hearted approach to political consistency was part of this: politics as a game of chess (which was how it struck Lady Randolph, listening to Fourth Party councils). A reputation,

---

[40] Dilke's diary, 9 June, 31 Dec. 1881, BL Add. MS 43924.

even if a rather rackety one, necessarily followed. Even Bradlaugh judged as early as August 1880 that 'in the present dearth of Conservative statesmen', Churchill would go far. At the end of the year, Gorst drew Churchill's attention to the amount of abuse he was attracting in the metropolitan and provincial press: 'one journal had the perspicuity to conjecture that you probably rather enjoyed it'.[41]

It was, indeed, a concomitant of his political style. His success in the House was not always as dramatic as his son claimed. But his bizarre mixture of courtliness, pious invocations, and appalling rudeness could be extremely effective. Few others would have gone out of their way to remark on the 'intolerable dullness' of an inoffensive speech from a well-meaning country member; few outside the Irish party entered so brazenly upon obstruction for its own sake. It was largely due to Churchill's efforts in the session of 1881 that a motion for adjournment at question time became a daily occurrence rather than a portentous emergency measure: though, in contrast with the previous year, he was less active in voting in 1881 than his allies.[42]

His conduct could inspire extreme feelings of repugnance; the *Daily News* in May 1881 referred to him as 'the chosen conduit-pipe of all the impure matter with which scandalmongers wish to flood the House of Commons, or the sink into which they pour their refuse and garbage'. But the *Pall Mall Gazette*, summing up the 'reputations of the session' some weeks later, decided only three men had achieved reputations *de novo*—Law, Healy, and Churchill; and if Churchill, like Healy, 'condescended to civilise himself', and acquired some moral weight, he would go far. Meanwhile, it was remarked in several places, his ostentatious frivolity about the ends of politics would tell against him.[43]

III

One can agree so far as to believe that detailed analysis of where the Fourth Party 'stood' on various issues of the day will not

---

[41] Gorst to Churchill, 27 Nov. 1880, RCHL i/30.

[42] In 1880 Churchill attended 116 divisions, Balfour 87, Wolff 87, and Gorst 84; in 1881 the tallies were 120, 188, 143, and 183 respectively.

[43] See article in *Fraser's Magazine* quoted in *Pall Mall Gazette*, 3 June 1881. Churchill's talents were marred by 'insolence' and 'a manner which produces the impression that he looks upon politics as a huge joke rather than a business which affects the happiness and welfare of millions'. For the remark about the conduit-pipe see *Daily News*, 24 May 1881. It went on graciously to assume that Salisbury's tribute to Churchill in the recess was occasioned by the latter's resemblance to the young Salisbury.

yield much in the way of enlightenment: since their priorities were tactical, and thus far ephemeral. But on what became from 1881 the issue of the day, their attitudes deserve closer attention. This was the Irish question, on which Churchill had ideas both more fixed and less predictable than on other issues. The period of the Fourth Party's rise to prominence saw the advent of conditions in Ireland that seemed—at least in England—tantamount to a social and political revolution. The agricultural crisis to which the Duchess of Marlborough had devoted her attention seemed to be bringing about the dissolution of the land system itself, and the social integument which it was thought depended upon it; the gentlemanly Home Rule rhetoric of Churchill's late guest at Phoenix Park dinners had been replaced by the implacable public face of what *The Times* would christen 'Parnellism'. And if Churchill knew more than most of his parliamentary contemporaries about the realities behind the Land War (such as the bankruptcy of the land system and the essentially clubbable nature of many of the nationalist leaders), he was also more deeply influenced by the robust, realistic, but essentially limited vision of his Dublin unionist friends who gathered at Howth.

For he had continued to cultivate his Irish contacts—returning to FitzGibbon's as early as October 1880, and spending Christmas there both this and the following year. Many of the questions upon which he consumed most parliamentary time were Irish: it was, as yet, his only area of special competence. One of his first major speeches was on the Landlord and Tenant Bill, on 5 July 1880; the first six speeches in Jennings's collection, covering the period up to Churchill's illness in 1882, deal with Ireland. Disraeli praised his Irish expertise to Wolff, and came to the Commons to hear Churchill speak on Ireland in January 1881. Behind the scenes, Churchill passed on FitzGibbon's advice to party leaders—even the despised Northcote; both Northcote and Disraeli referred to him on Irish affairs. In parliament he pressed causes like the Endowed Schools Commission, and was always ready to air his knowledge of local Irish details, from seditious utterances at Swinford to the need for improvements in Phoenix Park.

And to a surprising extent, Fourth Party campaigns in parliament were run on lines that coincided with Irish interests; the recurrent rumours of their breakup were often interpreted as a set-back to the Irish cause. Disraeli feared the results to the

party of their supposedly close identification with the Home
Rulers. But sympathies were not as close as they sometimes
seemed. The Fourth Party used Irish interests over, for instance,
the government's attempts to combat parliamentary disruption
by reform of procedure and introduction of closure in debate;
but they were equally capable of attacking the government from
an orthodox Tory angle like the accusation of not dealing with
the Irish malcontents strongly enough. However, they consistently escalated the political tempo in a way which the Irish
appreciated (and Northcote disliked). By the end of November
1880, Gorst proudly told Churchill that Charles Russell blamed
the Fourth Party for most of the threatening letters circulating in
Ireland. And in November 1881 their language was so extreme
that Northcote wondered whether Churchill might not be
arrested on his next visit to Ireland.[44]

What Churchill was actually saying was rarely as pro-Irish as
it seemed to be, though he asserted himself as an Irish expert and
referred on every possible occasion to his first-hand knowledge of
the country. Both Gorst and Wolff were more radical on the
question of Irish autonomy. Gorst had his own Irish connections,
including shady opportunists like Philip Callan. He toured the
country, sometimes with Churchill; he disliked Ulster Tories
and Southern landlords; he appreciated Parnell as an ally. On
occasion he got into trouble with the party respectables for his dislike of the Ulster interest, which he saw as hysterical and selfish,
'obsessed by crude ideas, hastily taken up as most in accordance
with what they imagine to be their own interest'. By 1883 he had
privately accepted the inevitability of Home Rule, and was
pressing on Churchill the need to 'shadow out in Parliament a
scheme which could free Ireland from what she regards as
thraldom, and unite all the English states in a common Imperial
bond'.[45] Wolff was similarly inclined in the early 1880s: popular
with the Irish members, he arranged liaison between Salisbury
and Parnell. Like Gorst, he accepted the inevitability of some
measure of separation for Ireland, and believed that if the
Conservatives could anticipate and appropriate this it would
work to their interest; he held no fears for the Protestant interest,

[44] Gorst to Churchill, 2 Nov. 1880, RCHL i/19; Northcote to Gibson, 7 Nov. 1881
(Ashbourne MSS, B/71/16).
[45] Gorst to Churchill, 29 Jan. 1883, RCHL i/105; also Wolff to Churchill, 15 Aug.
1883 (ibid. 157). On Ulster see Gorst to Smith, 14 July 1881, Hambleden MSS, PS/7/58,
and Gorst to Churchill, 18 Dec. 1882, RCHL i/89.

and was interested in the Hungarian parallel.[46] Churchill became interested in Wolff's ideas, which he 'often asked him to put on paper'; but neither he nor Balfour ever seem to have committed themselves thus far. This may reflect their personal expectations, compared to those of their older and less gilded allies. Gorst, for one, believed himself to be politically unambitious, and probably felt that his hands were comparatively untied. Balfour certainly doubted Churchill's solidarity on issues like the Land Bill, and disapproved of the extent of his Irish traffickings. In December 1880 Churchill (from Dublin) worried his allies by suggesting a policy of uniting with the Radicals and the Irish to renege on the Disraeli government's policy. He was capable in private of light-hearted references to the inevitability of Home Rule; numerous authorities, from Healy to Blunt and Labouchere, were to believe in 1885 that he had expressed unequivocal support for the principle.

This is to look too far ahead. But in the early 1880s, tactical arrangements between the Fourth Party and the Irish were common. F. H. O'Donnell referred grandly to Churchill, Gorst, and Wolff as his 'allies'; Parnell and Churchill came to reciprocal arrangements over support early on. By July 1880, Churchill was able to inform Northcote of the Home Rulers' intentions on parliamentary votes. William O'Brien later recalled the common ground between the Fourth Party and the Irish, and the inability of the Liberals to understand the warmth of a relationship which did not follow the normal course of British party politics. There was a frivolous and publicly displayed camaraderie: Churchill discussed political novels with McCarthy during dull debates, and made Mrs Jeune sing 'The Wearing of the Green' at dinner-parties attended by Northcote. He was friendly with Biggar and Healy, and had links with less savoury figures like Callan and O'Shea; his seat was directly in front of Parnell's at Westminster, and he sat with the Irish leader and Sexton in the lower smoke-room. Issues like the Indemnity Bill demanded by the Home Rulers against an Irish Protestant bishop for voting before taking his oath in the Lords gave rise to an elaborate parliamentary ballet.

By such manœuvres the impression of an alliance was created; numerous Conservative authorities concluded later that it was no more than that. But there was certainly an understanding;

[46] Wolff to Churchill, 28 May 1886, ibid. xiii/1514; also memorandum dated 9 Oct. 1885 (ibid. viii/961).

tactical as it was. Where Churchill did introduce an anti-Irish issue into debate, it was often simply to bring up a contentious point at a time when real discussion was impossible, or to create an isssue on which Northcote would have to beg him to relent. He took every opportunity of paying fulsome compliments to the Irish party: 'men of singular intelligence—of intelligence possibly equal to any which was in existence on the Treasury bench—and a most intimate and practical and accurate acquaintance with the feeling of the Irish people'.[47] When he spoke in a die-hard sense regarding Irish affairs, it was generally for the obvious purpose of accusing Forster, the Chief Secretary, of truckling to the extremists; when he described the Compensation for Disturbance Bill as 'dangerously near to Communism' his intention was so patent that Gladstone merely chided him for his frivolity. Even his support of coercion in January 1881 was so ambivalent that he still appeared as what Gladstone called him, the Irish party's 'single English ally': his reluctant assent to the measure being all but concealed in a line of attack which concentrated on blaming the Liberals for making it necessary.[48] It was part of a brief campaign whereby he attacked the government for leaving Davitt at large, ostentatiously fenced with the Irish members over points of order, and made a flying visit to the state trials in Dublin to store up further ammunition. But his approach was seen as basically anti-coercionist, and thus all the more embarrassing for the Liberals. The Irish did not particularly hold it against him; especially as he supported some of their amendments to the Bill, called for better treatment of political prisoners, and generally prompted one Irish MP to express his thankfulness that 'there was at least one Member who had been behind the scenes in Ireland'. The Liberals accused him of 'entire unacquaintance with and inattention to the cause of the debate', and of perpetrating a 'screaming farce'; but his points told against them, and for the Irish Party.

Many of his attitudes, however, were characteristic of enlightened Irish *unionist* opinion: from which, through his Dublin contacts, he was getting much of his inspiration. He railed against the introduction of special legislation, against the

[47] *Hansard 3*, ccliv, 678 (16 July 1880).
[48] Ibid., cclviii, 88, 1991. For Wolff's belief that the Tories should hang back from attacking the government on coercion see Wolff to Disraeli, 3 Nov. 1880, Disraeli MSS, B/xxi/W/495.

government's ignoring of Catholic educational demands, against their inability to use the existing law more intelligently: just as FitzGibbon and Morris did in their letters to him. He preferred the idea of Grand Juries organizing seed distribution in the West, rather than Boards of Guardians. His attacks on the Errington mission and his calls for grants to Irish fisheries, while supported by the Home Rulers, were equally in this tradition. Significantly, he scornfully repudiated Law's claim that the peasants of Mayo and of Donegal were 'the same people and the same race': already he had an eye to what he took to be the Northern interest.

Some of this was pure rhetoric (he was capable of interpreting an old woman's tenure of a cottage in a ruin as 'the occupation of Quinlan's Castle by a body of tenantry'); but over issues like land purchase he made serious private enquiries at the same time as indulging in extravagant oratorical fireworks. (He presented in parliament the unlikely argument that rural distress was caused solely by the unemployment consequent upon 'the exodus of landlords'—for which, of course, he blamed the Liberals.) And despite his many and manifest changes of front, Irish opinion continued to hold him in a curious affection. His consistent interest in Catholic education, and his continued cultivation of episcopal correspondents, helped ensure this. A full consideration of this would take us beyond 1882; but the syndrome was an important one as early as 1880.

IV

It was on the Irish issue that in the autumn of 1880 Churchill mounted the first of the national speaking tours which really made his name. In September 1880 he made his annual speech at the Woodstock Agricultural Dinner; though calling for 'freedom of contract' in all land legislation he was thought to be cultivating the agricultural labourers (as was Blandford, who also spoke). When Salisbury spoke at Woodstock in December, Churchill re-emphasized this commitment to the labourers, who provided half the 600-strong crowd. Some local opinion considered this was 'trickery', designed to dress up a basically reactionary view of tenants' rights: they may have felt vindicated by his violent denunciation of agricultural labourers in the Reform debates three years later.

On 18 November he spoke to a Conservative dinner at Portsmouth, Wolff's constituency. The government, he claimed, was overrun by Radicals and republicans; Gladstone put down Irish members like O'Donnell even when they were in the right; the closure rule was aimed at Tories, not Irish. And he repeated his point that the Liberals had caused the escalation of the Irish situation; the blood of the assassinated Lord Mountmorres was upon Forster's head. An uncharacteristic anti-Catholic note was also sounded, possibly out of consideration for the nature of his audience. The Woodstock meeting, which followed shortly, has been dealt with above. But it is worth recurring to his following appearance at Preston on 21 December, for here a new note was struck: exaggerated humour, baroque flights of fancy, an inspired use of epic and bathos. The Irish situation was portrayed as having introduced a lunatic dimension of Lewis Carroll proportions into public life: in this distorted world, various Liberal politicians tacked, veered, and lost their balance, trapped by their own hypocrisy and inconsistencies. Forster, abandoning a 'mild' Peace Preservation Act only to be forced into draconian coercion, was shown as a demented 'shuttlecock', buffeted between Dublin and London, sneered at and deceived in both, finally forced to announce that the Land League must be allowed 'a merry and gory Christmas'.

The venue for this oration was carefully chosen—Gorst was widely experienced in Lancashire politics, and told Churchill afterwards that his position was now vitally strengthened in the North. But such a splash created ripples which threatened Fourth Party solidarity. Churchill's attitude towards coercion was already very much his own; now, from Dublin on 27 December, he wrote to Wolff suggesting they take up Boer independence to embarrass the government. Wolff demurred, uncertain of the others' commitment (though Gorst was in fact keener) and preferring an informal alliance to a motion of condemnation. As this showed, Churchill was returning to his 1870s idea of co-operating with the Radicals and the Irish; another idea that occurred to him was some sort of joint action with Hyndman, which terrified even Gorst.[49] Churchill's idea of blocking the Coercion Act by a one-year amendment, uniting Radicals, Irish, and Conservatives to put the government in a

[49] Gorst to Churchill, 28 Dec. 1880, RCHL i/35. Also see W. S. Churchill i, 195–6; Wolff to Churchill, 28 Dec. 1880, RCHL i/34; Gorst to Churchill, 30 Dec. 1880 (ibid. 38).

minority, was rejected by Beaconsfield in early January; Balfour represented him as thinking he would bring the government down, but he hardly expected so much. Over Christmas, euphoric after the Preston success, Churchill was throwing out ideas for tactics and alliances like so many firecrackers. But despite the success that had seemed to be coming his way, his initiatives came to nothing. One effect of this was a readiness to consider a return to the ranks. At this time he responded to a friendly note from Northcote about Irish policy with an invitation to lunch, despite Gorst's injunctions to avoid being buttonholed. There seemed a chance that he might cut his ties, if circumstances allowed a productive realignment of forces.

But nothing of the sort came about. Churchill's disappointment was manifest, and his attitude to coercion sundered the Fourth Party, according to his son, until the renewal of the Bradlaugh debate in March. His line on parliamentary legislation to control obstruction—the so-called *clôture*—also opposed that of his party, and he crudely stated as much in Conservative councils. But with the resurfacing of Bradlaugh, and the Marlborough pension question, old alliances revived; 2 May saw the filibuster of James's projected Affirmation Bill, led by Churchill and supported by a significant number of Irish nationalists.

Ireland dominated the summer of 1881. The Irish Land Bill, a measure violently attacked by his father in the Lords, gave Churchill the opportunity for a series of highly coloured speeches, during which he compared the Land Courts to the Star Chamber and attacked the Bill as embodying draconian state interference; on nearly every clause he produced a series of obstructive and critical points, aggressively in the landlord interest, though his speeches on emigration drew some Irish support. On the third reading, his ironic speech congratulating Parnell called forth Gladstone's celebrated description of Churchill as the kind of flea 'whose office it is to bite, and who does not even produce in his victim the consciousness of being bitten'; by July 1881, his 'high-falutin' amendments to the Bill were considered a joke. His final proposed amendment was violent enough, and personal enough, to put him out on a limb. Smith begged him not to go ahead with it but Churchill publicly declared his intention to do so; Salisbury brought pressure to bear on him through Balfour; Gorst's son thought it was a plea from Marlborough that eventually stopped him, though his speech of withdrawal was as good as a motion.[50] But Tory-Democrat sympathizers like Wilmot appreciated the value of such a performance in embarrassing the Old Gang, who had decided upon a studiously moderate approach to the measure, and die-hards like Elcho liked its spirit. Public opinion, moreover, saw the move as intended to outface Northcote and bring a note of out-of-doors Tory extremism into the official opposition's studiously moderate tactics; while in the House, Smith blocked Churchill's grandiloquent motion, and Northcote ostentatiously removed himself from his seat.

Moreover, public opinion, and out-of-doors Toryism, increasingly constituted Churchill's audience. Gibes in the House had accused him of trying to attract the attention of a large urban constituency, and in the autumn he set off on tour once more, with a series of violent and scabrously entertaining speeches, concentrating on personalities and ridicule, the Irish question, and 'Fair Trade', or a system of commercial Protection. In September he delivered at Oldham a speech (unmentioned in his son's biography) where he came out firmly for Fair Trade. The speech also emphasized the social legislation of Disraeli's government, compared to the Liberals' empty promises: procedural reform in parliament being the final, unnecessary insult. As for the Irish Land Bill, while Gladstone brilliantly negotiated a tightrope trick above 'the rocks and rapids of Communism and revolution', social amelioration for the English remained ignored. 'There is a universal sense in the community of uneasiness, of discomfort, of diminishing resources; there is a knowledge that less employment is being afforded by the wealth and enterprise of the country to the working classes of the country, and that less employment is also marked by restricted wages.' Chamberlain and Radicalism ignored the real reasons for trade depression: Free Trade was a Liberal shibboleth brought off by playing class against class, and now proved insufficient. The urban classes must now help agriculture out of its depression: foreign markets must be forced open; increased customs duties must be levied at home. 'Protection' became the keynote of the

[50] Smith to Churchill, 27 July 1881 (RCHL i/45); Salisbury to Balfour, 29 July 1881 (Balfour MSS, BL Add. MS 49695): Gorst, *The Fourth Party*. The wording of the amendment ran as follows: 'That the Landlord (Ireland) Bill, as originally introduced and as amended in committee, is the result of a revolutionary agitation, encourages the repudiation of contracts, facilitates offences against individual liberty, is calculated to diminish the security of property, will not contribute to the peace and prosperity of Ireland, and tends to endanger the union between that country and Great Britain.'

speech's rousing conclusion; one account credited Churchill with demanding 'tax foreign iron, tax foreign silk, tax foreign calico, tax foreign linen'.[51] This was, Eardley Wilmot assured him, a 'trump card', and others believed it greatly helped the Conservative cause among working men—at whom Churchill's Oldham speech was specifically addressed. He himself drew attention in parliament to 'a movement among the working-classes hostile to Free Trade'; the *Morning Post* enthusiastically supported the cry. But the public identification of a rising party star with this dubious cause deeply worried senior party members like Cranbrook, Northcote, and Salisbury (Hicks Beach publicly declared his disagreement a few days later). Causing such annoyance was probably the extent of Churchill's serious intention. As the contraction of the economy became a political issue, the Conservatives had been flirting with Fair Trade since the summer; Smith had taken soundings about its viability as a cry to capture Lancashire.[52] Salisbury had thrown out public hints, and Churchill's friend Borthwick was prominent in organizing a Fair Trade meeting at Exeter Hall in August. Following Churchill, Northcote remained ambivalent on the issue at Hull and Newcastle in October; by the following January, he was disagreeing with Smith on the extent to which the party should publicly commit themselves on the issue. (Smith was receiving detailed reports about meetings in upstairs rooms in Soho, where 'women of the Annie Besant type' spoke of the masses' commitment to Protection.) And in general, the issue seemed attractive to the suburban elements at whom Conservative policy was increasingly pitched: though this often involved describing them, misleadingly, as the working classes.

All this was in the future; while such reactions probably pleased him, at Oldham in September 1881 Churchill's main requirement was met when the Fair Trade idea 'went down like butter', as he coarsely remarked to Balfour. All the local press noted it; the *Liverpool Post* decided Churchill was softening up a working-class constituency against the day when Woodstock should lose its representation. This was an idea which occurred at the same time to his leaders, who corresponded worriedly about the

---

[51] See *Morning Post*, 19 Sept. 1881. The final quotation is from *Pall Mall Gazette*, same date.

[52] See R. Mowbray to Smith, 10 Aug. 1881, Hambleden MSS PS/7/80; also Smith to Stanhope, several letters in October 1881, Stanhope MSS 0310, and Northcote to Cranbrook in HA 43 T501/271.

chance of Churchill standing for Preston at the end of the year. The divisiveness of the issue was noted by the Liberal press, who generally saw Conservative flirtation with Fair Trade in the recess as an anti-Northcote manœuvre, and no more; Lowther's success in North Lincolnshire on a Fair Trade platform having been a straw in the wind.

At Hull on 31 October, Churchill played the safer card of simple but vivid ridicule. Gladstone as a child crowing over the freedom of the city of Dublin, and his son as 'the resources of civilisation', created attractive caricatures; correspondents congratulated him on his 'offensiveness'. The Irish Land Courts provided much scope for invective; and his general message was that the Tory dispensation implied more liberty for the subject. Churchill, however, avoided any reference to economic questions, and restricted himself to his customary vision of Ireland as a black comedy, in which various Liberals were doomed to play ridiculous yet tragic parts. This was more acceptable to his moderate colleagues: letters of congratulation came from Gibson and Northcote, as well as Chenery (the editor of *The Times*) and FitzGibbon. On the other side, Chamberlain wrote to Escott that Churchill had 'made an ass of himself'; but, as Wolff remarked to Balfour in best Fourth Party spirit, the chief testimonial in the speech's favour was that it infuriated the Liberals.[53]

But Churchill saw these showy offensives as taking him further: as is shown by his next appearance at Manchester on 1 December. For in August he had been sounded out by Thomas Nash about meeting local Conservative notables there, avoiding 'ornamental nobodies': the overture had an obvious significance. The fact of this invitation was given prominent publicity. In October, Gorst advised Churchill not to pursue this connection; Churchill ignored the advice. He spoke to a large audience on 1 December and made a brief appearance at a bazaar the evening before, where he described himself as 'an obscure stranger' and spoke sentimentally of the natural Conservatism of Englishwomen. More to the point was the fact that W. H. Houldsworth, the leader of Lancashire Toryism, introduced him

---

[53] See Chamberlain to Escott, 2 Nov. 1881, Escott MSS, BL Add. MS 58777; and Wolff to Balfour, 17 Nov. 1881 (Balfour MSS, BL Add. MS 49838). Shortly before, the Hull Conservatives had 'actually thought [Northcote] dull!!!' on his speaking tour, according to Christopher Sykes (to Rosebery, 6 Oct. 1881, Rosebery MSS 10077).

in a very proprietorial way, that his public appearance originated from a private visit to this influential Tory Democrat, and that Churchill emphasized the importance to the Conservative cause in general, and to himself personally, of provincial Conservatism: which was already reviving the party and the cause. The major speech at Manchester, delivered in Churchill's most rollicking manner, attracted great attention. *Truth* remarked on the way that 'starring in the provinces' had become a new syndrome: 'the "I" is driving the "we" to the wall'. Invective, it was noted, was taking over from oratory. The *Manchester Examiner*, less analytical, found Churchill incoherent, mendacious, slanderous, and un-English: 'we need not be under the slightest apprehension that our Randolph Churchills will ever be permitted to hold power in this country'.[54]

This was wishful thinking. But the reactions to Churchill's speeches of this autumn are interesting, as they generally extrapolate from the actual performance a larger conclusion than mere offensiveness would warrant. Under the demands of the new national constituency the style of public life was changing, and Churchill was seen to be helping change it—in a way that inspired alarm and repugnance as well as amusement and admiration. His verbal style was almost literary (as at Preston the year before): it reproduced well. (His celebrated photographic memory for written evidence may have helped here.) His energy and outrageousness were remarkable; so, in private, was his cynicism and insouciance about his own apostrophes of causes like Fair Trade. And as he became used to the limelight, he played what looked increasingly like a single hand: a process that seems to have started with his frustrated initiative at Christmas 1880. On issues like the involvement of working-class candidates, and Fair Trade, he had begun his practice of anticipating his leaders by saying on public platforms what they cautiously discussed in private. While Conservative calculators were just beginning to think of suburbs, Churchill seemed to appeal beyond to the tenements.[55]

---

[54] *Truth*, 8 Dec. 1881, and *Manchester Examiner*, 2 Dec. 1881.
[55] See A. Egerton to Smith, 9 Apr. 1880, on his defeat at Manchester; he blamed it on the ignoring by canvassers of 'miles of new streets just outside of Manchester and other Boroughs . . . When the County and Borough Franchise is assimilated, which it will I suppose be this session, these suburban voters may very possibly strengthen instead of weaken the Conservative Party, as they are a very different class from the Working men householders in the Country' (Hambleden MSS, PS/6/580).

This radical impression was made all the more easily since public-speaking tours were still what Salisbury called 'a refined luxury': avoided by many, and disapproved of by others. ('What a horrid nuisance this speech-making is becoming', remarked Hartington to Rosebery that September.[56]) Only in recent years had any kind of a concerted effort been made to import leaders to provincial meetings. Churchill's acceptance of this trend made his name. By Christmas 1881, Lord Lytton was remarking that the attacks on Churchill from leading ministers implied he was a 'permanent political puissance'; and he featured in the Gilbertian salvoes of *Truth*'s Christmas number, though the squib emphasized that Churchill's parents' ambition for him was the motivating force behind his frenzied public activity. The Hull speech, referred to picturesquely by Liberal papers as 'the very vomit of faction', was still admitted to have established him as a power in the country; and he was also seen as having a certain value to the Tory leaders as a mouthpiece for statements they dared not make officially. Even Edward Hamilton, Gladstone's obtuse and pious private secretary, was forced to admit privately that Churchill was 'making a name for himself; it is sickening to think that a man of such unscrupulousness and with such utter want of seriousness should be coming to the front in politics and would on the formation of a Tory government be entrusted with governing this country'.[57]

The year 1882 began with a flurry of confused activity; after Christmas in Dublin, where Gorst caused some trouble with Kildare Street Club landlords, there were tensions within the Fourth Party and after some public disagreements Wolff had to coax Churchill from a temporary withdrawal with reports of his increasing reputation as a future leader. On 19 January, however, a Fourth Party demonstration took place, in the form of a meeting at Woodstock with Lord Lytton as guest speaker. Lytton, controversial ex-Viceroy of India, was a family friend, and Churchill had defended him in parliament; his appearance at Woodstock coincided with Churchill's efforts to work up his local interest, advocating Oxfordshire interests in parliament and forming a Conservative Association in the town. Lytton's address, full of zoological metaphors and anti-Liberal hyperbole, was in pure Fourth Party idiom; at further local meetings in the

[56] 28 Sept. 1881; Rosebery MSS, 10077.
[57] Bahlman, *Hamilton Diary*, i, 181.

following week Churchill reiterated the messages of parliamentary freedom and Fair Trade. At Tackley in early February he presented the Woodstock Conservative Association as a paradigm of the national situation, and Toryism as the party of popular liberty, the rights of the common man, and 'emancipation from monopolies and class privileges'; Gorst's teachings may have been taking effect. However, probably more significant is the fact that at this time two Manchester Conservatives, Houldsworth and Freston, approached him to stand in the city; Churchill refused on the grounds of expense, uncertainty, and his commitment to Woodstock. But he left several loopholes, and suggested a meeting in London; five months later he had still not come to a decision.

But such dilatoriness had been caused by factors outside politics. On 4 February he had been back in the House, 'as full of pluck and go as ever'; on 21 February he attempted to add an amendment to Labouchere's writ moving for a new Northampton election. Churchill wanted to add the words 'in the place of Charles Bradlaugh, who is disqualified by law from taking his seat in this house'. This did not pass; but when Bradlaugh administered the oath to himself, Churchill was the first to propose his expulsion. Another spurt of activity seemed promised. But this was his last appearance for many months. On 26 February his wife's diary records an unlikely luncheon party with Northcote, Gorst, Wolff, and Bentinck;[58] but the Conservative Party meeting in the Carlton the following month, where it was decided to moderate obstructive tactics, must have been made considerably more agreeable by the fact that by then Churchill was seriously ill, with an unmentioned ailment which incapacitated him by 3 March. No details are recorded of this illness, though Harcourt heard it was 'internal piles'.[59] The previous July a bout of 'seediness' had sent him to Trouville to recuperate; his health was already notoriously unreliable. Rosebery thought that the deteriorating illness which killed him manifested itself as early as 1885; indeed, by 1886 he had already become partly deaf. The evidence of Lady Randolph's correspondence with her sister, as well as the belief of his (admittedly rather ineffectual) doctors, leaves little doubt that Churchill's later debility was the result of syphilis; from the

[58] Lady Randolph's diary for 1882, CHAR 28/43.
[59] LHJ, 28 Feb. 1882, vol. 350, p. 42.

seriousness of his unnamed affliction in 1882 it could conceivably have been allied to this, but there is no evidence. All that is certain is that Churchill was incapacitated for months. Ill in London for seven weeks, he then travelled to America to recuperate on 23 April, returning, not much better, on 26 May. In early June his wife rented a house at Wimbledon, where he continued to convalesce; Lady Randolph recorded constant visits from Wolff, Bischoffscheim, Hirsch, and Borthwick. On 3 July Churchill went to Westminster 'for the first time'; on the 18th, the Churchills went to see 2 Connaught Place, where they were shortly to take up residence. But Churchill had not really regained strength; an operation was reported in the press in July, and Churchill declared to be recuperating once more at the Wimbornes' London house. It was not until October that he returned to parliamentary activity in any real sense: with a more fixed resolve, and a new sense of mortality.

Chapter 4

Insubordination Politics, 1882–1883

'But he is not what I call loyal. He cannot keep
himself from running after strange gods. What need
had he take up the Church question at Tankerville?
The truth is, Duke, the thing is going to pieces.
We get men into the House now who are clever,
and all that sort of thing, and who force their way
up, but who can't be made to understand that
everyone should not want to be Prime Minister.'
The Duke, who was now a Nestor among politicians,
though very green in his age, smiled as he heard
remarks which had been familiar to him for the
last forty years. He, too, liked his party, and was
fond of loyal men; but he had learned at last that
all loyalty must be built on a basis of self-advantage.
Patriotism may exist without it, but that which Erle
called loyalty in politics was simply devotion to
the side which a man conceives to be his side, and
which he cannot leave without danger to himself.

Anthony Trollope, *Phineas Redux* (1874)

I

Churchill's return to politics in late 1882 was at first halting and
cautious, and bedevilled by relapses into ill health; but marked
also by increasing anxiety, publicly expressed, about the position
of the party at large, and privately by the problem of re-
establishing himself. His new priority was urgent self-
aggrandisement. His absence had been swiftly used by Northcote
to change the direction of Opposition tactics: a meeting at the
Carlton Club was convened in March for this very purpose,
coming to cautious decisions about opposing the simple-majority
closure rule to restrict parliamentary debates, examining the
question of Irish coercion carefully, supporting the extension of
land-purchase clauses, and dropping obstructive tactics in the

Commons.[1] Even more important was the fact that in Churchill's absence had occurred two events, of tremendous symbolic as well as actual significance: the Kilmainham treaty whereby Parnell was released from gaol and the bombardment of Alexandria by the British fleet. One indicated a new departure in government relations with Ireland, the other an overt commitment to Egyptian involvement; and they reflected the two issues which Churchill was to make his own. The occurrence of these vital flash-points during his enforced parliamentary absence (as was to be the case with the fall of Khartoum and the Parnellite split in future years) left him with an additional length of parliamentary ground to make up: all the more pointed as such issues could be used rhetorically to signify both the loss of the government's initiative and the decay of the Liberal ethos. This tactic remained viable although the political effect of such crises helped Gladstone present the Liberals as a national party once more, and the economic recovery of 1882–3 further impeded the Conservative effort to take a class line in politics. Opposition to Gladstonian policy in Ireland and Egypt was not an easy line to follow for many of Northcote's party; the idiosyncratic slant which Churchill gave his treatment of these issues was as much the result of necessity as of eccentricity.

During his illness he had attempted to remain in touch with politics, through visits from friends, and such correspondence as he could manage; even before the bombardment of Alexandria he sent a scathing letter to the *Standard* about his own party's lack of a policy in Egypt.[2] They should not meet in 'hole-and-corner' venues like Willis's Rooms, dominated by bondholders; contradicting Salisbury, he advocated tactics of large open-air meetings with freely admitted audiences, and votes of censure within parliament. He visualized, in other words, making an 1876 out of 1882, and producing a Gladstonian appeal to the country on eastern affairs. The letter produced a simultaneous leader of approbation in the *Pall Mall Gazette*, which indicates that Morley may have been sent an advance copy: similar ideas, supporting the Egyptian nationalist leader Arabi, were being advanced by Churchill's old friend from Ireland, Sir William Gregory. On 17 July Churchill appeared in the House, for one of the very few occasions before October, in order to support

---

[1] Reported in *Pall Mall Gazette*, 18 Mar. 1882.
[2] 29 June 1882; unmentioned by either biographer.

Gorst's notice of a resolution censuring the government's treatment of Alexandria. Thus he had taken up, even before his
return, one of the stances which was to distinguish him in the
approaching session. He indicated another by his only other
appearance in parliament at this time, for the debate on
prevention of crime in Ireland: where he called for the use of
juries rather than Special Commission courts, in line with the
advice he received privately from Dublin.

Besides these two pressing issues, the state of the parties was
enough to disturb his convalescence. In the interim, 'hard-
headed Conservatives' had come to forecast a process whereby
the Irish would hold the balance at the next election and, with
the Conservatives, put the Liberals out: the Conservatives
declining to take office, Conservatives and moderate Liberals
would form a coalition under a respectable figure like Argyll.
This was exactly the scenario that Northcote desired and
Churchill feared. Northcote's own noticeably mild and bantering speeches in Scotland in the autumn gave a further indication: here he unworriedly remarked that the Liberal government was 'on top of the wave'. The whole process had been
aided by the third decisive event that occurred during
Churchill's illness: Salisbury's failure in July to carry a majority
of peers with him in his intention to oppose the Arrears Act in
the Lords, and his ignominious admission of the fact (which,
according to that astute juvenile, Loulou Harcourt, was 'thought
to be the most ill-judged and extraordinary speech ever made by
any leader of a party, and it seems probable that he will
resign').[3] Salisbury's call for an end to 'skedaddling' was also a
gage of opposition to Northcote and the faint-hearted; the
interesting thing is that Churchill was seen as 'flabby' on the
issue, along with his nominal Commons leader. However, this is
to ignore both his physical weakness at the time and the fact that
his opposition was grounded in the fact that he saw Salisbury's
line as tamely following that of the Irish landowners. Dublin
advice won out once more.

By the autumn he was ready for the fight again, writing to
Northcote to press for an aggressive line on Egypt, upon which
he felt that Radical and Irish support might be forthcoming.
Though Northcote had taken care to placate Gorst in Scotland,

[3] LHJ, vol. 351, p. 195 (10 Aug. 1882). On the significance of this see A. Jones, *The
Politics of Reform, 1884* (Cambridge, 1972), and P. T. Marsh, *The Discipline of Popular
Government: Lord Salisbury's domestic statecraft, 1880–1902* (Hassocks, 1978), pp. 21–5.

and Churchill in London, a fight with such allies was not to his liking. It was also obvious that Churchill, on his return to public life, was prepared to take up anything and everything in the autumn session that had been convened. In the event, the chosen topic happened to be procedure: the first day after the recess, he called attention to himself with lengthy observations on the adjournment of parliament: following a deliberately rhetorical line on the government's departure from parliamentary practice, forcing Northcote up to his pace, and boycotting a Carlton meeting convened to ensure unity of the Opposition. This indicates that he was determined to follow his own line in the debates on parliamentary procedure. Like many other Conservatives, including Salisbury, Churchill felt the closure should be limited; he had come out at a meeting at Disraeli's the year before against '*clôture* ad hoc', and been prepared to sit through the night to defeat it.[4] But the priority in October 1882 was to take a front place, and reinstate the ideas of separation from moderate Liberalism. Privately, he confessed to the Liberal Whip, he was ready to divide the House merely 'to see how many fools there were in it'. Churchill immediately used the debate on the new rules to traduce his colleague Raikes for being proud of his intimacy with political opponents when he was Chairman of Committees: 'what we want to know is where we are'. Decisiveness was all. The substantive issues were less important, and his general arguments in a sense irrelevant, since the principle of procedural reform was accepted by both parties. This, however, did not deter him. Obstruction was first of all defended as providing 'the safety valve of Irish rebellion': then he switched to accepting the *clôture*, but attacking the principle of the two-thirds majority proposed as an amendment by Gibson. Not only did this command a fair degree of respectful attention, but the chance of attacking Gibson himself added flavour: Churchill's old acquaintance from Dublin dinner-tables now being privately stigmatized as irredeemably 'Goaty', and even 'posing as a sort of leader'.[5] The speech against Gibson, much quoted by Churchill's biographers, was deliberately respectable, appealing to tradition and precedent, but using the

---

[4] Salisbury to Balfour, 15 Jan. 1881, BL Add. MS 49680; notes in Iddesleigh MSS, 22 Feb. 1881, BL Add. MS 50018.

[5] See Gorst to Churchill, 10 Sept. 1882, 14 Oct. 1882, RCHL i/76, 80. Gorst now grouped Gibson with Salisbury and Northcote in the 'ring' supposedly exploiting the party.

Irish party's case: the measure proposed would discriminate against them and was 'recommended, mark you, by an Irish member of the dominant class'. The real point came at the end. The Tories did not need a two-thirds closure rule as a 'little dyke' to protect them in opposition. They stood for more than 'coercion for Ireland and foreign war': the questions of franchise extension, tariff reform, and Ireland would have to be legislated upon soon in any case, and 'the attitude of the great Tory democracy, which Lord Beaconsfield partly constituted', would not merely be one of dogged opposition on this; in power they would need facilities for 'rapid legislation'.

Thus, after indicating an Irish alliance, Churchill held out a rather threatening promise of restored initiative from the Opposition, and foretold the restoration of sharp party lines in politics. *The Times* interpreted it thus. Northcote and Balfour quickly disassociated themselves from such a strategy, and in the division on the amendment only Ashmead-Bartlett and Percy supported the Fourth Party by being conspicuously absent. Churchill himself felt it necessary to assert, in a letter to *The Times*, that he was still firmly opposed to the principle of the closure. But more remarkably, he held out a direct invitation to Parnell—'a profound politician, who has shown conclusively his preference for and his belief in parliamentary action to redress Irish grievances rather than in a repetition of the efforts of '98 and '48'—to support him in his struggle against closure, with a view to forcing 'an appeal to the constituences'—in which, as an added bait, the Irish parliamentary party would be at least doubled.

Reactions to this bold move were varied. Tory Democrats like George Bowyer wrote hailing him as 'the coming man'. Houldsworth once more approached Churchill to stand for Manchester (to which Churchill pleaded his family duty to Woodstock). O'Shea, in the House of Commons, attacked Churchill for soliciting Irish votes as part of a campaign to advance himself to 'within measurable distance of a seat in some cabinet of the future: but whether as a Tory or as a Liberal, he would not profess to say'. The tone was set for Churchill's behaviour in the rest of the debate: gratuitously offensive to Liberals, wrangling about the frequency and viability of motions for adjournment, producing an endless battery of amendments, and constantly being accused of attempting to provoke a dissolution. He was frequently to be found defending the Irish

Party, remarking on one occasion that they above all people should be allowed to explain and withdraw statements, as they 'often used language to which they did not attach the same importance as their audience'.

It is surprising that nobody pointed out that the same applied to him. Occasionally he took an ultra-Tory line, opposing the necessity of the legislation which the Liberal policy was supposed to expedite, and thus directly contradicting his speech against Gibson's amendment. He and Wolff led many skirmishes of obstruction, which, Chamberlain remarked to his improbable confidante the veteran society hostess Lady Dorothy Nevill, merely played the Liberal game and sealed their own doom.[6] Certainly one point recurred again and again: that the government might soon be out of office. Some opinion linked this with the fact that Churchill knew early on of the departure to Australia of Schnadhorst, the Liberal organizer of victory, and wished to provoke an election in his absence. But perhaps more immediately relevant was another announcement of mid-November 1882: that Northcote's precarious health had failed him, and he had to retire abroad indefinitely.

II

For it is important to note that Churchill's speech against Gibson, which attacked one front-bench Opposition member and sundered Churchill from several others, coincided with the beginning of his open attack on the direction of the party, which prefigured an onslaught on the leadership. The questions thus raised were large ones. 'Lord Randolph Churchill's escapade speech, coupled with the Fourth Party articles in the *Fortnightly*', remarked *Truth* equably, 'merely show that parties in the House of Commons and out of it will have to be organised on new lines.' And the 'new lines' envisaged by Churchill, at least in public, followed the blueprint ceaselessly advocated by Gorst during Churchill's illness:

The time seems ripe for the rise of the Democratic Tory party, which was always Dizzy's dream, at the head of which you might easily place yourself. I want to write an article on the feebleness of the Conservative party as a political organisation, pointing out that it is led by and in

[6] 14 Nov. 1882; Chamberlain MSS, 5/56/5.

the interests of a narrow, oligarchic and landowning class, and that the people in whom the real Conservatism of the nation resides have no voice in the matter, nor are their interests ever consulted. But I doubt whether anyone would print it.[7]

This seems to have been the genesis of the composite article that appeared in the *Fortnightly Review* in November, under the title 'The state of the opposition' and signed 'Two Conservatives'. Balfour, writing to Salisbury, supposed them to be Wolff and Gorst; but Escott, editor of the magazine, records that Churchill was one of the authors.[8] The first section stated Gorst's thesis in its opening sentence: 'If the Tory Party is to continue to exist as a power in the state, it must become a popular party,' Coalition was meaningless; the various established powers could only be defended on the grounds of utility. Disraeli had seen the potential of the Lancashire election returns in 1868; out of power and disembarrassed of aristocratic lumber, he had built up a national organization. The cancer of 'class interests and privileges' had now grown up again; the interests of the boroughs were subjected to those of the counties, and 'selfish timidity' dominated parliamentary policy. Reorganization had to take place; the National Union of Conservative Associations was financially impotent, and corrupted by patronage on the local level, its work restricted to 'holding periodical demonstrations at which some member of the late Cabinet may exhibit his talents before the admiring crowd'. Unable to choose local candidates, the National Union merely enabled the masses to see, with ruthless clarity, the calibre of the 'privileged order' who pretended to represent them.

They listen to an idle resuscitation of the dead cabinet of 1880, which they would gladly forget, to a vain defence of its policy and virtues; they are wearied with minute criticism of foreign affairs knowing all the while that had the speaker been himself in office he would have done much the same as his opponents; they mark the satisfaction of the speaker at his own position, and his readiness to defend the rights of the privileged order to which he belongs; but they catch no word of

---

[7] Gorst to Churchill, 10 Sept. 1882, RCHL i/76.

[8] See his *Randolph Spencer-Churchill*, p. 158. Escott's correspondence shows that he ran with the hare and the hounds, criticizing this article to respectable Conservatives, but being taken to task by Mudford, the editor of the *Standard*, for varying his tone about Churchill depending upon his audience. The *Wellesley Index to Victorian Periodicals* attributes this article to Wolff and Gorst; but the style of the second section, as well as Escott's evidence, stamps it as Churchillian.

sympathy for themselves, nothing to show that it is their rights, their privileges, their liberties that he is zealous to maintain. He is a being made of a different clay, and living in a different atmosphere from theirs... Such speeches delivered by such men will never turn the hearts of people against the minister who is at present their idol and who, whatever may be his faults, always exhibits a passionate sympathy for the people.

This first section of the article reflects Gorst's preoccupation with the party at large, and implicitly outlines the policy of attack on the National Union which is generally attributed to Churchill nearly a year later. It appeared at a time when Gorst was still officially the agent of the party with responsibility for national organization; it probably lay behind the ensuing public criticisms of his loyalty which precipitated his resignation. His relations with the leaders had in any case reached a point of no return, not helped by his refusal to contest Preston when its representation was abandoned by Raikes. Gorst resigned his post with alacrity on 17 November; two days after Northcote's enforced withdrawal due to ill health had been announced, and just before the failing Goat left on a cruise of indefinite duration, waved off by W. H. Smith from the Dockyard Farewell Jetty at Portsmouth.

That same departure made the second part of the *Fortnightly* article all the more opportune. This section, differing in style from the first, reflected Churchill's preoccupations: entitled 'The Dual Leadership', it dealt with parliamentary tactics and political personalities. There was a highly coloured picture of Disraeli in old age, controlled by a rabble of 'Gil Blas and Figaros behind the scenes, guarding all the approaches to their chief's confidence with sordid assiduity'. His appointees were either blue-blooded nonentities or bourgeois placemen. Smith and Cross had administrative ability, but no real political experience. Hicks Beach was indolent, Lord George Hamilton and Stanhope talented but raw, Lowther brave but unfortunate. Gibson was singled out as hard-working and genuinely conservative, but too Irish to lead. Only Cranbrook or Northcote were left as Commons leaders; and Northcote was chosen, 'able and respectable, rich in information, experience and manners, good-tempered, astute, accomplished, a thorough man of business, and full of resolve; but too amiable for his ambition, which is great'. The end result had been the incoherent, confusing, and destructive dual leadership, leading to 'the sacrifice of the fortunes of the Conservative Party to an injudicious Irish coterie, insensible to any political motive outside Ireland'—the Irish landlords, who had tried to provoke Salisbury to dissolution over Arrears, and were now about to send the leaders off to Belfast to play to a gallery of 'Protestantism of the hottest type, fanaticism of the deepest orange'. This was the result of following Gibson's advice, and taking the Trinity College view, totally unrepresentative of English or even Irish political opinion. Although 'as yet there is no active disaffection towards him', Northcote was an unrepresentative leader, and the dual leadership a cause of indecision. 'Elijah's Mantle has been torn in two, and until the pieces are joined there can be no cohesion in the conservative ranks.'

This article of November 1882 presaged Churchill's more celebrated letters to *The Times* on the same theme the following spring: except that, added to the declaration of Northcote's inadequacy to lead the party at large, was the coda that he should not lead in the Commons either, and nor should any of his advisers. The deduction of a Salisbury–Churchill combination was not hard to draw. Similar criticisms, to a similar effect, were aired in Churchill's reply to a deputation from Manchester in November, which took the form of a violent attack on the Opposition leadership: another opportunity occurred when Edinburgh University students asked if in his opinion Northcote 'adequately represented' the Conservative Party, and Churchill replied with elaborate irony that 'if Sir Stafford Northcote does not represent the Conservative Party as adequately as it is possible for any human being to do, I am at a loss to know who is his superior in that respect'.[9] In the same week the editor of *The Times* asked him to write a letter and a signed article, the question of the leadership being ripe for discussion.

This was an indication of the general debate on the nature and direction of Conservatism which dominated the journals in the winter of 1882–3. Not all of it was Tory-Democratic. Balfour, Carnarvon, Lytton, Stanhope, Raikes, and Austin were circularizing leading Conservatives, in an effort to call into play the literary and political talent of the Conservative ranks in order to place a 'truly national' policy before the country. The *Nineteenth*

---

[9] *The Times*, 2 Nov. 1882. Peel and Disraeli, the argument continued, did *not* 'represent' it.

Century of January 1883 carried two articles by Raikes and Brodrick, entitled 'The functions of an opposition' and 'The functions of Conservative opposition' respectively. Raikes re-evaluated Disraelianism, and—while anti-Churchill in tone—implied severe criticism of Northcote. The importance of 'those who work outside the House of Commons' and 'popular approval' was emphasized. Raikes had, in fact, clashed badly with his party leaders over his decision to stand for Cambridge instead of Preston, and on occasion ostentatiously defied Northcote in the Commons. Brodrick had hitherto seemed impeccably orthodox, and his article was a more personalized assault on Churchill himself, as a temporary and destructive phenomenon, against whom the rest of the party tended to be unfairly seen as 'a sort of dull background'. The leaders inside parliament, and the party organization outside, needed to rediscover a decisive voice. Both writers analysed the record of Conservative opposition since 1880 in a way that implied a wider analysis of the party's *raison d'être* in general, in terms of the professionalization of politics and the new class nature of the electorate.

Indeed, even where the intention of publicists was Tory-Democratic, their arguments often had to embody a powerful if subdued identification with old Toryism: if only because an appeal to working-class voters had to avoid unalloyed materialism, which raised unanswerable questions of vested interest, and take refuge in a Panglossian version of Church, King, and Constitution as representing a truer form of English social identity than any Radical nostrum could hope to do. Thus Tory Democracy courted Orangeism as well as Protectionism. While it has not yet received the kind of historical analysis which it deserves, it is hard to see the Tory-Democracy movement as anything very much more coherent than the tag which Churchill gave it in private conversation: 'chiefly opportunism'.[10] Its avatars tended to operate in special circumstances. Liverpool,

---

[10] W. S. Blunt, *Gordon at Khartoum* (London, 1911), p. 414. For material about Tory Democracy see R. T. McKenzie and Allan Silver, *Angels in Marble: Working-Class Conservatives in Urban England* (London, 1968); W. T. Wilkinson, *Tory Democracy* (New York, 1925); and J. Robb, *The Primrose League* (New York, 1942). Recently R. E. Quinault, 'Lord Randolph Churchill and Tory Democracy', has brought a scholarly focus to bear on the problem, but analyses Churchill's position in terms which preclude a consideration of his shifting priorities in 1882–4. Some special circumstances are excellently delineated in P. Joyce's Oxford thesis, 'Popular Toryism in Lancashire, 1860–90' (1975).

Forwood's political base, had an exceptional record of working-class Tory activity; Houldsworth's victory in Manchester in October 1883, excitably taken as a proof that 'old-fashioned conservatism is entirely "played out" in all democratic constituencies', was won against a Liberal renegade, Dr Richard Pankhurst. As for Fair Trade, the economic wing of the Tory-Democratic campaign, leading politicians invariably saw it purely in electoral terms—Churchill included.[11] The fact that it reflected the effect of acute commercial depression was not generally alluded to. Protectionism was, none the less, closely connected with Tory Democracy. Churchill's friend Lord Dunraven was President of the Fair Trade League, and produced a Tory-Democratic manifesto in the *Nineteenth Century* in April 1883, possibly inspired by Churchill. This attacked the state of the party in the Commons, and advocated following the model of Chamberlain's 'caucus' in national organization. It was an interesting article, representing the essential base of Tory Democracy in that it identified Radicalism as implicitly 'communistic', and emphatically called for both Protectionism and imperialism. For Churchill, it was the beginning of a useful collaboration. He did not, however, identify himself with every manifestation of the new creed: later he was to refer slightingly to A. B. Forwood's candidature at Liverpool as a 'Tory Democrat' in December 1882, which brought the debate into public focus. Forwood's programme included Redistribution as well as franchise extension, sweeping local government for Ireland, extension of the Employer's Liability Act, housing reform, and redistribution of Church endowments (the 'hugger-mugger creed' of 'a political quack', remarked Liberal journals): not all of these planks were Democratic in the Liverpool context. He lost to a Liberal, but one of the Christian Socialist stamp.

Had Forwood won, Churchill might have championed him more openly. He represented a trend which could only work to Churchill's advantage. Forwood's campaign led Chamberlain to write to Lady Dorothy Nevill (in between comments about orchids and French novels) that 'the Whigs as a party are played out and the next great fight will be between the Tory Democrats

[11] See for instance Churchill to Northcote, 4 Nov. 1881, Iddesleigh papers, BL Add. MS 50021: 'I am informed on excellent authority that what with Fair Trade and the Irish vote we could win nearly every seat in Lancashire.' Also R. Brett to Chamberlain, 9 Dec. 1885, Chamberlain MSS, 5/6/3: '"Fair Trade" was the best card the Tories played [in the Plymouth election] and the "Authorised Programme" was no set-off to it.'

and the Democratic Radicals: it will never do for the latter to be outbidden, so you must be prepared for something drastic'.[12] Churchill was much involved in this process; the by now inevitable squib in *Truth*'s Christmas number forecast his taking office as a Radical minister. When the time came for him to define his own Tory-Democratic programme, he remarked that Forwood used the expression 'without knowing what he was talking about'. None the less, his close connection with Manchester Toryism remained; he received solicitations from countless local associations; rumours recurred in the press about his standing for some great working-class constituency. Conservatives like Smith saw this mounting activity as divorced from the larger issues to which Churchill and his allies constantly referred. 'Liverpool and Preston prove that men care more than we had supposed possible for themselves rather than for principles', he wrote disconsolately to Harrowby, 'and very much of the action of the 4th party and the Review and Newspaper articles are prompted by a resolve to push personal interests at all hazards. Who is to lead if Northcote ultimately fails?'[13] By Christmas 1882 the redefinition of Conservatism, called for by Gorst, accompanied by an attack on the leaders, broadcast in the press, seemed ready to take off. But at this point Churchill, unpredictable as ever, retired to North Africa for Christmas and refused to return.

III

The reasons were complex, and primarily personal. His father had planned a Mediterranean cruise, and Churchill had promised to join him in January; but it seems likely that his departure was advanced because of a bout of illness. The newspapers announced on 12 December that he had been ordered by his doctors to remain in the south until February; successive bulletins from abroad announced that his health compelled him to remain abroad and cancel political engagements. He travelled first to Algeria alone, only considering turning back when his wife fell seriously ill with typhoid. By early January he had returned as far as Monte Carlo, and met Gorst at Menton, but wrote to his wife on 5 January, 'I don't feel at all inclined to

[12] 28 Dec. 1882, Chamberlain MSS 5/56/5.
[13] Smith to Harrowby, 17 Jan. 1883, Harrowby MSS LIV/209.

begin politics again': a message repeated to Wolff with a threat
not to return for the opening of parliament, being 'happy in
Capua'. This was partly politic; he was bent on separating
himself from the leadership, alarming his allies by suggesting
they refuse the Conservative whip. The rift between Fourth
Party members was also allowed to widen at this time; Wolff
relayed ideas which were not to be shared with Gorst, while
Gorst pressed for initiatives on franchise extension, and even
Home Rule. But much of Churchill's delay seems to have been
due to his health, which dominates his letters to his wife in
London—though Wolff roundly accused him of 'lying perdu
somewhere in the purlieus of Nice with a woman'.[14]

Whether or not this was the case, Wolff's letters continually
wheedled Churchill to return, often by means of retailing the
golden opinions others held of him. From early January, the
tone becomes anxious; Churchill should not have given the
impression that he had retired: 'having routed all the goats, now
is the time for you to consolidate your strength ... I am sorry to
see you so much discouraged just at the moment when you might
not only make your own position but also the fortunes of the
party.'[15] It was certainly true that Churchill had withdrawn just
when the self-publicizing of the autumn session had paid
handsome dividends. He had reached a point where he was
'unquestionably the most popular speaker in the Conservative
party': Rosebery recalled that by this time he attracted greater
audiences than Gladstone. Denigrating the government in terms
of deliberate vulgarity was not his invention; it was, in fact, a
traditional Tory tactic. But public opinion at the end of the year
agreed that Churchill seemed deliberately to have given up
'trifling', and in doing so had won over a considerable number of
Tory rank and file from Northcote's side to his. Though his
parliamentary   pyrotechnics   were   written   off   as   sham
Disraelianism, they were reported none the less. His son saw
Churchill's capacity to get himself talked about as something
almost spiritual: 'a strange quality unconsciously exerted and
not by any means to be simulated'. It is more likely that his
position, lineage, vulgarity, and 'flash' had a great deal to do
with it, and his relentless cultivation of newspapermen even
more: besides Borthwick of the *Post*, Chenery of *The Times*,

---

[14] See Churchill and Mitchell, p. 117; Gorst, *Fourth Party*, p. 216 (a letter misdated in
W. S. Churchill, i, 165); and Wolff to Churchill, 8 Jan. 1883, RCHL i/93.
[15] 4 Jan. 1883, ibid. 183.

Gibson Bowles of *Vanity Fair*, and Labouchere of *Truth*, his intimate circle included by this stage Escott of the *Fortnightly* and G. W. Smalley, influential American correspondent of the *New York Tribune*. All corresponded with him, all wrote about him, all recorded in later years that they had been especially close to him (except Chenery, who died in 1884, whereupon Churchill immediately cultivated his successor, Buckle). Like Chamberlain, he was a master of the unofficial press leak; and Chamberlain claimed in the House of Commons that Churchill himself went so far as to contribute directly to *Vanity Fair*.[16]

When in the middle of February 1883 Churchill returned to London his health was restored; he had heard that Northcote's recovery was 'all humbug'; and he was in severe financial difficulties, having moved into his new house at Marble Arch leaving many bills unpaid.[17] His public activity was correspondingly frenetic. After the debate on the Queen's speech Gorst moved an amendment intended to exhume the Kilmainham Treaty issue, which Northcote unwillingly had to accept; Churchill then delivered a long and violent speech on Ireland, accusing Herbert Gladstone—with some prescience—of being a Home Ruler. He also attacked the government policy on Egypt, an issue which he had been working up since the previous November. The part FitzGibbon played regarding Irish affairs was filled for Egypt by the infinitely more naïve and self-important figure of Wilfrid Scawen Blunt, who supplied Churchill with ammunition from off-stage. Blunt, an aristocratic poet and colourful professional romantic, acted as avatar for several anti-imperial causes. From Churchill's side, it is likely that his immediate seizure of the Egyptian cause was dictated by his apprehension that it was, next to Ireland, the key issue upon which Liberalism contradicted itself.[18]

The Fourth Party, in any case, looked upon Blunt as something of a figure of fun; the important thing in February 1882

---

[16] *Hansard 3*, cclxxvi, 801.

[17] See Churchill and Mitchell, pp. 116–17, 120, for Lady Randolph's worries. Duns were met with half-payments only and the family solicitor instructed to find £15,000 in mid-January.

[18] *Hansard 3*, cclxxiv, 666. For an instance of local information, triumphantly used, see ibid., cclxxvi, 1445. According to Dilke, Gladstone was at this time in constant danger of resigning over the Egyptian policy (he, Bright, and Granville being initially the only supporters of the 'let alone' strategy): Dilke's diary, extract in Chamberlain papers, 8/2/1. But his belief that Arabi had set up the Alexandrian massacres turned him to belligerency. Blunt's first overtures to Churchill about Egypt began in 'November 1882', according to the Blunt MSS, 380/1977.

was that they were once again working closely together, Gorst and Churchill making a special issue of Transvaal affairs to attack the 'inhumanity' of the Boers, and Wolff joining in for a sustained campaign against the Board of Inland Revenue for its supposed interference with the House of Commons privileges. Churchill's choice of topics was as eclectic as ever, on one occasion urbanely implying that Gladstone liked nothing better than gambling at Monte Carlo. But the wider battleground of national opinion was also canvassed. At Woodstock in February he pressed a firm country-Tory line, identifying Conservatism with 'resistance to rebels' in social questions, attacking the priority given by the Liberals to metropolitan government ('who cares for the government of London?'), and warning his constituents of notorious plans afoot regarding land taxation.[19] Nothing could be further from Tory Democracy, and bearing in mind the audience this was unsurprising. But the battle-lines drawn up before Christmas were about to be breached. The articles by Raikes and Brodrick in the *Nineteenth Century* showed that the Fourth Party ran a risk of being outbid in the anti-Northcote game. In early March, Churchill provoked an issue which forced Northcote to open a correspondence with him about the Fourth Party's ostentatious insubordination. Northcote's letters were emollient, Churchill's replies rasping: his final letter to Northcote emphasized the intrigue of the leaders against the Fourth Party, and the numerous letters of support which he received from Conservatism in the country; also that he had 'no particular personal object to gain'. The point thus made was to be his keynote over the next months: that his campaign against the Commons leadership was not a mere power struggle; that it was backed by wider forces in the country at large; that it involved an aggressive redefinition of Conservatism; and that it required a single chief, Salisbury. Who would be Salisbury's lieutenant in the Commons was left open, but implicit.

The exchange with Northcote was the first step in this campaign. The second was apparent to readers of *The Times* a fortnight later, when a letter signed 'A Tory' appeared, complaining that in the projected celebrations over unveiling Beaconsfield's statue Northcote was to take the starring role. On 2 April, a letter signed by Churchill followed, which contrived to

---

[19] See *Morning Post*, 28 Feb. 1883.

insult as many elements in the party as possible. He took as his point of departure what he claimed was Gladstone's impending retirement, which would find the Conservative leadership 'in commission'. Northcote, Cairns, and Salisbury were all candidates. But Churchill's brutal animadversions on the general hopelessness and pusillanimity of the Opposition's parliamentary conduct made it clear where his sympathies lay. Further remarks about 'third-rate statesmen just good enough to fill subordinate offices while Lord Beaconsfield was alive' sharpened the point: so did the statement that Conservatives in the country had no patience with ' "bourgeois" placemen, "honourable" Tadpoles, hungry Tapers, Irish lawyers'. Salisbury himself was finally designated the obvious leader: Churchill even foisted upon him 'a policy rightly concerning and eloquently expressing the true principles of popular Toryism', and finally appealed to him not to let a misguided sense of loyalty sacrifice him to his 'useless' former colleagues.

Thus the letter was an appeal to Salisbury couched in terms which deliberately prevented him answering it: since it not only established for him in advance a policy which he had no intention of following, but also emphasized that he would be jettisoning his loyal supporters if he did so. The reaction in the newspapers was widespread, and very generally interpreted the main thrust of the letter as being Churchill's own bid for the Commons leadership. His son vividly described the backlash of opinion against Churchill, the flurry of support demonstrated for Northcote, the buildup of support for Churchill from Conservatism in the country, which followed. (There was also a curious positive effect, in that the general condemnation of Churchill often involved an assessment of how useful he was to his party when he did *not* go too far; but Churchill hardly calculated this outcome.) More immediately relevant was the fact that the concentration of attention upon Northcote's position in the Commons (aided by Gorst and Wolff among others) meant that for Salisbury, while taking up Churchill's challenge was out of the question, repudiating it publicly was not actually necessary. And he did not do so, though there were reports that he had privately reassured Northcote. Indeed, Churchill's appearance in this abrasive role, combined with his country-Tory speech at Woodstock, helped people to connect him with Salisbury: both devotees of what the *Spectator* happily called 'political epilepsy'. And Salisbury's silence left Churchill free to continue his campaign, which he did in a further, much longer, and still more offensive letter to *The Times* a week later.

Here he emphasized that the House of Commons repudiation of his last letter meant little to him; 'I was addressing the new rather than the old Conservatives.' The attack on Northcote became more personal: his 'more than usually apathetic' behaviour over the Arrears Bill, and his failure to support Salisbury, were brutally instanced (and Churchill's own stance on that issue conveniently ignored); he had also been ready to support the government over Bradlaugh. Finally, Churchill turned to what he claimed was the change of political tempo, infused by Radicalism. No longer were diplomatic, formalized arrangements to be made in parliament; the public platform and the stump speech formed the arena where 'the questions of the continuation of the monarchy, the existence of a hereditary legislature, the preservation of a central government for the three kingdoms, the connection between Church and state' would shortly have to be fought out on a democratic franchise.

Thus ultra-Toryism was mixed with an appeal to the country: and, in a much quoted phrase, to 'a statesman who fears not to meet and who knows how to sway immense masses of the working classes, and who either by his genius or his eloquence, or by all the varied influences of an ancient name, can "move the hearts of households"'. The tone of the letter combined maintenance of the constitution and anti-Radicalism with an appeal to democracy: and if the invitation to Salisbury was reiterated, the formula constructed could conceivably apply to Churchill himself as well. The letter involved less and less about Tory Democracy, and more and more about a take-over of leadership: while probably aimed at the destruction of Northcote's leadership in the Commons rather than as a challenge to Salisbury's over-all authority. It seems likely that this increasing self-advancement alienated Gorst—who was never as anti-Northcote as his colleagues, and who supported the testimonial to him raised by his colleagues after Churchill's first letter. Churchill's biographers underplay this change of emphasis in his second letter: Harold Gorst saw it as the essential point, and this probably reflected his father's view (which was also Balfour's). Wolff also put his name to the testimonial to Northcote. How much Churchill now needed his older allies is questionable. He had lost patience with Wolff at Christmas; he was on his way to parting with Gorst. But the latter had drawn his attention to provincial Conservatism, drafted the plan to capture the National Union, and probably educated Churchill in such ideas as he had about social reform. And the emergence of Churchill's drive for individual power, according to Gorst's son, was the rupture of a tacit contract: as was amply testified eighteen months later. The extent of Churchill's ideas on social reform was always limited; more often than not an attack on 'Whiggery' or an outrageous 'personality' distracted attention from the essentially restricted or even reactionary line which his argument was developing.

Moreover, Churchill continued to appear as the incarnation of doughty Conservatism, speaking on franchise extension at University College, London, a few days after his second letter in *The Times*: violently repudiating any idea that the agricultural labourers either wanted or deserved the vote, and pinning his faith instead on the extension of borough boundaries to en-franchise the suburbs. He also argued strongly against franchise extension to the counties in Ireland. This die-hard image was furthered by the Bradlaugh debate, which was renewed on 30 April. But these were essentially distractions from the campaign in hand: on 1 May 1883, the *Fortnightly* carried his article upon the recent unveiling of Beaconsfield's statue.

Churchill had already drawn attention to it as a symbolic event, and most newspapers took the opportunity to re-evaluate Disraelianism, usually emphasizing the late leader's social policy (in keeping with the current terms of Conservative debate) and moving on to demonstrate how the party had split without him. Thus far, Churchill's contribution followed similar lines to many. It embodied, however, a characteristic dash and *brio*. The title, 'Elijah's mantle', repeated the motif of his earlier letter (thanking the editor for the cheque, Churchill promised to use it 'to amuse myself for forty days and forty nights, like my great prototype'[20]). The article, written largely in Churchillian mock-heroic, celebrated Disraeli's flair and persistence, and castigated his successor's meek acceptance of defeat. To this was contrasted the basic 'recuperative power innate in the Liberal principle— the results of the longing of the human mind for progress and adventure'. But 'imperial rule and social reform', progressive policies both, should be appropriated by the Tories: instead of Northcote's quasi-Gladstonianism, which 'feebly imitated'

[20] Churchill to Escott, 2 May 1883, Escott MSS, BL Add. MS 58793.

Manchester economics, accepted Liberal favours, and 'prevented the realisation of that great eastern development of empire which had been the dream of Lord Beaconsfield's life'. (The writer's public stance on Egypt must have occurred to some of his readers at this juncture.) Throughout, the article was appositely and self-consciously Disraelian, both in its pervasive attack on Whiggery and in its construction and language.[21]

Indeed, numerous authorities, at the time and since, have painstakingly catalogued Churchill's political resemblance to Disraeli: which was no more than the former would have hoped for. But more significant in 'Elijah's mantle' was the criticism of Salisbury—who, Churchill wrote, betrayed his 'imperfect appreciation' of Disraeli in a recent speech.

[Salisbury] condemned in forceful language 'the temptation' which, he said, 'was strong to many politicians to attempt to gain the victory by bringing into the lobby men whose principles were divergent, and whose combined forces therefore could not lead to any wholesome victory'. Excellent moralizing, very suitable to the digestion of the country delegates, but one of those puritanical theories which party leaders are prone to preach on a platform, which have never guided for any length of time the action of politicians in the House of Commons, and which whenever apparently put into practice result in weak and inane proceedings. Discrimination between wholesome and unwholesome victories is idle and impractical.

Disraeli, with the young Salisbury himself, had even in 1866 carried off an alliance with the Whigs, 'whose principles are even more divergent from the modern Conservatives than the principles of the Radical party, and certainly any political victory in which Whigs bear a part must be to the last degree unwholesome and scrofulous'. As for the party leadership, Northcote's supporters claimed it should be exerted from the Commons. But Wellington, Derby, and Beaconsfield, under whom the party flourished, were in the Lords: 'I allude to these historical facts without wishing to attach undue weight to them.' None the less, the Lords, the monarch, and the party stood or fell together, and boldness in tactics, led from the Lords, was the recipe for

---

[21] The famous gibe about 'the old men who croon over the fires in the Carlton' may have been a conscious paraphrase of a passage from *Coningsby*: 'The Tory party . . . was held to be literally defunct except by a few old battered cronies of office crouched round the embers of faction, which they were fanning, and muttering reaction in mystic whispers' (Book iii, chapter 5).

Conservative success. The Lords could, and should, resist the Commons when necessary, even if an appeal to the country went against them—as might happen shortly.

This die-hard ovation, implicitly contradicting stances Churchill had taken in the past and would take in the future, dominated the article. Contrary to the impression given in his son's biography, an appeal to a policy of social reform and Tory Democracy did not come in until a final short paragraph: and then appeared more like a final Disraelian flourish than anything more considered. There was a hint that Conservatism could be encouraged in Ireland by an imaginative policy (just as Gorst had privately suggested to Churchill[22]): but this was 'so dangerous a subject that I pass from it with haste'. Where social reformism *was* indicated, Churchill once again identified it with Salisbury, to whom he attributed the cause of improving working-class dwellings, and included in the litany of social reformers Cameron (national insurance), Lawson (temperance), Bryce, and Collings for good measure: this was not Tory Democracy, and he took good care to repudiate the ideas advanced by Forwood at Liverpool. The article as a whole followed the progression of the three newspaper letters which had preceded it, in subordinating Gorst's Tory-Democratic ideology to Churchill's preoccupation with the man upon whom the mantle of Elijah would descend, 'whoever he might be'.

Most observers, indeed, saw it as a blatant advancement of self, nor was its emphasis mistaken.

Lord Randolph Churchill has written an article in the May number of the *Fortnightly* in which he comes forward as the advocate of Tory Democracy, and explains what this Democracy ought to be. The Premier is always to be a Peer, and the nucleus of the parties to be in the House of Lords. Under the paternal sway of this nobleman, aided and supported by his brother nobles, we humble folk are to be given, as an equivalent for political power, better houses, a compulsory scheme of national insurance, commons, parks, museums, libraries and workhouses, while an Irish policy is to be put forward 'to captivate the Celtic race'. The Tory Democracy, thus organised, is to put the Liberals into a minority as often as possible, and to assume office frequently for brief periods, in order to get what it can of the public spoil. We now know what a Tory Democracy is, what are its aims, and

---

[22] Gorst to Churchill, 29 Jan. 1883, RCHL i/105. This letter firmly identifies Gorst with an advanced Irish policy.

what the means are by which it proposes to attain them. 'Tory' it no doubt is, but why, in the name of reason, does Lord Randolph also call it 'democracy'?[23]

The Liberal press continued to see the Tory working man as an entertaining anomaly providing 'crowds' in single numbers, and dolefully spending bank holidays in earning piece-work wages by listening to Tory notables. In any case Northcote's outraged comment to Stanhope that 'we cannot go in for Democratic Toryism'[24] characteristically missed the point. Enthusiastic if rather incoherent writers like Standish O'Grady attempted from the 1880s on to give Churchill an ideology; O'Grady's *Toryism and the Tory Democracy* (1886) bears witness to the reactions of one confused acolyte who through Churchill's speeches in the early 1880s saw 'a mind travelling in an orbit of its own' and appreciated the rhetorical nature of his 'attacks' on certain interests which must, no matter how much abused, remain Conservative for self-preservation. But there was also an appreciation (especially after the franchise reform, long foreseen, of 1884) that much of this was a direct response to circumstances. 'Across the howling wilderness of modern Democracy Lord Randolph has to advance, flattering, coercing, inspiring, with his tongue much in his cheek, or much uttering cajoleries and unreal persuasions. Such is the law of the game as laid down by the democratic development of modern England.' And such apologias, as in O'Grady's case, produced very little in the way of a Tory-Democratic ideology which did not simply amount to the defence of property and an attempt to controvert Henry George. In many of Churchill's public pronouncements at this time, 'Tory Democracy' simply meant anti-Whiggery; which in turn was designed to cut out Northcote's supposed ideas of coalition. Moreover, he always went out of his way to inveigh against anything that could be called (in the parlance of the time) socialistic,[25] and never followed the tendency of some Tory Democrats to attack the Established Church as élitist. Whigs were, of course, another matter.[26]

[23] *Truth*, 3 May 1883.

[24] 26 May 1883; Stanhope MSS, U1590/0300.

[25] e.g. *Hansard 3*, cclxxxv, 1223, speaking on the Metropolitan Water Bill (11 Mar. 1884).

[26] See his attack on Algernon West, an amiable private secretary of Gladstone's who had been granted a Civil Service appointment, 1 June 1883; *Hansard 3*, cclxxiv, 1500. See Bahlman, op. cit., ii, 443.

The same trend is evident in the part Churchill played at this time regarding Bradlaugh's Affirmation Bill, upon which he delivered a speech of weight and sententiousness. This employed as a strong argument the idea that an increase in atheism would occasion a revolution among those at present enabled by the consolations of religion to 'toil their weary way through the world, content to tolerate for a time their less fortunate lot'. Churchill also appealed to the Disraelian tradition, and took the opportunity to deliver a fulsome encomium on Jews—not a question upon which many of his fellow-fighters supported him, as Labouchere ironically pointed out. The speech involved some considerable historical and contemporary confusion of fact, which following speakers capitalized upon, but it made its mark. After Bradlaugh's Bill was rejected Churchill attempted to press the matter further, with a resolution that would bind all future parliaments from allowing Bradlaugh to take the oath. Cairns violently protested that such an idea was 'as bad as well can be'[27] and Northcote appealed to Salisbury to stop him, but Salisbury stood back until Cardinal Manning also begged him to stop Churchill from spoiling the victory by pressing too far; then Churchill was reluctantly persuaded, via Balfour, to desist.

Despite such over-zealousness, his reputation was becoming more considerable, and a certain weight was beginning to attach to his name in mid-1883; Churchill cultivated this, prompting Gorst to ask James and Harcourt to invite him on to committees like that on Public Prosecutions. (Harcourt had renewed personal relations with Churchill at a chance meeting the previous September; by the spring of 1883 the kind of Liberals to whom he had been a distasteful political gamin were privately betting on how soon he would lead his party.[28]) In early June, Gorst imported him to Chatham, where Churchill defended their obstructive and aggressive tactics in parliament. Again, the note was restrained; personalities were avoided; the Liberals were given credit, in an indulgent way, for introducing some useful legislation, if not the 'state of elysian bliss' which they had promised. The chief point made was one upon which he had spoken in the Commons, the impeccable issue of a reduction in

[27] Cairns to Northcote, 15 May 1883, BL Add. MS 50021. For Northcote's anxious request to Cairns for aid see letter of 12 May 1883 in Cairns MSS, PRO 30/51/5: 'Randolph will try to embarrass us as much as he can.'
[28] See Gorst to James, 29 May 1883, James MSS M45/57; Bahlman, op. cit., ii, 436; and for Harcourt's *rapprochement* with Churchill, LHJ, 25 Sept. 1882, vol. 352, p. 12.

expenditure; except in naval matters, where an increase was necessary (welcome words for Chatham). Finally, he called for extrication from 'the Egyptian labyrinth'. 'We were not there for the civilisation of mankind, nor for real and tangible British interests'; the British had become oppressors, and their policy the plaything of the stock exchange.

This indicated the grounds upon which the Fourth Party had become reunited by May 1883, despite the increasingly lone hand played by Churchill in his campaign against the leaders: the question of Egypt. All three had an interest here. Wolff, who had much knowledge of and involvement in Egyptian finance, had long opposed increasing the English stake in the country, and interceded on Arabi's behalf the previous October; Gorst saw the whole involvement as a misconceived distraction of resources. No less important were tactical issues: the question was one upon which, as had already been shown the previous July, the Liberal government could come to grief.

Backstage Arabists included Chenery of *The Times* (an Arabic scholar in his own right), and both Sir William Gregory and his wife. But it was in the spring and summer of 1883, with General Hicks's advance into the Sudan, that Churchill's alliance with Wilfrid Scawen Blunt, begun by correspondence the previous November, became of paramount importance. Blunt had since 1880 seen himself as active in the regeneration of Islam, by means of agitation and negotiation as well as by poetry and horse-breeding. He had organized the legal defence of Arabi after the war, to which Churchill had contributed. In March 1883 they met at a chess tournament in the Strand, and Blunt was charmed by Churchill. 'Before the session [of 1883] was over', wrote Blunt in a characteristically self-inflationary mood, 'I counted him as already my disciple.' Blunt collaborated with Churchill over the latter's Egyptian speeches in parliament; and their co-operation was to extend to India, before coming to grief over Ireland. But the Fourth Party's view of Blunt (especially in Wolff's case) wavered between amusement and irritation; Gorst described him as somebody who had only got the right idea about Egypt by accident.[29] At this stage, however, Blunt's function was to provide embarrassing ammunition against the

---

[29] W. S. Blunt, 'Lord Randolph Churchill' in *Nineteenth Century*, Mar. 1906, p. 194; and Gorst to Churchill, 24 Dec. 1883, RCHL ii/230. For notes of a speech which Churchill was to deliver, see Blunt MSS 375/1977.

Liberal government. Most of this was welded into a correspondence carried on with Gladstone by Churchill, who detailed exhaustively his accusations against the Khedive of provoking the Alexandrian massacres, and various other crimes. (Gladstone's secretaries felt their chief paid too much attention to this, and to Churchill.) When these accusations had first been aired, Northcote had delivered himself into Churchill's hands by censuring him, and then belatedly taking up the cause himself. Northcote and Salisbury were accordingly sent copies of Churchill's correspondence with Gladstone: it also found its way into *The Times*. As he had established himself as an Irish expert in 1880, Churchill became an Egyptian expert in 1883; on 26 June he was prominent at a large Carlton meeting convened to discuss Egyptian policy. And, as with Ireland, this issue involved too many divided interests to break cleanly along party lines: Churchill's fulminations against 'bondholders' affected Conservatives as well as Whigs. However, the more immediate issue at this time concerned the judicial treatment of Arabi's vanquished supporters; and in campaigning about this, Churchill was able to cast back to the events of 1882 (when he had been absent through illness). As Blunt put it, 'he found it a pleasant fancy that he should array himself in the Grand Old Man's Midlothian garments, left as it were outside a tavern door . . .'[30]

Egypt, in fact, provided a kaleidoscope of advantages for the Fourth Party during the June debates. It attracted support from Biggar and O'Donnell, and gave Gorst the chance to harangue Northcote for never supporting initiatives from his own backbenches. It enabled Churchill to compile a formal statement against the Khedive which ran to eighty pages of affidavits and letters (when he disappeared to the Continent that summer, newspapers charitably credited him with going in search of further proofs against the Khedive with which to assail Gladstone in the autumn). His constant efforts to provoke a full-scale debate on Egypt were not to find fruition until the following year; but in June 1883, the question reunited the Fourth Party. It did not, however, find an echo in opinions either among the party at large or in the country; while revealing Churchill's desire for polarization it also demonstrated his isolation. And it also brought him back into eccentric

[30] Blunt in *Nineteenth Century*, p. 414.

company, at a time when he had been cultivating respectability. In doing so it added to his reputation in certain quarters; a journalist, visiting Arabi in his Ceylonese exile six months later, carried back 'salutations to Lord Randolph Churchill: he is, said Arabi, the friend of slaves'.[31] As always with Churchill, there was another side. At the very time that Arabi entrusted his greetings to the *Daily News*, Churchill was discussing his Egyptian speech at Edinburgh with Labouchere; he did not query the latter's remark that interest was waning and 'people wanted something more modern than Arabi and Tewfik; but he had taken it into his head that time ought to be occupied next session in any nonsense, so as to throw back the Reform Bill'.[32]

IV

But this is to anticipate; and a crowded six months intervened. Almost immediately after the June debates on Egypt, Churchill's personal life yet again forced upon him a retirement from politics. This time, the cause was the sudden death of the Duke of Marlborough on 4 July. This was a totally unexpected blow: he had very recently delivered a speech on the Deceased Wife's Sister Bill, described by Winston Churchill as 'perhaps the best he ever made', and by Henry Lucy, who heard it, as maundering, obtuse, and unintentionally hilarious.[33] Churchill had been in particularly merry parliamentary mood in early July, aiming smutty innuendoes at an agonized W. H. Smith and, on the night of the Duke's death, drawing attention to himself for being 'slightly drunk' in the House;[34] and his reaction to the sudden bereavement was intense. It is undeniable that he loved and revered his father; years before, in Dublin days, Ashbourne noticed how when Churchill entered the viceregal office in the morning 'he always put an arm round his father's shoulders and kissed his cheek'. At the Duke's funeral in July the same observer

---

[31] *Pall Mall Gazette*, 17 Dec. 1883.

[32] Labouchere to Chamberlain, 20 Dec. 1883, Chamberlain MSS 5/50/19.

[33] Probably not irreconcilable statements. See W. S. Churchill, i, 266; Lucy, *Diary of Two Parliaments*, ii, 348.

[34] *Hansard 3*, cclxxxi, 124. Smith had said in a debate on the Corrupt Practices Bill that torches, bands, etc. in an election contest 'only excited the women of the constituency'; Churchill 'hoped that although the right hon. gentleman's election for Westminster was marked by an overwhelming majority he would trust to other things than cockades, ribbons, bands, etc., exciting the women of the constituency'. For drunkenness, Bahlman, op. cit., ii, 436.

noticed Churchill kneel down beside the open vault 'and remain with his hands over his face for some time'.[35]

Shock and grief partly accounted for his withdrawal to Blenheim until late in the year. But there were also pressing family difficulties. His son wrote how through mourning the Duke, Churchill was drawn closer to his brother (still, and for the rest of his short life, called Blandford by the family); but this gives an erroneously placid impression. The new Duke's personality, combined with the family's financial position, led to a situation of mounting tension. His divorce case was looming at the time of his succession, and Blandford was known as the most disreputable of aristocrats. In the robust fashion of the day, newspapers described his record of 'ruffianly, brutal and profligate behaviour'; he was categorized as 'a foul-lived fellow, a ruffianly wife-beater, a man who, if many in both Houses of Parliament had their way, would have been subjected to the ignominious punishment of the lash'.[36] At least partly as a result of this social excommunication, Blandford had pursued a violently eccentric political course, appearing as an extreme Radical from time to time in 1881–2. Succession to the title made him inclined to veer back to the Conservatives; with the borough of Woodstock, as Churchill frankly told Northcote, 'completely controlled' by Blenheim, this was no unimportant matter. In July 1883 Churchill was detailed to overcome antipathy to his brother at the Carlton Club (an unlikely commission). For this cause he interceded with an immediately friendly Northcote who, however, according to Wolff, 'did not put his hoof down' about it.[37] Blandford was deemed unacceptable by the Conservative establishment. This infuriated Churchill, who felt his brother had 'publicly changed his politics, to please me more than for any other reason'; he took the rejection personally (or affected to). He had certainly gone out of his way to cajole Northcote into helping Blandford, sugaring his letters with 'little peeps into the camp of the enemy' regarding the Suez Canal Convention. Though in July 1883 Blandford was occupying himself in writing articles on Tory Democracy, by the following year he had appeared as a Liberal

[35] See memoir in Ashbourne Papers, A/1/1.

[36] Newspaper cuttings in Blenheim MSS, M/II.

[37] See Northcote to Churchill, 21 July 1883, Blenheim MSS K/IV; Churchill to Northcote, Iddesleigh MSS, BL Add. MS 50021; Wolff to Churchill, 3 and 5 Aug. 1883, Blenheim MSS L/IV.

once more, despite all Churchill's attempts to suppress news-paper speculation about his brother's politics.[38]

Though they nearly came to a *rapprochement* over politics, the brothers were soon sundered over money. Within weeks of his father's death, Blandford was planning 'a private transaction with some Vanderbilt' over the Blenheim pictures, as well as other deliberately offensive actions, driving his mother to a state of despair in which she relied totally upon her younger son; the Blenheim archives bristle with half-hysterical family recrimi-nations throughout the late summer of 1883. By the end of the year Churchill was attempting to stop Blandford and the family solicitor, Milward, from selling the pictures; this in turn led to a feud between the brothers, and Churchill's decision to give up the Woodstock seat.[39] When the case came to court, Blandford's argument was that he needed the money, since his income was claimed to be only £4,000 a year (probably the hereditary Marlborough pension attacked by Bradlaugh, which Blandford in fact commuted the following year for £100,000) despite a nominal rent-roll of £36,000.

On the surface, such comparative penury seems unlikely. But the terms of the late Duke's will supply some explanation. He had, up to his last days, continued frantically to realize assets: making £8,226 from a jewellery sale and attempting to sell a table of Marie Antoinette's for £6,000, only three weeks before his death. When his will was read, the Duke was found to have left £146,000 personalty. £2,000 went to his widow, with the contents of the London house and some Blenheim effects. The portions of his unmarried daughters were made up to £10,000. All unsettled real estate was to be sold; the proceeds of this, plus the residue of the personal estate, were to be held in trust for the Duchess until her death. And then it was all to come to Lord Randolph Churchill.[40]

Blandford was therefore left without anything that was not entailed, as much other property as possible having been converted into cash and put out of his reach. Despite his

[38] See Churchill to Escott, 9 July 1883, BL Add. MS 58793; *Pall Mall Gazette*, 10 Apr. 1884.

[39] See Duchess to Churchill, 'Aug. 1883', Blenheim MSS E/IV: 'You *must* be a little patient and not talk of giving up Woodstock.' Also letters of Feb. 1884 in ibid., G/IV. By March 1884, this was being widely canvassed in the newspapers; see *Pall Mall Gazette*, 9 Apr. 1884.

[40] See *Pall Mall Gazette*, 15 June 1883, 28 Sept. 1883, for Marlborough's finances and will.

succession, from the viewpoint of money-lenders he was no longer a creditworthy proposition. On the other hand, Churchill's prospects were much better than they had ever been. One of the most jubilant reactions came, understandably, from his much put-upon American father-in-law, who wrote to Lady Randolph: 'The Duke's action in regard to Randolph must make his brother furious, and they were anything but friends before. I am so glad to hear of R's good fortune. In course of time you ought to be very comfortable.'[41]

In course of time, so they ought to have been: 'in course of time' meaning, when the Duchess died. In October 1883 Churchill was considering investing, with Wolff, '20–25 thousand pounds' in the new Woodstock railway. The following February, he raised a loan of £31,000 from the Scottish Widows Life Insurance Office, on the strength of his mother's fortune.[42] But as his own health dramatically and notoriously declined, the chance of such large loans must have become more and more slight. Health and money, the twin themes that dominated Churchill's personal life even more than that of most people, were henceforward inextricably mixed.

Indeed, ill health and a deep depression rapidly followed these family worries. In August he took refuge at Pontresina and then Gastein; his letters from there reflect extreme anger and dis-illusionment regarding his party colleagues. Part of the reason was their rejection of Blandford (though the grounds of this seem adequate enough); but at least as important were the difficulties surrounding Churchill's own election to the Council of the National Union of Conservative Associations, which took place at this time (not a year earlier, as his biographers state). This election was only accomplished by the Chairman's casting vote, administered in gentlemanly fashion by Percy, Churchill's op-ponent. Though his election was welcomed by provincial leaders, De Worms and Henry Northcote promptly resigned, objecting to Churchill as someone who had repudiated the party leadership. Churchill's reaction was violent: De Worms and Chaplin, he told Wolff, would 'make the Tory party too hot to

---

[41] L. Jerome to Lady Randolph, 30 July 1883, CHAR 28/1.

[42] Wolff to Churchill, 23 Oct. 1883, RCHL i/189. The promoter, Waring, was later groomed as Churchill's successor at Woodstock, perhaps as a quid pro quo. But the deal appears to have fallen through, perhaps helping to account for Churchill's subsequent violent attacks on 'the railway interests' (*Hansard 3*, cclxxxvii, 11; ccxci, 1041, 1348–9). For loan see Blenheim, M/IV.

hold me'.[43] To his family, he threatened worse. His sister Rosamond wrote on 15 August: 'You mustn't indeed write such dreadful letters about politics and the future of the Conservative Party. I never heard such croakings and poor Mama takes it all to heart and for gospel truth.' At the same time his brother-in-law Lord Wimborne wrote in panic: 'The idea of your talking of going over to the other side!! I quite understand your leaving *this* party, but it will only be when you have made a new one.'[44] The equally disaffected Blandford, not yet sundered from Churchill, had joined him abroad, and it seems likely that they were meditating a joint initiative; a year later, discussing Churchill's reconciliation with his leaders, Blandford wrote: 'had he not quarrelled with me he would have been able, with Blenheim as a rallying point, to have raised his own standard and eventually, on the demise of the old country squire party, to have formed a strong party of his own in the country'.[45]

Churchill's antipathy to his party in the late summer of 1883 was thus principally caused by two personal slights. But the party news relayed to him by Wolff cannot have moderated his disillusionment. The Conservatives saw out the session in disarray. Parliament was prorogued on 25 August amid rumours that Northcote would give up the leadership (to the horror of Liberals). At the same time, there was much talk of Salisbury's wildness and unsuitability; the Duke of Richmond was publicly canvassed as a successor. Northcote's Commons tactics had been characteristically inept; after clashing in an untypically aggressive manner over the National Debt Bill, his critical motion about the government's abandonment of their agreement with the Suez Canal Company led unexpectedly to a great government victory. Wolff and Gorst wrote violently to Churchill about the fiasco: 'everyone feels it and everyone says it could not have happened except in your absence'.[46] Without him, his allies felt hampered; all they could do was skirmish about issues like the Scottish Local Government Bill, while party enemies like De Worms began to cut them out on Egyptian agitation. From

[43] W. S. Churchill, i, 165–6; T. Treadwell to Smith, Viscount Chilston, *W. H. Smith* (London, 1965), p. 180; De Worms's letter of explanation in *Daily News*, 10 July 1883; Wolff to Churchill, 3 Aug. 1883, Blenheim MSS L/IV; also *Truth*, 12 July 1883.

[44] Lady R. Fellowes to Churchill, 15 Aug. 1883, Blenheim MSS K/IV; Wimborne to Churchill, 14 Aug. 1883, Blenheim MSS K/IV.

[45] Blandford to Escott, 22 Aug. 1884, Escott MSS, BL Add. MS 58793.

[46] Gorst to Churchill, 29 July 1883, RCHL i/144, Wolff to Churchill, 3 Aug. 1883, Blenheim MSS L/IV.

Gastein, Churchill urged Blunt to 'egg on' Gorst and Wolff 'to make long and dangerous speeches against the Khedive'. Despite all his activity that year, he must have felt that both party and personal prospects had slipped back to the position of the previous autumn. But his own medical orders were, he claimed, to do nothing. 'In the winter by one or two speeches in the country I shall try to rub it all in.'[47]

In the meantime, he could brood on a reputation for cultivating new areas of Conservative support, and for taking an aggressive stance on the question of the party's leadership. He may not have been personally bent on displacing both Salisbury and Northcote at once; but the success of his publicity campaign on behalf of the former involved the chance of changing the Commons leadership as well, which is where his attention was principally directed. And his own name was more and more often canvassed as a potential leader; he cannot have been impervious to such blandishments. Other reactions to the prospect were less cheerful. Long afterwards Balfour begged a retired naval officer to write down his memories of Gladstone's table talk at Dollis Hill in 1882, wherein he himself had been praised as 'a young man of great ability and character, a high and true best type of English gentleman, and the future leader of the Tory party'. When his interlocutor had advanced the claims of Churchill, Gladstone 'fixed me with his glittering, hawk-like eyes—and said in his most emphatic manner—"*Never*. God forbid that any great English party should be led by a Churchill! There never was a Churchill from John of Marlborough down that had either morals or principles." '[48]

---

[47] Churchill to Blunt, 3 Aug. 1883, 14 Aug. 1883, Blunt MSS 303/1977.
[48] Memorandum by Capt. R. V. Briscoe, R. N. (ret.), written at Rome 8 Mar. 1913 at Balfour's request, Whittingehame MSS 74.

Chapter 5

Rapprochement Politics, 1883–1884

Mr Tuckham was at that moment prophesying the
Torification of mankind; not as the trembling
venturesome idea which we cast on doubtful winds,
but as a ship is launched to ride the waters, with
hurras for a thing accomplished. Mr Austin raised
his shoulders imperceptibly, saying to Miss
Halkett: 'The turn will come to us as to others—
and go. Nothing earthly can escape *that* revolution.
We have to meet it with a policy, and let it pass
with measures carried and our hands washed of
some of our party sins. I am, I hope, true to my
party, but the enthusiasm of party I do not share.
He is right, however, when he accuses the nation of
cowardice for the last ten years. One third of the
Liberals have been with us at heart, and dared not
speak, and we dared not say what we wished. We
accepted a compact that satisfied us both—satisfied
us better than when we were opposed by Whigs—
that is, the Liberal reigned and we governed: and I
should add, a very clever juggler was our common
chief. Now we have the consequence of hollow
peace-making, in a suffrage that bids fair to extend
to the wearing of hats and boots for a
qualification.'

George Meredith, *Beauchamp's Career* (1876)

I

In a sense Churchill's removal from the arena in 1883 differed
from his previous withdrawals in the summer of 1882 and the
Christmas of 1882–3; this time his political energies remained
engaged, and he maintained a close correspondence with Blunt
over Egyptian affairs. Popular opinion, indeed, credited him
with instructing the Fourth Party by telegram. Moreover, his
renewed anger against his own party had the effect of reviving
the aggressive policy which Gorst had shadowed out in the

spring. As early as 2 August Gorst was planning for Churchill to invade the National Union Council meeting at Birmingham where, in the absence of the front benches, they would 'have it all our own way ... if you really want us to become masters of the National Union'.[1]

Churchill's anger at the treatment accorded to his brother at the Carlton and to himself at the Council elections the month before had turned him aside from the paths of conciliation and respectability in which he had temporarily seemed to be treading. This is not to say, however, that his personal ambition was equally diverted, though the priority seemed to be once more the democratizing of Toryism. Wolff may have sensed this; he worried about Churchill's projected assault upon the party organization as a premature strategy. He decided they had run Salisbury too soon against Northcote; the leader in the Lords was now a 'broken reed'. 'I am quite ready', he assured Churchill, 'to upset the whole gang on the front bench whenever it is possible to do so ... to help you to develop a new Tory party, which already exists in embryo, and with which your name is already identified.' But these impeccable sentiments seem to have been intended more as reassurance than commitment; a fortnight later, Wolff had reverted to thinking Salisbury 'best for us'.[2] Possibly he felt that Churchill had reacted too readily to his previous encouragement.

There were, moreover, many crossed lines between factions and parties during the late summer of 1883. From the Liberal side, Henry James was pressing his friendship warmly on Wolff and Churchill. Raikes (whom Churchill cordially hated), a hitherto unfriendly follower of Northcote, was also amiable. As regarded the leadership stakes, with both Salisbury and Northcote temporarily discredited, Gorst feared that Smith was coming to the front. Against a battleground of insecurely held positions and shifting alliances, the campaign to wrest control of Conservative party organization from the Central Committee to the National Union of Associations was fought.

The ground had been well chosen. The Central Committee's functions were noticeably elastic, and those of the National Union correspondingly restricted. There had already been antagonism between the Central Committee and the National

---

[1] Gorst to Churchill, 2 Aug. 1883, RCHL i/146.
[2] See letters of 15 Aug. 1883, 28 Aug. 1883, ibid. i/157, 164.

Union Council in 1881, when the National Union had attempted to press Salisbury as leader; Henry Northcote, reporting back, blamed Churchill and Wolff.[3] From July 1883, the same combination pursued their aims. J. M. Maclean, ex-proprietor of the *Bombay Gazette*, and currently cultivating the representation of Oldham, was just one Conservative who found himself approached by Churchill, and unwittingly drawn into a campaign to make the Union financially independent.[4] As early as 20 September, Ashmead-Bartlett sent Northcote an extremely full report on the rebel plans; but Northcote held back. In the last week of September 1883, plans were laid for the National Union conference; Gorst privately emphasized that the Associations must be guided and flattered, and the desire of the local notabilities for recognition worked upon—the kind of recurring comment which acts as a reminder that the Union Council had very little to do with Tory working-men, or Tory Democracy. The Union itself, indeed, had had a striking tradition of deferential behaviour ever since its foundation in 1867.

The campaign was planned by Gorst and Churchill at this time; Wolff was later informed, and despite his earlier doubts responded enthusiastically to Churchill's audacity: 'you are really a compound of the following great men: Mirabeau, Lord Chatham, Pitt, Fox, Palmerston, Canning, Napoleon, Robespierre, and others'. Gorst and Churchill alone attended the Birmingham conference in October. This was, in a way, Gorst's moment. It can be seen as his riposte for his rejection as party agent in 1882, as well as the apotheosis of his attempts since the inception of the Union to move its Council in his direction. Churchill had only been a member since July; Smith had had to be assured that this would moderate and restrain him, and that it was a vital step on the way to his becoming 'to the Conservatives what Mr Chamberlain is to the liberals' rather than a destructive breakaway.[5] But this attractive development was not evident at Birmingham. The locale was significant: Churchill presented an alternative to the fabled Liberal caucus.

[3] H. Northcote to Northcote, 30 Apr. 1881, BL Add. MS 50040.

[4] J. M. Maclean, *Recollections of Westminster and India* (Manchester, 1902), pp. 65 ff. Maclean dates this as mid-1884, but the accompanying letters contradict this. Though not a National Union member, he was one of their most assiduous pamphleteers.

[5] J. B. Treadwell to Smith, 13 July 1883, Hambleden MSS PS/8/75. Treadwell was Bookstalls Superintendent in the Midlands and Manager of Birmingham House for W. H. Smith and Son in 1857–1900.

He took an openly aggressive line, denouncing the Conservative Central Committee as 'self-elected', and accusing them of financial corruption; he called for 'all finance to be collected and administered' by the National Union Council. This speech involved a return to the ideas of Gorst. 'The Conservative Party will never exercise power until it has gained the confidence of the working-classes; and the working-classes are quite determined to govern themselves and will not be driven or hoodwinked by any class or class interests'; he 'hoped before long to see Tory workingmen in Parliament'. Finally he proposed a resolution directing the Council to take steps for securing its 'legitimate influence'.

This made the kind of splash desired. Cranbrook publicly pointed out that the National Union was not itself representative of *all* Conservative Associations (a fact of which Gorst and Churchill were well aware, and had investigated behind the scenes); he privately reported back to Northcote. Gorst described the meeting as 'a real triumph', but this was chiefly with reference to the general reaction of the delegates; for a strong hostile element was present, and was represented on the Council. It has, in fact, been well shown how divided the various factions in Conservative organization circles were in 1883–4.[6] Though Churchill withdrew, well pleased, to Ireland, he was rudely shocked on his return: for Gorst accepted in early November an appointment which took him to India. He was a poor man, and the undertaking an extremely lucrative one: Churchill's desperate attempts to dissuade him were in vain. Though there had been recent tension within the Fourth Party, caused by Wolff's Liberal flirtations and Churchill's over-ready leaks to *The Times* via Chenery, Gorst had none the less provided advice, information, and strategy; his departure seems to have been caused by nothing more mysterious than the lure of £100 a week. To Churchill's pleas, he claimed that the Conservatives were already capitulating to Churchill, and would do so more readily without him.

Gorst's departure, however, meant a change in emphasis. At once Wolff counselled moderation to Churchill, and a deflection of his attention towards the country gentlemen, among whom were most of his 'secret admirers'. The organizational initiative got under way none the less; but it might have taken a different

[6] Feuchtwanger, op. cit., pp. 171–3.

path if Gorst had been present. Churchill created an Organization Committee, with himself as Chairman, to see Salisbury and discuss the funding of the National Union. The membership of this Committee concentrated his supporters on the Council but also included some of his opponents. At the same time, organization was pursued in a different sphere, and one in which Gorst's ideology counted for little enough. This was the Primrose League, first thought of in the previous April, which now really got under way. Wolff, Churchill, and Borthwick of the *Morning Post* were moving spirits; though Gorst had drafted the declaration of membership, he was largely uninvolved. This was not surprising. The League concentrated upon spectacle, titles, deferential ceremonies, and fulfilling the aspirations of provincial business men and their wives.[7] Salisbury met it at first with indulgent contempt, though his wife took active part; Northcote, by the beginning of 1884, was supposed to be terrified of it. The extension and organization of the Primrose League was closely associated with the intrigue on the National Union Council in December 1883; it had a particularly strong Birmingham chapter, recruited by Churchill himself; the most prominent figures in the national organization were his friends and relatives. His wife became a leading light, and used the League as a basis for door-to-door canvassing in the epic election campaigns of the next two years; she also spoke to factory audiences. In a newspaper interview, Lady Randolph emphasized the electioneering work of the Primrose Dames as a response to the restrictions imposed by the Corrupt Practices Act; her mother-in-law described the League 'as an engine for educating the masses', but this was a flourish for a Birmingham audience.[8] It provided a raucous but effective vehicle of propaganda, for Churchill as much as for Toryism.

In fact, exhortations to the party to organize were neither a novelty, nor a Fourth Party monopoly. 'Associate, associate, associate!', urged the *Standard* on 20 July 1882.

---

[7] See Burnaby to Churchill on the useful numbers of journalists joining the League: 9 Dec. 1883, RCHL ii/222a; Wainwright on its appeal in Lancashire, 2 Jan. 1884, ibid. 244; Robb, op. cit., *passim*. Loulou Harcourt on 19 April 1882 noted that no cabmen were wearing primroses 'and they are very good barometers of public opinion' (diary, vol. 350, p. 170). The Countess of Malmesbury in the *National Review*, May 1885, emphasized that the success of her Habitation was because she 'gave my whole time and energy to canvassing among the middle classes'.

[8] See interview with Lady Randolph and the Duchess of Marlborough at Birmingham in *Pall Mall Gazette*, 23 Nov. 1885.

Promote as much as possible political discussion and enquiry; bring distant associations together, and enable every Conservative to feel himself the member of a great and powerful and growing organisation. A healthy public opinion generated by these means would be contagious and soon spread beyond the ranks of party Conservatives. There is no time to be lost. The Conservative associations of the country must look forward ere long to another great political contest; let them remember the last, and on this occasion be prepared.

Salisbury himself said the same thing, at the same time; so did Northcote. In June 1883, Stanhope had belatedly proselytized on behalf of the Central Committee, trying to make it more representative and more active.[9] Nor was the drive to recruit among working-men any novelty. Balfour, no Tory Democrat, was sounded out from late 1883 to stand for Manchester; 'the political energy and intelligence of the *masses* in these Northern districts', he was assured by Thomas Freston, 'is far beyond anything to be met with in the South of England ... the future of English politics will be found to rest very much in these Northern constituencies—now these masses must be led by cultivated, self-denying, noble-minded men of power and position'. Balfour's indirect response was a contemplative magazine article which noted with faint surprise that social conditions rather than political constitutions now formed the main issue of contemporary political speculation.[10] But others were prepared to take the exhortations of men like Freston a stage further.

What Gorst had attempted to combine with this was a specific programme of welfare measures. Churchill, however, subordinated both the questions of provincial organization and social legislation to an urgent advancement of his personal position: as Cranbrook and others wrote in alarm to Northcote. Northcote, quite correctly, connected the energetic proselytizing and rapid expansion of the Primrose League with the National Union campaign; he feared 'a trap' and 'immense mischief'. Elsewhere he confided that if Churchill's National Union proposals were ignored, the League would be given 'the power of saying that the rich men of the party are stifling the energies of the workers, etc., etc.' This fear underlay Northcote's friendly exchange with Churchill following the latter's Christmas speeches at

---

[9] Salisbury, replying to the Littlehampton Conservative Association's address, in *Pall Mall Gazette*, 19 July 1882; Northcote at Hereford, reported in ibid., 19 Sept. 1882. Also see letter from Lytton in Stanhope MSS 0295 (8 June 1883).

[10] T. W. Freston to Balfour, 3 Jan. 1885; Whittingehame MSS, 28.

Edinburgh. Churchill had, indeed, been privately advised to treat Northcote gently, but on Christmas Day he remarked to Wolff that such accommodation must not go too far: 'it is not our policy to acquiesce in the Goat's movements unless they are in deference to our initiative'.[11]

None the less, Gorst's absence was further evidenced by the fact that Wolff pressed for asking Northcote and Salisbury to be trustees of the Primrose League, 'to attract subscribers and consequently funds'. This was always a priority, and the way that the League went about getting funds identified it irrevocably with Tory grandees. The Duke of Portland, approached by Churchill, 'had little doubt that I was invited because they were hoping for a good subscription'; he obligingly became a Knight Harbinger of the League, and for fifty years 'had no notion what that meant, except that I received an illuminated parchment certificate'.[12] This gimcrackery was characteristic, although the League began with a Tory-Democratic rubric, supposedly representing 'the alliance between the noble and the worker foreshadowed forty years ago in *Coningsby* and *Sybil*'. Its women's habitations were among the most successful; Liberal feminists fulminated against its appeal to 'ignorant and frivolous vanities' instead of 'the individual rights of women'.[13] Indeed, though Churchill had initially favoured something more like a secret society, the League went for public effect and an organization revolving round the fair-ground and the bazaar. Nor did the intended Tory-Democratic element flourish. Initially, the membership fee was a guinea; a lower class of 'associate members', who paid a shilling, was only introduced later. The League remains most notable as a characteristic if extraordinary manifestation of the more occult depths of the English class system. 'Just as Ulsteria is not so much an argument as a disease, so Primrosery is not so much a reasoned faith as a social cult.' Even when the membership became characterized by 'agricultural labourers and servant girls', deference remained the keynote.

For Churchill's part, he had little patience with the organization after its beginning. He disliked the prevalence of women's

---

[11] See Northcote to Stanhope, Stanhope MSS 0300, 11 Dec. 1883, 30 Dec. 1883; also to Cranbrook, n.d., Cranbrook MSS HA 43 T501/271; and Gorst, *Fourth Party*, p. 201.

[12] *Men, Women and Things: Memoirs of the Duke of Portland* (London, 1937), p. 175; Wolff to Churchill, 10 Jan. 1884, RCHL ii/251.

[13] Handbook for Liberal Women Workers cited in Robb, p. 1. See ibid., p. 89, for the extraordinary profusion and variety of entertainment laid on by the League.

'habitations', and warned them not to get above themselves.[14] In later years he pointedly ignored the organization, while the *Primrose Record* attacked his politics virulently. But at the end of 1883, the formation of the League seemed to augur a sinister initiative, leading Northcote to believe in the necessity of defusing the National Union campaign if at all possible. Stanhope, on the other hand, wanted a show-down; and Salisbury remained detached (possibly because National Union elements, when approaching him with the proposals for reform after October, had also unofficially sounded him out about assuming the sole leadership).

Moreover, Salisbury at this point took his own initiative. His article on the housing of the poor in the October *National Review* was widely seen as his manifesto on behalf of a revamped Conservatism. As part of a publicized national campaign, it led Chamberlain to remark privately by Christmas that 'just now public opinion is all on social questions'.[15] In November, it seemed likely that Salisbury and Churchill would come to a rapid accommodation over the National Union demands; Raikes and others declared support for what seemed to be the winning side. Such a prospect was inevitably gloomy for Northcote, who did not fail to notice that when Salisbury suggested Northcote should attend the meeting to consider the National Union's position, Churchill ignored him; by January he had come to feel 'it was a mistake not to fight'.[16] The terms of dialogue within the party were conspiring to exclude him; while Stanhope identified with local government and social legislation, and Salisbury and Balfour cultivated working-class dwellings, Northcote appeared more and more as a dislocated Whig. This had its own importance for Churchill. Salisbury's adoption of a housing programme seemed to the Fourth Party 'a leaf out of our book', and probably was more specific than anything Churchill had in mind; Blunt, asking him innocently 'whether he had any practical scheme for bettering the condition of the poor', was surprised to be told 'no, but Lord Salisbury has'.[17]

---

[14] Ibid., p. 113. 'Filthy witches', Sir Robert Peel shouted at electioneering Primrose Dames on the hustings.

[15] 'And free schools will attract more attention for the moment than foreign policy' (Chamberlain to Escott, 3 Dec. 1883, BL Add. MS 58777).

[16] Northcote to Stanhope, 16 Dec. 1883, Stanhope MSS 0300.

[17] *Nineteenth Century*, Mar. 1906, p. 407. Blunt added bemusedly: 'I do not take these offhand sayings of his as altogether seriously meant.'

II

But Churchill had, at the time, taken a step which allied him with the new Conservatism at constituency level. In early December he was sounded out to stand for Birmingham at the next election and had in turn approached the glamorous war hero, Colonel Fred Burnaby, to stand with him. Churchill already had financial interests in the city, and knew his Woodstock days were numbered; not only because of the quarrel with Blandford, but also because James had let him know the borough was doomed in any redistributive measure that might be drawn up. From thus early, his political manœuvres were defined and restricted by the concurrent discussions on parliamentary reform: a process that reached its climax the following autumn.

The attention Churchill was paying to Birmingham was evident at Edinburgh, where he monopolized the Christmas headlines with three speeches. These dealt with Egypt, with franchise reform, and with Ireland. They generally followed the pattern of what he had been saying at Westminster, except for a series of uncharacteristic anti-Semitic remarks about 'Jewish finances' and 'Jewish taskmasters' in Egypt. Arabi was to be liberated, and the 'horrible and shameful tale' of international stock-exchange politics terminated. Gladstone had backed the 'hideous and unimaginable vices of Oriental despotism' against 'a struggling people'. The incorruptible Arabi was contrasted with the subhuman desperado, Tewfik, a practitioner of the black arts and 'a dealer in human flesh and blood'. The evidence gleaned by Blunt's agents, Broadley and Beauman, was produced with a flourish; and Churchill demonstrated with grim humour how Gladstone first sent the cattle plague and cholera to Egypt, then 'a dozen doctors to assist at the funerals', then 'a dozen Dutch judges who at the present moment are all on leave endeavouring to learn the language from an elementary Arabic phrase book, wandering about Europe and waiting for their law courts to be built'. The performance ended with a violently anti-French peroration on foreign policy, and a personal attack on Gladstone's 'malignance'.

It was a reckless display involving several self-contradictions. Moreover, Churchill's outlined policy of recalling Arabi under an international protectorate was, as newspaper comment pointed out, 'as much opposed to the views of the opposition as to those of the government'. But Churchill was delighted with the general outrage felt at his mixture of levity and crudity, writing with elation to Blunt and promising him 'stirring times in the spring'. A certain euphoria may have pervaded his speech the following evening, to the Edinburgh Conservative Working-mens' Association, on the franchise. After preliminary per-sonalities (Chamberlain was 'merely a Birmingham citizen, the product after infinite labour and trouble of the Birmingham Corporation', and Hartington—apropos of women's suffrage— did not possess sufficient intelligence to distinguish between the sexes), the brunt of the speech was as at University College in April. There was, according to Churchill, no desire for assimi-lation of the county franchise, and any anomalies existing could be altered by extending borough boundaries and introducing Redistribution. James was quoted on the political illiteracy of agricultural labourers; Churchill reminded the borough voters that they had a preponderant influence and should not give it away to those 'inferior in wealth, independence and intelligence', whose interests so often clashed with theirs. The most important thing about this speech, besides its implication that he expected a dissolution soon enough to be held under the old dispensation, was that it gave Balfour and Elcho, who were on the platform, the opportunity to disagree publicly with the speaker about 'the intelligence of the agricultural labourers' and the assimilation of the county franchise. This was tactically welcome, but also genuine. Churchill's line was not one that many could embrace; Labouchere described it as 'an adaptation of the programme of the French communists to Great Britain', with the cities ruling 'by weight of votes' and the agricultural labourers 'remaining political pariahs for ever'. Though Churchill was later to change direction blatantly, one need not take seriously his claim that Balfour's interposition at Edinburgh was the cause; two months later he repeated the message just as violently.[18] The real reason was that he was still hoping to force an election in 1884. But Liberals made rhetorical capital out of it for years to come.

Churchill's third Edinburgh speech was on Ireland—the only issue besides Egypt, he had told his first audience, which really mattered. Here he brought in the question of franchise extension again, rejecting it as giving Parnell 100 MPs (though he had supported Irish franchise extension in 1877), attacking the

---

[18] *Hansard 3*, cclxxv, 171.

nationalists for wanting 'not Home Rule but national independence' (though he had praised Parnell's constitutionalism a few months before), and calling for material aid but no local government reform. Five years later Churchill apologized for his opposition to local government, claiming he had been preoccupied by the imminence of a national demand for independence, and the likelihood that Gladstone would respond to it. But at the time his emphasis was upon dire warnings about the Radicals and their difference from the old Liberal Party, to which there was so much gratitude due: Forster, Hartington, and Goschen alone were sound. And this, taken with his line on the Irish franchise, represented an obvious response to the crisis currently racking the Liberal Cabinet, threatened over Christmas with collapse over Hartington's resignation.

At Edinburgh, therefore, Churchill recurred to the message of Salisbury's 'Disintegration' article of two months before, abandoning his pro-Radical remarks of the previous session. Such a change deserves some explanation. The general aggressiveness of Churchill's die-hard tone at Edinburgh was probably connected with rumours current at the time regarding what Wolff called 'goaty coalitions' between Whigs and Tories planned both in the Lords and the Commons. Salisbury's leadership in the Lords had been seriously threatened at the end of October; Raikes warned Churchill before going to Edinburgh that Salisbury was planning coalition, with Smith as Commons leader.[19] Salisbury's visit to Argyll at Inverary was greatly publicized at this very time. But besides disrupting any projected coalition, Churchill's Edinburgh speeches were aimed at Birmingham: Bright being cut out over Egypt in the first, the urban interests being flattered in the second, and the die-hard opinions regarding Ireland, always held suitable for northern industrial audiences, being aired in the third. His Birmingham candidature was not made public until the end of January, and he had also been in contact with Houldsworth on behalf of the Manchester Tories, but either way, his line at Edinburgh was cast defiantly at the large towns. Equally in tune with the kind of support he was cultivating at this time was the Rossmore incident, which gave him the chance to appear in an Orange light by defending Lord Rossmore's alleged abuse of his position as a JP when he took part in an anti-nationalist demonstration in County Fermanagh. Churchill

[19] Raikes to Churchill, 15 Dec. 1883, RCHL ii/213, Wolff to Churchill, 1 Jan. 1884, ibid. 241.

sent a violently die-hard public letter to Lord Arthur Hamilton in support of Rossmore; he repeatedly brought up the matter in parliament, supported by Gibson but not Gorst. His Orange pose, allied with his record over Bradlaugh, led to his being approached shortly afterwards by a Church party seeking in parliament 'a bold, outspoken, clever speaker who will be ready at any moment to maintain the interests of Protestantism'; immense support in the North was promised. Churchill sent a pious but evasive reply, applauded by Wolff as 'a masterpiece of tact'.[20] But his public attitude—in marked contrast to Northcote's muted tour of Ulster that autumn—was highly coloured, demotic, and aggressive: reflecting the leadership struggle, his play for a new constituency, and the struggle for the National Union.

All these priorities can similarly be traced in his speech at Blackpool on 24 January 1884, hailed by previous biographers as the prime example of Churchill's oratorical style. The 'personalities' were marvellous; the picture of Chamberlain 'procuring a live earl' and with him 'flaunting his Radical and levelling doctrines before the astounded democrats of Newcastle' endures. Less personal, and more illuminating, was the image of Gladstone as one with the self-advertisers of Colman's mustard, Holloway's Pills, and Horniman's pure tea—a figure infinitely more theatrical than Disraeli. (Gladstone's secretary was outraged; Gladstone himself merely 'remarked that it was a curious fact that real vulgar abuse always and only emanated from scions of the highest aristocracy'.) The substance of the speech repeated the strictures made at Edinburgh. The Irish Invincibles were merely 'the more active section of Mr Gladstone's new allies'. Local government for Ireland meant 'Repeal', Egyptian policy was controlled by bondholders and 'a gang of Jewish speculators'. The 'classes' had gone wrong on Egypt; 'the people' must put it right. (This badly misinterpreted the real state of popular opinion regarding annexation.) In similar vein, he attacked the extravagance of public expenditure; the Foreign Office estimates must be reduced by two-thirds; the Army and Navy, while expensive, were ineffective and insufficient. The Radicals should put off 'legislation' and take up 'business'. Moreover, the state of trade required a great inquiry into revenue; the fearful depression in industry and commerce since

[20] Bishop of Liverpool to Bishop of Sodor and Man, 16 Jan. 1884, RCHL ii/268, sent by Spofforth to Churchill; also Wolff to Churchill, 30 Jan. 1884, RCHL ii/285.

1874 could be blamed circumstantially upon 'free imports'. In this and other matters, Churchill denounced Radicalism as a dangerous imposture. If Gladstone was assassinated, he implied, the Grand Old Man would have himself and his bloodthirsty policy to blame. The Tory party—'united, homogenous, patriotic and true'—would provide a government which would restore prosperity and peace; the Liberals were so riven between Whigs and Radicals as to be incapable. Both of these elements despised 'the people'; only the Tories would preserve 'the balance of Queen, Lords and Commons, and the established Church'.[21]

There was little, if anything, about Tory Democracy in this; more than any other of Churchill's speeches, it reflected Gorst's absence. The Fair Trade commitment was also against Wolff's private advice, though it reaped a promise of support from the Birmingham Fair Trade Union, a non-political organization which offered Churchill the services of some 'extreme Radicals'. Otherwise, the speech aroused comment by its tone rather than its content. The leader in the usually sympathetic *Pall Mall Gazette* was entitled 'Brutality in politics'; Churchill's 'disgusting' and 'indecent' excesses put him outside 'the ranks of civilised politicians', and represented an attempt to change the whole tone of public life. But it made the desired mark in Birmingham, where the *Daily Gazette* remarked that 'such a man obtains the touch of the people, and it but needs that he should become the representative of a great borough constituency to add considerably to his influence and likewise to his usefulness and his statesmanship'. Churchill obligingly announced at once his candidature for Birmingham.

The hopelessness of such a venture is evidenced by the fact that most of the encouraging letters he received came from covert enemies within his own party. At Woodstock on 29 January Churchill explained his decision: presenting Birmingham as a challenge which he could not honourably refuse, and rather disingenuously assuring his audience that Woodstock's representation would continue, no matter what the Liberals' ideas were. He went on to speak violently against the Birmingham Radicals, contemptuously dismissing the venerable Bright, and describing the Birmingham Liberal Association as 'an immense machine for hideous political corruption'.

---

[21] *Morning Post*, 25 Jan. 1884; Jennings has 'emissaries of the Irish party', and also deleted the wilder remarks about dynamite and the anti-Semitism.

III

Though mounting a die-hard parliamentary campaign on the Irish situation in early February,[22] the Birmingham candidature preoccupied Churchill: all the more because of the expectation he held, at least in public, of a fast-approaching general election. But his candidature was put by the chief local organizer in terms of how it would affect the party leaders; and this is how it was seen by Churchill as well. It coincided with an escalation in the war waged on behalf of the National Union—a campaign surveyed by many authorities. The meeting with Salisbury demanded by Churchill's Organization Committee was met by a deliberately dilatory approach (advised by Balfour). This, combined with Churchill's public stance in December and January, was noted by pundits: 'the Randolph–Salisbury ministry is postponed for the present', wrote Chamberlain ironically to Lady Dorothy in late January. Northcote was approached by Churchill for a meeting in late January, to which he acquiesced; but the only topic of discussion was Egypt, on which, he wrote primly to his son, 'I can't support his wild views.'[23] In early February, Churchill ousted Percy as Chairman of the Council of the National Union; thus fortified, he opened negotiations with Salisbury on 17 February for a definition of the National Union's powers. Salisbury delayed his reply until the 29th, and then returned a soothing and general letter (though urged throughout by Stanhope to crush Churchill). Dissatisfaction with Northcote's performance was at this time reaching one of its periodic high points; public discussion of the Tory leadership had become highly animated in private and in public.[24] Howorth, an important Lancashire Conservative, and Cattley in Southwark, had simultaneously come out with a call for a democratic leadership in parliament which was widely inter-

[22] One passage, in view of events two years later, deserves quotation: Churchill remarked that riots were inseparable from politics in Ireland, and Orangemen 'merely adopted the attitude now generally assumed by the Tory party in this country, of offering vigorous resistance to Radical and subversive doctrines, and describing those doctrines in extremely plain terms of speech. If language of that kind produced riots in Ireland, so much the worse.' *Hansard 3*, cclxxxiv 367.

[23] Chamberlain to Lady Dorothy Nevill, 27 Jan. 1884, Chamberlain MSS 5/50/22; Northcote to Henry Northcote, 27 Jan. 1884.

[24] See for instance Harrowby to Smith, 8 Feb. 1884, Harrowby MSS LXV, on the necessity for hard hitting in the Commons, and for an end to complimenting the government. Bradlaugh, Ireland, and other electric issues should be kept 'well to the front'. Such letters preached Churchillian tactics from the most unlikely pulpits, and were sometimes explicitly anti-Northcote.

preted as a Churchill cry, and certainly dovetailed with Churchill's advance to the chairmanship of the National Union. Howorth was, moreover, a dedicated Salisburyite, who frequented Hatfield. At this time, too, Churchill achieved his desire of a full-dress speech on the Sudan, working closely with Labouchere: for which Northcote implicitly censured him. His Egyptian speeches, backed by batteries of on-the-spot information, were impressive: only Dilke took him on in detail. Both his desire and his ability to displace Northcote were now obvious; steps like Howorth's implied that this might be done with Salisbury's tacit approval.

Others, however, realized with a slight shock in mid-February that Churchill could be out for higher stakes still. Looked at from one angle, Churchill's treatment of the National Union correspondence with Salisbury could be interpreted this way. His Organization Committee deliberately over-interpreted Salisbury's mildly encouraging letter on 29 February; on the strength of it they passed a resolution requiring funds from the Central Committee, though emphasizing that they had no ambitions 'to interfere with general policy in relation to public affairs'. Salisbury was privately informed of this, and attempted to clarify things with a letter on 6 March, pointing out that he had not meant the Union to take on such wide powers. Winston Churchill, by judicious quotation, presented his father's reply to this as fiery Tory-Democratic defiance. This ignores the fact that the main body of the letter was taken up by a denial that Churchill wanted the Union to take over the Central Committee's functions, and by a violent attack on Bartley, the principal agent at Central Office, whom Churchill assumed had leaked the offending resolution to Salisbury. (In fact, it had been Balfour, who had heard of it from Gorst.[25])

Indeed, the path of confrontation with Salisbury seems to have been embarked upon by Churchill with some ambivalence and hesitation: it was, in a sense, decided for him. At a Council meeting on 14 March, Percy attempted to have the Report adopting an extended role for the Union rejected, and failed. On 18 March, Churchill received an ultimatum from Bartley, requiring the National Union to leave the offices they shared with the Committee—though only if they had decided to embark

---

[25] The letter is given in full in Rhodes James. For the leak, see Salisbury to Balfour, 4 Mar. 1884: 'What you heard from Gorst makes me rather think that I ought to write privately to R.C.'—at once. BL Add. MS 49688.

on a completely independent line. This Churchill treated as a declaration of war. The next day, in the House of Commons, he ostentatiously supported Broadhurst's Leaseholders Enfranchisement Bill, declaring his pleasure at 'having crashed against the Pliocene and Miocene forms of antediluvian Toryism, the traces of which were, no doubt, occasionally to be found by the antiquarian or the archaeologist but which did not, and need not, in the least alarm any practical politician'.[26] Some at least of his listeners must have read between the lines.

Before Bartley's letter Satchell Hopkins, Churchill's main contact among Birmingham Conservatives, had tried to persuade him against making an open break; after the ultimatum, Maclean still urged him to make terms, possibly by getting co-opted on to the Central Committee. Stanhope, in fact, was attempting to arrange a *modus vivendi* on the 19th; Maclean's memory was that Churchill dismissed this as 'd-d nonsense'.[27] But all his decisive moves within the Union had been won by small majorities; he seems to have been ready for negotiations with Salisbury, and arranged a meeting with Gorst, Northcote, and Salisbury, for 21 March. Influences round him were all making for peace; he had been warned that provincial Conservatism would not support a complete breakdown in relations. Churchill's Organization Committee sent Salisbury a draft of the Report drawn up defining the Union's functions on 19 March; the arranged meeting took place on 21 March.

This remains somewhat shadowy. Certainly Northcote at least was intransigent, to judge by the memorandum he drew up for the meeting; while allowing the Union to stay in St. Stephen's and to receive a small sum, it was to have no say in choosing candidates. Salisbury's recollection was that Gorst and Churchill made clear that the Union's aspirations were essentially limited. Churchill later said that the leaders had given the impression that things were satisfactory, and had promised to communicate with the Union but had failed to do so. This was not true; on 26 March Salisbury wrote to Churchill clearly stating that disapproval of the Report had been expressed at the meeting, and reiterating it. At this point the Organization Committee

[26] *Hansard 3*, cclxxxvi, 24. For a different treatment of Churchill's commitment to the Leaseholders' Enfranchisement Bill see Quinault, 'Lord Randolph and Tory Democracy'.

[27] Satchell Hopkins to Churchill, 16 Mar. 1884, RCHL ii/319; Maclean to Churchill, 18 and 20 Mar. 1884, ibid. 322, 323.

amended their report (not before the meeting on the 21st, as Churchill's previous biographers state), and returned it to the leaders.

At this point too, Churchill's public behaviour became studiously moderate. Speaking in the City with Cranbrook on 25 March he very noticeably avoided every issue upon which he disagreed with his leaders—even referring to Egypt as 'the high road to India', an interpretation upon which he had poured scorn at Edinburgh. In the House of Commons on the same day, describing Gladstone's orders to Gordon as the last throw of a ruined gambler, he not only denied that he was trying to provoke a dissolution, but also gratuitiously stated that there was not the animosity between himself and the Opposition front bench that people supposed: 'such a statement was too idiotic to require comment'. On the 28th Northcote was visited by Gorst, whom he thought anxious to come to terms, and disapproving of much that had been done in his absence by Churchill. Gorst offered to arrange a new executive committee of the Union, and to work with the Central Committee: but the names suggested were almost exclusively Churchillite. This, combined with their reception of the amended Report, prompted Salisbury and Northcote to send a letter on 1 April conditionally withdrawing the 'notice to quit' and suggesting that the Party Whips should sit on the National Union Council.

Churchill at this point suddenly hardened. One reason may have been that he disapproved of Gorst's initiative; another, more tangible, could have been the fact that on 3 April the Opposition under Northcote failed ignominiously in an attempt to provoke the grand debate on Egypt so urgently desired by Churchill. In consultation with only Burnaby, Cotter, and Gorst (whom he referred to as 'the organisation committee'), he wrote a long and aggressive letter to Salisbury accusing the party leadership of intransigence, despotism, short-sightedness, and hypocrisy. He recurred to Bartley's notice to quit (contemptuously discounting Salisbury's withdrawal of it), and threatened to split the party. Salisbury took refuge in a lofty tone; 'fuss' was 'grist to R.C.'s mill', he assured Balfour, and he preferred not to enter into Northcote's over-excitement.

On 4 April, the day after sending this missive, Churchill presented the case to the Council: omitting Salisbury's attempted letter of clarification on 26 March, and trying to emphasize his own readiness to conciliate. Many members were, understandably, angry at the *fait accompli* perpetrated in their name; Churchill's attempt to draw up an Executive Committee to carry out the terms of the Report was opposed by some of the most influential names, though it passed eventually. His own position could not but appear destructive. Once again, outside events provide a clue. Explaining his intransigence to Lord Dartmouth, the President of the National Union, Churchill blamed Salisbury for trying to tie down the Union to the position which had been rejected at Birmingham in October—a curious interpretation of Salisbury's essentially conciliatory letter of 1 April. But he added, significantly, that he could not stand successfully for election in Birmingham unless the National Union was reformed in that sense. And a fortnight later he opened his campaign at Birmingham, unhampered by any commitments to the party leaders, and following a line of aggressiveness exceptional even for him.

IV

Churchill's Birmingham campaign—for that is the form it took, despite the fact that no election was at stake—during his visit in mid-April had various bizarre features. He was accompanied by the seven-foot-tall Colonel Burnaby, in many ways a curious running-mate. Though prepared to advocate Tory Democracy, and an indiscreet enthusiast for Fair Trade, Burnaby saw himself as representing 'what British officers and British soldiers have done in Egypt', and he was, if anything, a supporter of the Khedive Tewfik. However, the implicit disagreement with his colleague was evaded by the nature of Burnaby's speeches; after castigating the government's organization of military matters in Egypt, he invariably digressed into an engaging autobiographical ramble about one campaign or another—often at great length, and sometimes prolonging an anecdote through meetings held over two successive days. Churchill may have had occasional doubts about him, but his presence obviated the need for the senior candidate to turn up except at large meetings. In any case, Churchill's was the only voice Birmingham listened to in April 1884. At a preliminary dinner on the 15th he promised to represent 'the ideas of the influential residents of the town', and despite a Tory-Democratic flavour his speech was more interesting for an encomium on the Philosophic Radicals, and an implication that he had now accepted a full political Reform.

Otherwise, he presented Radicalism as 'humbug' in the light of its policies—which contradicted peace, retrenchment, and reform. In conclusion, he emphasized that, despite his reputation, he had not been 'personal or immoderate': he could not make very clear the party policy, as he was not in the confidence of his leaders, who were themselves bereft of a policy.

It was clear, therefore, that he had come among his new supporters as an outcast. In his speech the next day, he chose to emphasize the question of party organization and the need to 'argue and persuade . . . intelligent, independent and instructed masses' of electors. 'A very great field of work' remained open to Conservative associations. He would

take this opportunity of saying what I have for some time wished to say to a public meeting—that the National Union of Conservative associations is the centre of the nucleus of many of the Conservative Associations throughout the country—and the aim and ambition of the Council of the National Union . . . is to extend all over England, not only in other great towns but in our Counties, and also in our hamlets and villages, the popular principles of Conservative associations. The National Union is making great efforts in that direction; it does not meet with quite as much encouragement at headquarters as I should like to see. There is still a small knot of people whose minds dwell affectionately in the past still [*sic*] and they seem to look with some apprehension on the popular voice, but I have no doubt myself that all this will soon subside.[28]

Toryism should become 'a self-governed party'—by the exertions of influential business men, like those in his audience, who must set up clubs for the artisan classes. The whole speech was addressed to those middle-class provincials who appeared as National Union delegates; the celebrated phrases 'trust the people' and 'I have no fear of democracy', made much of by Winston Churchill, appeared in the context of Lord Randolph's defence of his record on reform and on the agricultural labourers (who, he had now decided, 'will never destroy the British Constitution').

In these speeches, Churchill gave maximum publicity not only to his assault on the Radical stronghold, but also to the Conservatives' internal split over organization. His private relations with Liberals also gave rise to reports that he would defect (he had been reconciled with Hartington in early April,

---

[28] Not in Jennings. See *Morning Post*, 17 Apr. 1884.

with maximum éclat).[29] The Birmingham speeches were seen as his first open bid for personal ascendancy in the party as well as in the Commons, to the despair of some of his correspondents. If biographers have seen them as a manifesto of democratic beliefs, what generally struck contemporaries was the implicit statement of his personal position. Nor was this true only of opponents; Burnaby, with military forthrightness, pointed out to Churchill that if he came to 'address the plebs' in places like Leicester, the only real point was to alarm Chaplin and Stanhope.[30] In other ways too, the viability of provincial Toryism as a power base was less effective than it seemed. Gorst had already investigated the actual state of the local Associations and found to his chagrin a very uneven pattern of affiliation to the National Union, whose representative nature was not all it claimed (a point made much of by Salisbury). Gorst had, in fact, instructed Churchill at Birmingham not to hint at the leader's opposition to the Union, but implicitly to try and cut out Salisbury by a general appeal to democracy. Churchill's speech did not follow these lines, though Gorst appreciated the performance just the same ('I thought your attitude as the humble and hardworking supporter of the party leaders who was not admitted to their confidence or honoured by their personal friendship was sublime'[31]).

After Birmingham, Churchill had both discovered the limitations of his provincial backing, and publicly warned his leaders of an open split; he was, by the end of April, ready for agreement. During that month, Percy had sent a circular letter to local associations, calling attention to Churchill's personal ambition as the real motivation behind the recent developments. Lord Abergavenny, who had sent the party agent Keith-Falconer to see Churchill before Birmingham, had warned Salisbury that their adversaries were sanguine about raising funds by an appeal through the country; but Churchill had also let him know that he did not intend to claim control of seat nominations, and was ready to accept the Party Whips on the Council, if the Central Committee was dissolved. Salisbury was ready to acquiesce in the long run. A Central Committee meeting on 29 April agreed to grant the National Union £3,000 a year;

---

[29] LHJ, 12 Apr. 1884, 30 Apr. 1884, vol. 358, pp. 58, 68.

[30] 8 May 1884; RCHL iii/371.

[31] See Gorst to Churchill, 15 and 17 Apr. 1884, RCHL iii/345, 347; also report in ibid.
344.

on 1 May a meeting was suggested to Churchill by Salisbury and Northcote via Rowland Winn.

But at a National Union Council meeting the next day, this delicate choreography seemed suddenly thrown out of step. J. M. Maclean, who had 'never contemplated the supersession of Lord Salisbury as leader of the party' and was now convinced that this was Churchill's aim, had put down a motion to compromise with the Central Committee. As Churchill's biographers tell it, the passing of this on 2 May came as a sudden shock. This ignores the fact that on 29 April Maclean wrote worriedly to Churchill pleading for *rapprochement* with the leaders, and refusing to believe what Churchill had told him— 'that [negotiations] would have ended in a satisfactory compromise if Lord Salisbury had not taken advantage of my notice of motion to break them off'. If his notice of motion *was* holding up negotiations, he offered to withdraw it before the meeting. Maclean was absolutely correct, for two days *later* Salisbury was still suggesting a meeting. Indeed, Maclean wrote again on 1 May, pleading that his motion did not indicate a want of confidence: he simply felt that the executive committee was too unrepresentative to come to an agreement with Salisbury.

On 1 May, indeed, Salisbury—who already knew about Maclean's motion—believed an agreement had been all but arranged.[32] Yet Churchill, for his part, refused to accept Maclean's offer to withdraw his motion: he simply reiterated that it evinced a want of confidence ('I could not treat it otherwise'[33]). He seems to have wanted the motion to proceed; and when it passed, he resigned his chairmanship.

Immediately, Churchill's exchange with Salisbury was given the utmost publicity by the appearance of his intransigent letter of 3 April in the *Standard*. Churchill denied having sent it; rumour claimed Maclean was responsible; either way, it did Churchill little harm. A further rumour that he had been expelled from the Union also worked to his advantage. Rothschild's gossip had it that it was Churchill's decision to engineer a rupture in negotiations, not Salisbury's; and the chronology of events seems to bear this out.

After the initial euphoria of his enemies, vividly described by Winston Churchill, a reaction set in in his favour in the party at

---

[32] Salisbury to Balfour, 1 May 1884, Balfour MSS, BL Add. MS 49688.
[33] Maclean, *Recollections* . . ., pp. 74–5; for his letters to Churchill see RCHL iii/353, 373.

1 Lord Randolph as a boy

2 Lord Randolph's mother

3 Lord Blandford

4 Lord Randolph and his father

5&6 Lord and Lady Randolph after their marriage

7 Sir Henry Drummond Wolff

8 John Eldon Gorst

9 Arthur James Balfour

10 Gerald FitzGibbon

SIR MICHAEL HICKS BEACH.

THE EARL OF CARNARVON.

THE MARQUIS OF ABERGAVENNY.

SIR STAFFORD NORTHCOTE.

THE MARQUIS OF SALISBURY.

MR. W. H. SMITH.

BARON DE WORMS.

LORD RANDOLPH CHURCHILL.

THE EARL OF IVITON.

MR. ASHMEAD BARTLETT.

MR. GIBSON.

MR. STANHAM.

St. Stephen's Review.

June 20, 1885.

June 20, 1885.

St. Stephen's Review.

11 The Conservative Leaders, June 1885

large. He had kept his eye on his provincial constituency throughout; at this very time, for instance, he came out in parliament and *The Times*'s letter columns as the defender of weekly wage-earners and savings-bank investors against Childers's light-coinage measures. His announcements at Birmingham were remembered; Chaplin's attempts to emphasize publicly that Churchill was 'not by any means alone in his desire to place the party on a wider and more popular basis', and that the point at issue in the National Union vote was the language used to Salisbury, were ignored. Not all newspapers took Churchill's position at his own valuation: the *Pall Mall Gazette* of 7 May carried an article by 'a Conservative candidate' which emphatically stated that the question of *party* leadership rather than Commons leadership had suddenly been brought into focus, cynically analysed Churchill's ability to present himself as 'a political Ishmael', and pointed out the contradiction between his private political relationships and his brilliant public presentation of them.[34] The *Standard* saw him as attempting a pseudo-Disraelian stroke and achieving a premature prominence through splitting the party at the very moment when unity was most needed. Provincial press opinion, however, reacted just as Churchill would have wished: he was seen as performing a great symbolic act, in rejecting, on behalf of the provinces, the Conservatism based on land, Church, and metropolitan grandees.

In fact the hierarchy, which had not wanted this split, was already suing for peace; on 7 May Stanhope (Churchill's 'hatred' for whom had seemed to Salisbury the chief obstacle) held out an olive branch. A Birmingham deputation led by Satchell Hopkins saw Salisbury the same day, and Forwood brought a group of provincial chairmen to Arlington Street on the 8th.[35] They called for an end to the quarrels regarding local

[34] 'Lord Randolph Churchill looks at the sea of upturned faces as if he really liked and was interested in every one of them. He has himself one of those striking faces which inspire interest, and he has an eminently sympathetic manner and voice which are the greatest contrast to the sardonic gloom and the wearied and wearisome frigidity of the Marquis . . . Added to this, our political Ishmael artfully fosters the idea that every man's hand is against him, that he is in disgrace at court, that his leaders won't speak to him, though in fact he dines with them frequently, and that he has nothing to trust to but the people's favour. When, therefore, he appears bareheaded before the populace, accompanied by his young and pretty wife, we have the perfect historical type of the aristocratic demagogue, "qui a bien etudié sa bete".'

[35] See RCHL iii/370 for Hopkins's comment on 7 May 1884 that he has seen Salisbury, 'most satisfactory', and also for the description of the deputation on the 8th.

affairs for the Union, and for the Whips to be appointed to the Council; while the leaders were to have control over 'general party finances, questions of public policy, and matters appertaining to the selecting of candidates'. There was nothing here very different from Salisbury's letter of 1 April, but Churchill responded favourably to it—informally on the 10th, formally on the 11th. By 12 May, Salisbury and Balfour were working on an organizational formula for peace. Churchill's tactics had veered extraordinarily. 'Randolph and the Mahdi have occupied my thoughts about equally', wrote Salisbury to Lady John Manners, reflecting the way the government's ill-advised Sudan policy was rebounding upon them. 'The Mahdi pretends to be half mad and is very sane in reality; Randolph occupies the converse position.'

Like the Mahdi, however, Churchill had the enemy in a particularly tight corner. All opinions were running by the end of April towards a belief that the government would fall. Churchill's support in the Commons was vital for Beach's motion of censure on the Sudan; Beach himself told Churchill so on 2 May. This also accounts for Beach's strong support for Churchill after his resignation. As early as 8 April, Walter Long and Lord Abergavenny were deputized to persuade Churchill to do his bit in the Sudan debate. He was also needed to arrange an accommodation with Parnell and Healy—the 'dirty trick' politics upon which the Conservatives had none the less come to depend.[36] Churchill had demonstrated his strength at a time when his party could not do without him. His publicized arrival at the Carlton Club meeting on the Sudan debate was the logical outcome: here he delivered a 'conciliatory, modest and reasonable speech ... urging complete union in the party'. It was reported that he had rescinded his decision to retire from politics, and would take an active part over the censure and franchise debates.

Who needed whom most was debatable. To some it appeared that Churchill's sudden *rapprochement* indicated that his support in the country had weakened. But he was himself desperately anxious for a dissolution over Egypt; moreover, Schnadhorst's absence and Bright's separation from the government enhanced his chances at Birmingham in the immediate future. In any case, his power in the Commons was unquestionable (even when their

[36] See Beach to Churchill, 2 May 1884, Long to Churchill, 8 May 1884, Abergavenny to Churchill, 12 May 1884, RCHL iii/355, 372, 381.

relations were at a nadir, at Christmas, Northcote had had to consult him over tactics regarding the choice of a new Speaker). Churchill obligingly produced a hyperbolic and violent speech in the Commons on the 13th, eulogizing Hicks Beach and going so far as to call for 'the taking over of Egypt under English protection and extending the might of Britain over that disturbed land for a time *and for all time*'. This volte-face indicates some quid pro quo with his party leaders. What Blunt thought of it is not recorded; but Churchill had to explain to him that 'it is only under the cover of a genuine and avowed British Protectorate that the National Party in Egypt can revive or that our unfortunate friend Arabi can be restored to his own again'. Blunt was hardly convinced. But Churchill's commitment to Egypt had always been based upon reasoning unintelligible to him. And it is perhaps symbolic that, though Churchill's biographers tell of him donating fifty pounds to Arabi's defence fund, Blunt's memoirs recorded the sum as five.[37]

V

Some Liberal newspapers hailed a 'Salisbury–Churchill' leadership as now a *fait accompli*; the compliment to Beach led to inferences that he was to appear as a compromise Commons leader; the *Spectator* was outraged at the party's acceptance of Churchill. Three days later, the National Union Council re-elected Churchill as chairman. His recovery of his position was caused less by the democratic revulsion in his favour chronicled by his biographers than by the oncoming censure debate, by his indispensable relationship with figures like Labouchere and Parnell (which appalled and terrified sincerely anti-Irish Tory Democrats like Forwood), and by tacit threats of desertion, such as he had employed with his family the previous summer. Burnaby begged him not to 'chuck up the whole thing and go over—that would not do—for you have a great future as leader of our side—and with the other lot you would only arrive at Derby's position'; Hicks Beach heard rumours he might secede at the same time; Rothschild was sounded out about his reception if he crossed over, and Churchill in fact took soundings whether Birmingham would support him as an independent if he

---

[37] Blunt MSS 465/1977, n.d.; indexed 23 June 1885, but probably 1884. Also see his *Secret History of the English Occupation of Egypt* (London, 1907), p. 544.

left the party.[38] Already his conversion to accepting the government's Franchise Bill, along with a specific date for redistribution, had been conveyed to the Cabinet via James—by now his chief contact with the Liberals. 'A snob at heart who loved swells', James took great care to advance Churchill's cause and reputation, often holding forth to incredulous Liberals: Churchill was also noted 'conversing very freely' over dinner with opponents like Harcourt.

Matters were still not entirely smooth on the Council; an important element would have preferred a more neutral chairman. Gorst felt the time had come to drive ahead on the executive committee, ignoring this residual opposition; he was worried that the much amended Report on the Union's functions had been referred to a committee of moderates run by Maclean. It was generally expected that a struggle would take place at the next conference in July. But this was to ignore the fact that Churchill was fast losing interest in the reorganization of Conservatism at large, and becoming preoccupied with how his unique position could be used to effect in the crisis over political reform now fast approaching: 'playing the game for his own hand entirely'.[39] His personal position now preoccupied everybody, including himself. As Stead put it, he had 'done his best to make himself impossible and failed'. The Scottish Conservative paper which confidently told its readers that Churchill was suffering from 'a cerebral infirmity', which explained all, was probably indulging in wishful thinking. For the moment Churchill continued to cultivate cross-bench friendships. His speaking record in parliament, on issues like leaseholders' enfranchisement and compulsory land sales, could be made to look Radical, though he may simply have been heeding the correspondent who authoritatively informed him that Tory Democrats were urban workmen who were 'Radical in home politics and Tory in foreign politics': scant comfort to Churchill, who, if anything, reversed these positions. Many observers must have felt at this time, as Derby wrote to Harcourt, that Churchill, being 'very clever' and unacceptable to the bulk of Conservatives, was 'keeping open a door between himself and the Radical section, to which if he has any real opinions he

---

[38] See Burnaby to Churchill, 8 May 1884, RCHL iii/371; V. Hicks Beach, i, 213; A. Jones, p. 135; and LHJ, 12 Apr. 1884, vol. 358, p. 58.

[39] Bahlman, op. cit., ii, 621.

ought to belong'.[40] In many ways, however, the argument is stronger for his attraction to moderate Liberals in mid-1884. On 18 May he was remarking to Liberal dinner-parties that men like Cross would be overthrown on the formation of 'his' government; on 20 May he demonstrated his various new allegiances by announcing his intention of voting *against* Brodrick's motion excluding Ireland from franchise reform. This was in complete contrast to statements such as that at Edinburgh, and caused jubilation in Ireland. His speech drew a bizarre picture of Irish farmers, 'replete with gain', settling down to enjoy the fruits of the Land War; it included the celebrated gibe at Smith about the mud-cabin vote, where Churchill superbly mocked suburban 'lords of pineries and vineries'; it also terrified Tory Democrats like Forwood. It was generally put down to a quid pro quo with Healy over the Irish support for Beach's Sudan motion. (Taunted with his inconsistency by Chamberlain two years later, Churchill merely remarked that he had been 'below the gangway then'.[41]) On 23 May Churchill violently opposed Stanley's amendment postponing the Franchise Bill, another volte-face from his many provincial speeches which had attacked its very principle. The step was taken as gratuitous defiance of his leaders: an impression amplified by Churchill's following attack on his front bench as covert anti-Reformers, which gave Bryce and others an opportunity to expatiate upon the divisions within Conservatism at large.

Despite his docility over the Sudan debate, therefore, Churchill remained difficult: Stanhope approached him in ostentatiously friendly terms, seeking a final settlement, on 28 May. But on the same day a letter from Churchill appeared in the *Morning Post* about metropolitan government, praising 'the spirit of progress, improvement, and wide popular control which is, I am rejoiced to say, characteristic of the present age'. And that night Churchill dined with Chamberlain, charmed unimportant Liberals, and professed 'a sovereign contempt for his front bench'. On 30 May he put himself out of reach, travelling

[40] Derby to Harcourt, 17 Apr. 1884, Harcourt MSS dep. 213 f. 31. He was accused of socialist tendencies by several correspondents; see for instance RCHL iii/395. But on the basically conservative nature of the leasehold enfranchisement issue see Quinault, 'Lord Randolph Churchill and Tory Democracy', loc. cit.

[41] *Hansard 3*, cccii, 621. Also see Brodrick, *Records and Reactions*, p. 162. Churchill had informed Harcourt of his intentions two days before; see Bahlman, op. cit., ii, 619.

to Paris and a private address, and sharing the city with an eclectic crowd of political holiday-makers, including Hartington, James, and Chaplin.

Churchill's tactics in June, while awaiting the annual National Union conference in July, continued to take the form of playing for time: on the understanding that he was indispensable to the party leaders for his Commons performances. He kept himself in the public eye, issuing public letters where he came out openly for Fair Trade, and explained his change of front on the Franchise Bill. It was, he wrote, a decision he had come to over the past five months, and not the result of 'one short debate'; if the government undertook not to make reform operative before Redistribution, convened an autumn session, and inserted a 'proper date' into the Bill, it should not be rejected. Thus he appeared as the voice of compromise.

What this implied in reality was that his priority had switched, from hoping for an early dissolution, to throwing his weight into the balance of the approaching crisis over Reform; and this was made to dovetail in with his strategy of aggression within the party organization. Throughout the summer of 1884, the great public issue was the fate of the proposed Franchise Reform Bill, and the extent to which Tory intransigence masked a desire to bargain over redistribution of seats. When on 17 June Churchill called for a Boundary Scheme to come into effect that year, he was met by a courteous if rambling affirmative by Gladstone. All this went with the middle ground where his campaign for personal supremacy had carried him. On 18 June he spoke at Aylesbury, 'posing as anti-Jingo and anti-Salisburian'; here he extolled 'liberal progressivism', and opposed the increase of empire, and of armaments; but, under the guise of an anti-French tirade, he called for 'a prolonged British occupation' of Egypt, acquiesced in by Europe at large—an important change, which must have appeared as both welcome to the Liberals, and worrying to the Conservatives. For, if Conservative strategy in late June was (in Beach's terms) to force a 'defeat on Egypt before the Lords could get to the Franchise Bill', Churchill was a vital counter. Both sides knew that, if Churchill split publicly with Salisbury, the government would survive; and splitting the party was what numerous correspondents, Tory Democrats as well as old parliamentary hands, begged him not to do. On 27 June he sent a noticeably frosty and intransigent letter to Akers-Douglas, ostensibly because of

Northcote's attitude to the approaching National Union Conference. Moreover, when the government was not defeated over Egypt, and the Conservative front bench determined in late June on rejection of the Franchise Bill in the Lords, this left Churchill in the comfortably centrist position he had publicized through letters and speeches since mid-May. He continued to make the most of this, after the Lords rejected the Reform Bill on 8 July: attempting, via Wolff, to co-operate with Goschen and Hartington beforehand. At the same time he ostentatiously removed himself from Conservative platforms, cancelling a Birmingham meeting on grounds of 'indisposition', and refusing Hopkins's pleas to support the Lords. He also cancelled meetings at Margate and Crystal Palace, to great annoyance, and took good care to make it clear privately that these refusals were purely diplomatic. By 5 July, he was threatening not to speak at Sheffield. He also refused social invitations, with what Lady Dorothy Nevill shrewdly surmised a 'Taper and Tadpole indisposition'. This policy reached its apotheosis in a particularly icy reply on 10 July to Northcote's request to speak on the franchise and Egypt. The message was clearly spelt out: if the party expected to use his talents, it would have to be on his terms.

This was evident in parliamentary debates on 10 July, when Churchill mounted an unnecessarily violent attack on Gladstone over his publicizing of private transactions with Salisbury regarding the Lords and franchise: for a moment, he was seen leading the Commons flank of an attack prosecuted by Salisbury in the Upper House. But even this clash with the Liberals ended with Churchill resuming a notably conciliatory tone and declaring that he would welcome any kind of compromise, and Herbert Gladstone saw it as 'a most wise and excellent speech, calling on the Tories to come to terms'. Outside parliament, he was in fact involved in several ill-fated attempts to bring about some arrangement, to Northcote's annoyance. Privately, he was told, both Chamberlain and Gladstone 'praised him up to the skies'. 'The Liberals are clever enough to appreciate you. It is only those jealous blockheaded Tories who run you down.'[42]

The 21st of July saw the working-men's march through London to demonstrate against the Lords' stance against Reform. It was

---

[42] Lady Dorothy Nevill to Churchill, 6 July 1884, RCHL iii/431. Also see Viscount Gladstone, *After Thirty Years* (London, 1928), p. 361. He sent suggestions to Salisbury via Northcote on 6 July (cited Jones, p. 158), and conferred at Blenheim with Wemyss on 12 July, before the latter's ill-fated attempt to impose a compromise (ibid., pp. 159–61).

watched sardonically by Churchill from the Carlton balcony, and the crowd favoured him with a particularly hostile demonstration. 'Lord Randolph's *sang-froid* was put down to injured pride; it really came from the meekness of injured innocence.'[43] Though he from time to time accused the Liberals of attempting to force a confrontation with the Lords, and could produce violent attacks on individual Liberals, it was known that this was for form's sake. Carnarvon was already pressurizing Salisbury to 'come to terms' with Churchill in order to take to a campaign of agitation on behalf of the Lords in the great towns, but Salisbury disagreed. Churchill, approached in the same sense by the party hack and future poet laureate Alfred Austin, was equally tough. They were both awaiting the outcome of the National Union Conference at Sheffield.

This was scheduled for 23 July. Northcote and Salisbury gave a dinner to the provincial press at the Criterion shortly before, a clumsy manœuvre which amused the metropolitan papers; on 22 July Salisbury was enthusiastically received at Sheffield. The Conference was closely observed, and seen as a trial of strength; but a significant body of opinion saw it, not as a struggle between democrats and despots, but between those who supported the Lords' policy on franchise and those who did not. It seems likely that from the beginning Churchill was prepared for compromise. He knew Northcote had wanted the Conference postponed: a development which terrified Percy, who told Balfour that his supporters were 'in fear and trembling—they dread the consequences of Randolph's vengeance, which he and his friends have not been slow to threaten them with, should he win the day'. Percy reiterated that he and his friends, who had borne the brunt of the struggle with Churchill, were now in danger of being abandoned by Northcote, Salisbury, and Beach, who feared an August dissolution and therefore needed Churchill.[44] Churchill's correspondence, however, shows him receiving constant intimations of slackening in his own provincial support. He had taken careful soundings of the number of local associations represented by his supporters in the unions and been 'vexed' at the result; he was also personally exhausted. His ally Wolff was, moreover, on the edge of a complete nervous

[43] *Pall Mall Gazette*, 24 July 1884.
[44] See Percy to Balfour, n.d., and Percy to Wortley (copy), 28 June 1884, in Whittingehame MSS.

breakdown.[45] None the less, he had prepared a strong campaign, scandalizing Forwood with a list of Council nominees which suggested a total gerrymander, and adamantly refusing to alter the Organization Report before circulating it. The Council elections gave Churchill's candidates a narrow victory. What followed was a rapid defusing, usually explained in terms of a slow realization that the election figures did not give the democrats the strength they had thought. Returning to London Churchill met Balfour and Akers-Douglas at the Carlton at 11 a.m. on 26 July;[46] Wolff saw Salisbury the same day at the Wimbornes' London house; finally Churchill and Salisbury met in the afternoon at a Marlborough House garden party. The speed and compression of negotiations was partly due to the fact that the election of a National Union Council chairman was hanging in the air, and partly due to the intransigent Gorst's fortuitous absence on the Isle of Wight. Churchill and Salisbury agreed that the Central Committee should be abolished (as had already been implicitly accepted, even by Salisbury); Beach was to be chairman of the National Union Council; the party Whips were to sit on the Council; the Primrose League was to be recognized officially, and Salisbury was to give a peacemaking dinner. The expectation of observers, that 'the much-abused "Caucus" would be introduced into the Conservative party', was not fulfilled. Gorst and Northcote were informed of this, by their respective allies, as a *fait accompli*. What seemed inescapable was the conclusion that Churchill's direct challenge to Salisbury had been bought off at an unnamed price.

One of the most striking features of the arrangement was the summary abandonment of Gorst—hitherto often seen, with good reason, as Churchill's *éminence grise*. His reaction was muted; tired and depressed, he declared his readiness to 'rest on our laurels'. But he had a private reason for giving way; Borthwick, closely involved throughout, told Loulou Harcourt on 10 November: 'Randolph had agreed that when the Tories came in he was to insist on Gorst being made Solicitor-General but this

---

[45] Regarding Wolff, Churchill's doctor, Robson Roose had diagnosed 'an exhausted nervous system' in early July (Roose to Churchill, 9 July 1884, RCHL iii/438). Roose's treatment may be given here, as a touching indication of an age when sympathy knew no bounds (and posts ran on time). Wolff was to telegraph to Roose at 2 p.m. every day, whereupon the doctor would write him 'a comforting letter' to reach him in the evening post and 'provide reassurance' to the nervous system.

[46] Chilston MSS F/11, diary for 1884 (a meeting unmentioned by W. S. Churchill or R. R. James).

arrangement of course falls through unless Gorst makes his submission to Randolph and the Tory party'—a significant if novel juxtaposition.[47] Gorst's formal reaction was that 'the autumn agitation will much change the face of politics, and we can look for fresh fields and pastures new in which to exercise political "influence"'. Indeed, he suited the action to the word; within a month he was preaching 'the land for the people' to the crofters of Scotland, in company with the erratic Professor Blackie. After Salisbury's dinner, Churchill took care to inform Escott that 'everything in the Tory party is now going on swimmingly, and it is a great relief to me for I was quite wearied and sick of the constant squabbling. Lord S. last night was amiability itself to all his guests.'[48] But Gorst had not been among them.

No one gave the same interpretation in later years of the speedy *rapprochement* on 26 July. Gorst felt abandoned, and his case was put with some bitterness by his son in *The Fourth Party*. Wolff rather ingenuously expressed surprise that this should be so. Balfour believed Churchill realized he had backed a losing horse, and got out while he could. Winston Churchill emphasized that Salisbury was forced to make an alliance with Churchill 'as an equal'. Churchill's most recent biographer believes that he had his hand forced by Salisbury breaking off negotiations in May, but was determined to withdraw honourably once he had 'democratised' the Union. Feuchtwanger's perceptive modern study of Conservative party organization emphasizes how little the constitution of the Union was actually changed. Only this last authority mentions incidentally the fact that Churchill's position between May and July had been greatly aggrandized by events outside the National Union: and this must be related directly to his decision after Sheffield. For by then, as will be seen, the negotiations over Reform had reached a stage which made him indispensable to his leaders. It is important too to note that it was Churchill, not Salisbury, who forced the pace in early May.

And it must be emphasized to what an extent provincial Conservatism felt let down by him: more than one local

---

[47] LHJ, vol. 361, p. 22.

[48] Churchill to Escott, n.d., BL Add. MS 58793: also Gorst to Churchill, 27 July 1884, RCHL iii/455. For Gorst's Scottish trip see *Pall Mall Gazette*, 27 Aug. 1884. He told them at Portree: 'I hold that the land belongs to the people, and that whatever may be the case with other descriptions of property, property in land must be held in such a way and be subject to such laws of restriction as shall be for the greatest good of the people.'

Association Chairman told Churchill after Sheffield that they would never have worked as hard if they had known this was to be the outcome. So little changed was the position of the Birmingham Association that by the end of the year they were sending obsequious requests for money to Bartley; and it is symbolic of Churchill's changed position that they asked him to intercede. Maclean much later interpreted the whole affair in pure provincial–Conservative terms. Reviewing Churchill's career, he saw the point of irrevocable failure as 1884, not 1886. 'Shattered' by his resignation in May, Churchill's overtures to the leaders in July were a sign of weakness, not strength. Maclean and others felt that Churchill had agreed to the 'euthanasia' of the National Union, and Democratic Toryism with it, and they never forgave him.[49] Blandford too, curiously, felt that Churchill's alliance with Salisbury was both a sell-out and a tactical mistake. But in Westminster terms, Sheffield and its aftermath had demonstrated that Churchill was 'a very heavy weight in the country indeed, however much he may be in need of ballast'.[50]

VI

The summer of 1884 established Churchill at the forefront of politics; 'the political sensation of England', as an American journalist put it, and something more as well. With political rehabilitation came social restoration; in the spring of 1884 he had been reconciled with the Prince of Wales. There had been a background of activity for over a year, involving figures as disparate as Wolff, Escott, the Rothschilds, and Charles Beresford: but the urbane James had sealed the reunion, to his own delight.[51] (Only a year before, Churchill had been pointedly attacking the estimates for the upkeep of Marlborough House as 'ludicrous and beyond credit', and receiving invitations to address Radical associations as a result.)

[49] Maclean, interestingly, claimed that Churchill had 'unlimited command of money, for the men who held the strings of the moneybags had secretly promised him support'. See his review of W. S. Churchill in *East and West* (Bombay), v (1906), pp. 192 ff.; also *Recollections of Westminster and India*.

[50] Pall Mall Gazette, 24 July 1884.

[51] See Knollys to James, 21 Feb. 1884, 26 Feb. 1884, James MSS M45/70, 72; Knollys to Wolff, 15 Mar. 1884, RCHL ii/317; Escott to Churchill, 6 Mar. 1884, 8 Mar. 1884, RCHL ii/308–9; Wolff to Churchill, 15 May 1883, RCHL i/119, 14–16 Jan. 1884, ibid. ii/256, 261. The reconciliation is misdated by a year in both W. S. Churchill and Rhodes James.

James's intercession is significant; for in the summer manœuvrings, Churchill had drawn close to him. Wolff frequently
reported overtures from James; Knollys identified James (a
bachelor with a houseful of illegitimate children) as Churchill's
closest respectable friend; they kept in constant touch. James
disingenuously told Harcourt that he 'refused to discuss [redistri-
bution] at all with Randolph lest he should gather any idea of
our views—but he constantly insists upon telling me his views':
an interpretation he repeated to Hartington. It is unlikely that
the traffic was as one-way as this; and only an Attorney-General
would have felt the need to reassure Harcourt thus. Hamilton,
listening in early August to Wolff and Churchill 'bandying
words freely' across a dinner-table with Harcourt and
Chamberlain, feared 'they exemplify the modern class of politician to which I suppose we shall have to accustom ourselves—
the politician who regards politics as a mere game'.[52]

For the moment, however, Churchill was playing by the party
rules. Salisbury had explained the *rapprochement* after Sheffield to
Balfour as 'a temporary retreat on account of the peculiar
circumstances of the moment, not compromising any future
action'; but this was to reassure his nephew and Churchill's
inevitable rival. The fact remained that Churchill had been
aggrandized, and was responding by overt acts of party loyalty.
On Egypt he took the unexceptionable Tory line of calling for
an extension of British commitment, which gave him another
change to explain. At a Manchester meeting in August where he
was accorded a phenomenal reception Churchill 'embraced his
leaders', in Stead's phrase, 'coldly but resolutely'; Labouchere
reported that he had 'given up having any opinions of his own'.
At the same time, however, Salisbury's hint that he might
countenance a simple population base for representation was
seen as a payment on his side for whatever bargain had been
struck with Churchill. In September, the *Fortnightly* published an
article by Churchill entitled 'An antidote to agitation'. This
called for a Redistribution Bill in the autumn session, and
reverted to Gladstone's 'significantly amiable' promise to institute a Boundary Commission; Churchill accused the govern-

---

[52] Bahlman, op. cit., ii, 67. For James's view of his Churchill dealings see letters
describing their trafficking like James to Harcourt, n.d., but 1884, Harcourt MSS dep.
86 f. 72; James to Hartington, Devonshire MSS, 340/1541. James in a private
memorandum in his papers repeats this strange analysis: implying here too that what
Churchill told *him* was to be taken as gospel, whereas anything he told Churchill was by
nature evasive.

ment of bad faith and vacillation, and warned Gladstone and
Hartington that if they provoked a general agitation against the
Lords, 'revolution and even civil war' would follow. Escott sent
proofs of the article to Gladstone, whose secretary replied: 'It
appears to be characteristic of the writer. His ignorance, his
grotesque and exaggerated style, his self-importance, show
themselves on every page. His position in his own party is a great
puzzle. Without experience, without knowledge, and without
manners, and yet he leads them—who can explain it?'[53]

Meanwhile the enigma in question had removed himself to
Scotland for the month of September, feigning a political illness.
Churchill did not care for shooting, telling newspapermen that
he infinitely preferred either going to Paris and living a
boulevard life, or going to Brighton and spending twenty hours
out of the twenty-four in bed.[54] But that autumn the moors saw
as heavy a concentration of politicians as of grouse. At the
beginning of September Smith and Northcote, cruising on the
Pandora off the coast of Ross, entertained Churchill to lunch.
Harcourt, moored nearby on the *Sunbeam*, 'chaffed' Northcote
brutally on the subject; Northcote, he recorded with satisfaction,
'did not seem to like it'. The Harcourts themselves, who
entertained Churchill, found him at his most forthcoming:
confidential and charming.[55] After family visits with the
Roxburghes he arrived at Sir Arthur Bass's, Glenquoich, where
he spent ten days in the company of Bright and James. Here he
discussed Reform intensely with James, who passed on the
negotiations to Hartington and Harcourt; Beach later remembered him as a moving spirit in the inter-party negotiations
which ended the deadlock.

Certainly, Churchill's freedom was circumscribed by the fact
that he had been reconciled expressly for the autumn campaign
on Reform. Thus though he privately wrote that the Lords'
rejection was 'an enormous blunder, but for which we should be
on velvet', a speech he delivered at Leeds when travelling south
on 3 October had to include a firm defence of the Upper House;
at Carlisle five days later, he sounded the same note of righteous
indignation on their behalf. At the same time he came out

---

[53] H. Seymour to Escott, 27 Aug. 1884, Escott MSS, BL Add. MS 58792. To judge by
Seymour's next letter, Escott pusillanimously agreed.

[54] *Pall Mall Gazette*, 27 Sept. 1884.

[55] See Harcourt to Childers, 1 Sept. 1884, Harcourt MSS 213 f. 68; LHJ, 31 Aug.
1884, vol. 359, p. 120.

strongly for 'a representation based solely upon numbers and which, while preserving the distinction between agricultural and manufacturing districts, creates, as a general rule, single-member districts'; and he emphasized Hartington's preparedness for compromise, and the Lords' readiness to be reasonable.

He was assumed in many quarters to be setting the public pace for Salisbury's private desires regarding county redistribution. Certainly, his reconciliation was part of the process whereby in October 1884 Salisbury seemed to observers as varied as Dilke and Beatrice Webb to be emerging as leader of hitherto divided Toryism; whereas Northcote could only hope to learn what both Gorst and Churchill thought about the Reform crisis by rumour. If Salisbury had retreated from his position of wanting a dissolution, while assuring his more militant colleagues that he had not, he needed Churchill; whether or not he was quite sure of him (when the government's Redistribution Bill was leaked to the *Standard*, Salisbury wrote urgently to Northcote to make sure that Churchill did not praise it). But at this time, Churchill's public appearances fortuitously provided an issue upon which he could demonstrate his antipathy to the Liberals. The Carlisle speech had been attended by violence, stone-throwing, and injuries; this was completely overshadowed by events at Birmingham a week later. Churchill and Northcote headed an enormous demonstration at Aston which, infiltrated by Liberals, turned into a violent free-for-all. Churchill had no opportunity to do more than deliver a brief eulogy of Northcote (which was, after all, the point). But he stayed on in Birmingham, making a round of speeches which defended the Lords in a true-blue sense; he attacked the politicizing of Trade Unions and, even when explicitly addressing artisans and dealing with the commercial depression, remained noticeably mellow towards his leaders; nor did he emphasize Fair Trade, unlike Burnaby. But he encouraged the 'young guard' of Birmingham Conservatives to break up Liberal meetings by force, and when taken to task by *The Times* accused that paper of 'goody-goody advice' and 'a stilted and impossible and ridiculous morality'.[56] He accused Chamberlain and Dilke of

---

[56] At Deritend Workingmen's Club; see *The Times*, 18 Oct. 1884. On 14 October he had told his audiences: 'It is in your power to collect and organise a body which by careful and assiduous attention at Liberal meetings will so conduct themselves that the Liberals at least will begin to perceive that they will do well to leave the Conservative meetings alone.' That night he exhorted more Birmingham Tories to resort to 'force'. See *The Times*, 15 Oct. 1884.

planning to institute a Republic and a Reign of Terror. He collected affidavits and statements from local organizers to draw a baroque picture of corruption, political espionage, and economic monopoly on the part of the Birmingham Liberal Association. Not surprisingly, he was himself threatened with personal violence. Most importantly, private collusion was masked by public rhetoric.

Chamberlain's complicity in the riots was never proved, but he was not averse to this acceleration of the political tempo, and the public row that followed horrified moderate opinion; it may have affected the Conservatives' bad showing in the Birmingham municipal elections the next month. The language used by Chamberlain and Churchill in their protracted public recriminations was taken as evidence of the declining tone of public life. Chamberlain hinted at Churchill's rackety extra-marital life; Churchill's more measured attacks covered the sphere of law and order, incitement to riot, and collective ministerial responsibility, as well as Chamberlain's abuse of hospitality to the stranger in his fief.[57] However, the whole affair also gave Churchill an opportunity to demonstrate his hostility to Radicalism (at a time when the exigencies of Reform were widely expected to divide politics along Conservative-versus-Radical lines); at a Coventry Radical demonstration he was burnt in effigy.

Despite the impression given by the icy correspondence quoted in Winston Churchill's biography, his father and Chamberlain were on speaking terms again before the end of October; and the inevitable James smoothed the way to a formal reconciliation. In public a year later, Churchill implicitly apologized to a Birmingham audience for his extremist stance. The whole affair added to Churchill's reconstructed aura of impeccable Toryism, which he preserved until the end of November—with the usual exception of his Irish alliance. The Irish members supported him against Chamberlain; Churchill attacked the government on Irish judicial administration so

---

[57] See *Hansard 3*, ccxciii, 356 ff., for Chamberlain's implication: 'I do not know what the domestic habits of the noble lord are. But I confess I am inclined to augur badly of him if he thinks it a matter of suspicion for a gentleman to stop at home with his family' [cries of 'oh!'].

warmly that he was accused of 'taking the Irish party under his patronage'; he recurred to his old love, denominational education, flattering the Irish for their peculiar ability to raise themselves through education. He also ran up a Fair Trade flag once again in a public meeting in early November. But on Reform he remained the soul of party orthodoxy; when Harcourt referred to the Lords as Sodom and Gomorrah, Churchill was the first to find the metaphor 'shocking and profane'. And on 7 November, when Gorst spoke in the old Fourth Party sense on Reform and the Lords as an implicit reproach to Churchill, Churchill rounded on him. It was 'a very painful surprise' to find him 'prostrating himself before the Prime Minister and counselling his fellow comrades to an ignominious surrender'. He appeared as the soul of Tory probity, even eulogizing the county members, and reproaching Gorst for his speeches to the crofters. It was the symbolic destruction of the last of the Fourth Party.

But his new allies were not to give him all he hoped. At this time, the beginning of November, the final steps to inter-party negotiation over Reform were taking place. Beach and Churchill shared a devotion to electoral districts, and worked closely together; James, Wolff, and Alfred Rothschild provided avenues to Hartington, suggesting bipartisan measures. It was the sort of activity in which Churchill revelled. But when it came to actual negotiations, he was not in the Tory delegation—carefully restricted by Salisbury, and reporting only to those who had been Privy Councillors. It may be thought he should not have expected to be involved at the highest level; it is certain that he wanted to be, and that he felt the arrangement come to with Salisbury in July meant that he should be. On 26 November, Salisbury met the party at large to announce the terms as negotiated.

To Beach, equally 'sore' at his exclusion, Churchill wrote a letter on 29 November counselling acceptance, in terms of pure tactical priorities, and showing that some of his old animus against Salisbury and Northcote had revived. He was, he summed up, 'disinclined to take any active part in the matter and to let things take their course [*sic*]'. He had, in any case, decided earlier that month that dissolution on the present terms would be fatally dangerous. As usual, his feelings were expressed in more visceral terms to FitzGibbon: 'our worthy leaders, who were effusively civil as long as the contest was severe, now that all danger is apparently averted, have very decidedly dropped me'.[58]

Churchill was already planning an extended journey to India; not departing in the odour of sanctity and the glow of a job well done, as his previous biographers state, but feeling decidedly let down. This is the genesis of his swan-song: a much trumpeted interview with E. T. Cook in the *Pall Mall Gazette*.[59] At Birmingham in October, he had denounced 'the activity and the extraordinary and fanatical zeal of the apostles of those wild and dangerous notions which have been denominated as socialism and communism ... which would, if taken up by our people, shake credit, frighten capital, and destroy national credibility'. But it had often been pointed out that a logical end to Tory Democracy was Bismarckian 'socialism', comprising protection, state regulation of industry, pension funds, and public works. In October, appearing as the ally of his leaders, Churchill had carefully disowned such ideas; in the *Pall Mall Gazette* on 27 November he did his best to reinstate them. After a strong and sweeping defence of representation based on numerically defined single-member constituencies, he produced 'his' programme for future legislation in the event of a Tory victory. Local government reform, with 'no Whig dodges', but based on an elective democracy; licensing to be controlled by these new bodies; working-class housing based on 'a large investment of public money and a large amount of state intervention for the benefit of the masses of the people'. The expenditure of the country must be boosted to £100,000,000; 'but we Tories have a great card in reserve in the Fair Trade movement'. This would have to be 'part of a general revision of the tariff in the interests of the revenue' (a tax on corn and a duty on imports, combined with reductions on tea and tobacco). '"In fact", said our correspondent, "you would proceed all along on the line of domestic policy in the same direction as Prince Bismarck, with State Socialism and customs revenue?" "Precisely", said Lord Randolph, "and does not Prince Bismarck know what he is about? He is the

[58] Churchill to FitzGibbon, 25 Nov. 1884, RCHL iv/498. The letter to Beach is given in Jones, p. 215. His reasoning was that, if the arrangement was upset and the government resigned, Salisbury and Northcote would come in—'a contingency too terrible to contemplate'. If it was opposed from within the party, there would be division on the eve of the election. Any combination to oppose the bill would be considered disreputable. He thought that Gladstone had helped Northcote to set aside Beach's views, hoping for just such an agreement.

[59] See Appendix 1.

biggest man in the world." ' Finally he described Imperial
Federation as 'moonshine', called for greatly increased expenditure on the Navy, and supported reform of the Admiralty
('simply an ingenious device for sending responsibility round
and round in a vicious circle'). Ireland needed a vast and
expensive programme of pacification, and Dublin Castle a
thorough overhaul: 'it is a nest of political corruption'. He ended
with a broad hint about universal suffrage. The over-all plan
was summed up elsewhere as 'Chartism plus Socialism'; it
contrived to cock a snook at nearly every bastion of respectable
Tory belief. There were tremendous repercussions in provincial
papers; the voice of Tory Democracy had been heard once
more, from what was by now an unexpected quarter. It seems
most easily read as a farewell nose-thumbing at the leaders who had
snubbed him. He did not attend the party conclave on Redistribution at the Carlton on 2 December, but wrote to Beach that
day describing the projected schedules as worthless, and briefing
him for the meeting. The next day he sailed for India.

The tactics Churchill used to win his way into the
Conservative hierarchy had not, in the event, relied upon Tory
Democracy, or even provincial Conservatism—despite his re-
discovery of this voice in late November. His eventual acceptance had been gained by his manipulation of a classic—and
classically collusive—crisis in late Victorian politics: the process
whereby in late 1884 the Liberals extended the electorate in an
initiative which was pressurized by the Conservatives to go the
way that suited them. From his efforts to play off the rumours of
Whig coalition attendant upon the Hartington resignation crisis
at Christmas 1883, and his occupation of a centrist position the
following spring, Churchill's path ostensibly deviated into internal revolt, backed by the Conservative Associations. At the point
of crisis, however, high politics provided his chance, and
Westminster was the sphere of action which enabled him to take
it. In the parliamentary brinkmanship, and the public and
private brokerage of political interests, which characterized the
autumn compromise, he had been a key element: reconciled for
this purpose by the still resentful party chiefs. And if the political
reform arrangements accepted from Gladstone's hands by the
Tories held important implications for the manner in which they
would retain their electoral strength, the discussions of July
which brought Churchill to heel were equally pregnant regarding the formation of the next Conservative government.

Chapter 6

Indian Politics, 1885

'And who in the meantime is to carry on the Queen's Government?' said Harold Smith, looking very stern. 'That should be left to men of lesser mark', said he of the *Jupiter*. 'The points as to which one really listens to a minister, the subjects about which men really care, are always personal. How many of us are truly interested as to the best mode of governing India? But in a question touching the character of a prime minister, we all muster together like bees round a sounding cymbal.'

Anthony Trollope, *Framley Parsonage* (1861)

I

Throughout 1885 there was a continuous theme in Churchill's political life, provided by India. He began the new year with his arrival in Bombay, travelled in the subcontinent until late March, and in June became Secretary of State for India in Salisbury's caretaker ministry: in the intervening period he relentlessly used Indian issues in speeches inside and outside parliament. The sequence of events cannot have been entirely fortuitous. Before writing his book, Winston Churchill believed the promise of the Indian Secretaryship must have been made before his father left England in December 1884, though he later revoked this opinion.[1] In any case, the position was a traditional one for a crown prince in politics, and this particular assumption a common one: Churchill was repeatedly referred to by the Indian press as 'a future Secretary of State for India'. And though he repeatedly stated that he was travelling purely for the good of his health (which was particularly precarious in 1885), his Indian schedule was hardly restful and embodies throughout a firm intention to get a grip on Indian politics.

---

[1] On the grounds that the sequence of events which led to a Salisbury ministry in June could not then have been foretold (Gwynn and Tuckwell, *Dilke*, ii, 72). But Loulou Harcourt had already heard that Gorst had been promised the Solicitor-Generalship.

This he did, to a surprising extent: and the story of Churchill and India is a tale of brilliantly liberal expectations and a traditionally reactionary outcome—a syndrome by now becoming familiar. This was heightened by the fact that 1885 was a vital turning-point in Indian history. On the one hand, the permanent threat of Russian advances on the North-West Frontier came to a crisis; on the other, the growth of native political organization reached a point of qualitative change, culminating in the formation of the first all-India Congress at the end of the year. With both processes, Churchill was intimately connected. India, like Ireland, was a country he experienced at first hand, and an issue upon which he constituted himself an expert. As with Ireland, he stood out initially against 'official' opinion; as with Ireland, local opinion backed him strongly; and as with Ireland, when he gained an official position he was seen as having executed a volte-face.

The process began with his three-month Indian visit in early 1885, usually presented as devoid of political significance: the letters home quoted by his biographers are devoted to the praises of tigers and elephants. This is a curious fact, since within three months of his return Labouchere could flippantly remark that 'Lord Randolph Churchill has just been through India with a paper collar and now rules that happy land'; and his letters to friends rather than family show a determined political priority, while he went to some trouble not only to meet officials but also to obtain introductions to less predictable figures via Wilfrid Scawen Blunt. His itinerary was closely monitored in the Indian press. Arriving at Bombay on New Year's Eve, he stayed there ten days before moving on to Sir Lepel Griffin at Indore, travelling by Gwalior; with Griffin he visited Agra, and then travelled to Lucknow on 21 January, reaching Calcutta on 7 February. After staying with the Viceroy, Dufferin, at Barrackpore, he travelled to Allahabad on 13 February. On the 22nd he arrived at Benares to stay with the Maharajah (here the fact that 'any Hindoo whose ashes are thrown into the Ganges goes right bang up to heaven without stopping no matter how great a rascal he may have been' gave him the idea that Gladstone should embrace the religion). A week at Rewah was followed by a brief return to Agra, then a visit to Hyderabad to stay with Salar Jung. He left India four days earlier than intended (although in early February he had resolutely refused all entreaties to return to England), catching the Marseilles steamer on 20 March, and travelling by land from Brindisi. On 7 April he arrived at Charing Cross, having travelled 22,800 miles.

His arrival in India had closely followed that of the new Viceroy, Dufferin, and the departure of Lord Ripon amid extraordinary and calculated demonstrations of affection; and this set the tone for official India during Churchill's connection with the country. The same period was marked by the tensions arising from Ripon's strategy to reverse Lord Lytton's noto-riously illiberal policies, and Dufferin's unsuccessful attempt to tread a path between the two. Politically, Churchill's image was more Riponite than Lyttonist; his support of Arabi was re-membered, and the native press greeted his arrival with mingled fear and admiration. Moreover, he at once showed his interest in local opinion, by declining an invitation to dine at the Bombay Club ('I did not come out to India to pursue politics or to make speeches'), but going to some trouble to arrange a well-publicized meeting with leading Indian politicians and intel-lectuals.[2] The meeting was set up by B. M. Malabari, editor of the *Indian Spectator*, and the newspaper accordingly praised Churchill's aptitude, readiness to learn, and courtesy; the subjects covered were those which were to recur throughout his connection with India, including the age-limit for admission to the Civil Service, and representation on legislative councils. For his part, Churchill deprecated the lack of interest in Indian affairs shown by parliament, and 'the absence of any organis-ation on the part of the natives to instruct the British public ... he thought that natives might with advantage send some of their representatives to England in order to acquaint members of parliament and others interested in politics with their wants and wishes', a suggestion which would be taken up sooner than he expected, and which infuriated representative Anglo-Indian opinion. His reactions were relayed in an en-thusiastic letter to Escott:

Race antipathies are greatly mitigated here, nor owing to the wise attitude of the Europeans have they been in any considerable degree aroused by the Ilbert Bill. The great demonstration in honour of Lord Ripon to bid him farewell has certainly been one of the most remarkable features in modern Indian history and its significance is, I think, scarcely appreciated by the officials ... What strikes me about it as most interesting is that it was undoubtedly the work of a perfectly

[2] Fullest report in *Bombay Gazette*, reprinted with comments in *Bengalee*, 17 Jan. 1885.

organised Caucus of leading natives, Brahmins, Mussulmans and other Hindoos all working together, having their headquarters at Poonah, their affiliated branches all over the Presidency, their travelling agents, organisers and orators all arranged upon the purest Birmingham principles. They produced the demonstration in Bombay and moved and controlled the people with the utmost ease and moreover brought up from various country districts upwards of 150 deputations with addresses. The demonstration was a pure political popular movement and nothing whatever to do with any personal qualities of Lord Ripon but was essentially the first real assertion on the part of the people of India of their claim, right and intention to exercise a more or less controlling influence over Indian Government. The immense success attained by the promoters had undoubtedly given them great confidence and courage; but having seen and conversed quite freely with several of the leading spirits I feel little doubt that their moderation and caution is equal to their intelligence and their knowledge. The name of the caucus is the Savajanih Sabha or People's Association I believe it means ... I never cease to rejoice that I was able to come out here. The novelty and variety of the people, their customs, their pursuits and interest are a source of intense satisfaction to one whose political appetite had been satiated *ad nauseam* by the drivel of the House of Commons ...[3]

This reflected a lack of understanding on several crucial points, but conveyed a characteristic enthusiasm.

Similarly at Calcutta Churchill discussed public questions with 'some of our ablest men', but refused a more formal session and also a public dinner given by the European community. In central India, with the racialist Lepel Griffin as his guide, he probably met few Indians; but in Agra he was once more taken over by local politicians, and gave an interview to a group of lawyers and journalists, returning later for a reception given by 'the élite of the native community'. Here he discussed the state of the ryots, technical education, local government, and native representation, and promised to appeal to other politicians to come and see India for themselves; he once again encouraged his listeners to travel to England and make their views known. At Benares at the end of February he met more local notabilities, and exerted some pressure on behalf of Indian interests.

The whole progress led to a tension which was perceived with some amusement by the press, and produced a covert com-

---

[3] Churchill to Escott, 8 Jan. '1884' (properly 1885), BL Add. MS 58793. He encouraged Escott to recruit Malabari and S. H. Chiplonkar, another prominent Indian nationalist, for articles in the *Fortnightly*.

petition between Indian associations and Anglo-Indian cliques to 'capture' Churchill. His encouragement of Indian deputations at Bombay was violently attacked by the governor, Sir James Fergusson, as 'meddling', and written up eulogistically in papers like the *Hindoo Patriot* and the *Bengalee* (though the vernacular press, which Lytton had shackled, was more cynical). In fact, his public actions (apart from exerting influence to prevent forcible impressment for frontier service at Benares) were few; his embarrassing Gladstone's government by telegraphing to the *Morning Post* details of their vacillation over Suakin, which he gleaned at Dufferin's dining-table, was more characteristic. But the novelty of his sounding out native opinion at all was what was remarked upon; and Anglo-India exerted itself to reclaim him.

Moreover, Churchill was careful to cultivate contacts here too. On 23 January he wrote to Dufferin in his most flowery style, rhapsodizing about India, Dufferin's appointment, and the qualities of his host Lepel Griffin, and asking to be received at Government House. When he arrived to stay, Lady Dufferin noted that he only just suffered such after-dinner diversions of the Raj as having his shadow-portrait drawn with his chin resting on a wineglass; his pastimes with Griffin would have been considerably less refined. The Viceroy, despite gracefully recalling years later that Churchill 'quite won my heart' when in India, was infuriated at the time by what he saw as 'the mischievous wretch's' troublemaking regarding those resisting the Bengal Tenancy Bill, encouraged by Churchill for admittedly party reasons; but, diplomat and Irishman that he was, he merely assured Churchill that it was extraordinary how much he had learned in India.[4]

This ambivalent relationship set a pattern for the future, as did Churchill's friendship with the eminent soldier Sir Frederick Roberts, whom he met for the first time at Rewah in February—though he had defended his record in parliament, and corresponded with him since 1881. Roberts—forceful, Irish, and a passionate forwardist as regarded frontier measures—became fast friends with Churchill, and was to influence his

---

[4] See Churchill to Dufferin, 23 Jan. 1885, in Dufferin Viceregal Papers, India Office Library (hereafter DVP), microfilm IOR neg. 4328; Hariot, Lady Dufferin, *Our Viceregal Life in India* (London, 2 vols., 1889), i, 55. For Dufferin's courteous recollection of Churchill see Dufferin to Lady Randolph, 14 Mar. 1895, in Cornwallis-West, p. 121; and for his anger at Churchill's interference on his visit, Dufferin to Kimberley, 13 Feb. 1885, DVP F 130/2, no. 11.

Secretaryship greatly. The same held true for Churchill's relationship with Sir Lepel Griffin, the Government Agent for
Central India: irascible, expansive, and womanizing, known as
a firm opponent of native initiatives, and a bellicose anti-
Russian. He and Churchill found themselves in fast agreement
on political issues, and within a month Griffin was wondering if
he might enter parliament as a follower of Churchill's; Churchill
wrote pointedly to Dufferin (who thought of Griffin as 'brilliant
but not first-rate') that the latter was 'one of the most attractive,
cultivated persons I ever had the good fortune to become
intimate with; if all Indian officials at all resemble him, I
imagine your Excellency's government will be well supported'.[5]

Such friends went oddly with the kind of Indians whom
Churchill cultivated. At Bombay he met a cross-section of
radical intellectuals and journalists, having been supplied with
introductions by Blunt, who assured him of 'a great future for
any statesman who will preach Tory Democracy in India'.[6] In
Calcutta his chief contact (and frequent future correspondent)
was the Maharajah Jotindro Mohan Tagore, whose British-
Indian Association was opposing the Bengal Tenancy Bill. In
Hyderabad, where he examined the army with great interest,
Churchill was deeply impressed by the Nizam's adviser Salar
Jung (an intimate of Gorst's from his own Indian visit), whom
he described to Roberts as superior to all other Indian ministers
and most European officials; he was astonished at the short-
sighted and shabby way in which the British treated him. By
this time, he had moderated his views on Indian politics:

I find nothing good in our position in India outside Bombay
(Presidency). I do not like the way the native mind, Hindoo and
Mohammedan, is working, particularly the latter. There is a movement, or rather I should say a buzzing which may precede a movement
(under certain favourable circumstances) which proceeds from causes
which the government ought long ago to have discussed, recognised
and dealt with. But the optimism and arrogance or rather self-
complacency of Indian officials is beyond all belief. Only recently I
have been altogether shattered by it. That there is a great gulf between

    [5] Churchill to Dufferin, as above. Also see Griffin to Churchill, 25 Jan. 1885, RCHL
iv/546. In 1889 Churchill promised him the reversion of his Paddington seat.
    [6] Blunt to Churchill, 1 Dec. 1884, RCHL iv/509. The Indians Churchill interviewed
were B. M. Malabari, Naroji Furdoonji, Dadabhai Naroji, Javerilal Umyshankar,
R. M. Sagani, Dinshaw Edulji Wascha, Badrudin Tyabji, and Kashinath Telang—all
influential in the Indian nationalist movement in 1885. For Malabari's description of
them see a letter in RCHL/iv/532.

the government and the natives, that the government know less than nothing of the native mind, that the government refuse to allow for a moment that anyone outside their circle can know anything or even get a passing glimpse of that mysterious mind, these are facts. I do not think there is any damage in the Russian advance if it stood by itself... [but] this is your position in India, that after a century or so of rule you have so little convinced (not the bulk of the people) but the leaders of the people of its excellence and merits that any great reverse from the Russians would leave you powerless.[7]

Less than a week after writing this, he left India. He had earned golden opinions from the Indian press for his attractive manner, keen interest, and open-mindedness, and had left an impression of liberal good intentions, obligingly summed up by Malabari: the official classes should be 'more just and tolerant', the educated Indians 'better united', the wishes of the Indian people more widely diffused, and the seat of government moved from Calcutta. 'If we have read his mind aright, he is not likely to allow his ideas to go to seed.'[8]

Similar impressions were left by newspaper interviews Churchill gave on his return, exhorting more politicians to visit India, and extolling the qualities of 'the intelligent native', 'equal to any European in information, extent of reading, and public spirit'. Throughout April and May his public speeches continued to reiterate his impressions of the country. But the issue which preoccupied him was increasingly 'how incredibly strong and at the same time incredibly slender, our position in India was'; and when he described Indian political organization to the House of Commons, it was with a deliberately sinister implication. This shift went unremarked in the Indian press; it presaged a disappointment to come.

II

Churchill returned in April to a mounting political crisis, as the Liberal government lurched to the end of its span. The climax to Gladstone's troubles had been the débâcle in Khartoum, where General Gordon's long-drawn-out agony at the hands of the

---

[7] Churchill to Roberts, 14 Mar. 1885, Roberts papers, 7101-23-21/6. For a similar note of disillusionment see Churchill to his mother, 22 Feb. 1885, RCHL iv/560; here he confessed doubts that British administration conferred any benefits on the natives, who probably preferred 'their own piggy ways'.

[8] *Indian Spectator*, 22 Mar. 1885.

Mahdi's besieging forces was directly attributed to the government's indecision. Churchill had missed the great debate on Gordon's death, though the Sudan affair had been the reason for curtailing his visit; but his value in such parliamentary circumstances was widely recognized, and the warmth with which he was greeted owed a good deal to his balance-holding qualities. He rapidly attempted to make up for missing the Gordon debate by trying to convert the debate on the Queen's message about the army reserves into a full discussion of the Sudan, for which he was attacked by Gladstone and cautioned by Northcote; this obviously rankled. Northcote had in fact used Churchill's absence to attempt a mild redefinition of his own position; in February he had presided over a Carlton meeting and announced that the party was ready to take office, implying that he would be the one to be summoned. But echoes of dissatisfaction and parliamentary disobedience continued none the less; rumours recurred that Hicks Beach (or Chaplin, or Lowther, or Smith) was about to relieve him of the Commons leadership. By the end of the month he had been unanimously attacked for 'feebleness' at a Carlton meeting which in Carnarvon's view 'virtually made Salisbury the Head of the Party'.[9] It was now generally accepted that he could not meet the tactical and organizational challenges posed by the new electorate; and Churchill's newspaper allies, Liberal as well as Tory, readily made the connection between Northcote's ineffectiveness and their favourite's absence.

Churchill acted up to the mark, opposing Cross's amendment on the Suez question on 16 April and carrying the House with him: a manœuvre which also involved defining himself against Northcote's leadership. A few days later he ostentatiously sided with Parnell over the Registration Bill, accusing the two front benches of 'a conspiracy ... to give each other as much latitude as they could'; at the same time his public and private relations with Liberals like James were notably bantering and playful. Rapidly, he resumed his position as the only prominent Conservative displaying political energy. His presidency of the Conservative News Agency, the fact that any speech he made was quoted verbatim, his physical well-being after his extended holiday, all helped to keep him in the public eye (ranking fourth in the *Pall Mall Gazette*'s canvass for 'Greatest English Humbug',

---

[9] See Carnarvon's diary, 24 Feb. 1885, BL Add. MS 60924; also reports in *Pall Mall Gazette*, 26 Feb. 1885, 17 Mar. 1885, and *Daily News*, 20 Mar. 1885.

but eighth in the same paper's stakes for 'Greatest English Statesman'[10]. Aggression continued unabated: throughout April and May he tirelessly hunted out parliamentary anomalies and danced on procedural pin-heads; he also, in some unlikely company, energetically pursued the chimera of the Tory working-man vote. (Speaking at Bow on Derby Day, he drew attention to the fact that a generation ago the entire Tory party would have been at the races; nowadays they were 'considering the prospects of our party and the condition of our country [while] the entire Radical party is at the present moment returning in a state of more or less exhilaration from Epsom Downs'.) This involved a recurrence, in less and less ambivalent language, to the desideratum of Fair Trade, especially when it was taken up by a conference of trade and labour organizations; his friend and ally Lord Dunraven had been campaigning assiduously for Imperial *Zollwerein* in his absence.

Principally, however, Churchill's political activity after his return revolved round his use of India; he had taken to heart Hicks Beach's injunction to him that 'no Englishman of any political authority' had articulated a coherent body of ideas on Indian affairs, and was increasingly advancing himself as Tory spokesman on the issue. His attack on the occupation of Suakin included portentous references to what he had heard in India; his warnings on the Russian threat were as sinister as Roberts would have wished. A celebrated address to a Primrose League banquet on 18 April, after eulogizing Disraeli and referring pleasantly to Childers's 'infatuated imbecility and drivelling idiocy', proceeded to a violent denunciation of the 'malignant' advance on the North-west frontier, and the superficial nature of British rule over a burgeoning sense of Indian self-consciousness. He was, moreover, being fed by regular, choleric letters from Roberts, as well as grievance-stricken epistles from Maharajah Holkar, and informative missives from Salar Jung. Most importantly, Lepel Griffin was invaluable to Churchill for planting out his ideas in indiscreet articles (though even Griffin baulked at writing the piece criticizing the Calcutta government's foreign policy which Churchill suggested to him in May[11]). What attracted most opinion in India was Churchill's

[10] 19 Jan. 1885. Greater humbugs were the Tichborne Claimant, Oscar Wilde, and General Booth.

[11] See Griffin to Churchill, 20 May 1885, RCHL v/611. 'However much I might enjoy this onslaught on the Foreign Office it is a luxury I must deny myself for the present, as I could hardly continue in the political service after its publication.'

open commitment to a comprehensive Parliamentary Inquiry
into the government of India, which he announced at Bow in
studiously democratic and non-party terms. Equally resonant
was the way that, in the same speech, he explained the extent of
his own change on the question of the British occupation of
Egypt in terms of Indian security—now 'most seriously men-
aced'. For the Russian advance to Penjdeh was treated by him as
a case for war, brought on by Liberal negligence; and when
Gladstone obtained a unanimous vote of credit on 27 April,
owing to Northcote's failure to take a firm line, it gave Churchill
the opportunity to raise the question of Northcote's inability to a
very receptive Salisbury.[12]

This exchange of ideas—confiding on Churchill's part, warm
and paternal on Salisbury's—led to Churchill's suggestion (at
great length) of revitalizing the Opposition by an extended
Fourth Party element, under Beach, and including Gorst, Wolff,
Raikes, Chaplin, Dyke, and Gibson: to press matters hard, and
use the Radical support passed up in the Penjdeh debate. For
himself, Churchill disclaimed all ambition; but he wanted this
reorganization done 'without any formal communication to Sir
Stafford Northcote', whom he described as having the effect of
'sewer-gas upon the human system—sickening, enfeebling,
enervating, and emasculating'. In other words, Beach was to take
over the Commons leadership. Salisbury's reply, approving in
principle, emphasized his inability to ditch Northcote; nevertheless, the pattern whereby the government would be overthrown
was now set, and Churchill's importance in the formation of
whatever ministry might follow guaranteed.

And significantly, the issues chosen by Churchill upon which
to demonstrate his own positive virtues were Indian security and
the Russian threat. In early May he delivered his celebrated
attack on Gladstone as 'the resuscitated Reschid Pasha', and
accused him of 'surrendering to Russia': a speech which saddled
him with a warmongering reputation that never entirely de-

---

[12] See W. S. Churchill, i, 381–3. On the vote of credit, both Churchill and Labouchere
(with whom he had been allied over the Egyptian and the Sudan votes) had been
convinced Northcote would speak during dinner-time (see Labouchere's interview in *Pall
Mall Gazette*, 2 May 1885). Curiously, Churchill absented himself to go first to a
Rothschild dinner-party and then on to the Turf Club—although he had written to
Salisbury that morning of his fear that Northcote might not fully use Irish and Radical
discontent: 'a delicate matter, which I could not myself even hint at to Sir Stafford
Northcote, who would probably suspect my motives' (27 Apr. 1885; Hatfield House
MSS 3M/Churchill/37).

serted him but was in fact atypical (as was the eulogy of Turkey which he found himself delivering at St. Stephen's on 20 May). In parliament, he threatened to obstruct supply votes; outside, when supporting Lionel Cohen's candidature for North Paddington, he recurred to the Russian threat in its most extreme formulation, quoting from letters he had received from India, accusing the government of truckling to Russia, and his own party of 'drifting'. Extremist tactics are also to be seen in his attack of the same time on Lord Granville, who had criticized inaccuracies in Churchill's speech of 4 May; Churchill savaged the inoffensive Granville in a letter to *The Times* marked both by exceptional brutality of language and an unmeasured attack on Whiggery. The points at issue were essentially minor ones of dating and diplomatic interpretation: the language was the important element, and the chance of posing as an irreconcilable Russophobe. Reactions were varied: indulgence from politicians, outrage from the press. The *Spectator* devoted a long article to what it saw, not as attention-seeking audacity, but as a fatal loss of self-control: 'political insanity' was the way Churchill was tending, and it would always prevent him leading. 'Insanity' was a word used more than once about Churchill at this time.[13] However prescient this may seem, it was part of the process which established him as a front-line spokesman on India, as he had already become on Ireland: the two areas where he was already being tipped for employment when the government should fall.

Indeed, when the government fell it was, appropriately, the Irish issue that preoccupied the prime movers; and, yet more appropriately, it was Churchill who drew attention to this. The Crimes Act was due to expire in August, and on 15 May Gladstone announced that the Liberals would at least partially renew it. Since early May Churchill had been straining for an issue upon which to press matters to a conclusion with the government and incidentally force into the open his own issue with Northcote. He was deeply absorbed in gleaning Liberal gossip and passing it back to Salisbury; by similar channels, he

[13] See *Spectator*, 16 May 1885; also Lord Derby's diary, 19 May 1885: 'Churchill, with all his remarkable cleverness, is thoroughly untrustworthy: scarcely a gentleman, and probably more or less mad.' (I owe this and other references to Derby's later diaries to the kindness of Professor J. R. Vincent.) Chamberlain, on the other hand, saw it as 'a mistake that will be forgotten in a week' (to Lady Dorothy Nevill, 17 May 1885, Chamberlain MSS 5/56/30) and Hartington brutally told Harcourt that every word of the letter was true (LHJ, 20 May 1885, vol. 369, p. 17).

let Dilke know on 17 May that the Conservatives would not renew the Crimes Bill—a commitment he made public at the St. Stephens Club on 20 May, thus appearing to seal the covert arrangements with the Irish party which made up so much of his parliamentary activity. Though Parnell called at Connaught Place more than once, these negotiations are untraceable—as is the evidence for Chamberlain's belief that at this time Churchill was ready to contemplate a future with the Radicals supporting him against his own party on a progressive Irish platform. Certainly some public manœuvres are consistent with this; at Bow he poured scorn on fellow-Conservatives like Bartley, praised Chamberlain and Dilke, and emphasized his own disagreement with his leaders, and was praised glowingly in a *Pall Mall Gazette* editorial. Such contingency plans, however, must have essentially depended upon how far an incoming Conservative government would meet his personal requirements. And an incoming government, in a minority in the House of Commons and unable to go to the country until electoral reorganization was completed in November, would depend on Irish support, for which Churchill was indispensable.

The arrangement revolved around the decision not to renew coercion, for which, in a memorandum written long afterwards, Churchill blamed Gibson: as the party's Irish adviser, Gibson allowed his own hunger for the emoluments of Lord Chancellor to overcome an impartial judgement. The decision once made, Churchill added, he himself could join; as 'it was well known that personally I would not have taken office had it been thought necessary by a Conservative government to attempt to renew the Crimes Act'. This ignores both the fact that Churchill himself was an Irish expert in the party (as was Beach, also opposed to renewing coercion), and the fact that Salisbury could not have formed a government without him. His own importance was positive, not negative. The fact that it was Churchill who first made public the party decision emphasized this. And, this stance once taken, the fall of the government was inevitable.

The budget amendment which precipitated it was framed at Balfour's house, with Beach, Gorst, Wolff, and Raikes in attendance; political journalists saw the whole manœuvre as a Fourth Party revival, and noted that Churchill was in his most obstructionist, Bohemian, and insubordinate form. When the government collapsed with some relief on 9 June, Churchill's delight was ostentatious, and much remarked. His colleagues were far more doubtful. Beach and Salisbury were stricken by doubts; two days later, after the decision to face office had been taken, Cranbrook was appalled to learn from Churchill the extent to which they relied upon the Irish. How far Churchill himself had private doubts is speculative. In his retrospective memorandum he presented himself as cautious, but at the time he appeared unequivocally in favour of taking office; his private papers show trial cabinets being drawn up in May. He may have exaggerated his readiness in order to push Salisbury (whose reluctance was freely confessed, and known to the newspapers) into a position where he could be seen to attempt to form a government and fail: thus repeating the Arrears Bill fiasco, and emphasizing yet again Churchill's own claims to the monopoly of positive initiatives. The decision to take office, however, favoured him in so far as he had to be included for the parliamentary viability of the ministry: and this gave him a bargaining counter which he used—and indeed over-used—to the full.

The strategy whereby Northcote was to be displaced had already been shadowed out in May; and it is significant that Beach once again was the vital figure in apposition to Churchill. Placement of the latter was at once seen as Salisbury's chief difficulty: first, in terms of where he could be safely located. The *Pall Mall Gazette* mounted an emphatic campaign to have him sent to Ireland, where he could be 'the real Governor': 'it will either make him or mar him, and it is about time that one or the other fate befell him'.[14] This reflected Stead's pro-Russian bent and his commitment to Dufferin: since the other office for which Churchill was at once tipped was of course the Indian Secretaryship. The object of speculation remained detached, insisting to Beach that he did not want to be accused of 'place-hunting'; his biographers portray him as staying aloof and detached, which he could well afford to, with Beach bargaining for his interests at Arlington Street. (It was also remarkable how speedily Churchill's stipulations became common currency in the newspapers.) Beach pressed Churchill's case to Salisbury on 10 June, and Salisbury responded by asking Churchill to call on him before anyone else; he decided to offer him India. Plans for an interview were altered by Salisbury's precipitate departure for Balmoral on the next day, but it seems likely Churchill was

[14] *Pall Mall Gazette*, 10, 13, 15 June 1885. Dilke believed this was the appointment most desired by Churchill; LHJ, 11 June 1885, vol. 369, p. 83.

indeed interviewed on 11 June, and made clear that he would not serve with Northcote.[15] At Balmoral, the way was made clear with the Queen for Churchill's appointment as Indian Secretary; on Salisbury's return Churchill was formally asked but refused; Northcote (still unaware of Churchill's stipulations) having been offered the leadership again. Beach also refused the Colonial Secretaryship. Four days of intransigence followed: Churchill, pressed by his mother and Henry James to be accommodating, remained immovable. On 13 June he refused to go to a meeting arranged at Salisbury's for the 15th, stating as his terms for attending that Northcote should be dispatched to the Lords, and Cross be excluded from the Cabinet: his attitude was seen by Manners and others as 'preposterous'. At this stage Northcote was still being kept in a fool's paradise, and Churchill correspondingly began to doubt his own tactics; he was noticed drinking heavily, abusing his leaders, declaring he would take nothing less than the leadership. Meeting with Rosebery at the Turf Club, he confessed himself uncertain and depressed ('in the last five years I have lived twenty'), declared he had lost all hope with the Conservatives, and refused a lightly proffered invitation to join the Liberals.[16] The momentum of an Old Gang ministry seemed temporarily under way.

However, at Salisbury's meeting on 15 June, unattended by Churchill, Beach withdrew his support from the party taking office at all, as did Lord George Hamilton; Northcote now heard of Churchill's demands (orally circulated, in the form that Richmond, Manners, Carnarvon, and Cross had to be excluded from the Cabinet and Northcote sent to the Lords). An impasse seemed evident. Salisbury announced 'with great warmth' that he would never give in to Churchill's demands; Beach defended Churchill's attitude as being vindicated by Northcote's ill health; Carnarvon supported Northcote's exclusion on the grounds of his 'torpidness'.[17]

[15] Rhodes James and V. Hicks Beach, following W. S. Churchill, claim that Churchill did not go to Salisbury (there is no reply from Churchill in the Salisbury papers); Cooke and Vincent surmise that he did (p. 262), and the fact that the Queen's journal for 12 June (the day after he would have seen Salisbury) records Churchill's determination not to serve with Northcote is strong evidence.

[16] See endorsement by Harrowby on Carnarvon's letter to Harrowby, 14 June 1885, Harrowby MSS L II/114; LHJ, 10 June 1885, 12 June 1885, vol. 369, pp. 77, 93; also Rosebery, *Churchill*, p. 42.

[17] See Salisbury to Harrowby, 15 June 1885, Harrowby MSS LIV, and a full report in Carnarvon's diary, 15 June 1885, BL Add. MS 60924.

At this point, even Goats like Harrowby began to agitate for Northcote to be sent to the Lords without further dithering. Though Salisbury assured Northcote that no pressure from Churchill or anybody else would make him suggest anything antipathetic to him, the weight of evidence (raked over in more than one painstaking study of the crisis) suggests that Salisbury was at least as preoccupied with ditching Northcote as with arranging a viable format for taking office; and here Churchill was more useful to him than he could decently admit.

Churchill's final manœuvre was to lead a Fourth Party revolt in the Commons on the evening of the 15th, on the question of an amendment of the Redistribution Bill; here he was supported not only by Wolff and Gorst but also by Beach. The latter strenuously claimed later that his action had been fortuitous; but it had the effect of escalating the movement to expel Northcote, and emphasizing Churchill's independent power. After the debate he told James that he had 'cooked Salisbury's goose' and congratulated Harcourt on retaining his place.[18] (At the same time, there was a countering tendency in that some Tory respectables were so annoyed by it that Churchill's subsequent softening may have been forced upon him by the realization that colleagues could not be treated as cavalierly in power as in opposition: a lesson he never completely learnt.)

That night Manners, warned by Gibson of the dangers of Churchill's intransigence, pressed Salisbury to treat with him; Balfour, by now his uncle's trusted emissary, emphasized their need to conciliate Churchill 'if we only consider the period up to the end of the next general election'; and Churchill himself, aroused by what seemed a weakening on Salisbury's part as to taking office at all, rapidly came to terms on the 16th, making no formal stipulation about Northcote (who was, however, effectively dropped by now) and giving way about Cross (not to mention his hopes of also seeing the last of Manners, Harrowby, and Carnarvon). He also obtained the Solicitor-Generalship for Gorst, and a special diplomatic appointment to Egypt for Wolff.[19] Northcote made some further difficulties about going to the Lords, but essentially had to take what he was given (the First Lordship and the Earldom of Iddesleigh). Churchill had

---

[18] LHJ, 15 June 1885, vol. 370, p. 5.
[19] Though he claimed in 1887 that the idea he had anything to do with Wolff's appointment was 'an abominable and malignant lie'; see *The Times*, 7 July 1887.

won, but at more of a cost than was recognized. Salisbury told Cranbrook that he was 'weary . . . above all of one forced upon him who played such pranks'; and the Old Gang was well represented in the Cabinet.

Moreover, Churchill continued to feel some ambivalence. As soon as formal arrangements were made, the chances of taking office at all were obscured by difficulties over receiving sufficient co-operation in parliamentary business from Gladstone. Several of Churchill's correspondents who were seeing him at this unsettled time assumed that he was bent on preventing the party accepting office; he himself spread uncertainty in the Carlton, and Dilke on the 19th was convinced that 'having shown his power by making himself Dictator, [he] now wishes for freedom'. However, in a meeting with the leaders on the 20th he urged a speedy settlement with Gladstone, and by the 21st was considered 'very anxious' for office. It has been suggested that he was still trying to trap Salisbury in a discreditable position, having fulfilled his real ambition of reconstructing his own position in the party;[20] however, it seems equally likely that Churchill now felt he had something to lose. (Had the prospective ministry collapsed, he would have been left in an anomalous position regarding Beach—consistent throughout against taking office—who would have gained most *vis-à-vis* Northcote.)

In his statesmanlike memorandum about the crisis, recollected in the tranquillity of the political wilderness, Churchill recalled that the example of Disraeli's refusal to serve in 1873 was constantly in his mind; but it is doubtful if he viewed matters in such an abstract way at the time. Colleagues like Cranbrook continued to suspect him of never really having wanted to take office: an analysis which seemed borne out by his constant threats of personal resignation. It is as likely that these were dictated more by the desire to test his own indispensability, and by a personal style which depended upon extreme statements of terms. In any case he was by now established in government: with, at least in the public eye, a corresponding aggrandizement in his personal position. This was not universally admired even among those who had been his allies; an old National Union supporter accused him of 'shelving . . . your ability to lead an

---

[20] Cooke and Vincent, *Governing Passion*, p. 268; also see Gwynn and Tuckwell, *Dilke*, ii, 147–8, for Dilke's impressions, and Carnarvon diary, 21 June 1885, BL Add. MS 60924.

advanced Tory party; we find you helping to place in power all those, and those only, whom we turned over at Sheffield'.[21]

III

The general politics of 1885 are dealt with below; but the theme which dominated Churchill's official activity was the urgent necessity to present a positive profile to the country in the limited time available to the government, and he emphasized this from the first Cabinet he attended. This is immediately apparent in his work at the India Office. Here too the Manichean duality of Riponism versus Lyttonism, which he had experienced in India, remained a continuing syndrome; and the expectations formed of him during his Indian visit, that he and Dufferin would follow a line reminiscent of Ripon's liberalism rather than Lytton's 'repressive measures and tinsel shows', were doomed to disappointment. Lytton had robustly seen the Indian question as 'our great problem of working efficiently a despotic executive in India without bringing it into collision with a democratic legislature in England'; Churchill followed this analysis, with its implicit rejection of increasing opportunities for Indian representation and the corollary of encouraging an 'aristocratic idea' of Indian government.[22]

Lytton was, moreover, a close personal influence on Churchill, who had violently defended the Viceroy's Indian record in 1880 (and attacked Ripon's 'want of foresight, military knowledge, and caution'). Lytton spoke at Woodstock for Churchill in 1880, and composed Primrose League anthems at Knebworth, where he had retired in 1880; disillusioned with politics (and democracy), he devoted his days to sham-Byronic verse and brooding over his repudiation. But he remained in touch with politics and though he distrusted Churchill he advised him closely on military appointments and on Indian finance. And the rehabilitation of Lytton's Indian policy, carried on relentlessly by his family after his death, was in a sense begun by Churchill in 1885.

---

[21] Staveley Hill to Churchill, 26 June 1885, RCHL v/652. It should be added that he was also a disappointed place-seeker.

[22] See S. Gopal, *The Viceroyalty of Lord Ripon* (Oxford, 1953); A. Seal, *The Emergence of Indian Nationalism: Competition and Collaboration in the Later Nineteenth Century* (Cambridge, 1971), p. 7; B. Martin, *New India 1885* (London, 1969).

Given this, his protégés in the Indian administration are illuminating. The most important was Roberts, whom Churchill appointed Commander-in-Chief against the Queen's wishes and Dufferin's advice.[23] Roberts was an unregenerate Lyttonist who opposed the admission of any Indians at all to the Civil Service and composed anonymous pamphlets with titles like 'The Russian Menace'; throughout his Indian service he 'dispassionately and without panic ... assumed the certainty of a struggle in Asia with Russia' and subordinated all military organization to this.[24] His remarks on the unreliability of Indian troops greatly impressed Churchill in India, and he quoted Roberts (though not by name) in parliament. As soon as he was appointed Churchill pressed Roberts's case for the command; in September 1885 he invited Roberts to the Wimbornes' shooting-lodge, and there they planned the massive (and expensive) military manœuvres which took place in India at the end of the year. Roberts's extravagant military ideas upset many old India hands, on the Council of India and elsewhere, but his 'tremendous' influence with Churchill made them despair: 'he has only to ask for anything he likes'.[25] Roberts's talent, decisiveness, originality, and Irishness appealed to Churchill and his influence was a prominent factor in Indian policy from the time of his accession.

Similarly, on his return from India Churchill had taken up the cause of Sir Peter Lumsden, recalled ignominiously from the frontier commission and known for his exaggerated view of the Russian danger; and with Churchill's appointment, Lumsden's influence was assured. In his first Cabinet Churchill poured scorn on the frontier as fixed, praising Lumsden; he and Owen Burne, Churchill told Salisbury, 'form my little private cabinet here on frontier matters, and both are undoubtedly most useful, wise and influential'.[26] More important still was Lepel Griffin, a figure seen by Indian opinion as violently reactionary: known as

[23] For Lytton's part see Lytton to Roberts, 24 July 1885, Roberts MSS 7141-23-37/116. For Dufferin's attitude see Dufferin to Churchill, 30 July 1885, DVP F 130/2, p. 123. After the appointment Dufferin wrote resignedly: 'The way in which your people had run him against Wolseley made his appointment a necessity' (5 Oct. 1885; ibid., p. 150).

[24] J. C. Morison, 'From Alexander Burnes to Frederick Roberts: a survey of Imperial frontier policy' in *Proc. Br. Ac.*, 1936, p. 27. Also see H. L. Singh, *Problems and Policies of the British in India 1885-98* (London, 1963).

[25] See Ashley Eden to Dufferin, 23 Dec. 1885, DVP F 130/21, no. 119.

[26] Churchill to Salisbury, 30 July 1885; quoted in Rose L. Greaves, *Persia and the Defence of India* (London, 1959), p. 75.

'the hammer of the baboos', he had supported Lytton's dis-
criminatory press laws and bitterly opposed Ripon's volunteer
policy. Churchill pressed his claims to a seat on the Council, but
Dufferin was completely alienated by Griffin's indiscretion,
rudeness, importunacy, and ostentatious carrying-on with 'light-
skirted women'.[27]

Churchill's attempted advancement of Griffin was an important counter in his effort to reorganize the Council of India in
order to enable him to overcome the influence of those who
supported the *Pioneer* and the moderately progressive ideas it
stood for. The whole question of his relationship with the
Council is instructive, since their interdependence was by nature
flexible: in theory consultative, in practice the Council had
powers of veto, but only at the discretion of the Secretary of
State (or because of his weakness). Secretaries like Salisbury had
been opposed to their Council (he had planned to restructure it
in 1880); Ripon had seen his as 'the most conservative body now
existing in Europe'.[28] Always cognizant of the discretionary
nature of his power over them, Churchill's strategy was charmingly to admit his inexperience, and carefully demarcate only
the issues which he intended to influence, silently assenting to
Council decisions on the rest. His accompanying tactic was heavy
reliance upon his permanent officials—one of whom, Godley,
provided a vast fund of Indian experience, and had known
Churchill since school-days.

His private secretary, A. W. Moore, was an Indian foreign-
affairs expert; more senior than most private secretaries, he
'supplied whatever was at first wanting to his chief', and Godley
privately described him as 'quite as much Secretary of State as
his master'. The influence of Salisbury himself was considerable:
he retained a close interest in Indian affairs (and an admiration
for Lytton). But the feature of Churchill's Secretaryship was the
affection in which he was held by his permanent officials. He had
a preference for the young and positive, believing like Salisbury
that there was 'a pitch of eminence at which men become
imbecile'; and more importantly, he won them over by listening

[27] Dufferin to Godley, 14 Apr. 1887, Kilbracken MSS, F 102/10.
[28] Singh, op. cit., p. 45. Also see Seal, op. cit., p. 4; also A. P. Kaminsky, 'Policy and
paperwork: the formation of policy in the India Office, 1883–1909, with special reference
to the permanent undersecretaryship of Sir Arthur Godley', Ph.D. thesis, University of
California, 1976, pp. 22–4: 'an uneasy truce, in which neither was supreme'. The power
of the Secretary lay in controlling Council procedure, marking some issues secret, and
very occasionally negating Council decisions.

to their advice rather than counsels from the field—even if the latter reflected Indian realities more accurately.

The style of India Office politics suited Churchill perfectly: 'a miniature government in itself', known to appeal 'to a minister who loves an arbitrary and singlehanded authority'. Politicians like Kimberley and Hartington clung on to the Office as much as possible, and were never really happy anywhere else; Churchill, had he known his limitations, could well have become one of their number. Nevertheless, there were lasting reservations—especially on the Council. 'I shall never forget how nervous and ill at ease he seemed to be at our first meeting', recalled Bertram Currie. 'His manners were not, as might have been supposed, at all presumptuous or assuming; he was very quick of apprehension and not overburdened with scruples, but I failed to detect in him that zeal in economy which he is said to have afterwards displayed at the Treasury. I never heard him express any large or statesmanlike views, and in my secret heart I thought him rather deficient in quality.'[29]

Though Dufferin assured Churchill that the Council was 'full of your praises' this was not initially likely; Churchill's popularity with his Council only increased in proportion to his intransigence towards progressivism in Indian policy. And Dufferin excelled in emollient missives. The nature of his viceroyalty closely reflected the character of the Viceroy himself: a self-conscious Irish *grand seigneur*, diplomatically adroit and skilful at public relations, ambivalent in political commitments as in much else, whose priority was 'to escape out of India ... without any very deep scratches on my credit and reputation'.[30] Despite the tensions of Churchill's Indian visit, in office the two achieved a warm epistolary relationship, compounded of elaborate flattery on both sides, and larded from Churchill's end with gossip. For his part, Dufferin's letters were convoluted, colourful, abounding in mixed metaphors, and extremely long ('he was just the same when he was a boy at Eton', remarked Salisbury caustically). And they emphasized from the beginning his readiness to concede that 'ultimate settlement of all important questions must of necessity be arrived at in London', as well as reiterating deprecatingly his own ignorance of all things Indian. Churchill countered that India must be governed *from* India, and that the India Office and

---

[29] B. Currie, *Recollections, Letters and Journals* (London, 1901), i, 196.
[30] Quoted in Seal, op. cit., pp. 170 ff.

Council must not be allowed to interfere with Dufferin's freedom of action: 'on all political questions, foreign or domestic, you have probably forgotten more than any member of your Council ever knew'.[31] It was his way to get on with Irishmen, Churchill remarked to Salisbury, 'to flatter and be flattered'; but it was also something more.

Such assurances were doubly important in the light of the uncertainty of relations between their two offices—regarding which, Dufferin assured Churchill, the latter's principles were 'far more liberal than any which have hitherto prevailed'. The relationship between Viceroy and Secretary—ambivalent, difficult, and discretionary—was evolving in the 1880s, with more and more decisions being referred back to London. While himself contributing to this process, Churchill contrived to assure Dufferin that he wished above all not to dictate to him; Dufferin's own desire to avoid trouble, as well as his background in diplomacy rather than politics, ensured that initiatives would inevitably come from London. And when Churchill warned Dufferin that 'you won't mind my occasionally, in my letters, falling back into a Tory or even reactionary groove',[32] it was exactly what Dufferin wanted to hear.

None the less, at the beginning the Viceroy was in some trepidation; he disliked above all else talkativeness and indiscretion and had marked in addition Churchill's political opportunism. He wrote privately to Godley about the new Secretary:

Hitherto circumstances have almost forced him to devote his chief attention to the mysteries of Parliamentary warfare, but with his new responsibilities and his great opportunities for becoming a useful public servant he may get to see that there is something better worth living for than party management and electoral victories. Nothing could be nicer or more considerate than are his letters and telegrams to me though, like a horse mounted by a new rider, I felt at first the effects of a somewhat uncertain and wayward hand. My great fear is—and I feel I can speak to you with the greatest openness—that he should be got hold of by the wrong people.[33]

Dufferin was principally worried about colourful militarists like Valentine Baker and Lumsden; and Godley's reply, categorizing Lumsden as 'impulsive, hot-brained, loud-mouthed and muddle-headed', cannot have eased his mind. Moreover, Godley added,

---

[31] Churchill to Dufferin, 1 Nov. 1885, DVP F 130/2, p. 161.
[32] 8 Sept. 1885, DVP F 130/3, no. 70.
[33] Dufferin to Godley, 12 Aug. 1885, Kilbracken MSS, F 102/10.

though Churchill's private secretary Moore was clear-headed and sensible, he too was dangerously influential, and 'had been born and bred in the hatred of Russia and in the faith of the "forward" policy'.[34] Dufferin was, however, unable to compete with these decisive counsels; and he only tried half-heartedly. His relations with Churchill, ostensibly successful, were fundamentally unsure. Churchill was privately to sum up Dufferin's viceroyalty as 'a great failure, a time of inaction and indecision and stagnation when the opposite elements were essential'. The most authoritative writer on the subject sees Dufferin as devoted to opposing Churchill's new ideas:[35] but seen in the context of Churchill's over-all retreat from Riponism, and the snowballing importance of electoral considerations from the autumn, the line followed seems to have been laid down in London.

In June this process had yet to define itself; and Indian opinion was distinctly favourable to Churchill's appointment, seeing the new Secretary as 'a prize for India' and 'a liberal in all but name'. A minority opinion expected Dufferin to resign over Churchill's appointment, and saw it as a 'satirical gesture' on Salisbury's part whereby he intended to convey his plan to dissolve the India Council; but the general expectation in India was of a liberal and imaginative term in office. In England, journals as different as the *Spectator* and the *Pall Mall Gazette* saw it as 'a sinister appointment', and reactions in political circles were equally tempered ('you may imagine the feeling of the old stagers here', wrote Kimberley to Dufferin from the India Office). Within the government, the consensus was that the India Office would provide 'a padded room for that restless being', but those within the padded room were at first extremely doubtful. Owen Burne recalled that Churchill was expected to tear the Office apart; but his hard work, ability to cut red tape, and political opinions soon made Burne an ally and then a fast

---

[34] 'As he knows every hole and corner of this office Lord Randolph naturally enough turns to him for some of the information which a Secretary of State generally gets from his Under-Secretary [Godley himself], and—equally naturally—he probably looks upon me as rather too much tarred with the Gladstonian brush to be taken much into his Councils'; Godley to Dufferin, 9 Oct. 1885, DVP F 130/21, no. 82. On Moore's death Godley wrote to Dufferin: 'He was a most remarkable man, extremely able and clear-headed, with "an infinite capacity for taking trouble", great experience and knowledge of his subject, and a very strong will. He was invaluable to Lord R. Churchill during his term of office; in fact he was, during those six months, quite as much Secretary of State as his master.' 4 Feb. 1887; DVP F 130/27A, no. 39.

[35] Martin, op. cit., p. 140. For Churchill's judgement on Dufferin see Churchill to Roberts, 9 Sept. 1888, Roberts MSS 7101-23-21/21.

friend. Many of his colleagues felt the same way, especially as Churchill's capacity *'for getting a thing done'* often involved doing what his staff already favoured.[36]

In public, Churchill's political style was swiftly adapted to office. Political correspondents noted with frank disappointment the moderation of his first statements; when baited in parliament about inconsistencies, Churchill blandly replied that he had 'no explanation whatever to give'. Gladstone was treated with politeness and compliments; they agreed on Afghanistan; he would not discuss Egypt, as he wished to avoid contention. At the same time, Churchill unveiled the government's general intentions in a sweeping, statesmanlike performance which should properly have come from the Leader of the House (adding to the very general impression that Beach was merely a front man for Churchill). Such an image must have seemed too good to be true; and it was.

From early on, Churchill realized that the financial problem was the main fact of Indian administration, due to the decline of the rupee and the increase in military expenditure: 'the presentation of the Indian Budget to Parliament will be no pleasant or easy duty', he warned Dufferin in early July. His characteristic tactic was to deflect attention from the realities of the case by an outrageous party attack, and he outlined this strategy to Dufferin three weeks before the budget was due to be announced, as well as pressing for advance figures reflecting the kind of military expenditure necessary for the next year. Dufferin sent some hurried calculations, begging Churchill not to disclose them in parliament; Churchill, after consultation with Lytton and others, framed his budget policy round the latter's recommendations about increasing tax, retrenching on public expenditure, and using the Famine Insurance fund 'for general imperial purposes'. When he unveiled his budget on 6 August, these provisions should have attracted most attention—implying as they did a reactionary shift in policy. But though the Secretary's financial expertise was admired by Liberal newspapers, the facts of his policy were ignored in favour of the vituperative party attack that accompanied them, and the savaging inflicted upon Ripon's administration, and Ripon himself. The picture of the

---

[36] See O. Burne, *Memories* (London, 1907), p. 272. Godley equally relished his 'complete straightforwardness, sincerity and absence of every kind of humbug and imposture ... candour such as this is, to the official mind, unspeakably refreshing' (*Reminiscences*, pp. 131–2).

high-minded Viceroy dulled and made sullen by the narcotic effects of Indian life was brilliantly funny: but the violent personal indictment that accompanied it was seen as a prostitution of departmental responsibility to party politics. This deflected attention from the fact that Churchill declared his intention to add to a large deficit by further military expenditure, to burden the Indian revenues, and to undertake expensive strategic railway construction, all policies he had attacked when out of office; his emphasis was that Ripon's 'criminally guilty' lack of prescience had thrown out financial expectations and swallowed up the Famine Fund. Moreover, the point this led up to was equally striking: Churchill claimed that 'if you have now in India economical, healthy and decentralised finance it is entirely the work of Lord Lytton'; his speech resolved itself into a eulogy of Lyttonist foreign and domestic policy. The violence of the language used against Lytton in 1880 had been unparalleled at the time; Churchill avenged him by launching even more virulent abuse at his successor. At the same time, old debts were paid off, with compliments to Irish members who had agitated on behalf of Indian interests; and Indian opinion was conciliated by remarks about the keenness and intelligence of those whom he had met, and—more concretely—the necessity for a Parliamentary Inquiry into the government of India. But a basic contradiction remained; for on his return from India Churchill had extravagantly praised Ripon more than once in private, declaring that 'nothing but the change from Lytton to Ripon saved us from a second Mutiny', and insisting that his policy towards Russia had been absolutely correct.[37]

The offer of an Inquiry distracted India, as the attack on Ripon had done in England; the Indian press, while expressing disgust at the denigration of Ripon and the contrast between Churchill's opinions as expressed in India and in England, still appreciated the implicit promise of governmental reform as a powerful antidote. The *Indian Spectator* even partially excused the attack on Ripon as 'infusing a lively interest into what had hitherto been a solemn farce'. But within a month Malabari was to give vent to 'a lurking suspicion that [Churchill] may have fallen into the hands of the Lytton-Strachey clique who did so

---

[37] LHJ, 10 Apr. 1885, vol. 366, p. 79, and 8 May 1885, vol. 368, p. 37. These record, not hearsay, but remarks in enthusiastic praise of Ripon's policy made by Churchill to Harcourt himself.

much harm to India'.[38] If so, this was a process implicitly outlined in the budget.

Overall, however, attention was deflected from uncomfortable questions like the increase in licence tax and the absorption of the Famine Insurance fund;[39] and even among Liberals reaction was not entirely hostile. Churchill himself crudely admitted the smoke-screen nature of the speech to Dufferin:

It was absolutely incumbent on me to divest the present Government of all responsibility for the heavy expenditure entailed upon India by the Russian advance, and this led me into a criticism of Lord Ripon's policy which was no doubt of a very controversial character and of which the other side strongly complained. But self-preservation is the first law of nature and of governments, and in view of the coming elections and of a possible second Midlothian campaign and of the extreme unscrupulousness of the Radical party in attributing every kind of foreign difficulty and of large expenditure to Tory Jingoism and extravagance I had no other course open to me.[40]

Even those who were most appalled at the speech, like Blunt (who had innocently acted as Churchill's go-between in obtaining information from Ripon himself), saw it as purely a party manœuvre. And in this, they tended to ignore the implications contained in its measures.

IV

The speech against Ripon was one strategy whereby Churchill defined himself in his new office; another was the celebrated process by which he fought off the Queen's attempt to have the Duke of Connaught appointed to the Bombay Command. Royal jobbery was a constant problem for late nineteenth-century secretaries of state, and the previous administration had had to resist the same suggestion. In Churchill's case, the issue was compounded by his dislike of the royal circle and the Queen's secretary Ponsonby: Connaught being a particular enemy from the days of his disgrace. The matter has been rehearsed in detail

---

[38] *Indian Spectator*, 30 Aug. 1885, 20 Sept. 1885.

[39] When instituting this, Lytton himself had declared: 'We have pledged ourselves not to spend one rupee of the special resources thus created upon works of a different character.' Quoted in *Hindoo Patriot*, 7 Sept. 1885. However, for the case that it was not, and could not by its nature be, inalienable, see Lady Betty Balfour, *Lord Lytton's Indian Administration (1876–80)* (London, 1899), pp. 496–7.

[40] 17 Aug. 1885; DVP F 130/3, no. 63.

by his biographers, but poses some interesting questions. When it arose first in late July, Churchill, who had remarked he 'was not equal either by position, age or experience to sustaining a difference' with royalty, implied he would abide by Salisbury's decision though he disagreed with the principle; on Salisbury remarking that the matter was for him to decide, he turned intransigent and sent letters to Dufferin violently opposing such an arrangement. Thus he had taken up a firm position when, in early August, Salisbury transmitted a message from the Queen to Dufferin about the Prince, causing Churchill to take offence and offer his resignation on 14 August. Salisbury humoured him, sent soothing letters, and promised 'to give up the right of communicating' directly with Dufferin (which was not in question); by 16 August Moore as emissary had reconciled Churchill and Salisbury. What is curious (and unmentioned by Churchill's biographers) is that on 18 August Churchill wrote to Dufferin remarking disingenuously that he had been 'compelled to make a gentle protest to Lord Salisbury' about the Queen's message, and not mentioning his threatened resignation:[41] which appears in this light as purely a tactical move between himself and Salisbury. This letter crossed with one of Dufferin's rather equivocally supporting the royal appointment; Churchill misrepresented it to Ponsonby as advice against the step, which caused the Queen to complain of his 'shiftiness', and made Dufferin feel generally hard done by.[42] Reay and Roberts were equally in favour of the measure; in mid-September Salisbury was still gently trying to persuade Churchill to agree; even after the Cabinet rejected the proposal unanimously on 9 October, the Queen and the Duke of Cambridge fought a rearguard action until Christmas.

In August, when the issue had been most critical, Churchill was ill and confined to home, telling Beach that he had 'no longer any energy or ideas and am no more good except to make disturbance'. (Buckle at this point suspected Churchill of send-

---

[41] DVP F 130/3, no. 65.

[42] Dufferin had written to Churchill that the removal of political duties from the Bombay Command would mean that any 'insuperable objections' to Connaught's appointment would no longer exist; Churchill merely repeated that the Viceroy saw political functions as an 'insuperable objection'. Dufferin wrote disconsolately to Ponsonby that this was 'the only respect in which my little master at the India Office has failed to treat me with exceptional kindness and consideration' (DVP F 130/21, p. 34; F 130/120, p. 31). The Queen expressed fury to Dufferin at 'the very *shifty* way in which she has been treated by Lord Randolph Churchill' (29 Oct. 1885, DVP F 130/21, p. 34).

ing anonymous anti-Salisbury letters to *The Times*.) But his resignation threat, in view of what was to come a year later, has a compelling interest; it seems to bear out the widespread belief that Churchill's commitment to office, and to the government, was lukewarm at best. More importantly, it indirectly reflected a deep-rooted clash over foreign policy, which would recur. But it is also likely that he knew Salisbury could not accept a resignation at such a time and on such embarrassing grounds: it was a safe form of self-assertion. Nor did it apply after August; the day before the Cabinet which finally decided the question in October, Churchill wrote to Dufferin that he was prepared to back down.[43] Resignation was a threat to make in the first weeks of the ministry, but not later.

Moreover, by October Churchill had become more immersed in other areas of Indian administration—where there were many difficult questions to inherit. One such issue was the age-limit for entry to the covenanted Civil Service; Indian opinion wanted this raised to enable them to compete on more equal terms, and Churchill initially took their part, thus reversing Salisbury's policy in the 1870s. However, when Dufferin hedged on the question Churchill did not press it; and Indians were left to compete on terms that merely gave them the 'freedom to fail'. Already an area of pressure which was launching future Indian nationalists on successful careers, the Civil Service Reform movement was abandoned by Churchill from October, when electoral considerations began to dominate his thinking.

On financial questions the same pattern imposed itself. From the autumn, his public speeches (especially in the depressed north of England) emphasized India as England's only great free foreign market; this popular priority forbade him to listen to Indian suggestions of imposing an import duty on English cotton goods. Moreover, as indicated in his budget, the defraying of increased military expenditure meant sharp reductions on civic buildings, roads, civil railways, and irrigation schemes.[44] Uneasy about this policy, Dufferin had pressed for increasing income tax instead of retrenching on public works, but Churchill had been obdurate. When Colvin, the Financial Secretary, produced

---

[43] 'I suppose if I was to press my objections to an extreme point I must get my way, but I am doubtful of the expediency of going so far.' Churchill to Dufferin, 8 Oct. 1885, DVP F 130/3, no. 75.

[44] See Churchill to Dufferin, 7 Aug. 1885, DVP F 130/3, no. 63. He wanted to save a million on railways and irrigation alone. For earlier attempts at such a policy see Greaves, op. cit., p. 13.

through careful trimming an outline plan which would prevent interference with the Famine Fund, Churchill countered with sweeping proposals for further retrenchment, restrictions on the financing of local government, suspension of the Famine Fund (a 'fetish'), and selling famine railways to private companies; future costs were to be met by a large Indian loan of £20 million on the London market (though he was warned against this by the Rothschilds). These statements provoked an anguished reaction from the Indian government; Churchill had to deny that he wanted to 'confiscate' the savings of local governments, 'break' provincial contracts, 'stop' famine relief, and 'abolish' the fund.[45] Dufferin emphasized that special measures would only be necessary in an 'unforeseen emergency such as a further fall of silver ... or a Burmah expedition'—both of which were in fact on the cards: war with Burma eventually pledged the Indian military expenditure to an increasing deficit. (Churchill was a remarkable Secretary in that, unlike his predecessors of both parties, he did not set himself against War Office and Treasury demands on India in matters of army finance.)

He had to fight his financial proposals through the Council by threatening to act without them; and the same elements objected to his railway plans, which were always a sensitive area. The question of famine-relief railways, and the priority accorded them, had been deeply connected with Ripon's viceroyalty. Churchill converted the Bengal–Nagpur railway into an investment proposition, and set up the Indian Midland Railway Company in July 1885, against fierce opposition. However, despite his constant proselytizing, and his attempt to interest the Rothschilds, the Company attracted a worryingly low level of investment; this was bad for Indian credit, and Churchill violently blamed the opposition of those on the Council who disapproved of profit-making, and of Churchill's own connections in the world of high finance.[46] By the end of the year, however, the Midland Company had placed nearly all its shares,

---

[45] Churchill to Dufferin, 8 Oct. 1885, DVP F 130/3, no. 75.

[46] See Churchill to Dufferin, 16 Oct. 1885, DVP F 130/3, no. 76. 'If I am at the office next year (which is very doubtful) when our loan is brought out I shall fight a great battle against Currie to place it in the hands of the Rothschilds, whose financial knowledge is as great as that of the Bank of England is small, and whose clientele is enormous.' Churchill also blamed Currie and Strachey for opposing private enterprise in Indian railway construction (DVP F 130/3, no. 60).

probably with the aid of the Rothschilds. The Burmese annexation the next month was to raise further opportunities; within a
week of its announcement a Rothschild company had applied to
a rather hostile Finance Committee to take over 'all Burmese
railways and construct lines to the frontier'. But by the time this
came up for consideration, Churchill was out of office.

In his intransigence over the Bombay Command, his relations
with colleagues, his sweeping financial proposals, and his general
style of government, Churchill can be seen accustoming himself
to his miniature despotism at the India Office. The sphere of
responsibility where this was most marked, and to which all
other considerations were to be subordinated, was foreign policy.
Here he acquired the taste for unilateral action, for interception
of dispatches, for private initiatives in the field, which were to
cause such difficulty in Salisbury's second government. Despite
his anti-Turkish posture in the 1870s, Churchill came into office
with the reputation of a fully fledged Russophobe: next to
Salisbury, the most extreme in the government. His own
presence in India at a time when war rumours were at their
height, and his cultivation of Roberts and Lytton, would seem to
fill out the picture. He had pressed on Salisbury the need for a
strong line on Russia a month before taking office. However, his
celebrated speech of 4 May had essentially been an effort to
recoup the missed opportunity of the previous week over
Gladstone's vote of credit; Churchill was concerned to attack
past Liberal policy rather than to reiterate the menace of Russia.
He rapidly denied that he was of the 'war party' and the
essential measures he called for were unexceptionable; a week
later he represented the Tories as 'the real Peace Party in this
country'. Even over present procedure regarding the frontier, as
Gladstone pointed out, he never suggested any alternative *modus
operandi*.[47]

And though Churchill's anti-Russian line led to reactions like
that of Roberts, who wrote immediately on his appointment to
press for a war policy, office brought with it a different priority.
For one thing, keeping reserves at the ready was financially
embarrassing; for another, Churchill feared that the Russians
might 'seek to influence the November elections and impair the
position of the Tory party': the kind of immediate political

---

[47] *Hansard 3*, ccxcviii, 727, etc. As recent scholarship has pointed out, Ripon's and
Lytton's frontier policies were not in fact greatly different (Gopal, op. cit., pp. 28–9).

priority which he reiterated to Dufferin.[48] Thus he determined
to come to a speedy settlement of the frontier question; a flow of
communications went from the India Office to the Foreign
Office, pressing for vigorous action, much to the pleasure of the
permanent India Office staff who had been advocating forceful
measures. The vexed question of the frontier demarcation, and
the Afghan occupation of the Zulficar pass, was already at issue;
Churchill expressed reiterated dissatisfaction with the way it
had been conducted, calling for insistence upon a regular treaty
with Russia which would tie them down, discipline the Ameer,
and 'have a good effect in Europe, Asia, and last but not least,
the constituencies at home'; he even drafted such a treaty
and sent it to Salisbury and the Queen, unabashed when the
Foreign Office poured cold water on the idea. The pattern of the
relationship between their two offices remained the same
through July: Churchill calling for a settlement *'one way or the
other* before Parliament rises', suggesting initiatives such as
arbitration via Bismarck, or backing the Shah of Persia to resist
Russia; while Salisbury procrastinated, preoccupied by raising a
new Egyptian loan, and Dufferin oscillated between support and
opposition—distrustful of Russian promises, but nervous about
Indian reaction to the increased taxation which a war policy
would mean. The result was that Churchill became increasingly
critical of Salisbury's dilatoriness, and what he saw as Foreign
Office obstruction. For his part, Salisbury's patience was sorely
tried by the flow of demands from the India Office. Roberts
provided a more sympathetic ear, and to him Churchill confided
that he did not think there was much chance of a Russian war,
but if there was, Russia could easily be attacked through the
Straits; what he really feared was a Russo-French alliance
encouraged by Bismarck.

Bismarck, in fact, was looming large in Churchill's heady
calculations. As early as 26 June he had decided that, regarding
Russia, 'the centre of action is Berlin'; he recurred to the

---

[48] He also feared Gladstone playing an Eastern policy card in the elections (Martin,
op. cit., pp. 138–9). For a general formulation of his fears see Churchill to Dufferin, 10
July 1885, DVP F 130/3, no. 50: 'I hope you may not think my anxieties as to possible
Russian proceedings in the autumn and winter visionary or over-alarmist. The Russians
without doubt have the most perfect information as to the state of parties in this country,
the nature of the political issues which have to be determined, and it stands to reason
that if they are of opinion, as they may be, that Russian interests may be promoted by a
change of government at the close of the year in this country they will work steadily, and
perhaps unscrupulously, to bring about that result.'

importance of overtures to Germany when defending to his colleagues the plan of a Rothschild-backed company to take over the Persian economy (the only member of the Cabinet to express enthusiasm for it). Influential as the Rothschild interest may have been here, the idea of joint operations with Germany in Central Asia was generally popular at the India Office and Salisbury himself was not averse to it, sending a tentative mission to Bismarck to ask for mediation over Zulficar. While avoiding open commitment, Bismarck sent Hatzfeldt to London as an earnest of closer relations. The new ambassador was an old friend of Lady Randolph's from Paris days, and saw much of the Churchills. Churchill continued to press the idea of German mediation, bringing Persia into the ambit of Indian diplomacy: 'Prince Bismarck would be very glad, so Rothschild tells me, to get the making of Persian railways into German hands and would not like to see all Persian development fall into the hands of Russia.' Rothschild passed on Bleichröder's information about Bismarck; Churchill saw Hatzfeldt, and then Count William Bismarck, in private discussions probably unauthorized by the Cabinet. But Salisbury continued to snub Churchill's plan for a broader Anglo-German understanding. 'Of course this would have been playing *gros jeu*', wrote Churchill disconsolately to Dufferin, 'but that style of game is, after all, in accordance with our policy in taking office, by which alone we risk a tremendous party stake.'[49] The German negotiations came to nothing in the end; Bismarck, always wary of the Liberals' return to power, cooled as soon as this seemed inevitable. Churchill noted this with annoyance. '*A nous deux nous pourrions gouverner le monde*', he remarked to Hatzfeldt; '*mais vous n'avez pas voulu.*' But the taste for *gros jeu* evinced in his letters of the time, and confirmed by this remark, was not to desert him.

Throughout August Churchill continued to press for a speedy foreign policy *coup* on the Russian question; increasingly, the fascination of geopolitics took over from more mundane Indian issues (as he frankly admitted to Dufferin). He pressed Salisbury to hold a Pacific squadron ready to bombard Vladivostok,

---

[49] Churchill to Dufferin, 2 July 1885, DVP F 130/3, no. 54. 'I was in favour of a bolder policy . . . pointing out certain ways in which it would be easy for England to be of the greatest use in promoting Prince Bismarck's policy and leaving to him with calmness to say to what extent, if any, he would be prepared to assist us to escape from a dangerous situation, not only in Central Asia, but in Egypt . . . Lord Salisbury, however, was not captivated either by my premises or my arguments.'

suggested that the India Office take over diplomatic relations with Persia and China ('Calcutta would become the centre of Asiatic politics'), and continually complained of the 'haphazard and unmethodical' manner of doing business at the Foreign Office; these attempts at interference were tolerated until he claimed the right to be present at interviews with the Russian ambassador, when they were abruptly choked off. On 11 August he opposed the whole Cabinet by wanting to retain troops in Egypt against Russia. These clashes on foreign issues had a continuing importance; rankling on both sides, they had much to do with Churchill's anger in mid-August and his preferred resignation at the time. He complained to Beach that he was not kept informed by Salisbury, who disliked and mistrusted him. What was referred to was not Indian affairs, but the less reasonable ground of foreign policy.

His official correspondence of the time was dominated by issues like the reliability of bizarre reports from a spy at St. Petersburg, found for Churchill by Lytton, who confided shaky but intriguing tales of conspiracy among the Grand Dukes; significantly, however, when solid news came in late August of Russia's desire to arrange a definite protocol about the frontier, it was relayed through Rothschild. With Salisbury in Dieppe, the new Russian initiative was discussed by Churchill and his inner circle at the India Office, communicating with Salisbury by telegram. Churchill told Dufferin that an important reason for speed was so that he could announce a Russian agreement to the Cutler's Feast at Sheffield on 3 September; this he did, with tremendous éclat, to a cheering audience. The speech involved a flowery eulogy of Dufferin, an emotional defence of the Ameer's loyalty, and a histrionic account of how the minority government, with all the odds against it, had successfully pressed forward a dangerous situation to an honourable and satisfactory conclusion. It was all Churchill had hoped for regarding the electioneering utility of foreign policy.

Ironically, by this point Dufferin had been coming round to a forward policy, involving a march on Candahar, and 'the permanent conquest of all Afghanistan on this side of the Hindu Kush and its incorporation with the Indian empire'; Churchill, explaining his precipitancy, assured the Viceroy that if it ever came to that, he would back Dufferin 'might and main ... but at the same time I wish to record my belief that such a policy would involve the bitterest Parliamentary struggle, and probably the fall of a government'.[50] By this point, electoral advantage was at a premium; frontier policy had been made to coincide with it as neatly as was practically possible. Privately, Churchill continued to worry about the Ameer's reliability and the 'flimsiness' of the frontier arrangements; publicly, all was well with the Asian world.

But foreign affairs remained a source of friction: particularly as the breakup of Eastern Roumelia and its absorption by Bulgaria happened simultaneously with the Russians' coming to terms on the frontier. At first furious at Britain's inability to protect Turkish interests (owing to the shock effect and the coming elections), Churchill then came to see—with the rest of the diplomatic world—that Russia was equally opposed to Prince Alexander's *coup*. At this point, he turned violently against Salisbury's 'ostentatious protection of Bulgaria, which is degenerating into an aggressive attitude against Russia'; to close colleagues, he fulminated against the uselessness of the Foreign Office and the malignant influence of the Queen. By the end of the year, his Russophobe image was reversed; he was now irritating Salisbury, not by calls to a warlike advance, but by appeals to stop exasperating Russia; and he was cultivating his own Russian contacts in the circle of the Duchess of Edinburgh.

V

Overall, in the Salisbury–Lytton tradition, Churchill 'subordinated Indian domestic policy to Indian external policy, and measured it by its appeal to the English electorate'; he constantly exhorted the Viceroy to keep military preparations up to a high level, assuring him that Smith and the War Office supported this policy too. The inevitable concomitant of this priority, seen from the Indian side, was the fear of increased taxation, and an identification of Churchill with Lytton and Roberts. Dufferin had noticed this, and blocked his more extravagant frontier plans; Churchill's preoccupation with as large and showy winter manœuvres as possible produced a worried and cautious response from the Indian government as regards expense; his pressing of new rifles on the army was opposed by Dufferin. This pattern of policy was bound to make Churchill's rule unpopular. In the Indian army itself, however,

---

[50] Churchill to Dufferin, 8 Sept. 1885, DVP F 130/3, no. 70.

there was room for a liberal policy which would redeem some of the lustre shed by his tour in early 1885; this concerned the question of Indian officers for Indian regiments, and the formation of an Indian Volunteer Corps. Since July Dufferin had been conscious of the extent to which the desire for volunteering privileges had become an implicitly political movement; Griffin's characteristic advice being that it was inspired by 'the two dissolvent forces of our Indian empire, the extreme Radical party in England who wish to run all Indian measures into English moulds, and the middle and lower class natives of India, who have received a more or less superficial English training and whose conceit is only surpassed by their ignorance'. Though a minority of progressive officials favoured allowing volunteering (on a selective and aristocratic basis), the general tenor of official advice linked the movement with the danger posed by press agitation, and Surendrath Banerjea's Indian Association. Dufferin faithfully represented these views to Churchill, advising against volunteering rights and recurring to the Lyttonist idea of giving aristocratic Indian youths commands in the Indian army.

Churchill, however, had already rejected this idea without consulting his Council; military opinion was against it, and Churchill had decided not to press the matter even before relations with the Duke of Cambridge were severed over the Bombay Command. To Dufferin's chagrin, Churchill therefore suggested that the Volunteer movement not be 'too sharply snubbed ... [but] tried cautiously on a small scale'. But he did not pursue the matter; as in the case of the Civil Service age-limit, tacit disagreement produced inaction. There was the added factor of Churchill's decreasing interest in domestic Indian affairs compared to the glamour of foreign policy. Possibly this was reflected in his final suggestion regarding army matters: that the government should 'pursue towards the native states a policy analogous to what Prussia carried out with the German states after the wars of 1866 and 1870'—feudatory armies incorporated in the general military resources, each state maintaining its quota, 'inspected by British Officers and brigaded with British troops': a policy which would gratify the Indian princes. This was Lyttonism incarnate, and faithfully represented the evolution of Churchill's Indian thought since his tour only six months before.

The shift thus indicated had been closely monitored by Indian opinion—brought, in 1885, to a highly analytical and sensitive point by the Indian press and the swelling political organization inspired by exactly the sort of Indians whom Churchill had cultivated in the spring. Moreover, at the same time as Indian preoccupations became dominated by foreign policy, the November elections in Britain approached nearer and nearer; and Churchill ruthlessly subordinated important issues of Indian development to British electoral considerations, especially in the area of trade—as his successors ruefully noted. Similarly his consideration of bimetallism was dictated by how popular it was in Lancashire, and the chance that it might rouse 'political party feeling as the Fair Trade movement does'. Where he did call for Indian initiatives, they were in the nature of 'a more generous and pleasing policy towards the native princes' and the encouragement of Indian entrants to Oxford and Cambridge. Nevertheless, there were commitments of a more far-reaching kind to be honoured: chief among them the question of a Parliamentary Inquiry into Indian government, which Churchill had called for before taking office, and repeated in his budget speech. It did much to dilute the resentment occasioned by other excesses, and Churchill was often reminded of it. At the end of his term in office he was still pressing it, on an inter-party basis; the terms of reference were drawn up by Sir Henry Maine, and Churchill wanted Hartington (to whom he sent military dispatches from the India Office) to be chairman. By the time these concrete proposals took place, however, the area to be surveyed was narrowly defined as the regulation of government machinery, and the membership overpoweringly Anglo-Indian.[51] In England, the idea was looked on with suspicion by both parties (Morley attacking it as a political gimmick); in India, where it had been expected to provide mechanisms for extended popular representation, the proposals were disappointing.

Before this development, however, the promise of the Parliamentary Inquiry had aroused great enthusiasm among Indian politicians; and it was a primary factor in the mission to England of three Indian delegates in late 1885, which provided the final confrontation between Indian expectations of Churchill and the actuality of his policy. The clash thus engendered led to

---

[51] The proposed members were Cranbrook, Lytton, Napier, Northbrook, Ripon, Hartington, Churchill, Goschen, Chamberlain, Temple, McCarthy, Fergusson, and Sir George Campbell; the legislation to be reviewed was the Government of India Act (1858), the Indian Council Act (1861), the High Courts Act (1861), the Civil Service Amendment Act (1861), and the Civil Service Legislation Act (1870).

Churchill's eventual outright rejection of the Parliamentary Inquiry; though he had told the Indian delegates 'he should support the inquiry whether in office or not', when the Liberals raised the question the following spring he took the leading part in blocking it.[52]

This Indian mission arose from the political ferment at a local level in India which made 1885 a landmark in the history of Indian nationalism. N. G. Chandavarkar, editor of *Indu Prakash*, M. M. Ghose, a barrister, and S. R. Mudaliar, a landowner and lawyer, came to England during the general election as representatives of the three presidencies, with the intention of declaring Indian support for those candidates of either party who embraced Indian reform (and particularly Churchill's Inquiry). Initially a moderate notion, the idea had been commandeered by elements with a more radical bias; the mission marked a vital step in the maturing of Indian nationalism, and also the final stage in Churchill's retreat from progressive ideas. On one side, he was warned against them by Anglo-India; on another, they were inevitably identified with the Radical lobby even before they left India. The manifesto of the delegates, entitled 'Appeal on behalf of the people of India to the electors of Great Britain and Ireland', though couched in moderate and non-party terms, stated Indian social and political grievances clearly. It opposed the 'forward' policy, and called for increased representation; it became rapidly identified with the mounting opposition to Dufferin's imperial ideas and Churchill's finance. Five years before, a political liaison between Lytton's Indian critics and the Liberal party in England had broken the non-alignment tradition and been interpreted as meaning that Indian politics had to be identified with one or other party line in England; and the delegates were inevitably brought into the ambit of Bright, John Slagg, and William Digby, all Radicals with a pro-Indian tradition.

The delegation's only Tory contact was the extravagant but ineffectual Wilfrid Scawen Blunt, ubiquitous in colourful and progressive circles. Blunt attempted to identify the Indians with his eccentric candidature at Camberwell, and arranged an interview with Churchill; but an election meeting organized by

---

[52] See Kimberley to Dufferin, 21 May 1886, DVP F 130/6, no. 25; Churchill to Salisbury, 24 Mar. 1886, 19 May 1886, Hatfield House MSS 3M/Churchill. He was pitted against Conservative peers like Cranbrook on the issue, and successfully persuaded every Conservative MP to resign from the Committee. Also see *Hansard 3*, cccv, 1161–2.

William Digby in South Paddington on 14 October firmly identified them with Liberalism, and indeed Riponism. In the very constituency being nursed by Churchill as an insurance against failure in Birmingham, two of the Indians launched detailed attacks on Conservative policy in India, specifying Churchill's sacrifice of economy to militarism: Blunt's appearance on the platform was robustly booed. With this background, the meeting of the delegates with Churchill the following day could hardly have been a success—though he had agreed to it against Indian Council advice and Blunt had assured the Indians that the Secretary was 'a sincere well-wisher', whose painful and surprising attack on Ripon had been merely a party manœuvre. The three delegates duly presented themselves with Blunt at the India Office—a meeting of which Chandavarkar has left a vivid account.[53] But Churchill, though charming and polite, took discretion to the uncharacteristic point of silence; to any political remark, he 'merely nodded'. Enquiries were made about Indian acquaintances, his intentions about a parliamentary inquiry repeated in studiously general terms, and expressions of goodwill exchanged. Already determined to withdraw, the activity of the delegates on a Radical platform in his own potential constituency made up his mind. He appeared almost at once on Lionel Cohen's platform in North Paddington to refute the charges made by Digby, who was running against Cohen in that constituency. Cohen, a relation of the Rothschilds, was a close associate of Churchill's and a generous contributor to party funds; Digby a prominent pro-Indian. The exchange snowballed into a general Indian wrangle, involving Lethbridge, Temple, and other unregenerate Lyttonists standing for parliament; the Indian delegates were pressed further and further to radical Liberalism. In Manchester, Churchill himself went out of his way to emphasize Indian issues in the contest between Fergusson, ex-Governor of Bombay (a severe critic of Churchill on his Indian journey), and John Slagg, Radical pro-Indian (an ally of Churchill's in his opposition days): he had come, in a sense, full circle.

Finally the three Indians appeared on Bright's platform at Birmingham on 21 November, and thus supported Churchill's own opponent in the Central Birmingham constituency. Churchill's riposte, at a speech at Bordesley, was brutal ridicule of a kind which Lepel Griffin himself could not have bettered:

[53] See Appendix 2.

There was no doubt about it that the Conservative party in the town had produced an alarming effect on the minds of the Radical party, and there was absolutely no expedient to which the managers of the Radical party, the caucus, would not condescend in order to avert the defeat which the efforts of the Conservatives were causing them to expect. Why, they had gone and done an immensely ludicrous thing. They had a meeting in the Town Hall that day and who had they brought down in order to support Mr Bright? They had brought down three unfortunate gentlemen who had travelled all the way from India, and who arrived in this country under the name of Indian delegates for the purpose of representing to this country at the present moment the views of the Indian people. He had nothing to say against these Indian delegates; no doubt they were very worthy and interesting persons, but they no more represented the opinions of India than he represented the opinions of Kamchatka. These people, owing to the anxiety of the Radical party, were having a very good time. He should not wonder if before the election was over they would not be asked down to Midlothian to support Mr Gladstone. He was afraid the Radical party were making fools of these poor Indian delegates—playing upon their ignorance and credulity. But what must be the desperation of the Radical party when, in order to secure the return of Mr Bright, they had to bring down on the platform of that great Town Hall three Bengalee baboos. (Roars of laughter and cheers.)

This was the envoi to Churchill's cultivation of the 'educated native' begun the previous January. It provoked a dignified letter from the delegation to *The Times*, expressing surprise at this hostility and disingenuously denying any party affiliation; it was left to the Indian press to remind Churchill of his previous promises that 'the opinions of educated natives will be heard in the next parliament'. The fortunes of India's 'Appeal to the British voter', like the electoral fortunes of those designated 'friends of India', came to an ignominious end. The 'New India' unveiled at the end of the year was set on a different course.

An important element in this process was the extent to which Churchill had become alienated. This was noted by Lytton, who wrote to Dufferin that the 'impudence' of the Indian delegates 'will have had the good effect, I hope, of curing Randolph Churchill of his *lubees* about "the highly educated native", and rendering him less credulous of all the nonsense poured into his ears by Blunt. He does not forgive these gentlemen their pilgrimage to the shrine of Bright and he now calls "The highly educated native"—"a beastly impostor".'[54] Dufferin did not

[54] Lytton to Dufferin, 'November 1885', DVP F 130/21, no. 105b.

have to take Lytton's word alone; Churchill wrote angrily of 'the impudence of these Indian delegates'. Significantly, he went straight on to remark that he had decided to pass over Sir William Wedderburn—a patron and founding father of the Indian National Congress—for a judgeship because of the latter's association with the Indian deputation. 'He never loses an opportunity of associating himself with native political movements; I consider that this deplorable habit of his constitutes a fatal qualification for the judicial bench.' Nor was this a fit of temporary pique: the next month he refused an appointment for G. T. Chesney on the grounds that he was 'too ardent a reformer, too fond of bringing himself before the public, too closely connected with [the] *Pioneer*'.[55] Most important, he felt no compunction about opposing the Parliamentary Inquiry when out of office. He had reverted to the Salisburian view of the educated Indian class as 'a deadly legacy from Metcalfe and Macaulay ... [who] cannot be anything else than opposition in quiet times, rebels in time of trouble'. The hopes he ended by fulfilling were not those of Malabari but of Lepel Griffin: who, writing to thank Churchill for his appointment as special envoy to China, offered his congratulations at the rout of 'Wilfrid Blunt and the whole band of fanatics and windbags'.[56] Indian opinion was correspondingly disappointed; a violent editorial in the *Indian Mirror* following Churchill's Birmingham campaign accused him of being 'ignorant of India, utterly wanting in common candour, reckless of assertion'; he had become 'a cuckoo, only repeating the cry of his Council', and playing upon the Birmingham industrial interests by openly admitting how they relied upon exploitation of India. Most of all, he stood finally revealed as the rehabilitator of Lytton—'a second-rate poet employed to work out the visionary plans of a second rate novelist in India'.[57]

[55] Churchill to Dufferin (telegram), 4 Dec. 1885, DVP F 130/17, p. 175. For Churchill's attack on Wedderburn see Churchill to Dufferin, 27 Nov. 1885, DVP F 130/3, no. 80. He continued: 'The natives are sure to raise an angry cry if one of their idols is set aside, but for my own part I should attach little importance to their views as to judicial capacity.'

[56] Griffin to Churchill, 8 Dec. 1885, RCHL x/1150. For Salisbury's view see Salisbury to Lytton, 9 June 1876, in *Letters of Lord Lytton*, ii, 22.

[57] *Indian Mirror*, 27 Nov. 1885. Cf. Dufferin to Northbrook, 16 Oct. 1886: '... if we take native opinion as it now exists, we should find it hostile to the annexation of Burmah, to the increase of the army, to the railways and fortifications of our North-West frontier, to our subsidies to the Ameer, and indeed to every class of expenditure which is likely to increase expenditure without bringing in an obvious and immediate return'. B. Chandra, *Nationalism and Colonialism in Modern India* (Bombay, 1980), p. 288.

VI

This process had been counterpointed by the only action of Churchill's Secretaryship to be examined—and then in a ritual way—by his biographers: the conquest and annexation of Upper Burma. This undertaking was grandly described in 1945 by the doyen of British authorities on the subject as 'rather a cheap little tragedy', revolving round the personalities of the Burmese king and queen: 'a weakling, already a gin addict, ruled by a little tigress who would stick at nothing in order to maintain her position'. Most modern historians, however, take the involvement as a classic case of commercial pressure dictating imperial expansion at a time when domestic markets were contracting and no one needed to feel guilty about the process.[58] From Churchill's side it represented a triumph of British electoral and commercial pressure over Indian opinion, and sealed his reconstruction into a classic Tory Secretary of State.

Since the British annexation of Lower Burma, the upper province had been a desirable sphere of commercial influence; its nominal independence under King Theebaw was seen as immaterial in terms of trade, and any infiltration by other powers was taken as a direct danger to trade between British Burma and the Kingdom of Ava. This claim to exclusive influence had worried the government of Upper Burma since the 1860s; they had pressed for recognition of their diplomatic independence in London, and had exerted several royal rights and monopolies over British traders. Questions of diplomatic protocol also rankled, as well as the homicidal practices of aristocratic Burmese power-groups. After the withdrawal of the British Resident in 1879 the Burmese opened diplomatic relations with Italy and France, signing a commercial convention with Ferry's government in January 1883. The Rangoon Chamber of Commerce had agitated for intervention on behalf of British interests; Gladstone and Dufferin refused. By mid-1885, however, increased French penetration of the region, and Theebaw's generally haphazard rule, had inflamed opinion on the spot.

---

[58] See especially D. R. SarDesai, *British Trade and Expansion in South-East Asia 1830–1914* (Columbia, Missouri, 1977). The best accounts are in A. T. Q. Stewart, *The Pagoda War: Lord Dufferin and the Fall of the Kingdom of Ava 1885–6* (London, 1972), and Martin, op. cit. For a classical contemporary rationalization see J. Nisbet, *Burma under British rule—and before* (London, 1901). The quotation about the gin addict and the tigress is from D. G. E. Hall, *Europe and Burma* (London, 1945), p. 170.

The results in Britain proceeded with Pavlovian predictability. In the early 1880s, pressure exerted by the Manchester Chamber of Commerce on the Indian government had prevented Theebaw farming out the raw cotton monopoly; Lytton, moreover, had pressed for severe measures in the 1870s, arguing for annexation in 1878 and 1879. Economic and imperial motives interacted; besides immediate Burmese factors, the British fear of French influence in South-East Asia was affected by the desire for an overland route to China. One of the first deputations received by Churchill as Indian Secretary was from Chambers of Commerce representing Burmese trade interests and worried about *rapprochement* with France; they called for outright annexation. More direct pressure was applied by the Bombay–Burma Trading Corporation, who saw their teak interests as threatened by the Burmese court, which had accused them of bribery and—whatever the truth of the accusation—imposed fines on them that were exorbitantly crippling. The British Burmese authorities refused to intervene; the Corporation brought its case to London, claiming that Theebaw was looking for an excuse to withdraw their privileges because he had promised them to France.

In fact, the letter from Ferry produced as evidence of this was a forgery, a fact suspected by many British officials; and an expanded Franco-Burmese arrangement was implausible politically, economically, and for engineering reasons. But in Cabinet Churchill emphasized every rumour about French banking and railway initiatives in the province; the Rangoon Chamber of Commerce, aided by the British press, kept up the pressure for annexation. The India Office was already well disposed to such representations; Moore produced memoranda for Churchill showing that trade with Britain had not progressed since Theebaw's accession, and those on the spot sent analyses in the most reductionist terms.[59] Churchill assiduously drew Salisbury's attention to rumours of Franco-Burmese treaties, and relayed commercial complaints to Dufferin; but Indian official opinion remained anti-interventionist, especially on financial grounds. Here, however, Churchill's increasing militarism was aroused,

---

[59] See H. Soltau, a missionary, memorandum, 22 Oct. 1885, RCHL viii/936: 'There is no doubt about the trade. It will simply flow down the Irrawaddy, and even if the Chinese trade does not rise to the anticipations of the most sanguine, Upper Burma alone will provide ample room for English capital and English brains to find a harvest.' For Moore's memorandum see RCHL vii/843.

and though he assured Salisbury and Dufferin that he would avoid 'to our utmost' any policy implying annexation, this was disingenuous; a virtual ultimatum was issued to Mandalay in early September.

Churchill was strongly supported in this by his inner ring at the India Office; Burne had been looking for what he straightforwardly called 'any pretext to annex Burma' since Lytton's day, and Moore was similarly convinced.[60] Bernard, Chief Commissioner of British Burma, and Durand, Under-Secretary of the Indian Foreign Department, had long been anxious for action. Against this pressure, and a well-orchestrated press campaign, Dufferin's initial doubts could not be sustained; moreover, Churchill had already made up his mind. His priorities were essentially political, and oriented towards British public opinion: 'a government never fails to derive a certain amount of credit for successful military operations', he reminded the still doubtful Dufferin on 18 November. And though he opposed annexationist policy in Malaya and Siam, the annex-ation of Burma was decided upon by him from an early stage; he exploited rumours of Franco-Burmese treaties to sabotage Salisbury's notion of a joint initiative with France which might culminate in the demarcation of spheres of influence, though both Salisbury and Freycinet favoured the idea. (His allies Moore and Burne omitted to inform Dufferin of the notion.) Over and over again Churchill emphasized the priority of trading interests and the fact that a forward policy in Burma would mean that 'the large commercial interests in this country will be warmly on [our] side': a case he also made for sending an unpopular mission to Tibet. The exigencies of Birmingham rhetoric dictated 'a larger, bolder, policy towards China, Siam and Burma'; the same priority made annexation a foregone conclusion.

Dufferin's recalcitrance was partially overcome by the pro-mise that a Burmese war would remove the Council's objections to the Viceroy's expedients for raising money: Salisbury's procrastination finally gave way, on the grounds that Burmese relations were an Indian affair and very little to do with them need be referred to Cabinet. The arrival on 13 October of Theebaw's refusal to accept the Bombay Company's version of the teak dispute provided Burne's 'pretext'; Dufferin responded

---

[60] SarDesai, op. cit., p. 212. For militant memoranda by Burne about Theebaw, Burma, and the French see PRO CAB 37/16/59, 37/18/23.

with an ultimatum demanding sweeping influence for a British agent and trade concessions. Churchill, impatient already, wanted no hesitation; he gave Buckle the text of the ultimatum and his latest telegram to Dufferin, and *The Times* obediently produced an annexationist editorial which implied that Churchill, Salisbury, and Dufferin were unanimously determined on a 'forward' policy, provoked beyond endurance by Theebaw. The ultimatum was to reach Mandalay by 30 October, British troops having already embarked for Rangoon. On 23 October Churchill announced a probable war, with certain benefits accruing to British trade, to a cheering crowd at Birmingham.

Dufferin, still prey to doubts, was by now driven on by Churchill to a policy which not only upset Indian finance but irrevocably identified his administration as revived Lyttonism. Early November saw bids for a diplomatic settlement by the Chinese in London as well as the Burmese in Paris, and also a last French initiative; all blithely ignored by Churchill. Theebaw's evasive reply to the ultimatum on 8 November began the Third Anglo-Burmese War, a sad and unnecessary undertaking. The pathos of this strange little war, conducted on the Burmese side by indolent officers under golden umbrellas and ending in the miserable departure of the (perfectly sober) king and his much traduced queen from their red and gilt palace, forms a set-piece of imperial expansion. On a different level, it sabotaged Dufferin's viceroyalty, alienated Indian opinion, and ironically came just too late to affect the Tory electoral fortunes, the capture of Mandalay being announced on 1 December.

The aftermath of the war was unexpected, and tragic; on Churchill's instructions, Dufferin ordered a forward drive into the Shan States, pushing the new Chinese border to the Salween river—far to the east of the initially chosen treaty port of Bhamo. Guerrilla resistance turned this into a running sore; nearly 35,000 British troops were involved by 1888, operations lasted for several years, and cost ten times Dufferin's original estimate. This was yet to be perceived in 1885, and what preoccupied Churchill most was the fact that a *Times* correspondent, treated badly by General Prendergast on the spot, was making trouble in London; Churchill had him reinstated, where he created immense embarrassment for the reputation of the British in Burma. This was not forgotten, and army opinion there dreaded Churchill's return to office in 1886 'as he backs the newspaper people so shamefully'. The time Churchill devoted to the embroilment is symbolic of the chief importance he attached to the whole affair, which was publicity. None the less, by late 1886, the campaign up the Irrawaddy had become so tarnished that Dufferin was driven to producing a privately printed pamphlet for circulation among his influential friends attempting an exculpation of himself for the Burma policy. But by then Churchill was no longer responsible.

As soon as the outcome of the campaign was known, the London Chamber of Commerce and the Liverpool Brokers' Association pressurized Churchill directly for annexation; and he himself had made no secret of his eventual preference since before the war. 'I feel sure the Burmah enterprise will be a most remunerative investment', he wrote to Dufferin on 27 October; 'at Birmingham last week I made no concealment that we intended annexation ...'[61] In fact, Dufferin was very doubtful about 'intending' any such thing. He regretted 'being driven into the Burma business'; though sometimes favouring annexation, he was worried by Bernard's advice against it, and by the end of the expedition favoured a protectorate. As late as 22 December he was still floating the idea of a puppet prince. Burne later recalled how he and Churchill dragooned 'the unwilling Viceroy' into the decision; Churchill later told Roberts that he received 'no help from Lord Dufferin', and at the time complained to Salisbury that the Viceroy was 'impotent to take the smallest responsibility on himself; we have to decide everything and he gets all the credit'. Royal opinion was stridently annexationist also, and Dufferin gave way—while always making clear to commiserating Liberals that Churchill had forced his hand.[62]

This was no less true for the fact that Churchill was himself advised against annexation by local authorities who pointed out that Theebaw was not a tyrant, and that the financial advantages of the case were exaggerated; but his reaction was to argue that the French danger, the current distractions in eastern

---

[61] The words he used were: 'We are threatened with a war with the King of Burma. The result of that war, unless the King of Burma yields in time, will probably be annexation, or at any rate some arrangement in the nature of annexation' (laughter and cheering)—*The Times*, 24 Oct. 1885. In fact, Churchill had told Carnarvon on 19 October 'Burmah will be annexed' (Carnarvon MSS, PRO 30/6/55).

[62] See Northbrook to Dufferin, 28 Jan. 1886, DVP F 130/249, no. 17; Gladstone to Dufferin, 17 Nov. 1886, ibid., no. 240. Also Churchill to Roberts, 22 June 1894, Roberts MSS 2102-23-21/29; O. Burne, *Memories*, p. 270, and A. Stewart, op. cit., p. 115.

Europe, and most of all the fact that 'public opinion is fully prepared for it', all made an immediate take-over imperative. Further emphatic evidence against annexation from those on the spot was equally snubbed; 'believe me', wrote the Governor of the Punjab grimly to Dufferin's secretary, 'the annexation of Upper Burma is not a thing to be undertaken by Lord Randolph in the easy-going, jaunty way in which he seems to have announced it'. Nor was it. But when the annexation was announced, Churchill's chief regret was that it 'could not have taken place a month earlier', and thus helped the Conservative results in the boroughs.

In December, the last loose ends were tidied up. A potential difficulty over Chinese claims was steamrollered over by the India Office, who felt some annoyance with the Foreign Office for listening to China experts; embarrassments like the continued presence of Burmese envoys in Paris, where they had arranged railway concessions, were avoided by Burne's diplomacy and a large Rothschild loan. That ubiquitous family speedily put in a proposal for control over the ruby mines as well as railway interests in Upper Burma, relayed by Churchill to Dufferin and Salisbury, but did not meet with success.[63] The annexation was announced on 1 January 1886 as 'a New Year's gift to the Empress and her subjects'—highly unwelcome as it was to those subjects in India who had to pay for it. Churchill, in FitzGibbon's house at Howth for the auspicious day, drank a cheerful toast to it with his Irish Tory friends.

Far from Dublin, the reaction was different. Military expenditure was always a key question in the polarization of Indian opinion, directly linked as it was to taxation and financial policy; and from the beginning the Burmese involvement was condemned in India as both unnecessary and expensive. Churchill's ex-ally Malabari remarked that the only 'interests' represented were those of 'a company of chauvinist monopolists' and accused the Indian Secretary of using the issue to make an electioneering bid; the Burmese affair was condemned unanimously in the Indian press as expensive, jingoist, and Lyttonist, a criticism also aired at Westminster. 'King Cotton' was seen

---

[63] Churchill to Dufferin, 14 Jan. 1886, DVP F 130/6, no. 1; Churchill to Salisbury, 28 Dec. 1885, Hatfield House MSS 3M/Churchill/221, where he crudely remarked that Rothschild was 'as keen as nuts'. See Stewart, chapter 12, for the complex story of the ruby mines. Later, the government having refused Rothschild's proposal, Churchill opposed the idea of their entering into any other contract; *Hansard 3*, cccvii, 98.

as the true policy-maker behind it, and Churchill's personal ambition linked to his use of the issue of depressed British industries. Even in Anglo-India, Dufferin's council resented the large loans on a depreciating currency necessitated by Churchill's Burmese policy. The fact that Ripon had laboured to prevent war with Theebaw, and was inexorably opposed to annexation, helped to point up the moral of Churchill's progress from 'friend of India' to unrepentant forwardist. The debate on annexation in parliament was, as might be expected, sharply conducted and raised pertinent questions as to financial and military liabilities; but by then the Secretary of State answering them was a Liberal.

Burma had been seen by Churchill as a key issue in the November elections, and on platforms throughout the country he used Indian affairs to bravura effect. The promised Parliamentary Inquiry was presented as a progressive measure pressed upon him by his contacts among 'educated natives' and opposed by hypocritical Radicals; but a more characteristic note was struck by his reiterated attacks on Ripon's 'ostrich-like stupidity ... which lost no opportunity of exciting hatred between the Europeans and the natives in India'. His industrial audiences were promised that the annexation of Burma would lead to a revival of trade, illustrating the interdependence of 'your Imperial domination and your commercial supremacy'.[64] In the same sense, a warlike attitude to Russia was defended on the grounds of protecting India as 'the one great free and open market for British goods'. In India, such statements sealed the disillusionment of progressive opinion; the final touch being given by his Birmingham jeers at the 'three Bengali baboos', which completely destroyed the image of 'a gift to India' with which he had embarked upon office.

For the Viceroy's part, when the government fell after Christmas he thanked Churchill 'for earnestly and energetically advocating [his colleagues'] views and fighting their battles with your Council'; but he welcomed Kimberley back to office in a

[64] 'If you neglect your Imperial domination you will undoubtedly lose your commercial supremacy ... If you allow a ridiculous person like the King of Burma to plunder your subjects and to persecute them, perhaps to murder them, and generally to pursue an unjust, hostile and aggressive attitude against your trade interests, if you allowed that to go on with impunity and took no notice of it, what do you think would be the conduct of the powers more powerful?' 20 Nov. 1885, at Birmingham; see *The Times*, 21 Nov. 1885 (not in Jennings).

private letter which expressed delight and relief.[65] Posterity was to judge Dufferin harshly: 'I do not believe', George Hamilton wrote bitterly in 1900, 'he has been in any single place of responsibility and authority in which he did not more or less purchase popularity by leaving to his successors unpleasant legacies.'[66] For different reasons and on a different level, the same was true of Churchill in 1885. Overall, what is most striking about the official relationship of the two men who ruled India in what was to seem in retrospect a most important year is their joint inexperience—often bewailed by Dufferin, not greatly worried about by Churchill. This gave free play to the more decisive advisers in the India Office. It also contributed to the way in which Churchill's Indian orientation shifted steadily and with increasing rapidity from ostensible Riponist progressivism to a Lyttonist reaction—a process dictated in great part by immediate pressures and electoral priorities. An analogous process could be traced in the development of Churchill's stance regarding his other area of special competence: Ireland. And it was Ireland which had, by the end of his term at the India Office, come once more to dominate the political world.

[65] Dufferin to Kimberley, 14 Feb. 1886, DVP F 122/5, p. 15. For Dufferin's farewell letter to Churchill, 2 Feb. 1886, see DVP F 130/5, p. 7.
[66] To Curzon, 17 May 1900; quoted in Singh, op. cit., p. 75.

Chapter 7

Crisis Politics, 1885–1886

It is the necessary nature of a political party in this
country to avoid, as long as it can be avoided, the
consideration of any question which involves a great
change. There is a consciousness on the minds of
leading politicians that the pressure from behind,
forcing upon them great measures, drives them
almost quicker than they can go, so that it becomes
a necessity with them to resist rather than to aid
the pressure which will certainly be at last effective
by its own strength. The best carriage horses are
those which can most steadily hold back against
the coach as it trundles down the hill. All this
Phineas knew, and was of the opinion that the
Barrington Erles and Ratlers of his party would not
thank him for ventilating a measure which, however
certain might be its coming, might well be postponed for a few years. Once already in his career
he had chosen to be in advance of his party, and
the consequences had been disastrous to him.

Anthony Trollope, *Phineas Redux* (1874)

I

The great dislocation of political forms which constituted the
Home Rule crisis of 1885–6 provided Churchill with a political
context within which he used his talents for balance-holding,
brinkmanship, and bluff to the full; it was, in a sense, the high
point of his career. His apprenticeship in office, surveyed in the
last chapter, conferred an added weight upon his public image;
newspaper correspondents, in the inevitable public-school jargon
of political journalists, noted that he was now taken seriously by
'good boys' like Stanhope and Hartington. He was determined
to stress the positive role of the government, and in Cabinet
emphasized continually the urgency of doing this in the limited
time available to them, and the necessity of driving home as
publicly as possible the supposed errors of their predecessors: a

strategy he himself enthusiastically applied to the records of Northbrook at the Admiralty, Spencer in Ireland, and Ripon in India. But from the beginning he also called for positive initiatives—the abandonment of the Liberals' proposed new taxes, the rejection of their Afghan boundary line—and he reclaimed an old Irish pledge by working up an Irish Educational Endowments Bill with FitzGibbon in the last days of the session. Overall, Churchill's energy in office was notable for the diversity of the areas in which it was exercised: much as he took his India Office duties to comprise an extraordinary degree of interference in foreign affairs, he took his position of supremacy in the Commons as licensing a wide range of individual initiatives. And where this led him to attack Spencer's administration and side with the Irish over the Maamtrasna inquiry, it involved (as did his attack on Ripon) breaking an important political rule, and carrying into public a disagreement aired in Cabinet. It was the use of opposition tactics prolonged into office which made him an impossible colleague for those who (unlike Beach) had not accepted his inevitable supremacy.

The shifting balances of minority government allowed this latitude, which was one reason why Churchill pressed his position so far in 1885–6. Another had to do with more immediate causes: his personal life dictated its own urgent priorities. From 1885, his pace of living was frantic, his patience more easily exhausted than ever; a sense of time running out seems to have pervaded his calculations. A statesmanlike pose could be summoned up on occasion; at a Windsor visit (which he privately categorized as 'deadly') the Queen found him 'very quiet' and 'talking sensibly'.[1] But short-term priorities tended to interfere with long-term strategies, here as everywhere else. And problems of health and marriage wound the pace up further.

With his advancement to office, Churchill's beautiful wife became a more political lady than she had hitherto been. His appointment meant that another Woodstock election had to be fought, and though Chamberlain dissuaded Joseph Arch from contesting it, a less impressive Liberal entered the lists. Churchill privately confessed himself 'very anxious and worried' about the election. Added to his recent record on agricultural interests, and the fact that since the reform legislation the borough had

---

[1] *Letters of Queen Victoria*, 2nd series, iii, pp. 683–4, and Churchill to Duchess of Marlborough, RCHL vi/733. He claimed that the smoking room was '6¾ miles' from his bedroom.

nothing to lose in a final gesture of independence, there was the more important fact that he was now on bad terms with Blenheim. He was, however, unable to campaign himself; so his wife did, with characteristic panache, initially against the opposition of Blandford as well as of Corrie Grant, the Radical candidate. The enterprise attracted characteristically Churchillian publicity; though she was not the first political wife to campaign for her husband, the newspapers took up the contest with eagerness, especially when Grant imported his own, less exotic, Liberal women supporters.[2] The seat was successfully defended, and Lady Randolph, already a celebrated hostess, was now an important political adjunct. Though never a political manipulator in the mode of Mrs Jeune or the Duchess of Manchester, she was fully prepared to speak on platforms and give interviews; she was prominent in Birmingham later in the year, organizing 'phalanxes of lady canvassers' and giving interviews in the press; she remained one of the chief organizers of the Primrose League, and appeared at provincial meetings with Churchill in the campaigns of 1886.

In many ways, however, their marriage was by now more an alliance than a love affair; 'though he gets on pretty well with his wife when they are together', wrote Labouchere to Chamberlain at the end of the year, 'he is always glad to be away from her'.[3] While their letters remain affectionate until the summer of 1886, at that point a severe estrangement occurred and rumours of separation were rife by the end of that year. The chief importance, politically speaking, is that at this period of frenzied activity, Churchill had no real personal base upon which he could fall back and recoup his strength. Blenheim was unwelcoming, his wife's London life revolved round the socially exhausting world of the Prince of Wales, his only recreations, apart from fishing in the autumn, were gambling and racing. His frequent week-ends in Paris were supposed to involve womanizing; but they may simply have provided a much needed rest.

To judge from his family correspondence, money was also a particular worry in 1885–6. Neither he nor Lady Randolph was capable of economizing; their pastimes were the most expensive possible; the loans raised on the reversion of his mother's fortune were soon exhausted. As early as January 1885 there was talk of

---

[2] Corrie Grant's canvassers at Woodstock were not Girton ladies, as often claimed; one was a Newnham girl, the other not a student at all. See *Pall Mall Gazette*, 6 July 1885.

[3] Labouchere to Chamberlain, 25 Dec. 1885, Chamberlain MSS, 5/50/54.

getting rid of horses, selling the lease on Connaught Place and going to live with the Duchess in Grosvenor Square.[4] His associations with the world of high finance were now manifold; the Rothschilds and their circle loomed larger and larger in his private and public life. Churchill resigned from the St. Stephen's Club, with maximum publicity, because they blackballed his friend Wertheimer; Lady Randolph campaigned for L. H. Isaacs at Walworth; Lionel Cohen, an influential financier, was a close associate of Churchill's in the Paddington constituency. Less reputably, he and Wolff were still involved with the railway financier Charles Waring, whose plans for Egyptian finance they pressed on Salisbury, and whose family were to be conciliated by social advancement through the Marlborough connection.[5] The world of Trollope, never far from Churchill, here moves from *Phineas Finn* to *The Way We Live Now*. And in analysing Churchill's actions in 1885–6, a simple but important factor that should not be forgotten is the importance of an official salary.

Behind all this was the increasing worry of his health. Colleagues flooded him with warnings in the late summer of 1885 about the danger of his nerves giving way; James, Dilke, and Chamberlain shared information in September about Churchill's debility; Labouchere sent a highly coloured account to Rosebery. 'R. Churchill is in a very bad way, the action of his heart has given way, and he takes a lot of digitalis. He says that he must knock up if he has to sit up in the House of Commons, as he cannot sleep after 6 in the mornings and breaks down if he does not go to bed early. This he says he does not want to do, it will delight his colleagues who are civil but who all hate him cruelly with the exception of Hicks Beach.' In August and again in November he was confined to his bed with illness; platform-speaking, he confided to Dufferin, entailed extreme strain and illness ('and the constant necessity of trying to say something new makes one a drivelling idiot').[6]

---

[4] Duchess to Churchill, 8 Jan. 1885, Blenheim E/IV/65. It is interesting also to find him presenting himself as one with the poverty-stricken London middle class, unable to afford a law-case to prevent the Metropolitan Railway from interfering with his holding; *Hansard 3*, ccv, 865.

[5] See Wolff to Churchill, 25 Jan. 1886, RCHL xi/1328, and Churchill to Salisbury, 25 July 1885, Hatfield House MSS 3M/Churchill/62.

[6] See RCHL viii/892, 897, 901a, 913. Also Dilke to James, 14 Sept. 1885, James MSS M45/119. 'I told Chm. of the bit in your . . . letter as to R. Churchill. He is *very* sorry to hear it and so am I.' Also Labouchere to Rosebery, 25 Nov. 1885, Rosebery MSS 10041, and to Chamberlain, 18 Oct. 1885, Chamberlain MSS 5/50/28, for a similar letter. Churchill remarks on his own ill health in a letter to Dufferin, 27 Oct. 1885, DVP F 130/3, no. 77.

But there were more deep-rooted causes than this; his incurable disease had now taken firm hold, and Churchill was under the constant care of Dr Robson Roose, a fashionable Brighton gout specialist who was an expert on debilitating neurological disorders. Roose's popular works, which bore titles like *The Wear and Tear of London Life* (1886) and *Waste and Repair in Modern Life* (1897), made frequent examples of the killing pace of life suffered by 'politicians and statesmen' under his care. His more academic work, *Nerve Prostration and Other Functional Disorders of Daily Life* (1888), dealt with neurasthenic diseases, which in many instances (ranging from headaches and constipation to neuralgia and epilepsy) he attributed to hereditary or contracted venereal disease. It is possible that he misdiagnosed Churchill: many of whose symptoms could equally well have indicated a brain tumour, or multiple sclerosis. However, he certainly believed Churchill to have syphilis—a far more common affliction at this time—and he ministered to him accordingly.[7] By 1885, Roose had passed Churchill on to Thomas Buzzard, a specialist in this area. But he continued to treat his distinguished patient; and given that his prescription for the disease was the popular one of potassium iodide and mercury, the progress of the patient was inevitably downhill. It was realized that mercury treatment could lead to increasing debility and tremors, but it was the only known antidote. Retrospective diagnosis by amateurs is unproductive, but it might be noted that classic symptoms of this treatment like darkened skin-colour, diminution of hearing, vertigo, and hoarseness were all repeatedly noted by Churchill's friends from the mid-eighties.[8] Less harmful were the constant injunctions to give

[7] 'The possibility of syphilis being at the root of a given nervous disorder should always be borne in mind': *Nerve Prostration*, p. 19. Also see pp. 133, 195, 199, 219, 274, 588.

[8] See J. Hutchinson, *Syphilis* (London, 1887), p. 71, for a reference to Buzzard's expertise. He saw Churchill as early as autumn 1885. For contemporary treatments and their effects see T. Robinson, *The Diagnosis and Treatment of Syphilis* (London, 1886), Roose, *Nerve Prostration*, D'Arcy Power and Murphy (eds.), *A System of Syphilis* (5 vols., London, 1914). Also C. C. Dennie, *A History of Syphilis* (Springfield, Ill., 1962), W. A. Pusey, *History and Epidemology of Syphilis* (London, 1933), and J. Cleugh, *Secret Enemy: the History of a Disease* (London, 1954). Belief in the treatment of syphilis lasted virtually unchanged for four centuries until the development of serum testing and the isolation of the virus organism in the early twentieth century. See Mitchell and Churchill, *Jennie*, p. 129 for 'giddiness'; Rosebery, *Lord Randolph Churchill*, p. 113, for early manifestations of the disease; T. P. O'Connor, *Memories of an Old Parliamentarian*, i, 65, for his curious skin-colour; and various references in Churchill's own letters (e.g. W. S. Churchill, ii, 359) for remarks about his increasing deafness. One might add that T. Robinson remarks as a very common symptom the slight paralysis of the eyelid muscles, resulting in lowered lids: a marked feature in later photographs of Churchill.

up alcohol and tobacco (recurring resolves of Churchill's), and to take long sea-voyages to favoured spots like North Africa; but neither remedy was adopted consistently. The cardiac weakness which accompanied the disease was treated by increasing doses of digitalis; the late nights and frantic activity continued. The febrile energy alternating with apathetic despair, the lapses of judgement, the violent rages which characterized Churchill's behaviour, while always inseparable from his tense and moody persona, became more marked from the mid-eighties; and all are, coincidentally, concomitants of the same malady. Lady Randolph's biographer believes that his separation from her at this time arose from the diagnosis of his disease, and that their eventual reconciliation came through his telling her about it. The secret remained closely guarded up to his death; 'up to now the General Public and even Society does not know the real truth', his wife wrote to her sister in 1895, 'and after *all* my sacrifice and the misery of these 6 months it would be hard if it got out. It would do incalculable harm to his political reputation and memory and be a dreadful thing for all of us.'[9] (There were whispers in ensuing years, but the fact that the only authority to put the statement in print was Frank Harris rather detracted from its credibility than anything else.)

This was an additional pressure upon someone whose life was by now irredeemably a public one. He himself contributed to this by his cultivation of the press. He had worried in early 1885 about the tractability of Buckle and *The Times*, but by the end of the year was able 'to inspire the first two articles' in a single issue;[10] Lucy's taking over the *Daily News* in January 1886 led to a sudden change in that paper's presentation of Churchill, who was now seen as serious and statesmanlike. Personal contacts apart, however, he was in any case a favourite topic. The Central News Agency graded his speeches as 'Class 1', for verbatim reporting—a privilege shared only by Chamberlain, Gladstone, and Salisbury.[11] Churchill himself worried incessantly about the reporting of his speeches, and took issue with Lucy and Routledge over the printing of an unauthorized version; even before Jennings's laundered edition of 1889, Edward Arnold produced a selection of Churchill's speeches

[9] A. Leslie, p. 173, quoting Lady Randolph to Leonie Leslie, 3 Jan. 1895.

[10] Churchill to Salisbury, 1 Dec. 1885, Hatfield House MSS 3M/Churchill/195.

[11] See *Pall Mall Gazette*, 3 Nov. 1885. Dilke, Granville, Hartington, and Spencer received one column; Beach, Childers, Cross, Harcourt, and Trevelyan half a column; Northcote was 'ploughed'.

entitled *Plain Politics for the Working Classes*. His presidency of the Conservative News Agency echoed this preoccupation; and his manipulation of publicity was seen as one of his hallmarks, leading to frequent comparisons with other stars of the broadsheets like Sarah Bernhardt. Those visiting London at this time, after a long absence, found 'people talk of him as they talked of Disraeli thirty years ago'.[12]

At the same time, the possession of office, respectability, and a salary enabled him to spread his wings; one of the few general statements of his political philosophy (apart from characteristic asides in official memoranda, such as that 'persons more than principles determine political events'[13]) comes from this period. It took the form of a speech to the Cambridge University Carlton Club, just before he took office. Here he emphasized the fortuitous, pragmatic, unpredictable nature of political discourse: the expectation that a politician had to be everywhere, know everything, produce 'every variety of vituperation' upon his opponents, and keep up with a vast quantity of correspondence. 'In such a state of things, how can you expect on any subject anything like political thought?' Much of his argument was designed to back up his campaign for reforming parliamentary procedure (Grey, Russell, Peel, Canning, and Disraeli, he pointed out, attended fewer public meetings, held fewer Cabinets, and sat in shorter sessions than men did now). But his basic issue concerned the death of political thought. 'It is essentially an age of action, but action based rather on instinct than on logic or reason or experience.' Government was an empirical science, yet experience seemed of little help: 'the study of history in our present case is almost useless'. Over an empire of 300 million there presided a monarchy and two Houses of Parliament, all ancient institutions, 'intensely conservative in their procedure'. Yet they were founded on a new basis, of five million totally unpredictable electors. The state could be being swept to a political Niagara, or be carried gently to 'some

---

[12] G. F. Bowen to Dufferin, 9 Aug. 1886, DVP F 130/24B, no. 160. The Bernhardt comparison occurs in *Truth* and the *Pall Mall*, picked up in Escott's *Society in London*, and on one occasion echoed by the Norwegian *Dagblad*. 'He has some of the genius, some of the strong feelings, of the combination of opposing qualities, which the great actress possesses. Like her, he can be violent, energetic, flighty. Like her, it is impossible for him to say what he will do under given but uncommon circumstances. The love of the glittering and the beautiful is developed in both to the same degree. Both are the children of passion and of whims . . .' Quoted in *Pall Mall Gazette*, 11 July 1885.

[13] RCHL v/620.

undiscovered ocean of superhuman development'. Political analysis and political thought alone could show, and they were at a discount.

Being Churchill, the speech continued with a series of gibes at 'personalities', including several leading Cambridge figures; but the over-all message comes through with curious effect. What passed for 'ideas' in politics was the 'arrant trash and falsehood' peddled by the Radicals to the agricultural labourers; Cambridge Toryism might produce a substitute, but for his own part he must confess bewilderment. 'My state of mind when these great problems come across me—which is very rarely—is one of wonder, or perhaps I should rather say of admiration and of hope, because the alternative state of mind would be one of terror and despair'; he could only trust in 'the evolution, by some process or other which I do not exactly know, and cannot determine, of the higher and nobler humanity'.

The speech is interesting for treating general ideas in a way usually foreign to Churchill's visceral and instinctive approach. It also reflects something of his state of mind in the period just before the Conservatives took office; a state of mind which led to difficult relationships with his colleagues once they had arranged themselves in power. At Bow on 3 June he had savagely attacked Bartley for remarking that the party did not have a policy, and had gone on to outline one: this embraced procedural reform, Irish and English local government legislation, revenue and fiscal restructuring, a parliamentary inquiry into Indian administration, and reassessment of the Afghan frontier boundary. The striking thing about this list is that they can all be seen as non-party issues; the appalled *Spectator* took the analysis further, describing it as an endorsement of the whole Liberal programme. Either way, such an outline was a warning to Salisbury; and the tension implicit in such an approach lasted throughout the ministry. Salisbury wished, in everything, to play for time until after the November elections; Churchill wanted to make a splash. The psychological relationship between the two evolved in these terms as well, and can be traced through their copious correspondence: Churchill eager, importunate, confiding, verbose; Salisbury's responses urbane, dry, humouring, but concealing a mounting impatience. From late July, the honeymoon was effectively over; mid-August saw Churchill ill, surly, ready to threaten resignation, being pleaded with by Beach. By now he was convinced that Salisbury as well as his other colleagues disliked him, and had instigated the violent attack that appeared in the *Standard* after the Maamtrasna debate. On 12 August, already ill and two days before his threatened resignation over the Bombay Command, he gave a curious speech at a rainy Dorset agricultural fête. To a background of heckling, he defensively rehearsed the accusations heaped on him of having 'disgraced the character and betrayed the interests of the great Tory party', and in a rambling exegesis stood by his record on Maamtrasna and denied contracting 'a profligate alliance' with Parnell. It was a strange performance, indicating how deep and public Cabinet divisions had become.

These developments were exacerbated by Salisbury's bizarre style in Cabinet, expatiated upon at length by Lady Gwendolen Cecil. Ostensibly vague and compliant, the Prime Minister was privately complaining to friends like Carnarvon how difficult it was to manage Churchill, and how much more difficult it would be in the future.[14] Here it must be remembered to what an extent the Cabinet was still dominated by the 'Old Gang'; to assume that Northcote was relegated to complete obscurity rather begs the question of how he re-emerged as Foreign Secretary the next year (a very ostentatious form of obscurity). Cranbrook and Richmond complained to the Queen of Churchill's 'wrong and bumptious' tone in Cabinet. Beach, whom Salisbury worriedly believed to be under Churchill's thumb, was his chief ally in tactics and in policy; but he was not always as reliable as he seemed ('the manners of a pirate and the courage of a governess', said Balfour—for whom the epigram could be reversed[15]).

It is against this background that Churchill's legislative energy must be seen. The caretaker ministry was described by Winston Churchill as 'a Parliamentary paradise ... in the midst of a political inferno', and it brought in legislation on a broad front; but Churchill would have added initiatives to do with taxation, Temperance, and a non-interventionist foreign policy, first seeking Bismarck's support and then angled towards Russia. Most of all he chose to occupy the rather surprising ground of procedural reform of parliament. He had introduced the topic

---

[14] Carnarvon MSS, BL Add. MS 60821, pp. 117–19; also diary entry for 1 Aug. 1885, Add. MS 60925.

[15] Quoted in L. P. Curtis, Jr., *Coercion and Conciliation in Ireland 1880–92: a Study in Conservative Unionism* (Princeton, 1963), p. 26. For Salisbury's worry about Beach and Churchill see Carnarvon diary, BL Add. MS 60925, 1 Aug. 1885.

both at Cambridge and at Bow, accusing Gladstone of taking it up 'in a party spirit, directed solely to party aims'; the Conservative approach, as he outlined it, would be broader, altering the hours of parliamentary business in the interests of public men, and handing much of the business of the House over to committees. There was a variety of private reasons behind this; the control of the inevitably much increased Irish party after the elections, Churchill's own impatience with the 'nauseous drivel' of the Commons, his own ill health, and his doctor's orders of regular early nights. He told Loulou Harcourt the new rules were 'especially made to suit his own constitution'.[16] But most importantly, it could be interpreted as a non-party issue (indeed, Gladstone emphasized it as a priority in September); as well as carrying the practical implication that restructured Grand Committees might be used to hive off the kind of legislation otherwise planned for delegation to National Councils by Chamberlain. When he finally aired the topic in Cabinet at the end of the year, Churchill marshalled his reasons for reform in an immense memorandum, supposedly drawn up 'at the request of the Prime Minister', in which his emphasis throughout was anti-Irish and inter-party.[17] By then it was being played as a counter for continuing in office in the post-election dispensation; it was also made the occasion for yet another dramatic resignation threat on 15 December. Churchill's resolutions were eventually referred to a Committee of both Houses, and he had to give up his more drastic closure proposals. But when his plans were announced in January 1886, *The Times* accurately remarked that such sweeping ideas could hardly be carried by Churchill alone 'in the present state of parties'; the Liberal press noted their close similarity to Gladstone's ideas; and everyone thought there was a chance

---

[16] '. . . as he could not sit up after 12 o'clock at night and liked to get away to Scotland in July'. LHJ, 24 Jan. 1886, vol. 377, p. 4.

[17] The reasons were the 'flight of members' from mid-July, the abandonment of government measures at this time, and the hasty approach necessarily taken to important business, as well as the ensuing encouragement given to obstruction. A regular autumn–winter session would have to be accepted, with late sittings curtailed by extension of closure powers. Business was to be expedited; Grand Committees were to take over much of the consideration of legislative details. Much Private Bill legislation would have to be referred to tribunals like the Railway Commission or 'existing local bodies, or to local bodies which the legislature may call into existence'. His memorandom ended by threatening that any government which did not embrace proposals of this kind would be unresponsive to public opinion, would lay itself open to being stymied by the Irish, and would cast doubt on the sincerity of its legislative intentions (PRO CAB 37/18, no. 19). For the eventual resolutions drafted by Beach see PRO CAB 37/18, no. 48.

they would delay discussion of the Irish question for weeks. The attraction of the issue for Churchill was its adaptability; personal priorities and political tactics fused. It was an instance where the tension set up by his private and his public life could be creatively used.

II

This tension, however, led to trouble in other areas: notably that of cross-bench relationships. Churchill's friendship with Chamberlain was ostentatiously paraded, even at the height of his attempt to win Bright's seat in Birmingham; in May 1885 Chamberlain privately believed that Churchill contemplated a separation from his leaders and a union with the Radicals. Certainly he closely cultivated both Chamberlain and Dilke at this time, telling them as early as 17 May that there was to be no coercion from the Tories, and in his speeches of late May and early June referring to both as men of common sense and ability, unlike the tricky and 'casuistical' Gladstone. Gladstone himself read this as a threat, and warned Chamberlain that the sight of Churchill 'in the bosom and to a great extent in the leadership' of the Tory party was a sign of such political demoralization that the Liberals *must* remain united. Chamberlain, none the less, by November was describing Churchill to Dilke as 'a man I really like and who might be—and perhaps will be—on our side some day'.[18] A third Radical connection was the inevitable Labouchere. *Truth* had long been an ally of Churchill's, Labouchere believing in 'puffing individuals' even when he abhorred their politics; they co-operated over issues like Egypt, and getting Wolff returned again for Portsmouth (in which they failed). Though Labouchere enjoined Churchill not to mention 'that I ever say anything to you about politics',[19] he hardly meant it; Churchill used him as a sounding-board, as did everybody else, and Labouchere obligingly told everyone everything; his chief importance was to be for future political historians. But the connection was valuable at the high point of

---

[18] 13 Nov. 1885; RCHL ix/1058. It was evidently sent to Churchill by Dilke. At Hawarden in October Gladstone remarked that Chamberlain was 'far the most conservative of the two'; he 'anticipated more danger from extreme doctrines' from Churchill. LHJ, 22 Oct. 1885, vol. 372, p. 63.

[19] RCHL x/1158.

the 1885–6 crisis, since it gave Churchill direct access to disaffected Liberals—and he used it thoroughly.

Labouchere was part of Churchill's Bohemian life, centred on Brighton, Paris, and backstage at Henry Irving's theatre; in the *beau monde* his chief Liberal contact was Henry James, at once urbane and secretive (his social successes being threatened with vitiation by persistent rumours of a secret illegitimate family). James sent Churchill emotional little notes expressing joy in 'one of the most valued friendships I have', visited him often, and shared Whig gossip with him: a political association begun over Reform, in which both men saw further potential.

Such connections were an inheritance of Churchill's peculiar position in the late 1870s, preserved into respectability; and the same could be said of his much more potentially alarming Irish relationships. These still embraced Callan and O'Shea as well as the designated parliamentary leaders. The question of 'alliance' between Tories and Irish in 1885 has been exhaustively canvassed, at the time and since; there was certainly an entente, and equally certainly Churchill had more to do with it than most. The celebrated interview with Parnell before the 1885 elections was thus described by Churchill to Hamilton three years later:

Parnell told him that a Tory Government would have a great chance in Ireland if they dropped coercion, and would be secure of the Irish vote at the coming election which would make a difference to them of 50 seats. R.C. undertook in reply that he would not join any Government that proposed coercion; and, Parnell on his side undertook to support a modest land purchase Bill which subsequently took the shape of the Ashbourne Act.[20]

Dick Power, who arranged the meeting, had already approached him about Parnellite support over legislation like the Labourers' Act. Newspaper gossip reported that Healy and Churchill arranged the vote whereby the government fell. But less obvious emissaries, like Wolff and even Winn, had dealings with the Irish over the terms of their support. Though Healy told Labouchere there was no formal contract, despite Churchill's 'vague talk of Home Rule', there was a general belief in political society that a bargain had been struck (and certainly the legislation of Salisbury's brief ministry represented

[20] EHJ, 12 May 1889, vol. xxi, p. 122, BL Add. MS 48650.

quite a generous payment on account). Much of this was, however, a House of Commons arrangement; and government ministers like Cranbrook were appalled at Churchill's frank statement of the understanding in Cabinet. The implication was that it involved him, but not them; which, given the importance of Churchill in the formation of the government, was not realistic.

He certainly kept an avenue open—to the annoyance of Blandford, who complained the following spring that his brother 'always refrained from burning your boats with those Irish'.[21] Similar irritation was felt by the general constituency of Tory Democracy: a typical working-men's deputation congratulated him on 'determined resistance to the selfish theories and quixotic panaceas of faddists and caucusmongers for Ireland's supposed ills', and such bodies had warmly approved his Orange stance over Lord Rossmore; through 1885 letters from provincial Conservatives begged him openly to deny the Parnellite alliance. (This he obligingly did, on several occasions.) However, issues closer to their hearts predominated before 1886: such as protectionism, which Churchill openly advocated at Cambridge in June.[22] And in other sections of the party, a countering idea persisted: that the Tories *could* settle Ireland. An initiative in this direction was mounted in the journals by Irish conservatives like Henry Bellingham and Gavan Duffy; an influential lobby within Parnell's party was held to prefer the idea of a Conservative scheme (largely because of their educational ideas). The argument, so attractive to Gorst and Wolff, that Home Rule meant the opposite of Repeal, was an enduring one; the idea that the Parnellites would become 'a section of the Conservative Party' was advanced to Churchill as late as December 1885. The fact that the principal avatar of Tory Home Rule was the inept Wilfrid Scawen Blunt, passionately imploring Churchill in June to come out openly for an Irish parliament, and to let Blunt be his follower, should not conceal the fact that many better judges thought along similar lines. As it was, Churchill merely advised

---

[21] 14 Apr. 1886; Blenheim MSS G/IV/8.

[22] On his visit to the University Carlton, he also attended a meeting of the local Fair Trade League, where he accused Gladstone of trying to force 'filthy' foreign wines down the throats of Britons instead of English beer, and called on them to 'consider favourably whether the moment has not arrived for a tax upon foreign manufactures': the state of the economy being such that Peelism was outmoded, and an increased duty on corn would not necessarily raise the price of bread.

him to 'soften down the precision of your views as regards an Irish parliament'.[23]

From the Liberal side, Irish sympathizers like W. H. Duignan saw Churchill as likely material for a Conservative Home Rule initiative, and many Liberals believed in the summer of 1885 that they had to raise the bidding to Parnell in order to compete with Churchill's offers; two days before the Hawarden Kite, not only Churchill's dealings with the Irish but also the declared wish of many Conservatives for a large Home Rule measure were topics of conversation at the National Liberal Club. After the dust of the first Home Rule Bill had settled, Justin McCarthy declared that Tory Cabinet members had discussed Home Rule with him; but by then no one was very interested any more. As even a partisan Tory historian has put it, the fact that the Conservatives represented Home Rule as a national issue only after pinning Gladstone to it may have been tactically adroit, but did not make it morally exculpable, nor any the less embarrassing in after-years.[24] It was, however, of a piece with the instinctual politics preached by Churchill at Cambridge and practised by him with unique insouciance.

From the first days of the government he was identified as a friend to the Irish: defending them from Radical attacks in the House, and making it clear in Cabinet that he would not uphold Spencer's policies. He had given many hostages to fortune, notably in his condemnation of Dublin Castle in the *Pall Mall* interview of December 1884, and he was frequently reminded of them. Publicly, he was identified with the Tory abandonment of coercion. But his language under this head was particularly careful. It is well known that in his St. Stephen's Club speech of 20 May he announced that the Tories would not feel it necessary to renew coercion, but less often remarked that at Bow on 3 June he cautiously recanted the commitment, accusing the Liberal press of 'deliberately misconstruing' his remarks: 'I pronounced no opinion whatever . . . do not press these remarks of mine too

[23] See Blunt MSS 389/1977. For his unfailing belief that Churchill had declared for Home Rule in 1885 see *The Land War in Ireland* (London, 1912), pp. 1, 18, 20, 24, 34, 140, 143; *My Diaries* (2 vols., London, 1919–20), ii, 128; and his article in *Nineteenth Century*, Mar. 1906. Also see G. Birdwood to Churchill, 5 Dec. 1885, RCHL x/1138. Earlier a memorandum of Moore's dated 31 October had pointed out that the views of the Irish representatives deserved dispassionate consideration, as they were *not* rebels: an Irish parliament, even with tariff reform, would not necessarily threaten the imperial system.

[24] E. A. Akers-Douglas, 3rd Visc. Chilston, *Chief Whip: the Political Life and Times of Aretas Akers-Douglas, First Viscount Chilston* (London, 1961), p. 61.

far.' In the same speech he reiterated the Tory mission to preserve the Union; but with deliberate inaccuracy he identified the Irish party with a policy of total repeal, a rhetorical safeguard which he was to use repeatedly over the next six months. His stance on coercion, however, was what mattered immediately, and here his position was pivotal. In his retrospective memorandum, Churchill blamed Gibson for the decision to abandon it, and portrayed his own attitude as unsullied by calculation; but he had been testing the ground out for himself, he was well supplied with statistics from Ireland which tended to demonstrate the decrease of major crimes, and Lytton's account to Dufferin summed up what everyone knew: 'he had undoubtedly committed himself with Parnell, not, as was reported, to propose or support any sort of concession in the direction of Home Rule, but to oppose any policy in the direction of coercion'.[25]

Given this, and given Churchill's statements in Cabinet, the Maamtrasna incident was inevitable. In October 1884 Gorst and Churchill had taken up the cause of those accused of murder at Maamtrasna: the Irish motion to reverse the previous administration's decision gave Churchill, Hicks Beach, and Gorst the chance to mount an attack on Spencer. It also, as Winston Churchill pointed out, 'thrust the Whigs for a space back upon Mr Gladstone' (as well as allegedly converting Spencer to Home Rule).[26] Responses on Churchill's own side were probably more extreme than he bargained for; the Queen's virulence was predictable, but Gorst's attack on 'reactionary Ulster members' also led to an infuriated reaction from the Hamiltons and others. Salisbury was less angry at Churchill than anyone else, defending him as having to square the circle between opposition pledges and government duties; what really worried him was the evidence it gave of Churchill's ascendancy over Beach. Carnarvon, who had anticipated the difficulties of Churchill's position but expected his 'cleverness' to extricate him, was deeply embarrassed, but found himself bemusedly accepting Irish congratulations on the event.

Churchill himself, however, was shaken. He complained to

---

[25] Lytton to Dufferin, 22 May 1886, DVP F 130/24A, p. 38. Long afterwards, Churchill stated baldly that the only reason they did not bring in coercion in the summer of 1885 was because they couldn't (*Hansard 4*, x, 1266, 27 Mar. 1893).

[26] James to Gorst, 31 Oct. 1884, BL Add. MS 44218, ff. 173–4; W. S. Churchill, ii, 441; Brodrick, *Records and Reactions*, p. 63; Sir John Ross, *The Years of My Pilgrimage*, p. 177.

Labouchere that Parnell had sprung the incident on him as a surprise, unallowed for in their agreement; George Hamilton thought him unnerved by the strength of die-hard reaction, and he certainly made a rapid attempt to mend his Ulster fences with a glowing tribute to the Ulster members in a speech at Sheffield. But the immediate result was a powerful revolt against Churchill's growing ascendancy; two colleagues refused to share a political platform with him, leading to a cancelled meeting at Liverpool, and provincial Conservatives who still resented his Sheffield capitulation in 1884 used this occasion to repudiate him publicly. Most important, the *Standard* on 31 July subjected Churchill to an extraordinarily vehement and wide-ranging attack. He was accused of having risen to the top by assiduous cultivation of newspapers, backed by a shaky combination of public bluster and private opportunism; his ignorance and crudity must be measured at their worth, and the fact faced that he had been ruinously overrated. Speaking for Toryism, the *Standard* declared: 'We will follow Lord Salisbury, but we will not be governed by a sort of overgrown schoolboy, who thinks he is witty when he is only impudent, and who really does not seem to possess sufficient knowledge even to fathom the depths of his own ignorance of everything worthy of the name of statesmanship'; the popular belief that he was, 'like his brother', at heart a greater Radical than Chamberlain, was right. This was far more hostile than anything which appeared in the Liberal press; given Alfred Austin's position at Hatfield, it was easy for Churchill to believe that it was inspired by Salisbury, especially as he knew the paper was refusing to accede to moderating pressure behind the scenes.[27] His public defence of his action was disingenuous: the government had 'sternly and in the most uncompromising manner' refused Parnell's actual demand for an inquiry, merely reminding the Irish of their constitutional right of appeal to the Lord Lieutenant. But privately he knew this demonstration of sympathy had jeopardized his Commons position, and incidentally put paid to any hopes of the government backing an Irish University measure, in which he and Ashbourne had warmly supported Carnarvon.

This was all the more important because with office Churchill had recurred to his old ideas of Irish educational reform, working closely with the ebullient FitzGibbon. At FitzGibbon's suggestion, they drafted an Educational Endowments Bill, sal-

---

[27] See B. L. Cohen to Churchill, 7 Aug. 1885, RCHL vi/777.

vaging a Liberal measure against Dyke's wishes and, in FitzGibbon's words, 'giving some legislative effect to our happy labours of 1878–80'. This involved much coming and going with Sexton and Healy, soothing the claims of emissaries like Dwyer Gray, and responding to frantic bulletins from Howth when the hierarchy played cat-and-mouse with Molloy, their well-meaning but innocent nominee on the commission. Churchill was never closer to FitzGibbon than during this summer; FitzGibbon wrote continually, worrying about Churchill's health as well as about educational politicking. 'I did so wish', he wrote when Churchill postponed his September visit, '. . . that I could get the chance of doctoring you! The Eye [Ireland's Eye], the Sea, the Air, less Fire, less Smoke, no Work, some Walk, more Talk, such would be my prescription in monosyllabic form for a week, to be repeated—if found endurable—with Father Healy . . . for spirituals.' A more sardonic and hilarious note was struck in his running commentary on the doings of Lord Carnarvon, the gullible and ill-starred Viceroy.

On Friday 'His ex' had a fine field day—he began by presenting an Albert medal to a 'valorous' dispensary doctor, then for an hour discoursed to the Moderator and other Representatives of the Presbyterians on the beauties of 'mixed education', and finally gave himself an appetite for his dinner by a tête-à-tête with Archbishop Walsh. I told him he deserved to have ended his labours by presenting himself, amid applause and with appropriate remarks, with another Albert medal . . . His powers of gushing are unimpaired, and he makes steady progress in the affections of any who keep such articles for the representatives of alien oppression.

Their work on the Educational Endowments Bill provided a constant point of reference; FitzGibbon shared every twist and turn of commission politics with Churchill, angry with obstruction from Presbyterians and Catholics alike. The idea of denominational education encouraging a sound and conservative Irish middle class pervaded their correspondence; 'I think', wrote FitzGibbon, 'of casting about for a means of allying the clever lay nationalists with the orders in demanding at least one Irish school to compete with Ushaw, Edgbaston and Stonyhurst.'[28]

This kind of collusion was the stuff of Carnarvon's honeymoon period; it led to discussions over university education, which the hierarchy seemed anxious to settle with the Tories, and which FitzGibbon urged Churchill to use as a carrot—so much so that

[28] 1 Sept., 18 Oct., 9 Sept. 1885; RCHL vii/855, viii/985, vii/883.

Churchill worried about FitzGibbon alienating Walsh by setting less nationalist clerics against him. 'It is to the Bishops entirely to whom I look in the future to turn, to mitigate or to postpone the Home Rule onslaught', he wrote in October. But by November FitzGibbon was telling Churchill that the intractable Walsh 'desired to accelerate the National Movement, and to *keep back* the settlement of all burning questions until he can put them into the crucible of Parnell's parliament. A pleasant prospect for moderates of all creeds, particularly Protestants!'[29] This tone took over after the elections, which gave the Parnellites the balance of power, and it did not go unheeded.

None the less, in December a draft Irish University Bill was circulated to Churchill and others, and he warmly approved of it; he would even have added a Catholic College in Armagh. He showed a similarly Howth approach to the question of land purchase, since he was ambivalent about 'clearing Parnell's path with British gold'; FitzGibbon continually denounced the policy of 'the landlords getting out at the expense of the rest'. But Churchill conferred about land-purchase schemes with George Fottrell, an influential nationalist solicitor, on his visits to Dublin (and, according to Fottrell, talked Home Rule to him as well).[30] He remained merrily dismissive about boycotting, assuring Salisbury that it would disappear through 'boredom', that newspaper reports of Ireland were unreliable, and—apropos of Parnell's demands, articulated in late August—that the demand for 'Repeal' was rhetorical and 'as old as the hills'. Speaking at Sheffield shortly after Parnell's statement of terms, he ostenta- tiously made no reference to them. And in letters to Dufferin in July and August he represented Parnell as a moderate, though he feared trouble from Davitt, and he saw any real threat as coming from landlords and Northern Protestants rather than nationalists: 'but as you know that has ever been so in Irish history'.[31]

[29] 10 Nov. 1885, RCHL ix/1045. For further details see Carnarvon MSS in PRO 30/6/58–9, and for a fuller treatment, Foster, 'Northern Counties Station', loc. cit.

[30] See Dilke's diary, 27 May 1885, Chamberlain MSS 8/2/1. Fottrell had been negotiating between Parnell and Dublin Castle and had, in conjunction with Chamberlain, published articles on Irish local government in the *Fortnightly*. as well as handling legal business for the National League.

[31] Churchill to Dufferin, 24 July 1885, 28 Aug. 1885, DVP F 130/3, nos. 60, 67. On the other hand, he saw Gladstone's election manifesto as extremely ominous. 'If people would have the patience, intelligence or courage to read between the lines they would perceive that there is no political or social change which that document does not easily admit of. I fear we are approaching a period of great confusion in English politics . . .' Same to same, 22 Sept. 1885, ibid., no. 73.

All this was extremely appealing to Carnarvon. He too had entered office a convinced anti-coercionist; he too felt that neither boycotting nor the spread of the National League could be contained by special legislation; he too had wished to give an undertaking about Irish university education from the outset. He was also ready to discover supporters in the ministry, Salisbury having told him on 6 July that though he would only go as far as Provincial Councils for Ireland, many in the party would accept very forward views. Carnarvon over-interpreted this, as he also over-interpreted comments of Salisbury's such as that the failure of the Munster Bank 'brought into startling relief . . . the utter hopelessness of managing England and Ireland together'.[32] And he rapidly formed great hopes of Churchill, sending him leaders from the *Freeman's Journal* and copies of memoranda of the state of Ireland, and encouraging him to confer with Ashbourne at Boulogne in August. Carnarvon pressed him to visit Ireland from late August, with mysterious promises of 'something which I think you may be interested in hearing', and agreed with Churchill that the newspapers exaggerated the agrarian situation. Churchill, however, principally opposed coercion as 'ruinous *to our party*'; Carnarvon was meditating a wider scheme.

By September, in fact, the Viceroy was in an altogether transfigured state. 'It is a most unhappy country', he wrote to Cranbrook, 'dowered—as in a fairytale—with great gifts and great misfortunes. Very little is really known or understood of it in England . . . The Orangemen seem to me sometimes to be demented.'[33] Carnarvon's brief infatuation with Churchill coincided with his discovery of Ireland. Churchill, for his part, was glad to slip over to Dublin in early October after a recuperative fishing holiday in Scotland. In Ireland he was extremely popular (rumours that he might be appointed Chief Secretary had been ecstatically greeted), and indeed something of a favourite son. After visits to Holmes, the Attorney-General (an adherent of the Howth circle, in whom FitzGibbon placed great confidence), and FitzGibbon himself, Churchill arrived at the Viceregal

[32] 22 July 1885; BL Add. MS 60825, p. 38. Carnarvon marked this passage. The earlier reference is also here. It was easy to make such mistakes (if they were mistakes). Lytton, staying at Hatfield in November, 'gathered from [Salisbury's] remarks that if he could see his way to the efficient protection of the loyalists he would not feel much alarmed at any form of Home Rule'; Lytton to Dufferin, 'Nov. 1885', DVP F 130/21, no. 105b.

[33] 2 Sept. 1885, Cranbrook MSS, HA 43 T501/262.

Lodge on 1 October. The company seemed enervated after Howth: 'it is very dull, very proper and very respectable here', he complained to Salisbury. 'I feel rather like a fish out of water and am always afraid of saying something which may shock these most truly excellent people.'[34] He added that he found Carnarvon, who was cosseting his health, evasive and hard to pin down. But from his side Carnarvon was dazzled by his brilliant guest, confiding to his diary:

He gives one the idea of being frank in saying what he thinks—and it seems to me as if Salisbury was gaining an influence with him—he showed me a letter from Salisbury to him entering at some length into the present position of foreign affairs and evidently written for the purpose of pleasing him—Randolph, in speaking to me of Salisbury, said that he was an enigma to him—that at times Salisbury was so open and intelligible; that at another time he dropped a veil over his thoughts. He told me another thing, which I had certainly never heard before— viz. a story that Disraeli was the real father of Dufferin—and he declared that when he was in India and saw much of Dufferin, Dufferin said and did many things which indicated or bore secret evidence to the relationship. Curious!

But their conversation hardly stopped there. Five years later Churchill recalled 'walking up and down on the terrace in front of the house, hearing Lord Carnarvon's confessions' about Home Rule.[35] With newspapers openly prophesying a Tory–Parnellite scheme of Imperial Federation plus Home Rule, focused on Churchill, with Wolff pressing just such an initiative on Churchill the month before, with Dublin Castle memoranda emphasizing the conservatism of Parnell and his allies, the Viceroy felt sure of support; at the Cabinet of 6 October everyone realized his Home Rule proclivities. Up to a month later, he was being assured by Gavan Duffy that it was generally known in St. Stephen's that Churchill, Beach, Cross, and most younger Conservative MPs agreed with him.[36] And after his

[34] 1 Oct. 1885; Hatfield House MSS 3M/Churchill/152.
[35] Carnarvon diary, 1 Oct. 1885, BL Add. MS 60925. Also EHJ, 5 Apr. 1892, vol. xxviii, p. 109, BL Add. MS 48657. Churchill recalled: 'And though there was Lord C. committed and Lord S. sitting on the fence, not a word was ever mentioned in the Cabinet . . .'
[36] Carnarvon diary, 2 Nov. 1885; Cooke and Vincent, *Governing Passion*, p. 287. Also see *Pall Mall Gazette*, 3 and 7 Oct. 1885, and Wolff to Churchill, RCHL viii/961, 962. He denied there were any real grounds for the fears of Protestants and landlords, and went into great constitutional detail to show the feasibility of Home Rule within the Empire. For Jenkinson's memorandum for the Cabinet, in very similar terms, see PRO CAB 37/16, no. 52.

advocacy in Cabinet of a forward Irish policy on 6 October, he dined with Churchill and found him 'very amiable'.

The results of the elections were to change the terms of this potential alliance; and at the end of November, Churchill was appalled to discover through Labouchere that Carnarvon had seen Parnell. Though by 10 December Churchill was writing to Salisbury that Carnarvon must go, as late as January Carnarvon was still corresponding with Churchill, agreeing that neither Cabinet nor party understood the realities of the case. But by then Churchill had tactically boxed the compass, and set his sails to the North.

III

The election of 1885 was, for Churchill as for every other platform politician, a venture into unknown territory; Lepel Griffin coarsely commiserated with him about 'attempting to convince the Great Unwashed by arguments which it will take three generations of education for them to understand'. Working-class Conservatism remained a doubtful quantity, grouping on issues like liquor rather than ideology. Churchill's rhetorical strategy revolved round avoidance of Ireland, and he advised Salisbury to work up issues like Church Disestablishment, with a view to splitting Whigs and Radicals: Liberalism versus Socialism remained a key Tory card, though Disestablishment took pride of place by the end. Churchill's own election address concentrated upon the danger to Empire and colonies abroad, and Church and freedom at home. (Ireland occurred as an incidental issue, and was then promised conciliatory and fair legislation.) A foretaste of his approach was provided by the immensely long speech at Sheffield on 5 September in which he revealed the settlement of the Afghan frontier. He also made the most of Whig–Radical divisions, and ended with the celebrated exhortation to Hartington to 'come over and help us'. Concentration on this phrase obscures the fact that the major part of the speech comprised a merciless satire of Hartington as an inept leader and a politician bereft of ideas: even a 'debased opportunist'. Harcourt was similarly pilloried. But Chamberlain, though 'no-one disagrees with him more than I do in every one of his political principles', was according to Churchill honest and straightforward. The 'invitation' to Hartington, expressing the belief that he had 'not been true to liberalism' and that the Tories now stood for the principles of Palmerston, was hardly anything that could be responded to; it is worth noting that Churchill privately believed in October that Hartington was by now so far separated from Chamberlain that he would soon retire from politics. (Chamberlain's speech at Warrington three days later, on the other hand, was phrased as a reply to Churchill: a dialectic maintained throughout the election campaign.)

The avoidance of Ireland was for Churchill, as for others, the cardinal strategic point. He emphasized both to Salisbury and to Dufferin the importance of not breaking silence ('the nationalists do not expect us to do so and do not want us to do so. Perhaps it might be indicated that perfect similarity of treatment between the two countries as regards local government is our platform, but negatives would I think be most ill-timed'[37]). As the campaign got under way, other Conservatives too found themselves treading the path of quasi-Liberal nostrums in order to emphasize Liberal divisions and attract the new electorate: Salisbury's Newport speech on 6 October, which he grimly described as an 'egg-dance', was the ultimate example. Churchill affected great admiration of this ('never was there before a public pronouncement more comprehensive in its scope, arranged with more consummate skill, or imparted in a manner more likely permanently to impress'); with Akers-Douglas and others, he henceforth cast himself in the role of keeping Salisbury 'up to Newport'.[38] On 19 October, he performed his own egg-dance at King's Lynn, opposing the candidature of Joseph Arch, where he was subjected to violent heckling. His own record at Woodstock was instanced as an earnest of Tory good intentions towards the agricultural interests; Bright was taken as authority for a Panglossian picture of the condition of agricultural society, and Chamberlain's description of exploitation dismissed as urban ignorance. A theme throughout was Bright's disagreement with Chamberlain's supposed ideas. On larger issues, the dance became distinctly faltering. A Protectionist kite was flown in the assertion that the import of foreign grain had brought down agricultural wages; free and compulsory education was criticized on the grounds that it would 'deprive many a struggling

---

[37] Churchill to Salisbury, 1 Oct. 1885; Hatfield House MSS 3M/Churchill/152.

[38] See Churchill to Salisbury, 8 Oct. 1885, Hatfield House MSS 3M/Churchill/155. Akers-Douglas to Churchill, n.d. but Nov. 1885, RCHL ix/1056, which shows them attempting to get Salisbury to repeat the performance.

cottage home of the earnings which might be afforded to it by the labour of a healthy boy or girl', but a compromise payment of a penny a week suggested. Allotments were supported on principle, but the 'folly and absurdity' of the three-acre scheme were demonstrated, as hypothetically applied to Norfolk. Chamberlain, as the cleverest man in public life, must know this; which demonstrated the 'intense dishonesty and flagrant immorality' of the Radicals. Churchill himself, however, believed in local bodies being entrusted with restricted powers to purchase smallholdings, without compulsion.

At the same time, he described himself as a frequent supporter of Radical suggestions, and *The Times* saw the whole speech as deliberately outbidding Chamberlain: an analysis subscribed to by Chamberlain himself, in public and private. ('R. Churchill is funny,' he wrote to Dilke, 'dead against free schools and proposing board schools. Dead against the local authorities and then giving them all the powers if they go through the form of provisional orders. It is a sign of weakness to follow us so closely and yet not to dare to go all the way.'[39]) This approach was dictated, not only by the tactic of emphasizing Whig–Radical divisions, but also by the fact that Churchill was challenging Chamberlain on his own ground in Birmingham. He had also agreed to stand for South Paddington, as a favour to the local association, who were trying to avoid an embarrassing clash between two rival candidates—one of whom, Churchill's friend L. L. Cohen, was persuaded to stand instead for North Paddington.[40] But Churchill made it clear that he could take no part in the London contest, and all his attention was directed to Birmingham: he solicited honours for local Tories from Salisbury, visited the constituency repeatedly, and worked hard to capitalize upon the populist Conservative recovery which temporarily dominated the city's politics in the late 1880s (though the pairing of Conservative with Liberal municipal wards enabled the Liberals to retain all seven parliamentary seats).[41] His public references to Bright were always laudatory and sometimes eulogistic, though Bright chose never to mention

[39] Chamberlain to Dilke, 20 Oct. 1885, Chamberlain MSS 5/24/440. For the speech, much of which is not printed in Jennings, see *The Times*, 20 Oct. 1885.

[40] Carnarvon was the go-between in this arrangement; see his diary for 26 Feb. 1888, BL Add. MS 60924, and correspondence of the time in BL Add. MS 60857.

[41] See C. Green, 'Birmingham's politics, 1873–1891: the local basis of change', in *Midland History*, 2, pp. 84–98 (1973–4).

Churchill at all. Chamberlain was presented time and time again as the real Liberal leader, with Derby, Goschen, and Hartington as his 'sulky followers' (on one occasion, he omitted to mention Gladstone altogether). Industrial depression was a frequent theme, and the protectionist hints dropped at Bow and Cambridge were amplified in Birmingham, notably in his reply to a labourers' deputation complaining of unemployment. Newspapers saw him as playing for the middle ground, and emphasizing issues susceptible to party co-operation; in his first Birmingham speech he emphasized the recent change in the nature of parties and what they stood for. The Tories had become the party of the great towns, the Radicals of Continental-style Socialism and state dictatorship; 'the Tories have changed for the better and the Radicals for the worse'. The Radicals opposed Imperial federation, and dissembled their predatory intentions towards the Church and the Lords. Birmingham had its special requirements; but the same messages were repeated at Worcester on 4 November, of Chamberlain's supremacy and the threat to the Church.

By this point, Churchill was confiding to amused audiences that if the press did not report him, he would give the same speech everywhere: otherwise, the search for novelty was liable to produce incoherence. (Perhaps this inured his listeners to the odd reversal whereby he was now emphasizing that Egypt could not be evacuated, while Gladstone was calling for speedy withdrawal.) The real message came in his delineation of the Tory programme as embracing local government reform, franchise extensions, and procedure (which he went into in detail, while not mentioning closure): all to be dealt with in a manner 'to excite the co-operation of all parties'. Ireland was conspicuously unmentioned. In the inevitable answering speech, Chamberlain pointed this out, asked what had happened to Churchill's suggestions about leasehold enfranchisement, Fair Trade, and allotments, and reminded the eulogist of Bright that the year before he had referred to him not only as calculating and mean, but also as squalid and corrupt.

Perhaps this public response, which also drew attention to Churchill's decorum and dullness since his elevation to office, helped spark off the speech at Manchester on 6 November in which Churchill launched his famously offensive attack on Hartington and Whiggery. After some insider taunts about Childers and Rosebery offering Home Rule to Ireland, and the

Irish reaction to Dilke's and Chamberlain's projected visit, he moved on to Hartington's 'disreputable evasions, stammerings and stutterings and haltings and hesitations', while Chamberlain forced plans for unequal taxation and compulsory division of land down his throat. Going to Belfast 'to hunt up Irish Whigs', the Marquis had endeavoured to strike a number of bargains in fuddled after-dinner speeches, hinting at coalition with the Tories and at the same time accusing them of allying with Parnell—this from an author of the Kilmainham treaty, who shifted ground on every policy, 'doggedly swallowing bit by bit all the great morsels of political programme which Mr Chamberlain chucks at him'. This violent attack culminated in the breathtakingly offensive image of Hartington as a force-fed boa constrictor. The whole attack hung on the rather inadequate grounds of Hartington having recently accused Tory Democracy of lacking political principles: Tory Democracy which, according to Churchill, had taken the place of the Whigs in the political spectrum, and stood for peace, retrenchment, the retention of Church establishment, and—much less emphasized—social and administrative reform.

Hartington's violent personal reaction to this attack is usually stressed, but the effect of the speech deserves more analysis. It was certainly brought about in part by Churchill's exhaustion of ideas, and his boredom with the restraint he had been practising at Birmingham; but it was also of a piece with his taunting of Whiggery at Sheffield: by contrast Radicalism was, once again, 'straight forward and honest'. The fact that he was addressing Lancashire Tories was also important: Churchill cast himself as the defender of Tory Democracy against Hartington's 'scurrilous' aspersions. Most of all, it was a public attack on an electoral tactic by which Churchill was privately preoccupied, the supposed Tory–Whig co-operation over seats in Ulster threatened by the Nationalists. As with all Churchill's speeches in the latter part of the campaign, it not only avoided the Irish issue, but also avoided confronting directly the issues raised by Chamberlain's 'unauthorised programme'. At Manchester he made far less capital out of the Disestablishment threat, the great Conservative cry of the election, than might have been expected: especially as he pressed the issue hard upon Salisbury in private. The exigencies of his Birmingham candidature had produced a situation where there seemed almost a public collusion between Chamberlain and himself.

The terms of public rhetoric were defined after 11 November by the commencement of Gladstone's Midlothian campaign, and this provided the material for Churchill's speech when he returned to Birmingham on 13 November: the Scottish journey was brilliantly pictured as the final staging post of an exhausted theatre troupe on tour. More significantly, Gladstone was attacked for declaring (in Churchill's view) an intention to 'silence the Irish voice' in the next parliament, a voice which now spoke unanimously for the first time. In retrospect, this is more striking than the concentration upon Church and state which distinguished both this and Churchill's final speech in Birmingham (a direct response to Gladstone's attempt on 11 November to remove the issue from the political arena). In his final performance, Churchill recurred to the essential similarity of Conservatism and moderate Liberalism; he apologized to the Birmingham Corporation for his language about them at the time of the Aston incident; reform of local government and land tenure was promised for the future; an imperial foreign policy was solemnly pledged. Chamberlain figured as the real Liberal leader, a leader to whom Bright and Cowen were as opposed as was Churchill himself; yet again, 'the Tory party, which in old days may have been misguided, may have been too unwilling to contemplate change, may have been too reluctant to move with the times, has taken the place of the Liberal party'. And he finally came out for protection, blaming free trade for the lengthy economic depression, and instancing France and Germany as examples of countries with elaborate protectionist systems and a low cost of living. Empire and trade were indispensable: foreign policy should stake out new markets, and domestic policy protect them. Ireland was only touched upon in order to make the point that events had proved coercive legislation unnecessary.[42] Chamberlain riposted in the kind of open dialogue which had been a feature of the campaign throughout: as was the spirit of his reply, conveying appreciation of Churchill's ability and amusement at his inconsistency.

The results of this election, fought with indulgence towards Radicals and virulence towards Whigs, were as traumatic for Churchill as for any other Tory: the narrowness of his own defeat in Birmingham reflected great gains in the boroughs, but this was soon followed by the disillusionment of the county

---

[42] See *The Times*, 21 Nov. 1885 (not printed in Jennings).

returns. This was seen as the outcome of a brilliant confidence-
trick by the Radicals epitomized in the slogan of 'three acres and
a cow'. 'The yokels in Dorsetshire and some parts of Norfolk are
already beginning to smell a rat instead of the cow', wrote Lady
Dorothy Nevill gaily to Churchill; 'the last report is that our
J. C. [Chamberlain] is to give £400,000 for Houghton, all the
Prince of Wales's servants and labourers voted *en masse* for Arch!'
Churchill put it more compactly to Roberts: 'we have been jolly
well sold by the counties'.[43] The parliamentary result, with the
Parnellites holding the exact balance between Liberals and
Conservatives, produced an equally succinct conclusion in a
note from Labouchere to Churchill: 'we shall have to cut you
out with the Irish'. From early December, Churchill impatiently
awaited the announcement of a Home Rule initiative by
Gladstone.

At the same time, his restless mind and febrile political energy
canvassed strategies and policies with anyone who would listen.
In October he had told Labouchere that the divisions among
Liberals would give the Conservatives two or three years in office
even with 280 seats. Carnarvon nervously recorded in early
December

a very remarkable conversation with R. Churchill, the principal
features of which were his great cleverness and a certain grasp of his
whole case. But his rashness mingled with great ignorance on certain
points was very alarming. His present plan is to reply himself on the
Address to the opposition if Beach will agree, to give a conciliatory *non
possumus* to Home Rule, then if successful to proceed with procedure
rules which will spend five or six weeks, during which time he expects
outrages and outbreaks not to fill up my place, but to govern by Lords
Justices and then when things grow bad send out Wolseley.[44]

Regarding Ireland, this remained more or less the core of his
strategy: FitzGibbonism triumphant. In terms of party balance
at Westminster, the picture is more blurred. The main piece of
evidence, much used by his biographers, is an immense memorandum drawn up by Churchill before all the election results
came through, and sent to Salisbury on 3 December. This
argued for coalition with Whigs on the basis of a new programme; authorities like Gwendolen Cecil and Winston

---

[43] Lady Dorothy Nevill to Churchill, n.d., RCHL xi/1234; Churchill to Roberts, 11
Dec. 1885, Roberts MSS 7101-23-21/17.

[44] Carnavon MSS, dated '29.11.85?' in BL Add. MS 60825.

Churchill pointed out that all his suggested policies were calculated to facilitate fusion, including as they did abolition of intestate primogeniture, enfranchisement of future leaseholds, and universal extension of local government powers, with purely popular election by ratepayers. Such ideas were gently and inevitably rejected by Salisbury as either insubstantial or unnecessarily offensive. How far Churchill intended a Whig coalition at the time is, in fact, debatable, though he declared himself prepared to stand down in order to make way for it. He admitted that the Whigs would probably have to refuse places in the government at the moment; he himself had done his best, in his election speeches, to make it impossible for men like Hartington and Goschen (the very names he suggested to Salisbury) to come over without appearing to be utterly absorbed. More important is the order of priorities regarding policy in his memorandum to Salisbury: parliamentary procedure, departmental reform (economizing and rationalizing all public departments), and his Indian Inquiry, could all be approached on an inter-party basis *without* coalition, and thus gain time. A policy of 'progressive measures' in the spheres of land, local government, and education was attractive, and pressed on him by Tory Democrats in early December; but as Churchill knew, the Whigs could at the moment only refuse. James knew of these ideas, and thought 'the mode of proceeding' not feasible, but 'the substance not impossible'; he was himself more inclined towards co-operation than many others.[45] The Whigs whom Churchill approached were those who were already in his circle. ('It is odd that you and I should have at the same moment the idea of negotiating for a coalition through Rothschild', wrote Wolff on 7 December; 'it is a development of this new Bhuddism [*sic*].') At the same time as making these overtures, Churchill was visiting Labouchere in Brighton, and misleading him about schemes to make Beach Speaker and Churchill himself Leader; he also declared to Labouchere a *non possumus* for Home Rule, and a desire for Hartington's support. The first week of December was devoted to such feints and soundings.

At the same time, a positive line on Ireland had to be produced; and here advice from across St. George's Channel played a peculiar part. Notably, a closely reasoned letter from

[45] James to Churchill, RCHL x/1127; n.d., but written from Blankney, where Chaplin was trying to sound him out (see Chaplin to Churchill, 8 Dec. 1885, ibid., 1153).

Chief Justice Morris on 5 December counselled that 'now a put-down-your-foot-and-stand-no-nonsense-policy is impracticable', and suggested an inter-party committee including Parnell to consider a solution within the imperial framework. Churchill framed a reply in impeccable *non possumus* terms, arguing that the Irish issue was deadlocked, and even if a dissolution on a Gladstonian Home Rule Bill eventually returned a parliament committed to 'Repeal', this was as it should be: 'the Disraeli epoch of constant metamorphoses of principles and party has passed away. Radical work must be done by Radical artists, thus less mischief will arise.' He kept a copy of this letter, which was written in terms more formal than his usual exchanges with Morris; it seems to have been scheduled for possible publication, and interestingly, Morris's letter was sent on to Salisbury, with a strong recommendation of Morris's wisdom and foresight; a copy of Churchill's answer, of which Salisbury warmly approved, followed later. Similarly on 10 December, in a pious letter about Carnarvon's perfidy, Churchill none the less promised Salisbury to support 'whatever course you finally decide upon . . . no matter what may be the result'.

Thus some options were being left open; but it is likely that he was influenced considerably by a powerful letter from FitzGibbon on 7 December, advising him to open parliament with strong initiatives in the spheres of foreign affairs, Indian administration, and Irish education, but as regards 'the National Question—*for Heaven's sake don't touch it! It is red hot.*'[46] The argument from Howth continued with a reasoned, sceptical, and intransigently unionist rationale against doing anything positive in the nationalist direction: a line more or less followed by Churchill from this point on, though this and other letters of the time imply that Dublin Tories had doubts about their ally's soundness. FitzGibbon's emphasis was against any idea of a Tory scheme, and in favour of pressing hard the University outline delicately tested out with Molloy and Walsh in Dublin; Churchill amplified such ideas to Salisbury, notably in his memorandum, which reads very much like a deliberate demonstration of Churchill's ability for executive power in Ireland. By the time this was written, it had become clear that Carnarvon must go; the idea for his replacement was a firm Chief Secretary with a Cabinet base, the part for which Churchill was shortly to cast himself.

[46] RCHL x/1149. For a full quotation see Foster, 'Northern Counties Station', p. 264.

In terms of party politics, by the first Cabinet meeting on 14 December he had heard from Labouchere and others that Gladstone was 'mad to come in', that Chamberlain felt Home Rule was not a horse to back, that Parnell now felt there was little to be expected from the Conservatives. The position, fluid since the election, was setting hard. 'Kites' declaring Gladstone's commitment to Home Rule were flown in the *Liverpool Post* and the *Daily News* on 11 and 12 December; by 14 December, the *Pall Mall Gazette* categorically stated that he was at work on a scheme. As regarded the immediate question of whether to stay in office and meet parliament, and if so on what grounds, Churchill knew Salisbury wanted to starve Gladstone out by avoiding an early resignation. Most important, on 9 December Salisbury had replied doubtfully to Churchill's memorandum offering a programme to attract Whigs and stay in office, and Churchill had interpreted the answer as expressing an ill-considered preference 'to make your programme rather rigidly orthodox Tory, with a view of expanding it into Whig heresy when the time for a fusion should seem to have arrived'. In a long letter on 9 December, Churchill presented himself as the voice of conscience, calling Salisbury back to 'the Newport programme' and 'an active, progressive—I risk the word, a democratic policy, a casting off and burning of those old, worn-out aristocratic and class garments from which the Derby–Dizzy lot, with their following of county families, could never, or never cared to extricate themselves'. If Salisbury repudiated the announcement of such a policy Churchill declared he would accept the decision, but felt it made immediate resignation a matter of necessity: a step he advised again the next day, this time on the grounds of Carnarvon's now declared Home Rule sympathies. This was the policy with which he was identified by the time the Cabinet met on 14 December.

From this first assembly, colleagues like Cranbrook assumed Churchill's priority was to break up the government before meeting parliament, and thus free his hands for mischief: and in many ways his actions bear this out. At meetings on 14 and 15 December, the Cabinet rejected Carnarvon's recommendations for a committee to consider a devolutionary measure and considered Churchill's proposals for procedural reform. When these were put aside on 15 December, Churchill astounded his colleagues by offering his resignation (though not all of them heard it at the time). In a letter to Salisbury the next day, he

effectively withdrew it in a lengthy, hectoring outburst, declaring
that he had been shattered by Salisbury's repudiation and
Beach's 'treachery' on the issue; he concluded with a blatant
threat to disrupt proceedings further, veiled as an attack on
Beach ('Beach shall soon discover that in the House of Commons
he cannot stand alone, not even with the help of all the holy old
men, or holy young men'). Akers-Douglas was sent an equally
despairing salvo the same day. Salisbury, understanding the
implication, sent a carefully worded letter of reconciliation
(going so far in his original draft as to suggest holding Cabinet
meetings in a room where Churchill could smoke). 'Believe
me—you cannot be more anxious to be "free" than I am', he
wrote, adding that procedural reform had not been ruled out,
and would be recurred to. Churchill took this as acquiescence,
and characteristically over-interpreted it: within a few days he
was circulating his procedural ideas among colleagues, and
informing them that this was being done at Salisbury's request.
Procedure can be taken, in this context, as a mechanism for
inter-party co-operation. In the meantime, however, he had
done his best to quarrel, not only with Salisbury, but also with
Beach; he had told James that there was no longer any chance of
Whig coalition;[47] he told Dufferin that the government would
go out on an amendment vote of confidence as soon as
parliament met. Carnarvon judged his resignation offer as an
unpremeditated personal outburst,[48] but Churchill may have
been attempting to clear the way towards playing a lone hand.
In any case, if he was temporarily nursing any tactics towards
disruption, they were pre-empted by Herbert Gladstone's revelation on 17 December, which effectively identified Gladstone
with Home Rule. The latter's sounding-out of Balfour about a
bipartisan solution, contemptuously rejected by Salisbury, was a
further indication of increasing fluidity. Parnell's reaction to the
sudden movement of the glacier on 17 December characterized
the general expectations held out of the Secretary of State for
India; 'it will set Randolph on the look out for some new deal'.[49]

---

[47] See Hartington to Duchess of Manchester, 15 Dec. 1885: 'H. James told me that he
saw R. Churchill at the Oppenheims' in a very bad humour. He said that he was to
understand that all that he had said to him before was completely at an end; and that
now their only object would be to harm us.' A. B. Cooke and J. R. Vincent (eds.),
'Ireland and party politics 1885–7: an unpublished Conservative memoir', part iii, *Irish
Historical Studies*, xvi, no. 64, p. 457.

[48] Carnarvon to Cranbrook, 19 Dec. 1885, Cranbrook MSS HA 43 T501/262.

[49] William O'Brien, *Evening Memories* (London, 1925), p. 99.

Chapter 8

Die-hard Politics, 1886

Clithering was much worse off than Alice. In her
story all the cards came to life, and though the
unexpectedness of their behaviour made things
difficult for her there was a certain consistency
about the whole business. A card player might in
time adjust himself to a game played with cards
which possessed wills of their own. But poor
Clithering had to play with a pack in which one suit
only, and it not even the trump suit, suddenly
insisted that the game was a reality. The other
three suits, the Liberals, the Conservatives, and the
Irish Nationalists, still behaved in the normal way,
falling pleasantly on top of each other, and winning
or losing tricks as the rules of the game demanded.
The Ulster party alone—Clubs, we may call them—
would not play fairly. They jumped out of the
player's hand and obstinately declared that the
green cloth was a real battlefield. The higher court
cards of the suit . . . Clithering felt himself able to
control. It was the knaves, . . . the tens, the sevens,
and the humble twos which behaved outrageously.
   And Clithering was not the only player who was
perplexed.

George A. Birmingham, *The Red Hand of Ulster*
(1912)

I

The news of Gladstone's initiative did not, in fact, set Churchill
to renegotiating terms with the Irish: as he let both Justin
McCarthy and Blunt know at once.[1] His decision to adopt the
'British Philistine' view instead was tied closely in with the
advice he had been receiving from Howth, as well as the current

---

[1] See J. McCarthy and Mrs Campbell Praed, *Our Book of Memories* (London, 1912), p.
28: 'His party thought they had no chance with Home Rule after Gladstone had taken it
up, and they had therefore better drop it and take to the British Philistine view.' Also
Churchill to Blunt, 26 Dec. 1885: 'If you want Home Rule you had better go to Mr
Gladstone; we cannot touch it.' Blunt MSS 306/1977, also quoted in *Land War in Ireland*;
and Churchill to Roberts, 18 Dec. 1885, RCHL x/1186 (copy).

of opinion he had plumbed within the party. His own position similarly required speedy clarification. The area within which he chose to exercise his own initiative was Ulster: a traditional place of resort for Tory politicians temporarily needing to make a figure or to demonstrate their probity. In Churchill's case, these requirements coincided with his own knowledgeable but limited dimension of Irish unionism; and the story of his Orange Card demonstrates not only how a rhetorical gesture came to be apprehended in terms of reality, but also how the ensuing political situation limited Churchill's future opportunities for the sort of instinctual politics with which he had come to be identified.

This pattern did not declare itself immediately. On 18 December he wrote of Gladstone's initiative to Roberts, adding 'we shall certainly go out of office about the 20th of January ... we ought to be in opposition without loss of time'. With Gladstone preserving his own silence, however, nothing was yet fixed; on 20 December Brett thought Churchill was still planning for an eventual Tory Home Rule scheme to dish Gladstone. The days before Christmas passed in a frenzy of negotiations, with Churchill in continual contact with Labouchere and Rothschild, and involving the Whigs in the government's agonized discussions about the terms on which they would meet parliament in January. The extent to which these confidences were calculated is impossible to gauge; certainly, decent Liberals were shocked by Churchill's disclosure to Labouchere of Gladstone's approach to Balfour ('a breach of confidence of the first order'). For his part, Labouchere was able to tell Churchill on 23 December that Chamberlain reckoned on a majority of Liberals defecting from Gladstone: which Churchill took as evidence for arguing that the government should precipitate events by resigning when parliament met. Salisbury was unconvinced; and by Christmas Eve Churchill felt the government might succeed in hanging on.[2] (His constant reiteration to Labouchere of Conservative readiness to call a dissolution on Home Rule may have been, as Healy surmised, largely bluff.) Churchill told Lytton on 26 December that Gladstone's rashness would keep them in: 'our attitude will be ... orthodox above all suspicion'.[3] Salisbury's dilatory style of

[2] Churchill to Dufferin, 24 Dec. 1885, DVP F 130/3, no. 84.

[3] Lytton MSS, Herts. Record Office; my thanks to the archivist, who kindly supplied me with this quotation.

government, and the dearth of Conservative colleagues who could or would hypothesize politically in an untrammelled way, gave Churchill few other outlets; the drawback was the risk of being fed rank inaccuracies, like Labouchere's allegations that Gladstone was going to support a Home Rule amendment on the address. But Labouchere's urgent Christmas message was probably calculated to appeal strongly to Churchill: 'My object is simply this. I am as sick of great principles as Charles Surface was of his mother's sentiments and I want to squelch the last of these great principles and place the G.O.M.—before parliament meets—in the position that he knows officially that the Conservatives will not deal with Home Rule. This suits me—it may suit you.'[4]

This is the authentic currency of Churchillian discourse; whether it was the normal private medium of exchange among other politicians is debatable but not implausible. ('His political action was guided purely by party consideration', wrote Holmes, the Irish Attorney-General; not in disapproval. 'But in this respect he did not differ from his contemporaries and while he was more capable, he was not less honest than they.'[5]) He had already begun to float the idea of using Protestant feeling in Ulster and Lancashire against a Liberal Home Rule initiative; when he travelled to Dublin for the Howth symposium on 27 December, this strategy was reinforced by a meeting which Holmes arranged between Churchill and the markedly eccentric leader of the Ulster Unionists, Major Saunderson. He was also brought into contact with the Howth circle when they were at their most uneasy. The ethos of Dublin legal Tories, if they had ever been able to consider a devolutionary initiative in a dispassionate way, was by Christmas 1885 rapidly turning Orange, and the process would be completed by Archbishop Walsh's threat to Trinity College the following month: which seemed to FitzGibbon to give the lie to Churchill's strategy of diverting nationalism by an educational alliance with the bishops. For his part, Churchill was in a state of high nervous energy, terrifying the Viceroy in a two-hour conversation on New Year's day. 'He is very clever and ingenious and has many far-reaching thoughts,' wrote Carnarvon in his diary; 'but he is over-rash and if he guides the chariot of the Sun he may easily set our English world on fire. He has an attractive side to his

[4] Labouchere to Churchill, 25 Dec. 1885, RCHL x/1206.
[5] Cooke and Vincent, 'Ireland and party politics', i, *Ir. Hist. Stud.*, xvi, no. 62, p. 163.

character and is open to the influence of counsel and prudence. But—.'⁶

It was after his return from Howth at New Year that Churchill began to float FitzGibbon's ideas for 'permanent legislation for the preservation of social order' in Ireland rather than temporary coercive expedients, 'special' in nature and useless for curbing either the League or boycotting. Otherwise, his energy was chiefly devoted to finding out from Labouchere what Gladstone's expectations of support were, information for which he traded titbits about the Conservative plans for the Queen's Speech. Expectation succeeded expectation, and Churchill's letters to Salisbury bristled with conflicting gossip; contacts like Buckle and Escott (whose rooms Churchill used on visits to Brighton) were worked to the full; but one of the few accurate pieces of information to be vouchsafed him did not come until 12 January, when Chamberlain told him of the plan to engineer an anti-government majority on Jesse Collings's amendment. By then, in any case, a definite approach to Ireland had to be settled upon, and this had dictated Churchill's manœuvres. In Cabinet on 9 January he had traduced Ashbourne's description of the bad state of Ireland as 'vague and unsatisfactory', complaining violently to Carnarvon afterwards; 'I spoke out strongly against the Cabinet being influenced by anything but facts and figures.'⁷ He was at the same time infuriated by his colleagues' lack of imagination over introducing a local government bill ('a large good bill, probably as good as any other measure which the other side could produce'): he had previously wanted a measure for Ireland prepared. Similarly, he had pressed his plans for procedure once more: possibly as a vehicle for staying in office. But on 9 January, he told Rothschild of his anxiety to resign, and James relayed messages to Harcourt about his readiness to give way to coalition.⁸ By the time of his dinner with Chamberlain and Labouchere on 12 January, impatience and restlessness were

---

⁶ Carnarvon diary for 1 Jan. 1886, BL Add. MS 60926.

⁷ Churchill to Carnarvon, 9 Jan. 1886, BL Add. MS 60825.

⁸ Rothschild told Harcourt of Churchill's desire for resignation, and Harcourt told Hartington (Devonshire MSS, 340/1877); and James told Harcourt of Churchill's readiness to give way to Hartington, and his apology. Harcourt then dressed James down for cultivating such an 'unscrupulous' person as Churchill, giving rise to the supposition he was 'in Randolph Churchill's pocket'. 'James replied "He never gets anything out of me and I get a great deal out of him", a remark which I should think is very wide of the truth' (LHJ, 10 and 14 Jan. 1886, vol. 376, pp. 31, 68).

taking over. His general conclusion from this meeting was that Gladstone would 'try conclusions with us immediately'; the next day he embarked upon a flurry of activity. A letter went to Hartington, apologizing for the Manchester speech and using the India Inquiry as a counter to re-establish relations (though, this priority achieved, Hartington was assured that the Inquiry might come to nothing). The news of Carnarvon's resignation leaked out that day (it had been confided by Churchill to FitzGibbon well before): and in Cabinet Churchill joined Cranbrook in pressing for a tough appointment (Wolseley) to succeed him. On the 13th also, Bradlaugh was permitted by the speaker to take the oath in the newly opened parliament, confounding Churchill's and Beach's plan for an Affirmation Bill debate. And probably on the same day, Churchill informed a scandalized Holmes of his plan simultaneously to arrest all the nationalist members on a charge of high treason and proclaim the National League.

This idea had been outlined a few days before to Blunt by Algernon Bourke, but Churchill had been described as opposing it; Blunt, who while lecturing Churchill about Ireland on 8 January had apprehensively noticed 'an odd mischievous look' cross his face, was not so sure. On 14 January Churchill, despite his opposition to Northcote's wish for a coercive clause in the Queen's Speech, and his criticism of Ashbourne's lack of information on 9 January, was writing to Dufferin that the state of Ireland was very grave and needed strong measures; on 15 January, he pressed his draconian plan on the Cabinet, accompanied by the embarrassed Holmes. Though it received a considerable amount of support, the initiative was rejected.

Superficially this adoption of an extreme policy seems to indicate a change of direction, but it can represent an underlying consistency, if seen as directed towards staying in office. Churchill's assurances to Liberals of his desire to get out in early January tended to follow Cabinet defeats, and need not be implicitly believed; though he disagreed with Beach's 'preposterous' idea of playing for time by a three-week adjournment, their basic plans ran closely together. The scheme for suppression of the League makes more sense in tactical terms when it is linked with the measures for land purchase and local-government reform in Ireland with which Churchill wished to accompany it; and all the more when it is remembered that he told Holmes that he himself was prepared to go to Ireland as

Chief Secretary to carry it out (an idea he also floated to Salisbury). Carnarvon, appalled at Churchill's plan, thought it merely bluffing: 'a sort of feint to cover all proposals'. But it was perfectly in line with the advice of FitzGibbon and other Irish friends, to use the criminal law for outlawing combinations, rather than temporary or arbitrary measures: 'precedents are to be found in the laws of every turbulently inclined country except our own'.[9] This opposition to 'coercion', as the phrase was understood, was based on its inability to cope with the League, and the parliamentary impossibility of sustaining a defence of the policy based on 'outrage' figures, which had declined considerably since October. Even after parliament opened, he described the policy of suppressing the National League and introducing a Land Bill as 'the only method of averting defeat on Jesse Collings'; indeed, some Liberal opinion thought it 'very difficult for us to oppose a scheme of this kind'.[10] He still had hopes of taking up a month with procedure, which he and Beach continued to press. And, again with Beach, he stood out against a traditionally conceived 'Coercion' Bill, implicitly pointing out to Salisbury in a long letter on 16 January that the success of such a policy in parliament depended upon his acquiescence, and that he could not see his way. Though Churchill weakened under pressure on 17 January, he and Beach continued to object to coercive legislation, for which opposition Salisbury blamed the weakness of the Queen's Speech. When he finally agreed to a coercive measure in the Cabinet of 23 January, it was probably (as he told James) because he had realized the Whigs were for it too. But he must have expected Whig support by his speech of 21 January, when parliament opened: he ironically dared Parnell to raise a Home Rule amendment, pointing out that the Queen's Speech contained a passage of 'so indubitable a form' as to give him no choice. Topics like Burma and Jesse Collings's amendment were irrelevant; a debate on Ireland, or failing that a straightforward inter-party discussion of procedure (instigated by Beach the day before), would enable the government 'to fulfil their duty ... on reasonably honourable terms' (laughter).[11] He also held out the promise of Irish local government in the future: thus he played for time in public as well as in private. He had by

---

[9] FitzGibbon to Churchill, 18 Jan. 1886, RCHL xi/1355; Carnarvon diary, 15 Jan. 1886, BL Add. MS 60926.

[10] LHJ, 24 Jan. 1886, vol. 377, p. 4.

[11] *Hansard 3*, cccii, 173.

now, however, got the 'feel' of the new parliament, and two days later he and Beach succumbed; on 26 January a coercion Bill was announced, Collings's amendment debated, and the government defeated at 1 a.m. the following morning.

In the final debate, curiously, Churchill and Beach contributed to a miscalculation whereby Collings's amendment came on sooner than Salisbury wished; a mollifying counter-amendment which Salisbury had arranged to buy more time was cut out by Churchill's prematurely taking the floor. This was probably unintentional; it would certainly have been inconsistent for him to cut short the government's life, though as he kept telling Balfour at this time, 'in politics there is no looking beyond the next fortnight'. Certainly, going out of office was not the unalloyed pleasure which it seemed to his colleagues, though his high spirits were noted at the Carlton supper after the division. By 30 January, in any case, he knew not only that the possibility of a Hartington–Salisbury government, which he had hypothesized to Rothschild on 27 January, would not present itself; but also that Parnell would no longer be fobbed off with a Land Bill.[12] At the Prince of Wales's on 3 February Rosebery found Churchill angry at the Irish and disillusioned with his career. Of the journey to Osborne to hand in the seals on 6 February Harrowby recorded: 'we had a cheerful luncheon, all very bright; but Randolph was low, and said he feared Gladstone was in for 6 years'. A newspaper correspondent on 8 February was struck by his moody figure, glowering behind a Carlton window at a rowdy demonstration below.[13]

He had cause for reflection. In the few weeks since the solidifying of Gladstone's known intentions before Christmas, Churchill had—unlike most Conservatives—cultivated the opposition, hypothesized about potential combinations, worked out strategies for staying in power, visited Ireland, conceived an initiative which would disrupt the position of the Irish at Westminster, reintroduced his gambit for inter-party action, and made himself deliberately difficult in Cabinet. A recurrent wish to have his hands untied conflicted with his enjoyment of office, his aggressiveness in Cabinet, and his need of money. Once set free, and sure of the direction of Liberal dissidence, he was ready

---

[12] Blandford to Churchill, 30 Jan. 1886, RCHL xi/1349.
[13] *Weekly Irish Times*, 13 Feb. 1886; also Harrowby MSS, LV/201 (memorandum of visit to Osborne, 6 Feb. 1886). The Queen told her outgoing ministers to 'agitate in every village' over the Irish question.

for a feint in the die-hard direction; and the fact that this took him to Ulster was helped by the increasingly embattled nature of the advice he was receiving from Howth.

II

This, in fact, repeated a pattern of many years' standing: two years before, FitzGibbon had inveighed against Churchill's 'party views of the "Irish Nation"':

'Give the devil is [*sic*] due' and admit that, in return for a very unenlivening and frequently repeated repast of cold potatoes, the Northerners have in honour of Capricorn asserted their own existence and their determination not to be cast off by English politicians ... No doubt the Orange Flag is given to frightening otherwise steady horses, but it is the only one which gathers any *rank and file* together in Ireland who would not cut all you Britishers adrift tomorrow if they could, and cut all *our* throats the day after.[14]

The message was not lost on Churchill, but his public image had always been distinctly antipathetic to what he called 'foul Ulster tories'. His desire to make 'an inflammatory speech in Ulster' in 1880 had been moderated by 'fear of Kane', an extreme Orange clergyman; his shifting stance on the Irish franchise had infuriated Ulster: Maamtrasna had seemed the logical culmination of this development. But there was a countering tradition. His mother was a Londonderry; the Bradlaugh affair had identified him with unreconstructed Protestantism; his stance on the Rossmore incident had been impeccably Orange; his speeches in Scotland had rung out hard-line Protestant unionism. The Orange card seemed discounted by the Tories in the formation of the caretaker ministry, but the results of the election predicted a different development.

Ulster unionist opinion had been solidifying since early 1885; by the end of the year, both its parliamentary organization and its public rhetoric had reached a new pitch. On 30 December, Saunderson called for armed resistance and a civil war if the government yielded to the Parnellites; the Ulster view of the government, always jaundiced, had become antagonistic in a way that worried Beach, Salisbury, and Churchill, who corresponded on the matter in tones of distaste. But with the deadlock of December, the importance of Ulster unionism to the

---

[14] FitzGibbon to Churchill, 11 Oct. 1883, RCHL ii/181.

Tories escalated—as it always did in a crisis. (As FitzGibbon pointed out to Churchill, they stood to the Conservatives in the same relation as the Fenians to Parnell, or the Whigs to Gladstone: the unimaginative orthodoxy from which, in calmer times, the leadership liked to feel able to deviate.) In December, Churchill floated to Hawarden via Labouchere a threat to agitate Ulster; after Christmas he met Saunderson in Dublin; on 21 January he offered himself to Saunderson for a speaking engagement; by early February his intention to visit Belfast was known.

Strategic opportunism obviously played a large part, but his appearance as a leader in the Rossmore agitation, and the influence on him of beleaguered Dublin Toryism, should not be forgotten. Nor should the pattern of contacts which comes into focus when considering the background to this involvement. His wife's much loved sister had married into a notably Orange Monaghan family, the Leslies (and her husband accompanied Churchill to Belfast). Lord George Hamilton, though he did not like Churchill, was a close political associate, anxious for him to visit Ulster; even the colourful Major Saunderson had a marginally Churchillite record as leader of a parliamentary ginger group determined to 'give it hot to Northcote', though he distrusted Churchill and told him so at their Dublin meeting. Most of all, the breakdown of FitzGibbon's overtures to Archbishop Walsh, and the latter's threat to the bastion of Irish Ascendancy interests in mid-January, inevitably turned Churchill from intriguing with Catholics to cultivating Orangeism.

It is notable that in Churchill's public declaration of violent unionism on 13 February at Paddington, Walsh was prominent in the Protestant demonology conjured up by the new convert. Though Wolff saw it as 'Fourth Party form, toned down by the caution of the ex-minister',[15] it is hard to see where the caution came in. Throughout, the word 'Protestant' was unequivocally used instead of 'loyalist' or 'unionist': 'England will not leave the Protestants of Ireland in the lurch.'

They are essentially like the English people, a dominant and an imperial caste. It was only Mr Gladstone—it was only the insanity which was engendered by the monstrous and unparalleled combination of verbosity and senility—it was only Mr Gladstone who could for a

[15] Wolff to Churchill, RCHL xii/1393.

moment imagine the Protestants of Ireland would yield obedience to the law, would recognize the powers or would satisfy the demands of a parliament in Dublin—a parliament of which Mr Parnell would be the chief speaker and Archbishop Walsh the chief priest.

Gladstone's policy was really Repeal, and forced the Protestants of Ireland into a policy of civil war: they could only be 'conquered by force of arms'. On his forthcoming visit to Belfast he promised to assure the Protestants that 'there were hundreds and thousands of English hearts, and also hands, ready when the moment of trial came'. This was fair warning: in fact, it was more categorically inflammatory than anything he actually said in Ulster. It was followed by a campaign in the Liberal press to have him arrested for incitement, while Tory pundits saw it as a restoration of Conservatism to its proper public role. Churchill followed it up with a public letter to a troubled Catholic correspondent, arguing that Catholics were given full freedom in Ireland since 'all vestiges of Protestant ascendancy have been swept away', but that the nationalist struggle had aligned creed against creed. Repeal meant 'the most bitter and terrible oppression of Protestants by Catholics'. 'What wonder that I as a Protestant should cast in my lot with my co-religionists in Ireland?'[16]

It was easy to write this volte-face off to ready opportunism, which is what Irish opinion did; and to retrospective judgement, the deliberate exaggeration of religious antipathies may seem the most reprehensible aspect of the manœuvre. In contemporary terms, however, the striking element in the speech is its evasion of substantial criticism of the Home Rule principle; a vague definition of 'Repeal of the Union' enabled him to take refuge in 'constitutionalist' and religious rodomontade, of a type calculated to appeal to Lancashire Tory Democracy as much as to Ulster revivalism. Much of the speech was, in fact, a demonstration of the popular and national nature of Toryism, and was designed to reassure his audience that the Conservative strategy on Irish coercion was purely consistent, and in no way linked to calculations respecting the Irish vote. He also revealed that the Salisbury government had been prepared to grant 'measures which would to a large extent have met the legitimate aspirations of the Irish people', in local government, land, and higher education. As the first ex-ministerial utterance of importance

---

[16] Churchill to John O'Shea, 18 Feb. 1886, RCHL xii/1387.

since the government's resignation, it was as much an apologia for their uneasy course on Irish policy as an earnest of what was to come.

It is interesting that Churchill wrote to *The Times* to moderate its first report of the speech (including a reference to O'Shea and Galway which described the new member as one considered 'loathsome and repugnant from every point of view'—a broad hint about his private position). But it set the tone for other Tories; on 17 February Salisbury delivered a die-hard speech on Ireland, emphasizing that the Protestants were threatened with 'absolute slavery' under Parnell. The necessity for demonstrating unimpeachable sentiments on Ulster was further shown by a violent Carlton meeting on 19 February, where Churchill was attacked publicly for his Irish flirtations having landed the Conservatives in perplexity. He was defended by his new ally, Saunderson, who brusquely told a protesting Catholic Conservative peer that 'all Protestants might now be considered to be ranged on one side of the question, and all Catholics on the other'.[17]

This may have been something of an embarrassment for Churchill, but worse was in store. The plans for his Ulster meeting went on apace, under the management of the uncomfortably bellicose Dr Kane and William Johnston of the Orange Order, who determined early on to impose upon Churchill's visit a distinctively Orange colour.[18] Others involved in the organization included Lord Arthur Hill, Lord Deramore, W. E. McCartney, Lord Rossmore, and Saunderson. Churchill's arrival in Ulster and journey to Belfast on 22 February provided the occasion for vast scenes of Protestant demonstration, and an ecstasy bordering on hysteria. His own peculiar position regarding Irish affairs was evaded, or ingeniously presented: addresses at Larne and Carrickfergus and his reply to them emphasized his father's viceroyalty as a golden moment in the country's troubled past. His exhortations were less belligerent than at Paddington: while reminding those who greeted him that their privileges might be 'worth fighting for', he added that such a trial was unlikely to be put upon them. Responding to Orange Lodge addresses, he emphasized his own Ulster ancestors rather than contemporary

---

[17] *Pall Mall Gazette*, 19 Feb. 1886.
[18] See *Weekly Examiner and Ulster Weekly News*, 13 Feb. 1886. Kane had previously declared, regarding Churchill's supposed nationalist sympathies, that if he ever set foot in Ulster, 'things would be made very unpleasant for him': ibid., 6 Feb. 1886.

divisions. In his principal speech, a more die-hard tone appeared: he attacked the Roman Catholic threat to Trinity College, recalled the shadows of 1641, and accused Parnell of dictatorship on an unrepresentative basis. Regarding religion, however, he carefully skirted the kind of identification he had made at Paddington, denying that 'from an English point of view' resistance to Home Rule should be identified with any creed, and disclaiming any wish to stir up religious strife. The corollary of this was that Catholics who were 'loyal' should stand up and be counted, and combat their clergy's support of the National League. If this unlikely appeal failed, however, he 'would be no party to cripple the efforts of the cause which I am anxious to support by any undue or hysterical indulgence of the sensibilities of timid and nervous persons'. If Catholics would not align themselves with Protestants, he had to confine his hopes to the latter, 'and essentially to the Protestants of the great province of Ulster'. If their fate was left in their hands, they should remember 'no surrender', and give practical meaning to the 'forms and ceremonies' of Orangeism. For the moment, they might remain orderly in their demonstrations; the storm might blow over; but 'if my calculations should turn out to be wrong, then I am not of the opinion, and I have never been of the opinion, that this struggle is likely to remain within the lines of what we are accustomed to look upon as constitutional action'.

Whatever subdued attempt the speech included to moderate his Paddington message was swamped in his conclusion, and in the speeches that followed—Saunderson promising another Boyne, and advocating the use of force, and Johnston pledging the audience to fight in a Protestant army. The disturbances that started outside the hall, continued throughout the next weeks, and culminated in the riots of the following June, represented the Ulster response to a rhetoric which had always meant what it said. It is doubtful if Churchill understood this, at the time or later. No more did most English opinion; Salisbury congratulated him on his adroitness in avoiding giving offence to Catholics, *The Times* felt the sectarian nature of the speech was necessary for the circumstances, the Liberal press saw it as a spiteful revenge on the Irish for having declined whatever bargain Churchill had offered, and also a necessary blood-letting for someone 'reverting to the aboriginal type of the Tory rapparee': 'after his seven months of sobriety in office he needs a political debauch'. Even the nationalists in parliament tended to amusement rather than anger ('I daresay you Irish gentlemen will never forgive me for Belfast'—'We are too sorry for you to be angry, you ought to have had a better fate'.[19]) Though an effort was made by Sexton to have him impeached for treasonable incitement, it did his image (as Salisbury pointed out) no harm: in Lancashire as well as Ulster. Those who were most scandalized were those who felt they had been led into the wilderness by Churchill himself—Blunt and Carnarvon.[20] The general view of the political world was that hesitantly expressed by his father-in-law to Lady Randolph: 'I was startled at first and thought he was wrong, but as usual his mistakes turn out to be the right thing after all; I hate religion in politics but I have no doubt in the present instance it is justifiable.'[21] The temperature of politics out of doors in the first six months of 1886 had been raised to an extraordinary level; Churchill's Belfast visit was one of the high points of the Home Rule fever. Its effect was to bring the Ulster unionist case to the forefront of political attention; Churchill himself, his fellow-speakers, and all the Belfast papers dwelt on the previous ignoring of Ulster by Westminster politicians, and predicted that henceforth this could no longer be the case. Nor was it; and the extent to which Churchill himself was identified with this most inflexible of causes cannot have been entirely comfortable for him. His Ulster contacts like Saunderson, Deramore, and Rossmore pursued him indefatigably, demanding favours, extorting support, claiming misrepresentation, complaining about nationalist 'infiltration' in Belfast; unlike his other supplicating correspondents, they never apologized for bothering him. He was Ulster's champion; and his attitude to Ireland could never resume its old flexibility. Much of what he said in Belfast and in his public letters on the question contradicted his previous statements; and it is likely that his private views were closer to Wolff's breezy opinion that in a Home Rule Ireland the Protestants would use their minority guarantees and economic advantages to secure for themselves the whip hand. Nor did he rule out devolution for Dublin. The letters from ultra-Protestant fanatics which flooded on him from Scotland and India as well as Ireland cannot have been

[19] An exchange recorded in William O'Brien, *Evening Memories*, p. 113.
[20] Blunt, *Land War in Ireland*, pp. 31–2; Carnarvon to Harrowby, 27 Feb. 1886, Harrowby MSS LII/87. For Salisbury's reaction see letter of 27 Feb. 1886, RCHL xii/1394a.
[21] L. Jerome to Lady Randolph, 28 Feb. 1886, CHAR 28/1.

welcome; his airy statement in early March admitting that he had 'for a considerable time hoped to be able to work in alliance with the Irish Party' may have been a deliberate attempt to scare such support off.

But the convulsions of 1886 led to a state of affairs where, by May, the Ulster leaders were announcing the preparation of an army of 100,000, and the likelihood that Wolseley and 1,000 defecting British officers would join them; at the same time Churchill was defending his Belfast stance in parliament on the grounds that Ulster's allegiance would be abrogated by the passing of Home Rule legislation, which would inevitably lead to civil war. Though Parnell exonerated Churchill from intentional incitement to bloodshed, Healy quoted Saunderson's statement that Churchill had privately 'asked what force we could raise if it came to civil war'. He was by now inescapably tarred with the Orange brush. By September, with the situation defused, he was complaining to colleagues about 'those Belfast beggars' in his pre-1886 mode, and attempting to silence Saunderson in the House.[22] But the aura of Protestant champion could not be thus easily dispelled.

This was no disadvantage in the eyes of the Tory Democracy, who sounded him out immediately after Belfast with invitations to address working-class audiences in March; their worries about his contacts with the Irish, never really allayed, were for the moment set at rest. Churchill himself did his best to emphasize the separation, violently taking issue with the *Daily News* on 3 March for claiming that he, Carnarvon, and Ashbourne had drafted a Home Rule measure before the ministry fell (an idea spread by Gladstone among others). In this, as in his public letter of 7 May which coined the phrase 'Ulster will fight; Ulster will be right', Churchill described his own record of consistency against 'Repeal of the union', which he carefully defined was what Home Rule meant 'at the present day'. Also on 3 March—the same day as Salisbury spoke at the Crystal Palace—Churchill addressed a large meeting at Manchester in a lengthy speech which vividly reflected his position after Belfast. His opening remarks about the Tory weakness in Commons debate, and his wildly inaccurate state-

---

[22] R. J. Lucas, *Colonel Saunderson, M.P.: a Memoir* (London, 1908), p. 113; Churchill to Gibson, 30 Sept. 1886, Ashbourne MSS B/32/4; Churchill to Morris, 6 Sept. 1886, in Wynne, op. cit.; and Churchill to the Queen on Saunderson's 'deplorable' behaviour, 3 Sept. 1886, Royal Archives B 37/103.

ments about the November election results, gave the opposition
some gratuitous ammunition; but he then proceeded to represent himself as Protestant deliverer, and his address as an
answer to the 'envenomed' assaults on his probity and consistency which had been heaped on him since Belfast. The
Conservatives had never trafficked with Home Rule. The election had been artificial, fought on false issues, with the urban
electorate's wise decision outweighed by the 'less intelligent'
voice of the counties. Gladstone, who had promised in the
election campaign to unite the Liberals and not to consider
Ireland unless he had an independent majority, had proceeded
to split the Liberals and take up Ireland. The British parliament
had been captured by 'Irish repealers and Scotch radicals'; and
he called on Hartington and James to come over with other anti-
Gladstonians and join a new, 'essentially English', party of the
Union, defined against the Separatists (amongst whom he numbered Chamberlain, supposedly meditating his own scheme).
Over the whole speech keynote themes were, as in the election
(and indeed at Belfast), the Empire, India, imperialism, and the
threat to commerce; a kite was flown for bimetallism; increased
army and naval expenditure was demanded (ironically, in view
of the future), the annexation of Burma defended, and the Tories
presented as the party of national unity. It was a classic mixture
for Tory Lancashire, embracing imperialism, commerce, and
chauvinism; but there was no real treatment of Home Rule,
outside Gladstone's alleged plan of 'Repeal'.

The Times, which found the performance prolix and unconvincing, set the tone of reaction by concentrating on the
invitation to coalition. But it was over-ingenuous to separate the
two halves of the speech. For the language Churchill used about
Gladstone's frauds, and his apostrophizing Salisbury as the one
champion who could vanquish the Grand Old Man, made it all
the more difficult for Gladstone's ex-colleagues to join such
company; and his emphasis on his own devotion to, and work
for, the Tory party (not, as *The Times* tartly remarked, for his
country) implied that coalition would mean absorption. As even
the anti-Home Rule Liberal press pointed out, Churchill's new
party on examination turned out to be the old Tory party under
a new alias. Newspaper opinion went on to stress exactly what
Churchill remarked to Salisbury in private a week later: 'there
would be a fusion *if it were not for me*'.[23] In the view of Stead,

[23] My italics. Churchill to Salisbury, 9 Mar. 1886, quoted in R. Rhodes James, p. 235.

what Churchill blocked the way to was any Whig–Tory coalition; the most likely future fusion being 'a party of Despotic Socialism', headed by Chamberlain and Churchill. 'His instincts are democratic and socialist and he is capable of anything, even of coming out as a red-hot Repealer the day after tomorrow if his present bid for the Union meets with no response.'[24] This was an extreme reading: what can be inferred from his speeches is a wish to prevent fusion in any predictable form. But if Churchill's Orange card in February 1886 restored him to the canon of orthodoxy in some Conservative circles, in other areas his opportunism and unreliability seemed more clearly demonstrated than ever; and his own over-reaction in repudiating attacks on this front, his infelicities at Manchester and elsewhere, and some uncharacteristic parliamentary ineptness in the weeks ahead, are further evidence that he had overplayed his hand and placed himself in a more restricted political position than he could occupy with comfort.

III

His parliamentary tactics in the weeks leading up to the Home Rule debate were accordingly irreconcilable, and designed to emphasize above all the purity of the Tory record on Ireland. On 4 March he pressed Holmes to bring on a 'futile' motion to refuse supply, supposedly as a tactic to force Gladstone to debate Ireland. This was widely criticized on his own side but Churchill, 'wild for an Irish row', was insistent. When the initiative proved a fiasco, he unashamedly blamed Holmes's 'voice and manner', and defended the attempt to Salisbury.[25] From his own point of view it had indeed succeeded, as it had given him the opportunity publicly to deny any imputation of electioneering calculation in the Tories' recent Irish record, and to use the debate for a long and rather embarrassing discussion of Tory attitudes to Ireland and his own position in this regard as well as that of others.[26] After admitting that the late

[24] *Pall Mall Gazette*, 4 Mar. 1886.

[25] 9 Mar. 1886; Hatfield House MSS 3M/Churchill/250.

[26] He asked if it were really believable that Salisbury, Cranbrook, Carnarvon, and Northcote were 'so utterly lost to all considerations of political honour and to every consideration of political honesty that they are influenced and only influenced by the meanest and most corrupt motives [cries of "Yes"]'. *Hansard 3*, cccii, 1977. Newspapers interpreted the performance as Churchill 'doing penance in a white sheet'; or alternatively, as breaking under the strain of Sexton's expected impeachment (*Evening Mail*, 4 Mar. 1886, and *Weekly Freeman*, 13 Mar. 1886).

government 'blundered' in its presentation of the Irish situation in January, he said that he had no reason to conceal that he had once wished to work with the Irish party; he hoped to do so again, since the Tories were best equipped to deal with land and education. They had simply never dreamt that Gladstone would go for 'Repeal', or that the National League would become so powerful. And he carefully rehearsed the evidence for Irish order and disorder, and the inability of ordinary coercion to deal with 'a society divided against itself': the Tories had to stand firm against the handing over of the country's administration to the National League. Thus for Churchill's purposes the failure of Holmes's motion to draw Gladstone was only secondary; he had had his chance to deliver his own apologia, and in the process to portray Gladstone's scheme as the extreme of anarchy and Repeal, reserving constructive Irish policy for the Tories. Irish newspapers took it as a full confession; Ulster opinion was correspondingly infuriated.

Otherwise, his strategy in parliament throughout March was curiously uncertain. He took an irreconcilable line on the government's India inquiry, inherited from his own initiative, though Cranbrook tried to persuade him not to. In the Home Rule debate he was to press the Liberal Unionists to the front, leaving them to make the running; but in the previous month he handled Hartington badly, despite their personal *rapprochement* in mid-January. Churchill's parliamentary attacks on the new government concentrated upon Hartington's absence from it, demanding explanations; this was probably as unwelcome to Hartington as to Gladstone (who saved him from having to make a statement by himself replying to Churchill's debate on the address). By April, Churchill was sending anxious notes to keep the Whigs up to the mark in the Commons; Hartington was not particularly receptive, and generally took a line of lofty distaste for Churchill's partisanship. In all this, it is notable that Churchill acted as *de facto* Leader in the Commons; he in fact found Beach 'too polite' and yielding in his treatment of Hartington, and complained of this to Salisbury.

As usual, his relations with Chamberlain are instructive: despite the latter's far more anomalous position, Churchill was much closer to him, sharing criticism of Hartington and plans for Irish strategy. Even while still in Gladstone's government, Chamberlain continued to confide in Churchill: their intimacy was much noted by the press, which may have occasioned

Churchill's covering himself by public gibes at Radicals like Jesse Collings. By the end of March, just out of the government, Chamberlain was transmitting versions of Gladstone's plans to Churchill; Churchill, bringing him together with Salisbury, urged him to avoid floating alternative Irish schemes, to which Chamberlain replied on 6 April: 'as regards National Councils, I certainly shall not put them forward as an alternative. The day has gone by for them and we must try something new.'[27] But the implication of an initiative was soon lost in the organization of debate, which Churchill once again managed, rather than Beach.

On 8 April Gladstone introduced his Home Rule Bill, in a scene that was a great set-piece of Victorian political iconography; Churchill's speech on the first reading came four days later, at a time when backstairs negotiations had still not clarified the degree of dissent within the Liberal ranks. This may have partially accounted for Churchill's moderation, but the tone was still, for him, extraordinarily muted. He concentrated almost entirely upon the technical details of Gladstone's Bill, following closely an immense memorandum on the subject contributed by FitzGibbon. Though Smith had advised him to go in for 'word painting in strong colours, which you know how to use', he first concentrated in legalistic language on the absurdity of two orders sitting together, and the bad deal Ireland was offered in giving up the no-taxation-without-representation principle for a mere £1,400,000 per annum. The central point in his speech was, yet again, that 'the principle of the bill is Repeal': Ireland had no say in, for instance, a monarchy crisis in England; Irish members were excluded; Parnell could coerce Ulster without control. As for the areas reserved, if he were Irish he would feel his patriotism 'wounded and affronted'. Moreover, the Irish party as it stood had no right to impose its will on the imperial parliament in which they were a minority. The speech was notably restricted to such technical points; it praised Gladstone kindly, and gave Morley full credit for sincerity. Even the analogies used were hardly hostile: Ireland, according to Churchill, *would* be a nation after this Bill—like Italy after Austrian domination, or Bulgaria after Turkey. These were curious parallels for an anti-Home Ruler.

This strangely subdued performance was generally interpreted

[27] RCHL xii/1452: 6 Apr. 1886.

in one way. Whitbread, following, pointed out that Churchill 'kept a remarkably open mind' and never 'put his foot down' on the principle of the measure. Churchill interposed that he put his foot down on the Bill itself, but Whitbread reiterated that 'nothing fell from him that would justify me this time next year, supposing the noble lord propounded a liberal scheme of federation or anything else, referring to his speech tonight as being inconsistent with his doing so'. Churchill's repeated assertion that 'I have pronounced over and over again against repeal' was hardly the point; as Morley remarked privately to McCarthy, 'we all declare against repeal, and we put whatever meaning we like on the declaration'.[28]

A similar evasiveness can be traced in his performance on the second reading. This concentrated first on a number of historical points (constantly challenged and usually wrong) and then on the question of the constitutional propriety of Gladstone's wish to obtain a vote on the Bill's principle and then withdraw it. What stayed in people's minds was the surprisingly modest stance taken from the first, which was much remarked on. Essentially he was following the line of Jesse Collings, who confided to him: 'I and Chamberlain are home rulers; they are *repealers* and *separationists*', or of the *Pall Mall,* which always supported Home Rule but opposed Gladstone's Bill.[29] It may be that Chamberlain's unexpectedly floating notions of 'federation' in his speech of 9 April expressed ideas shared by Churchill, for which the door was being kept open. Possibly the fact of his own apologia on Holmes's motion, and the public assertions of Irish members like O'Connor regarding 'certain transactions' with their party,[30] tied his hands; his own statement that he had to make a moderate speech in order not to alienate his new allies may have explained his courtesy to Gladstone, but not his silence regarding the principle of Home Rule itself.

His other public pronouncements of the time are no more enlightening. He refused to attend the Unionist rally of 14 April, describing it privately as 'a piece of premature gush': though,

---

[28] Cooke and Vincent, *Governing Passion*, p. 77 (note). Gladstone's verdict on Churchill's speech was recorded by Lewis Harcourt: 'He was in his pseudo-statesman vein but made no practicable suggestion of an alternative policy—his only idea is to return to the "policy of Mr Smith", of "the 26th of January".' LHJ, 12 Apr. 1886, vol. 378, p. 78.

[29] Collings to Churchill, 11 Apr. 1886, RCHL xiii/1472.

[30] *Hansard 3*, cccvi, 883.

when addressing the Beaconsfield Club the same night, he called
it 'a concurrence ... unparalleled in the annals of English
history ... the germs of a coalition based upon one great
principle, the safety and integrity of our Empire'. Much of this
speech was Primrosery incarnate, attacking Gladstone's 'malignant personal ascendancy ... poisoning the political life of
England'. An odd note for the Beaconsfield Club, however, was
heard in his statement that he himself, despite his 'rigid fidelity'
to Toryism, believed 'a united Liberal party was essential to the
life of England', to 'control and restrain' the tendency of Tory
principles to 'imperfection and deterioration'; even more eccentric for his audience was his expressed belief that the alternative
to Gladstone's measure was not 'Cromwellian coercion', but the
application to Ireland of the same principles as suited England,
avoiding 'any vast or organic change' but 'gradually introducing
wise and salutary law'; thus liberty, property, and social order
would be restored, and the League wither away. This was very
far from Salisbury's deliberate appeal to an unconstructive Irish
policy a month later: a contrast which cannot have escaped
either.

Churchill attended a meeting of Liberal Unionist peers at
Derby's house the next day, and then departed to Paris on 20
April; he kept a low profile for the rest of the session. This was
partly due to the sensitivity and uncertainty of relations with the
Liberal Unionists; he believed, like most people, that on 8 May
Chamberlain had been 'cornered' by Gladstone, and feared that
if Gladstone did opt for retention of Irish members the only Tory
course would be a motion for adjournment. Salisbury's die-hard
speech to the National Union of 15 May was an added worry—
seen by Labouchere as exposing the real nature of 'unionism',
and demonstrating the reality of 'Randolph's private promises'.[31] However, on 18 May Hartington announced his *non
possumus* at Bradford; Churchill reopened communications about
parliamentary tactics on the second reading, and helped trap
Gladstone into denying any intention to reconstruct his Bill. But
he seemed 'surly and uninvolved' on 29 May in discussions of
James's scheme for walking out on the second reading. At a City
Conservative Club dinner on 2 June he refused to talk about
Home Rule at all, on the rather tendentious grounds that it
would give the government ammunition to prolong the debate;

---

[31] Labouchere to Chamberlain, 17 May 1886, Chamberlain MSS 5/50/108.

he denied that it signified 'a malignant and sinister intention' to surrender his principles. An added reason for his public silence, as well as for his rudeness to James, was that he was involved in a severe parliamentary quarrel with the latter over James's accusations that Churchill's Ulster incitements made him 'half a traitor'. Thus, on many levels, his Irish involvements combined to tie him down in late May and early June; even at the climax of the debate on the second reading, Parnell's indirect reference to the Carnarvon interview was generally taken as aimed at Churchill. His retirement to Labouchere's river-side house on 4 June, to join Ellen Terry and others for a weekend party, can only have provided scant comfort.

By then, however, the uncertain course of Chamberlain and his allies was clear; by 8 June the Bill was lost and dissolution decided upon. On 20 June Churchill published his extraordinary election address, making up for recent moderation by abusing Gladstone in violently exaggerated language; newspapers which saw it as 'the inimitable *champion comique* of the parliamentary stage' bounding back with a broad gesture to pit and gallery were probably right. But, besides providing much ribald amusement, the address had a powerful function to perform, for Churchill had determined several days before to remove himself to Norway during the election, after a modicum of public activity. Piqued and poor, he had accepted a fishing holiday with his friend Tom Trafford, which he hoped would cost him next to nothing. Salisbury, in fact, believed Churchill would have preferred a Whig government, with no dissolution, for the sake of saving money.[32] His decision to play a minor part was not affected by the fact that he was unexpectedly opposed in Paddington, where he addressed his constituents at a closed meeting on 26 June. Here the villadom of Bayswater gathered to admire Churchill and his wife, turned out in the height of fashion; their hero stood by his address, speculated on Gladstone's sanity, sounded a patriotic drum, and talked more specifically about Ireland than he had done for weeks. Rather sketchy historical parallels were adduced to show that no Irish parliament had ever worked; the basic divide between Protestant ascendancy and Catholic peasantry was irreconcilable except within the framework of Empire; 'this is the Irish

[32] Cecil, *Salisbury*, iii, 298; also see Churchill to Duchess of Marlborough, 16 June 1886, RCHL xiii/1531. He appeared, however, at three public meetings; not two, as stated by both biographers.

question, and there is no other'. He also claimed the country was more prosperous than much of England, and that English administration of Ireland under the Union was 'a conspicuous and glowing success' (which he had denied on many previous occasions). The whole performance was tactically analogous to his address; extreme and sweeping, it also embodied much received wisdom from his Irish contacts (the insolubility of the Irish question being a central theme). An observer noted that he was on top of his form; fluent, brilliant, imperturbable, never referring to notes, damning 'Yankee gold' with his American wife beside him on the platform, moving from a grandiose call to the spirit that fought Blenheim to an appeal for the votes of the Paddington bourgeoisie, speaking with 'the infallibility of a Pope and the readiness of a cheapjack'. [33] But this was the high point of his campaign. Three days later he spoke at a meeting of Cohen's, where he repeated the threat to Protestant Ireland, advertised the classless nature of Toryism, and lightly accused Gladstone of being funded by millionaires; but his only other appearance was at Manchester on 30 June, where the Orange note was sounded, Gladstone flayed as a 'maniac', and the public-spiritedness of Toryism towards their 'temporary allies' apostrophized: they would allow Liberal Unionists to win seats uncontested, no matter what the latter might go on to do.

In fact, he had been influential behind the scenes in fixing such arrangements, at Birmingham and elsewhere. At Birmingham, too, his protégé Henry Matthews preached an obediently Churchillian line on Ireland, calling for similarity of treatment with England. Socially, Churchill continued to spend more time in Liberal company, staying at Waddesdon with Chamberlain and Hartington for a weekend in the middle of the campaign. Public attention concentrated on his position in the election, as someone who had frankly steered an inconsistent course, and as one of the primary disturbing forces of politics; but tantalizingly little was seen or heard of him. The ground which Salisbury and Gladstone had chosen to take up on the issue, of classes versus masses, was fundamentally antipathetic to him, and may help account for his displeasure with the leadership expressed in letters of the time. And in all of what he had said over the past weeks, as Parnell pointed out caustically at

---

[33] See Appendix 2. It is a telling description, not least in the affectionate and proprietorial tone adopted by many Liberal newspapers towards Churchill.

Chester, Churchill 'did not shut himself out from joining a future government by proposing something of the same kind [as Gladstone], because in his published utterances he has been very careful only to say that he could not support repeal of the Union; and repeal of the Union is not the question at all'.[34]

As recent historiography has elaborately shown, politicians of all varieties were engaged at this time in squaring the circle in order to prove past consistency; not least Parnell himself, who in the same speech poured scorn on Grattan's parliament, which he had previously postulated as the only solution. Churchill had steered a wilder course than most, and correspondingly kept quieter. Two days after Manchester, he left Hull for Norway, and there remained. Where the extraordinary events of 1855–6 had left him remained to be seen. His reputation for opportunism and immorality in politics had seemed confirmed by Belfast. 'No man in a responsible position had ever done a wickeder act than was committed by Randolph Churchill when he advocated a breach of the law in Ulster', Gladstone told Hamilton; 'he ought to have been struck off the list of Privy Councillors and never to be admitted again as an adviser of the Crown.'[35] History, and hindsight, might confirm this. But he had advanced to the practical leadership of the Tories in the Commons, and proved his skill in office; even the damage done to his personal position on Ireland by his own rashness and Gladstone's devastating initiative could not take away from that. The principal Tory casualty was, of course, Carnarvon; at Portofino in the spring he had read Churchill's speeches dealing with his Irish viceroyalty and concluded 'it is not easy to frame a given number of sentences which are more inconsistent with fact'. By the autumn, all the ex-Viceroy's previous allies had deserted him. 'The lesson which I am rapidly learning', he confided to his diary, 'is that the popular belief in England that no trust is to be placed in Irish character is not far wrong. They are very clever and plausible and attractive; but they are not true; and for their own purposes they can be utterly false.'[36] Churchill might have agreed with him; while the Irish certainly would have applied

---

[34] *The Times*, 30 June 1886. In fact, Churchill's only specific reference to 'Home Rule' rather than 'repeal' came at Manchester, after this taunt; and he then referred to the 'insolubility' of setting up 'a co-ordinate and subordinate parliament at Dublin'. Insoluble indeed, by anyone's definition.

[35] EHJ, 16 July 1886, vol. xv, p. 71, BL Add. MS 48644.

[36] Carnarvon diary, 16 Feb. 1886, 8 Sept. 1886, BL Add. MS 60926-7.

the same description to Churchill. The metaphor which Churchill used for Chamberlain's negotiations with Gladstone, 'diamond cut diamond', would serve equally well here; but it remained to be seen if Churchill's game of bluff with the Irish question in 1885–6, and the extraordinary parliamentary reversals of that year, had really strengthened his personal position with his party.

Chapter 9

Official Politics, 1886

But perhaps the most wonderful ministerial phenomenon—though now almost too common to be longer called a phenomenon—is he who rises high in power and place by having made himself thoroughly detested and also—alas for parliamentary cowardice!—thoroughly feared. Given sufficient audacity, a thick skin, and power to bear for a few years the evil looks and cold shoulders of his comrades, and that is the man most sure to make his way to some high seat. But the skin must be thicker than that of any animal known, and the audacity must be complete. To the man who will once shrink at the idea of being looked at askance for treachery, or hated for his ill condition, the career is impossible. But let him be obdurate, and the bid will come. 'Not because I want him, do I ask for him', says some groaning chief of a party—to himself and also sufficiently aloud for others' ears— 'but because he stings me and goads me, and will drive me to madness as a foe.' Then the pachydermatous one enters into the other's heaven, probably with the resolution already formed of ousting that unhappy angel. And so it was in the present instance.

Anthony Trollope, *The Prime Minister* (1878)

I

The results of the 1886 election, while depleting the Gladstonian forces, left the Conservatives effectively imprisoned by their Liberal Unionist allies: and within the party, Churchill's position was equally circumscribed. The demonstration of Tory probity made necessary by the loss of the Irish alliance had hedged him in; his own meteoric rise had alienated old intimates like Gorst, now relegated to junior office. Moreover, his health was causing more and more anxiety, as were his financial affairs.

One of his first reactions to the prospect of office was that 'we want the £5000 a year badly ... I cannot understand how we get through so much money'; and in September, his mother was annoyed to find him yet further into debt, and borrowing heavily. His poverty was, moreover, well known, with a much publicized collection within his constituency to pay his election expenses, and gossip freely recording his debts. 'Natty [Rothschild] told us a curious bit of Randolph's private affairs with great indiscretion', recorded Loulou Harcourt late in the year;

though he said that as Randolph made no secret of it he did not see why he should. Andrew Montagu with his solicitor came to see Natty one day on business, and the conversation turning on R.C., Natty said to Montagu 'I know you are always thinking you are going to die and I also know that you have lent Randolph £500. Now if you were to die he would be called on to pay it and I know he would not be able to do so. Will you take steps to prevent him from being called on to pay it in the event of your death.' Montagu at once told his solicitor to sit down and draw out a codicil to his will to that effect, which he did.[1]

His marriage was also under public scrutiny, for sound reasons: he and Lady Randolph were practically separated for much of the year, with Churchill referring to himself as 'living at the Carlton'. Throughout 1886, a year when Dilke's affairs and Lady Colin Campbell kept divorce on everyone's mind, rumours continually had the Churchills in the courts.[2] They were appearing together at country-house parties by the end of the year. But Lady Randolph's liaison with her husband's friend Count Kinsky, a Viennese diplomat, continued to be well known in society, where it was referred to jokingly as 'the Austrian alliance'.

This situation was allied with Churchill's fast declining

---

[1] LHJ, 28 Dec. 1886, vol. 380, p. 29.

[2] See Churchill and Mitchell, ch. 7; Churchill to Salisbury, 7 Aug. 1886, Hatfield House MSS, 3M/Churchill/276. Also EHJ, vol. xvi, p. 4 (BL Add. MS 48645) and LHJ, 6 Jan. 1886, vol. 380, p. 107: 'Morley sent us a report this morning which he has from a press man that proceedings are going to be entered at once in the divorce court by Lady Randolph Churchill against Ld. R. C. and Lady De Grey and by Ld. R. Churchill against Lady Randolph and John Delacour. I can hardly believe it as Lord Randolph would not be fool enough to commence proceedings and I don't believe Lady R. could make out a case against Lord R. and Lady De Grey. They have been very intimate for some time but I believe it has been purely intellectual and not physical. Lady De Grey has always appeared to me to be absolutely passionless.' For references to the 'Austrian alliance' see ibid., pp. 189–90, and vol. 381, p. 153.

health, generally remarked upon; Hartington noticed in September how worried Churchill was about his health, and Blunt at the end of the year found him, at thirty-seven, 'aged, like a man who has had a stroke'. His colleagues continually feared a complete breakdown, nervous as well as physical. Churchill's manner was increasingly withdrawn, moody, and ostentatiously rude; too many stories of the time, too often told, bear this out, as does his son's early autobiography. The sense is of a fuse getting shorter and shorter: his presentiment of an early death, reinforced by the knowledge of his disease, was confided to friends as diverse as Rosebery and Escott. He had become a dreaded as well as sought-after dinner-guest; his violence in society was compounded by a solitary private life. He was estranged from his wife (whom he abused to his friends), and unable to confide fully in his mother; his closest friends were unable to support him through his frantic political work. Though reconciled with his brother, Blandford was preoccupied (along with most of society) with the Lady Colin Campbell divorce case (in which he figured notably, despite his brother's attempts to intercede with James). FitzGibbon was in Ireland, Wolff in the Near East, Rosebery travelling at length abroad. Rothschild, by now one of his closest friends, was not involved in public politics; and in fact, the company Churchill sought for relaxation was that of unpolitical social drones like Harry Tyrwhitt and Tommy Trafford, or even Charles Kinsky, with whom he escaped to Paris. He was close to celebrated hostesses like Lady Dorothy Nevill, Mrs Jeune, and the Duchess of Edinburgh, and rumour linked him with Lady de Grey and Ellen Terry; but it is unlikely that he had a consistent mistress (he told a sister-in-law that he only liked 'rough women who dance and sing and drink—the rougher the better—great ladies bore me'). His private life, as his public one, was largely dominated by politics.

Even on his retreat from the elections to Norway, Churchill was plied with telegrams from Rothschild, who alone knew his address. The picture rapidly emerged of a Conservative government determined upon 'Resistance', insecure in the Commons, but unprepared for coalition. Churchill knew this before his return, and was probably disappointed; as Blandford pointed out, he would by now have been a key figure in such an arrangement (Eddy Hamilton, perennially innocent, had been surprised to learn that Hartington had 'no objection in sitting in

the same cabinet with R. Churchill').[3] The decision against it
was a Tory one, based on general party feeling, and on
Salisbury's making it clear that he would only take Hartington
without Chamberlain. But deprived of Hartington by himself,
the Commons leadership inevitably devolved upon Churchill.

Returning to England on 24 July, Churchill went at once to
Arlington Street; after a second meeting on 28 July, Smith wrote
to Harrowby that he would have the lead in the Commons.
Beach supported the step, an act generally seen as magnanimous; but he had been unpopular, and Churchill had acted
effectively as Leader in the last session. Moreover, he acted as
such in July; bombarding Salisbury with rather peremptory
suggestions for the new government, irritating men like Cross by
holding 'a daily sort of Cabinet at the luncheon table at the
Carlton', and conferring continually with Chamberlain. Old
enemies like Cross and Stanhope were argued against; already
trouble was forecast. 'Salisbury's cabinet is not yet formed',
wrote Carnarvon in his diary, 'and he must have a not very
pleasant time. Randolph is already a rival that can compel, or
thwart, or drive, or hold back. At any moment he can force
Salisbury's hand in the House of Commons; and in cabinet-
making he is taking a very strong part.'[4]

However, the pattern that emerged demonstrated as much
Salisbury's powers of resistance as Churchill's aggression. Cross
got India, against Churchill's wishes; Stanhope was not rejected.
Ashbourne remained in Cabinet. And Iddesleigh emerged as
Foreign Secretary, a post which was originally offered to
Cranbrook and which Churchill urged Salisbury himself to
keep: 'the real safe solution, at any rate for a time'. Powerful
rumours attributed a wish for this post to Churchill himself, and
Blandford urged him not to be 'humbugged out of it'; had he
been appointed, it would not have been under Salisbury's
tutelage, as was the case with the other two candidates. As it
was, he retained ambitions in that sphere. Meanwhile, after
being canvassed for Ireland, he was appointed Chancellor of the
Exchequer: which added to the general impression that he had
supplanted Beach. FitzGibbon's reaction was characteristically
perceptive: feeling that the job was ill-suited to Churchill and
his reputation, he wrote suggesting that Goschen (whom

    [3] Blandford to Churchill, 9 July 1886, Blenheim MSS G/IV; EHJ, 22 July 1886, vol.
xv, p. 79, BL Add. MS 48644, and note 26 below.
    [4] Carnarvon diary, 1 Aug. 1886, BL Add. MS 60927.

Churchill had thought of bringing in to cut out Stanhope) be suborned for the part.

'Ministries to a great extent make themselves', wrote Salisbury wearily to Harrowby, refusing him Cabinet rank with the Privy Seal. 'That is, one or two appointments exacted by some external circumstances have a long chain of quite inevitable consequences. It has so happened in this case. Beach was evidently the necessary Secretary for Ireland; but that involved Churchill having the lead in the Commons; and that made both Cross and Stanley think that a migration to the Lords would be more comfortable for them.' To himself, he added, the separation from Harrowby and Carnarvon was 'a very painful as well as a very irksome task'. But in fact, Churchill's glittering elevation apart, the ministry was strongly Old Gang in flavour: despite a concerted campaign in newspapers for widespread reconstruction from the ranks, and the wishes of men like Raikes to 'clear out the superfluous veterans'. The ministry was essentially 'packed' against the new Chancellor from the beginning. As Forwood correctly wrote to Churchill, 'in the composition of the ministry an overpowering weight is being given to land, property, and status, to the exclusion of bankers, manufacturers, and traders, the backbone of the country' (and of Tory 'Democracy').[5]

How much Churchill himself worried about this is debatable; he later claimed that 'all through the old, and not the young, Tories have been my best friends; it was Beach and the Duke of Rutland who made me leader'.[6] But his clients and supporters within the government were not impressive. Henry Matthews, the embarrassing Home Secretary, was a 'discovery' of Churchill's: an erratic QC who had prosecuted Dilke, and whose re-election in Birmingham led to Churchill forcing Chamberlain to withdraw support from a Radical Unionist opponent. This was all the more embarrassing as Matthews had once embraced Home Rule; and, as a Roman Catholic, his appointment led to a public clash between Churchill and Orange bigots in Scotland. More importantly, it also angered both the Conservative old guard and Tory Democrats like

---

[5] Forwood to Churchill, 31 July 1886, RCHL xiii/1606. He went on to ask for 'broad, generous measures' on the domestic front, sketching out something very like the Dartford programme. Raikes supported Churchill's policies, but never forgave him personally for advancing Matthews to the Home Office.

[6] H. H. Asquith, *Fifty Years of Parliament* (2 vols., London, 1926), i, 150.

Howorth. Matthews was soon a figure of fun, mishandling several important *causes célèbres* before he was pensioned off. Ritchie at the Local Government Board was also well-disposed towards Churchill; so was Clarke, the Solicitor-General (Gorst having moved to an under-secretaryship at the India Office, after—to Churchill's annoyance—declining to 'jump at' a judgeship). But the only heavyweight offices where anything like a Churchill cave existed were in Ireland, where FitzGibbon had advised 'an ornamental, affable and openhanded figure head to the Castle, with a strong *Maire du Palais* in the Chief Secretary's office'.[7] Both requirements were met, Beach being accompanied by Churchill's young cousin Lord Londonderry. The combination represented an informed and conciliatory line on Ireland. But Churchill failed to complete the desired triumvirate by replacing Ashbourne with FitzGibbon; and events in Ireland and elsewhere would conspire to alienate Beach from him by the end of the year.

He was, in fact, very much alone; and in a position which attracted almost as much censure as admiration. The hostile reaction is best expressed in a pamphlet by J. M. Crozier published the following year, which saw Churchill as a phenomenon created by the press, which he cultivated both in public and in private. 'It was the sub-editors and reporters who made Lord Randolph': however hostile a paper's editorial line might be, the simple fact of being reported, 'by the mere echo and reverberation of his name in the public press, surrounded him in the mind of the multitude with an aureole of real but vague and indefinable superiority'. Certainly, his publicity machine was pervasive; he struck even Matthew Arnold at this time as remarkable for 'vitality, audacity, and a spirit of revolt against used-up routine'.[8] However, though those outside the inner circle greeted the prospect of Churchill as Leader with consternation, within the government even longstanding enemies like Cranbrook reacted philosophically, recognizing the appointment as inevitable. Another old opponent, J. M. Maclean, was gracefully conciliated by being asked to second the Address in answer to the Queen's Speech. The session got under way in August with a great deal of attention focused upon him.

Both Churchill's style as Leader, and the arrangements of business, reflected the difficult nature of the government's composite

[7] 20 July 1886; RCHL xiii/1568.
[8] *Pall Mall Gazette* interview, 5 Sept. 1886.

majority. Churchill took a firm line from the beginning that the government would prorogue parliament after the financial business instead of reconvening in October; this involved blocking private members' bills, and set the new gamekeeper against old poachers like Labouchere, Parnell, and Bradlaugh. There were some piquant reversals: Churchill, the ex-traducer of private secretaries being given government appointments, now defending such jobs against Labouchere (whom he stigmatized disdainfully as 'a society journalist'). But the larger issues raised great difficulties. As Salisbury pointed out when suggesting that they avoid a party line on private measures, the reform of procedure was not yet in operation; and the arrangement of time at the government's disposal led to Churchill promising Parnell a day for his Tenant Relief Bill, as a clear-cut tactical decision to minimize obstruction on the estimates. The uneasy nature of the government's majority was emphasized by the fact that Churchill had not previously consulted the Liberal Unionists, and had desperately to line up Hartington: Parnell's bill was, moreover, cleverly constructed to split the Liberal Unionists from the government. The eventual outcome was a behavioural trauma for the Liberals, with Chamberlain and his Radicals abstaining on Parnell's Bill, and Hartington supporting the Conservatives in going against it.[9] At the same time, Churchill infuriated old guard Tories by promising Bradlaugh a committee on perpetual pensions. It is little wonder that the newspaper correspondents noted his extreme nervousness in the House.

In a particularly exhausting session, he was forced to face many of the inconsistencies of his own past career in parliament; and he was not in the health to stand it. Though enabled by his domestic difficulties to dine in the House every night, his obsessive attendance was considered unnecessary by colleagues, most of whom warned him in early September that he was overdoing it. Churchill himself compounded the impression by sending a desperately worded letter to the Queen about the doomed state of the party in the Commons, which led to a

---

[9] For Churchill's defence of the step to the Queen as 'a choice of evils' in a letter of 3 Sept. 1886, see Royal Archives, B 37/103. He also pointed out to her that giving Parnell a day *after* supply put him in the position of not being able to delay supply without contradicting his own assertions about the urgency of the Irish case, whereas if he allowed the estimates to pass he forfeited an opportunity for revenge 'in the certain eventuality of his bill being rejected'.

predictable flurry of enquiries and explanations.[10] The strain was obvious, culminating in his celebrated abuse of Beach in front of Lord George Hamilton. He was, in fact, the most difficult of colleagues; a fact which had been partially concealed by the separateness of the India Office, but was now thrown into sharp relief. Nor did he conceal impatience: a note passed to Balfour during the first Cabinet on the Local Government Bill was carefully preserved at Whittingehame. 'Very Private. How d-d dull this is. I am getting sick.'

The correspondence between Churchill's colleagues during the uneasy days of the government's establishing itself continually adverts to his behaviour; the fullest report, which may stand for the rest, was sent by Smith to Cranbrook at Balmoral after the commotion caused there by Churchill's despondency in early September, and probably reflects more sympathy than most.

You might find men in the party who hold different opinions, but the general sentiment is that Randolph Churchill has done his work this session—which has been exceedingly difficult—with great skill and success, and there is really no ground to apprehend 'checks and defeats or disaster to the government' . . . He is very highly strung, very easily excited, and he is pursuing a very bold course, but I think a right one. It is however a violent strain upon him and he is very far indeed from being strong. The result is alternations of feeling—at one moment confidence, at another despondency, and these conditions, varying with a kind of feverish attack, produce results such as the Queen has seen in his letters and as we find in our conversations with him—but there is no expression of this variation of feeling in his attitudes in the House, as the newspaper reports testify. He may be a little hotter and sharper at times in his retorts on his opponents at one time than another, but there is no sign of despondency or of uncertainty. He has been very poorly this week but although we may be all kept here for some time before we finish the estimates we shall suffer no serious check or disaster and the session will close with Randolph confirmed in his position of leader, unless there is some extraordinary outburst which I do not anticipate.[11]

---

[10] His reports to the Queen generally emphasized the personal nature of the Irish attacks on him, the irresponsibility of Harcourt, the nobility of Chamberlain, and the brilliance of Matthews (who on 20 September supposedly 'demolished Mr Gladstone in a fashion not seen in the House of Commons for twenty years'): Royal Archives, B 37/115. For the despondent letter see ibid., B 37/99 (31 Aug.).

[11] Smith to Cranbrook, 3 Sept. 1886, Cranbrook MSS, HA 43 T501/260. Also see W. Gregory to Dufferin: 'Randolph Churchill has astonished everyone by the high qualities he has *as yet* shown as leader, but he is irritable and far from strong in health. If he cannot get to bed by 12 o'clock he is unable to sleep. Labouchere, his friend, says "we shall work him out by Easter"' (4 Nov. 1886; DVP F 130/24B, no. 231).

This should not conceal the fact that some of Churchill's publicized insecurity was politic: a letter to Hartington on 13 September, begging him not to go to India and describing the government as 'a rickety infant requiring the most careful handling', and himself as 'awfully alone in the House of Commons and glad to grasp at an opportunity of placing things before you', is a very careful production indeed. Hartington refused to be drawn, avoiding in his reply any response on the level of political personalities or government prospects. More and more, Churchill's diplomatic energies were being channelled towards the Liberal Unionists: to an extent which far transcended the simple need for majorities on the floor of the House. His relationship with Chamberlain, still a figure high in Old Tory demonology, was a worry to colleagues: especially as it was often aired in Cabinet meetings, where Churchill's attitude was at its bullying worst. As Salisbury expressed it to his private secretary, Churchill tended 'to put before us the dilemma of accepting his views or endangering the Union with Ireland': and this carried most weight when Churchill's views were Chamberlain's as well. The alliance, like others outside the government, was also trumpeted abroad; Brett heard by the autumn that 'Churchill and Natty Rothschild seem to conduct the business of the Empire in great measure *together*, in consultation with Chamberlain.'[12]

It was hardly a combination guaranteed to excite Salisbury's approval; moreover, by early November, Churchill had addressed a series of violent remonstrances to his chief, largely centred on the static nature of the government's legislative intentions, and culminating in a celebrated and petulant outburst:

I am afraid it is an idle schoolboy's dream to suppose that Tories can legislate—as I did, stupidly. They can govern and make war and increase taxation and expenditure *à merveille*, but legislation is not their province in a democratic constitution ... [Chaplin] is the natural leader of the Tories in the House of Commons, suited to their intellects and their class prejudices. I certainly have not the courage and energy to go on struggling against cliques, as poor Dizzy did all his life.

A threat of secession could hardly be more clearly worded. Salisbury's soothing reply, equally celebrated, was also con-

[12] See J. P. D. Dunbabin, 'The politics of the establishment of County Councils', *Hist. Jn.*, vol. vi (1963), no. 2, p. 239, and M. Hurst, *Joseph Chamberlain and Liberal Reunion: the Round Table Conference of 1887* (London, 1967), p. 99.

structed to carry a deliberate message. After defining the purpose of Conservatism as not offending the masses and retaining the support of the classes by maintaining their confidence, he firmly deprecated the desirability of passing 'drastic symmetrical measures ... trusting to public meetings and to democratic forces generally, to carry you through'. And this was an exact description of the tactics which Churchill had adopted by the late autumn of 1886.

II

Such a hiatus arose directly from the nature of Salisbury's government and its position with regard to legislation, which raised fears and expectations evocatively defined at the time by Goschen in a private letter.

At present, so far as I can see, everything looks very black. The fact is, the first principles of Government have been shaken in every quarter and new forces, new principles, new men are governing the country. I needn't tell you that a Conservative Government with Churchill as the leading spirit is practically a new force, incalculable by experience; and as for the Gladstone, Parnell, Labouchere opposition, it is as unlike any previous party or any previous opposition, as *hitherto* a French opposition has been to an English one. Startling propositions of the gravest character, striking at the structure of society altogether, are not laughed out of court, or rejected with indignation, but are played with, and treated as we used to treat the ballot and the six-pound franchise or the Irish Church twenty years ago. It is possible that these new forces may govern the country satisfactorily, but they have to learn some very bitter lessons in the course of their apprenticeship. Even the Trades Union Congress, which for several years past surprised me by its comparative good sense and moderation, was extremely socialist and subversive this year. First principles will have to be defended *à outrance*, or they will go to the wall, and no one cares to defend them, many from indolence, many from cowardice, and many (whom I call the flunkeys) from a resolute disbelief in very serious changes being in progress. 'We have heard all this before.' You know the style ... Will a Conservative majority arrest this tendency? I doubt it. Randolph Churchill will utilize it for democratic Tory purposes ...[13]

Goschen underrated Salisbury's determination to mark time; but Churchill was soon committed in a different direction. As early as 5 August he had consulted Chamberlain about the

---

[13] Goschen to Dufferin, 10 Oct. 1886, DVP F 130/24B p. 65.

programme; at breakfast that day Chamberlain suggested procedural reform in the following February, no autumn session,
and a flexible approach to Ireland (including a Land
Commission and an inquiry into the possibility of equitable rent
arbitration and public works). Though Smith and Salisbury
were less enthusiastic, Churchill a week later promised
Chamberlain 'an army of Commissions'.[14] His general responsibility for policy, as Leader of the House, was soon pressed
further than heads of other departments liked. Nowhere was this
more true than Ireland.

The general Cabinet committee on Ireland (Salisbury, Beach,
Churchill, Matthews, and Smith) confronted a situation of
deteriorating agricultural conditions and a redoubled recession
in late 1886; but wishful thinking at first led them to believe that
the parliamentary defeat of Home Rule had had the effect of a
healthy purgative. This was reflected in the declaration by
Churchill of the government's intentions towards Ireland: a
firm, positive line, dealing with social, agricultural, and governmental questions on the principle of equality and 'simultaneity'
with England. Fisheries, communications, and drainage were to
be dealt with; 'a genuinely popular system of local government'
to be worked up; General Buller was dispatched to the troubled
districts. Though annoying Tory Democrats and others, this was
less sweeping than it seemed. Churchill was demonstrating his
own respectability on the Irish issue (at a time when, besides the
interminable repercussions of the Belfast riots, his name was still
occurring in detectives' reports in Dublin, as backing scurrilous
pamphlets, and intriguing with the likes of Callan).[15] But he was
also obeying FitzGibbon's advice not to commit himself to any
definite Irish policy until he saw how the land lay. The large-
scale investigative commissions promised to Chamberlain were
duly delivered, but the latter found his ally hard to interest in
the facts of local government or land-law reform. Following
speakers in the debate on the Queen's Speech interpreted
Churchill's declarations as a do-nothing policy, and Irish reactions were unimpressed. But efforts to raise a debate on the new
Leader's past language, and recriminations about disorder in
Belfast, were foiled by his elaborate parliamentary politeness.

Attention was fixed forward, towards harvest and rents.

---

[14] Churchill to Beach, 5 Aug. 1886, RCHL xiv/1637; Churchill to Chamberlain, 12
Aug. 1886, Chamberlain MSS 5/14/22.
[15] 'Secret Reports' in St. Aldwyn MSS PCC/46.

Salisbury, uneasy about the outcome of the Land Commission under Cowper, hoped eventually for coercive legislation; Churchill and Beach did not. The cautious opinion of advisers was that the Irish situation was settling. But by the end of August, resistance to evictions was noticeable; and October saw the promulgation of the Plan of Campaign, whereby tenants whose landlords refused to reduce rents withheld the amount towards an organized community resistance. By then, Churchill counselled Salisbury against speedy proceedings to outlaw it; though Beach was ready to take action. Here as elsewhere, FitzGibbon was in the background, continually advising against 'the old played-out game of arbitrary but temporary and inconclusive coercion'. But on the land question, which lay behind this dilemma, Churchill found himself aligned against the Chief Secretary: a conflict which was to have lasting results.

Here also FitzGibbon had given Churchill caustic and realistic advice in July.

The land question will continue to settle itself by the natural disappearance of rent. It is now really impossible to obtain (apart altogether from the League's work) any return from land equal to the judicial rents of four years ago, and the landlords are aware of this, and consequently are realising that evictions and the like are useless. But in any case the Irish landlords, as you well know, are neither personally nor politically worth the money or the labour which it would require to preserve them from the, *I* believe, inevitable operation of the economic laws which are crushing them.[16]

But with office, Churchill was no longer in a position to act upon this analysis; on this as on issues such as the nationalization of Irish railways, he argued against Beach, and on the same side as Salisbury. Churchill's attention to the House of Commons view, and his fear of alienating landlords, led him to declare publicly against revision of rents by state interposition; Beach's firsthand experience, and his knowledge by the end of August of the worsening agricultural situation, aligned him against this. As early as 21 August, meeting in a country house, Beach unburdened to Churchill his dissatisfaction with the government's refusal to accede to the tenants' demands; two days later in parliament, he implied sympathy with their side. On 27 August George Hamilton as go-between warned Churchill of Beach's dislike of his position, his nerviness and antagonism, and his

[16] 20 July 1886, RCHL xiii/1568.

readiness to resign and break up the government; he was especially opposed to Churchill and Salisbury over the question of a state guarantee of rents, and was angered by the discrepancy between his and Churchill's speeches in the Commons. This was the background to Churchill's furious dressing-down of Beach, described in Hamilton's memoirs and in a letter from Churchill to Hartington on 13 September: 'it may be interesting to you to know that the difference led to an explanation between me and him of so extremely frank and candid a nature that for a short time the existence of the government was in much danger'. Churchill went on to represent himself, Smith, and Hamilton as keeping the peace between Beach and Salisbury on Irish issues— Beach requiring constant advice and stiffening. The main point of the letter was to flatter Hartington and to overcome ill feelings caused by Parnell's Tenant Relief Bill, but it reflected a conflict which had far-reaching repercussions.

On Parnell's Bill, which was constructed to extend the 1881 Act to leaseholders, revise judicial rents, and prevent evictions if half the rent was paid, Beach's attitude was hostile; but he was at first in favour of accepting the provision to check evictions. It was much noted in early September that Beach's and Churchill's public statements on Ireland often clashed. And while Churchill considered Beach too radical on the land issue, he found him 'sluggish' on the questions of Irish Commissions to deal with public works. By October, with the drawing of battle-lines in the Irish countryside, Beach's tone had moderated: he asked Churchill to put in a good word for the landlords in his Bradford speech at the end of the month. But their bitter disagreements in August and September reflected a changed dispensation. Similarly, though Churchill was still closely in touch with the FitzGibbon circle over educational politics, corresponding with English Catholics over schemes for an Irish university, and using O'Shea as a link to conservative Irish bishops, he could no longer involve himself in his old free-wheeling way: parliamentary majorities and the sanctity of the Union intervened, despite FitzGibbon's enthusiastic letters about intrigues on the Commission for intermediate education and his promise in late November that 'Howth looms tranquilly in the near and brilliant future.'

The Union, indeed, remained a combustible issue, liable to be set alight by the most unexpected flare. When Churchill made a brief declaration on 15 September that the functions of the

Board of Works and the Local Government Board would be developed 'in accordance with Irish ideas and desires', placing them 'in the hands of the Irish people', it was at once interpreted in some papers as 'the white flag of Home Rule'; and Chamberlain believed that it indicated that 'the Government had determined to accept National or Provincial Councils', going on to suggest to Churchill with elaborate casualness that municipal government for Ireland should be brought in anyway, 'leaving the larger questions of Home Rule, Provincial Assemblies, Dublin Castle, etc., for another session'.[17] Churchill himself may have been prepared to slide by easy stages into the dangerous terminology of devolution; around this time he sent Salisbury a sweeping memorandum from a 'Unionist' Irish correspondent which suggested giving 'six-sevenths of what is meant by Home Rule' to new local authorities and two provincial assemblies in Belfast and Dublin—rejected sharply by Salisbury as 'too much like real Home Rule'.[18] On 9 October the *Daily News* had 'details' of a Unionist Home Rule Bill, supposedly planned by Churchill and Chamberlain, and involving four provincial councils and a Canadian-type constitution. This may have reflected no more than the fact that the government had started discussing local government; but the facility with which such kites took to the sky forced Churchill to be particularly careful about remaining earth-bound.

If Ireland put considerable stress on the government, the question of local-government reform strained it to breaking-point; and here too Churchill was prominent in exerting pressure. The issue had bedevilled the Liberals in the early 1880s, but discussion of the extent of representative innovations had been side-tracked by the questions of political reform and Ireland. When it returned to haunt Salisbury, the explosion of the Irish issue affected the question; Hartington, for instance, believed that to deal with the matter in Ireland first would create an attractively conservative precedent for England, an approach opposed by Churchill, who was in this above all else representing Chamberlain as well. In Cabinet, he fought violently and aggressively for extensions of popular power, which aligned him against Salisbury. The clashes were well known, and leaked assiduously by Churchill and Chamberlain to

---

[17] See *Pall Mall Gazette*, 16 Sept. 1886; Hurst, op. cit., p. 108; Chamberlain to Churchill, 2 Oct. 1886, RCHL xvi/1865.

[18] RCHL xiv/1683, xv/1808.

Liberal friends (they are closely monitored in Loulou Harcourt's diary); Salisbury, for his part, complained continually to correspondents about Churchill's obstructiveness. His ideas on the subject had been outlined to the Prime Minister in his memorandum of the previous December, and involved purely popular election by ratepayers and large and liberal measures of local legislative powers: education and poor-law management were to be left as they were, but all Quarter Sessions business, sanitary matters, vote registration, land surveys, and registration of titles were to be given to local boards, which should also advance money on the security of the rates for the purchase of smallholdings and allotments. Salisbury had demurred at thus far 'showing our hand', and a polite wrangle had followed, with Churchill earnestly pressing the need for 'a redistribution and relief of burdens, to which every man in our party is deeply pledged, [and which] is without doubt anxiously expected by the constituencies'. Much of this was in the realm of abstract hypothesis, given the political conditions of late 1885, and Ireland and a change of government had come between; but the matter rankled, and with Chamberlain now behind him, Churchill could only go further, especially on matters like Poor Law control—to democratize which was to Salisbury like 'leaving the cat in charge of the cream jug'.

Moreover, on this issue as on Ireland, Churchill and Beach were on different sides: Beach had in the front of his mind the position of the impoverished English country gentry, being himself an archetypical example. 'If the owners are to have half the taxation, they should have half the representation too': in other words, he pressed hard for weighted electoral representation in the new bodies, being prepared to call Chamberlain's bluff by defying his pressure outright. This plan was, in fact, abandoned by C. T. Ritchie at the Local Government Board; by the end of November he produced a scheme of county and district councils to be elected by household suffrage, with the powers of the old Highway and Sanitary Boards, Boards of Guardians, and the administrative powers of the Quarter Sessions. It was the idea of handing over Poor Law administration 'to the agricultural labourers' which Salisbury objected to: and he was supported by all the Cabinet except Churchill who, Salisbury wrote gloomily to the Queen, would produce 'all the obstacles his official position enables him to offer'.

Churchill, moreover, was here representing Chamberlain,

whose association with local-government reform was well known: it had come to be an important component in the machinery that drove the Unauthorised Programme. And Salisbury, for his part, enlisted Hartington's advice—against Churchill, who was forced to agree to exclude Poor Law administration because of Hartington's wishes. This was done with an ill grace; and his reaction to Hartington's idea of a preliminary Irish measure on restricted lines was also hostile. Throughout November, he attempted to pressurize Hartington to drop this (using the invaluable Rothschild as a go-between). The local government impasse led to Churchill's outburst of 6 November about the Tories' inability to legislate; he also made the gaffe of speaking his mind to the Queen, who passed it on to Salisbury. Finally, at the end of November, Salisbury persuaded him to a *modus vivendi*. But Beach rejected the scheme, worried that the precedent of the owners paying half the county rate would be extended to the Poor Rates. Rather than see this happen, he preferred a limited scheme confining both rating and representation to occupiers. Thus matters stood in early December, with Chamberlain abroad and Churchill increasingly isolated.

The third major issue, not to do with his own department, upon which Churchill diverged from his colleagues was, inevitably, foreign policy. From the summer of 1885, in private conversations with foreign envoys, he had been taking a strong anti-French and pro-German line, going so far as to float ideas for reciprocal treaties. At the end of that year, Hatzfeldt had been much impressed by conversations with him tending to the same end. Churchill's emphasis was the Indian priority; the lack of British interest in Eastern Europe; and a frank admission that Salisbury did not agree with him, but that he would 'exert all his influence' to carry his views. Bismarck was sceptical of Churchill's ability to deliver all he promised, and dismissed as naïve his expectations that Austria would set a pace in controlling Russia, which Britain could merely approve; but Hatzfeldt was surprised to note that Churchill was in the position of defining policy to the Russian ambassador, and Herbert Bismarck believed that Churchill, as Leader in the Commons, had more influence over foreign policy than Salisbury.[19] (Nobody mentioned Iddesleigh; least of all Churchill.)

[19] See *Grosspolitik 4*, nos. 784, 780, 789; also comment on Reuss's letter to Bismarck, 14 Dec. 1886, reproduced in Dugdale, *German Diplomatic Documents 1871–1914*, i, p. 267.

Certainly, Churchill chose to believe that part of his duties involved foreign affairs, and here he pursued a line—Boswellized in the dispatches preserved in the *Grosspolitik* documents—that was far more consistent than elsewhere. To diplomats he continually emphasized the interaction between Conservative hegemony at home and a peaceful foreign policy abroad (the connection he was to gamble upon in his budget at the end of the year). He also expansively described his disagreements with Iddesleigh (as Northcote had become) and Salisbury—a curious, and to Salisbury repellent, mode of diplomatic behaviour. While assuring Salisbury that he presented his opinions to Hatzfeldt as 'mere House of Commons views, for his own private information for whatever they were worth, not to be considered in any other light', the envoy did not take this impression away.[20] In September the ambassador at Berlin, Malet, faced by Herbert Bismarck with a report of Churchill's statements to Hatzfeldt, 'became very red' and burst out into invective against Churchill: his intimacy with Russophil Radicals, his revolutionary ideas, his opportunism and self-advancement. 'When a statesman refrains, on Parliamentary grounds, from carrying out a policy which he knows to be right, he is acting unconscientiously.'[21] Thus the Foreign Office view of Churchill; shared, if in less ingenuous terms, by Iddesleigh and Salisbury.

For his part, Churchill presented himself to Hatzfeldt at the end of November as engaged in trying to influence the Cabinet against France, and in favour of joint action with Austria, in order to please Germany: the point being not to 'strengthen the position of Lord Iddesleigh, who today is without influence', and

---

[20] Churchill to Salisbury, 23 Sept. 1886, Hatfield House MSS 3M/Churchill/343. For varying versions of one interview on 24 September compare Churchill's account to Salisbury, largely reprinted in W. S. Churchill, ii, 158–9, with Hatzfeldt's in Dugdale, op. cit., pp. 153–5.

[21] Dugdale, p. 246. In a dispatch the following year Malet summed up Churchill's ideas on foreign policy as retailed to Herbert Bismarck. 'I found that he held views which were entirely opposed to those which I understood Lord Salisbury to hold. He said that England need only provide for the safety of India, that you should do your utmost to strengthen your position there, and that it was worthwhile to buy off the aggressive tendencies of Russia in that direction by giving her free hand [*sic*] with regard to Turkey. He considered that neither Turkey in Europe nor Asia Minor signified in the least to you and he asserted that the British taxpayer would never again be induced to pay a penny towards defending them in the interests of the Sultan. He attached little importance to Egypt being in your hands and urged that the Cape route to India was the surest route and would be sufficient.' Malet to Salisbury, 23 Dec. 1887, Hatfield House MSS 3M/A/61/57.

Hatzfeldt being enjoined not to tell Salisbury of their conversation. These notions had a purely hypothetical significance; Berlin never believed England would back Austria in a forward policy in the East, as Churchill kept suggesting, and the chancellery there was fully aware that Churchill 'was in no position to give or fulfil assurances; for the moment that he retires from or is driven out of the Cabinet, the situation is entirely altered, and every pledge given by him is null and void'. What mattered was that it represented another area of government in which Churchill attempted to seize an initiative: and that happened to be the area most cherished by Salisbury himself. ('In 1886, it is true', wrote Salisbury's daughter grimly much later, 'Lord Randolph Churchill experimented in an independent foreign policy. But it was only for a few weeks, and while Lord Iddesleigh was Foreign Secretary.'[22]) It was, moreover, an initiative taken in public as well as in private; in parliament he had delivered scathing pronouncements about the Radicals' affectation of 'high moral positions' and 'purposely impractical principles' regarding foreign affairs, and his ideas about allowing Russia a free hand in Eastern Europe were linked with his emphasis on a firm Afghanistan policy. ('I think sometimes our policy (foreign) is too European, and not sufficiently Asiatic', he had told Salisbury in November 1885; 'we have no European interests.'[23])

By the time of the 1886 ministry, he was converted to a practically pro-Russian policy, having told the Russian ambassador that the Tories were 'not their hereditary foes'.[24] This went with a carelessness about the fate of Constantinople, and a callousness about the luckless Prince of Bulgaria (deposed by Russian infiltration at the end of August). Such attitudes were partly to please Liberal Unionists, partly the result of encouragement towards a German–British alliance from the Rothschilds and Bleichröder, and partly dictated by a Treasury dislike of incurring expensive entanglements; but they were also guaranteed to align him directly against Salisbury, Northcote and (less importantly, but not negligibly), the Queen. Similarly, his line on Egypt—where he was increasingly intransigent in public

---

[22] Cecil, *Salisbury*, iii, 173; also see Dugdale, pp. 234, 263.

[23] *Hansard 3*, ccciii, 1408; Churchill to Salisbury, 9 Nov. 1885, Hatfield House MSS 3M/Churchill/176.

[24] Churchill to Dufferin, 24 Dec. 1885, DVP F 130/3 no. 84.

about the need for an indefinite British sojourn—led to a definitely anti-French stance, further alienating the Premier and Foreign Secretary (though not the rest of the Cabinet). None the less, in private Churchill continued to canvass the possibility of arranging a withdrawal, which worried Wolff, diplomatically involved on the spot. But such ideas were, quite correctly, deemed too unpopular for public consumption. While Iddlesleigh saw Bulgaria as a moral issue, being met apathetically ('I toss and turn the question of our proper course over and over in my mind'), Churchill not only intrigued with Hatzfeldt but called Cabinet meetings where he stood out for a pro-Russian policy (supported by Hamilton and Smith).[25] From early September, he plagued Salisbury with bitter complaints about Iddesleigh's carelessness about giving commitments in Eastern Europe; while Salisbury may not have been displeased at this evidence of his Foreign Secretary's incapacity, he cannot have approved of the news in mid-September that Churchill had casually 'hinted' to de Staal (the Russian ambassador) at an understanding which would involve aid in Egypt and Afghanistan in return for giving Russia a free hand in the Balkans. A week later, reporting a discussion with Hatzfeldt, Churchill suggested that if Germany and Austria took the lead against Russia, England could support them against France. Salisbury's attempts to throw cold water on the idea were met with truculence from the Treasury: 'it was supposed that Lord Iddesleigh would act under your direction'.

At the same time, Churchill took every opportunity in the Commons of pronouncing magisterially upon foreign policy; opponents tried to tempt him into saying openly that Britain had no interest in who controlled Constantinople. Also in September, his planting-out of his opinions in *The Times* was not missed by the Queen, who drew Salisbury's attention to it; he similarly inspired articles in the *Morning Post*. While Salisbury interpreted the general thrust of Churchill's policy as being anti-Constantinople, it may principally have been anti-Iddesleigh. By the end of September, it had reached campaigning pitch, orchestrated with letters to the press from Brett arguing that a Palmerstonian policy towards the Straits had been obsolete since

---

[25] See Salisbury to Queen Victoria, 11 Nov. 1886, PRO CAB 41/20/20 and Northcote to Cranbrook, 20 Oct. 1886, Cranbrook MSS, HA 43 T501/271. Also same to same, 31 Aug., 7 Sept. 1886, ibid.; and Cecil, *Salisbury*, iii, 314.

1870, and that Russia was Britain's natural ally.[26] Matters were at a head by the time Churchill made his celebrated speech at Dartford on 2 October: and he gave Salisbury fair warning two days before. 'Really', he had written on 30 September, 'if it was from not wishing [*sic*] to cause you any annoyance, I would put such a spoke in old Iddesleigh's wheel when I speak on Saturday as would jolt him out of the F.O.'

To Salisbury, who had withdrawn to Dieppe fully expecting 'monkey tricks' from Churchill, this was hardly reassuring. Moreover, just before Dartford, an incident occurred which must have tipped the scale. As described by Rothschild to Loulou Harcourt, Iddesleigh decided to appoint the violently anti-Russian Condie Stephen to the delicate diplomatic post at Sofia, and then sent Stephen to Rothschild to ask for a £400,000 loan for the Bulgarian defences against Russia. Rothschild, astounded, refused the money (on the grounds that no guarantees were being offered); he sent Stephen away and telegraphed to Churchill, who was in the country. Churchill came up to London, blocked Stephen's appointment, and sent a telegraph to Salisbury in Foreign Office cipher, signed 'Iddesleigh' (probably by the clerk), complaining about the matter. The result was commotion in the Foreign Office, bewilderment at Dieppe, and severe annoyance on the part of Iddesleigh and Salisbury. Faced with it by the latter, Churchill merely took up his ground in a long and ranting letter against Iddesleigh, sent the day after his Dartford speech.[27] The science of making himself impossible could hardly be taken further.

This marked, for the moment, a high point; his language towards Iddesleigh became temporarily modified, and he even communicated directly to him an interview with d'Aunay in Paris later that month. But the report of the conversation, where Churchill took a stridently anti-evacuation line over Egypt, must have made Iddesleigh's ears burn. Moreover, in reporting the

[26] See P. Fraser, *Lord Esher* (London, 1973), p. 75. For Herbert Bismarck's view of the state of affairs see a conversation recorded by Rosebery in March 1887. 'Randolph wished to be Foreign Secretary but Salisbury would not have him. He used to say one thing one day and one another and Hatzfeldt used to say "What *is* the policy of this government!" Iddesleigh did nothing and when he went to the Cabinet allowed himself to be overruled by his colleagues . . . Hatzfeldt always went to Salisbury.' Rosebery MSS 10176.

[27] 3 Oct. 1886; Hatfield House MSS 3M/Churchill/318. The incident is also recorded in LHJ, vol. 380; Iddesleigh to Salisbury, 1 Oct. 1886, 2 Oct. 1886, and Salisbury to Churchill, 1 Oct. 1886, in Hatfield House MSS 3M/Churchill; also Rothschild to Churchill, 27 Sept. 1886, RCHL xvi/1844.

same conversation confidentially to Hatzfeldt, Churchill represented the Foreign Secretary as a cipher, whose pro-French
leanings were irrelevant: 'nothing could be done without him
(Churchill)'. As for Germany's satisfaction over Zanzibar, if 'due
to the misunderstood zeal of subordinate civil servants in the
Foreign Office any difficulty should arise', Hatzfeldt should
'approach him or Salisbury immediately'.[28] Despite Salisbury's
expressed disapproval, Iddesleigh was to be treated with brutal
disrespect. By November, Churchill had consistently encroached
upon foreign policy to an extent which, taken with his didacticism
in other spheres, could only imply that he cherished expectations
of total capitulation.

III

This determination to claim for himself a wide area of jurisdiction distracts from Churchill's performance in the office to which
he was appointed: inevitably, because a forward policy was
what was most disliked at the Treasury, and Churchill here as
elsewhere soon took on the colour of his surroundings. This was
traditional. As Cosmo Monk told Phineas Finn regarding a
similar appointment, 'a bright financier is the most dangerous
man in the world'; and as Derby told Disraeli in 1852, 'you
know as much as Mr Canning did. They give you the figures.'
'They' gave the new Chancellor the figures, and much else
besides.

This was not immediately apparent. Churchill began his
tenure choosing rather to take advice from Rothschild and
Cohen, as well as floating ideas from entrepreneurs like Waring;
the reaction to his appointment among the officials was trepidation about the possibility of working with 'one whose breath
was agitation, and his life a storm on which he rode'. The spectre
of Fair Trade was raised against him at once (his father-in-law
devoutly believed him a protectionist 'at heart'[29]); so were his
opposition attacks on Civil Service salaries, and 'gangs of Jewish
speculators'. However, just as at the India Office, he won over
his officials, principally Eddy Hamilton, West and Welby: who
remembered him as 'one of the best Chancellors of the

---

[28] My italics. See Dugdale, p. 229, and *Grosspolitik*, no. 804. Also, for a similar
emphasis in November, Dugdale, p. 232—which shows Hatzfeldt acting as a medium
direct from Bismarck to Churchill, and Iddesleigh not being shown certain memoranda.
[29] L. Jerome to Lady Randolph, 20 Aug. 1886, CHAR 28/1.

Exchequer who ever came to the Treasury'. To some he seemed
'a tool in the hands of his permanent officials'; Welby described
him as 'a minister of the type that civil servants appreciate'. This
often meant principally that he was 'singularly free from
affection of knowledge which he did not possess'; along with his
absorption, decisiveness, imagination, and light-in-hand touch
went a deference to the experts and a contempt for detail.

In the Commons early on, Churchill was continually put on
the spot, and continually admitted his ignorance: he was the
butt of loaded questions trying to flush out protectionist sympathies. His defence was a full adoption of Treasury orthodoxy:
which happened to be Gladstonian orthodoxy. At their first
meeting, Hamilton was amazed to hear Churchill declare he
would welcome an international inquiry rather than pay anything more to keep the army in Egypt;[30] he also declared at once
his determination to restrict spending on the buildings for the
War Office and Admiralty. The same Gladstonian sense of
economy was exercised in the realms of carriage of specie, secret-
service money, departmental costs, and the Irish railway system.
In this, he was following a general trend: 'what strikes one most
about the three major Conservative or Unionist Chancellors—
Northcote, Goschen and Hicks Beach—during this period is the
extent to which their financial roots and assumptions were as
Gladstonian as those of their Liberal counterparts'.[31] Or, as
Harcourt characteristically put it at the time, 'like a woman who
is married I forget all I ever said when I was single'. Harcourt,
indeed, saw Churchill early on in order to instruct him in 'the
comprehension of the duties of the Exchequer and of the
condition and prospects of the revenue', and may have been
strongly influential. He certainly thought so: 'my advice was
"Be *orthodox* and be *economical*: these are the only virtues of a
Chancellor of the Exchequer!" I also told him that I had got
£3,500,000 off the estimates of War and Admiralty by tendering
my resignation.'[32]

Thus Churchill early sounded a note of reassuring probity:
'every alteration or reform or modification of a Department
which would involve an increased charge possesses in my eyes an
incurable defect'.[33] This was a popular line (Welby noticed,

---

[30] EHJ, 3 Sept. 1886, vol. xv, p. 105, BL Add. MS 48644.

[31] D. Kynaston, *The Chancellor of the Exchequer* (London, 1980), p. 34.

[32] See Churchill to Harcourt, 29 July 1886, Harcourt MSS, dep. 215, f. 118; also
Harcourt to Chamberlain, 24 Dec. 1886, Chamberlain MSS, 5/38/55.

[33] *Hansard 3*, cccviii, 1734; debate on appointment of a minister of education.

regarding Treasury policy, how much 'ahead of his contemporaries' he was in closely monitoring public opinion). Much
of the detail of Churchill's policy, however, was simple continuity. Beach, seeing Harcourt at the last change-over in
February 1886, had told him that the outlay on the Army and
Navy must be kept down, taxes kept low, light coinage taken
into account, and the issue of one-pound notes considered:
Gladstone agreed, and Churchill therefore carried the latter
principle into an aggressive Cabinet memorandum of early
December, suggesting raising the perpetual annuity needed for
light coinage by an issue of one-pound notes which would
'replace the half-sovereign in waistcoat pockets': and this plan
was later favoured by both Goschen and Gladstone. The recall
of the half-sovereign had an additional importance, as Churchill
was also examining proposals for the extended use of silver in
coinage to help the Indian economic situation: but here too his
bias was setting towards a flinty orthodoxy.[34] Similarly, as early
as 7 August Churchill suggested a commission to inquire into the
costs of the public departments; this was announced on 13
September and appointed a week later, mostly staffed by
representatives of the business community like Sir Edward
Guinness and the ubiquitous Rothschild. On the same day he
laid down the principle that the Public Accounts Committee and
the controller, acting together, had *at least* the authority of the
Treasury; as was pointed out, this meant that 'the great
spending departments' would have to listen to them. Orthodoxy
reigned: even when the private reasoning was quintessentially
Churchillian (the state purchase of Irish railways was presented
to Salisbury as enabling 'strategic movements of troops and
police, patronage, and bribery by reduction of rates and
construction of new lines').[35]

Moreover, orthodoxy publicly expressed itself in the
Churchillian mode: with maximum publicity effect, and a
marked degree of deliberate offensiveness towards established
interests. One instance was his giving government mail contracts
to commercial steamer companies; another, his removal of the
coal and wine dues in London from the City and the Board of
Works, who had previously split the profitable monopoly. The
principle of the octroi duty had been much condemned by
Liberal economists like Courtney; Churchill decided to abandon

[34] See PRO CAB 37/52.
[35] Churchill to Salisbury, 2 Dec. 1886, Hatfield House MSS 3M/Churchill/341.

it, announcing the decision in Cabinet on 16 November and meeting a deputation from the Corporation and the Metropolitan Board two days later. He harangued these staunchly Conservative bodies in purely Gladstonian terms, condemning 'a tax on a necessary of life' as 'involving a principle of taxation which we in this country have long sought to get rid of', discriminating against the lower paid, and deleterious to 'any standard of financial economy'. The Board of Works was stringently criticized for its indebtedness, and 'the propertied classes' assured that an increased rate would not be necessary if a financial overhaul was undertaken. Moreover, the question was particularly grave because of 'the absence of representative municipal government in London', which should be remedied.

A full text of this speech—a series of calculated snubs—went to *The Times*, and caused the desired outcry. The *Standard* furiously called upon Salisbury to disown Churchill; letters from protectionists like Lowther drew the conclusion that food duties would be instituted to replace the coal dues; angry memorials were still arriving at Churchill's office when he resigned. By clearing the decision in Cabinet beforehand, he had tied Salisbury's hands; by announcing the principle in the way he did, he ensured the maximum outburst. 'R. Churchill has stirred up great opposition by his reply to the Board of Works and the City', recorded Carnarvon; 'the worst part of his speech was his apparent conversion to the creation of one great municipality for London—the thing to which the Party as a whole were steadily opposed—to say the least it is very unnecessary—and if Salisbury does not take care will turn many friends into enemies.'[36] Thus a Treasury decision was keyed into the campaign which Churchill mounted at his Dartford speech on 2 October. To Hamilton, it seemed Gladstonianism pure and simple: the deputation 'went away dumbfounded'. The manner of delivering the judgement, rather than the judgement itself, was to have endless future importance: not least because one of the deputation's leaders was Fardell, the strong man of Churchill's power base in South Paddington.

Within the Cabinet, too, Exchequer policy was presented in a way which emphasized its divisive potential rather than its

---

[36] See Carnarvon diary, 19 Nov. 1886, BL Add. MS 60927; for the Cabinet decision beforehand, PRO CAB 41/26/27, Salisbury to Queen Victoria, 16 Nov. 1886. Full report in *The Times*, 19 Nov. 1886.

fundamental orthodoxy. Churchill declared an intention to restructure the charges on the National Debt and thus to avoid increasing income tax, otherwise made necessary by the 'great growth of expenditure and stagnant, indeed shrinking, revenue'. The Debt charge was to be reduced, and only suspended by parliamentary consent in case of emergency. A Cabinet memorandum of 9 December emphasized the Chancellor's desire to decrease income tax by $2\frac{1}{4}d$. and to construct 'if possible, a larger margin than usual between the estimated expenditure and estimated income of the year'. It was serving fair notice of his budget, which would take its place in the public campaign of self-aggrandizement to which he had devoted the autumn.

This was inaugurated by the celebrated Dartford speech of 2 October; which in turn should be related to Chamberlain's efforts throughout September to cement his influence upon the Cabinet, and Churchill's use of him as a bogey. Salisbury's absence in Dieppe was relevant: still more so was Chamberlain's projected departure for the Near East on 7 October, and his meetings with Churchill before. The day before Dartford, Chamberlain told Dilke 'that Randolph would give him all he wanted, and leave Hartington and Salisbury in the lurch. Randolph had promised him to have an anti-Jingo foreign policy, leaving Turkey to her fate, and to pacify Ireland with the National Councils scheme, modified into two Councils, or into Provincial Councils, to pacify Ulster; and Churchill had also promised him procedure reform—that is, a sharper closure—and a three acres and a cow policy for England.'[37] The next morning, an inspired article appeared in the *Morning Post* attributing similar views to Churchill. And that afternoon, Churchill delivered to an immense crowd what essentially amounted to a substitute Queen's Speech: the ultimate in politics as defined by what the public wanted.

All the themes of the previous weeks found expression—his attempts to redirect foreign policy, his conversion to Gladstonian finance, his use of Liberal Unionism. A positive government policy was recapitulated, with their four Commissions for Irish land, Irish industrial development, currency reform, and departmental expenditure; to this was added a declaration of intentions regarding allotments and tithe-law reforms, local-government extensions with licensing powers, the reduction of

---

[37] Gwynn and Tuckwell, *Dilke*, ii, 265.

taxation and expenditure, the reform of railway rates, and the extension of elementary education (amounting to free schools). A later authority has seen it as exploiting the 'political capital to be made out of minor changes':[38] Churchill defined the programme more pregnantly as 'matters which ought not to excite party controversy'. For the Liberal Unionists were ostentatiously apostrophized and it was, indeed, their programme. 'We must not dwell too fondly on the past', Churchill told his Conservative audience. 'Politics is not a science of the past; politics is the science of the future. You must use the past as a lever with which to manufacture the future. Politics is not a science, it is not a profession, which consists in looking back; it is not a profession which consists in standing still; it is in this country essentially a science and a profession of progress.' Appositely, this judgement was followed by encomiums upon the Liberal Unionists and the 'union of the Unionist party'. 'We consider it is our duty as a Government so to adapt our policy as to prove to the British people that the Unionist Liberals were right in the course which they took and were justified in the great political sacrifices which they made.' This was, of course, just what many Conservatives did not consider their duty: including the Prime Minister. And the shock of this concealed the fact that much of what Churchill outlined was not, in substance, particularly radical (or Radical).

An examination of the speech reveals many ambivalences and omissions. Social insurance on the Bismarck model was never hinted at (though it would have cut out the Liberal Unionists). The country gentry were not really threatened, and indeed soon conceded all they were asked; in fact, some opinion saw Churchill's Dartford opinions on land as pillaging the poor to pay off the landed classes. The sale of glebe lands for allotments was attributed to Salisbury as his 'special interest', and plans for facilitating land transfer were credited to Halsbury; the increased taxation of personal property necessary to pay for local government was emphasized as a consensus measure. Similarly, ideas such as licensing powers for local government had already been aired in parliamentary answers. The first priority in the programme (dropped in the printed version, which creates a false impression) was procedural reform and a defence of the simple closure: a marked reversal from his position in earlier years, but not particularly controversial. Ireland was played

[38] C. Howard, 'Lord Randolph Churchill', *History*, xxv (1940), no. 2, p. 37.

down, as having monopolized too much time already; but dual ownership, Churchill announced, must give way to single, and the landlords' justice and moderation was warmly praised. And in foreign policy, though his blatant appeal to Austria to take over the lead in the Bulgarian embroilment attracted much attention, Churchill was very careful in his exposition of Britain's position: he defined the nature of her interest, and denied that she was completely uninvolved. Two days later he informed Chamberlain that 'the foreign policy of this country has undergone a complete change ... closely approximating to what were your ideas in 1876–8', a statement which has been roundly categorized as 'a lie';[39] but it is as likely that he believed that at Dartford he had consolidated his attempt to cut out Iddesleigh throughout the previous month.

Certainly the public reaction must have encouraged such expectations. Both the *Pall Mall* and the *Spectator* noted that he spoke 'as in England only the head of a Government speaks, as if he had either consulted his colleagues or intended to press his proposals on them in a manner not admitting of demur ...' As a corollary, the speech was seen at once to highlight the anomalous position of a Prime Minister in the Lords; and, despite Churchill's reiteration in private and in public that Salisbury had approved the substance of the speech in advance, it could only be assumed to be an attempt to displace his leader. (Churchill himself wrote sarcastically to his wife that the reaction would make Lady Salisbury fear for 'Robert'.[40]) Inevitably, his refusal to attend a Guildhall banquet shortly afterwards was seen as dictated by disinclination to play second fiddle to Salisbury; though the Prime Minister himself waited to speak out until late November, the 'Dartford programme' was attacked publicly by Stanley and Chaplin. (Smith, however, sent an approving letter to *The Times* of 30 October which bore out Churchill's claim that the speech had been made with the full assent of his Cabinet colleagues.) The main significance of the Dartford speech was as an articulation of reforming Unionism rather than resistance Unionism: which did not stop simple Liberals like Eddy Hamilton interpreting it as a new

[39] Rhodes James, p. 54; J. P. D. Dunbabin, 'Politics of establishment of County Councils', p. 247.
[40] 8 Oct. 1886; Churchill and Mitchell, p. 151. See Carnarvon's diary, 4 Oct. 1886, BL Add. MS 60927, for a reading of the speech as an unequivocal challenge to Salisbury; repeated by Hamilton, and nearly every political journalist.

Tamworth manifesto, and 'a complete Tory capitulation'. Gladstone expected it to cause 'a *superfoetation* of Radical ideas on our side'; and it strengthened Chamberlain's position just as it weakened Hartington's. The Liberal press saw it, depending upon the editorial politics, as either a transformation scene or a clothes-stealing exercise: 'slavish dependence on the Liberal Unionists', outrageous expediency, or pure bluff. More surprisingly, apart from the *St. James's Gazette*, most Conservative newspapers applauded it, especially in the provinces,[41] and *The Times* described the programme as 'reasonable, temperate and practical', which in many respects it was.

Even in terms of foreign policy, some opinion interpreted Churchill's message as a declaration that Britain would *not* abandon Bulgaria to Russia; but more generally, the speech served to float publicly the arguments Churchill was presenting privately to Salisbury and Hatzfeldt. The French press angrily inferred an understanding between London and Vienna, and an anti-French bias; the German papers approved Churchill's 'statesmanship'; the Russians were disdainfully hostile. All took the speech as addressed to Europe, 'while Lord Iddesleigh is silent, and Lord Salisbury is withdrawn with his secrets to his villa at Dieppe'.[42] Iddesleigh himself hastily assured his correspondents that the speech was not made over his head: Churchill came to see him beforehand, 'and [we] found ourselves very fairly in accord, though he was terribly afraid of England's taking too forward a position...'[43] Once again Churchill had cleared the substance beforehand, and relied upon the style to provoke the effect. And this effect was consolidated by the unconvincingly 'incognito' journey he undertook to the Continent immediately afterwards.

This had been announced since 24 September, and should have provoked no embarrassment; but the combination of the crisis in Bulgaria, the ripples after Dartford, and Churchill's insistence upon a transparent pseudonym, led to severe annoy-

---

[41] The *Pall Mall Gazette* of 2 Oct. 1886 listed as coming out in support the *Manchester Courier, Liverpool Courier, Sheffield Telegraph, Scottish News, Yorkshire Post, Birmingham Gazette, Dublin Express, Bristol Times and Mirror, Western Mail, Globe, Standard,* and *Quarterly Review.*

[42] *Kölnische Zeitung.* This and other quotations come from the *Pall Mall Gazette*'s report of foreign newspaper reactions on 6 October.

[43] 'He told me his main object was to maintain the Unionist party and he would accept no line of policy which was likely to break it up': Iddesleigh to Cranbrook, 5 Oct. 1886, Cranbrook MSS HA 43 T501/271.

ance. French diplomatic sources believed he had gone to Berlin
to line up Bismarck for a new step in Egyptian policy, but had
been advised against it; his every movement was detailed in the
international press. These activities involved visits to theatres,
museums, and boulevards, and seem to bear out his repeated
statements that the visit was a purely private one. But, interestingly, he never made this clear to Malet, the ambassador at
Berlin; he managed a conversation with the Austrian military
chief at Vienna; and a hitherto unpublished letter to Rothschild
from the same city shows that he had an interview with Kalnoky
and pressed once more for joint action with Germany in the
Near East, promising the support of the British fleet.[44] While
embarrassment may have been his primary aim, diplomatic
intrigue was not ruled out altogether.

On Churchill's return to England, he was due to star at the
National Union's conference at Bradford, which caused some
trepidation; he was warned by Smith not to pledge too much in
the way of economy, and by Beach not to mention Ireland,
where the situation was stable but delicate. Churchill's performance on 26 October is generally seen as an unrepentant
reiteration of Dartford, but was subtler than that: it amounted
to both a personal apologia, and a pious identification of his
ideas with Salisbury's 'Newport programme' of the previous
year. It was well suited to a National Union audience (who were
asked to show their approval of Dartford by their welcome to
Churchill): he was surrounded by supporters and intimates, and
completely in control. At a preliminary morning meeting, he
countered an aggressive anti-Russian resolution from a Carlton
delegate by calling for abstentionism in the Near East, and then
delivering a flowery tribute to the Liberal Unionists and their
alliance. His main speech made mock-rueful references to his
having 'troubled the repose of politics' at Dartford; he went
straight on to Ireland, in rank disobedience to Beach. The social
situation was described in rosy terms, and the landlords praised

---

[44] 16 Oct. 1886. After describing the theatres and women of the town, Churchill relayed
diplomatic gossip from Paget and discussed the likelihood of the Hungarians pressing
Austria to war with Russia, and the irritation of the Emperor and Kalnoky with
Iddesleigh. 'I told the minister, whom I saw yesterday, that if Austria, supposing that an
occupation was threatened, chose to address an ultimatum to Russia, we would join, and
send our fleet through the Dardanelles to Varna simultaneously with the ultimatum,
assuming always that Bismarck was privy to this movement and consented to it—that the
open and direct participation of Germany was not absolutely essential but her
connivance was.' I owe this reference to the Hon. Miriam Rothschild and Dr Charles
Lane, in whose possession the letter is.

(three days after the announcement of the Plan of Campaign);
but the possibility of special legislation for certain districts was
sketched out, and a direct challenge issued to Parnell. On
foreign affairs, the Dartford position was reasserted, with—it was
claimed—Salisbury's and Iddesleigh's assent. In a similar mood,
Churchill claimed Dartford was not 'Radicalism', but 'a mere
repetition' of Salisbury's 'great historical speech at Newport': in
fact, the culmination of 'what every sincere Conservative
speaker of any position or intelligence has been explaining to the
country for the last six years'. While denying that they had
embraced 'three acres and a cow', he declared that they had
approached the problem of the agricultural labourer under
Collings's tutelage, in order to satisfy their new allies (a passage
dropped from the printed version, and offensive to many Tories).
And though declaring against any intention of a back-door
scheme of Home Rule, and ingeniously describing the *Daily
News* report on the subject as a canard arising from Lucy's
mixing up a leader proof with some copy for *Punch*, he
committed the government to a local-government scheme for
Ireland. The rest of his speech was devoted to procedure, on
which he 'frankly and fully admitted that he had changed his
mind'; but he defended the virtues of inconsistency, and the
necessity to control the Irish at Westminster.

Again, there was a variety of reactions. *The Times* emphasized the new hard line on Ireland, Chaplin attacked the closure
proposals, Clarke earned his promotion by coming out strongly
for 'the reform that saves', Smith wrote a public letter pledging
government support to Churchill's programme. The general
journalistic view was that of a new era being opened by
Churchill's recognition of the democratic constitution of parties.
But it would have been odd if he had not emphasized this angle
to a National Union conference in the North. And behind the
scenes, matters were crystallizing against him from the beginning of November. Smith, Manners, and Cranbrook moved to
stiffen Salisbury against Churchill in Cabinet; Cranbrook especially addressed a number of remonstrances to him on this score.
Balfour, elevated to Cabinet in mid-November, saw himself as
filling a similar role. Salisbury generally returned evasive
answers to accusations of pliability; but to Cranbrook he admitted
the impossibility of 'leading an orchestra in which the first fiddle
plays one tune and everybody else another' (a classical encapsu-
lation of the difference between Conservative and Liberal

approaches to government). On 18 November, when Churchill
was giving his deliberately provocative answer about the coal
and wine dues, Salisbury delivered a speech at the Mansion
House which equally deliberately contradicted much of the
Dartford ethos. On 21 November Smith found the Premier
depressed, ostensibly over the local-government wrangles regarding the rates, Poor Law administration, and the control of
county police. 'But behind all', Smith reported to Cranbrook, 'I
could see there was a great depression which he said in a joking
way partook of the weather (we have the vilest fog I can
remember), and a sense that one most important member of the
Cabinet was at issue with himself and the other members of the
Cabinet on many if not on most questions ... we shall see what
we shall see.'[45]

By the end of the month, a powerful element in the government had coalesced against Churchill; on 30 November,
Salisbury replied to Alfred Austin's remonstrances about 'the
projects of R.C. to take my place', with a veiled threat that
Churchill would not last long. Nor was the Leader in the
Commons always the popular figure recalled by his biographers;
Carnarvon heard in December that he was 'very violent in his
language in the House of Commons—swears at members of his
own party and is said to be unpopular—also that there are
intrigues—Raikes being one of the conspirators—and that H.
Matthews wishes to exchange his secretaryship of state for a
judgeship'.[46] The last were two of Churchill's few supporters
within the government, but Raikes had borne a grudge since
Matthews's elevation; another, Beach, had been increasingly
alienated by their disagreements over Ireland, culminating in
the Bradford speech, and over local government, where Beach
heartily disapproved of the Chamberlain–Churchill line. As
Churchill's star rose even higher in the politics of publicity,
where he was a past master, an ominous aspect was being cast in
the sphere of official politics: where he was, as yet, a tyro.

IV

Moreover, when the crisis came, it was on official grounds; if
Churchill had hoped to precipitate a confrontation over a great

[45] Smith to Cranbrook, 24 Nov. 1886, Cranbrook MSS HA 43 T501/260.
[46] Carnarvon diary, 8 Dec. 1886, BL Add. MS 60927. For another account of
Churchill's rudeness as leader, Raikes, op. cit., 170.

public issue he was baulked, and in the event Salisbury chose the ground. From an early stage, Churchill had planned his budget. In September Hamilton had put the financial situation before him, emphasizing that they had to deal with the largest peacetime estimates on record and allow for advances on the Land Purchase Act; this would force heavy reliance upon the income tax, and extra borrowing. By early November, faced with the Chancellor's plans in outline, Hamilton found them 'slap-dash': Churchill wanted to reduce income tax from 8*d.* to 4*d.* (unless 'a Russian dash on Constantinople' brought on war). He also declared his intention to reduce Sinking Fund payments, abolish tea tax, and increase the succession duty. Though these ideas were modified in the draft that had evolved by early December, Hamilton still feared that he would 'fly too high'. The basic design revolved around the idea of reducing income tax as a great popular *coup*, linked with the expected reforms in local-government death duty; house duty and corporate duty were to be increased, and taxes instituted on horses and wine. The death duty was, in fact, to be restructured into a graduated tax on real estate, varying by the personal legacy, not the whole estate: another bid for popularity, but principally advantageous to 'small inheritors from a great estate'. Stamp duty was to be levied on joint-stock companies, a step later adopted by Goschen. Reductions were arranged by withholding local grants-in-aid, by decreasing the debt charge by four and a half million, and by several direct economies. The ensuing surplus was to be devoted to local government (five million plus liquor-licensing powers, including the proceeds of horse tax, house duty, and a penny of income tax); the rest would be absorbed by reductions in tea tax, tobacco tax, and income tax (eventually reduced by 3*d.*). Despite Winston Churchill's description of 'a vast financial revolution', what is most striking is the element of continuity; Harcourt had floated the ideas of graduating death duty, lowering the Sinking Fund contribution, and substantially reducing income tax, the previous February, and Goschen later adopted several of these measures. Where Churchill did propose a revolution was in the minefield of protection; he sounded out West with the idea of duties on all imported food, but was forcefully warned against it, and true to his usual practice, Churchill at once accepted the official view.[47]

[47] See LHJ, 10 Feb. 1886, vol. 377, p. 132, for Harcourt's plans. Regarding food taxes, West told Churchill that everyone would realize 'that such a tax was only the thin end of the wedge of Protection': 7 Dec. 1886, RCHL xvii/2122.

Hamilton, told of Churchill's ideas in November, was impressed by their ostensible audacity but warned him that they might break up the government and leave him without a party; however, when they were first put to the Cabinet in mid-December, the reaction was muted. Cranbrook, Smith and others were nonplussed, and wanted time to think them over; Churchill told Cranbrook 'he had been surprised there had not been much more hesitation, and that he never expected so much acceptance as he had met with'.[48] None the less, he was prepared for a struggle, leaking the details to Chamberlain and Brett, and probably Rothschild, as an insurance. This reflected the fact that the budget plans were inextricably connected with the sweeping local-government reforms upon which Chamberlain and Churchill were bent. Different ideas about the rating power of the projected new local authorities provided a thorn in Salisbury's side; while Churchill inexorably pressed for adoption of Chamberlain's views, Salisbury remained preoccupied with the necessity of saving the pockets of the country gentry. Indeed, Salisbury's immediate reaction to the budget was to confer with Balfour and calculate how much the magnates of Hertfordshire would lose under Churchill's schemes, balancing increases in succession duty against the subventions offered to the poor rate; Salisbury, in deeply hostile terms, worked out that they would carry an extra burden of ninepence in the pound.[49] Smith, whose own enquiries to Churchill received a spectacularly rude and offhand answer, remarked to the Prime Minister that the budget 'has found out so many corns on which it jumps that there is great danger it may be beaten in detail'. His own position as Secretary for War was a particularly sensitive one: for Churchill's calculations heavily depended upon keeping the estimates of the Admiralty and War Office down. And in refusing to listen to his requests Churchill was making a constitutional as well as a tactical mistake. His colleagues had every right to vet fiscal matters; and by implicitly denying it, Churchill was making yet more impossible the combination judged vital for winning a budget through Cabinet, that between Chancellor and Prime Minister.

The initial hardening of battle-lines over the budget must, moreover, be seen against the revived difficulty of local-government reform, and the desire of many in the party to assert

[48] Cranbrook to Richmond, 25 Dec. 1886, Cranbrook MSS HA 43 T501/16.
[49] Salisbury to Balfour, 18 Dec. 1886, Whittingehame MSS 29.

resistance values after Dartford and Bradford. On 8 and 9
December Salisbury delivered speeches in the City emphasizing
that the Conservatives were as conservative as ever; on 15
December Walter Long announced that the majority of the
government expected local-government reform to be both limited and in the gentry's interest. This made public the disagreement precipitated by Beach's intransigence; at the very time
when Chamberlain returned from his travels, Churchill was
seeing defeats in the Cabinet over questions like *ex officio*
representation. At dinner together on 17 December, after
presenting his budget to the Cabinet, Churchill told
Chamberlain a crisis was coming; on 19 December, he instructed him to pressurize Salisbury by a public declaration on
local government; meanwhile, the card of 'splitting the forces of
the Union' was repeatedly played to Salisbury by Chamberlain,
Rothschild, and Churchill. By 22 December, according to Brett,
a compromise was worked out on the basis of a democratic
franchise, restraints on the rates, and the subvention promised
by the budget. If this was so, Churchill probably felt he had
managed to dictate from a position of isolation; and it may help
explain his other actions that day. It should also be noted that
since early December the Liberal Unionists had been taking
cautious soundings about reunion in Chamberlain's absence,
though only on a tentative basis and only among second-string
politicians. Churchill, monitoring this process closely, heard on
20 December that Gladstone proposed abandoning Home Rule
to help consummate the event. Such a happening would leave
the way open for Liberal reunion, and Conservative doom. And
the fact that Churchill relayed the rumour at once to Salisbury
can be seen as an implicit warning, or a threat: since the events
of the past month left Churchill not only isolated within his own
party, but also in a position where the only issue upon which he
ostensibly differed from the Liberals was Ireland.

It is in this context that the issue upon which confrontation
came must be considered: the question of reducing military and
naval expenditure.

The fact that Churchill's record the previous year had been
repeatedly in favour of increasing these very estimates is not
particularly relevant here;[50] the point is that once in office, it

---

[50] See his interview in *Pall Mall Gazette*, his speech at Wimborne in August 1885, and
his speech at Manchester on 3 Mar. 1886. At Sheffield on 5 Sept. 1885 he had even
suggested paring down the Civil Service in order to increase military expenditure.

was an inevitable issue. In August the question of naval economy was drawn to his attention; and he soon conformed to the Treasury norm. Due to party government, 'the curse of modern England', remarked General Wolseley, every minister attempted to build 'a claptrap reputation' by reducing the estimates; and Churchill's papers show that he was considering economies in the military service from the beginning of his tenure. This was simply to take his position in a time-hallowed ballet involving Chancellor, Prime Minister, and spending departments. In Churchill's case, he was trying on behalf of the Treasury to reassert a control which had lapsed by 1874: as his successors Goschen and Beach were to admit, both of whom gave way over service estimates—though the hostility endured. In this struggle, the Treasury Gladstonians may well have encouraged him. Eddy Hamilton and Gladstone had privately agreed in September that 'it is the Army and Navy expenditure to which the Government of the day can only look for effecting sensible reductions'; Hamilton subsequently told Churchill that heavy autumnal borrowings were necessary because of the largest peacetime estimates on record (a typical Treasury way of putting it). Harcourt had remarked to a correspondent in October apropos of the government's commissions: 'All the economy talk is for the "gallery" and not real business. The real truth is there has been much growth of work and little growth of expenditure in the Civil Service of late years. If anything is to be really done it must be done by big reductions of Army and Navy and that only a Tory government can attempt'; he then told Hamilton he would support Churchill in pressing for reductions.[51]

On the other hand, the Naval Defence Act of 1885 had appropriated five and a half millions to shipbuilding and to fortifying coaling-stations; and since Smith's warning before Bradford, Churchill knew that the War Secretary opposed any reductions. Throughout November, as he became increasingly alienated from the leadership over foreign affairs, local government, and the repercussions of Dartford, he was also involved in negotiation with Smith over the estimates. On 20 November he sent a particularly offensive letter, referring—with many exclamation marks—to 'frantic departmental extravagance' and

[51] See EHJ, 22 Sept. 1886, vol. xv, p. 128, and vol. xvi, p. 16, BL Add. MSS 48644-5; also his memoranda of 8 and 10 Sept. 1886, RCHL xv/1775, 1800; and W. V. Harcourt to E. Ruggles-Brise, 6 Oct. 1886, Harcourt MSS, dep. 729 f. 116.

implicitly threatening to resign. Smith's reply was conciliatory but firm. From the Admiralty, George Hamilton warned Churchill of the danger of breaking up the government; he managed to pare off £500,000 from his own estimates, but practically made up for it by requiring extra munitions money via the War Office. On 7 December Churchill had a long interview with Salisbury; on 14 December Smith (with whom Hamilton had been staying) refused to drop anything. Churchill sent an intransigent letter on the 15th ('if I cannot get my way I shall go'). Smith offered to resign instead. Churchill warned Salisbury in a letter of 15 December of an approaching crash; Salisbury arranged a meeting for the 16th, adding 'the Cabinet, happily, not I, will have to decide the controversy between you and Smith'.

So far, this exchange merely represents the annual pre-budget manœuvres; Harcourt had danced the same steps the year before. It seems likely that Churchill was playing it this way. His letter of the 15th to Salisbury is a curious, jumpy mishmash. Its prime emphasis was first to arrange a meeting with Salisbury and pass on a recent conversation with Hatzfeldt, secondly to convey that his own influence with Chamberlain continued undiminished, and thirdly to complain about Iddesleigh; his threat to resign over the estimates follows as a casual inclusion, seized upon by Salisbury. Churchill then weakened his own position by not bringing the estimates question to Cabinet—probably because he knew that he would not have the Prime Minister's support. On 17 December, with the estimates dispute still festering, the budget was unveiled to the Cabinet: Salisbury played down the meeting in his report to the Queen.[52]

After the Cabinet there was a general dispersal to country houses; Churchill remained in town to entertain Salisbury, Goschen, and others to dinner with the Prince of Wales on the 18th. Immediately afterwards, Salisbury reported to Balfour in Scotland about a 'curious scene' there.

R.C. came up after dinner to me and Goschen and gave us a long speech in the most open way, announcing the differences there had been among us on the subject of local government and informing us that Chamberlain was irreconcilably hostile to any kind of representation of owners. Goschen took my view—R.C. admitting our logical position but insisting that Joe's [support] was worth buying and could

---

[52] 17 Dec. 1886; PRO CAB 41/29/28.

only be bought at this price; and that if he was not bought he would go over to G.O.M. The barque looks crazier and crazier—and the chances of her floating diminish day by day.[53]

This serves as a reminder that at this very point the local-government issue was at an impasse, and Churchill was forcing Chamberlain upon the Cabinet. By the 18th also Salisbury and Smith had given Churchill firm notice that they would stand out against the budget proposals: and when Smith requested a printed memorandum of Churchill's scheme, he received a brutal and frivolous snub.[54] Churchill wrote to Chamberlain on 19 December, enjoining him to press the government hard; he met again with Smith on the 20th. At this interview, Smith told Cranbrook, 'I adhered to my view and he then said he should resign as he said he was sure I should be supported by my colleagues';[55] he wrote to Salisbury immediately afterwards. 'It comes to this—is he to be *the* government?' A warning followed that Churchill intended to resign on matters of general policy. Meanwhile Churchill travelled to Windsor for the evening of the 20th, meeting George Hamilton, First Lord of the Admiralty, *en route*, and confiding lightly to him his intention to resign; later he forced Hamilton to witness his drafting a letter on the Castle notepaper, an incident dramatically told by George Hamilton in his memoirs, and often repeated since. Thus the background to Churchill's first letter of resignation.

To consider the intention behind it is necessary to emphasize that, constitutionally speaking, such a move was extraordinarily premature: contemporary practice held unequivocally that in such a conflict as that between Churchill and Smith, the appeal was to the Prime Minister and to the Cabinet,

[53] Letter in Whittingehame MSS, 29, dated 18 Dec. 1886.
[54] 18 Dec. 1886; printed in Rhodes James, p. 284. 'How can you be so unreasonable as to require me to write a "short" memorandum on the Budget proposals? Changes so large cannot be set out in "short" documents; they require a regular budget speech arranging all the arguments in favour and I have neither time nor energy to do that until I [word missing] it is absolutely necessary for H of Cms purposes. Really, considering your frightful extravagance at the War Office you might at least give me a free hand for "ways and means". If the Cabinet want further information on the proposed budget I am ready to be cross examined, but I could not possibly produce the document you demand. I assume for all practical purposes that the Cabinet have consented to the outline of the budget. The permanent officials are now hard at work on elaboration of details and I shall not trouble my head about it any more until a week or ten days before it is to be presented to Parliament.'
[55] Smith to Cranbrook, 24 Dec. 1886, Cranbrook MSS HA 43 T501/260.

and the most recent authorities agree.[56] Salisbury made much
capital out of Churchill's refusal to put the matter to the
Cabinet, and Cranbrook agreed that this meant Churchill was
determined to force the issue. Gladstone—a good authority—
believed that Churchill was wrong in assuming the Chancellor
had the right to rule over defence estimates: if he did, 'he would
be the master of the country'. Salisbury on this subject agreed:
he was celebrated for not supporting his Chancellors in Cabinet
disputes. When the Chancellor was Churchill, the result—as the
latter well knew—was a foregone conclusion.

The letter of 20 December was probably an attempt to
circumvent a show-down in a Cabinet where he had no support.
In it Churchill briefly restated the disagreement with Smith, and
to a lesser extent George Hamilton, and announced that he therefore begged to take his leave. Interestingly, the only other issue
raised was foreign policy: 'if the foreign policy of this country
is conducted with skill and judgement, our present huge and
increasing armaments are quite unnecessary, and the taxation
which they involve perfectly unjustifiable'. For throughout
November and December, his interference in this sphere had
escalated: 'I cannot get my ideas on foreign policy attended to',
he had told Salisbury in a letter of 8 November, continuing with
a torrent of abuse against Iddesleigh ('quel crétin!'). His
complaints about what he saw as the mishandling of Austria
continued; he had maintained his unauthorized conversations
with Hatzfeldt, whom he informed of his 'confidential' discussions in Vienna. But, he informed Hatzfeldt on 4 December, no
arrangement with Austria would be possible until Karolyi and
Iddesleigh were removed (towards which end Wolff was supposedly intriguing in London at this time). He was also, as a
juxtaposition of diplomatic dispatches shows, giving a different
angle to envoys from that provided by Salisbury; by early
December he was enjoining Hatzfeldt not to mention their

---

[56] See Welby's definition of Treasury control to Goschen in 1887, referring to the
question of War Office estimates. 'If in the exercise of these functions he is completely at
issue with a colleague, the appeal lies to the P.M. and to the Cabinet.' Quoted in Sir
Horace Hamilton, 'Treasury Control in the 80's', *Public Administration*, 33 (1955), p. 14.
Also see Disraeli to Derby in 1867: 'The Admiralty is beyond the control of the
Chancellor of the Exchequer ... it is the P.M. alone who can deal with that department', quoted in Kynaston, op. cit., p. 64. The latter states unequivocally that a
disagreement between War Office and Exchequer was inevitably put to the Cabinet; see
also W. S. Hamer, *The British Army: Civil and Military Relations, 1885–1905* (Oxford, 1970),
p. 64.

discussions to the Prime Minister.⁵⁷ Hatzfeldt none the less repeated much of his conversations with Churchill throughout December to Salisbury, who delicately deprecated Churchill's views on Russia: what he thought of Churchill's assurance to the Germans that France was their common enemy, and must be crushed, can only be guessed at.

Such conversations were being held with Hatzfeldt up to the confused Christmas of 1886; indeed, it is a curious if fortuitous coincidence that on the fateful evening of 20 December Churchill sat up late at Windsor with, of all people, the deposed Prince Alexander of Bulgaria. The letter which he wrote that night was, as has been indicated, to be part of the same process whereby he had tried to cut Iddesleigh out of foreign affairs, and to force Chamberlain's ideas upon the Cabinet; the unstable condition of the Liberals at the time, which threatened the union of the Unionists, seemed to give him added leverage. (It is not unlikely, given his surroundings, that he remembered the unfortunate Duke of Connaught and the Bombay Command.) In after years, Churchill consistently said in private that this letter was over-interpreted. Chamberlain's version to Dilke at the end of December, after seeing Churchill, is worth quoting for its terse survey of the essentials. 'At last he resigned once too often, as of course it was on the wrong subject: Salisbury jumped at it, and accepted it in a cool letter when Churchill did not mean it in the least. It was only the classical annual resignation of a Chancellor of the Exchequer against his colleagues in the Army and Navy.'

Salisbury, in calling Churchill's bluff, probably saw the weakness and unpopularity of the restricted ground taken up by Churchill in the letter of the 20th, and determined to fight on it. Letters from Smith and Hamilton strengthened his will; he sent copies of Churchill's letter to his colleagues; his note to Balfour conveyed an uncharacteristic tone of glee.⁵⁸ Balfour's reply was equally enthusiastic, and grasped at once the point of letting

⁵⁷ See report of their conversation of 4 December in *Grosspolitik*, no. 874 (not translated in Dugdale version).

⁵⁸ 'New sensation! Randolph meets Smith on Monday—and after two hours' discussion goes down to Windsor, from where he writes me a letter of which I enclose you a copy. I have replied expressing effusively my very deep regret—but stating that I fully concurred with Smith and Hamilton; and that I should regard it as the gravest responsibility to refuse in the present state of Europe the funds necessary for protecting our ports and coaling stations. I have written to Smith and Beach—when I know more I will let you know.' Salisbury to Balfour, 21 Dec. 1886, Whittingehame MSS, 29.

Churchill go on an unpopular issue. Salisbury's next priority was to neutralize Beach. This he did by sending a particularly vague and misleading account of the situation to Ireland, as Rhodes James has effectively shown. But in any case, Beach was no longer Churchill's staunch ally.

Churchill returned to London on 21 December, seeing Smith that day and the next; by the 22nd he knew from the latter that Salisbury would accept his resignation. He had not told his wife of the situation, and she continued to plan a large reception (ironically, at the Foreign Office); only Wolff was confided in, and possibly Brett.[59] On the evening of the 22nd Salisbury's reply arrived, stating conclusively that he accepted Churchill's resignation. Probably with a view to publicity, it emphasized national defence: 'The outlook on the continent is very black. It is not too much to say that the chances are in favour of war at an early date; and when war has once broken out we cannot be secure from danger of being involved in it. The undefended state of many of our ports and coaling stations is notorious ...' This theme of the coaling stations was reiterated, and Churchill's attitude represented as unpatriotic: 'no-one knows better than you how injurious to the public interests at this juncture your withdrawal from the Government may be'. The rough draft in the Salisbury papers shows that the words 'formidable' and 'disastrous' were rejected, and a reference to Salisbury's 'help-lessness' deleted. Such changes symbolized the Prime Minister's decision to represent the defection as a wounding, but not a fatal, blow.

On reception of this bombshell, Winston Churchill recorded with superb disingenuousness that his father sent to Salisbury from the Carlton 'a letter of farewell'. In fact, the letter he composed on 22 December was a desperate attempt to broaden the ground of disagreement, with a view to strengthening his position in the public eye. It began with the statement that 'foreign policy and free expenditure upon armaments act and react upon each other', moved to the issue of domestic hardship under high taxation, and finally asserted that 'the character of the domestic legislation which the Government contemplates in my opinion falls sadly short of what the Parliament and the country expect and require'. Again a Liberal Unionist, in this

---

[59] See Brett to Harcourt, 22 Dec. 1886: 'R.C. is unwell, knocked up by the excitement. He thinks Salisbury means to fight it out.' Harcourt MSS, dep. 729, f. 124 (copy).

12 Churchill on his travels in India, with his secretary, Frank Thomas

13 Churchill at work in the India Office,

ENGLAND·CANNOT·DESERT·THE·PROTESTANTS·OF·IRELAND·

THE MEETING IN THE ULSTER HALL, BELFAST

IN THE STREETS

CHAIRED

14 Sketches of Churchill in Belfast, February 1886

15 W. H. Trafford, 'Natty' Rothschild and Churchill on the lawn at Tring, 1890

16 Churchill and his Dublin friends at one of his last Howth parties, Christmas 1892
Seated, from left to right: David Plunket (Lord Rathmore), Benjamin Williamson,
Frank Lynch, Lord Morris. Standing: Lord Randolph and Gerald FitzGibbon.

17 Lord Randolph after his return from Africa

case Brett, recorded his reasoning most neatly: 'R.C. had not intended his letter to be a formal resignation but in receipt of Salisbury's letter wrote to him justifying his conduct and put in other reasons besides finance such as local government and foreign affairs, peace, etc.' What had begun at Windsor as a tactical exertion of pressure had to be converted in mid-course into an effort to break up the government. Churchill showed this letter to Lord Harris in the Carlton smoking room, declaring 'I never was so certain that I was right as I am on this occasion',[60] set off to the theatre with his wife and Wolff, and in the interval called round to *The Times* and gave the paper notice of his resignation.

A point not sufficiently stressed in attempts to explain this bizarre step is that he had with him a copy of the letter he had just written, or maybe even the original (which did not reach Salisbury until one in the morning): and it seems likely that he wanted Buckle to publish it, written as it was expressly to present his case to the public. Certainly he expected some quid pro quo in the way of editorial support; but he did not get it. Rumours exist of a sharp exchange with Buckle; and when the paper announced his resignation the next morning, it merely added a paragraph stating: 'we believe that other circumstances have combined in the past few weeks to make Lord Randolph Churchill regard his position in the ministry as a false one. He has not been satisfied with the shape which the legislative measures for Great Britain have assumed after discussion in the Cabinet. They do not appear to him adequate to the requirements of the country.' But this was so vague as to be useless for Churchill's purpose, and the leader of the same page contrived to discount the importance of any reason beyond the estimates; the next day, it stated baldly that Churchill had resigned 'on the economic question alone', all other rumours being red herrings. Buckle's course was set; he continued indefatigably to preach that this was not a fatal blow, that public opinion was entirely with Salisbury, and that the inclusion of Hartington in the ministry could save the country. Churchill's attempt at premature publicity misfired dreadfully. Salisbury, receiving the Carlton letter in the middle of the night at a ball, kept it until the next morning, when the news of the resignation was made known to the Queen and country by courtesy of Mr Buckle's centre pages.

[60] Harris to W. S. Churchill, 12 Feb. 1906, CHAR 8/24.

(Such were Churchill's relations with his wife that this was the first she heard of it too.) This miscalculation set the pattern for what was to follow. Personal debility, constitutional impatience, the enmity of his colleagues, a determination to force capitulation before his time ran out, and an overpowering belief in his own ability to capture, at least rhetorically, the middle ground in reforming politics had led Churchill out on to a dangerous limb. His attempt to fight back would equally be characterized by these elements, and by whatever alliances he could construct from his isolation.

Chapter 10

Resignation Politics, 1887–1888

'I always observe', said Madame Max Goesler,
'that when any of you gentlemen resign, which you
usually do on some very trivial matter, the resigning gentleman becomes of all foes the bitterest.
Somebody goes on very well with his friends,
agreeing most cordially about everything, till he
finds that his public virtue cannot swallow some
little detail, and then he resigns. Or someone,
perhaps, on the other side has attacked him, and in
the mêlée he is hurt, and so he resigns. But when he
has resigned, and made his parting speech full of
love and gratitude, I know well where to look for
the bitterest hostility to his late friends. Yes, I am
beginning to understand the way in which politics
are done in England.'

Anthony Trollope, *Phineas Finn* (1869)

I

The outcome of the days before Christmas was that the initiative
had passed to Salisbury; and with him it remained. Churchill
failed to control or define the context within which his resignation was interpreted—originally because he had not prepared
the ground, and then because he failed to gain publicity. The
terms of the public reaction were those of preserving the Union,
not of economy, social legislation, local government, or even
foreign policy. This rallied the party to Salisbury. All (except
Beach) advised against fusion with Hartington; all disapproved
of any idea of the Commons leadership going to Goschen. The
priority became to show that the government, having refused to
capitulate to Churchill, need not capitulate to anyone else. And
capitulation was seen everywhere as Churchill's real aim: as
Smith wrote to Cranbrook, and said to everybody, 'the real
truth is, I think, that it is not possible for him to yield his opinion

or mould it so as to co-operate with his colleagues. He must rule; and my estimates have only been a pretext.'[1]

This was certainly the position from 22 December, even if it had not been Churchill's original plan; and the public reaction was accordingly hostile. All the important newspapers abandoned him, except the *Morning Post*. The foreign press, interestingly, never mentioned the estimates question, assuming Ireland, Bulgaria, Egypt, or Radical ideology to have been the proximate question: but here too the issue was converted into a tilt against Salisbury. Inevitably, attention shifted to how the Prime Minister could preserve his government and his majority: and thus to Hartington, who was travelling in Italy. Churchill's great object, spectators decided, was 'to prevent Hartington from joining Salisbury, in order that Salisbury should take him back on his own terms'. The other cynosure was Chamberlain: if he unequivocally withdrew support from the government, Churchill's position was saved. And Chamberlain's response to Churchill's step was the celebrated speech at Birmingham on 23 December, holding out the chance of Liberal reunion, and generally seen as a farewell to the Conservatives; to that extent, collusion with Churchill was suspected. The political situation in Christmas week hinged on the Liberal Unionists; and it could take almost any direction. Gladstone, for one, suspended all judgement and hypothesis and abandoned himself to pleased surprise; he was struck by the vision of Churchill as 'a Treasury man ... in that capacity a better man than Dizzie ever would have been'.[2]

While Hartington, telegraphed by Salisbury, made his slow way back from Rome, Churchill's priority was to consolidate his position: and here he failed. There was no support, even from his creatures within the government. The pusillanimous Matthews, realizing on 24 December that Churchill's position was 'irremediable', never thought of resigning; the only government member who did so was Dunraven, who gave up an undersecretaryship too late to be of any use (despite Churchill's encouragement). Beach reacted to Salisbury's dilatory letter of 21 December in an equally unhurried way; Irish land, local government, and the fact that Churchill had not consulted him about procedural reform had probably nearly exhausted his patience, and he assumed Churchill could be talked round. It is

[1] 24 Dec. 1886; Cranbrook MSS HA 43 T501/260.
[2] Gladstone to E. Hamilton, 29 Dec. 1886, quoted BL Add. MS 48645, f. 69.

noticeable that no Cabinet ministers wrote to Churchill during Christmas week, while he was living on his nerves between the Carlton and Connaught Place: Beach's visit on 28 December was the first to break the silence. His correspondents numbered professional intriguers, disappointed Tory Democrats, bemused back-benchers; though supporters like Henniker Heaton assured him that forty of the younger MPs were his supporters, this was insubstantial comfort. Alone of the friends whom he saw regularly, Rothschild told him the truth—he had made a mistake and must get back. Labouchere and Chamberlain assured him the government was doomed, the latter adding that 'we must re-form parties on a new basis': but without a concerted plan having been set in advance this was as shadowy as Henniker Heaton's forty back-benchers. It was, as Harcourt noted, 'now a game in which anything and everything is on the cards'.

It was also, for Liberals, a spectator sport, and described as such ('very amusing, and breaks up the monotony of the former situation, which was beginning to be tiresome' ... 'a very amusing crisis ... Hartington at Monte Carlo is perfect, so like the idea of *Milord Anglais* in a French play').[3] The Tories saw things more grimly, Salisbury calling a Cabinet on 28 December, where he restricted the issue to the estimates, and did not even read out his correspondence with Churchill. Beach, taken by surprise, had come over from Ireland for the meeting, where he alone counselled resignation, and also refused to take over the Leadership of the Commons in the event of a Hartington coalition. When he called on Churchill after the Cabinet (the first of his colleagues to do so), and was shown the letters, 'he said he had no conception how strong his case was and that if the Cabinet had been told the decision might have been very different';[4] but the next day he returned to Ireland, having done his rather half-hearted best. Salisbury had continued to dictate the terms of reference: the public statement after the Cabinet was a masterpiece of obfuscation.[5] Moreover, on 24 December

[3] Exchange between Harcourt and Brett, 23 and 25 Dec., Harcourt MSS dep 729, ff. 125, 127.

[4] LHJ, 28 Dec. 1886, vol. 380, p. 32.

[5] It described his reply to Churchill's Windsor letter as 'answering Lord Randolph's arguments and stating that he would not take the responsibility of refusing the heads of the War Department and the Admiralty', not as accepting his resignation. Thus the initiative seemed to rest with Churchill. Churchill's reservations about the government's legislative programme, mentioned in *The Times*, were dismissed: '[Salisbury] was much surprised at this, inasmuch as Lord Randolph Churchill has never before alluded to this subject to him in connection with his resignation'.

Churchill had requested permission to publish his letters of resignation, which had been refused unequivocally: according to Salisbury, for this to be done before the explanation in parliament would require royal permission. He then postponed the opening of parliament until 27 January.

Churchill's spirits must have been raised by Beach's telling him on the 28th that the Cabinet would not accept a coalition; the next day Lady Randolph was announcing that her husband would rejoin the government. But three days later Salisbury knew that Goschen would join the government as Chancellor with no need for reconstruction; and the crisis was over.

Historians have hypothesized about it as much as contemporaries did; there is a favourite game of drawing parallels with Palmerston in 1853 (down to a snowstorm and the Eastern Question), or Curzon in 1923, or Mosley in 1930. Winston Churchill presented his father's action as a selfless sacrifice for economy; Mr Rhodes James, in the best chapter of his book, identified it as a forcing tactic that misfired when Salisbury took it literally. This much is verifiable, since Churchill himself said so over and over again. Neither biographer sees it as a bluff turning into a bid for leadership, which is how contemporaries interpreted it. Certainly, Churchill had not prepared the ground by 'lobbying'; but, bearing in mind that his attention was fixed on the Liberal Unionists, he may not have felt this to be necessary. Hartington was away (and both he and Goschen had recently reaffirmed the Liberal faith in public). Chamberlain may have been squared: he was certainly warned on the 19th that a crisis was coming. (Hartington, Smith, and even Brett, who knew a good deal, believed he had encouraged Churchill to make a stand).[6] And certainly, a prime motive in Churchill's attempt to broaden the grounds of his resignation after the 22nd was to make it impossible for the Liberal Unionists to stay in Salisbury's government, by branding it as reactionary on a wide front.

However, Salisbury's effective muzzling of him left public attention concentrated upon the estimates question; interpretations behind the scenes rarely looked further than foreign affairs. Here, there was a broad consensus that Churchill had really resigned in an attempt to shift British policy away from an anti-Russian stance, and thus oust Iddesleigh from the Foreign

---

[6] LHJ, 23 Dec. 1886, vol. 380, p. 1; Hurst, op. cit., p. 114; Chilston, *Smith*, p. 100.

Office.[7] In the vacuum of Churchill's own silence, theories abounded. The most perceptive reading came from FitzGibbon who, after failing to persuade Churchill to retire to Howth, decided he should be left 'within reach of the olive branch', and soliloquized: 'I can't understand your firing the mine *now*: more than a year ago I *expected* you to do it, and conveyed as much ...' His argument, which showed how well he knew his friend, was that Churchill's ordained place was in leading the respectables.

I wish from the bottom of my heart that you may at least agree in this, that there are but two possible governing parties in any State, the party of solid stolid slow moving respectability, and the party of scrambling scurrying tinkering disturbance. The former never has leaders enough and seldom any whom it does not bring in from outside (*teste* Dizzy), the latter always has too many. Properly led the power of the first is great, not led they are only a mask for plunder. *You* are their only hope, don't go over to the enemy.[8]

So much of Churchill's strategy at this point had to depend on waiting and seeing that it is difficult to evaluate his own reactions: but some judgements can be drawn. With his bluff called, and his attempts at publicity suppressed, he could only wait for Hartington's reaction. Hartington's entry into the ministry would have been fatal to Churchill; but if Salisbury had to give way to a Hartington government, Churchill would in all likelihood be asked to join, and it is worth noting that, as the government struggled through crises in the autumn, a Hartington ministry had frequently been on Churchill's mind. The other chief counter to be played involved Chamberlain: so carefully aligned against Salisbury by Churchill in the days before his resignation, and connected inextricably in the minds of onlookers with that step. Chamberlain's public reaction took the form of his kite for reunion at Birmingham, which deserves examination. Not only did it work to Churchill's advantage by threatening Salisbury's position: Chamberlain also represented Churchill as a Liberal in all but name, driven out by reactionary Conservatives. He detailed the issues on which Churchill had taken a Liberal line and emphasized the paragraph in *The Times*

---

[7] Derby to Hartington, 26 Dec. 1886, Devonshire MSS 340/2073, Northbrook to Dufferin, 7 Jan. 1887, DVP F 130/27A, no. 7, Waddington to Flourens, 11 Jan. 1887, *Doc. Dipl. Fr.*, 1st ser., ii, no. 13, Blunt to Churchill, 30 Dec. 1886, Blunt MSS 394/1977, letters from the Crown Princess of Prussia and Rowton to the Queen in Royal Archives B 38/1, 2, all make the assumption that the resignation was purely a foreign-policy crisis.

[8] 2 Jan. 1887; RCHL xviii/2291.

that indicated Churchill's wider disagreements with his colleagues. But he went on to adduce that Liberal Unionists now had to look to Gladstone; they had a great common ground of agreement, '*even upon Ireland*'. Home Rule was no longer necessary, if the land was treated properly.

The last clause was what attracted opinion; but the whole tenor of the speech, made though it was before Churchill could confer with Chamberlain, is compatible with a scenario whereby Churchill might have been counting on some kind of Liberal reunion on the basis of forgetting Home Rule: the only ground upon which he could join them, and capitalize upon their agreement regarding foreign policy, economy, local government, agriculture, and education. Beach, and nearly everyone else, hypothesized about a Chamberlain–Churchill combination at once: the Birmingham speech, upon which Churchill immediately congratulated Chamberlain, implied it. Their exchange of letters was warm and conciliatory. And Churchill, who had allowed Wolff to begin negotiating with Hatfield on 23 December, almost immediately withdrew his support from the initiative, and looked to Birmingham.

But Churchill was only part of Chamberlain's calculations; and he was not prepared to co-operate fully with him, or indeed treat with him frankly. Though he assured Churchill on 29 December that he would not enter a Unionist coalition government, he told Edward Heneage three days before that he would support such a move, and he was supposed to be pressing Hartington to join Salisbury. To the Gladstonians, he represented himself as urging Churchill to rejoin the government. He was rapidly absorbed in what were to become the Round Table negotiations for Liberal reunion: if these were to retain any semblance of viability, he could not afford to play too close to Churchill. Churchill realized this a month later, and publicly retaliated. But in late December he lost some valuable time while waiting for Chamberlain to conjure up a new opening.

Meanwhile, there was even less to be hoped for from the Conservative side. 'The matter is very critical but by no means desperate and may drag on indefinitely for some days', Churchill wrote to his mother on 28 December, probably after hearing the Cabinet had rejected an offer to Hartington. For the moment, he brazened it out; 'he banged into the Carlton a day or two after his resignation', recorded an acquaintance, 'and lay all the afternoon on a sofa, reading a French novel, while all round him were groups of men, mad with rage, cursing him up hill and down dale'. However, all the evidence shows that he was nonplussed at the extent to which his support had fallen off.[9] At a celebrated luncheon party given by Mrs Jeune on 26 December, Churchill told the company that he never expected Salisbury to accept his resignation; Fitzjames Stephen (who like FitzGibbon saw Churchill as a bulwark against 'Jacobinism') talked to him seriously and afterwards wrote to Salisbury asking him to be forbearing. Salisbury's reply (knowing his man) instanced Churchill's great fault as forcing the Cabinet to take Chamberlain 'as our guide in internal politics'; he also complained of his impulsiveness, variability, and bullying.[10] Wolff's attempts at arranging a compromise were deflected with equal adroitness; Salisbury, again suiting his response to his audience, took the line of remarking delphically that 'more astonishing things have occurred than that in a government formed by Lord Hartington, I and Lord Randolph Churchill should have office'. This was a scenario in which Wolff also managed to interest Goschen; it remained a solution attractive in terms of mathematical logic but not materially practicable.

In essence, Hatfield House never deviated from Balfour's initial advice of letting Churchill go on an unpopular issue, 'in obvious alliance with Joe'; and Salisbury continued cleverly to restrict the issue publicly to the estimates, while in private letters to colleagues he widened the ground wherever it would weaken Churchill. To Hamilton he instanced Churchill's 'incessant interference' in foreign policy; to Cranbrook, taken completely unawares, he gave a highly inaccurate impression of his letter accepting Churchill's first resignation. ('I answered, *arguing with him* . . and received that night, at one in the morning, his letter resigning.'[11]) Salisbury had also effectively destroyed any sup-

---

[9] West Ridgeway to Mackenzie Wallace, 31 Jan. 1887, DVP F/130, 27A, no. 33. For Churchill's surprise at his lack of supporters, see especially comments in Cornwallis-West, ch. 9.

[10] The Jeune luncheon and its aftermath is treated in detail by R. Rhodes James, pp. 303–4; it is also fully described in a letter from Sir William Gregory to Dufferin, DVP F/130 24B. 'He admitted that he hardly thought Lord Salisbury would have taken him at his word, and not accepted some further compromise, but he said he always had the Cabinet against him, and that his position was hopeless.' Mrs Jeune also described Churchill's case to Carnarvon on 28 December. 'He is low—saying that he has no friend in the world—that there was an intrigue in the Cabinet against him—that Salisbury at last joined against him and then he had no chance . . .' (BL Add. MS 60927).

[11] A. E. Gathorne-Hardy, *Gathorne Hardy, 1st Earl of Cranbrook: a Memoir* (2 vols., London, 1910), ii, p. 268. For Cranbrook's surprise at how far things had gone see Cranbrook to Richmond, 24 Dec. 1886, Cranbrook MSS, HA 43 T501/16.

port Churchill might have at court, by ensuring that the Queen did not receive her Chancellor's resignation until well after *The Times*; the Prince of Wales's attempts to present Churchill's apologies to his mother were met by torrents of vituperative abuse. Smith was equally assiduous, writing to his colleagues repetitive letters which emphasized Churchill's overweening ambition and his covert alliance with Chamberlain.[12] Akers-Douglas obligingly pledged full support; moreover, he and Captain Middleton had plumbed constituency opinion, and confirmed that feeling towards Churchill was highly antagonistic. Alfred Austin and the *Standard* (to whom Churchill was convinced Salisbury had shown his letters) emphasized usefully demotic points like Churchill's rudeness to the Queen. There is also more than a hint of inspiration in a letter from Howorth, a *habitué* of Hatfield, which was written to *The Times* with suspicious alacrity on 23 December declaring that 'Mr Goschen is the man' to replace Churchill and offering him his seat. To Churchill's fury, Salisbury even sent his own version of the Chancellor's resignation to E. T. Cook of the *Pall Mall Gazette*, enjoining him 'not to let it be seen that I have been in communication with you'.[13] Ironically, the gentlemanly Salisbury faction contrived to beat Churchill hands down on his own ground, that of manipulating publicity.

This was partly to do with the fact that he was physically unwell: Mrs Jeune, Brett, and others record him as being 'knocked up' in Christmas week, through debility as well as excitement, and his wife thought he resigned in a manic state: 'in the bottom of my heart I sometimes think his head was quite turned at the moment and that he thought he could do *anything*'. His marriage was also going through a stormy passage, with open and violent quarrels, and renewed rumours of divorce;

---

[12] The letter to Akers-Douglas is a model. 'I am very sorry about Churchill, but the real truth is estimates are a pretext—not the real cause. It was really Salisbury or Churchill and if Salisbury had gone, none of us could have remained—not even those who are disposed to go with him on allotments and local government rather than with Salisbury. He dined with Joe on Friday, and that I think settled it . . .', 24 Dec. 1886; Chilston C/25, quoted in *Chief Whip*, p. 100. A nearly identical letter went to Balfour (Whittingehame MSS 29 and Chilston, *Smith*, p. 227: 'if he is in a government he must be Chief Supreme—a Bismarck') and to Cranbrook.

[13] I owe this information from the Cook papers to the kindness of Professor Stephen Koss.

Hamilton heard that 'he was dared to do it by his wife'.[14] But, whatever the reason, Churchill's facility for gaining the public ear, and gambling on a winning issue, had deserted him. His old tutor Mandell Creighton utterly misread Churchill's intention when he congratulated him for deciding to educate the public to a policy instead of intuiting one from their supposed wishes. Churchill was convinced that the 'new democracy' would not stand the expense and responsibility of war, and had declared as much repeatedly.[15] Chamberlain also believed at this time that 'fighting can never again be *popular* with the people, with the masses'; but he was to change his mind. Churchill, however, remained convinced, and certainly felt that the issue of belligerency was one to emphasize. In September he had told Hatzfeldt he was prepared to resign rather than support an anti-Russian policy; in December he told Maclean that this was exactly what he had done, and disagreed when Maclean tried to argue it was not a popular line. Coming as it did shortly after Bismarck obtained large army increases in December, and with Boulanger Minister of War in France, logic was on Maclean's side; but Churchill failed to see it.

Another miscalculation arose regarding the reaction to his step within the party: Churchill failed to realize how violently his wrecking tactics would be greeted, because he failed to share the paranoiac insecurity of his colleagues. Convinced though he was from time to time in December that the government was headed for a smash, he did not see that eventuality in the same terms as, for instance, Cranbrook, who can be found in a private letter (chosen at random) referring to Gladstone as 'an infamous and degraded joiner of assassins, fawning upon traitors': and this to a colleague who considered him too liberal.[16] Churchill

---

[14] See Lady Randolph to Leonie Leslie, A. Leslie, p. 122. For rumours about a sensational divorce between them see Hamilton to Rosebery, 13 Jan. 1887, Rosebery MSS 10032; F. A. Villiers to Rosebery, 31 Dec. 1886, ibid. 10080; Ridgeway to Mackenzie Wallace, 31 Jan. 1887, DVP F/130/27A, no. 33. See also Lord Derby's diary for 19 Jan. 1887: 'Letter from Lady S [probably Sefton or Sackville] who tells me among other matters that R. Churchill is taking steps to get rid of his wife, whom he accuses of playing tricks with four men. A pleasant disclosure of manners in that set.'

[15] See Goschen to Dufferin, 26 Nov. 1886, DVP F/130 24B, no. 251. Also Waddington to Flourens, *Doc. Dipl. Fr.* 6, ii, p. 149. 'Il est convaincu, il me l'a dit lui-même, que la nouvelle democratie anglaise s'intéresse de moins en moins aux guerres d'influence et d'équilibre, qu'elle redoute d'être mêlée aux luttes du Continent, et qu' elle désire par-dessus tout l'allègement des charges budgetaires. Il veut être le porte-drapeau de cette democratie et, en lui donnant satisfaction, la rallier au parti conservateur.'

[16] 3 Apr. 1887, Cranbrook MSS HA 43 T501/16 (Cranbrook to Richmond, copy).

simply did not see political divisions in such apocalpytic terms, once he had stepped off a public platform; and he probably never realized how far he had damned himself in the eyes of colleagues by so nearly bringing the government down. He was also, in a sense, inured from such a realization by the soothing hypocrisies which characterized the interaction of high society and high politics; when Churchill's mother, visiting Dublin in early February, was told by Ashbourne that he, Smith, and Hamilton 'would do anything to get him back' and that Salisbury 'was very fond of him', she enthusiastically retailed the opinions to her son.[17] But they are far more indicative of how Ashbourne talked to duchesses than of how his party viewed their ex-Chancellor.

II

Faced with this well-orchestrated opposition, Churchill quickly realized that the longer he delayed publicizing a wide platform of reasons for his desertion of the government, the less likely he was to obtain a hearing. As one of his constituents put it in a letter to *The Times* on 30 December, 'Lord Randolph Churchill may have taken a line which was the only one open to him as a man of honour and as a consistent politician. If this be so, he is in this position—that he has withheld from the public every rag of evidence which could lead them to that conclusion.' Similarly, the Duchess found among Churchill's old friends in Dublin a bewilderment as to his motives, and a desire for enlightenment.

As early as 23 December Churchill attempted to fix things in high quarters with a letter to the Prince of Wales; baulked by Salisbury of the opportunity to publish his letter of resignation, he resorted to other expedients, such as writing to indefatigable gossips like Labouchere and Brett;[18] and a full report in the *Pall Mall Gazette* of 29 December giving the reasons behind his resignation seems obviously inspired. This detailed how Salisbury had tied Churchill's hands by refusing him the right to a full explanation, and emphasized local government, foreign

---

[17] 2 Feb. 1887; Blenheim MSS, E/IV.

[18] He wrote to the Prince of Wales that divergence and a split were inevitable, and sent him copies of the letters to and from Salisbury. The letter to Labouchere is now lost but Labouchere to Winston Churchill, 27 Sept. 1905, CHAR 8/20, shows that Labouchere's letter to Churchill of 23 December, quoted in W. S. Churchill, ii, 253, was actually a *reply*.

policy, and Democratic Toryism as the real context of Churchill's decision. The *Pall Mall Gazette* had asked him for a statement immediately after his resignation; and what they received amounted to a paraphrase of the document with which Churchill attempted once more to broaden his case.

This was a lengthy letter to Akers-Douglas dated 1 January which, though described by Winston Churchill as 'a private letter', was to all intents and purposes a public manifesto; Cross referred to it as a letter 'which Lord Randolph's friends prevented him publishing'. Douglas realized this, remarking to Salisbury that Churchill probably intended to publish it; and it was so assiduously leaked that by 5 January Buckle actually asked Churchill for the text to put in *The Times*. By then, however, it had been sent to the *Pall Mall Gazette*, where a full paraphrase appeared that evening. The letter emphasized the need for popular support for a popular Tory party, and put foreign affairs at the head of the government's failures. Churchill declared his intention to support Salisbury, but also left his hands free to join any 'coalition, fusion or reconstruction ... which by its composition and its policy will be an earnest and a guarantee to the country that a period of peaceful, progressive administration has in reality set in'. He constructed this letter to replace his second letter to Salisbury; it was indefatigably circulated to the Prince of Wales, Jeune, Dunraven, and others. Akers-Douglas, however (who had decided party feeling was unanimous against Churchill, and had warned Salisbury not to 'magnify' Churchill's position), kept it strictly private: except to show it to Salisbury, who complained to the Duchess that Churchill's broadcasting of this and other evidence of their disagreements made any reconciliation extremely difficult.[19]

At the same time Churchill's constituent Burdett was used as a link to the newspapers: writing indefatigably, trying to cultivate the *Telegraph*, settling for the *Morning Post* and *Lloyd's News*; but his attempts to draft terms of reconciliation with Smith and

[19] 'Made the breach unbridgeable,' in Churchill's words. For the full letter from Salisbury to the Duchess (which was much longer than the extract given in Rhodes James) see RCHL xix/2314. For royal reaction to the Akers-Douglas letter see Royal Archives B 38/8, 9, T 9/84, I 55/59. Ponsonby dismissed it, and Cross pointed out to the Queen that 'the reasons are wholly beyond those given to Lord Salisbury for his resignation'; similarly, Ponsonby had emphasized that Churchill's remarks to the Prince about a general divergence between him and Salisbury were 'a new revelation' (Royal Archives, C 38/85).

Ritchie led to a snub from Churchill, whose priority was still to present his case to the public. On 6 January he wrote to the Cambridge Carlton, abusing Goschen and calling for a progressive and peaceful policy; on the 11th he complained to a Primrose League deputation that he was 'rigorously denied a public personal explanation'. At the same time, he sedulously emphasized to private contacts that he had left the government on larger issues than the estimates. To Brett 'he gave out plainly and evidently wishes it to be known that his chief cause of quarrel with Salisbury has been in foreign affairs': Salisbury was determined to reinstate Alexander and fight Russia. 'I left the government really on foreign policy, though this cannot be stated in public', wrote Churchill to Roberts on 2 February: 'I wanted peace and friendship with Russia ... but I could not effect this change. The estimates was a pretext, and a good one.' On the same day he sent a full account to Morris:

I left them because I had ceased to have the smallest influence with them. I wanted them to adopt a policy of rational Liberalism in Home and Foreign affairs. They preferred an easy matter, the 'principles'? of stupid Toryism.

As I was perfectly aware of the speedy result of that course of action if persisted in, and as I could not modify it from the inside, out I went, as I did not choose to share the responsibility of their folly. Now you have it all, and you will see that all this talk of reconciliation is supremely silly. I differed with them on everything except their Irish policy. I approached every subject from a different point of view. I kept steadily looking to the next General election. They confined their attention to expedients which they thought suitable for the moment.

In addition to this there was a mischievous meddlesomeness in their foreign policy which may at any moment land us in with Russia. In a word it was 'Jingo redivivus'.[20]

This was Churchill's fullest private exposition; and the date upon which it was delivered is significant, for by then he knew that the government, failing with Hartington, had succeeded in obtaining Goschen. ('They shot at the pigeon and killed the crow', remarked Churchill coarsely to Morris.) Though it became a cliché to say so, Churchill hardly 'forgot' him: as a quasi-Liberal of high intellectual calibre he had figured in every coalition hypothesis for years; as well as being a candidate for the very

[20] Wynne, *An Irishman and His Family*, p. 119; Churchill to Roberts, 2 Feb. 1887, Roberts MSS 7104/23, R/21/25; LHJ, vol. 380, p. 21.

post of Chancellor in 1882 and 1886. Churchill himself had suggested him for the Home Office in November 1885, and finding him a seat since his defeat in July had been one of his preoccupations as Leader. Moreover, 'forgetting' him was a useful retrospective rationalization, often indulged in by Churchill, and as often religiously recorded by anecdotage. Goschen's importance as a rescuer is less striking when it is considered that Salisbury was prepared to press on without him, giving W. H. Smith both of Churchill's posts instead of simply the Leadership. (It would inevitably have killed Smith, but would have demonstrated the Conservatives' utter determination to have done with Churchill.)

The accession of Goschen, with Iddesleigh being unceremoniously shuffled out of the way, and an attempt to bring the Whigs Northbrook and Lansdowne into the Cabinet with the new Chancellor, drove Churchill to more extreme tactics. He had already tried to convey to Salisbury he would support him if he appointed a Conservative successor, but not otherwise;[21] now he drafted a violent letter to the *Morning Post*, vilifying Goschen's accession, attacking the granting of places to the Whigs as a betrayal of the party, jeering at Iddesleigh's displacement, and announcing that these steps 'release me from any pledge and sever every tie which might have bound me to my late colleagues'. The letter continued with an extraordinarily abusive attack on Salisbury and his government, and a rallying-cry to Tory Democracy.[22] The letter, however, was never sent; and has therefore been ignored by biographers. It shows how Churchill's mind was working on 5 January, when the possibility of the offers to Northbrook and Lansdowne was made public knowledge. By 7 January, it was known that they would not be joining the government; and Borthwick probably advised against printing the letter in this form. And any possibility of publishing it was put paid to on 12 January by the sudden death of Iddesleigh at Downing Street.

This was an event which shook Churchill deeply: coming as it did hard upon the Foreign Secretary's demotion, it caused a great public stir, and led to a virulent newspaper campaign against Churchill, at whose door the event was practically laid by the *Standard*. Churchill himself was badly upset, sending a

[21] Via Alfred Austin; see Austin to Salisbury, 29 Dec. 1886, Hatfield House MSS 3M/Austin.
[22] See Appendix 4.

contrite letter to Salisbury (and receiving an extraordinarily magnanimous message from Iddesleigh's widow). All thought of a violent onslaught on his ex-colleagues had temporarily to be abandoned.

Salisbury was equally shaken by Iddesleigh's death, but in practical terms it eased his difficulties: removing an embarrassment, creating sympathy for the government, and stirring up a renewed outburst against Churchill. Moreover, Smith's assumption of the Leadership in the Commons, initially greeted with hilarity, proved passable; his patent ill health and much advertised humility helped him accomplish the transition, and old Tories congratulated him on 'raising the character of the leadership and the House of Commons and checking the degradation which was coming over the House' under Churchill.[23]

Churchill's star, however, was now irretrievably in decline. Already his friends had noted that he realized the extent of his mistake. This realization impelled him to direct his attention once more to his Liberal Unionist friends—and also to Gladstonians. It was the dream of Labouchere to bring Churchill into a reconstructed Liberal alliance and solve Ireland by allowing Ulster separate representation; and Gladstone had since early December been taking soundings about reunion on the basis of moderating or postponing Home Rule.[24] Gladstone's reaction to Churchill's resignation had been merrily to wonder if 'Randolph had not a conscience after all'; he joked pointedly to Harcourt about becoming 'a joint in his tail' if he went in for economy.[25] The delicate manœuvres set in train by Chamberlain's reunion kite of 23 December distracted attention from Churchill's relations with the Liberals; but on 10 January, when he was meditating his no-holds-barred attack on Salisbury's reprieved ministry, Churchill sent a public letter to E. R. Russell of the *Evening Post* which was widely taken as aimed at Gladstone. This missive called for a return to economy and 'the better financial practices which prevailed before 1874'. Gladstone's reaction was that this 'did Churchill credit', and might be 'of political importance': he himself sent a public letter to Russell. But

---

[23] Harrowby to Smith, 25 Sept. 1887, Harrowby MSS LXV/476.

[24] See Labouchere to Churchill, RCHL xviii/2274, 2289, 2279; also J. K. Lindsay, 'The Liberal Unionist Party until December 1887', Ph.D. thesis, Edinburgh, 1955, pp. 291 ff.

[25] LHJ, 26 Dec. 1886, vol. 380, p. 13.

Iddesleigh's death intervened; and on 18 January Churchill replied, to an enquiry whether his *Evening Post* letter signified approval of Gladstone, with a blast against the financial administration of 1880–5.

He was probably open to offers; but none came. Dining with him on 14 January, Chamberlain found him—according to Loulou Harcourt—

rather depressed. He says he is going to make the Government's life a burden to them, and will especially direct his 'attention' to Goschen, with whom he is furious as his (Goschen's) acceptance of the Exchequer effectually prevented any reconciliation with Randolph, which up to the last moment he (R.C.) was expecting and hoping for. Chamberlain thinks Randolph is only too anxious and willing to come over to us now and says that with very little encouragement he would actually cross the floor of the House and come and sit below our gangway ... Neither Chamberlain or P [W. V. Harcourt] have the least wish that Randolph should 'come over and help us' as they think he would be a mischievous element in our party and would not damage the Tories nearly so much from our side of the House as from theirs.[26]

James, Brett, and other Liberals testified to this as well ('may God defend us from such a Coriolanus!'); though Chamberlain recorded elsewhere that Churchill actually asked him 'Shall I come over?', it was unlikely he would be invited. The resignation grounds foisted upon him by Salisbury made his policy ideas anathema to Chamberlain, who told him frankly in mid-January that as regarded economy 'he personally would give him no support and the he hated economy, etc.';[27] while Gladstone feared Churchill's propensity for a forward social policy at least as much as his opportunism. Though in the *Pall Mall Gazette* of 19 January Brett obediently floated the idea of a Hartington–Churchill ministry on the lines of 'Bismarckian frankness' in foreign policy, and Wolff at the same time was canvassing a combination of the two that might be stretched even further, it was becoming clear by late January that the Liberals would have little to offer him.

This affected his plans for his first public exposition of his reasons for resigning, due to be delivered on 27 January when parliament opened; and so, even more, did the news that came through on the 26th—Goschen had been beaten in his attempt to gain a parliamentary seat at Liverpool. This was generally

[26] Ibid., 15 Jan. 1886, vol. 380, p. 58.
[27] Ibid., 16 Jan. 1887, vol. 380, pp. 163–4.

taken as a more severe blow to Salisbury's efforts to stay afloat than it seems now; and it was probably decisive in arousing another hope of reconciliation and moderating Churchill's intention to hit the government hard. In December he had confided to Chamberlain that he 'believed if he made his statement in the House of Commons on the causes of his resignation he would smash Salisbury and have a rally of the Tory Democracy to himself in the country'.[28] But the day before he was due to deliver it he wrote gently to W. H. Smith of his desire to avoid controversy; and the speech, as it transpired, was a weak performance, avoiding the issues of foreign policy and legislative programmes and concentrating on the estimates. Brett believed that Iddesleigh's death 'prevented Churchill from making a great deal of his explanation which related to foreign affairs', but its anodyne quality stemmed from more immediate circumstances than that.

None the less, the speech contained some interesting indications. 'It would be idle to deny', Churchill added to his remarks about the estimates, 'what is very well known, that there were other matters of grave importance on which it was my misfortune to hold opinions differing from those of Lord Salisbury.' The estimates themselves he expressed in terms of what they meant for taxation; and he claimed that he would have accepted reductions of as little as half a million (thus weakening his whole case). He had not resigned on the budget as a whole; but the question of a peaceful foreign policy was linked to the estimates issue. He had early been committed to retrenchment, warning Smith and Salisbury in October that he would have to resign if it was not attempted: when that eventuality occurred, he was determined 'to resign at such a moment as to give to Lord Salisbury the most ample margin of time to make any arrangements that were necessary before Parliament met': 'the suggestion that my action has been taken in a hurry is entirely wrong'. This was followed by a pious invocation of his duty to his public:

The relations which exist between a Minister and the people are nowadays so direct and very close, and owing to the practice of great and large mass meetings, which have become so usual and so common, a Minister or the Leader of the Opposition is brought into close contact with the people. He discourses with the utmost freedom, without much

---

[28] Ibid., vol. 380, p. 71.

qualification, on public affairs. The practice may have its advantages and its disadvantages, but the practice exists; and I can conceive nothing more disastrous and ruinous, or more fatal to the healthy tone of our English political life, than that the people should take it into their heads that a Minister or Leader of the Opposition, whoever he may be, when he comes down to address them, thinks of nothing but exciting a moment of passing cheer and leaving the meeting straightaway without remembering what manner of man he is. I hope it will never be imputed with accuracy or justice to me that I knowingly or intentionally contributed to such a belief.

(Some at least of his listeners must have remembered his performances on Fair Trade, Ireland, and the franchise.) Churchill then read his letters of 20 and 22 December, and Salisbury's of the 22nd, which he presented as the crucial break, with an implicit criticism of Salisbury's alacrity: 'this was a letter which brought things to a conclusion'. The reactions were mixed; both Harcourts found the speech impressive, Sir William cheering many of the points, and his son finding it contained 'some very nasty blows at the government', but did not make the most of them: others judged that 'no-one ever gave worse reasons for resigning'. The provincial Conservative papers, some of which had been giving him the benefit of the doubt for the past month, uniformly found the grounds of the resignation inadequate and disappointing. Churchill's friends privately criticized the speech; and the government did not react with the gratitude he expected. Within days he was privately declaring his intention to 'make up for the shortcomings of his explanation by a warm attack on the government'.[29]

This came on 31 January. The day before, at Birmingham, Chamberlain had once more held out hopes of reunion with the Gladstonians, after disappointing them by making gratuitously

---

[29] Ibid., vol. 381, pp. 55, 62–3, 68. For witnesses of the speech see A. Pease, *Elections and Recollections* (London, 1932), p. 154, and LHJ, 27 Jan. 1887, vol. 381, p. 40: 'He was very calm and dignified, showed no spite, arrogance or excitement, and his blows at the Government, which were very nasty ones, were delivered entirely through the medium of his correspondence with Lord Salisbury. The little he said about foreign policy was very strong, clearly pointing to a dangerous policy of indiscriminate intervention. I think he made a tactical mistake in laying so much stress on the coaling stations defence, but on the whole his ground was good. His speech after the first word was received in absolute silence by the Tories, and with occasional bursts of cheering from our men. His attempt to minimise his economy by saying he would have been willing to accept a reduction of only half a million was a mistake and became almost absurd. There was a sentence in Salisbury's letter of December 22nd about the danger of immediate war in Europe which seemed foolish and dangerous and might with advantage have been omitted.'

anti-Irish remarks at Hawick a week before. Churchill used the opportunity to make what was ostensibly a speech in support of Tory Unionism, and an attack on the Liberal Unionists: in reality, it was geared to weaken the government by making it impossible for the Liberal Unionists to support them. He represented himself as always having gone out of his way, while Leader, to accommodate the Liberal Unionists; but he 'frankly admitted' that they were simply a 'crutch' to be used until the Tories could walk alone. The Irish landlords were defended and a hyperbolic tribute paid to Beach; but while appealing to unreconstructed Unionism, and to anti-Chamberlainism on all sides, Churchill's speech was also directed far more forcefully against the government than his performance of four days before. He launched an attack upon Goschen, insisted that the Queen's Speech demonstrated that the government was following the Dartford programme, and claimed that Salisbury would never have been connected with the cause of economy except for Churchill. In connection with his own resignation, Salisbury was stigmatized as 'a master of the art of tactics'; Churchill passionately denied that he had resigned over the issue of keeping up the coaling stations, and accused Salisbury of adroitly pinning this identification upon him by sleight-of-hand. He reiterated that he had left the government over retrenchment, linked to a pacific foreign policy and low taxation. Besides declaring ominously that he did not want to have to spend much time 'worrying and attacking the Government on minor points', he ended with an open threat:

Any little political influence which I may possess—any little political strength which may have been given to me—has not hitherto been drawn, for any practical or permanent purpose, from within the walls of this House, or from within that circle whose centre is the Treasury Bench. No, Sir; it has come from outside, and I appeal on this question to Caesar—to the just and generous judgement of the people. I know that I have sought for nothing—absolutely nothing—except to protect and promote their most material interests, and on this great question of economy and retrenchment I patiently wait for the judgement of the people.

Though a rambling, catch-all, and clumsily metaphorical performance, the speech was the kind of stand many of Churchill's friends had been urging him to take; FitzGibbon was delighted by it, and correctly described it as 'the second edition of your *apologia*', while (equally correctly) accusing Churchill of 'a soupçon of cl–p-tr–p' in his rhetoric about economy. 'With very great ability', Smith told the Queen, 'he suggested reasons for his retirement which were intended to place him in a better position before the country.'[30]

Chamberlain's complaint about the 'crutch' reference was private, and essentially moderate: 'Why will you insist on being an Ishmael—your hand against every man?' They 'must agree in private', he told Churchill via Lady Randolph, 'as to the amount of public abuse they were to shower on one another'. Churchill's reply was friendly, claiming that he had to warn the Tories not to be duped by Hartington. This arose from the fact that on 2 February Hartington had given one of his occasional virtuoso performances at Newcastle, where he expressed support for Liberal reunion and changes in Irish local government, but also contrived to stand by the Conservatives, reject Home Rule, and support coercion. No obvious political realignment was on the way; and the same day, Churchill suddenly decided to leave England.

It was a snap decision, involving the cancellation of social arrangements made less than a week before, and precipitated by a sense that he had mishandled his parliamentary chances ('scrupulousness and generosity are the signs of a political fool', he wrote in his farewell letter to Mrs Jeune). His departure was so immediate as to lead to a flourishing rumour that he had not left England at all, but was in hiding somewhere. But Churchill had, indeed, set sail for North Africa, pausing only in Paris to collect some letters of introduction from his new friend, General Boulanger.

Despite the hilarity and bravado of his letters home, and his assurance to Rothschild from Italy in March that he was 'quite satisfied with the progress of events', he was frequently deeply depressed; nor were politics always far from his mind. He wrote a lengthy and cheerful letter to Akers-Douglas, obviously keeping a line of communication open; and, encountering Rosebery at Naples on his journey home, they enjoyed long and frivolous conversations about public affairs. Churchill talked lightly of how near he had been to becoming a Liberal in 1885. 'But I thought seriously of it then, and it is impossible now.' During his absence, which lasted nearly two months, his position had declined. Sir William Gregory had some claim to be Churchill's

[30] FitzGibbon to Churchill, 1 Feb. 1887; RCHL xix/2384. Also Smith to the Queen, 31 Jan. 1887; Royal Archives B 38/5.

oldest political supporter, having believed in his star since the viceregal days in Ireland; he at first thought Churchill's resignation would inevitably bring him back as prime minister. But in late March he wrote to Dufferin:

When I wrote to you some time ago I was under the impression that Randolph Churchill was likely to play a great game. He had fine cards, in spite of the anger caused by his retirement, but he has completely thrown away his chance by ill-temper and indiscretion and now he is no longer missed and talked of. He writes to his mother in his wanderings in Southern Italy that politics have become utterly distasteful to him. I suppose he sees the gravity of his errors. Colleagues will stand a good deal from a man on whose steadfastness and loyalty they can rely, but these are precisely the qualities wanting in Randolph.[31]

III

Churchill returned to England on 27 March, 'much improved in health', and announced an ambitious speaking-programme: in which one of the first engagements was a public explanation to his Paddington constituents on 3 April, which was generally also interpreted as an attempt to put himself right with his party. Here he stressed his ill health and his desire to support the government, with whom he agreed 'on many questions of public interest'. He had resigned, he said, to precipitate an inquiry into the inefficiency and extravagance of War Office administration (a slight but perceptible change of ground): ambition had nothing to do with it. 'Why, good God, if I had consulted motives of personal ambition alone, I had only to keep and stay where I was.' He denied that he had wanted to bring in a 'popular' budget, and emphasized his financial probity and the savings he had forced upon the estimates. Peace, retrenchment, and reform (though not in these words) were what the people wanted. The weight of the speech was on the ethos of Peel, 'the greatest Tory minister this century had produced', and on Tory Democracy. Salisbury, 'a great statesman', was now following the Dartford programme—policies 'enough to make the Duke of Wellington and Lord Eldon turn in their graves'. As for himself, he was careless of praise or blame. Finally, he ended with a violent attack on Gladstone as the ally of Irish assassins and a

---

[31] Gregory to Dufferin, 21 Mar. 1887, DVP F/130/29A, no. 66.

peroration in favour of coercion: 'the whole social life of Ireland has become utterly rotten and putrifying, and nothing but the sternest, boldest and most deep-going remedy can restore health to that diseased and putrifying organ'.

Though much of the speech was pointed and ironic, and much else patently failed to carry conviction, it was friendly towards the government: which was only politic. Churchill's eroded position was symbolized by those who appeared on his platform in support: an eclectic assortment of second-rankers, composed of Fair Traders, Tory Democrats, local worthies, and family. Even Cohen sent an excuse. Within the circles of power, he was still a pariah. Though Akers-Douglas and Middleton tried to prevent criticism of him being too openly expressed during his absence, the Salisbury circle remained implacable. Lady Salisbury, whom Churchill believed had influenced her husband to accept his original 'resignation', denounced him at dinner-tables for selling Cabinet secrets to the Rothschilds.[32] Moreover, in his absence the government had suffered another set-back due to Beach's retirement from the Irish Secretaryship through ill health in early March. Though warned in advance by their mutual doctor, Roose (breaking the Hippocratic Oath for a quid pro quo to a valued client), Churchill had not returned for the crisis. Yet again, he had been absent when a fortuitous event could have been turned to advantage: and the advantage was taken by Balfour, whose appointment in Beach's place was to be the great unexpected success of the ministry.

In April, however, the state of affairs was still uncertain; both Tories and Liberal Unionists had suffered reverses, and were anxious to avoid a trial of strength. Churchill at first played the game, suggesting to Chamberlain collusion with the government over the Crimes Bill: 'he seemed to be very impressed with the

[32] For this implacability see Akers-Douglas's letter to *The Times* in Chilston, *Chief Whip*, p. 121. For Lady Salisbury's part, Redesdale, *Memories*, p. 686, and Curzon to Churchill, 4 Feb. 1887, RCHL xix/2391. H. Bismarck said she told him in 1888 that 'many of their present cabinet were dull, but that they could all be trusted, and then launched out against Randolph who communicated everything to Natty Rothschild, and hinted that people did not give great financial houses political news for nothing' (Rosebery MSS 10176, memorandum of a conversation with Herbert Bismarck, 7 Mar. 1888). Also see E. Hamilton to Rosebery, 13 Jan. 1887, ibid. 10032; he wrote that trouble might in any case have come from 'the excessive intimacy of a man occupying the post of Chancellor of the Exchequer with a certain great financial house'. Lady Salisbury had cause for resentment; at a Hatfield dinner in November Churchill had been heard remarking 'bad dinner, cold plates, beastly wine' and had to apologize. Blunt, *Land War*, pp. 198–9.

danger to our Party institutions arising out of the present situation', wrote Chamberlain in his unconvincingly decorous memoir. But this solicitude did not last. On Primrose Day, speaking at Nottingham, he produced a far less respectable performance than the Paddington speech of a fortnight before. Though Ireland was the theme (the Pigott forgeries having appeared in *The Times* to coincide with the second reading of the Crimes Bill the day before), the Tory-Democratic drum was beaten, their cause identified with Liberal Unionism, and snide references made to the party leadership. It is likely that he was warming up for the introduction of Goschen's budget two days later.

This announced increases in stamp duties, reduced the Sinking Fund payments by two millions, brought income tax down a penny, decreased the tobacco duty, and granted subvention to the local rates. Given its moderate resemblance to his own plans, Churchill's fury was reasonably described by Eddy Hamilton as 'sour grapes'. He had sounded out Hartington about a joint attack; and in the Commons he launched a long and bitter denunciation, claiming that if he had suggested similar expedients he would have been traduced, comparing Goschen's scheme unfavourably to Harcourt's last budget, and expressing virtuous abhorrence of the Chancellor's 'paltry and frivolous' reasons for raiding the Sinking Fund. Goschen's reply effectively demolished him. Leaving the House, he furiously attacked the budget, as dishonest and undemocratic, to anyone who would listen.[33]

Churchill's reaction to Goschen's budget was the preliminary to the campaign upon which he was to expend most of his effort for the year: that of economy. Expenditure had already been moderated, by Goschen and others; but a parliamentary committee on the estimates, which Churchill had suggested in his speech of 31 January, had been accepted by the government, and Churchill—with many complaints about the length of time it took to get under way—agreed to chair it. He confided to Hamilton his expectation that it would become a great public issue, and lead to a campaign in the country; he also expressed an ambition to go to the War Office and drastically reorganize it. This seems to have remained his belief: which indicates, yet again, his failing grasp upon the reality of the day. For one

[33] EHJ, BL Add. MS 48645, f. 56. Churchill claimed to Hamilton that the budget was aimed against increasing the powers of local government.

thing, any question of restricting the army, and more especially the navy, was not a popular issue: the *Pall Mall Gazette* had for two years been campaigning about inefficiency in the navy, and the need for extending its powers. And—another stroke of ill luck for Churchill—from the beginning of 1887 the economy entered a phase of temporary but marked recovery, which lasted through nearly all of Goschen's Chancellorship and was fully realized at the time. The times were out of joint for the rhetoric of retrenchment, and the exposition of industrial recession to Tory-Democratic audiences: both of them Churchillian stocks-in-trade.

The new campaign was none the less taken to the country in a speech at Wolverhampton on 3 June: an immensely long performance, much criticized for extravagant attitudinizing and violent language. The deplorable condition of the army and the navy, and the necessity for their reorganization, was emphasized: and this mundane task was presented as the foundation of an extraparliamentary campaign. 'I am going to try and speak a word tonight which I hope will make the ears of some people tingle.' Revelations were promised, Wolseley and the 'army ring' roughly attacked, specific instances produced of sinecures, bungled contracts, and inadequate defence arrangements. (These were often mistaken, and silently corrected in the printed version of his speeches prepared a year later: the most amended production in that much-amended collection.) Goschen's budget came in for further attacks: much of the rhetoric was aimed at the government rather than the departments. 'I want, if possible, to make you perfectly sick of that state of things. I want to make you as furious and angry against that state of things as I am myself. I want, if possible, to bring down upon those who are responsible for that state of things the anger and even the vengeance of the British people.' The real point came at the end, where he described his personal fate as a 'victim' of the system, at the hands of 'the P.M., the First Lord of the Admiralty, and the Secretary of State for War': he had been sacrificed to 'the audacious humbug of the official ring'. While claiming he 'did not particularly blame the present Parliamentary ministry', he attacked their dilatory approach towards appointing a committee to review the estimates, and accused Salisbury of finding domestic affairs 'intensely dull'. Finally he announced the existence of a 'plan' of sweeping reform, to be unveiled when he saw that the British people were prepared to support him; the party in London refused to listen about expenditure; only the country Tories could be relied upon. This appeal to the 'British democracy' was compounded by a significant gloss (omitted from the printed version):

The French chamber has just done a very sound thing. It seems to have been convinced that the French democracy was travelling along the high road to national insolvency and that they had better try and put up; and I do not think they set a bad example to the House of Commons at all. What did they do? They turned out of office the Government which refused to retrench and placed in office the Government pledged to retrench, and placed at the head of the Government the man who was principally responsible for inducing the French Government to adopt a policy of retrenchment. [Cheers].

This speech coincided with his most open attacks yet on Salisbury's government. He refused to address a meeting in Sutherland because he disapproved of Conservative policy, a point he reiterated throughout the summer. At the same time he sounded out the possibilities of joint action, not with the determinedly uneconomic Chamberlain, but with Gladstone. Churchill's brother-in-law Marjoribanks arranged a discreet meeting at Dollis Hill in July. All the overtures had come from Churchill, and Gladstone's account to Hamilton was restrained: Ireland had never been mentioned, finance alone was discussed, Churchill and Gladstone had agreed that the professional elements in the army needed more responsibility. Privately Gladstone recorded in his diary that Churchill, who 'was not at his ease', began by touching on Ireland. It is likely, however, that Gladstone's summing up to Hamilton accurately reflected his general approach. 'But though he was heart and soul with R.C. on the question of economy, and would co-operate with him to the best of his ability on the subject of expenditure, he was too old to go into details.'[34]

Thus the public was prepared, and a private alliance sounded out: but the issue of economy in naval and military expenditure merely led into an unproductive public debate. Churchill was vociferously supported by the naval constructor Sir Edward Reed in attacking Sir Nathaniel Barnaby, the former's chief professional rival; he had, probably unintentionally, blundered into a violent internal controversy. His sweeping criticisms, which left

---

[34] EHJ, 22 July 1887, BL Add. MS 48646, f. 107. I am indebted to Dr H. C. G. Matthew for looking at the apposite entry in Gladstone's diary (13 July 1887) for me.

out the context within which expenditure had fluctuated over
the previous period, as well as his technical inaccuracies and
violent personal attacks, were shuddered at by ex-colleagues,
naval and military circles, and *The Times*.[35] Churchill continued
to identify himself with the issue; in supply debates during July
and August, he continually pressed for reductions, supported by
Liberals like Childers and Bradlaugh. He called for a refusal of
supply until his criticisms had been answered, and produced
figures and details: but many of his imputations were argued
from hearsay and authoritatively contradicted, while the personal tone of his attacks on Stanhope also detracted from the
effect. The issue never swept the country in the manner
indicated by Churchill at Wolverhampton. Though his select
committee on military estimates sat throughout the summer, and
led to many revelations, it failed to capture the public imagination. The publication of the War Office Accountant-General's
evidence was a *coup*, showing as it did the inflated costs of preparing figures; the lack of control exercised by parliament over the
estimates was fully demonstrated, and Churchill's close and
hostile questioning and 'cruel pertinacity' widely reported.[36] But
those criticizing the expenditure were incongruous allies—
officers fighting civilian control and Radicals seeking retrenchment. Rifts were inevitable, for what the military element were
seeking to implement was reorganization rather than economy.
Criticism was increasingly directed at excessive centralization,
changes in auditing, and administrative inefficiency: economy
was slowly forgotten. Eventually, Churchill's committee 'drew
conclusions contrary to the original purposes of the enquiry' by
demonstrating not the extravagance of the War Office demands,
but the deficiencies in its methods of raising money caused by
political mismanagement, and the need for a radical new
approach to mobilization. (In fact, it led indirectly to greatly
increased expenditure on items like barrack construction.)

Moreover, by the end of the year Churchill himself had
fully adopted the army view, deciding that politicians were to
blame for the large expenditure without commensurate returns,
and that what was needed was professionalization, not restriction of expenditure; his instinctive predisposition towards

[35] See Richmond to Cranbrook, 18 June 1887, Cranbrook MSS HA 43 T501/257;
Penrose Fitzgerald to *The Times*, 8 June 1887; Churchill to *The Times* (in response to a
hostile leader), 21 June 1887.
[36] See *Pall Mall Gazette*, 29 July 1887, 5 Aug. 1887, for full reports of evidence.

'Prussianization' won through, in this as in other spheres. To anticipate, his select committee was replaced in 1888 by a Royal Commission chaired by Hartington, to inquire into the 'Civil and Professional administration of the Naval and Military departments, and the relation of those departments to each other and to the Treasury'. This reflected a general debate on national defence, which had led to reorganization in the army in 1888: leaving financial control in civilian hands, but involving the military as professional advisers. In 1890 Hartington's Report came out for a General Staff, eventually moderated into a War Office council; but Churchill dissented from it. He called for two professional advisers, grand War and Naval ministers, who would be non-party officers, appointed for a five-year term with Cabinet membership; and for the finance of army and navy to be entrusted to one Secretary of State. This was, in fact, a close approximation to the plan of the Wolseley 'ring', and epitomized how far he had come from economy and retrenchment: by early 1888, he was being accused of having abandoned economy. However, he was still absorbed in the evidence of his committee, which seemed to observers like Hamilton to have reached the proportions of a mania with him. It also served to distance him from Chamberlain, who believed and said that economy and army reorganization were unpopular issues, not worth spending time on: a disagreement fully realized by Churchill, who none the less persevered.[37]

In other spheres, however, the events of the summer brought him close to Chamberlain again: notably the issue of Irish land. The situation had continued to deteriorate, and the report of the Cowper Commission vindicated Parnell's rejected Tenant Relief Bill; the government had to introduce a bill in July which repeated its provisions. Churchill and Chamberlain were discussing the prospects of collusion at this time; and Chamberlain's objections to the limited concessions of the Land Bill threatened the Unionist alliance with disaster. Salisbury in the Lords had made the Bill a question of the government's survival; the fact that Churchill joined Liberal Unionists and Ulster tenant-farmer representatives in demanding a provision for judicial revision of rents must have looked threatening indeed. On 14 July Churchill delivered a speech in parliament on the subject,

---

[37] The disagreement was discussed in a conversation recorded by Hamilton in his diary, 6 Aug. 1887, BL Add. MS 48645, f. 116. Also see W. S. Hamer, *The British Army: civil and military relations, 1885–1905*.

well advertised in the papers. '[The government] expected him to bless it—he cursed it and tore it to shreds, and they did not cheer when he sat down', noted an observer.[38] In fact, his performance was more adroit than this. He first commended the government for introducing the measure and declaring an interest in the tenants' case, and then attacked nearly every clause—the exclusion of leaseholders, the carelessness of the financial drafting (a gibe at Goschen), the potential for extravagant legal jobbery (a dig at Ashbourne), the doubtful ethics of the bankruptcy clauses, and 'the utter want of finality of the whole thing'. Balfour was 'trying to build up a great system of national credit on a widespread foundation of national insolvency'. Churchill called for judicial powers of composition of equitable rents, for land courts to revise rents nationally in line with price movements, and for a review of mortgage charges on estates which had reduced rents. It was one of his most powerful and damaging speeches, warmly welcomed by Harcourt, who described it accurately as a surgical operation—eviscerating the Bill under an anaesthetic which gradually wore off. He declared support for 'the Bill drafted by the noble Lord'; Parnell similarly thought the government must withdraw their Bill in the light of Churchill's 'very important and able speech'; Gladstone found it 'admirable'.

Churchill's correspondence at this time shows that he wanted to put the government out; and, coming as it did at a time when the Conservatives were badly weakened in by-elections, this attack seemed to have a profound effect. If Salisbury stayed intransigent he would have to go to the country, and rumours abounded of a centrist ministry under Hartington, including Churchill as Irish Secretary. But the government eventually backed down on the question of judicial revision of rents, with dire warnings of the need to preserve the Union; the Bill was withdrawn for reconsideration, and remodelled in the Churchill mode; when it was reintroduced at the end of July he welcomed it in an emollient speech emphasizing his own friendship to the government. However, Balfour's reaction was frosty; and Churchill continued, as of old, to co-operate with the Irish party, praised by Healy and Parnell, and declaring that the landlord could no longer be seen as the creditor of the tenant, but his 'partner': a reneging on 'high Tory doctrine' which led

[38] Pease, *Elections and Recollections*, p. 184 (from his diary). Also see *Pall Mall Gazette*, 14 July 1887.

to a sharp exchange with Chamberlain on 1 August, represented by Churchill to his mother as a deliberate demonstration that he was acting independently of Birmingham.

Ireland came between Churchill and his potential ally in other ways too. From March, Salisbury had openly embraced coercion rather than 'platitudes and rosewater' for Ireland; it was a symbolic stiffening of policy, and with only Matthews advocating the Churchillian idea of a bill which could apply throughout the United Kingdom, an exceptional measure was soon drafted. It involved special juries, summary jurisdiction, the suppression of associations, and a change-of-venue clause (eventually dropped under Liberal Unionist pressure). It was introduced in March, and though Chamberlain strongly opposed it Churchill—as part of his rehabilitation on his return from abroad—took a firm line of support ('because he has the intelligence to see that any other line would at this moment be fatal to his political influence and prospects', wrote Lytton cynically).[39] In the summer, however, his commitment wavered; and when the government used their new powers to proclaim the National League in August, Churchill approached Hartington about joint action against them. This highlights the fact that from early summer he had, along with his anti-government campaigns over economy and the Land Bill, been floating plans for fusion with one or other section of the Liberal Unionists.

As early as 3 April, leaving Mrs Jeune's with Chamberlain, he had 'proposed a Chamberlain–Hartington–Randolph league against both parties', and at Nottingham on the 19th he aired the idea publicly: 'I do not see much difference in the present day between a Liberal Unionist and a Liberal Conservative, nor do I see the difference between either and a Tory Democrat.' Here also he took the opportunity to recant his 'crutch' speech: 'nothing was further from my mind' than to cast any slur on the Liberal Unionists, and he indeed had wanted the alliance made 'more permanent and practical'. To this end, he had administered 'a dose' intended to restore their union. Early summer saw a deliberate duet played out; following Churchill's threats to the government at Wolverhampton, and on the same day as he demolished their Land Bill, Chamberlain's speech at Willis's Rooms canvassed a Centre Party on the basis of the

---

[39] To Professor Tyndal, 16 Apr. 1887; *Letters of Lord Lytton*, ii, 316. Churchill also sent a letter to *The Times* in firm pro-government terms (19 May 1887) and told Beach he thought the Bill first-rate. For his speech in parliament see *Hansard 3*, cccxcvi, 345.

Dartford programme. Four days later, at Trowbridge, Churchill again called for closer union with the Liberal Unionists: they could not return to Gladstone, and must now be welded into 'a great National party', which would form an administration prepared to go forward with the positive and progressive measures that should have followed the political reforms of 1884–5. Chamberlain, he declared, had discovered the 'fund of popular sympathy' within the Tory party, which no 'class prejudices or fossil opinions' could dampen: their policies could fuse. A similar message was hammered home by Churchill when opening a Conservative club on 2 July. In these speeches of June 1887, Churchill used the language of Tory Democracy far more unequivocally than in his campaign for the National Union four years before; much of the retrospective interpretation of the earlier period was heavily influenced by the rhetorical form taken by his fusionist manœuvres of this summer.

Hamilton, visiting Blenheim the same month, found high hopes among the family of seeing Chamberlain serve under Churchill; but the public attention paid to their collusive debate about a National Party should not obscure the important point that they could not constitute it by themselves. Much of the talk of Centrism was intended, in fact, to prepare the way for a Hartington ministry which would include both Churchill and Chamberlain.[40] And Hartington would not always listen. Lady Randolph's celebrated story of the yachting party where he monosyllabically froze out Chamberlain's pushing overtures on behalf of a Centre Party may reflect no more than Hartington's annoyance at being interrupted in a tête-à-tête; but it serves as a reminder that, for all the Wolverhampton rhetoric, cultivation of Whiggery was a necessary concomitant of fusion. Churchill was well aware of this: besides his representations to Hartington over coercion, he is to be found in August telling Chamberlain they had to stick close to Hartington and assuring his mother that Hartington, not Chamberlain, held the key to power.[41] Similarly, after the government's defeat at the Spalding by-election in early July, which caused him 'undisguised joy', he approached Rosebery about taking the post of Foreign Secretary in a projected Hartington ministry; Rosebery, who had the year before remarked to Hamilton that Churchill would 'sell his own

[40] Lindsay, 'Liberal Unionist Party until December 1887', p. 396.
[41] Churchill to Chamberlain, 22 Aug. 1887, Chamberlain MSS 5/14/367; Churchill to Duchess (copy), RCHL xx/2624a.

soul' for a political advantage, recorded his own reaction as a high-principled negative.[42]

This coincided with the crisis over the Land Bill, when hopes ran high; but by late August the chance had receded. By late August, too, the chances of co-operation in opposition had diminished. A Hartington–Churchill combination, while not excluded by past rhetorical excesses, would have required delicate manœuvres; Churchill was never sure of Hartington, feeling in 1887 that the Marquis 'hated him politically and ignored him socially', while James had taken care to tell Hartington in late 1886 that Churchill would never serve under him. Looking in the other direction, Chamberlain disliked Churchill's obsession with economy; and he also affected to find Hartington too impossibly reactionary to work with. He later explained his incompatibility with Churchill on the grounds of the latter's readiness to endanger the existence of the government, while he himself refused to go so far; which runs counter to the fact that in August it was Churchill who vetoed (via Hartington) Chamberlain's plan of a modified Home Rule scheme, as impossible for anyone in the government to support. 'It would be fatal to the prospects of a coalition or of a national party, to which he still looks forward, though he sees greater difficulties than he did in the way of any combination which would not include Lord Salisbury.'[43]

In fact, Churchill's readiness to change direction, his bias towards Hartington, his views on coercion, and much else, had effectively separated him from Chamberlain by the end of August. According to Winston Churchill, who probably had it from Chamberlain himself, they decided to end their efforts

[42] Crewe, *Rosebery*, i, 302; for an earlier reference see EHJ, 6 Oct. 1887, BL Add. MS 48645, f. 128. Hamilton's dog-like devotion to Rosebery and suspicion of Churchill is well expressed in a naïve description of Ferdinand Rothschild's account of an Ashridge house party in 1887. 'He was delighted at seeing Rosebery and R. Churchill together. They had chaffed each other freely and bandied words in great good humour. Neither got the better of the other in conversation, but the contrast between the two was striking—R. Churchill eaten up with inordinate vanity and always putting down everybody as a fool, Rosebery always modest about himself and never saying an ill-natured word of a soul. Rosebery and R. Churchill always had a mutual admiration and liking for each other from Oxford days. They saw a great deal of one another at one time years ago' (Ibid., 21 Dec. 1887, BL Add. MS 48647 ff. 94–5).

[43] Hartington to Chamberlain, 15 Aug. 1887, in Holland, *Devonshire*, ii, 192–4. Also see *A Political Memoir*, p. 279. In April the ever hopeful Blunt had been told by Churchill that if coercion did not work, '"there is no middle ground, and Home Rule it will be". I should not be surprised, from the tone in which he said this, if after all he were to do the thing himself.' *Land War in Ireland*, p. 248.

towards parliamentary co-operation during a friendly walk in St. James's Park during that month. By the 31st, it was generally known that Chamberlain had 'lost all desire for coalition'.[44] By this point, Salisbury was learning to use Chamberlain to show that the cause of resistance could have a populist face; and in the autumn Chamberlain left for America on a government mission, leaving Churchill free to indulge in his own very different kind of Irish schemes, which involved an abortive plan to bring in an Irish denominational education bill as a private member. The story of his attempts to form a consistent front with Hartington, or Chamberlain, or both, need not be pursued further; though it was obviously canvassed at race-meetings and dinner-parties throughout the summer, and an indefinite number of straws in the wind can be discerned in letters and diaries from the political world. To assemble the clues into a plot is not worth the detective work; the point is that Churchill had now too little to deliver, either in terms of political leverage or ideological strength. 'Oh, no!', wrote Henry James to Harcourt, 'we shall not court Randolph. We are Foxite Whigs, not Burkeans.'[45] Another Liberal Unionist intimate of Churchill's, Brett, later summed up the result of 1887 to Chamberlain in a piece of political psychologizing, which recalled the other Henry James.

Under the existing state of things the two ablest administrators, except Gladstone, in England, yourself and Randolph, will find yourselves, the one by act of the Unionists, the other by act of the Tories, excluded from office. Why did the intrigues and negotiations for reconstruction of the government fall through in the autumn? For two reasons. 1. Because the personality of Randolph was thought too dangerous. 2. Because the same view was taken of your opinions.[46]

IV

Moreover, the dangerousness of Churchill remained an axiom in most political calculations (the Queen, for one, confided to anyone who would listen that she would do 'all I can to prevent

[44] Lady Frances Balfour to Gerald Balfour, 31 Aug. 1887: 'He was hot for it two months ago—a 'national' party. I asked [E.B.] Finley if he had ever heard who Chamberlain wished as P.M. of the National Party and he laughed and said he had not defined anything except that he and Randolph were to be the National Party.' Balfour MSS at Whittingehame, 28.

[45] Harcourt MSS, dep. 86, f. 86 (n.d.).

[46] 13 Feb. 1888; Chamberlain MSS, 5/6/12.

such a catastrophe' as his return to the government). The chances of the Conservatives taking him back are more briefly told. In February, with Churchill away, Akers-Douglas had sounded out his brother-in-law and political apprentice George Curzon about his resuming the India Office: but Churchill had professed lack of interest. Throughout the summer, his view had been towards a Liberal reconstruction; but in the autumn, he began to look once more towards the Tories. This was largely because of Beach's position. According to Holmes, his closest political associate, the Irish Secretary's resignation in March had been caused as much by disgust as by his bad eyesight: certainly his recovery was miraculously fast, and though he had remained connected with the government, his biographer records that by October he was 'in substantial agreement with the Liberal Unionists and strongly opposed to Salisbury'. This development was connected with a *rapprochement* with Churchill; at the end of that month Beach came to Smith and openly proposed a reconstruction, bringing Churchill back to the War Office, where he was prepared to behave well and 'get on very well with Goschen'. Smith feared that Beach and Churchill were implicitly threatening to go openly against the government if their initiative was not accepted: and he thought 'Salisbury was not so strong against it as he has been'.[47] These hopes persisted; the next month Churchill was still writing to Beach about the chances of government reconstruction, and the entire Churchill family's correspondence remained obsessed with the subject of Salisbury's health. In public, Churchill's utterances from the autumn took a sudden pro-government turn. But the view from Hatfield remained cynically unchanged. 'The only unfavourable symptom in the present situation, to my eyes', wrote Salisbury after reading one of these effusions, 'is that Randolph is supporting us so zealously. The Archfiend is getting light-headed.'[48]

Indeed, the record of Churchill's speeches from September showed an obvious desire, as Salisbury pointed out to Smith, 'to come back'. At Whitby on the 24th he preached the gospel of the Union, patriotism, and order. Irish land had received enough attention, and Irish legislation should be halted; the real success of the session had been the Coal Mines Regulation Bill, 'the most valuable piece of unsentimental lawmaking any parliament ever

[47] Smith to Akers-Douglas, 28 Oct. 1887, in Chilston, *Smith*, pp. 265–9.
[48] Salisbury to Balfour, 26 Oct. 1887, quoted in Curtis, *Coercion and Conciliation*, p. 206.

produced'. In this the message of Tory Democracy was fused with loyalty to the Union and praise of the government. At Sunderland on 20 October he offered the same composition. Though he claimed to Chamberlain that he hated speaking when out of office, as it was 'making bricks without straw',[49] his free hands enabled him to borrow the Liberal Unionist programme *in toto* (one man one vote, registration by paid local officials, compulsory employers' liability, sweeping local-government reform with the grant of licences to the new authorities, and departmental economy). This, however, was by way of a riposte to Gladstone's statement the night before that Ireland blocked the way to reform: as a finesse, Churchill claimed that Toryism offered a Gladstonian programme without the obstacle. And while admitting that he went further than many of his party in this, he also emphasized his own connection, past and future, with Toryism. The same message was reiterated at Chester-le-Street two days later: the cause of the Union must be identified by 'the masses' with progressive legislation. Again, the tone was specifically Tory-Democratic, with the attendant anti-Irish and anti-socialist overtones; this reflected both his audiences and the company on his platforms (Jennings, Beckett, Wombwell, Curzon, and Byron Reed: avatars of Tory Democracy, determined to keep their wayward champion on the right path).

At the same time he emphasized his probity on the Irish issue: cast in doubt by a campaign of O'Connor and McCarthy at this time to identify him yet again with Home Rule two years before.[50] The police brutality at Mitchelstown was fervently defended by Churchill in parliament (though he had initially called for a judicial inquiry): he evolved a curious doctrine that no citizen had 'any right whatever' to resist a policeman, and declared that 'subject to reasonable limitations there is nothing in reason which a government cannot do'. These statements, and indeed Churchill's whole unreconstructed image of the autumn, were best encapsulated in his speech at Newcastle on 22 October, where he was accompanied, ironically, by that Lord Durham whom he had so brilliantly mocked as Chamberlain's captive 'live earl' in his palmy days. 'The coercion of the Protestant community of Ulster', declared Churchill, 'is a far

---

[49] Churchill to Chamberlain, 10 Sept. 1887, Chamberlain MSS 5/14/37.

[50] See T. P. O'Connor in *The Times*, 31 Oct. 1887, and J. McCarthy's speech at Hull in December.

more wicked, far more unjustifiable, and a far more brutal coercion than any which the present government can be supposed to be guilty of ... Are we to be squeamish? Are we to use nothing but milk-and-water methods in dealing with secret societies which are formed for no purpose but the commission of murder and outrage of every kind? ... Meet these ruffians, these fiends in human form, with their own weapons.' In the best Tory-Democratic ethos, this was linked with the menace of socialist organizations, 'which exist for no other purpose than causing riot and disorder'. Both varieties of revolution must be suppressed; working men should realize they threatened enterprise, commerce, and the welfare of the masses ('capital can take to itself wings and fly away'). Later in the day he attacked the idea of state interference: 'You must not look to the State always to protect you, to the State to assist you and do this, that and the other for you. You must be, in the first place, prepared to do everything for yourself and to take any assistance which you may get from the State as a bit of luck which you had no right to expect.' The speech ended with a Gibbonian peroration on the death of empire, which would follow the dissolution of the Union.

This was almost embarrassingly supportive for Salisbury; at one point, Churchill went so far as to refer to 'we, the Government'. His bouquets to the Liberal Unionists, which were many, were designed to disassociate them from Radicalism. Bright and Chamberlain were presented as law-abiding, collusive figures, running the country with the Tories; independence, self-sacrifice, and close co-operation were the keynotes of the two addresses he gave in the town.[51] At Stockton two days later the message of Ireland and the Union was repeated, with brutal relish: histrionic and approving accounts of the carnage with which troops treated Irish riots in America raised much laughter. Here too Churchill observed Liberal Unionist susceptibilities by finally identifying himself against Fair Trade (which he had hinted at accepting in June at Wolverhampton). Liberal Unionist opinion had been severely ruffled by Conservative feelers on the issue at this time, and Churchill preached a reassuring message: inaccurately claiming that the government's commission on trade depression had discovered overproduction to be the cause, and identifying free trade with 'political

[51] See *The Times*, 24 Oct. 1887 (there are many excisions in the Jennings version).

stability' and a general working-class commitment to Toryism. This raised some outcry; though Churchill left several loopholes, the Fair Trade League attempted to reconvert him with a lengthy public letter to *The Times*.[52]

But these exhibitions of probity brought him no nearer to rehabilitation. The speeches were severely criticized in the press for their verbosity, repetitiousness, and egocentricity: criticisms which must have hurt him, since he often adverted to them in public. He travelled further north for his annual autumn holiday; Hamilton found him with the Roxburghes at Floors in November—affable but reserved, spending his days fishing or sitting in his room, completely determined upon 'working out his economical ideas', and planning drastic reorganization of all government departments.[53] In December he stayed with Hartington for a shooting party, where he did not shoot. In his last major speech of the year, at Stockport on the 15th, he reverted to hostility towards the government. Their foreign policy continued dangerous; they had not implemented the Dartford programme; they must move themselves to carry out 'large and liberal legislation'. Economy, which had not been much mentioned in his conciliatory speeches of October, was threateningly referred to: finance must be brought back to pre-1870 standards. In reply to the vote of thanks, he emphasized his own 'perfect fidelity and loyalty' to the Tory party: and, despite it, his repeated conflicts with those who held high positions therein. But his faith was placed in large audiences like the present, and their support encouraged him in his struggles. The Tory-Democratic message of Sunderland here regained its old aggressive emphasis.

His final initiative of the year was an oblique venture into foreign policy: and here, too, the chief conclusion to be drawn was his reduced importance. With Churchill out of office, and Iddesleigh dead, Salisbury's hands had been free to construct the Mediterranean agreements of February and March; the curious division of responsibility which had enabled Churchill to make his bid for the redirection of foreign affairs no longer existed, and his stock in Continental chancelleries had plummeted. A recent

[52] 2 Nov. 1887. He said at Stockton that he could see nothing wrong in principle in 'a system of protection which should involve a duty on food . . . if there was a great, strong national demand'; he was not a fanatical Cobdenite. But Protection, he claimed, was 'a frightful burden to France and Germany' (having asserted the opposite on more than one occasion in the past).

[53] EHJ, vol. xxv, p. 53, BL Add. MS 48654.

intimacy with Boulanger had not helped his reputation either; Churchill's great French friend, the Marquis de Breteuil (model for Proust's Breauté) was an ardent supporter of the General; after several meetings in Paris Churchill entertained Boulanger in London. But the French presidential crisis in December 1887, for which Churchill travelled to Paris, disappointed him as much as everything else that year. The emergence of Carnot depressed him: 'a sort of French W. H. Smith; the present age seems to be the age of Smiths'.[54]

His own final, un-Smithlike gesture was a grand journey to Russia at the end of the year. As in October 1886, he guaranteed maximum publicity by surrounding it with mystery, pretending until the last moment that he was going to Spain. Russia was the most sensitive of destinations, especially for the pro-Russian Churchill, and the government was correspondingly embarrassed: the Foreign Office was constrained to issue a formal disclaimer that Churchill's visit had any official purpose (though the French ambassador reported back that it was a preparation for his take-over as Foreign Secretary). He travelled in style, accompanied by Breteuil, Trafford, and Lady Randolph (who had, the foreign dispatches remarked, 'private reasons' for visiting Berlin, Kinsky having been posted there). His reception in Russia, closely described by his son, was flatteringly warm; he had prepared the way well with Morier, the English ambassador, with whom he had worked closely the year before.[55] He was granted a long interview with the Tsar, enjoyed the snow and the spectacle, and travelled back slowly via Berlin and Paris. Despite the aggressive publicity, Churchill probably hoped to make out of his visit some potential for conciliation; he drew up a lengthy memorandum for Salisbury of his meeting and conversation with the Tsar, and the Prince of Wales arranged an interview for him with the Prime Minister on his return.[56] But this report, with its anti-French tone, and vague-

---

[54] Churchill to Duchess, 5 Dec. 1887, RCHL xxi/2762.

[55] See Morier to Churchill, 22 Sept. 1886, RCHL xv/1825. In his anti-Russian days, ironically, Churchill had thought Morier 'a most unfortunate appointment' (Churchill to Dufferin, 7 Aug. 1885, DVP F/130, 3, no. 63). The Ambassador was considered so pro-Russian by the Queen that she refused to see him in December 1886 (Derby to Hartington, 26 Dec. 1886, Devonshire MSS 340/2073).

[56] For the memorandum see W. S. Churchill, ii, 359–66 (which excludes a characteristic enquiry from the Tsar about Goschen's Jewish origins). For Churchill's long reports to the Prince of Wales, and the latter's arrangement of an interview with Salisbury, see letters of 29 Dec. 1887, 30 Dec. 1887, 11 Feb. 1888 in Royal Archives, T 9/102–4.

ness about Constantinople, hardly had the desired effect. Salisbury played down its importance to the Queen, and dismissed the value of Churchill's impressions to those diplomats who asked ('c'est un esprit fantasque et ses conseils n'ont pas grande valeur'); to Lytton he complained that Churchill's visit had actually done harm.[57] In fact, Salisbury began overtures to Russia for an amicable arrangement regarding Persia less than a month after Churchill's return; but Churchill was not thanked.

Churchill paused in Berlin in early February, where he was similarly fêted; his opinions were expressed less sweepingly than of old, and he took care to let Paget know that he now felt Britain had to defend Constantinople.[58] In a light exchange with the French ambassador there, who described him as 'un libre esprit', Churchill gaily asked: 'Qui sait ce que nous réserve l'avenir?' But a conversation also recorded at Berlin by his friend Herbert Bismarck, the Chancellor's son, gives a better impression of Churchill's realization of his position by the end of this disastrous year. Bismarck, who planned to set out for England at the same time, suggested they travel together,

as it would ensure me a good reception. He made a curious face and said, 'If you think that being with me will ensure you a good reception from the classes among whom you are naturally thrown, I suspect you are mistaken, but if you mean the masses that is another thing, your being with me would certainly ensure you the best reception from them.' My impression from this speech and other things which he said is that his views have become even more radical than they were, and that worship of the popular breath has taken complete possession of him. He believes that to be the key to Power in England and his personal ambition outweighs his patriotism. He does not see far enough ahead to understand the danger to England of a policy of isolation, but he fancies that it will suit the popular feeling and in this indeed he may be right with regard to the masses, for they are ignorant of foreign affairs. I said to him that it was the duty of a statesman to guide popular feeling, not to be led by it. He replied that it might be all very well in other countries, but in England it merely meant being driven from power.[59]

---

[57] Salisbury to Lytton, 8 Feb. 1888, Hatfield House MSS 3M/A59/76. Also de Laboulaye to Flourens, 12 Jan. 1888, *Doc. Dipl. Fr.*, 1st ser., 7, no. 11, and Waddington to Flourens, 10 Feb. 1888, ibid., no. 42.

[58] Paget to Salisbury, 2 Feb. 1888, Hatfield House MSS 3M/A48/74.

[59] A memorandum of Malet's to Salisbury, 23 Dec. 1887, Hatfield House MSS 3M/A61/57. This conversation took place on Churchill's way to Russia.

Chapter 11

Wilderness Politics, 1888–1895

In this Olympus partners are changed, the divine
bosom, now rabid with hatred against some opposing deity, suddenly becomes replete with love
towards its late enemy, and exciting changes occur
which give to the whole thing all the keen interest
of a sensational novel. No doubt this is greatly
lessened for those who come too near the scene of
action. Members of Parliament, and the friends of
Members of Parliament, are apt to teach themselves that it means nothing; that Lord This does
not hate Mr That, or think him a traitor to his
country, or wish to crucify him; and that Sir John
of the Treasury is not much in earnest when he
speaks of his 'noble friend at the Foreign Office' as
a god to whom no other god was ever comparable
in honesty, discretion, patriotism, and genius. But
the outside Briton—and this description should
include ninety-nine educated Englishmen out of
every hundred—should not be desirous of peeping
behind the scenes. No beholder at any theatre
should do so. It is good to believe in these friendships and these enmities, and very pleasant to
watch their changes.

Anthony Trollope, *Can You Forgive Her?* (1864)

I

A treatment of Churchill's career lends itself to a cyclical form.
The early period, though broken by several withdrawals from
the scene and experimental changes of front, forms a recog-
nizable pattern overall, and can be treated in a more com-
pressed form than the high point of 1884–7; and the same is
true for his last years out of power. His son's picture of him at
this time presents an exiled tribune, at the height of his abilities,
exerting a considerable influence upon a resentful government:
moderate, consistent, and never acrimonious. Not surprisingly,

this view is not easy to sustain. His bitterness became more and more marked; and his powers declined from the first steps he took into the wilderness. Even the issues upon which he took a stand tended to be those where he had already accumulated a bank of knowledge to draw upon—Egypt, economy, and Ireland.

The state of his health was measured by his increasingly furious temper, celebrated bouts of anger now alternating more and more frequently with flashes of his old zest and brilliance. (Even on his visit to Russia, people had taken his jovial companion Trafford for his doctor.) He took refuge in further and more frequent journeys abroad, spending long interludes in the South of France in the summer of 1888, Monte Carlo in the following winter, Norway in May and June 1889, France and North Africa in the winter of 1890–1 (as well as the usual retirement to Scotland in the autumn). On his visits to Monte Carlo he gambled heavily, and his extravagance remained undiminished in other spheres: sharing a racing stables with Lord Dunraven meant large outlays, a house at Newmarket, and constant attendance at Doncaster, Sandown, and Goodwood. He was more closely connected than ever with the world of financial speculation, often in the company of the celebrated Colonel North; Eddy Hamilton found him becoming 'over-civil to millionaires'. His account ledgers at Rothschilds show large flutters on South American mining companies and the like, and his debts to the bank had reached £11,000 by the end of 1891. At his death they stood at the astonishing sum of £66,902.[1]

It is not, therefore, surprising to find him angling for appointment to embassies abroad from 1889 (and even for the Viceroyalty of India). But no paying job materialized, and in the autumn of 1892 the Churchills had to give up their tenure of Connaught Place and move in with the Duchess in Grosvenor Square. In this adversity, their marriage revived, though 'she always grates on his nerves', wrote Churchill's brother-in-law when Lord and Lady Randolph embarked upon their last journey together in 1894. While her love affairs continued to provide much material for gossip, and Churchill complained to

---

[1] See EHJ, 5 Nov. 1889 (vol. xxii, p. 124), BL Add. MS 48651; Rothschild Archives (London) Main Ledger Series 10/76–10/85 (1886–95) and RAL South Africa Letters 38/244A (1889–95). For details of Churchill's bank account I am most grateful to Lord Rothschild and the trustees of N. M. Rothschild and Sons, who kindly granted me access to the bank's archives.

his friends about them,[2] her loyalty to him in his decline was
fierce and touching; her own serious illness in late 1892 united
them further. For himself, Churchill continued to make frequent
visits to the Parisian house he shared with Trafford, on what
Wolff termed his 'missions of enquiry into the higher education
of women'.[3] But his correspondence with his wife from the late
1880s returned to the affectionate superscriptions of their early
marriage, and they missed each other's company when apart.

In his public life, Churchill also attempted at first to regain his
old footing: from the time of his return from Russia in February
1888 he appeared as an authoritative figure in parliament,
issuing weighty pronouncements about procedure, and expressing horror at obstruction and disrespect towards the Speaker.
This did not, however, imply support of the government; he
often worked with Radicals, and though he praised the general
trend of affairs (and even Goschen's finance), his over-all
demeanour was threatening. At Birmingham on 9 April he spoke
of the need for reforms in Irish local government, land law, and
education; and, even more ominously, of 'the dream of Tory
democracy', which—for once—he defined: as a democracy which
supported a Tory government 'acting with lofty and liberal
ideas'. At the same time, the Irish party were praised for their
'essentially parliamentary conduct': as a reward, the next session
of parliament should be devoted to the amelioration of Irish
grievances. He had already gained vociferous Irish approval by
opposing Balfour's plans in a long speech on the Irish Land
Commission on 27 March; and Ireland again provided the
material for his first parliamentary attack on the government on
25 April. Balfour's attempt to laugh out a Parnellite Bill for Irish
local government drew a baleful speech from Churchill, who
declared his own commitment, and that of the government, to
Irish local government in 1886. Ireland was not an 'inferior
community', and must have equal privileges; the Tories were
committed to progressivism, not reaction. His own position was
emphasized throughout: 'though honourable members do not in
the least object to my winning applause at great mass meetings

---

[2] See LHJ, 9 Aug. 1892, vol. 384, pp. 107–8. 'Randolph Churchill talking of his wife to
Natty Rothschild said the other day "I suppose you know she is living with Freddy
Wolverton". Natty told us this himself.' For further references to this relationship, which
replaced her much deeper attachment to Charles Kinsky, see Churchill and Mitchell,
pp. 167–9. Also see LHJ, 1 Nov. 1892, vol. 387, p. 28, where he finds Churchill at
Jeune's, 'inclined to abuse his wife, though her life is still said to be in danger'.

[3] Wolff to Churchill, 19 Jan. 1890, RCHL xxv/3381.

in the country, there seems to be a considerable difference when I carry these opinions to a practical conclusion'.

As Chaplin pointed out in a letter to *The Times* the next day, and as Churchill had privately emphasized at the time, the commitment to Irish local government in 1886 had been strictly conditional;[4] but this embarrassing restatement was taken by the Gladstonian press as a milestone on the way to Home Rule, and caused considerable disturbance. It was an especial embarrassment to the Liberal Unionists, as Churchill intended; Chamberlain's agreement with Balfour that land reform had to come first was, in Churchill's view, welshing on their joint commitment. Chamberlain's and Hartington's discomfiture was evident, as was the pleasure of Gladstone and Parnell. However, Churchill had abstained on the vote, rather than support the Parnellites outright; and when he reiterated at Preston on 16 May the need to 'build from the base' and 'educate and train the Irish people by degrees in the art of self-government', his real emphasis was upon his own position. He was 'not politically dead yet': the government was following his Dartford outline willy-nilly (while still not touching economy and handing out sinecures); though Salisbury 'would not say more in my praise than he could possibly help'. His position, he said, was to chastise the government for its own good; Ireland, it might be inferred, provided a convenient nest of scorpions.

Thus the public profile; and for the rest of the summer Churchill seemed to keep uncharacteristically low, though he engineered a government defeat on a minor issue involving Matthews in July and the vote of twenty Conservatives against the government on the issue of departmental reform was a cause for private jubilation. He was generally absent from newspapers and from *Hansard* in the summer of 1888; the Bribery Prevention Bill, which carried Churchill's name, was largely managed by his aides. He himself was living in a rented house at Egham, much involved in racing schemes, and his plans for extended travel in the next session aggrieved his officious helpmate, Louis Jennings. However, the Irish issue had not dropped out of his private consideration; and, though he reacted with 'terror' to suggestions of joint action from O'Connor,[5] from early 1888 he was receiving discursive, questioning, and slightly depressed letters from FitzGibbon on the need for a new initiative. In reply

---

[4] See for instance Churchill to the Queen, 19 Aug. 1886, Royal Archives B 37/92.
[5] *Memories of an Old Parliamentarian*, i, p. 65.

to Churchill's request for some 'new views' on Ireland for a speech at Oxford in February, FitzGibbon had pleaded a lack of inspiration: 'perhaps because I can't bring myself to believe in the reality of anything on either side'. It was an approach that matched Churchill's mood. FitzGibbon described Balfour's decisive and draconian rule in Ireland as a strait-jacket, removal of which would bring on an uncontrollable fit; both Ashbourne and the Chief Secretary were criminally insouciant regarding 'constructive and conciliatory measures, for which all this repression ought to have given favourable opportunity'. This was the background to Churchill's attacks on the government on Irish local government in April; the following month, FitzGibbon prepared a venture in their traditional joint sphere of intermediate education, which aimed at adapting the Royal Schools for extension into a denominational framework.[6] Churchill passed this on to Balfour; but he came up against Protestant objections, and was further delayed by Archbishop Walsh's absence and Churchill's own social distractions (for which FitzGibbon took him to task). In June, the web of Howth diplomacy was tangled by the discovery that Balfour had been making his own representations to the bishops regarding higher education; though Churchill continued to apply pressure to Beach about approaching Balfour with his and FitzGibbon's ideas, the reception was cool. In the summer of 1889 Balfour's public initiative regarding Irish education was uncharacteristically inept enough to put the question out of court. Balfour, who confessed he 'could never make up his mind whether he disliked the Orangemen, the extreme nationalists, the political dissenters, or the Roman Catholics the most',[7] was hardly equipped to take on the Byzantine world of Irish Church politics, in which FitzGibbon had instructed Churchill with such peculiar effect; but it is likely that his suspicion of the Lord Justice and his embittered ally prevented his accepting their advice in 1888.

Irish education remained a possible sphere of intervention for Churchill; FitzGibbon continued to preach to him that here was a chance for a 'practical step in Irish legislation ... through

---

[6] See FitzGibbon to Churchill, RCHL xxii/2823, 2879, 2917, 2920; also Balfour MSS, BL Add. MS 49695. Churchill continued to press for government aid for the Christian Brothers, even when he was turning up in parliament for nothing else; see *Hansard 4*, ix, 750.

[7] Quoted in M. C. Hurst, 'Joseph Chamberlain, the Conservatives and the succession to John Bright, 1886–9' in *Hist. Jn.*, vii (1964), no. 1, p. 91.

mutual, friendly and "national" co-operation of Protestants and Catholics—a style of Local Government of which you have a claim to be the exponent'.[8] But Churchill's obediently attempted initiatives, like the plan to add amendments to the 1890 Local Taxation Bill in the interests of Irish national education, were advised against by his diminishing band of parliamentary allies, as politically unwise in face of government opposition at a time when he was negotiating for readmission to the government. For FitzGibbon's part, his attitude was one of increasing despair at the refusal of either side to listen to his advice: the politics of pragmatic consensus were no longer possible. In Ireland, the rhetoric of irreconcilability which had been preached from Howth in 1886 had already set hard into reality.

In England, none the less, ideas of an Irish initiative were kept alive: by Chamberlain's calls for a 'new policy' in 1888 and 1889, and by Churchill's manœuvrings at a less public level. In 1888 he had pressed the idea that 'Balfourism is played out and the time is come for a "generous policy"', not only on the Chief Secretary himself, but on figures as diverse as Beach, Lytton, and Lord Roberts;[9] he had publicly aired the issue in a clever and considered speech to the Oxford Union in February 1888, revolving round the 'insolubility' of the Irish question, and the irrelevance of constitutional parallels. Butt came in for praise as 'a sound Tory' and so, more interestingly, did the Buttite tradition; the whole question was reviewed in a more considered and enquiring way than was usual with Churchill in public, though his general conclusion was that all Irish 'movements' were transient by nature. Such statements paralleled Chamberlain's concurrent explorations of the question, though Churchill did not plan a joint action with him; and in April 1889 (just after a severe quarrel with Birmingham) he approached a more significant potential ally. Lord Carnarvon's diary for that month records a series of sounding-out visits from Churchill and FitzGibbon, presenting an anti-Balfour line, calling for a new departure, and generally raising seductive visions of the heady days of 1885. Carnarvon was surprised at how far they had come since then; FitzGibbon was 'evidently quite prepared for self-government in its subordinate features

---

[8] FitzGibbon to Churchill, 16 May 1890, RCHL xxvi/3552.
[9] See Churchill to Beach, 23 Mar. 1888, RCHL xxii/2850; Lytton to Lady Betty Balfour, 28 May 1888, *Letters of Lord Lytton*, ii, 351; Churchill to Roberts, 9 Sept. 1888, Roberts MSS 7101-23-21/24.

and institutions—he would not I think object to Provincial Councils provided they do not assume the character of Parliaments', and Churchill told him he would grant 'everything short of a parliament'.[10] They suggested a joint initiative in this sense in both Houses; Carnarvon was attracted, but insisted on first sounding out Hartington for support. Discussing the past, Churchill was as interesting and attractive to Carnarvon as ever: he admitted his conferences with Parnell in 1885, 'but this was before he was in office—and he seemed quite aware that at that time Salisbury was quite open to consider terms with the Home Rulers'. Thus confirmed in his own view of history, Carnarvon was well on the way to falling under Churchill's spell once more.

Events, however, conspired against any decisive step. FitzGibbon believed that an open pronouncement in the Commons would result in Churchill being beaten, and 'thrown into the arms of the Gladstonians'; he preferred the idea of declaring his initiative at 'some public meeting'. Initial soundings showed that Salisbury would take an unalterably hostile line, though Beach and Smith were friendly. While Hartington was seen, and discussed ideas (preferring two 'Provincial Councils', one at Belfast), he proved as adept at holding off as ever. Churchill refused to involve Chamberlain, virtuously condemning him as untrustworthy and self-interested. He continued to call on Carnarvon and confer with him closely; the memorandum they drew up in May 1889 shows their ideas extended to Provincial Councils with eventual control of police and Resident Magistrates, as well as educational measures, a peasant proprietary, and the development of resources. In May, however, Carnarvon fell ill; Churchill went fishing; Balfour's popularity in the House made any movement seem inopportune. Churchill used his answer to an invitation to contest Bradford as an opportunity to call for a new Irish policy on 24 May, and spoke at Birmingham on 30 July in the pro-Irish sense agreed with Carnarvon. But the effect was muted by the anger aroused by his speech on the licensing question at Walsall two days before, and was not publicly co-ordinated with any larger initiative. His meetings with Carnarvon continued, but they principally discussed the past; and by now neither really occupied a position which would make the implementation of a FitzGibbon initiative practicable or even newsworthy.

[10] See Carnarvon diary, BL Add. MSS 60932-3 (entries for 4–7 Apr. 1889 and 10 Nov. 1889); also Churchill to Carnarvon, 7 Apr. 1889, BL Add. MS 60830.

II

Churchill's reasons for not involving Chamberlain in his Irish soundings of April 1889 may seem trivial; but in fact his overtures to Carnarvon followed hard upon one of the most serious of his recurrent ruptures with Chamberlain, and may well have been occasioned by it. This was the celebrated incident of Churchill's abortive candidature for the Central Division of Birmingham in April 1889. He had retained close links with the Conservative party in the city (which continued to be split into Churchillite and anti-Churchillite factions); from early 1888, he had exerted himself to press for honours for local supporters. Bright's increasing debility provoked much discussion about the succession to his seat. In May 1888, Chamberlain promised Churchill his support in that eventuality; by December, Churchill was offering the reversion of his Paddington seat to Lepel Griffin. Churchill's line, however, was invariably that he would only leave Paddington for a completely assured succession at Birmingham: in other words, if both Liberal Unionist and Conservative parties in the division agreed. This raised the eternal problem of Unionist co-operation, traditionally problematic in Birmingham; and by the time Bright finally died, in March 1889, Chamberlain felt safe enough to argue that Churchill had become so unpopular that the local Liberal Unionists (and even some Conservatives) would not accept him.

The story has often been told of how on 2 April a deputation from Birmingham called on Churchill and asked him to stand; and how, against all expectations, he deferred the decision to a committee of Chamberlain, Hartington, and Beach—which was, as Labouchere caustically told him, like Christ leaving the decision about crucifixion up to Pilate, Caiaphas, and Doubting Thomas.[11] Chamberlain's version was 'we unanimously advised him not to stand, although I again told him that if he did I should feel myself pledged to give him any support in my power': Churchill's, that he was told 'my candidature would not be supported by the Liberal Unionists and if persisted in would probably result in the loss of the seat to the Unionist Party'. If this was so, however, it seems conclusive that Chamberlain had arranged it. Though the Liberal Unionists were not represented in the deputation to Churchill on 2 April, their local chief

[11] Labouchere to Churchill, 3 Apr. 1889, RCHL xxiii/3089.

Powell Williams had supported the idea up to 29 March, when Chamberlain had told him Churchill would not stand; on 31 March he had asked Akers-Douglas to exert pressure on local Conservatives in favour of the potential Liberal Unionist candidate, Albert Bright. And while Churchill had told Chamberlain on 26 March that he would not contest Birmingham if it was 'a doubtful chance', this was no more than he had always said.

All the evidence shows Chamberlain's implacability; though he had written to his son on 3 December 1888 'if Randolph wants to stand we must back him', by the 15th he was unequivocal: 'I am not surprised that the Tories should be sore with Randolph, but I wish he would himself say openly that he would not stand. If he thinks he ought to be selected he may make trouble for us.'[12] On Churchill's side, Beach later interpreted it to Winston Churchill as 'intended to be a personal attack on Joe', which would be repudiated by Smith and Salisbury and isolate Churchill even further: success *or* defeat at Birmingham would thus keep him out of the government, where Beach wanted him to return.[13] But Beach had a retrospective axe to grind, having played the part of Doubting Thomas. And the basic question remains why Churchill voluntarily submitted himself to a committee judgement—if he really wished to stand for Birmingham, and was not simply being chivvied into it by local politicians and Tory-Democrat friends. There is some evidence for the latter interpretation.[14] But his reactions at the time were uncharacteristically indecisive, probably reflecting his own debility.

The results in Birmingham nearly destroyed the Unionist compact in any case: a furious row developed between the local parties, embarrassing Chamberlain, and deliberately fanned by Churchill. Similar tensions followed in contests at Rochester and Bradford; the Unionist alliance underwent a considerable internal strain in the late spring of 1889. Churchill and Chamberlain indulged in a much quoted public correspondence; but the real issue—as Churchill's letters implied—involved the situation of

[12] Chamberlain to Austen Chamberlain, 3 Dec. 1888, 5 Dec. 1888, Chamberlain MSS 5/12/4.

[13] Beach to W. S. Churchill, 18 Sept. 1904, CHAR 8/19.

[14] There was some forcing the pace by Jennings, and a long letter to *The Times* from 'A Tory M.P.' (5 April) delineated in great detail, and from an inside stance, the background to the decision.

the local constituency party, rather than his own position. Also made manifest was the extent of the Cecil family's enmity to the renegade, which brought Chamberlain yet closer to Hatfield. Salisbury assured him privately of his support; Chamberlain told an approving Balfour that if Churchill declared any further intention to contest Central Birmingham, 'he should regard this as a Declaration of War between Randolph and himself... His position in politics largely depended upon his position in Birmingham.'[15]

In fact, Churchill, discovering decisiveness too late, did tell a Birmingham audience on 29 July that he was ready to stand for the city if they wanted him; he also called for 'no more three-cornered arrangements', and declared the Liberal Unionists should come clean and join the Tories. But his backing-down over the candidature, and his recent flouting of Tory doctrine over Temperance, had eroded his influence in the city to such an extent that the pronouncement was not made particularly much of. This local unpopularity was instanced by Chamberlain in October 1889 when Smith, wishing to get rid of the disastrous Matthews by promoting him to the Court of Appeal, again floated the idea of a Birmingham seat for Churchill; Chamberlain's reply was as flinty as ever.[16] It was part of the strategy whereby he retained six out of the seven city seats for Liberal Unionism until he formally joined the government. And whatever the extent of Churchill's private commitment to the idea of representing Birmingham, in public he was thought to have acted pusillanimously. The constant comparisons drawn between him and Chamberlain were by now inevitably to his detraction—'soft metal against hard steel', according to Harcourt; 'cool vindictiveness has far more staying power than passionate spite'.

As this incident demonstrates, Churchill's relations with the government became no easier. In the late 1880s, he occasionally sent ministers like Smith or Goschen long letters of paternal advice, while remaining capable of attacking them in public. But despite a closely orchestrated campaign with Wolff and the

[15] Balfour to Salisbury, 2 June 1888, quoted in Rhodes James, pp. 335–6. Salisbury wrote to Chamberlain: 'Apart from all questions of compact, I think that the success of such a programme as Churchill has put forward would reduce political life very far below the level it occupies in any other country, even the U.S.'

[16] See Churchill to Chamberlain, 23 Oct. 1889, Chamberlain MSS 5/65/12; Chamberlain to Smith, 25 Oct. 1889 (copy), ibid. 16; also Middleton to Smith, 28 Oct. 1889, in Chilston MSS CL P/1, p. 437 (Middleton's letter-book).

Prince of Wales, Churchill was unable to interest Salisbury greatly in his report from Russia in early 1888, and the Prime Minister's attitude continued implacable. (Wolff, the eternal go-between, was told sharply by Salisbury in October 1889: 'What I have never been able to get either you or him fully to appreciate is that many of us work at politics for the purpose of promoting and defending certain ideas, and that co-operation with a politician who from time to time does his best to extinguish those ideas is greatly hindered, not to say more.'[17]) With Churchill's encouragement, Beach returned to office in February 1888: practically an admission that it was too dangerous to allow him to combine with Churchill.

The party left to Churchill embraced tyros and malcontents—Lord George Curzon, Ernest Beckett, Henniker Heaton, Dunraven—led by the egregious Louis Jennings, an embittered littérateur and part-time journalist who appointed himself Churchill's Achates in early 1887.[18] Fussy, irritating, addicted to feuds and plots, Jennings was unpopular with Churchill's older friends: 'while he was a born intriguer', wrote Beach to Winston Churchill long afterwards, 'he was just the man to magnify himself ... with all his abilities he was anything but a good adviser to your father and I thoroughly mistrusted him'.[19] Jennings was, moreover, the archetypical Tory Democrat—a middle-class villa-dweller, rabidly anti-Irish as well as anti-Cecil, hating Chamberlain, and determined to reclaim Churchill from those more dangerous pastures into which he instinctively strayed. Though indispensable to Churchill for political (and journalistic) purposes, he was never a boon companion; his endless letters to Churchill frequently imply disapproval of his ally's social jaunts, and on one occasion he actually pursued him to the Riviera to discuss the publication of Churchill's speeches—where his arrival was hardly welcomed. Jennings was not privy to Churchill's negotiations with

[17] Wolff to Churchill, 8 Oct. 1889, quoting a letter of 1 Oct. from Salisbury; RCHL xxiv/3290.

[18] Writing to Churchill on 14 June 1888, Jennings described the twenty Conservatives who voted with Radicals and Irish on his resolution about reorganization in the public departments as Churchill's followers. These were: G. C. T. Bartley, A. A. Baumann, E. W. Beckett, Lord Charles Beresford, M. W. Mattinson, J. H. Heaton, F. C. Hughes-Hallett, H. S. Cross, Baron K. Dimsdale, F. Duncan, R. Gent Davis, W. T. Goldsworthy, C. F. Hamilton, R. C. Mayne, E. S. Norris, F. T. Penton, T. B. Royden, T. H. Sidebottom, and W. Sidebottom; tellers L. Jennings and Major Rasch. See RCHL xxii/2922; *Hansard 3*, cccxxxvi, 1945–6; *Dod's Parliamentary Companion*.

[19] Beach to W. S. Churchill, 18 Sept. 1904, CHAR 8/19.

Carnarvon and Hartington in 1889 (he frequently begged Churchill to abandon Ireland in favour of 'the decent English workman'); indeed, Carnarvon felt Churchill at this time wanted a friend badly, but would throw him over if circumstances demanded it. 'He said rather sadly, I have no friend to whom I can talk.'[20] Jennings could not be talked to, at least in the free-wheeling Churchill style; for one thing, he took nearly all Churchill said at face value.

He was, however, preoccupied with the presentation of Churchill to posterity. A plan for a Tory-Democrat paper in Paddington, backed by Churchill, fell through because of lack of funds; but Jennings took over the editing of Churchill's collected speeches, which covered the period up to the end of 1888, and appeared in March 1889. Jennings searched out endless newspaper reports, and as indefatigably pored over what to omit; he contributed a highly tendentious introduction about Churchill's relations with the party; he wanted to include the letter to Akers-Douglas of January 1887, and the memorandum on the formation of the government in 1885.[21] His frequent letters to Churchill emphasized the importance of the production as 'a material portion of contemporary history', to be culled by 'future historians', and the contents were gauged accordingly. The strident tone of the introduction and notes did not add conviction; and the work was in commercial terms a fiasco, only selling 250 copies in the first month after its appearance.

It also added to the generally antagonistic attitude towards the government preserved by Churchill in 1888–9. In a long letter to Goschen of March 1888, outlining his plans for army and navy reform, he emphasized that he did not care if the government was placed in a minority; this was followed by public attacks on the estimates (though he disappointed the Radicals by the extent to which he had abandoned economy in favour of efficiency). He expected Gladstone's regained strength and the situation in Ireland to bring the government down in the early autumn;[22] in November he applied pressure by calling (in front of an unimpressed audience of the Paddington bourgeoisie) for an urgent domestic programme dealing with Temperance, sweating, and the importation of foreign labour.

---

[20] Carnarvon diary, 14 July 1889, 9 Nov. 1889, BL Add. MS 60933.

[21] See Jennings to Frank Thomas, 1 Dec. 1888, RCHL xxiii/3022; also Jennings to Churchill, ibid. 3029. For sale of speeches see ibid. 3118.

[22] Churchill to Roberts, 9 Sept. 1888, Roberts MSS 7101-23-21/84.

The same month saw a series of skirmishes with ministers in parliament, often with Irish backing, and a notably anti-government speech on supply using Jennings's researches. On 1 December he delivered a celebrated frontal attack, in a powerful speech on the occupation of Suakin; he 'only carried one man with him', according to Smith, but, as Morley wrote to Rosebery, the weight he brought to the Liberal side was measured in more than numbers. 'His first vote against his friends: I wonder what his last will be.'[23]

Three days later, he went much further, springing a motion for adjournment on a thin House, supported by Gladstone, Harcourt, and Childers. Quoting 'the highest military authorities', Churchill called attention to the inadequacy of the English forces at Suakin and the danger they stood in—embarrassing both Smith and Stanhope—and ended with a histrionic and sentimental appeal to Bright, 'a great Englishman' on his bed of affliction. Only Chamberlain, Hartington, and their followers saved the government. 'You may well say the Randolphian business was fishy', Morley told Rosebery; 'Pray, believe ... *One who Knows*.'[24] This was only one climax in Churchill's protracted attack on the government during November and December; on the 17th, in reply to Chaplin's invitation to bring a vote of censure, he retorted 'give me a day and I will do it'. It was a safe threat, coming as it did at the end of the interminable session. But the whole sequence belies his son's interpretation of the Suakin attack as an isolated outburst.

More or less bereft of support, however, there was little he could do; and the positive issues upon which he could attack the government were not numerous. Foreign policy under Salisbury was no longer a weak link, though Churchill privately disapproved of the Mediterranean agreements and told an Oxford audience on his return from Russia that Europe stood on the brink of 'a rupture of peace such as we have not seen since 1815'. However, he praised Salisbury's policy in public, telling Lytton that 'he hoped to obtain the eventual adoption of his "own policy" by means of private persuasion'.[25] This policy, as outlined to Hartington in early 1888, involved an informal

---

[23] 2 Dec. 1888; Morley to Rosebery, Rosebery MSS 10045.

[24] Same to same, 10 Dec. 1888, ibid.

[25] Lytton to Lady Salisbury, 14 Feb. 1888, *Letters of Lord Lytton*, ii, 337. For Churchill's views on the Mediterranean Agreements see his letter to Prince of Wales, 30 Dec. 1887, Royal Archives T 9/103.

understanding with Russia, and detachment from the Central Powers; he had now moved from his idea of a German alliance, and went so far as to attack Germany's 'aggressive colonial policy' in 1885–6 (a policy he had vociferously condoned at the time). He had also returned to preaching the evacuation of Egypt, and his inclination towards Russia involved benevolent neutrality towards France: though, understandably, he did not always remember this.[26]

It was over France, moreover, that his unreliability for office in the Foreign Service manifested itself: for Churchill's close relationship with Boulanger gave rise to extreme embarrassment. He was convinced the General would take over the government in the summer of 1889; he had him to dinner with the Prince of Wales in London; friendly with ardent Boulangists in Paris, he preached the cause in London with indefatigable fervour.[27] This told against him in his anglings for a diplomatic appointment— which commenced in November 1889 with Wolff sounding out Salisbury about replacing Lytton in Paris with Churchill. Salisbury refused, but countered with a tentative offer of St. Petersburg, which Churchill, after much agonizing, decided to accept. But nothing came of the idea, though Churchill reminded Wolff to keep Salisbury up to it. When Lytton died in 1891, Churchill anxiously requested Paris, supported by Balfour; but his attitude towards Egypt, and his connection with Boulanger, made it impossible.[28]

Thus by the autumn of 1889, Churchill was prepared to exile himself to Russia; the spring of that year had been, as described earlier, devoted to Irish negotiations behind the scenes, and in the summer he remained detached, refusing invitations to

---

[26] His Channel Tunnel speech, celebrated by his biographers as a *tour de force* but thought by James 'the weakest thing he has done' (James to Chamberlain, Chamberlain MSS 5/46/21), was in fact based on a stern warning of the dangers of French belligerence.

[27] See Carnarvon diary, 14 July 1889, BL Add. MS 60933; *Letters of Lord Lytton*, ii, 379; Churchill to Prince of Wales, 8 Apr. 1889, Royal Archives T 9/120; Tyrwhitt to Churchill, 25 Apr. 1889, RCHL xxiii/3148. Also EHJ, vol. xxi, pp. 73, 109, and xxii, p. 119, where at a Rosebery dinner-party on 26 Oct. Churchill was 'delightfully naïve about Boulanger. "There was a chance of Boulanger's success. Had it been fulfilled, I should have been in great favour in France; I should always have had a bed at my disposal at the Elysée, and all you fellows would have said how clever I had been. But there he is—done for; and so I have done with him." '

[28] See Carnarvon's diary, 9 Nov. 1889, 10 Nov. 1889, BL Add. MS 60933 (Churchill confided in Carnarvon and asked his advice). Also Wolff to Churchill, RCHL xxiv/3264, 3276, 3282, for scattered references. For the reasons (relayed by Balfour) why Paris was impossible in 1891 see letters from Lady Randolph in Blenheim MSS, H/IV.

Conservative dinners. His speech of 26 July on Royal Grants was, as he told the House, his first for a long time. He used it to define himself against Bradlaugh, an embarrassingly frequent ally the year before, and his sentiments were admirably loyalist. Shortly afterwards, however, he took a public initiative which set him against many Tory elements and incidentally challenged Chamberlain on his own ground. At Walsall on 28 July he delivered a covert attack on the apathy of the government and parliament compared to the dynamism of provincial Toryism, and called for the breaking-up of large estates among small proprietors; the adoption of working-class housing schemes by local authorities, using compulsory purchase; and, what mono-polized all attention, licensing reform.

In some ways this traditionally difficult question was a surprising departure for Churchill; as recently as 1886 he had hotly defended the right of parents to send their children to buy beer as 'one of the few pleasures available to the working-classes', and derided 'fanatics belonging to temperance societies'.[29] The cause of temperance, however, had—even in Conservative circles—an urban and Orange flavour; and his correspondence shows he had been taking soundings for an initiative since late 1888. When it came, however, the delicacy of his own position, and the extreme language he used, roused more or less unanimous suspicion and hostility. The 'destructive and devilish liquor traffic', 'a disgrace to English civilisation', must be curbed and controlled; moreover, the brewers and distillers, with their 'enormously powerful political organization', had no right to compensation: 'not one sixpence'. This extraordinary statement was instantly attacked from the floor of the meeting, and Churchill hastily added that he would recognize their claims 'in a fair and judicial way': but with the traditionally Conservative liquor interest attacked, and the sacred principle of compensation endangered, the damage was done. There were dissentients from the vote of thanks at the end of the meeting, rumbles from the Birmingham Tories, and for once Wolff and Jennings agreed in disapprobation. It is possible that Churchill wanted to point up a classic area of disagreement between Liberal Unionists and Conservatives, by driving the latter to

---

[29] *Hansard 3*, ccciv, 667. In his speech on his licensing bill, however, Churchill made great play with the image of small children exposed to the horror of public houses (ibid. cccxliii, 1698 ff.).

take an irreconcilable line on licensing reform; but it backfired, by concentrating all the recriminations on his own head.

Churchill persevered with the issue, publishing newspaper articles on it, and in April 1890 introducing a Licensing Amendment Bill which was quite favourably looked upon by the government, but was dropped after the first reading. It had been drafted with the aid of Liberals like Harcourt, Livesey, and James, and gave powers to county councils to reduce the numbers of public houses as instructed by District Committees appointed by them; total abolition was possible in an area where two thirds of the ratepayers were in favour. This angered the Conservative side, while the extreme temperance advocates decried the commitment to the principle of compensation, though Churchill claimed it could not be properly legislated for by a private bill. None the less, Sir Wilfrid Lawson, the veteran temperance politician whom Churchill had consulted, saw the Bill as a triumph, and both Ritchie and Harcourt glowingly eulogized it in debate;[30] but it did not reach a second reading, since the government's Local Taxation Bill, which reached its second reading on 12 May, embodied clauses on licensing and compensation. Churchill then concentrated on adding amendments to this; but it was racked by crisis, and when the government majority sank to four on 19 June, the licensing clauses were dropped. Churchill, not surprisingly, later accused Goschen of sabotaging the whole issue.

Thus his speech at Walsall in July 1889 staked out one line of advance, though it did not in the event amount to very much; and his following performance at Birmingham on the 30th, besides outbidding Chamberlain in democratic stakes, took up another gage. This was the long-planned declaration of Irish policy, as arranged with Carnarvon, to whom he confided that 'he intended to speak out, telling his audience he could not speak freely in the House of Commons'.[31] But the message did not come through as clearly as initially planned: largely because no detailed plan of local government, with Hartington's and

---

[30] Introduced on 29 May 1890. Lawson said privately: 'the voice is the voice of Randolph, but the words are the words of Lawson' (F. C. Channing, *Memories of Midland Politics* (London, 1918), p. 102). For correspondence about drafting it see Churchill to Harcourt, 24 Jan. 1890, Harcourt MSS, dep. 218, f. 5.

[31] 14 July; BL Add. MS 60933. Carnarvon wrote on 1 August that he largely agreed with all Churchill said, and applauded his non-committal line; all they might disagree upon was Egypt. This letter implies that Carnarvon was thinking in terms of a wider co-operation than merely over Ireland (RCHL xxiv/3230).

Carnarvon's backing, could be produced. On 'Repeal' Churchill was as gnomic as he had ever been: 'the idea is inadmissible because the construction is impracticable and the construction is impracticable because the idea is inadmissible, and that idea has guided me since the commencement of this great Home Rule controversy and will continue to guide me till the end. But short of that I would go a long way, I frankly confess.' This 'long way' involved representative local government, decentralization of administration, and 'the creation of a great peasant proprietary all over Ireland', with the aid of £100 million, raised on the rates by the new agencies of local government. This plan, for linking further land reform to local-government extension rather than furtherance of the Ashbourne Act, was also adopted by Chamberlain; Churchill articulated it at length in three long letters to the *Morning Post* in April 1890.[32] At Birmingham the idea was expressed in terms of politics: it would dissipate the political energy in Ireland by redirecting it to a local, material base, which would in turn institute a natural division of parties—Conservatives against Radicals instead of tenants against landlords. The Conservatives, Churchill promised, would have a large preponderance, as both Irish people and Irish Church were naturally Conservative. This was pure FitzGibbonism;[33] and the 'brilliant Irishman and Tory Unionist' whom Churchill quoted in the course of his speech can only have been him. Equally characteristic was the following attack on the spirit of 'Podsnappery'—Philistine English complacency and chauvinism towards Ireland, rather than a generous and imaginative attitude which could culminate in equal institutions. It was not, however, a message popular in Birmingham; nor in Wales, where it was substantially repeated in early September. And, more importantly, it did not lead to the kind of general new departure planned in April. By October 1889, speaking at Perth, Churchill had reverted to historical platitudes on the Union (as well as deliberately offensive

---

[32] The originals of which are in the National Library of Ireland, MS 2080. See also letter to *The Times*, 27 Nov. 1888, and *Hansard 3*, cccxxx, 1853 ff.

[33] See for instance FitzGibbon to Churchill, 30 Nov. 1889, RCHL xxiv/3339. 'A wise measure giving Ireland the power to buy off all her own landlords, at her own risk and cost, giving her in return the power of managing her own domestic affairs, when, but only when, she has dealt fairly, on prescribed terms, with all vested interests, would not touch the English or Scotch pocket and would make the ability to exercise it the condition of Ireland's earning comparative independence.' Churchill's letters to the *Morning Post* the following April repeated this message at great length.

remarks about the laxness of Scottish Conservative organization). Such a speech made no waves at all, except for involving
him in leisurely epistolary arguments with Harcourt on recon-
dite historical points to do with the Union. In this correspondence, Churchill privately disclaimed all admiration for Pitt;
but, he added, 'in public Tory gods must be adored'.[34] It was a
lesson painfully emphasized by his experience in the wilderness.

III

It was, therefore, in the logic of Churchill's position in 1888–9—
covert hostility to the government, and a frustrated Irish
initiative—that he should violently attack his party over the
outcome of the Special Commission on *The Times* forgeries,
which in 1887 had attempted to implicate Parnell in the Phoenix
Park murders. There was, at the same time, a consistent record
on Churchill's part of opposition to the commission; though it
should be noted that at Nottingham in April 1887 he had
delivered a lengthy harangue on 'Parnellism and Crime' (excised from Jennings's version), where he called on the Irish to
start libel proceedings if *The Times*'s statements were untrue, and
concluded: 'we must assume that there is truth in it if the Irish
cannot disprove it'. He had also been ready to suggest to Smith
ways of embarrassing the Parnellites by a libel prosecution
against *The Times*, and had annoyed the Parnellites by a similar
challenge. But the idea of covering the whole area of the Land
League's activities with an investigatory commission, suggested a
year later when a libel case revived the charges, offended him
deeply; his Irish Tory friends like FitzGibbon and Morris
inveighed bitterly against it. In July 1888 Churchill produced a
long memorandum for Smith, closely following their arguments,
and condemning the idea of an 'extra-constitutional' tribunal as
being both politically biased and potentially dangerous. The
record of the commission bore out all his misgivings; the final
act, with the forger's suicide in a Madrid hotel, approximated to
one of the French novels with which Churchill beguiled his
leisure hours, and the mass of allegations regarding Land League
activities destroyed any climate of opinion which might have
made his Irish initiative possible. The debate on the commission
report, where Churchill (on FitzGibbon's advice) deviated from

[34] Churchill to Harcourt, 5 Dec. 1889, Harcourt MSS, dep. 217, f. 87; also see
Harcourt to Churchill, 30 Nov. 1889 (copy), ibid., dep. 729, f. 403.

Jennings's planned amendment to launch his own attack, has been dealt with in detail by both biographers; Rhodes James has pointed out that Jennings knew well in advance of Churchill's intention to speak on the main question, but persevered none the less. There had already been rumours of a quarrel between them; and Churchill's speech separated him from his fussy follower for good.

This speech condemned government and commission alike: the description of Pigott, final product of the 'mountainous parturition', as 'a ghastly, bloody, rotten foetus' was uniquely offensive. Ironically, however, this helped the government off the hook by affording a general distraction: and it altered the embarrassing line which the debate was taking, towards the perennially awkward question of the Tory–Irish alliance in 1885, which Churchill was as anxious to avoid as were his ex-colleagues.[35] The performance was seen by most as an exercise in the politics of egoism; it led to a flurry of cancelled meetings, and resignation threats in Churchill's constituency association, though there is surprisingly little in his correspondence reflecting its effect. Newspaper publicity was swiftly resorted to; the *Morning Post* loyally published his 1888 memorandum to Smith. Churchill in an uncharacteristically forthcoming interview to the *Evening News* of 20 March poured scorn on the *Standard*, spoke dismissively of Jennings, and used the occasion to deplore Balfour's Irish administration and the government's reactionary social policy. Thumbing his nose at a more elevated level, he gave a large dinner-party five days after his speech for the Prince of Wales at which the guests were either Irish Tories or English Liberals, and where the tone was probably celebratory.

There was all the more reason for this as the government was lurching to a particularly low point in mid-1890: Churchill had believed in late 1889 that another session under Smith's leadership meant 'smash', and the fluctuating barometer of by-elections seemed to rock the Unionist alliance so badly as almost to capsize it. His own episodic attempts to build up a countering position on Irish land and local government, as well as his attacks on the Army estimates and Goschen's licensing scheme, helped push the government to the brink. By the end of June 1890 Salisbury, the Queen, and many others felt Smith must be

[35] See P. Marsh, p. 158. It might also be noted that Chamberlain, who followed, saw the speech—and all attacks on the commission—as at least partially aimed at him, because of his close involvement in inspiring it (*Hansard 3*, cclxii, 524).

replaced; his blunders over introducing attempted changes in procedure, and his abandoning the Land Purchase and Titles Bill until the next session, publicized his increasing illness and incapacity. After a revolt of the party respectables against Smith's proposal to hold over bills from one session for enactment in the next, there was a great deal of talk of reconstruction in June 1890.

Moreover, it puts Churchill's April performance in perspective when it is noted that these rumours none the less involved him as well as Hartington—even in the perennially hostile columns of *The Times*. The most direct evidence that negotiations actually lay behind the rumours comes in a long letter from George Russell to Henry James, describing the breakdown of Smith, the government's perilous state, and Russell's opening of overtures to Churchill: who agreed to break his practice and campaign for the Conservative candidate at the Barrow by-election, 'provided it was the desire of the Government'. According to Russell, Smith and Balfour approved of thus identifying Churchill with the government, and opening negotiations for his return; but Salisbury 'held aloof', and the expected pressure from Hartington on Churchill's behalf never materialized.[36] An interview between the Duchess of Marlborough and Salisbury found the latter as impossible to pin down as ever.[37] However, in June Churchill dropped his hostile amendments to Goschen's Bill dealing with local taxation, for which he was duly thanked by Chaplin and Smith; at the end of the month he travelled to Barrow and spoke in favour of Wainwright—which, he told friends, meant that in three weeks he would have rejoined the government. The speech was violently anti-Radical, praised Salisbury's foreign policy, and presented a powerful party case; it received a first leader in *The Times*, pointing out the significance of Churchill's supporting the government against Caine (an ex-Liberal Unionist and fellow temperance advocate).

But the government delayed on their half of the bargain. On 23 July Churchill delivered another noticeably pro-government

[36] See Russell to James, 28 June 1890, James MSS M45/409; Russell to Churchill, 14 July 1890, RCHL xxvi/3616. The rumours became so prevalent in July that several of Churchill's correspondents wrote to him congratulating him on his readmission to the government, and it was reported in diplomatic dispatches (see Waddington to Ribot, 9 July 1890, *Doc. Dipl. Fr.*, 1st ser., 8, no. 169).

[37] See RCHL xxvi/3576 for a typed account. Salisbury insisted that Churchill's time would come, and that he himself was 'nearly played-out'.

speech, praising their policies, minimizing his 'occasional differences' with them, and receiving heavy hints from fellow-
speakers about services he would perform for the government 'in
the future'. By then, however, *The Times* merely pointed out the
clumsiness of his attempts to return, and instanced his Irish ideas
and congenital instability against the notion: as well as, more
damningly, the fact that he was losing his grip on provincial
audiences. In fact, he had backed the government at their lowest
point, and was now finessed; and though he told Henniker
Heaton he would hold aloof from the 'final flurry' of a
government that had so long ignored his advice, the final flurry
never came. Instead the Parnell divorce hearing, only a few days
before parliament reassembled in November, gave the
Conservatives a completely fortuitous new lease of life.

   In fact, Churchill had become increasingly disillusioned; the
opening of the session found him in Monte Carlo, *en route* for
Egypt. Old allies had dropped off; in 1888 he had been asked to
stand down as patron of the Cambridge Carlton, in 1890 he had
failed to gain re-election to the Council of the National Union.
'Parliament exists for no other object than that of wasting time',
he wrote to Hicks Beach in 1890, 'and we fail when we try to
force its nature and divert it from its real purpose.'[38]
Increasingly incapacitated and exhausted, he gave up speaking
at Westminster altogether from May 1890 until the summer of
1892. He was drifting into a political limbo: sustained only by
his powerfully united family, whose letters to him continued to
harp on hopes of a government disaster, and optimistic inferences of a breakdown in Salisbury's health.

   The winter was spent on the Nile and the Riviera; on his
return in February 1891 he represented himself to the
Paddington voters as independent and unambitious. 'My differences with the Government are not altogether exhausted.' He
had privately drafted an immense letter resigning his seat, which
instanced his disagreements with both parties; one sentence,
deleted in the rough version, declared that he would have
crossed over to the Liberal party in early 1887 if it had not been
for Home Rule, an impossibility because of the 'two races and
two religions' in Ireland. Ten pages concerned his differences
with the government over Ireland; he also instanced as areas of
controversy expenditure, licensing, the eight hour day, im-

---

[38] Churchill to Beach, 14 July 1890, St. Aldwyn MSS, PCC/82.

perial customs-union, and foreign policy. This statement, as well
as much else at the time, broadcast an intention to 'practically
withdraw from political life'.[39]

This memorandum was never acted upon; but he settled
down for the moment to being a 'London member'. He had
already identified himself with causes like unemployment in
Paddington, and a polytechnic institution for education (towards which he had raised large sums of money from financier
friends); in 1888 he mounted an attack upon corruption on the
Metropolitan Board of Works. In this he was acting as the
mouthpiece of T. J. Fardell, the most prominent figure in his
constituency association; and when Fardell graduated to a seat
on the new London County Council, Churchill took a particular
interest in its doings. This was possibly dictated by the fact that
Salisbury deeply disapproved of the institution, and advised his
lieutenants not to have anything to do with it. Churchill, by
contrast, made it a special cause, and attempted to set up a
'London League' of democratic Tories who would oppose the
Progressives on the LCC: he publicly blamed Rosebery as a
'Machiavelli' who had plotted its take-over by the Liberal party.
Rosebery, who liked the idea, took to signing his letters with the
sobriquet.

Along with this collusive banter, however, Churchill was
exploring the new range of interests which enabled his son to
present him later as a lost labour leader; and though he may
have been conscious of the increasingly Marxist resolutions of
the TUC from 1893, or the potential of the new ILP, it is more
likely that this new identification was a result of his own acute
sense of the flow of public opinion, crystallized by the need to
outbid the Progressives on the LCC. In many speeches and
letters from 1891, he pointed out that organized labour was the
coming heavyweight force in politics: 'we are now come, or are
coming fast, to a time when Labour laws will be made by the
Labour interest for the advantage of Labour ... personally I can
discern no cause for alarm in this prospect'.[40] But his recurrent
emphasis was that Toryism could absorb this, and a correspondent who asked if he supported 'a distinct but not separate
party of Labour within the Conservative ranks' received a
broadside: 'We Tories have ever been content to leave fantastic

---

[39] RCHL xxvi/3691; undated, but the context is February 1891.
[40] Letter to Arnold White, *The Times*, 2 May 1892, partially quoted in W. S.
Churchill, ii, 459.

groupings of individuals for the promotion of various forms of fads and hobbies to our political opponents.' The Tories would take on the Labour cause, giving 'practical effect by legislation to much of what Labour asks for'; but this must be consonant with 'a just regard for legitimate rights of property, for due individual freedom of action, and for the protection of the general commercial interests of the State'.[41]

His embracing of the Eight Hours' Bill is equally illustrative; though he declared his conversion to the coal-miners' case, he was opposed to it as a general national principle. The fact that he opposed Bradlaugh on the issue was seen as symptomatic of a new line of political division: politically Conservative state interventionism versus old-style individualist Radicalism.[42] Churchill's presentation of the eight hours principle to Balfour was not as the thin end of a socialist wedge, but as evidence of a new trades unionism which could be friendly to Conservatism; such measures would probably result in 'a return towards protection, which may take the form of an inter-colonial customs union: a result agreeable to all our party traditions'.[43] Though Winston Churchill inferred that his father would have become a 'Tory-Socialist' in the twentieth century, this seems unlikely. He certainly read, and praised, articles by Sidney Webb; he and Dunraven had characteristic hopes of H. H. Champion, and tried to raise money for his newspaper ('though he calls himself a Socialist he hates Radicals and does his best to fight them').[44] But time and again he defined social reform as anti-socialist; and while he preached on behalf of housing of the working class by local authorities, and declared that crime and drunkenness were conditioned by living-circumstances, his panaceas remained private ownership and private initiative. (He attacked State aid for hospitals, for instance, as a pernicious foreign abomination.) At Walsall he warned that when a revolution came it would be brought about by the condition of the masses in the great towns;

---

[41] *The Times*, 17 Oct. 1892.

[42] See *Spectator*, 1 Mar. 1890, and for the debate, *Hansard 3*, cccxii, 1119 ff. Rosebery in 1885 had been seen as a leader in the 'race towards state socialism' because he embraced work-hours regulation (*Pall Mall Gazette*, 29 Sept. 1885).

[43] Letter quoted in Fraser, *Chamberlain*, p. 230. Churchill repeated this analysis regarding protection in his letter to White, above.

[44] Dunraven to Churchill, 31 Jan. 1890, RCHL xxv/3391. This may be the origin of rumours that Churchill was floating a Tory–Democrat paper in Paddington. For his praise of Webb see Churchill to Ayrshire Miners' Unions, 9 Dec. 1889, RCHL xxv/3344; for Winston's hypothesis, see vol. ii, p. 486.

but he later denied, correctly, that this speech had anything to do with socialism; or that he had said 'anything original' beyond the fact that Conservatism was the party of social rather than organic reform (a distinction he kept perfectly clear).[45]

In reality, what he was doing in 1890–1 was recurring to the Tory-Democratic line, far more coherently and consistently than in 1883–4, but still avoiding specific social panaceas except on certain occasions like Walsall. It was a genuine preoccupation, not only in public; in a long conversation with Carnarvon in November 1889 he talked much of social reform, and the need to win the masses by including their representatives in government. But this represents no more than the insecurity evinced at the same time in Tory tracts like the novels of W. H. Mallock. On another occasion he turned round Harcourt's 'we are all socialists now' to 'we are all more or less philanthropists now': social rather than organic reform once more.[46] In February 1891 he told his Paddington audience that political power was in the hands of the labouring classes: 'what are you going to do for them?' A war between Capital and Labour was developing, which must be avoided by State arbitration in industrial disputes; nor should Conservatism automatically take the side of Capital. Villadom cannot have been unduly sympathetic; but Churchill by this stage was past caring. He would have privately agreed with what his friend Lady Sykes wrote to him in 1892:

There is a great deal of what I call 'middle-classness' and bourgeois humbug on the surface of English politics still—but I cannot help thinking that the *real* electorate nowadays—i.e. artisans and labourers—don't care a button for any of those 'old institutions' which, unless they are perfectly sound and doing some practical work, are all doomed to disappear. Tant mieux, I much prefer real democracy to the tyranny of the petite bourgeoisie.[47]

But in the speech at Paddington, as in much else of Churchill's social-reform pronouncements of the time, he was recurring to Fourth Party as well as Tory-Democrat manners: he even quoted Gorst, who had recently attended an International Labour conference at Berlin. And the envoi at Paddington, as

---

[45] See speech in Wales, 6 Sept. 1889. He also denied that he supported the eight hours principle. (The next day found him hotly defending the Established Church in Wales at a fête organized by Lady Londonderry.)

[46] See *The Times*, 11 Jan. 1890; also Carnarvon diary, 9 Nov. 1889, BL Add. MS 60933.

[47] 'Sept. '92', RCHL xxviii/3996.

with so much of the ethos of the Fourth Party and Tory Democracy, was cast in terms of pure Toryism, and the politics of personalities rather than of ideas: Conservatism must use its strength in capital and among the employing classes to buy off the nascent Labour organizations and outbid Gladstone, 'the most extraordinary man whom this century has produced'.

IV

Moreover, Churchill's involvement with politics in early 1891 was short-lived: by April of that year, his plans for a large-scale expedition to South Africa were announced. This was presented rather grandiloquently to his constituents as a mission to search out suitable areas for the depressed British working-man to emigrate to, but his son defined his objects more accurately as 'sport, gold and peace'. His priority was gold, though he consistently evaded reporters' questions on the issue; family letters refer repeatedly to the possibility of his coming back with a fortune. Indeed, his relations had more than a passing interest in such an eventuality. Churchill's expedition was organized by a syndicate, who held their capital at Rothschilds': in this he held £5,000, and Lord and Lady Wimborne (from whom he had borrowed this stake) £2,000; another sister, Lady Sarah Wilson, invested £1,000, as did the Duchess. Other shareholders, with similar stakes, included intimates like Borthwick and Breteuil, and financial acquaintances like Hirsch, Neumann, Colonel North, and H. H. Marks (editor of the *Financial News*). The total capital held was £15,994.[48] Churchill with difficulty kept his wife's brother-in-law Moreton Frewen, enthusiastic inventor of a patent gold-crushing machine, out of the venture, though the newspapers instantly connected him with it: but the Rothschilds loomed in the background, providing one of their mining engineers (H. Perkins) for the expedition, and a close connection existed between Churchill and the magnates of the British South Africa Company and De Beers', Rhodes and Beit. Beit travelled in the expedition, avoiding publicity; Churchill, already a shareholder in Rhodes's company, stayed with him in Cape Town, and in his public letters home resolutely advocated the Rhodes argument about the unification of South Africa and the position

[48] See B. Roberts, *Churchills in Africa* (London, 1970), pp. 11–13; Guest to Churchill, 4 Dec. 1893, Blenheim MSS K/IV. Also a long conversation with Churchill in EHJ, 27 Mar. 1891, vol. xxvi, p. 40, BL Add. MS 48645.

of the Uitlanders. Though this relationship later went sour, it was much emphasized by newspapers, and played down by both principals as much as possible.

The publicity accorded to Churchill's ostentatious and unwieldy expedition was considerable. (His personal equipment alone cost £1,750; the general outfit resembled 'the commissariat of a continental army', according to the contemptuous Percy Fitzpatrick.) The attention it gained was compounded by Churchill's own reports, furnished to the *Daily Graphic* for 2,000 guineas and later published in a volume entitled *Men, Mines and Animals in South Africa*. These were widely attacked for their contentiousness and alleged vulgarity; so, more reasonably, were Churchill's increasingly careless interviews—criticizing Salisbury openly, involving himself in an international incident about Delagoa Bay, and praising Gladstone's conduct towards South Africa in the early 1880s. He was, in fact, less and less in control of himself. In South Africa he was rapidly identified by his famous bad temper, and violent attacks on everything Boer (including, laudably, their treatment of black Africans), which eventually embarrassed Rhodes. Too many stories of his wilfulness and rudeness, and the violent but petty controversies which followed his tour, have been catalogued to need repetition.[49] Worst of all, he found Mashonaland (whose terrain was ill adapted to his vast equipage) a hell on earth; his reports lowered the share-prices of the British South Africa Company and De Beers, and led to an open quarrel with Rhodes, whom Churchill abused ever after.

The wider results of his South African tour were to discourage prospective emigration and investment, to affect adversely Rhodes's plans for South African expansion, and to annoy Boer opinion by a further display of British high-handedness. But the personal outcome was more productive. 'No more unwise or unsafe speculation exists than the investment of money in exploration syndicates', Churchill had written in his *Daily Graphic* letters; however, he made many small investments in stock like Jumpers and Transvaal Silver; he invested, with Beit, in the disappointing Matchless Mine at Hartley Hill; and he also, on Perkins's advice, put £5,000 into the Witwatersrand mines being opened up by deep-level mining techniques. On his

---

[49] Roberts, op. cit., *passim*. For his indictment of Mashonaland see *Men, Mines, and Animals in South Africa* (London, 1892), pp. 198–9, 289 ff.; his violent attacks on the 'degraded' Boers are too numerous to catalogue.

return, the syndicate became a limited company, with a capital of £30,000; and though Churchill was forced to sell some of his Rand shares after his return, the residue of his holdings realized £70,000 after his death.

On his return from Africa, the mood of disillusionment with politics which had gripped him in February continued. In October at Mafeking, he had heard of Smith's death and Balfour's succession to the Leadership, which he greeted with a letter to his wife which Rosebery has called 'tragic'. 'I have waited with great patience for the tide to turn, but it has not turned, and will not now turn in time ... I am quite tired and dead-sick of it all, and will not continue political life any longer.' The personal priority was, as ever, to the fore; and he had, in fact, declared at Paddington the previous February that he no longer cared about political influence and had no remaining ambition. But there was also, as this letter shows, a sense that his time had run out. His health was to break down noticeably in 1892; already signs of slurring in speech, vertigo, and palpitations were becoming marked. What would follow, in the inevitable pattern of General Paralysis, were the euphoric delusions which would lead to such embarrassments in the terrible last two years of his life.

None the less, the ambition remained for an honourable retirement; it was in November 1891, on his way home, that he telegraphed to Balfour asking for the Paris Embassy, 'the one thing I have longed for [for] years', and rather pathetically promised to 'obey all instructions'.[50] But this was not possible. Through early 1892 he sustained his intention to retire; he continued to shun parliament, and Lady Dorothy Nevill, meeting him 'quite beaming' in the street that summer, astutely felt 'the excuse was South African mines, not politics'.[51] Churchill gave up racing this summer, however, probably for money reasons, and also moved out of Connaught Place. In May he was negotiating with the German government about setting up another expedition, this time to Damaraland, which would have brought him £10,000 and concessionary rights; but nothing came of it. He took private bets that he would never make another public speech, and his reply to a request for a statement on policy in April bitterly castigated his ex-colleagues for refusing to listen to his 'liberal and progressive ideas'; he had, he

[50] Telegram in Balfour MSS, BL Add. MS 49695; see also n. 28 above.
[51] Lady Dorothy Nevill to Chamberlain, '4 M.', Chamberlain MSS 5/56/77.

said, decided never to repeat the experience again and would decline all opportunities.[52]

This detachment enabled him to cultivate Liberal society even more than previously. His work on the Army and Navy Commission had brought him close to Hartington; his campaign against expenditure involved working with Harcourt; his Bribery Prevention Bill had been backed by Whitbread and James. He frequently said in private that only Home Rule kept him from crossing over ('not that he had any scruples about it', according to Rothschild, but because he believed it impracticable).[53] He visited Malwood and Chatsworth, and moved in a sphere above party differences, where politicians of different sides took pleasure in assuring each other that what mattered most in politics as in life was that one should not be 'dull'.[54] In such company, he was noticed at a Liberal dinner-party, 'a little afraid of Gladstone', but holding forth on Wallace, Darwin, and 'the origin of all things'; in 1888–9 he took to seeing Gladstone frequently, who was always entertained by his 'nimble-mindedness' but feared 'he has not a single grain of conviction in him except in the abstract'. None the less, the Duchess took to entertaining the Gladstones, and pressing Churchill upon them.[55] In the summer of 1892, he was Boswellized as a gay dinner-companion by Rosebery, whom he visited frequently; this was in his best mood, not seen by everybody. Rothschild remained the closest of friends: 'R. Churchill turns to N. Rothschild for everything', Hamilton noticed, but 'Rothschild, who is R.C.'s chief mentor, is giving R.C. up as a hopeless politician.' And even Rothschild was at times so angered by Churchill's conduct that he had to leave the room.[56]

[52] Mrs Nicholson to Churchill, 17 Feb. 1893, RCHL xxix/4078, reclaiming a bet; and Churchill to Lionel Holland, 6 Apr. 1892, in possession of Rosenbach Foundation, 2010 Delancey Place, Philadelphia.

[53] EHJ, 21 Aug. 1888, vol. xx, p. 27, BL Add. MS 48649.

[54] Harcourt confessed to Balfour in July 1890 that he 'hated the dull dogs on both sides'; Balfour playfully replied that 'in this bad world where so many people are dull and so many are spiteful, you and I who are neither are owed a debt of public gratitude. We shall not be payed.' Balfour MSS, BL Add. MS 49690.

[55] See E. Hamilton to Rosebery, 11 Apr. 1891, Rosebery MSS 10031; EHJ, vol. xx, p. 23, xxi, p. 73, BL Add. MSS 48649-50; and A. Ponsonby, *Henry Ponsonby, Queen Victoria's Private Secretary: His Life from His Letters* (London, 1942), p. 261. Hamilton's diary has numerous references to Gladstone's opinion of Churchill—always impressed at his 'extraordinary cleverness' but depressed by his lack of morals.

[56] EHJ, 21 Aug. 1888, vol. xx, p. 47, and xxi, p. 20, BL Add. MSS 48649-50. Also see an incident at Tring (where Churchill abused Rhodes), reported in LHJ, 23 Jan. 1893, vol. 380, p. 80.

Holding such views, and keeping such company, it is unsurprising that Churchill steered clear of political activity in the election campaign of July 1892. His constituency association publicly doubted his commitment to the party, and in his one passionate speech at Paddington, on 2 July, Churchill represented himself as 'one who for the last five years or more has occupied the position of an outcast from the Unionist Party, publicly reviled by them'. Otherwise he avoided involvement, except for some oracular pronouncements on labour. But there were more sinister reasons than mere pique. He told FitzGibbon 'I have a great and increasing horror of anything in the nature of speeches and functions'; in August, when he finally returned to public life after the Liberal victory, he found himself unable to speak in the Commons. 'His real reason he admitted to us [at Tring]', Brett recorded: 'his nerve has gone and the new House, full of strange faces, appalled him.'

In November, he was further unnerved by Blandford's death (having recently married a rich American widow, he had remained a social outcast, and in pure Gothic tradition was found dead in his laboratory at Blenheim 'with a terrible expression on his face'). The same month, at Lady Jeune's, Loulou Harcourt heard Churchill reply to Lucy's suggestion that he take a leading part in the Opposition: 'Oh! No; I am quite out of politics now and besides I shall see far less to oppose in the measures of the present government than I did in those of the last.' In early 1893, he was recorded as more bitter than ever against his own party ('I ought to have stuck to [Northcote] and not to Salisbury'), and heard remarking: 'I am the greatest philosopher going now. I live on reminiscences ... Nobody ever played so high a political game as I did. Rosslyn's gambling on the Turf is nothing compared to what my gambling in politics was. I threw away a great fortune, and I admit very recklessly.'[57]

None the less, his acceptance by his ex-colleagues in Opposition, and the treacherous optimism which accompanied his disease, helped galvanize him into a campaign against Gladstone's second Home Rule Bill, and he returned to public platforms in a series of speeches, in early 1893, more violently anti-Home Rule than those of 1886: though the treatment was

[57] EHJ, 20 Jan. 1893, vol. xxx, p. 90, BL Add. MS 48659. Also see LHJ, 1 and 3 Nov. 1892, vol. 387, pp. 28, 38; 23 Jan. 1892, vol. 389, p. 80. Churchill also assured the ever hopeful Blunt that he was as opposed to the Conservatives as ever on issues like Egypt; 26 Mar. 1893, Blunt MSS 964/1977.

usually historical, his language on personalities caused controversy, and some of the imagery used echoed his palmy days.
(The *Spectator*, though always hostile, thought this campaign was
re-establishing him as a public figure.) But his speeches, increasingly diffuse, rambling, and inaudible, were less and less
reported; by November *The Times* simply carried summaries.
There is nothing more graphic in Churchill's decline than the
way in which he simply fades out of the newspaper columns
which had done so much to make him what he once was.

He continued to attack Home Rule, and defend the Lords
('fighting for no class motives'), on whose obstruction he
produced a pamphlet. For his speeches on the Bill itself he was
backed, as ever, by endless memoranda from FitzGibbon; this
time he was totally dependent on them. His performance,
agonizingly described by Winston Churchill, showed how terrible the deterioration had become. As early as his speech on
local government in April 1888, journalists had noticed his
'indistinct utterance'; he was now hardly capable of getting
through a speech and apologized continually for his bad hearing
and articulation. In the early summer of 1893 Dr Buzzard—who
had seen him first in October 1885—decided that General
Paralysis was commencing in earnest.[58]

Though Winston Churchill saw the content of his father's
speeches in 1893 as having lost little in cogency and brilliance, it
is hard to agree; and to judge by his correspondence, only
FitzGibbon, writing from Dublin, and Wolff, who was in
Madrid, continued to hold out expectations of him. Those who
saw him regularly knew better. FitzGibbon, indeed, told
Winston Churchill later that in his father's last years 'his
prescience and the activity of his intellect were often absolutely
unimpaired': in January of that year, new proposals of Irish
policy from Churchill aroused his apprehensive interest. In July
1893, FitzGibbon was inspired by reading Rosebery's *Pitt* to
dream of Churchill combining with Rosebery to complete the
Union by a progressive Irish policy; Churchill, writing shakily to
Rosebery from the German spa where he was trying to recruit
his health, hinted at the same idea, and received a gentle
answer. Another strange collusive ploy at the time was his idea
of founding a Junior Reform Club with his impeccably

[58] For inarticulacy in 1888 see *Pall Mall Gazette*, 25 Apr. 1888; for remarks about the
onset of General Paralysis in 1892 see report in *Lancet*, 29 Dec. 1894. Also see Buzzard–
Roose correspondence in R. S. Churchill, *W. S. Churchill*, i, Companion volume.

Gladstonian brother-in-law, Marjoribanks.[59] But such ideas were really manifestations of the bouts of euphoria which increasingly characterized his manic states. Furious at 'gossip' about his health, refusing to follow his doctors' advice, he insisted that he was recovering while remaining obsessed with his failing speech; old friends who encountered him in Germany that autumn were shocked by his condition.

The autumn holiday was intended to set him up for a new political initiative: he had accepted an invitation to contest Central Bradford in July 1893, clearing the decision with Paddington and overcoming the objections of Liberal Unionists, which he blamed on Chamberlain ('If I contested the Orkneys he might still have moments of uneasiness').[60] A long autumn campaign created scenes of awful embarrassment; local newspapers cruelly described his candidature as 'farcical'. Before Christmas, he wrote to Akers-Douglas from the South of France that he would have to give up public speaking 'for some time';[61] he then travelled to Howth for the last Christmas house party. Rambling letters continued to appear in *The Times*, and he made further visits to Bradford in early 1894, helped out by Balfour and Chamberlain; but his candidature evaporated in a welter of misunderstandings and offence, compounded of Churchill's unreliability and the hysteria of the local agents at his open admissions of a 'growing inclination towards Liberal Unionism rather than Conservatism'.[62] There were some fearful last appearances in the Commons, witnessed in many memoirs; 'R.C. terrible', wrote James briefly to Chamberlain in April, and the *Times* parliamentary correspondent recorded that 'nothing more tragical has been seen in the House of Commons in our generation'.

This terrible public death was finally ended by a journey

---

[59] See Marjoribanks to Churchill, 7 and 8 Sept. 1893, Blenheim MSS I/IV, K/IV. Also see FitzGibbon to Churchill, 9 July 1893, RCHL xxx/4277. 'You and Lord Rosebery could *amalgamate* Ireland, complete Pitt's work, reform the Irish "Departments" root and branch, and build up Liberty and Local Government from the bottom.' Also Churchill to Rosebery, 2 Sept. 1893, ibid. 4325, from Kissingen, appealing to him to withdraw his support from Home Rule, far more sinister now than in 1886. 'The dream which often comes upon me [is] that some day not very remote I may have the gratification of finding myself in the same party and holding the same opinions as you will hold. I do not even draw the line against speculation as to being, if the fates are kind, even your colleague.'

[60] Churchill to Hartington, 12 June 1893, Devonshire MSS 340/2824.

[61] 19 Dec. 1893; Chilston MSS 1/128.

[62] See Colefax to Churchill, 12 Mar. 1894, RCHL xxxi/4471. The local party finally questioned his mental capacity for standing.

round the world in June, its ultimate destination never in doubt. He continued a social life to the moment of departure (his last letter to Rosebery was about getting Asquith into the Jockey Club stand at Epsom); in moments of lucidity on his tour through America, Japan, and the Far East he wrote laborious, interminable letters to old friends. But despite recurrent violent outbursts he was fading all the time and on his return in late December 1894 was in a state of coma; he recovered slightly, but most of his powers were gone. Lingering a few weeks, often in great pain, he sometimes regained consciousness; a letter read to him from FitzGibbon caused him to laugh and make an unintelligible joke about lobster fishing in Dublin Bay. But there was, as his wife wrote, 'not a glimpse of hope', nor had been for many months. He died on 24 January, and his funeral attracted vast public attention; his will, made in July 1883, left £500 and his effects to his wife, with the income from the rest of his estate. The capital, held for his sons, came to £75,971 gross thanks to the South African investments, but was practically all swallowed by debts.

Lady Randolph had been with him throughout the last six months, during which her own private life had also crashed into ruins. She left for Paris, and a new beginning: not before writing to FitzGibbon a letter which reflected the family attitude to her husband's life and death. 'I know you will agree with me that Lord S. has much to answer for. There was a time, a few years ago, when a generous hand stretched out would have saved everything, and he would now be with us as he was. But Lord S. and the others were too jealous of him. I feel all this deeply and hope one of these days it will be known.'[63] The same message was repeated in a terrible letter sent by the distraught Duchess to Salisbury himself:[64] expressed with more or less restraint, this

[63] 4 Jan. 1895; RCHL xxxi/4526. The very last letter in the huge Churchill archive is her farewell letter to FitzGibbon on 18 February, sending him Randolph's backgammon board. 'Goodbye dear Lord Justice—don't forget me *quite*—if you ever had time to write me a letter I should be proud.'

[64] See R. Rhodes James, pp. 369–70. 'The Iron entered his soul. He never said so. He never gave a sign even to me of disappointment but for Days and Days and Months and Years even it told on him and he sat in Connaught Place brooding and eating his heart out and the Tory Press reviled him the Tory Party whom he had saved abused and misrepresented him and he was never the same . . . He had the greatest admiration for you and you might have done anything with him. But he was young and I sorrowfully admit—he was wrong—He has suffered for it and as for me my Heart is broken . . . Its all over now. My Darling has come Home to die and oh it seems such bitter mockery that *now* it is too late he seems to be understood and appreciated.'

interpretation would survive along with the analysis of Churchill as a preacher of 'progressivism' before his time.

On the opening of parliament, however, the tributes were principally to a great performer in that enclosed world. Balfour gracefully indicated his affection for 'a friend with whom almost all the events of my public life are intimately bound up'; Harcourt and Hartington gave affectionate testimony from his opponents. The newspaper obituaries on 26 January took a more censorious tone: except on the Continent, where his death attracted great attention, and expectations of his return to power had never ceased to be canvassed. *The Times*, in a full-page notice, set the style of hostile future commentary; though the tone was personally friendly, it emphasized Churchill's political inconsistency, his self-advancement, his evasiveness on issues like Ireland, his malleability to the ideas of permanent officials in the India Office and the Treasury, his resignation on the grounds of ambition rather than economy. His adoption of social issues in later years was caused by his 'exclusion from the field of *la haute politique* by the peculiarity of his position'; on the labour issue, he was 'lured forward when he saw Mr Gladstone hanging back'. The over-all image was populist, Napoleonic, imperious, and unintellectual. 'He was no political thinker. He never went below the surface of any subject. He had no hold, intellectual or moral, upon principles.' He was no Machiavelli: demonic in a Puckish rather than a Mephistophelian sense. As a final, feline blow, the obituarist pointed out that though he liked to talk intrigue, he was not as good at it as any of his Fourth Party colleagues. The *Spectator*, more openly deprecatory, read as a lapidary condemnation:

Born of a great house, he had very considerable powers, could make himself understand any political question, was the best music-hall orator of recent times, and had a capacity for getting up details which surprised both the Treasury and the India Office. He had perfect audacity, untiring energy, and a gift of acquiring popularity; but all his qualities were marred by a strain in his character which we can only describe as instinctive rowdyism. He charmed rough audiences from the platform, but he overwhelmed political enemies with abuse, snubbed and deserted political allies, and in all crises of his career played visibly, sometimes even cynically, for his own hand. He had occasional flashes of political insight and rose fast, but his colleagues never trusted him; and when in 1886 he resigned, hoping that the Cabinet would fall, the Cabinet stood—and he was thenceforward politically a nullity. It is probable that there was some deep taint in his blood, and that for many of his impulses he was irresponsible; but England escaped, in his failure to become Premier, very serious dangers.

Except for one or two angrily committed pieces in journals like the *Saturday Review*, no one said Churchill was a 'great elemental force in British politics'. This was left, eleven years later, to his ebullient and brilliant son, only coming to know his father in his last years, but already cultivating his father's friends and fated to build the orthodox family view of Lord Randolph's career into a great work of art and politics. This would tend to obscure by its magnificence something grasped by contemporaries—that what was represented by Churchill's career was a self-made phenomenon: the ability of a raw but dazzling politician to grasp the shifts of power and rhetoric from day to day, and to utilize and even in a sense create the locomotive of publicity in an age which was just beginning to invent it. He had an erratic but notable talent for spotting a winning issue; his analysis of many aspects of policy to do with Ireland, the Empire, and the new age of democratic politics was ruthlessly cogent and often highly prescient. But these remarkable talents were used in a political context dominated almost exclusively by ephemeral considerations. 'What brings men to the front', he fiercely told a silenced dinner-party in 1889, 'is much more opportunity than character.'[65] This was made manifest over a very few years when both the collusive nature and the materials of crisis in British politics were extraordinarily well adapted to his own knowledge and to his own capacities. And his success was first amplified, and then shattered, by his blatant genius for working in public as others, of fewer talents but labouring under less pressure, operated in private.

[65] EHJ, 5 Nov. 1889, vol. xxii, p. 124, BL Add. MS 48651. 'He thought there was great nonsense talked about its being necessary for success in politics that men should (what is called) possess the confidence of their party. What great politician had ever been universally trusted? Had Sir Robert Peel always possessed the required confidence? Lord Palmerston? Disraeli? Mr Gladstone? Lord Salisbury? No—such confidence had all been forfeited at times by these statesmen. Their parties had been obliged to accept them notwithstanding . . .'

Epilogue:

The Politics of Piety

Neither the public nor the historian will permit the
statesman moods. He has from the first to assume
he has an Aim, a definite Aim, and to pretend to an
absolute consistency with that. Those subtle ques-
tionings about the very fundamentals of life which
plague us all so relentlessly nowadays are supposed
to be silenced. He lifts his chin and pursues his Aim
explicitly in the sight of all men. Those who have
no real political experience can scarcely imagine
the immense mental and moral strain there is
between one's everyday acts and utterances on the
one hand and the 'thinking out' process on the
other. It is perplexingly difficult to keep in your
mind, fixed and firm, a scheme essentially complex, to keep balancing a swaying possibility while
at the same time under jealous, hostile, and stupid
observation you tread your part in the platitudin-
ous, quarrelsome, ill-presented march of affairs ...

H. G. Wells, *The New Machiavelli* (1911)

I

Political biography in the first generation after the Victorians
was not the province of Lytton Strachey: the ministers of
Gladstone's and Disraeli's governments found commemoration
in monumental works produced by their own sons and daughters. Such acts of filial piety could be almost unreadable
(Gathorne-Hardy on Cranbrook), stridently self-pitying (H. St.
J. Raikes on his father), useful but unconvincing (Crewe on
Rosebery), or at once ponderous and sketchy (Lady Victoria
Hicks Beach on Sir Michael); they could also use personal
knowledge to add brilliant flourishes which sometimes contrived
to obscure rather than illuminate (Lady Gwendolen Cecil on
Salisbury), or to dispute the views of the inevitable journalistic
observers outside the family circle (Herbert Gladstone on his
father in *After Thirty Years*). Of this strange genre (which will

inevitably lead to the invention of psychohistoriography as a sub-discipline), no product is more interesting than Winston Churchill's extraordinary *Life of Lord Randolph Churchill*.

No filial relationship of that age (or any other) has been so closely examined by historians; the fact that the doomed and embittered father alternately ignored and actively disliked his eldest son is borne witness to in volumes of pathetic letters. On his father's death in 1895, Winston wrote much later, 'there remained for me only to pursue his aims and vindicate his memory';[1] this was certainly a maturing ambition. Within seven years of his father's death, Churchill was an MP, a South African war hero, a writer, a rising man: still poor, raw, and insecure, but afflicted with a sense of destiny and on his way to becoming brilliant. In the latter capacity, he could only remind his father's old friends of Lord Randolph, in his prime and on the make. 'In mind and manner he is a strange replica of his father', noted Wilfrid Scawen Blunt in 1903, 'with all his father's suddenness and assurance and I should say more than his father's ability. There is just the same *gaminerie* and contempt of the conventional and the same engaging plain spokenness and readiness to understand. As I listened to him recounting conversations he had had with Chamberlain I seemed once more to be listening to Randolph on the subject of Northcote and Salisbury . . .'[2]

Rhodes James's perceptive study of Churchill's early career has pointed out the effect on the young politician of concurrently studying his father's life: he rebelled against the tyranny of party, formed ginger groups, stormed against his leaders, indulged in violent and rather crass 'personalities' in his speeches, and 'seemed intent upon re-creating his father's career'.[3] Equally to be considered, however, is the effect of what was happening in his own career upon the way he wrote his father's biography. For if Churchill's political actions were in some ways intended as a vindication of Lord Randolph's life, the converse may also be true: that the *Life* was at least partially intended as a vindication of the political somersaults being executed by the author at the time of writing it.

---

[1] W. S. Churchill, *My Early Life* (London: 1959 edition), p. 62.

[2] Blunt, *My Diaries*, p. 489.

[3] R. Rhodes James, *Churchill: a Study in Failure 1900–1939* (Harmondsworth: 1973 ed.), p. 19.

For in 1903–4, Churchill was negotiating the change of party which his father never accomplished (though some of his allies and intimates had done so since his death). For Winston Churchill's purposes, the priority was to show that such an idea never entered his father's head, except as a glancing notion at the beginning of his career: through his own fidelity and constancy to the party which rejected his teachings, Lord Randolph condemned himself to a lonely wilderness, while they condemned themselves to political impotence. It was a careful thesis, worked with close attention; as he told Chamberlain, 'my own change of party is an additional reason for care on my part'.[4] The political echoes of days gone by were all around him as he wrote, and his own actions were repeating many of his father's patterns. In the summer of 1902, when beginning work on the biography, he was cultivating Rosebery as his father had done: 'I should like to bring you and Beach together', he wrote in October; 'there lies the chance of a central coalition. "Tory-Liberal" is a much better name than "Tory-Democrat" or "Liberal Imperialist"; and certainly neither paradoxical nor unprecedented. The one real difficulty I have to encounter is the suspicion that I am moved by mere restless ambition: and if some issue—such as Tariff—were to arise that difficulty would disappear.'

Thus the fact that at the very time this issue obligingly materialized Churchill was charting his father's tergiversations on the issue of Protection in the 1880s was sensitive. One Birmingham correspondent wrote that Lord Randolph had remarked privately at a meeting, 'within these walls I am a Fair Trader, outside I don't know anything about Fair Trade; when the masses shout for Fair Trade, then I shall be willing to take up and champion the cause'; the supplier of this information received short shrift, and the anecdote did not find its way into the biography.[5] But in less disreputable ways, the parallels were useful in 1903. Friends feared Churchill's propensity to Fourth Party initiatives on the issue; old colleagues of Lord Randolph's like Ernest Beckett, J. E. Gorst, and Hicks Beach found themselves sounded out by Winston Churchill on the Protection issue: in October, still a Conservative MP, he raged: 'I am an English Liberal. I hate the Tory party, their men, their words

---

[4] W. S. Churchill to Lady Randolph, R. S. Churchill, *W. S. Churchill*, ii, Companion volume, part 1 (henceforth *WSC*, ii Comp. I), p. 453.

[5] *WSC*, ii, Comp. I, p. 170.

and their methods.'[6] He seemed to be becoming possessed by the spirit of his father (seen by so many as demonic): there was even, in 1904, a terrible moment when he forgot his words and had to abandon a speech in the Commons, giving rise to dark suppositions about heredity. More significantly, his belabourings of Balfour in 1903 not only recalled his father's treatment of *his* leaders in the early eighties (while Balfour's deliberate misapprehension of Churchill's position was worthy of Salisbury at his best); but the picture he drew of the young Balfour in his father's biography was one which would, to the impartial onlooker, seem to excuse such treatment.

History repeated itself, or was made to do so: Churchill not only negotiated for a Centre Party pivoting on Hartington, but also played with the idea of contesting his father's old battleground of Central Birmingham (where people were saying, as they had said of Lord Randolph, 'that man may call himself what he likes, but he's no more a Tory than I am').[7] Ghosts were all around him, but this should not obscure the fact that he assiduously called them up. 'You will have to look back twenty years to find equal bitterness', he triumphantly told Morley in October 1903; 'when I think how easy the Conservatives made the path of the Liberal dissentients in 1886, and how enormously they profited by their aid, I wonder at the tightly locked door with which we seem confronted.'[8] Others helped in this; when Churchill's own front bench ostentatiously walked out on a speech in March 1904 it was Gorst who upbraided them, in the memory of Lord Randolph, 'who of all men in the world deserves well of his party, who was the ornament and leader of that Party in the House of Commons at one period of his life'. But, if Churchill wished to provoke the passions of his father's heyday, he also wished to retain the curious collusiveness of high politics which had characterized the age: 'that line of half-chaffing, half-candid intercourse which prevails between people who know each other though on opposite sides, in this country almost alone of modern countries'.[9] And this, as with Lord Randolph, led easily to accusations of unprincipled opportunism.

The writing of the book and the change of party proceeded

---

[6] R. S. Churchill, *W. S. Churchill*, vol. ii (henceforth *WSC*), p. 71.
[7] *WSC*, i, Comp. I, p. 274.
[8] Churchill to Morley, 16 Oct. 1903, BL Add. MS 60391AA.
[9] *WSC*, ii, 92.

together; both climaxed in January 1906, with the publication
of the two volumes and Churchill's successful campaign for
Manchester as a Liberal. In letters to old friends of his father's,
literary details arising from proof-reading are mingled inextricably with the political business in hand. During the
Manchester election, he announced:

I admit I have changed my party. I don't deny it. I am proud of it.
When I think of all the labours Lord Randolph Churchill gave to the
fortunes of the Conservative Party and the ungrateful way in which he
was treated by them when they obtained the power they would never
have had but for him, I am delighted that circumstances have enabled
me to break with them while I am still young and still have the first
energies of my life to give to the popular cause.[10]

Privately, he wrote to Lord James: 'This election is the justification of my father's life, and points the moral of my book. The
one crowning irretrievable catastrophe which he always dreaded
has now overtaken the old gang, and with them, the great party
they misruled.'[11] The fact that he held this analysis is important
for the turn his political career took; but it is equally important
for the way that the book was written.

II

That Lord Randolph's life was matter for a great biography had
been noted as early as his obituary notices; brief accounts and
reminiscences appeared in many journals during the later 1890s.
The essential materials for a major work, however, were located
in the vast collection of political correspondence and memoranda left in the care of Lord Howe and Ernest Beckett, two of
Lord Randolph's last political followers as well as his literary
executors. With the help of Rosebery's intercession, Churchill
obtained full access in the summer of 1902; while demanding
'fullest liberty and discretion', he agreed that the executors
should have the right 'to withhold from publication documents
that they might consider injurious to Lord Randolph's memory
or injurious to others'. This clause was, understandably, not
called into play.

By the late summer, Churchill was convinced that 'there

[10] Ibid., p. 123.
[11] W. S. Churchill to Lord James, 18 Jan. 1906, James MSS M45/1432.

emerges from these dusty records a great and vivid drama':[12] at the simplest level, he was not only making the acquaintance of a father who had always repelled his efforts to know him, but also interpreting the politics of the age. Helped in his arrangement of the papers by his brother Jack, he was also in close contact with his father's brothers and sisters: notably the Tweedmouths and the Wimbornes, all now prominent Liberals. No less important were those intimates of his father's private life who still wielded political and social power; Mrs Jeune, now Lady St. Helier, entertained Winston Churchill as constantly as his father (and introduced him to his future wife); in September he visited his father's old hosts Edward VII at Balmoral and Rosebery at Dalmeny. Travelling up the Nile that Christmas he found himself with the Cassels, the Connaughts, Gorst, and Hicks Beach, who discussed the biography in detail. He wrote the bulk of the book at Blenheim and at Sir Ernest Cassel's villa; the people and the places took him on a voyage of discovery, and his idealization of Lord Randolph was compounded with an abiding regard for the abilities of his father's contemporaries. As late as 1937 he named 'the four most pleasing and brilliant men to whom I have ever listened' as Morley, Chamberlain, Rosebery, and Balfour:[13] an impression first formed in the years when he discussed with them his father's dazzling career.

Their reactions were vivid and characteristic. Chamberlain co-operated at once, if on his own terms: he entertained Churchill at Highbury after the latter's break over Free Trade, and provided lengthy and partisan reminiscences on the subject of his troubled relationship with Lord Randolph. ('I must have had a great many more real talks with him than I ever had with my own father', wrote Churchill.) Rosebery and James were even more intimately involved in the production; Beach, Hartington, and Salisbury provided letters. Balfour wrote charmingly in 1902 claiming to have lost all Lord Randolph's letters; Louis Jennings's widow wrote extracting a promise that Churchill's account of their quarrel should be fair to both sides, and then produced a memorandum of the incident kept by her husband. Old official colleagues, like West and Godley, were closely consulted; Godley—like Beach, James, FitzGibbon, and Lord George Hamilton—provided long written accounts to

---

[12] To Lady Randolph, 15 Aug. 1902; *WSC*, ii, Comp. I, p. 436.
[13] W. S. Churchill, *Great Contemporaries* (rev. ed., London, 1939), p. 97.

clarify his reminiscences, suitable portions of which were built into the completed edifice. Goschen was courteously evasive about overtures from Lord Randolph in June 1885 ('I do not, I think, have an inaccurate memory of events; I simply forget'). Brodrick, though a political enemy of father and son, was helpful in obtaining permission to quote India Office material; Iddesleigh's heir gave a frosty permission to publish his father's letters. Morley, who published his *Gladstone* in 1903, provided constructive suggestions as well as interceding with Chamberlain. This indefatigable process of cultivation produced at least two vital collections of Lord Randolph's letters which have since been lost, those to Wolff and to FitzGibbon: tantalizing portions of which remain enshrined in Lord Randolph's monument.

Of the politicians he approached, the most ambivalent reaction came, appositely, from Rosebery. Churchill thought of him as 'my father's greatest friend ... I inherited this friendship, or rather the possibility of renewing it in another generation. I was anxious to cultivate it for many reasons, of which the first was to learn more about my father from his companion. With some at least of those feelings of awe and attraction which led Boswell to Dr Johnson, I sought occasions to develop the acquaintance of childhood into a grown-up friendship.'[14] That the 'many reasons' referred to also included Churchill's ambition to integrate Rosebery into a Centre Party alliance adds an additional flavour to the campaign. But Rosebery, so helpful in the initial stages, soon proved recalcitrant. Though his correspondence with Lord Randolph contains a vast and possibly significant gap from their youth to 1889, he had written some notes on his friend in the form of an elegant and resonant personal memoir; when Churchill pressed to incorporate sections in his work, Rosebery first claimed that the manuscript had been burned, then that it was unsuitable for inclusion. This is the story told by their correspondence, though in 1937 Churchill wrote that Rosebery had asked him to include his memoir and he, for reasons of artistic integrity, had demurred. Possibly this had been his initial reaction, afterwards recanted, and Rosebery had taken offence in his inimitable way; he had perfected the technique of suddenly withdrawing into hauteur, or 'going up like a balloon', in a contemporary's vivid phrase. Whatever the reason, he refused to have his memoir incorporated, and it appeared, in an extended version, some

[14] Ibid., p. 14.

months after Churchill's great work: a brilliant mixture of character appreciation, monograph, and review, rather disingenuously described by Rosebery to Churchill as 'an advertisement for your book'.

One final figure from Lord Randolph's life was summoned in the process of political table-turning: the raffish Frank Harris, first drawn to Lord Randolph's attention when editor of the *Fortnightly* as a useful political aide, and a firm admirer of his. Winston Churchill used him as literary agent, and Harris was responsible for obtaining £8,000 advances from Macmillan on his behalf. This was all the more laudable, because Harris had in fact wanted to write the book himself.[15] (The fact that his reminiscences of Lord Randolph were to form a scurrilous passage in *My Life and Loves*, including an almost completely unlikely assertion of the manner in which he contracted syphilis, should not conceal the fact that in 1905 his connection with both Churchills was both genuine and appreciably close.)

The collection of papers left by Lord Randolph, and the letters and reminiscences provided by his friends and contemporaries, were constructed by Winston Churchill into a monument which was in many ways a triumph of art. The style was oratorical, but had not yet become flatulent; though deliberate and grand, it had not yet descended into what Evelyn Waugh categorized as 'sham Augustan, where the antithesis fall like hammers'. This was partly avoided through the quantity of lengthy interpolations built into the text from other sources; his great difficulty, he told Rosebery, was 'the graceful weaving of numerous original documents into the regular narrative'.[16] This not only diluted a stylistic flavour whose fullness often approaches rotundity: it also ensured the work's lasting importance as a repository of contemporary correspondence and memoranda. The fact that both style and content were adapted to the production of a definite thesis makes them both of additional importance.

For Churchill, confronted with his father's reputation for unconcealed opportunism and embarrassing levity, determined to scale his story up to the dimensions of Greek tragedy. Other filial biographies of dead politicians told pious tales of deserved

[15] See E. Beckett (Lord Grimthorpe) to W. S. Churchill, 26 Oct. 1905, CHAR 8/21. For Wolseley's recommendation of Harris to Lord Randolph as a 'useful political follower' see RCHL xxiii/2972.

[16] *WSC*, ii, Comp. I, p. 438.

success; Churchill sought out 'the pattern of failure ... I find it—physical and political—in every page of the story I am writing'.[17] Moreover, where others might see Lord Randolph's failure as a visitation of hubris for the sin of self-seeking, Churchill took exactly the opposite view. 'It is easy to deal with men whose motive is self-interest', he wrote; 'others can cypher out the chances too.' But Lord Randolph was a mystery, in his son's eyes. 'A veil of the incalculable shrouded the workings of his complex nature. No-one could tell what he would do, or by what motive, lofty or trivial, of conviction or caprice, of irritation or self-sacrifice, he would be governed.'[18]

Such an interpretation was aired early on in the rendering of Lord Randolph's career; it was to reach its apotheosis in Churchill's treatment of his father's political virtue in not changing party after his resignation. And it involved taking on many of his father's old enemies. 'There is something touching about the fidelity with which he continues to espouse his father's cause and his father's quarrels', wrote Blunt in 1904.[19] The subtlety with which they were presented in print masked an unforgiving attitude. (A correspondent complaining of Churchill's political attacks on Balfour, 'one of Lord Randolph's dearest friends', received an unequivocal denial: 'I feel bound to declare, after a study of the very extensive evidence which has been placed before me, that such a statement seems to me extravagant.'[20]) Thus it was important to identify Balfour as an integral member of the Fourth Party in *Lord Randolph Churchill*, though most authorities (including Balfour himself) went to some trouble to show that he was not;[21] his defection to the family camp could therefore be implicitly seen as pusillanimous (while strenuously denying any such implication). For all the ostensibly sympathetic presentation of Salisbury, the reactionary and nepotistic qualities of Cecil government were drawn in a way which could, to a discerning reader, reflect directly upon the present; and when Beach, on reading the proofs, tried to suggest more emphasis upon the personal incompatibility which separated Salisbury and Lord Randolph, Churchill firmly insisted upon retaining the stress on 'deep and wide chasms of

---

[17] W. S. Churchill to Hugh Cecil in *WSC*, ii, Comp. I, p. 349.
[18] W. S. Churchill, *Lord Randolph Churchill*, ii, 128.
[19] Blunt, *My Diaries*, p. 518.
[20] 14 Apr. 1905; *WSC*, ii, Comp. I, 388.
[21] See for instance H. Gladstone, *After Thirty Years*.

political differences'. They were, indeed, the essence of his argument.

That argument was presented all the more adroitly for using the evidence to hand in a way which conceded unimportant points in order to claim a wider case. This strategy was employed in dealing with Lord Randolph's pungent and irreverent correspondence which, on the surface of things, would seem to state the case for opportunistic cynicism with unanswerable effect. Others feared that this would be the case. FitzGibbon wrote: 'You must exercise your best judgement, and great caution, in deciding the effect which the publication of his views, as disclosed to an intimate friend, would have upon the public estimate of his statesmanship. The cynical, if not Machiavellian, tone of many of his letters to me needs to be discounted by my own propensity in the same direction.'[22] But by and large, Churchill let the irreverence stand: some friendly critics, including the Duke of Marlborough, felt that the 'cynical and flippant' side of Lord Randolph's character came through too clearly—'the reader forms the idea that levity played too large a part in his nature'. But this reflected another aspect of the biographer's approach: to quote as freely as possible material that would show similar levity and ruthlessness on the part of others. Much of this was deleted at proof stage. From the Foreign Office, Lansdowne insisted on dropping comments in Salisbury's correspondence that showed too crudely Iddesleigh's position as a rubber stamp, or the FO view of Bulgaria. Balfour worried intensely about the presentation of Gladstone's approach to Salisbury, via his good offices, in December 1885. Lord James recorded in his diary how he 'excised freely' in his copy of Churchill's proofs to save the feelings of those still alive. This encountered an increasingly aggressive reaction from Churchill; he finally told the over-emollient James that he himself retained the copyright power to publish any of Lord Randolph's letters, no matter how indiscreet or hurtful, and was quite prepared 'in the ultimate resort' to use this power 'as a leverage to procure the liberty to publish' those written by others. 'My dear Lord, I am not a damned fool—nor do I wish to offend great people who have been kind to me. I anticipate no difficulties whatever; even when I remember that no account which is not in part disagreeable to someone is ever likely to be

---

[22] *WSC*, ii, Comp. I, p. 446.

amusing or true.'[23] But polite blackmail remained an eventual possibility.

In the event, in its general lineaments Churchill's view of his father survived these injections of discretion; and the effect of his attribution of far-ranging and consistent strategies was, if anything, reinforced by the flippant pungencies included from Lord Randolph's letters. The political picture of the 1880s formed an unmistakable outline. The Fourth Party were more than free-lance musketeers: they had a general purpose. Chapter six of volume one, on 'Tory Democracy', could be read as a manifesto of Winston Churchill's in 1904; and Lord Randolph was identified as 'a Tory Democrat' as early as 1878[24]—a concept which he was presented as having invented, other Tories being uninterested in working-class possibilities[25] (the rhetorical pedigree in Young England was barely mentioned). Thus Lord Randolph 'hesitated' about supporting Salisbury in the early 1880s because of the latter's 'lack of liberalism' (the fact that the Fourth Party was in practical terms a front-group for Salisbury in the Commons was thus conveniently lost). The country Tories, according to Churchill, liked Lord Randolph's style but disagreed with his opinions[26] (in fact, given the often ultra-Tory implication of many Fourth Party nostrums, the reverse was often true). He triumphed in the cause of giving the National Union a voice in party organization, and then made peace on equal terms (the very general interpretation of a sell-out in return for elevation to the hierarchy, reiterated after 1906 in a number of publications, was superbly ignored). Overall, bearing the democratic fire out of which sprang up a new Tory electorate, Lord Randolph saved his party.

In truth, at this crisis in their fortunes, the Conservative party was rescued in spite of themselves. A very little and they would never have won the new democracy. But for a narrow chance they might have slipped down into the gulf of departed systems. The forces of wealth and rank, of land and church, must always have exerted vast influence in whatever confederacy they had been locked. Alliances or fusions with Whigs and moderate Liberals must from time to time have secured them spells of office. But the Tory party might easily have

---

[23] See typescript diary extracts in James MSS, M45/1824, and W. S. Churchill to James, ibid. 1201 (17 Nov. 1902).

[24] W. S. Churchill, *Lord Randolph Churchill*, i, 105.

[25] Ibid., 274.

[26] Ibid. i, 272.

failed to gain any support among the masses. They might have lost their hold upon the new foundation of power; and the cleavage in British politics must have become a social, not a political division—upon a line horizontal, not oblique ... [Lord Randolph Churchill] accomplished no mean or temporary achievement in so far as he restored the healthy balance of parties, and caused the ancient institutions of the British realm once again to be esteemed among the masses of the British people.[27]

Consistent throughout, in Winston's view that very consistency was Lord Randolph's undoing; 'always an economist', he left the government on a noble issue. And then he was rejected: the issue returned to again and again by Churchill, possibly because it provided a psychological reason for his own rejection by his embittered father. The chosen comparison becomes, instead of the Younger Pitt, the older Charles James Fox. Rejection was made easier by Lord Randolph's romantic commitment to his party: but this condemned him, according to the carefully argued peroration that closed the work.

Lord Randolph's name will not be recorded upon the bead-roll of either party. The Conservatives, whose forces he so greatly strengthened, the Liberals, some of whose finest principles he notably sustained, must equally regard his life and work with mingled feelings. A politician's character and position are measured in his day by party standards. When he is dead all that he achieved in the name of party, is at an end. The eulogies and censures of partisans are powerless to affect his ultimate reputation. The scales wherein he was weighed are broken. The years to come bring weights and measures of their own.

There is an England which stretches far beyond the well-drilled masses who are assembled by party machinery to salute with appropriate acclamation the utterances of their recognised fuglemen; an England of wise men who gaze without self-deception at the failings and follies of both political parties; of brave and earnest men who find in neither function fair scope for the effort that is in them: of 'poor men' who increasingly doubt the sincerity of party philanthropy. It was to that England that Lord Randolph Churchill appealed; it was that England he so nearly won; it was by that England he will be justly judged.[28]

Again, the tone is that of an election manifesto; the arguments those with which Churchill went into battle for Manchester as a Liberal, the month his book was published.

---

[27] Ibid. i, 300–1.
[28] Ibid. ii, 488–9.

III

The question of evidence omitted in the cause of this presentation is an interesting one; a preliminary laundering of the record had already taken place in 1888, with the appearance of Jennings's highly tendentious edition of Lord Randolph's speeches—many of which had had long sections of abuse or inconsistency skilfully deleted. A certain amount of editing of letters was obviously necessary (Lady Iddesleigh could not be expected to bear with references to her husband as a 'cretin', an 'old muff', or a 'species of earthworm'); but what Churchill was prepared to print, especially in his father's correspondence with Salisbury, was quite exceptional. Salisbury's son blue-pencilled much of the personal abuse contained in letters described with rather suspect *naïveté* by Winston Churchill as 'good-humoured'.[29] The names of those invaluable go-betweens like Brett or Rothschild, who in a pre-telephone age passed verbal messages too subtle or incriminating for commitment to paper, were similarly excised. But from the beginning of the story, a more calculating and interpretative censorship was also at work. The more cynical comments in Lord Randolph's letters to his fiancée about the Woodstock election in 1874 are dropped, perhaps reasonably; less reasonable seems the complete silence about Disraeli's anger with Churchill in July 1875 over a letter the latter sent to *The Times* regarding the Prince of Wales's visit to India. In the treatment of Churchill's campaign against Bradlaugh, no mention is made of the fact that Bradlaugh made an issue of an attack on perpetual pensions, especially the Duke of Marlborough's. A blatantly anti-Northcote letter of Churchill's to the *Standard* on 29 June 1882 is ignored; so is an article in the *Fortnightly* showing plans for an assault on the National Union a year before it started. These details may have escaped the author, but he must have known about Churchill's newspaper interview in November 1884, a Tory-Democratic manifesto which puts a very different complexion upon his withdrawal to India three days later. The discussion of political reform in 1884 is played down, perhaps because of Churchill's several blatant changes of front on the issue; so are the non-official aspects of his Indian Secretaryship, such as his approval of Riponism on his visit to the country and the disappointment

---

[29] See especially the letter from Churchill to Salisbury of 15 Dec. 1886, referred to by W. S. Churchill in ibid. ii, 230.

of the hopes held of him by Indian politicians when he took office. Selective quotation of a letter from Dufferin is given as evidence that the Viceroy supported Churchill's stance over Connaught's command; in fact, the original reads in a directly contrary sense.[30] The same sorely tried Governor's doubts and worries about the annexation of Burma are ignored, as are the widespread criticisms of the step and its bloody and expensive outcome. Ireland was another area of great potential embarrassment, carefully skirted; and though Blunt's correspondence with Churchill shows that he gave him access to those portions of his diary identifying Lord Randolph as a covert Home Ruler in 1885, no mention of them enters Churchill's treatment. (Blunt tactlessly published them in the *Nineteenth Century* as soon as the book came out.)

On personal details, an equally thorny path lay before the biographer. The unhappiness of Lord Randolph's marriage could not, obviously, be mentioned, but the precariousness of his finances could: it was a subject which Churchill believed 'biographers of eminent persons' should not 'slur over'.[31] He did not, however, mention Churchill's growing intimacy with Rothschild, to whom he 'turned for everything' by 1888, to whom he entrusted Cabinet secrets, the interests of whose firm he pressed in Persia, India, and Burma, who was—to general discomfiture—his closest adviser as Chancellor of the Exchequer, and to whose bank he owed £66,000 when he died. Rothschild, in fact, rates no index mention at all.

To such omissions of fact are added countless textual omissions. A letter to Salisbury reading 'the only reason I accepted Iddesleigh was because it was supposed he would act under your direction' becomes (with no evidence of elision) 'it was supposed Lord Iddesleigh would act under your direction':[32] the phrase may have been dropped to ease the Iddesleigh family's feelings, but also conceals Churchill's didacticism. A quotation is given 'from a letter to his constituents, never published', in 1891: it is not mentioned that this draft letter expressed his decision to resign his seat and leave politics, in one of his recurrent fits of furious pique (and also admitted his intention in 1887 of joining the Liberal party). Throughout, the attempt to convey *gravitas* is made by polishing the language actually used in Churchill's

---

[30] See ibid. i, 516, cf. original in RCHL vii/815.

[31] *Great Contemporaries*, p. 288.

[32] W. S. Churchill, *Lord Randolph Churchill*, ii, 161, cf. R. Rhodes James, p. 272.

letters: 'I shall get everything out of [Chamberlain]' for example becomes 'I shall learn more'.[33] Purely trivial; but through such tiny, solicitous amendments, the chosen over-all portrait of Lord Randolph survived the apparently contrary trend of much of the evidence.

The integral composition of the work, moreover, added greatly to this effect. Churchill showed a brilliant talent for compartmentalization; the Reform arrangements in 1884 were kept strictly separate from the outcome of the National Union controversy (which they helped decide); the Egyptian issue was sharply divided from the other parliamentary campaigns with which it interacted. Lord Randolph's rocking of the precarious ministerial boat in 1885 by threatening resignation over Connaught's appointment is relegated to the chapter on India (practically an appendix to volume one). To define a theme, or drive home a message, quotations are chosen from letters and speeches ranging over five years; the deliberate abandoning of the day-to-day dimension conceals the fact that Lord Randolph's priorities were very often tactical, and to see his career from 1881 to 1884 as more or less one phase ('the *enfant terrible*') is simply wrong. Such careful demonstrations meant that, where opportunism had to be faced, the author could afford to defend it in the ringing tones of Lord Randolph himself ('an unchanging mind is an admirable possession—a possession which I devoutly hope I shall never possess'). Consistency was at best a bourgeois virtue. A. G. Gardiner attributed to Churchill 'that scorn of concealment which belongs to a caste which never doubts itself':[34] but it was, in terms of the construction of his father's apologia, only selectively true.

The interpretation, in fact, had to be consistently loaded. The Fourth Party's intervention on the Employers' Liability Bill had to be presented as in the interests of the work-force, which it self-confessedly was not; quotations were artistically selected to show Churchill's struggle over the National Union as far less tentative and tactical than it was.[35] Recurrent themes of ultra-Toryism in Lord Randolph's speeches and public letters are invariably dropped or ignored. And where Lord Randolph's desire to establish Salisbury as sole leader is dealt with, there is no

---

[33] See W. S. Churchill, *Lord Randolph Churchill*, ii, 78, cf. RCHL xii/14386.

[34] Quoted in Rhodes James, *Study in Failure*, p. 17.

[35] Notably in the 'close corporation' letter partially quoted by W. S. Churchill, i, 317, to give an erroneous impression of implacability.

mention of the conclusion drawn by all contemporaries: that this would inevitably necessitate a new leader in the Commons.

Similarly, at the crisis point of his career, Lord Randolph's virtue with regard to Irish Home Rule is fiercely defended. There could never have been a compact with Parnell, it is argued, as there is no written evidence: and 'nothing that related to politics, whether creditable or not, whether important or petty, seems to have been excluded from his archives'.[36] (This did not, however, prevent a good deal of judicious weeding before the papers were bound up into the blue and gold volumes now in Churchill College.) Churchill could not, in any case, make a deal with Parnell, since 'the chances of his joining a Conservative administration were undetermined': which contradicts all that has been implied about the position he had attained in mid-1885. Salisbury was similarly exonerated from any trafficking with the Irish devil in 1885 (though in fact Carnarvon and Lord Randolph liked to agree in the late 1880s that he had been prepared to go as far as anyone). And though Churchill's visit to Ulster in February 1886 is neither analysed nor defended, the epigraph to the chapter which deals with it implies a condonation.[37]

On foreign policy, the impression is given throughout that Lord Randolph consulted his superiors; and though Churchill did not have access to the collections of diplomatic documents which amply disprove this, he did have a copy of his father's letter to Lord Roberts about his resignation detailing foreign policy as the reason and remarking that the estimates were 'a pretext, but a good one'. In the days following his resignation, Churchill described his father as holding aloof from intrigue— his second letter to Salisbury, a patent attempt to broaden and publicize the grounds of disagreement, is interpreted as 'a letter of farewell'; and though Churchill knew that Labouchere's letter of advice on 23 December was in reply to one written by Lord Randolph at the very first instant after his resignation, this would not be guessed by the reader.[38] Nor is the obvious fact, that his subsequent letter to Akers-Douglas was written for publication and in fact was leaked to the papers, ever referred to; as throughout, the fact that Lord Randolph cultivated

---

[36] W. S. Churchill, *Lord Randolph Churchill*, i, 394.

[37] 'Vote it as you please. There is a company of poor men that will spend all their blood before they see it settled so'—Carlyle, *Cromwell*.

[38] See Labouchere to W. S. Churchill, 27 Sept. 1905, CHAR 8/20.

journalists and gossips is ignored, in favour of the inference that publicity attached itself to him in a manner both miraculous and fortuitous. Lord Randolph's patent manœuvres against the ministry in 1887 were similarly left aside ('during the whole of 1887 Lord Randolph had regularly supported his late colleagues'). Sending Churchill material for the biography, Hartington (by then the Duke of Devonshire) had impressed upon him the need for 'caution as to those [letters] of 1887': and this was sedulously obeyed. As Churchill wrote: 'Never did he contemplate alliance with the Liberal Party.'[39] The resignation had to be shown as totally unplanned: no alliances were tested, no friends were informed, no support was invited. Again, a pattern of tiny textual changes accompanies the thesis. Quoting a letter from Lord Randolph to his mother, 'I should give anything to form a government' becomes, more modestly, 'I should like to form a government'; in reproducing the sentence 'altogether my action is not unjustified by events and the public will soon see it', the latter clause is carefully dropped.[40] The real point of speeches like that of 31 January 1887, a well-advertised and damaging attack on the government, is ignored. The emphasis on Lord Randolph's giving up the Fair Trade cause instead of making an issue of it evades the fact that his doing so was a response to a Liberal Unionist scare; the protracted and punishing nature of his attacks on his ex-colleagues, over issues like Egypt and the Irish Land Bill, is ignored. It is also implied that all social contact with Salisbury ceased, which is untrue; and the long account of a conversation with the Tsar in January 1888 which Lord Randolph 'left' in his papers was in fact written for Salisbury's benefit, and was part of an attempt at ingratiation.

Some inaccuracies arose from the paucity of material available in 1902–5; when Churchill wrote that his father never considered joining the Liberals in 1887, or when he wrote that by 1890 Lord Randolph 'had never made a personal attack on any of his late colleagues, nor can I discover any unkind or acrimonious word used about them',[41] he knew nothing of diaries like those of Eddy Hamilton and Loulou Harcourt which so amply contradict him. Similarly, the inaccuracies in repre-

---

[39] Devonshire to W. S. Churchill, copy, Devonshire MSS 340/2893/4, and W. S. Churchill, *Lord Randolph Churchill*, ii, 307.

[40] See RCHL xix/2402a, 2414a, for copies of originals.

[41] W. S. Churchill, *Lord Randolph Churchill*, ii, 442.

senting parliamentary scenes, the conflation of some letters, and the important errors of dating are not to be included in any deliberate over-all plan.[42] But the pattern which evolves overall is carefully stressed, and conforms closely to what Churchill's emotions wanted to be true, as well as to what suited his politics; a great weight of minor alterations and major emphases combined to produce a portrait in the painting of which Churchill not only discovered his father, but also refashioned him in his own image.

IV

Constructed as an epic tragedy, often beautifully and always interestingly written, filled with high drama and incisive characterization, and containing as its principal characters many figures still on the political stage, Churchill's life of his father could not fail to be a success; the additional factors of Lord Randolph's fascination and his son's current notoriety made that success all the more assured. The publication of the two volumes in January 1906 attracted widespread attention; the book sold 2,306 copies in the first week after publication, and did not flag. As the numerous reviews preserved in the Chartwell archives demonstrate, it had a tremendous critical reception. While it would be pointless to quote from these, the recurring impression was that Churchill had produced something very different from the usual work of piety; though the *Times Literary Supplement* saw the work as filially biased, it judged it to be politically impartial and to embody—considering its heredity—surprisingly few lapses of taste. The maturity and grandeur of style caused some eyebrows to be raised, but was generally admired; so was what was seen as an extraordinary impartiality and self-effacement on the part of the biographer.

Rosebery was one of the few who demurred at this: while

---

[42] e.g., for the quite different accounts in *Hansard* of Churchill's jeers about amendments on 'dirty bits of paper', and Gladstone's actual remarks on 'that which the locust spared, the caterpillar devoured', see *Hansard 3*, cclxxiv, 1453, 1511. But Winston Churchill may have preferred to follow the accounts of newspaper correspondents. For conflation of letters see for instance Salisbury to Churchill, 29 Mar. 1886, in vol. ii, pp. 73–4, which has a last paragraph that does not appear in the original (RCHL xii/1438c). Important misdatings occur in i, 164, where Churchill's letters should be dated 1880 and 1883, not 1882; regarding his reconciliation with the Prince of Wales, which was in 1884, not 1883; his election to the National Union council by Percy's casting vote was in July 1883, not 1882; he was not a 'minister of the Crown' when he spoke to the Cambridge Carlton on 6 June 1885.

generally admiring, he thought the narrator was not enough of an unseen wire-puller; the subject of the material should tell his own story. Some guessed that, in the subject's words, the tale might be rather different. J. M. Maclean wrote a particularly interesting piece, taking issue with Churchill on those episodes in which he had been involved, and stressing in a friendly way Lord Randolph's unashamed lack of principle and ability to change sides; Frank Harris, who wrote admiringly of the work at the time, later dismissed it as 'two stout volumes, an admirable official Victorian biography, distinguished by the remarkable fairness used to explain every incident in his political career, a politician writing of a politician'; more perceptively he added that Winston Churchill 'probably would have written a real life, had not Randolph been his father, and had he not his own political career to consider'.[43] Generally, those who found fault with the portrait were exceptions, and did so for odd reasons: such as the *Telegraph*'s argument that Churchill had written about Lord Randolph too frankly ('there are passages in this book which most English sons would have hesitated to write about their fathers'). In private, some reactions were as hostile while being less naïve. Theodore Roosevelt wrote:

I dislike [*sic*] the father and dislike the son, so I may be prejudiced. Still I feel that, while the biographer and his subject possess real farsightedness, especially in their appreciation of the shortcomings of that 'Society' which had so long been dominant in English politics ... yet they both possess or possest [*sic*] such levity, lack of sobriety, lack of permanent principle, and an inordinate thirst for that cheap form of admiration which is given to notoriety, as to make them poor public servants ... A clever, forceful, rather cheap and vulgar life of that clever, forceful, rather cheap and vulgar egoist.[44]

Generally, Lord Randolph's old friends expressed delight (with an implication of relief). FitzGibbon wrote that the Irish press was delighted with its impartiality and good taste; Rosebery, who had criticized some of the style and production, eventually 'could not find a fault'; Chamberlain felt he had 'allowed the facts and the letters to tell their own story'. Others had slight reservations; Blunt, deeply admiring, still slightly resented the underestimation of Churchill's Home Rule commit-

---

[43] Frank Harris, *My Life and Loves* (1964 compendium edition), p. 471.
[44] See E. Morison *et al.* (ed.), *The Letters of Theodore Roosevelt* (Cambridge, Mass., 1952), v, 409, and vi, 1329. I am indebted to Mr Owen Dudley Edwards for these references.

ment in 1885 (his own belief in which had got him into such trouble). Tim Healy wrote shrewdly: 'The impression which your quotations from his speeches leave on me is that they were often selected in vindication of his policy rather than in exhibition of his powers.'[45] Lord Tweedmouth, choosing his words carefully, assured Churchill 'it gives a very real and faithful presentment to his friends and the public of the best side of your father'.[46] But balancing these are the considerable number of letters to Churchill from acquaintances of Lord Randolph's, announcing that Churchill's rendering of his father's career had changed their opinions of the events of twenty years ago.

For the general reaction was to the book's political content ('no-one who cares for politics will willingly put it down when it is once in his hands. People who do not care for politics had better not touch it'[47]). This is reflected in the general consensus that the book got better as it went along, and that the early, 'personal' chapters could do with pruning. The political difficulties that had been circumvented were equally noted; as Rosebery put it:

A son, who hardly knew his father as a public man, or not at all, writing his father's life: the story only ten years old, and full of delicacies and resentments; many survivors of those times, whose toes it was impossible to avoid treading upon, still in existence . . . And the author had normal animosities by leaving his party, and had to write with delicacy about both parties in view of past and present connections.

This was, indeed, the point; and this was Churchill's triumph. Lord Londonderry reacted perfectly when he wrote to Churchill that after reading his book what he most admired in Lord Randolph was the way he never thought of changing his party.[48] Rosebery's monograph, appearing some months later, pressed home the point forcefully indicated by Churchill's two volumes. That point was defined by one solitary commentator, writing a year later, on another subject: 'he has endeavoured throughout his story to persuade his readers that, if Lord Randolph had been guided by the logic of his convictions, he would have deserted the Conservative fold and embraced Liberalism; that,

[45] 16 Aug. 1906; CHAR 8/24.
[46] 10 Sept. 1905; CHAR 8/20.
[47] *TLS*, quoted in *WSC*, ii, 136.
[48] 28 Jan. 1906; CHAR 8/21.

at any rate, is the impression which the book leaves on their minds ... [He has] perverted [Tory Democracy] into a justification for joining the Liberal ranks.'[49]

The political effect of the book was increased by its rapidly gaining the status of a literary classic, if sometimes in rather ill-judged company (Hugh Kingsmill pointed out that the critic who said it ranked with Morley's *Gladstone* and Boswell's *Johnson* was 'trying to give an idea of a horse by saying that it is fit only for the knacker's yard and a certain Derby winner').[50] *Lord Randolph Churchill* was at once pirated for a host of inferior political biographies, and even 'memoirs' of the period. As well as provoking a debate in the journals on Tory Democracy contributed to by Hugh Cecil, Herbert Vivian, and others, it directly or indirectly contributed to the genesis of Rosebery's *Lord Randolph Churchill*, Harold Gorst's *The Fourth Party*, and Balfour's *Chapters of Autobiography*. Gorst tried to present his father as the real inspiration of Tory Democracy; Balfour denied a close connection with the Fourth Party and attributed to Lord Randolph the desire to oust Salisbury from the early eighties; Rosebery amplified Churchill's case for his father as a Liberal *manqué*, putting the case far less equivocally (as befitted a man who had himself kept his political virtue). This helped to carry through Churchill's real message: that there was no place in the Tory Party for men of ideas, then and now. True or false, this obscured the fact that what ideas were actually possessed by Lord   Randolph—that   most   instinctive   and   febrile   of politicians—had often been grounded in pure Toryism.

Nearly half a century and two world wars later, Churchill prepared a new edition of the great *Life*; and by then his priorities had changed. Once more a Conservative, he wrote in the preface to the 1951 edition that 'the Tory Democracy of which [Lord Randolph Churchill] was the exponent, has enabled the Conservative Party to preserve its inherent strength and vitality, and to hold its position in spite of world convulsions and ceaseless domestic change; I believe he could take his place in the House of Commons today with less sense of disharmony than any of his contemporaries'. But the original thrust of his two volumes of special pleading remained. It was not greatly

---

[49] See Fabian Ware, 'Conservative opportunism and Imperial democracy' in *Nineteenth Century*, no. 361 (Mar. 1907), pp. 405–18.

[50] See 'Winston Churchill's War Memoirs' in *New English Review*, 1945 (reprinted in M. Holroyd (ed.), *The Best of Hugh Kingsmill* (Harmondsworth, 1970), pp. 282–3).

dislodged by the only subsequent biography of Lord Randolph. While a remarkable production for a very young man, and adding to the picture by pioneering work in the Northcote, Salisbury, Smith, and Balfour archives, Rhodes James's study left the general portrait of Lord Randolph's career substantially unaltered. (Significantly, in a more controversial and highly perceptive study of Winston Churchill written ten years later, the same author wrote far more ambivalently of his father's achievement.) *Lord Randolph Churchill* endured, in the same whitewash that had dazzled those who beheld it in 1906: and that glare had conveniently been refracted on to the architect standing beside. This achievement had, however, led to a removal of Lord Randolph from his contemporary context. 'His political action was guided purely by party consideration', wrote an Irish lawyer who worked with him; 'but in this respect he did not differ from his contemporaries, and while he was more capable, he was not less honest than they.' Churchill represented his father immortally as a misunderstood Prometheus; hostile opinion retaliated by seeing in him a thwarted Lucifer. But to depict him in either image is, in fact, to elevate him too far above his political fellows.

Appendices

Pall Mall Gazette, 27 November 1884

THE TORYISM OF TOMORROW
An interview with Lord Randolph Churchill.

On hearing of Lord Randolph Churchill's intention to leave England for some months' holiday, we sent one of our representatives to wait upon him with the object of putting the country in possession of his views on the present and his hopes for the future. The following is a report of the conversation that took place on the occasion:

'I am going to India', said Lord Randolph Churchill, 'because I hate the cold weather, and the political ground is perfectly clear for a holiday and I am tired of work. The Reform question will be practically settled and done with by the end of this year, and next session the Government will merely be living on sufferance until the boundaries are readjusted and registers are ready for a general election.'

'Then you do not agree with Mr Morley, who has no great faith of the proposals working to the end that is hoped.'

'Decidedly not', replied Lord Randolph: 'both parties are pledged too deeply to allow the negotiations to fail. What the arrangement is to be is more than I can tell you, for I am not arranging it; but I can tell you roughly what the scheme is that I should like to see. The two essentials are that urban and rural districts should be separated, and that representation should be based on population. There is no difficulty about the application of these two principles whatever. I have seen a scheme drawn up by a young Conservative that takes 53,000 as the number entitled to a member, and find the sum works out as easily as possible. The whole country is mapped out in single member constituencies, each with a population of 53,000. Purely agricultural boroughs beneath 10,000 should be merged in the counties; small boroughs which are really urban should be grouped. The scheme I have told you of shows how this can be done all over the country without any of those geographical difficulties with which Mr Bright tried to frighten the Eighty Club.' Our representative here asked whether Lord Randolph would apply his principles with equal rigour in the case of counties and of London. 'Yes, certainly', was the answer. 'London should have its full quota of seventy members, or whatever it might be. Why not? There is no objection to it. On the contrary, there is the strongest possible reason in favour of giving London its utmost due; for that is the only way of redressing the balance between the north and the south. As for the centrifugal theory, who would ever have thought of it, and who would ever be found to believe in it, except Mr Gladstone? I am for giving town and county each its due, neither more nor less. Certainly I have no desire to rob London or any other town to pay the counties more than their due, for I do not believe that the agricultural labourers will vote Tory. On the contrary, if, as I hope and believe, the farmers vote Tory, their labourers, you may be sure, will vote Liberal. And besides, the Church of England, which is a great political force on the Tory side, is not nearly so strong in the counties as in the towns—all the best energy of the Church is spent nowadays in the towns. To the counties, then, I should certainly not be tempted to give more than their due. They should be split up into single-membered divisions, just as large boroughs into single-membered wards. Single-membered constituencies are the soul of the whole concern; they afford the only working system of minority represen-tation. As for the old two-membered county constituencies, they are simply a survival from the days before railways, when the two members were wanted to protect each other "from robbers by day and ghosts by night". There is nothing whatever to be said for them any longer.'

Nothing, our representative admitted, except that, as Mr Bright would say, they are 'on the old lines'.

'The old lines', Lord Randolph replied, 'simply mean the old Whig dodges. The Whigs are playing just the same game now that they played in 1867, and they ought to be met in the same way as they were then. They went on prating about six-pounders and seven-pounders, and so on, until Lord Beaconsfield went down to the firm ground of principle in household suffrage. And that is what will have to be done now—we must go down to the principle of population. The "fancy" scheme in the *Standard*, even if it had survived my examination of it in Birmingham, would never by any possibility have passed the House of Commons—if only for this reason, that it raised an infinity of debateable details. Still less would it afford any basis for an agreement between the two parties now. But if you go on the basis of population there is much less room for dispute, and that is why some such scheme as I have sketched out to you will have to be adopted.'

Our representative, as a good Radical, only hoped that it would be.

'Well, if the Radicals like it so much the better. All I can say is that I regard the arrangement of the Reform question as infinitely good for the Tories and infinitely bad for the Liberals. Why, the whole sting will have been taken out of the agitation against the Lords, and there will be quite as much credit on our side as on the other from the Reform business. This being so, I can see no reason whatever why we should not win the next election.' Our representative here ventured to suggest that even an easy victory required a body of fighters, and that 'our only general' on the Tory side was retiring to India. 'But', rejoined Lord Randolph Churchill, 'we do not need to show any fight just now; our strength is to sit still. A Government that is in on sufferance never has a good time; it has no opportunity of accomplishing anything, but only opportunities of being harassed. And Mr Gladstone's Government will have a ghastly array of questions to face next year before it dies— Ireland, Egypt, South Africa, and ghastliest of all, a bankrupt Budget. "Mr Gladstone is a host in himself." No doubt; but are you quite sure that you will have Mr Gladstone to fight the next election for you? Are you certain that he will not do as he has so often hinted, and retire from public life as soon as he has seen the Reform Bills through? And if you have no Mr Gladstone, but all Mr Gladstone's post-obits, how do you think you will fare at the polls?'

Our representative gladly admitted the probability of a Conservative victory for the sake of learning from Lord Randolph Churchill 'what will he do with it?' 'That depends entirely on the composition of the Conservative Cabinet; and I can only speak for myself of what I would like to see. Even so you will hardly expect me to unfold a complete programme for you; but let me ask you whether you have considered how many of Mr Gladstone's subjects in that celebrated article of his in the *Nineteenth Century* have never been touched at all, and what Tory democracy would do with them. There is the reform of local government, for instance. I would approach that question just as I have approached parliamentary reform. I would have none of the Whig dodges, with their half-and-half dilutions of the representative system, and their indirect voting, but I should like to see frankly elected and democratic local bodies. I do not believe the country gentleman would really lose so much influence thereby as is supposed; they can always serve as elective guardians, for instance, now when they choose, and they would win at least their fair share of representation if all such bodies were purely elective. Licensing is a very difficult question; but I agree with you that if we only had county boards such as I have described, it would practically be impossible to keep licensing out of their hands. But I do not say that the licensing would be well done. The unpaid magistracy, however, I should maintain, principally as a matter of economy. Then there is the housing of the working classes; no question is more important than that, and I believe the Tory party will be capable of dealing with it in a very large way. We are not hampered by any devotion to imaginary dictates of political economy, as the Whigs are, and we should not shrink from a large investment of public money and a large amount of State intervention for the benefit of the masses of the people.'

The obvious reflection suggested itself that all this would want money. 'Decidedly it would, and you must be prepared before many years are over—especially if the *Pall Mall Gazette* has its way about the navy—to see the expenditure of the country up to £100,000,000. That is a serious outlook: but we Tories have a great card in reserve in the fair trade movement. I am not at all disheartened by the Hackney election, for I recognise quite clearly that it will require a good deal of time to bring the boroughs round to fair trade or a tax on corn. When the truth comes to be known—here, for instance, what Sir John Macdonald has to say of the actual working of the thing in Canada—I am not at all sure that fair trade will continue to be regarded as so much of an economical fallacy. But I look on these things, and have always done so, solely from the point of view of revenue. Now what can be more flagrantly immoral than Mr Gladstone's new addition to the income tax—restricting the area of taxation at the very moment when he is about to enormously enlarge the area of representation? But even Mr Gladstone could not go on adding to the income tax for ever, and for new expenditure you must go to new sources of revenue. No one need think of putting a tax on corn and a duty on imported manufacture just by themselves; fair trade would be part of a general revision of the tariff in the interests of the revenue. What, for instance, if we greatly reduced the duty on tobacco and on tea? That and things like that would cover a multitude of new duties. The restrictions would be immensely popular with the working classes, and would, moreover, I do not doubt, bring in an increase of revenue itself.'

'In fact', said our representative, 'you would proceed all along the line of domestic policy in the same direction as Prince Bismarck, with State Socialism and Customs revenue?' 'Precisely', said Lord Randolph, 'and does not Prince Bismarck know what he is about? He is the biggest man in the world.' 'And as to foreign and colonial affairs?' 'Well, I need only make one remark, and that is, that the *Pall Mall Gazette* is doing an excellent service by keeping the question of the empire above the region of party politics. This is most important in the matter of the colonies, although all the present talk, by the way, about Imperial federation is mere moonshine. The scheme is altogether premature, and it is the greatest mistake in the world to suppose that the fussy self-constituted representatives of the colonies here represent public opinion out there. As to the navy, if all the *Pall Mall Gazette* says is true, then nothing short of an immediate expenditure on an adequate scale can be thought of. I am bound to say that all I have heard entirely bears out "The Truth about the Navy", and I shall be much surprised if the debate in the House of Commons does not conclusively make in the same direction. The Conservative front bench is every bit as much to blame as the Liberal: they have been in a conspiracy of ignorance and optimism together. Still, there is less to hope for now from the Liberals of the two. The present Government is bankrupt and will not dare to spend as largely as is necessary. Even worse than nothing would be a wretched million or two, which would do no good but an infinity of harm in hanging the whole question up. For my own part, if "The Truth about the Navy" be admitted, then a large expenditure spread over a number of years should be incurred; and I should not hesitate for a moment about it, for I believe it would be as popular as it would be patriotic. The one other thing needful about the navy is the rout out of the Admiralty; there is neither rhyme nor reason in the present arrangements, which are simply an ingenious device for sending responsibility round and round in a vicious circle.'

One other question our representative ventured to put before leaving, 'What about Ireland? Is there a lesson to be learned from Bismarck there also?' 'If a large expenditure of money by the State or public works is Bismarckian, yes. There would be an immediate and an enormous manner of pacification. And alongside of that it is of primary importance to reform the Castle. It is a nest of political corruption—of more kinds than one; and when next the *Pall Mall Gazette* wants a new sensation it could not do a better public service than by telling us "The Truth about Dublin Castle". Let me say this in conclusion. You have said the schemes I have been telling you about sound as if they were learned in the school of Bismarck. Well, when Prince Bismarck first propounded his domestic policy, everybody said it was absurd, and the English newspapers in particular conspired to ridicule it. Yet Prince Bismarck seems to be getting on pretty well, don't you think?—and there is universal suffrage, remember, in Germany.'

Appendix 2

TWO ACCOUNTS OF CHURCHILL'S INTERVIEW
WITH THE INDIAN DELEGATES, 15 October 1885

1. From W. S. Blunt, 'Randolph Churchill: a personal recollection' in *Nineteenth Century*, Mar. 1906.

He had promised me to see certain native delegates sent from India, as representing the three Presidencies, to advocate advanced native views of a Home Rule kind. 'Moore's face', I had written, 'was a picture when he told him of this decision; but in his light-hearted way Randolph would hear of no objection, and so it is settled.' Now two days later the interview was to take place, and I find the following account of it:

Randolph was quite charming, putting them at their ease at once. There was nobody else present but ourselves, and the face of the office messenger when he showed us in was even more comic than Moore's had been two days ago. The expression was exactly that of the old steward in the 'Mariage a la mode'. Mon Mahon Ghose did most of the talking, and he asked Randolph about the Parliamentary enquiry and what subjects it would include. Randolph said it would depend on them to make it a useful one. They must send over their very best men to give evidence, and take care they were absolutely accurate about facts, as there were plenty of old-fashioned people who did not want existing things disturbed, and who would pick holes where they could. He said Sivaprasad had informed him that a royal order to come to England would override caste difficulties, and that the Benares divines would decide it in this sense. But Chandavarkur [*sic*] objected to this that Benares could not lay down the law for the whole of India. Still he hopes it might have some effect. Mon Mahon Ghose wanted to know whether the enquiry would include the judicial system, as that was what was giving rise just now to most ill-feeling; and Randolph said that if it depended upon him it should. His colleagues had been most amiable about this inquiry, and if the Conservatives were in office the inquiry would be a full and impartial one. He was against members of the government sitting on it; but those should be chosen who had most title to consider Indian affairs, independent men of all parties. He should support the inquiry whether in office or not. The enquiry would also include the revenue question. Ramaswami explained to him the enhancement grievance. He begged them to address him again on any special points they required to make known connected with their respective Presidencies; and at the end of three-quarters of an hour they went away, highly delighted.

2. From N. Chandavarkar, *English Impressions* (1887), pp. 44–5.

On Thursday the 15th October at 4 p.m. we were taken by Mr Blunt to the India Office—a massive building or, I should say, several buildings rolled into one, presenting from the inside a somewhat dreary spectacle, where a stranger is apt to lose himself as in a labyrinth. But the Secretary of State's room—that where Lord Randolph was seated and received us—was of modest pretensions. One or two cupboards containing books, a few chairs, a table, and a large map of India—that was about all the furniture I remember to have seen there. Nothing could have exceeded the grace and kindliness with which Lord Randolph shook hands with us. I do not wonder that they make a hero of him on Tory platforms. A good appearance is a great advantage to a speaker in England, and Lord Randolph has it even more than either Mr Bright or Mr Chamberlain. He has all the polish in his manners and speech of the Frenchman, with the ceaseless activity of his own race. His moustaches, at which his opponents point their finger of scorn, give grace to his animated countenance and heighten the effect of his vivacity which is the marked feature of his eyes. There is also a kind of melody in his voice—and when he speaks, words, to use an Oriental figure of speech, flow like honey. In introducing us Mr Blunt told him that he had advised us not to identify ourselves with any particular party. Lord Randolph merely nodded. Mr Man Mohan Ghose said we should be glad to remain neutral. Again a nod of approval from his lordship. Lord Randolph apparently thought that it was a question on which it was prudent he should not speak but might as well convey his meaning by his silence. He spoke of his visit to India, said how much he liked all he had seen, and made some enquiries about Raja Siva Prasad of Bengal, whom he described as 'a very nice gentleman'. That over, we talked politics. He said that he was very earnest about his proposal for a Parliamentary enquiry into Indian affairs. He had spoken about it to his colleagues in the Cabinet before introducing the Indian Budget into the House of Commons in July and they had all approved of it. But what the Liberals would do if they should come into power, he said he could not say. He indeed thought it was probable, if they got into office, that they would carry out his proposals, but it was equally probable they would try to limit the scope of the enquiry. His own settled conviction on the subject was that the enquiry should be thorough and lead to something practical. The committee should examine carefully the way in which the country was being governed; and it should consist of *the best men available in Parliament.* Mr Morley, he continued, had opposed his proposal on party grounds more than from any settled convictions on the subject. His speech had surprised his lordship considerably.

Our interview lasted a little more than half an hour. Before parting, Lord Randolph said he would be glad to hear from us again on any subject specially appertaining to our respective Presidencies. We bowed our thanks to his lordship and parted. Thus commenced an acquaintance which, however, was not subsequently kept up in the good spirit in which it had begun.

Appendix 3

Pall Mall Gazette, 28 June 1886

THE MIDLOTHIAN OF THE METROPOLIS
LORD RANDOLPH AT THE TORY CAUCUS

(By Our Special Commissioner.)

The fight has begun. Lord Randolph fired the first shot on Saturday night, or rather took his preliminary canter, for the scene of his fulminations was a riding-school. Somehow or other the fighting man of the Tory party, or his friends, declined to open the arena to all comers. The school is not even in the street. It is hidden at the bottom of a slight decline which leads to the mews of which the school forms one side. Then if you discovered the mews, as you might by its smell, a number of gentlemen in evening dress barred your entrance to the hall unless you were provided with a ticket. What with the smell and the distribution of seats, a sightseer ignorant of the occasion would have thought he was going to a circus. There were white tickets for one circle, blue tickets for another, but without a ticket there was no admission. I need not tell you then that a charming unanimity characterized the noble lord's reception. It is a pity that Lord Randolph—(with all his faults I love him still—he is one of the very best platform speakers of the time)—condescends to these precautions. Every cock can crow on his own particular midden, but it takes a very game cock indeed to crow on another cock's property. I should like to see Lord Randolph call a meeting of Tory working men this week, say at Mr Charrington's hall. I do not say this because I wish to see the descendant of the great hero of Blenheim's (of whom he bragged later on in the evening) head broken. I say it in all honesty, because I think that out in the East he might make a few 'verts, while in a mews-and-corner meeting such as Saturday's he doesn't influence a single individual. The villadom of Paddington, some two thousand of whom were thrilled by Lord Randolph's eloquence and fascinated by Lady Randolph's magnificent bonnet, would swear at Lord Randolph's bidding—aye, and believe they were swearing the truth— if he had told them that Paddington was situated in Yorkshire, and that Yorkshire was in South Africa. Such devoted followers make a solid foundation for the seat in which Lord Randolph sits. Mr Page Hopps has undertaken a forlorn hope when he promised to storm the Paddington fort, which is held by soldiers so loyal that they will fight with their eyes bandaged and their ears stuffed with wool, through which the din of battle cannot penetrate to the brain.

The meeting was admirably managed: there was no confusion, and none of those rows, no legs of chairs, etc., in the air, which tend to make a meeting lively. By half-past seven the riding-school was full, but the crowd amused itself by watching the brilliant array of ladies and gentlemen on the platform. The whole audience was eminently respectable and well-to-do, composed chiefly of that middle class whose vanity Lord Randolph tickled late in the evening. But the platform glowed with gay dresses and flowers. The men were mostly in evening dress, and the show of heavy gold chains and jewellery was remarkable. I must not forget to mention the Primrose orders which dangled at the bosoms of men and women alike, knights and ladies, squires and dames, of different degrees of picturesqueness. It was natural that this other National League should be well represented. The windows behind the platform were thrown up, and had become as boxes at a theatre. There were strips of red and white drapery, and a sort of Royal box, lined with red stuffs, which also over-looked the platform, and was full. The temperature was cool, though the closing of the main entrance afterwards led to two or three slight interruptions. 'I am well aware that political discussion on these warm June evenings is not agreeable. But don't blame the warm June evenings, but Mr Gladstone,' said Lord Randolph, to whom an interruption is naturally an irritant. On looking at the leaflets with which every one was provided one was struck by the line:

These proceedings will commence with 'Rule Britannia'.

And that there should be no mistake about it a tall gentleman, with a moustache which rivalled his master's, got on his feet about 8, and led off the first stave of that well-known air. This is just the sort of person who is required at Gladstonian meetings, and I would strongly recommend to Mr Hopps to engage half a dozen gentlemen with sonorous voices, not necessarily with Randolphian moustaches, to control the harmony at their meetings. They should have a tuning-fork or some such musical instrument, or they may begin a few notes too high, like Lord Randolph's musical gentleman. However, I do not complain. It was amusing to hear:

This was the charter of the land,
And guardian angels sang the strain.

At this point his voice breaks and he starts again in another key which produced anything but angelic sounds. Lady Randolph looked imposing, or rather her bonnet did. It was a wonderful contrivance of abnormal proportions, like a headdress of a century or two past. I could not describe its complicated details.

Put shortly, Lord Randolph told his audience that the Empire was in danger; that Mr Gladstone was a liar and a madman; that the Irish problem was insoluble; that if the English withdrew from Ireland the Anglo-Saxon Protestant and the Roman Catholic Celt would fall to and destroy each other. He was in capital form. Lord Randolph is an accomplished platform orator. In face and manner he is a small echo of the great Macdermott. If he failed as a politician he could turn to the music-hall with every hope of a distinguished career. I can readily fancy the unction with which the brother of the Duke of Marlborough would sing, say, a verse from 'God Save the Queen', as, for example, it was paraphrased for Saturday's audience:

O Lord our God, arise,
Scatter his enemies,
  And make them fall;
Confound their politics;
Frustrate their Fenian tricks;
On Thee our hopes we fix;
  God save us all.

His voice is full and sonorous, though he sometimes lisps and clips his words—Anticyram, for instance, became Antithyram—which had quite a funny effect. He is beautifully dressed, his linen is glossy, and evidently carefully superintended in the best laundries, his gold chain has the solid appearance of real 18 carat, his tiny shoes, rosettes, and silk socks are the daintiest of their kind. His manner is typified by his own phrase:

'COME ON',

which he has perhaps inherited from that Marlborough, his great ancestor, who it is believed is the only person for whom he has any reverence. Lord Randolph keeps himself well in hand. When he says Mr Gladstone is a liar, or that Mr Gladstone is mad, or compares him to Nebuchadnezzar, he hurls it at his audience, and then throws himself back as though he were a painter contemplating a fresh touch to the picture on his easel. Sometimes he walks about the platform as though it were really a stage, or he puts his hands in his pockets, leans against the table, and condescends to be colloquial. His voice reaches far, and a rather monotonous delivery is varied by little relapses into pathos, or grave or scornful, as occasion requires. He seldom smiles, or if he does the moustache hides it. This moustache is to Lord Randolph much as the whiskers are to a cat. Without it he would lose half his force. But its glories are not likely to be shorn, for it helped him on to fame, and one credits Lord Randolph with a sense of gratitude. He denies that he has literary aptitude, and deprecates the idea that he burns the midnight oil over his manifestoes and his metaphors. But his bitterest enemy would credit him with a trenchant style, with a complete mastery of the vocabulary of abuse, a fluency which is still emphatic, a ready command of telling figures, and an imperturbability which nothing can break down. He steps up to the footlights, never stumbles, sends every shaft right to its mark, and seldom refers to written notes. His adjectives are never exhausted. They are like the widow's cruse. He appeals to his God with a fervour which would have procured him high place in another hierarchy. He speaks with the infallibility of a Pope and the readiness of a cheap Jack. Nothing abashes him. He denounces Yankee gold as though he would scorn to stain his fingers with it. He conjures up one Blenheim, but conveniently forgets another. His five bogies amused his gaping audience, and his description of 'our prisons large enough, our gallows numerous, our hangmen to be had in any numbers, and cheap rope', was the signal for a great guffaw. His fervid question to these Primrose squires and dames as to what course Mr Gladstone and Mr John Morley would have pursued if they had had to deal with the Spanish Armada, or the French at Blenheim, or the domination of Napoleon, brought down the House, though its effect was spoiled by the immediate appeal by which it was followed, to the electors of Paddington. Paddington after Napoleon was not happy. Lord Randolph does not often descend to such bathos.

Appendix 4

Churchill's draft letter to the *Morning Post*, *c*.5 January 1887 (RCHL xix/2366).

An introductory paragraph declared his intention to explain what had caused his resignation after all; despite his original intention, as outlined in his letter to Akers-Douglas, to give the government 'cordial and steady support'. The letter continued:

The appalling intelligence however which appears in this morning's papers as to the reconstruction of the Government in my opinion releases me from any pledge and severs every tie which might have bound me to my late colleagues.

Mr Goschen, we are informed, is going to join the government as a 'Liberal', wrapping his Whig robe tightly round him lest he should be at all contaminated or defiled by the Tory pitch.

This might have been tolerated, and although no doubt popular sympathy is not Mr Goschen's strong point yet a strong infusion of a certain kind of liberal principles might probably have acted as a tonic on the cabinet constitution.

But alas! the reformation does not stop here. Lord Iddesleigh and Lord Cross are to resign from their respective offices. Here again adverse criticism is not essential for it may well be that the two noble lords after many years of public life see nothing unattractive in well-earned repose.

But in what manner does the leader of the Tory Party, the successor of Wellington, Peel, Derby and Beaconsfield, supply their places?

By agreeing with Mr Goschen, so we are informed, to take into the Cabinet two Whig peers.

Two Whig peers who have nothing to recommend them save their names and wealth, who have done nothing whatever for the cause of the Union, who could not if they tried get five hundred electors to listen to them for quarter [*sic*] of an hour in any part of the country.

To carry out this appalling arrangement men like Sir H. Holland, Mr Ritchie, Mr Jackson, representing large constituencies, in full touch with the people, of first-rate administrative ability, are left mouldering in minor offices, other members of our party who would have filled with signal credit the offices vacated by the above-named gentlemen are condemned to continue plodding idly through the lobbies at the call of the whip, though by bringing them into the Government the people would have been directly represented in the administration and much new Tory talent would have been brought to light.

Never was there such an insult passed upon a party by its leader; all the hard and biting contempt which has been poured forth on us by our foes is assented to, and exceeded by this action of the trustee of the honour of the Tories. Here we have it proclaimed on high authority that the Tory party, which many of us not without success have been striving to induce the British people to place confidence in, are unable from among ourselves to fill with credit or capacity the ranks of office, but that if a Tory Government is to have a chance of life it must be permeated by hungry Whig office seekers.

I protest loudly. Certainly if I could have dreamed that a Tory noble would thus betray his party's interests, would thus sacrifice their future, I would have undergone any amount of humiliation, any amount of imputation of violated or forgotten pledges, rather than by my resignation have prepared for or precipitated such a calamity.

As one who has worked for the Tory party as hard and continuously as it is possible for man to work, who has had concentrated upon him the most virulent and malignant abuse of political opponents, and who has borne it gladly, as one who though only for a brief period has had the immense and memorable honour of leading in the House of Commons a political association the separate, peculiar and proud traditions of which go back into the past for two hundred years, I protest against this contemplated arrangement being further proceeded on.

I denounce it as a stab in the back for the Tories, as a sudden and traitorous but certain death blow, as the prostitution of the power and virtue of a popular party to the lowest purposes of class intrigue.

I care not a scrap for the indignation of the classes and the clubs which this protest will call forth. I despise and defy in anticipation the aspersions of false and base motives which will be heaped upon me, and I call upon all those many thousands I believe in the country who have faith in the future of a regenerated Toryism as the best security for popular liberty and happiness to make their voices heard loudly now, and heard in time, to prevent this immeasurable calamity.

If I protest in vain, if this exclamation finds no responsible echo, if Whig pedigrees are to be the sole qualification of office and representation of great constituencies, the possession of first-rate abilities, long record of hard work among the people themselves for the prosecution of our principles direct disqualification, then indeed it will be apparent me [*sic*] that all my ideas and hopes as to the great party with which I have been connected have been foolish, illusory and false, and that the proud and unconquerable spirit of the Tories, the sole hope for Britain, has for ever died away.

Sources

The contemporary memoirs, journals, articles, and records which I used
are fully recorded in the footnotes, as are the relevant secondary works. I
have therefore listed manuscript sources only.

Balfour papers (British Library and Whittingehame)
Beaconsfield papers (Bodleian Library)
Blunt papers (Fitzwilliam Museum)
Cabinet papers 1885–7 (Public Record Office)
Cairns papers (Public Record Office)
Carnarvon papers (Public Record Office and British Library)
Chamberlain papers (Birmingham University Library)
Chartwell Trust papers (Churchill College, Cambridge)
Chilston papers (Kent County Record Office)
Churchill family papers (Blenheim Palace)
Lord Randolph Churchill papers (Churchill College, Cambridge)
Cranbrook papers (East Suffolk Record Office)
Devonshire papers (Chatsworth)
Dilke papers (British Library)
Dufferin papers (India Office Library)
Escott papers (British Library)
Hambleden papers (W. H. Smith and Son Ltd.)
Hamilton diaries (British Library)
Harcourt papers (Bodleian Library)
Harrowby papers (Sandon Hall)
Iddesleigh papers (British Library)
James papers (Hereford Record Office)
Kilbracken papers (India Office Library)
Roberts papers (National Army Museum)
Rosebery papers (National Library of Scotland)
Rothschild papers (N. M. Rothschild and Sons)
Royal Archives (Windsor Castle)
St. Aldwyn papers (Gloucestershire Record Office)
Salisbury papers (Hatfield House)
Stanhope papers (Kent County Record Office)

Index

Peers are listed under titles, unless they generally appear in the text under their family name. Churchill's sisters appear under their married names. Throughout, 'Churchill' refers to Lord Randolph.